Rick Steves®

BEST OF
GERMANY

Contents

Introduction 7
   The Best of Germany 8
   Travel Smart 24

South Germany

Munich 33
   Munich in 3 Days 34
   Orientation 34
   Tours 35
   Munich City Walk 40
   Sights 56
   Experiences 80
   Eating 82
   Sleeping 89
   Transportation 94
   Near Munich:
      Dachau Memorial 98

Salzburg, Austria 103
   Salzburg in 1 Day 104
   Orientation 105
   Salzburg Town Walk 112
   Sights 123
   Music 133
   Eating 135
   Sleeping 139
   Transportation 144

Bavarian Alps 147
   Bavarian Alps in 2 Days 148
   Füssen 149
   The King's Castles 164
   Wieskirche 174
   Oberammergau 175
   Linderhof Castle 180
   Zugspitze 182

Rothenburg &
the Romantic Road 187
   Rothenburg & the
      Romantic Road in 2 Days . . . 188
   Rothenburg ob der Tauber 189
   Near Rothenburg:
      The Romantic Road 214

Best of the Rest 217
   Würzburg .217
   Nürnberg 223

West Germany

Rhine Valley 231
   The Rhine Valley in
      1 or 2 Days 232
   Rhine Blitz Tour 234
   Bacharach 244

St. Goar. 255
Marksburg Castle
    in Braubach 262
Near the Rhine Valley:
    Burg Eltz 266
    Cologne. 268

Best of the Rest 275
Baden-Baden. 275
Frankfurt 282

North Germany

Berlin 291
Berlin in 3 Days. 292
Orientation. 293
Berlin City Walk. 299
Sights. 313
Experiences. 336
Eating 338
Sleeping 343
Transportation. 347

Best of the Rest 352
Dresden 352
Hamburg 361

German History 368

Practicalities. 372
Tourist Information 372
Help! 372
Travel Tips. 373
Money. 373
Sightseeing 376
Eating 377
Sleeping 381
Staying Connected. 385
Transportation. 386
Holidays & Festivals. 400
Conversions & Climate. 402
Packing Checklist 403
German Survival Phrases 405

Index. 407

Map Index 417

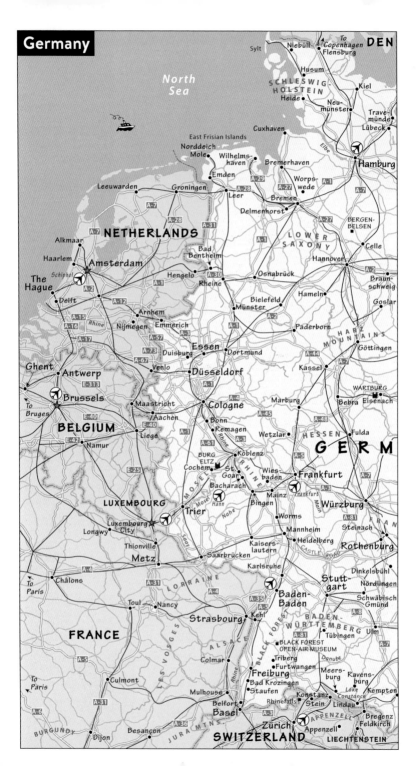

Germany

Introduction

Germany is blessed with some of Europe's most spectacular scenery—the jagged Alps, flower-filled meadows, rolling hills of forests and farmland, and the powerful Rhine River. Its many castles range from evocative ruins to sturdy fortresses to Romantic-era palaces fit for a king.

In contrast to these beautiful images, the country has a troubled 20th-century past. Throughout Germany, you'll see respectful acknowledgment of this tumultuous time, with thought-provoking museums and somber memorials.

As a nation, Germany is less than 150 years old ("born" in 1871). It was split into East and West after losing World War II. After the Berlin Wall fell, Germany was officially reunited in 1990, resulting in both euphoric joy and growing pains.

Today Germany is at the forefront of human progress, with high-tech trains, gleaming cities, and world-class museums. A founding member of the European Union, Germany leads the way in creating a stable, prosperous Europe for the future.

Yet the country nurtures its culture and traditions. You can visit idyllic half-timbered villages, enjoy strudel at the bakery, or sip a stein of beer while men in lederhosen play polka tunes.

With medieval castles, speedy autobahns, old-time beer halls, shiny skyscrapers, and the best wurst, this young country with a long past continues to make history.

THE BEST OF GERMANY

This book focuses on Germany's top destinations—its most fascinating cities and intimate villages—from powerhouse Berlin to sleepy Bacharach. A focused 14-day trip highlights lively Munich, musical Salzburg (just across the Austrian border from Munich, it's too convenient to pass up, even in a book about Germany), the castle-studded countryside of Bavaria, the medieval walled town of Rothenburg, quaint villages along the mighty Rhine, and the fascinating, ever-changing capital,

Berlin. And when there are interesting sights or towns near my top destinations, I cover these briefly (as "Near" sights), to help you fill out a free day or a longer stay.

Beyond the major destinations, I cover the Best of the Rest—great destinations that don't quite make my top cut, but are worth seeing if you have more time or specific interests: Würzburg, Nürnberg, Frankfurt, Baden-Baden, Dresden, and Hamburg.

To help you link the top stops, I've designed a two-week itinerary (see page 26), with tips to help you tailor it to your interests and time.

North Sea

DEN.

Baltic Sea

Hamburg

NETHER-
LANDS

POLAND

100 Kilometers
100 Miles

Berlin ⊛

GERMANY

Cologne

Rhine

Dresden

BURG
ELTZ

Rhine
Valley

**The Rhine
Valley**

St. Goar
Bacharach

Frankfurt

Würzburg

CZECH
REPUBLIC

LUX.

Rothenburg

Nürnberg

**Rothenburg and
the Romantic Road**

Baden-
Baden

Danube

Bavaria

Danube

FRANCE

NEUSCHWAN-
STEIN

Munich

Rhine

Bavarian Alps

Oberammergau

Salzburg

Füssen

Zugspitze

SWITZ.

AUSTRIA

THE BEST OF MUNICH

Lively, livable Munich has a compact, pedestrian-friendly core that welcomes strolling. The city is awash in convivial beer halls, beautiful gardens, stately churches, fancy pastry shops, and fine art museums. The crown jewels at the Residenz and the oompah bands at beer halls remind visitors that Munich has long been equally at ease hosting royalty and commoners alike.

❶ *The towering **New Town Hall** presides over Munich's main square, Marienplatz.*

❷ *The **Viktualienmarkt**, a fun open-air market with cheap eateries, sports a Bavarian maypole.*

❸ *A guide proudly introduces visitors to the palatial **Residenz**, home to Bavarian royalty for centuries.*

❹ *At **beer halls**, oompah bands play "Roll Out the Barrel!" to crank up the fun.*

❺ *The **Chinese Tower** in the English Garden is a landmark near a popular beer garden.*

❻ *Ride the rapids at the south end of the **English Garden**, where the surf's always up.*

❼ *Time to order another!* **Prost!**

❽ *A statue of Mary and an ornate glockenspiel (with daily shows) overlook **Marienplatz**— Mary's Place.*

11

THE BEST OF SALZBURG

Just across the German border in Austria, delightful Salzburg has a charming Old Town, splendid gardens, Baroque churches, and a hill-capping medieval fortress. The city's sights and soundtrack are a mix of Mozart (he lived here) and *The Sound of Music* (so did the Von Trapp family). At night, there's always music playing and the town is beautifully floodlit.

Salzburg's charisma and proximity to Munich make it irresistible to tuck into a Germany trip.

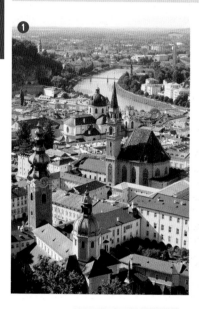

❶ *Salzburg's compact **Old Town** is an inviting maze for visitors to explore on foot.*

❷ *The **New Residenz,** where prince-archbishops once partied, hosts a glockenspiel and museums today.*

❸ *The **Mirabell Gardens** anchor a soaring view of Salzburg's old-town spires and hill-capping fortress.*

❹ *Walk or bike along the **Salzach River,** or just admire the city view from the bridge.*

❺ *Grave sites are lovingly tended at **St. Peter's Cemetery.***

❻ ***Fountains** add a splash of artistry in this lively city, brimming with music and culture.*

❼ *Festooned with old-time signs, the street called **Getreidegasse** entices shoppers and photographers.*

THE BEST OF THE BAVARIAN ALPS

This region boasts fairy-tale castles, lovely churches, thrilling luge runs, and cozy villages such as Füssen (a handy home base) and adorable Oberammergau.

Straddling the border with Austria, the towering Zugspitze offers mountain thrills, with high-altitude lifts, trails, and view cafés.

❶ Growing up in **Hohenschwangau Castle** inspired "Mad" King Ludwig to build castles of his own.

❷ The ceiling of the **Wieskirche** opens up to the artist's view of heaven.

❸ Visitors admire **Linderhof Castle**, "Mad" King Ludwig's smallest, most intimate home.

❹ Bavaria's **Lüftlmalarei**—colorful painted scenes on houses—raise the bar for house painters everywhere.

❺ To avoid long lines, order **timed tickets** to tour Neuschwanstein and Hohenschwangau Castles.

❻ Swooping downhill on a **luge:** Wheee!

❼ **Füssen** makes a cozy home base for visiting nearby castles and sights.

❽ The stunning **Neuschwanstein Castle** is King Ludwig's masterpiece and swan song.

THE BEST OF ROTHENBURG AND THE ROMANTIC ROAD

Photogenic Rothenburg, encircled by a medieval wall, has half-timbered buildings and cobbled lanes lined with tempting bakeries, pubs, shops, and museums. It's my favorite stop on the Romantic Road, a scenic route linking cute towns and divinely beautiful churches in the serene, green countryside.

❶ *Vineyards and forests blanket the hill topped by* **Rothenburg,** *Germany's best walled town.*

❷ *Half-timbered buildings, arches, and towers contribute to the* **picturesque charm** *of Rothenburg.*

❸ *Rothenburg's* **main square** *draws locals and tourists alike.*

❹ *In this Middle Ages* **altarpiece,** *the master wood-carver, Tilman Riemenschneider, brought wood to life.*

❺ *Walk the narrow,* **roofed wall** *of Rothenburg early or late for maximum medievalism.*

❻ *If you go for Baroque, visit the gardens of* **Weikersheim Palace,** *along the Romantic Road.*

THE BEST OF THE RHINE VALLEY

The mighty Rhine River is steeped in legend, where storybook villages (including the quaint home-base towns of Bacharach and St. Goar) cluster under imposing castles. Touring the Rhine by boat, train, or bike, you'll pass vineyard-draped hillsides, vintage castles, slow barges, and the massive cliff of the Loreley along the way.

❶ Costumed soldiers evoke **feudal times,** when lords and robber barons vied for control of the Rhine.

❷ The village of **Bacharach,** nestled on the Rhine, is fun to stroll.

❸ Ferries **cruise** up and down the Rhine, taking passengers on a joyride.

❹ Visitors can clamber up and down the ruins of **Rheinfels Castle,** enjoying Rhine views.

❺ **Cologne**'s grand Gothic cathedral is impressive day or night.

❻ The Rhine Valley produces **fine wine,** which can be sampled in tastings at wine bars.

❼ Castles have built-in chapels, ranging from plain stone to decorative, with fine **stained glass.**

❽ **Burg Eltz,** in the Mosel Valley, wins Europe's best-furnished castle award.

THE BEST OF BERLIN

The most happening place in the country—from avant-garde architecture to vibrant nightlife—is Berlin. Germany's capital also features evocative monuments and memories of the Wall that once divided the city and country. The modern dome topping the old Reichstag exemplifies how the city has melded its complicated past with its exciting future.

❶ Along the **Spree River,** crowds come out with the sun.

❷ Dating from 575 BC, the **Ishtar Gate** (detail shown) from Babylon graces the Pergamon Museum.

❸ Sunset highlights the dome topping the **Reichstag,** Germany's historic parliament building.

❹ Berlin's stocky **cathedral** is just over a century old, built under the reign of Kaiser Wilhelm.

❺ The **Brandenburg Gate,** once separating East and West Berlin, is now a powerful symbol of freedom.

❻ Segments of the former **Berlin Wall** are decorated with graffiti.

❼ The lively **Hackescher Markt** neighborhood with its shops and eateries—is fun to explore.

❽ The quirky little **green man** (Ampelmann) on the stoplight is a nostalgic reminder of communism.

THE BEST OF THE REST

With extra time, splice any of these destinations into your trip. **Nürnberg's** Old Town invites browsers while its Nazi sites fascinate historians. Walkable **Würzburg** has a palace fit for a prince-bishop, while **Baden-Baden's** baths are just right for spa lovers. Amid a forest of skyscrapers, **Frankfurt** has a pleasant old-time square and popular riverfront park. **Dresden's** impressive museums and rebuilt church are inspiring. Germany's largest port, **Hamburg,** offers a harbor tour that shows off the city's stunning architecture.

❶ Hamburg, Germany's most important port, has a huge harbor that even landlubbers enjoy touring.

❷ In **Dresden,** a cyclist joins the Parade of Nobles, a mural made with 24,000 porcelain tiles.

❸ In **Baden-Baden,** it's fun to make waves at the Baths of Caracalla.

❹ Nürnberg, largely rebuilt after World War II, has a sweet Old Town and powerful Nazi sites.

❺ Modern **Frankfurt** has skyscraping towers and down-to-earth parks.

❻ A **guard** stands watch in Dresden.

❼ The Residenz Palace is just one reason to visit **Würzburg,** filled with atmospheric wine bars.

TRAVEL SMART

Approach Germany like a veteran traveler, even if it's your first trip. Design your itinerary, get a handle on your budget, make advance arrangements, and follow my travel strategies on the road. For my best advice on sightseeing, accommodations, restaurants, and transportation, see the Practicalities chapter.

Designing Your Itinerary

Decide when to go. Peak season (roughly May-Sept) offers the best weather, long days (light until after 21:00), and the busiest schedule of tourist fun. Late spring and fall generally have decent weather and lighter crowds. Winter can be cold and dreary, but Germany's famous Christmas markets brighten main squares from late November until Christmas.

Choose your top destinations. My itinerary (described later) gives you an idea of how much you can reasonably see in 14 days, but you can adapt it to fit your timeframe and choice of destinations.

Fun-loving Munich is a must for anyone, with its engaging mix of beer gardens and world-class art. If castles spark your imagination, linger in Bavaria and on the Rhine. Historians appreciate Nürnberg, Dresden, and Berlin. For music and Mozart, settle in Salzburg (Austria). If you like medieval walled towns, make tracks for Rothenburg. To feel the pulse of 21st-century Germany, head to Berlin. Hedonists luxuriate in the baths at Baden-Baden. Hikers love to go a'wandering in the Bavarian Alps, and photographers want to go everywhere.

Draft a rough itinerary. Figure out how many destinations you can comfortably fit in your time frame. Don't overdo it—few travelers wish they'd hurried more. Allow enough days per stop: Count on at least two or three days for major destinations (and at least three for sights-packed Berlin).

Staying in a home base (such as Munich) and making day trips can be more time-efficient than changing locations and hotels. Minimize one-night stands, especially consecutive ones; it can be worth taking a late-afternoon train ride or drive to get settled into a town for two nights.

Connect the dots. Link your destinations into a logical route. Determine which cities in Europe you'll fly into and out of; begin your search for transatlantic flights at Kayak.com. If you fly into Frankfurt (a popular arrival point), note that the airport has its own train station to easily get you to your first destination (the Rhine villages are just an hour away).

Decide if you'll travel by car or public transportation, or a combination. Trains connect major cities easily and frequently. Trains in Germany are either fast and pricey (book ahead for discounts, or use a railpass), or they're slow and cheap (even cheaper with one of several day passes). Long-distance buses are inexpensive, though it's wise to book several days in advance.

A car is useless in big cities, but it's helpful for exploring countryside regions, where train and bus connections are relatively infrequent and time-consuming.

For the best of both worlds, use trains to connect major cities, and rent a car strategically (or take a regional bus tour) to explore the countryside, such as the Bavarian Alps region, which has many scattered sights.

Allot sufficient time for transportation in your itinerary. Whether you travel by train, bus, or car, it'll take a half-day to get between most destinations.

To determine approximate transportation times, study driving times (see the map in Practicalities chapter) or train schedules (Germany's Deutsche Bahn, www.bahn.com). If Germany is part of a bigger trip, consider budget flights; check Skyscanner.com for intra-European flights.

Plan your days. Fine-tune your itinerary; write out a day-by-day plan of where you'll be and what you want to see. To

help you make the most of your time, I've suggested day plans for destinations. But check the opening hours of sights; avoid visiting a town on the one day a week that your must-see sight is closed. Research whether any holidays or festivals will fall during your trip—these attract crowds and can close sights (for the latest, visit Germany's national tourism website, www.germany.travel).

Give yourself some slack. Nonstop sightseeing can turn a vacation into a blur. Every trip—and every traveler—needs downtime for doing laundry, picnic shopping, relaxing, people-watching, and so on. Pace yourself. Assume you will return.

Ready, set... You've designed the perfect itinerary for the trip of a lifetime.

Trip Costs per Person

Run a reality check on your dream trip. You'll have major transportation costs in addition to daily expenses.

Flight: Frankfurt has the most convenient, cheapest flights from the US,

though Munich is affordable and a more charming starting point. A basic round-trip flight from the US to Germany can cost about $1,000-$2,000, depending on where you fly from and when (cheaper in winter).

Public Transportation: If you're following my two-week itinerary, allow $350 per person; it'd be worthwhile to buy a German Flexipass with five train days (to use for longer trips between major destinations) and purchase point-to-point tickets for short, cheap, regional trips (e.g., between villages on the Rhine). German

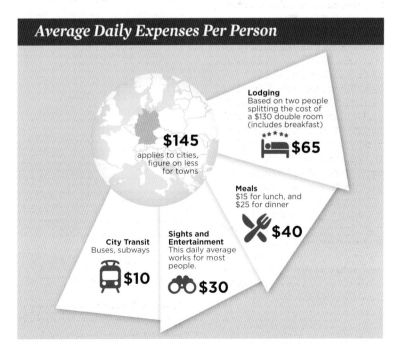

Average Daily Expenses Per Person

$145 applies to cities, figure on less for towns

Lodging Based on two people splitting the cost of a $130 double room (includes breakfast) **$65**

Meals $15 for lunch, and $25 for dinner **$40**

Sights and Entertainment This daily average works for most people. **$30**

City Transit Buses, subways **$10**

THE BEST OF GERMANY IN 2 WEEKS

This unforgettable trip will show you the very best Germany has to offer, with a special guest appearance from Austria.

DAY	PLAN	SLEEP IN
	Arrive in Munich	Munich
1	Sightsee Munich	Munich
2	Munich, half-day trip to Dachau in morning	Munich
3	Munich, late afternoon to Salzburg (1.5 hours by train)	Salzburg
4	Salzburg	Salzburg
5	Leave early for Bavarian Alps (4 hours by train). Visit Neuschwanstein Castle (make reservations for later in the day or tomorrow morning)	Füssen
6	Choose from Bavarian sights (easy by car or bus tour): Wieskirche, Linderhof Castle, Oberammergau, Zugspitze	Füssen
7	Travel to Rothenburg (5 hours by train)	Rothenburg
8	Rothenburg	Rothenburg
9	To Bacharach (4.5 hours by train)	Bacharach
10	Short Rhine cruise to St. Goar, return by train	Bacharach
11	Travel to Berlin (5.5 hours by train)	Berlin
12	Berlin	Berlin
13	Berlin	Berlin
14	Berlin	Berlin
	Fly home	

This trip can work by train or car. Or use trains to connect major cities and rent a car for the countryside. For example, following this itinerary, rent a car in Füssen on the morning of Day 6, explore Bavaria, drive the Romantic Road to Rothenburg, then visit the Rhine (including Burg Eltz); you could drop the car in Frankfurt (or Cologne) on the morning of Day 11, then take the train to Berlin.

Here are other options: You could stay longer in Munich, using it as a home base for day trips to the Bavarian Alps (by bus tour or public transit) and even to Salzburg (by train). Or you could fly into Salzburg, start your trip there, then continue to Munich, the Bavarian Alps, Rothenburg, the Rhine, and Berlin.

Join a walking tour to learn from a local expert.

rail passes are sold at most train stations in Germany.

Car Rental: Allow roughly $250 per week, not including tolls, gas, parking, and insurance. Rentals and leases (an economical way to go if you need a car for at least three weeks) are cheaper if arranged from the US.

Budget Tips: You can cut my suggested average daily expenses by taking advantage of the deals you'll find throughout Germany and mentioned in this book.

City transit passes (for multiple rides or all-day usage) decrease your cost per ride.

If using trains, opt for the cheaper slow trains, and use day passes for further savings (most cost-effective for groups of 2-5).

Avid sightseers buy combo-tickets or passes that cover multiple museums. If a town doesn't offer deals, visit only the sights you most want to see, and seek out free sights and experiences (people-watching counts).

Some businesses—especially hotels and walking-tour companies—offer discounts to my readers (look for the RS% symbol in the listings in this book).

Book your rooms directly with the hotel. Some hotels offer a discount if you pay in cash and/or stay three or more nights (check online or ask). Rooms cost less outside of peak season (May-Sept). And even seniors can sleep cheap in hostels (some have double rooms) for about $30 per person. Or check Airbnb-type sites for deals.

It's easy to eat cheap in Germany. Restaurants offer among the most reasonable prices in Europe. You can get tasty, inexpensive meals at bakeries (many sell sandwiches), department-store cafeterias, and fast-food stands. Cultivate the art of picnicking in atmospheric settings.

When you splurge, choose an experience you'll always remember, such as a concert, spa, or alpine lift. Minimize souvenir shopping; focus instead on collecting wonderful memories.

Before You Go

You'll have a smoother trip if you tackle a few things ahead of time. For more information on these topics, see the Practicalities chapter (and www.ricksteves.com, which has helpful tips and travel talks).

Make sure your passport is valid. If it's due to expire within six months of your ticketed date of return, you need to renew it. Allow up to six weeks to renew or get a passport (www.travel.state.gov).

Arrange your transportation. Book your international flights early. Figure out your main form of transportation within Germany: You can buy train tickets online in advance, get a rail pass, rent a car, or book a cheap flight. (You can wing it once you're there, but it may cost more.)

Book rooms well in advance, especially if your trip falls during peak season or any major holidays or festivals.

Reserve or buy tickets ahead for major sights, saving you from long ticket-buying lines. Reserve ahead for Neuschwanstein Castle. For a Munich BMW factory tour, sign up at least two months in advance. To visit the Reichstag dome in Berlin, reserve a free entry slot online a week or two in advance. To see Dresden's Historic Green Vault, book your tickets online well in advance, or take your chances and line up early for same-day tickets. Tickets for the music-packed Salzburg Festival (mid-July through August) go fast; buy tickets far in advance (on sale in January).

Hire guides in advance. Popular guides can get booked up. If you want a specific guide, reserve by email as far ahead as possible.

Consider travel insurance. Compare the cost of the insurance to the cost of your potential loss. Check whether your existing insurance (health, homeowners, or renters) covers you and your possessions overseas.

Call your bank. Alert your bank that you'll be using your debit and credit cards in Europe. Ask about transaction fees, and get the PIN number for your credit card. You don't need to bring euros for your trip; you'll withdraw euros from cash machines in Europe.

Use your smartphone smartly. Sign up for an international service plan to reduce your costs, or rely on Wi-Fi in Europe instead. Download any apps you'll want on the road, such as maps, translation, transit schedules, and Rick Steves Audio Europe (see sidebar).

Pack light. You'll walk with your luggage more than you think. Bring a single carry-on bag and a daypack. Use the packing checklist in Practicalities as a guide.

Travel Strategies on the Road

If you have a positive attitude, equip yourself with good information (this book), and expect to travel smart, you will.

Read—and reread—this book. To have an "A" trip, be an "A" student. Note opening hours of sights, closed days, crowd-beating tips, and whether reservations are required or advisable. Check the latest at www.ricksteves.com/update.

🎧 Stick This Guidebook in Your Ear!

My free Rick Steves Audio Europe app makes it easy for you to download my audio tours of many of Europe's top attractions and listen to them offline during your travels. For Germany, these include major sights and neighborhoods in Munich, Rothenburg, the Rhine Valley, and Berlin, plus Salzburg in Austria. Sights covered by audio tours are marked in this book with this symbol: 🎧. The app also offers insightful travel interviews from my public radio show with experts from Germany and around the globe. It's all free! You can download the app via Apple's App Store, Google Play, or Amazon's Appstore. For more info, see www.ricksteves.com/audioeurope.

Be your own tour guide. As you travel, get up-to-date info on sights, reserve tickets and tours, reconfirm hotels and travel arrangements, and check transit connections. Upon arrival in a new town, lay the groundwork for a smooth departure; confirm the train, bus, or road you'll take when you leave.

Give local tours a spin. Your appreciation of a city or region and its history can increase dramatically if you take a walking tour in any big city or even hire a private guide. If you want to learn more about any aspect of Germany, you're in the right place with experts happy to teach you.

Outsmart thieves. Pickpockets abound in crowded places where tourists congregate. Treat commotions as smokescreens for theft. Keep your cash, cards, and passport secure in a money belt tucked under your clothes; carry only a day's spending money in your front pocket or wallet. Don't set valuable items down on counters or café tabletops where they can be quickly stolen or easily forgotten.

Minimize potential loss. Keep expensive gear to a minimum. Bring photocopies of important documents (passport and cards) to aid in replacement if they're lost or stolen. Back up photos frequently.

Guard your time and energy. Taking a taxi can be a good value if it saves you a long wait for a cheap bus or an exhausting walk across town. To avoid long lines, follow my crowd-beating tips, such as making advance reservations, or sightseeing early or late.

Be flexible. Even if you have a well-planned itinerary, expect changes, closures, sore feet, bad weather, and so on. Your Plan B could turn out to be even better. And if problems arise, keep things in perspective. You're on vacation in a beautiful country.

Attempt the language. Most Germans—especially in the tourist trade and in cities—speak English, but if you learn some German, even just a few phrases, you'll get more smiles and make more friends. Practice the survival phrases near the end of this book and bring a phrase book.

Connect with the culture. Interacting with locals carbonates your experience. Enjoy the friendliness of the German people. Ask questions; many locals are happy to point you in their idea of the right direction. Set up your own quest for the best beer-and-bratwurst, castle, or cathedral. When an opportunity pops up, say "yes."

Germany...here you come!

Welcome to Rick Steves' Europe

Travel is intensified living—maximum thrills per minute and one of the last great sources of legal adventure. Travel is freedom. It's recess, and we need it.

I discovered a passion for European travel as a teen and have been sharing it ever since—through my tours, public television and radio shows, and travel guidebooks. Over the years, I've taught thousands of travelers how to best enjoy Europe's blockbuster sights—and experience "Back Door" discoveries that most tourists miss.

This book offers a balanced mix of Germany's cities and villages. I've also included Salzburg, just over the border in Austria. The book is selective—rather than covering dozens of castles along the Rhine, I focus on the best: Rheinfels and Marksburg. And it's in-depth: My self-guided museum tours and city walks provide insight into Germany's vibrant history and today's living, breathing culture.

I advocate traveling simply and smartly. Take advantage of my money- and time-saving tips on sightseeing, transportation, and more. Try local, characteristic alternatives to expensive hotels and restaurants. In many ways, spending more money only builds a thicker wall between you and what you traveled so far to see.

We visit Germany to experience it—to become temporary locals. Thoughtful travel engages us with the world, as we learn to appreciate other cultures and new ways to measure quality of life.

Judging from the positive feedback I receive from readers, this book will help you enjoy a fun, affordable, and rewarding vacation—whether it's your first trip or your tenth.

Gute Reise! Happy travels!

Rick Steves

Munich

Munich ("München" in German), often called Germany's most livable city, is also one of its most historic, artistic, and entertaining. Also known as "Germany's biggest village," Munich is big and growing, with a population of 1.5 million.

Until 1871, it was the capital of an independent Bavaria. Its royal palaces, jewels, and grand boulevards remind visitors that Munich has long been a political and cultural powerhouse. Meanwhile, the concentration camp memorial in nearby Dachau reminds us that eight decades ago, Munich provided a springboard for Nazism.

Orient yourself in Munich's old center, with its colorful pedestrian zones. Immerse yourself in the city's art and history—crown jewels, Baroque theater, Wittelsbach palaces, great paintings, and beautiful parks. Spend your Munich evenings in a frothy beer hall or outdoor *Biergarten,* prying big pretzels from buxom, no-nonsense beer maids amid an oompah, bunny-hopping, and belching Bavarian atmosphere.

MUNICH IN 3 DAYS

Day 1: Follow the "Munich City Walk" laid out in this chapter, visiting sights along the way. After lunch, tour the Residenz.

On any evening: Try a beer hall one night and a beer garden on another. Stroll through Marienplatz and the core pedestrian streets. Have a dinner picnic at the English Garden.

Day 2: Visit the Dachau Memorial in the morning. Later, if the weather's fine, rent a bike to enjoy the English Garden. Or tour the top art museum, the Alte Pinakothek.

Day 3: Take your pick of these fine sights: Egyptian Museum, Lenbachhaus (German art), Nazi Documentation Center, Munich City Museum, or—away from the center—the Nymphenburg Palace and BMW-Welt and Museum.

With extra time: Day-trip options include a day-long bus tour to see "Mad" King Ludwig's Castles (covered in the Bavarian Alps chapter) or even a visit to Salzburg, Austria (1.5 hours one-way by fast train).

ORIENTATION

The tourist's Munich is circled by a ring road (site of the old town wall) marked by four old gates: Karlstor (near the main train station—the Hauptbahnhof), Sendlinger Tor, Isartor (near the river), and Odeonsplatz (no surviving gate, near the palace). Marienplatz marks the city's center. A great pedestrian-only zone (Kaufingerstrasse and Neuhauser Strasse) cuts this circle in half, running neatly from the Karlstor and the train station through Marienplatz to the Isartor. Orient yourself along this east-west axis. Most of the sights and hotels I recommend are within a 20-minute walk of Marienplatz and each other.

Tourist Information

Munich has two helpful city-run TIs (www.muenchen.de): in front of the **main train station** (may be closed when you visit while station undergoes renovations; Mon-Sat 9:00-20:00, Sun 10:00-18:00, tel. 089/2339-6500—answered Mon-Fri 9:00-17:00), and on Munich's main square, **Marienplatz,** below the glocken-spiel (Mon-Sat 9:30-19:30, Sun 10:00-18:00; sometimes closed Sun off-season). Pick up the *Discovering Munich* brochure, which describes transportation options, and the free, twice-monthly magazine *In München,* which lists movies and enter-tainment (in German, organized by date).

EurAide Train Assistance: At counter #1 in the train station's main *Reisezen-trum* (travel center, opposite track 21), the eager-to-help EurAide desk is a godsend for Eurailers and budget travelers. EurAide makes reservations and sells tickets and sleepers for the train at the same price you'd pay at the other counters (May-Oct Mon-Fri 8:30-20:00, Sat until 14:00, closed Sun; Nov-April Mon-Fri 10:00-19:00—except Jan-Feb 8:00-13:00, Sat 10:00-12:00, closed Sun; www.euraide.com). A line can form at this popular service; do your home-work and have a list of questions ready.

Rick's Tip: *Supposedly* **"free" walking tours are advertised all over town.** *Tip-ping is expected, and the guides actually have to pay the company for each person who takes the tour—so unless you tip more than they owe the company, they don't make a penny. Expect a sales pitch for the company's other, paid tours.*

Helpful Hints

Museum Tips: Museums closed on Mon-day include the Alte Pinakothek, Egyptian Museum, Lenbachhaus, Munich City Museum, Nazi Documentation Center, and the BMW Museum. The art museums are generally open late one night a week.

Your ticket to the Jewish History Museum, Munich City Museum, Nazi Documentation Center, or Lenbachhaus gets you half-price admission to any of the others up to two days later (e.g., show your €5 Nazi Documentation Center ticket to get €5 off your €10 Lenbachhaus ticket).

Laundry: Waschcenter is a 10-minute walk from the train station (self-service daily 7:00-23:00; drop-off Mon-Fri 7:00-19:00, Sat 9:00-16:00; English instructions; Paul-Heyse-Strasse 21, near intersection with Landwehrstrasse; U-Bahn: There-sienwiese, mobile 0171-734-2094).

Taxi: Call 089/21610 for a taxi.

Private Driver: Reliable **Johann Fay-oumi** speaks English (€70/hour, mobile 0174-183-8473, www.firstclasslimousines.de, johannfayoumi@gmail.com).

TOURS

🎧 To sightsee on your own, download my free **Munich City Walk audio tour** (see sidebar on page 29 for details).

WALKING AND BIKE TOURS

Munich's two largest conventional tour companies, Radius Tours and Munich Walk, run comparable walking and bike tours in Munich, and day trips to Dachau, Neuschwanstein Castle, and other places. Both offer RS% discounts to my read-ers. Just show your book and ask at the time of booking (online reservations not required).

Radius Tours has a convenient office and meeting point in the main train sta-tion, in front of track 32 (tel. 089/543-487-7740, www.radiustours.com). Consider their city walking tour (€15, at 10:15, 2.5 hours), "Birthplace of the Third Reich"

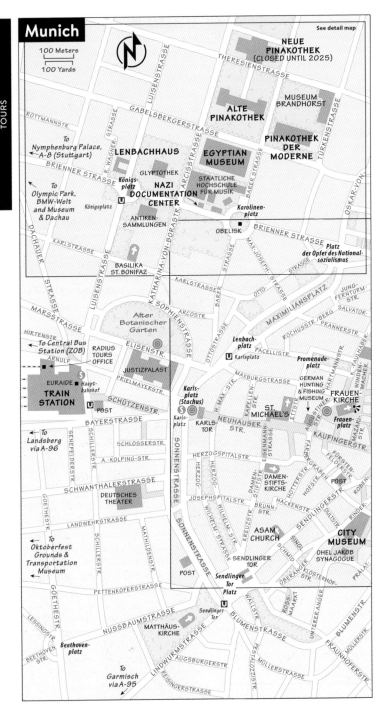

Munich

See detail map

100 Meters
100 Yards

NEUE PINAKOTHEK
(CLOSED UNTIL 2025)

THERESIENSTRASSE

ROTTMANNSTR.

GABELSBERGERSTRASSE

ALTE PINAKOTHEK

MUSEUM BRANDHORST

To Nymphenburg Palace, A-8 (Stuttgart)

LENBACHHAUS

EGYPTIAN MUSEUM

PINAKOTHEK DER MODERNE

BRIENNER STRASSE

GLYPTOTHEK

To Olympic Park, BMW-Welt and Museum & Dachau

Königs- platz

NAZI DOCUMENTATION CENTER

STAATLICHE HOCHSCHULE FÜR MUSIK

Königsplatz

ANTIKEN- SAMMLUNGEN

KARLSTRASSE

Karolinen- platz

OBELISK

BRIENNER STRASSE

Platz der Opfer des National- sozialismus

BASILIKA ST. BONIFAZ

KARLSTRASSE

JUNG- FERNTURM- STR.

MARSSTRASSE

Alter Botanischer Garten

ARCOSTR.

MAXIMILIANSPLATZ

SALVATOR

HIRTENSTR.

To Central Bus Station (ZOB)

RADIUS TOURS OFFICE

ELISENSTR.

Lenbach- platz

PACELLISTR.

Promenade- platz

ARNULF

EURAIDE

Haupt- bahnhof

JUSTIZPALAST

PRIELMAYERSTR.

MAXBURGSTRASSE

GERMAN HUNTING & FISHING MUSEUM

FRAUEN- KIRCHE

TRAIN STATION

Karls- platz (Stachus)

ST. MICHAEL'S

Frauen- platz

POST

SCHÜTZENSTR.

Karls- platz

KARLS- TOR

NEUHAUSER STR.

KAUFINGERSTR.

To Landsberg via A-96

BAYERSTRASSE

SCHLOSSERSTR.

HERZOGSPITALSTR.

FÜRSTEN- FELDERSTR.

POST

A.-KOLPING-STR.

SCHWANTHALERSTRASSE

DAMEN- STIFTS- KIRCHE

ROSEN-

DEUTSCHES THEATER

JOSEPHSPITALSTR.

HACKENSTR.

SENDLINGERSTR.

LANDWEHRSTRASSE

To Oktoberfest Grounds & Transportation Museum

ASAM CHURCH

CITY MUSEUM

PETTENKOFERSTRASSE

SENDLINGER TOR

OHEL JAKOB SYNAGOGUE

POST

Sendlinger Tor Platz

NUSSBAUMSTRASSE

Sendlinger Tor

BLUMENSTRASSE

MATTHÄUS- KIRCHE

Beethoven- platz

To Garmisch via A-95

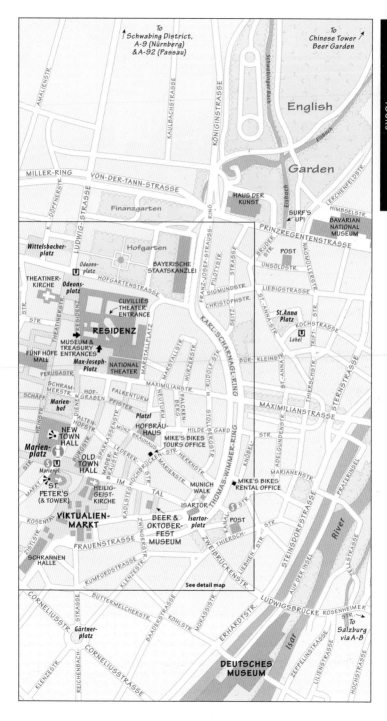

To
↑ Schwabing District,
A-9 (Nürnberg)
& A-92 (Passau)

To ↗
Chinese Tower
Beer Garden

English

Garden

MILLER-RING

VON-DER-TANN-STRASSE

Finanzgarten

HAUS DER
KUNST

SURF'S
↙ UP!

HIMBSELSTR.

BAVARIAN
NATIONAL
MUSEUM

PRINZREGENTENSTRASSE

POST

UNSÖLDSTR.

Wittelsbacher-
platz

Hofgarten

BAYERISCHE
STAATSKANZLEI

LIEBIGSTRASSE

Odeons-
platz

THEATINER-
KIRCHE

Odeons-
platz

HOFGARTENSTRASSE

St.Anna
Platz

KOCHSTRASSE

CUVILLIÉS
THEATER
ENTRANCE

Lehel

RESIDENZ

MUSEUM &
TREASURY
ENTRANCES

FÜNF HÖFE
MALL

Max-Joseph-
Platz

NATIONAL
THEATER

BÜR- KLEINSTR.

PERUSASTR.

SCHRAM-
MERSTR.

HOF-
GRABEN

FALKENTURM

MAXIMILIANSTR.

SCHAFF

Marien-
hof

FALKEN-
BERG

MAXIMILIANSTRASSE

Platzl

NEW
TOWN
HALL

HOFBRÄU-
HAUS

MIKE'S BIKES
TOURS OFFICE

Marien-
platz

OLD
TOWN
HALL

HILDE-GARD

MARIANENSTR.

Marienpl.

MUNICH
WALK

MIKE'S BIKES
RENTAL OFFICE

ST.
PETER'S
(& TOWER)

HEILIG-
GEIST-
KIRCHE

TAL

ISARTOR

VIKTUALIEN-
MARKT

BEER &
OKTOBER-
FEST
MUSEUM

Isartor-
platz

POST

SCHRANNEN-
HALLE

FRAUENSTRASSE

See detail map

River

CORNELIUSSTR.

BUTTERMELCHERSTR.

Gärtner-
platz

LUDWIGSBRÜCKE

ROSENHEIMER
STR.

To ↘
Salzburg
via A-8

CORNELIUSSTRASSE

ERHARDTSTR.

Isar

DEUTSCHES
MUSEUM

MUNICH AT A GLANCE

In the Center

▲▲**Marienplatz** Munich's main square, at the heart of a lively pedestrian zone, watched over by New Town Hall (and its glockenspiel show). **Hours:** Glockenspiel jousts daily at 11:00 and 12:00, plus 17:00 March-Oct; New Town Hall tower elevator runs daily 10:00-19:00; Oct-April Mon-Fri 10:00-17:00, closed Sat-Sun. See page 41.

▲▲**Viktualienmarkt** Munich's "small-town" open-air market, perfect for a quick snack or meal. **Hours:** Market closed Sun; beer garden open daily 10:00-22:00 (weather permitting). See page 46.

▲▲**Hofbräuhaus** World-famous beer hall, worth a visit even if you're not chugging. **Hours:** Daily 9:00-23:30. See page 53.

▲▲**The Residenz** Elegant palace awash in Bavarian opulence. Complex includes the Residenz Museum (lavish apartments), Residenz Treasury (Wittelsbach family crowns and royal knickknacks), and the impressive, heavily restored Cuvilliés Theater. **Hours:** Museum and treasury—daily 9:00-18:00, mid-Oct-mid-March 10:00-17:00; theater—generally Mon-Sat 14:00-18:00, Sun from 9:00, longer hours Aug-mid-Sept. See page 57.

▲▲**Alte Pinakothek** Bavaria's best painting gallery, with a wonderful collection of European masters from the 14th through the 19th century. **Hours:** Wed-Sun 10:00-18:00, Tue until 20:00, closed Mon. See page 66.

▲▲**Egyptian Museum** Easy-to-enjoy collection of ancient Egyptian treasures. **Hours:** Wed-Sun 10:00-18:00, Tue until 20:00, closed Mon. See page 69.

▲▲**Lenbachhaus** Three stages of German art: 19th-century, Blue Rider, and post-WWI—most important for its Blue Rider collection. **Hours:** Wed-Sun 10:00-18:00, Tue until 20:00, closed Mon. See page 69.

▲▲**Nazi Documentation Center** Thoughtful look at Munich's role in the rise of Nazism. **Hours:** Tue-Sun 10:00-19:00, closed Mon. See page 71.

▲**Munich City Museum** The city's history in five floors. **Hours:** Tue-Sun 10:00-18:00, closed Mon. See page 64.

▲**Asam Church** Asam brothers' private church, dripping with Baroque. **Hours:** Sat-Thu 9:00-18:00, Fri from 13:00. See page 49.

▲**English Garden** The largest city park on the Continent, packed with locals, tourists, surfers, and nude sunbathers. (On a bike, I'd rate this ▲▲.) See page 71.

▲**Deutsches Museum** Germany's version of our Smithsonian Institution, with 10 miles of science and technology exhibits (main branch). **Hours:** Daily 9:00-17:00. See page 72.

Outside the City Center

▲▲▲**Dachau Concentration Camp Memorial** Notorious Nazi camp, now a powerful museum and memorial. **Hours:** Daily 9:00-17:00. See page 98.

▲▲**Nymphenburg Palace** Impressive summer palace, featuring a hunting lodge, coach museum, fine royal porcelain collection, and vast park. **Hours:** Park—daily 6:00-dusk; palace buildings—daily April-mid-Oct 9:00-18:00, mid-Oct-March 10:00-16:00. See page 73.

▲**BMW-Welt and Museum** The carmaker's futuristic museum and floating-cloud showroom, highlighting BMW past, present, and future. **Hours:** BMW-Welt showroom exhibits—daily 9:00-18:00; museum—Tue-Sun 10:00-18:00, closed Mon. See page 79.

tour (€17.50, April-mid-Oct daily at 15:00, off-season daily at 11:30; 2.5 hours), "Bavarian Beer and Food" tour (€36; April-mid-Oct Mon-Sat 18:00, off-season Tue, Thu, and Sat at 18:00; 3.5 hours), or 3-hour bike tour (€29.50, April-mid-Oct daily at 10:00).

Munich Walk uses Marienplatz as its meeting point (tel. 089/2423-1767, www.munichwalktours.de). Check out their city walking tour (€14, year-round at 10:45, May-Oct also daily at 14:45, 2 hours), "Third Reich in Munich" tour (€16, daily year-round at 10:15, 2.5 hours), "Beer and Brewery" tour (€30, May-mid-Sept Mon, Wed, and Fri-Sat at 18:15, less frequent off-season, 3.5 hours), or 3.5-hour bike tour (€25, daily 10:45, no tours Nov-March).

HOP-ON, HOP-OFF BUS TOUR

Gray Line Tours has hop-on, hop-off bus tours that leave from in front of the Karstadt department store at Bahnhofplatz, directly across from the train station. Choose from a basic, one-hour "Express Circle" that heads past the Pinakotheks, Marienplatz, and Karlsplatz; or the more extensive "Grand Circle" that lasts 2.5 hours and also includes Nymphenburg Palace and BMW-Welt and Museum—a very efficient way to visit these two sights (both tours depart 3/hour, 9:40-18:00). Just show up and pay the driver (€17 Express tour—valid 24 hours, €22/€27 Grand tour—valid 24/48 hours, daily in season, tel. 089/5490-7560, www.stadtrundfahrten-muenchen.de).

Rick's Tip: *If you're interested in a* Gray Line bus tour *of the city or to nearby castles, such as Neuschwanstein,* get discounted tickets at EurAide *(cash only). They also sell* Munich Walk *tour tickets.*

LOCAL GUIDES

I've had great days with two good guides: Georg Reichlmayr, who has helped me generously with this chapter (€200/3

hours, mobile 0170-341-6384, www.muenchen-stadtfuehrung.de, and Birgit Stempfle (€180/3 hours, mobile 0171-718-1465, www.sightseeing-munich.de).

TOURS TO NEUSCHWANSTEIN

While you can do many day trips from Munich on your own by train, going as part of an organized group can be convenient. Gray Line Tours offers rushed all-day bus tours of Neuschwanstein that also include Ludwig's Linderhof Castle and 30 minutes in Oberammergau (€54, does not include castle admissions, RS% at EurAide, daily, www.stadtrundfahrten-muenchen.de). Radius Tours runs all-day tours to Neuschwanstein using public transportation (€49, €42 with rail pass, RS%—use "student rate" when you book online, does not include castle admission; daily April-Dec, Jan-March tours run Mon, Wed, and Fri-Sun; reserve ahead online, www.radiustours.com). Of these options, I prefer the guided private bus tours because you're guaranteed a seat (public transport to Neuschwanstein is routinely standing-room only in summer).

MUNICH CITY WALK

Munich is big and modern, but, with its pedestrian-friendly historic core, it feels a lot like an easygoing Bavarian town. On this self-guided walk, rated ▲▲▲, we'll start in the central square, see its famous glockenspiel, stroll through a thriving open-air market, and visit historic churches with lavish Baroque decor. We'll sample edibles at a venerable gourmet deli and take a spin through the world's most famous beer hall.

Length of This Tour: Allow two to three hours for this walk through a thousand years of Munich's history. Allow extra time if you want to tour the museums along the way—details in "Sights," later.

🎧 Download my free Munich City Walk audio tour.

⦿ Self-Guided Walk
• *Begin at the heart of the old city, with a stroll through...*

❶ *Marienplatz*

Riding the escalator out of the subway into sunlit Marienplatz (mah-REE-en-platz, "Mary's Square," rated ▲▲) gives you a fine first look at the glory of Munich: great buildings, outdoor cafés, and people bustling and lingering like the birds and breeze with which they share this square.

The square is both old and new: For a thousand years, it's been the center of Munich. It was the town's marketplace and public forum, standing at a crossroads along the Salt Road, which ran between Salzburg and Augsburg.

Lining one entire side of the square is the impressive facade of the **New Town Hall** (Neues Rathaus), with its soaring 280-foot spire. The structure looks medieval, but it was actually built in the late 1800s (1867-1908). The style is "Neo"-Gothic—pointed arches over the doorways and a roofline bristling with prickly spires. The 40 statues look like medieval saints, but they're from around 1900, depicting more recent Bavarian kings and nobles. This medieval style was all the rage in the 19th century as Germans were rediscovering their historical roots and uniting as a modern nation.

The New Town Hall is famous for its **glockenspiel.** A carillon in the tower chimes a tune while colorful figurines come out on the balcony to spin and dance. It happens daily at 11:00 and 12:00 all year (also at 17:00 March-Oct) and lasts about 10 minutes. The *Spiel* of the glockenspiel tells the story of a noble wedding that took place on the market square in 1568. You see the wedding procession and the friendly joust of knights on horseback. The duke and his bride watch the action as the groom's Bavarian family (in Bavarian white and blue) joyfully jousts with the bride's French family (in red and white). Below, the barrel makers—famous for being the first to dance in the streets after a deadly plague lifted—do their popular jig. Finally, the solitary cock crows.

At the very top of the New Town Hall is a statue of a child with outstretched arms, dressed in monk's garb and holding a book in its left hand. This is the **Münchner Kindl,** the symbol of Munich. The town got its name from the people who

New Town Hall

Glockenspiel

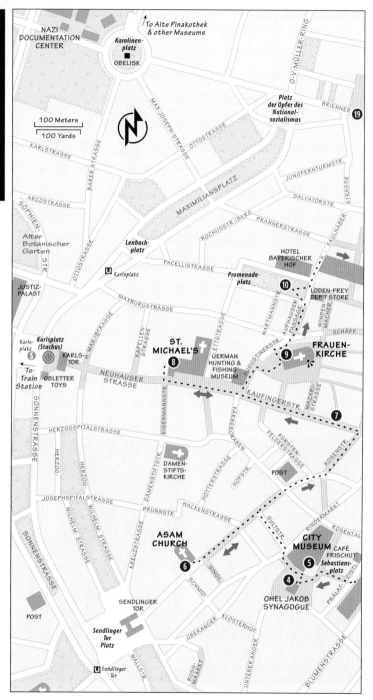

NAZI
DOCUMENTATION
CENTER

To Alte Pinakothek
& other Museums

Karolinen-
platz
OBELISK

O-V-MÜLLER-RING

Platz
der Opfer des
National-
sozialismus

BRIENNER

19

MAX-JOSEPH-STRASSE

OTTOSTRASSE

100 Meters
100 Yards

N

KARLSTRASSE

JUNGFERNTURMSTR.

BARER STRASSE

MAXIMILIANSPLATZ

SALVATORSTR.

STRASSE

ARCOSTRASSE

ROCHUSSTR./BERG

PRANNERSTRASSE

K. FAULHABER

SOPHIEN-
STR.

Alter
Botanischer
Garten

OTTOSTRASSE

Lenbach-
platz

PACELLISTRASSE

HOTEL
BAYERISCHER
HOF

U Karlsplatz

Promenade-
platz

10

LODEN-FREY
DEP'T STORE

WINDEN
MACHER

JUSTIZ-
PALAST

MAXBURGSTRASSE

HARTMANNSTR.

AUFHAUSER
PASSAGE

SCHÄFF

Karls-
platz

Karlsplatz
(Stachus)

S

To
Train
Station

KARLS-
TOR

OBLETTER
TOYS

H. MAX-STRASSE

KAPELLEN-
STRASSE

ST.
MICHAEL'S

8

AUGUSTINERSTR.

9

FRAUEN-
KIRCHE

NEUHAUSER
STRASSE

GERMAN
HUNTING &
FISHING
MUSEUM

EISENMANNSTR.

KAUFINGERSTR.

MAZARI-
STRASSE

7

SONNENSTRASSE

HERZOGSPITALSTRASSE

FÄRBERGRABEN

FÜRSTEN-
FELDERSTRASSE

ROSENSTR.

HERZOG-

DAMEN-
STIFTS-
KIRCHE

HOTTERSTRASSE

HOFSTR.

POST

JOSEPHSPITALSTRASSE

DAMENSTIFTSTR.

BRUNNSTR.

HACKENSTRASSE

WILHELM-STRASSE

KREUZSTRASSE

DULTSTR.

RINDERMARKT

ROSENTAL

SONNENSTRASSE

ASAM
CHURCH

6

SINGL.

CITY
MUSEUM

5

CAFÉ
FRISCHUT
Sebastians-
platz

4

PRÄLAT-ZISTL.

POST

SENDLINGER
TOR

SCHMID

OHEL JAKOB
SYNAGOGUE

Sendlinger
Tor
Platz

OBERANGER

KLOSTERHOF

UNTERANGER

BLUMENSTRASSE

U Sendlinger
Tor

ROSS-
MARKT

WÄLLSTR.

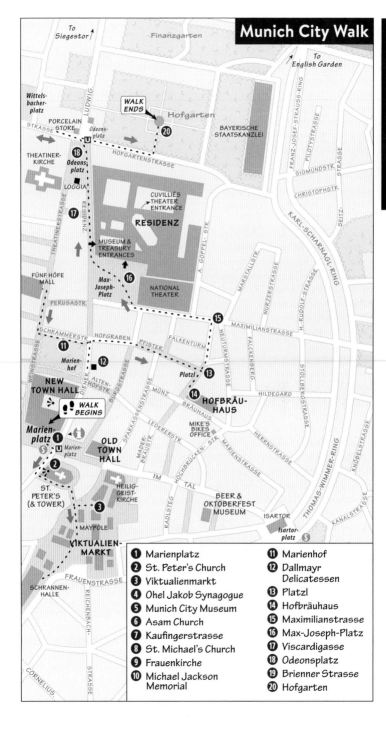

43

Munich City Walk

To Siegestor

Finanzgarten

To English Garden

Wittels-bacher-platz

WALK ENDS

Hofgarten

20

BAYERISCHE STAATSKANZLEI

PORCELAIN STORE

STRASSE

Odeons-platz

HOFGARTENSTRASSE

18

THEATINER-KIRCHE

Odeons-platz

LOGGIA

CUVILLIÉS THEATER ENTRANCE

RESIDENZ

17

MUSEUM & TREASURY ENTRANCES

FÜNF HÖFE MALL

16

Max-Joseph-Platz

NATIONAL THEATER

PERUSASTR.

SCHRAMMERSTR.

HOFGRABEN

PFISTER

FALKENTURM

15

MAXIMILIANSTRASSE

11

Marien-hof

12

Platzl

13

NEW TOWN HALL

WALK BEGINS

14

HOFBRÄU-HAUS

Marien-platz

1

Marien-platz

OLD TOWN HALL

MIKE'S BIKES OFFICE

2

ST. PETER'S (& TOWER)

HEILIG-GEIST-KIRCHE

3

IM TAL

BEER & OKTOBERFEST MUSEUM

MAYPOLE

Isartor-platz

VIKTUALIEN-MARKT

FRAUENSTRASSE

SCHRANNEN-HALLE

STRASSE

CORNELIUS-

1 Marienplatz
2 St. Peter's Church
3 Viktualienmarkt
4 Ohel Jakob Synagogue
5 Munich City Museum
6 Asam Church
7 Kaufingerstrasse
8 St. Michael's Church
9 Frauenkirche
10 Michael Jackson Memorial

11 Marienhof
12 Dallmayr Delicatessen
13 Platzl
14 Hofbräuhaus
15 Maximilianstrasse
16 Max-Joseph-Platz
17 Viscardigasse
18 Odeonsplatz
19 Brienner Strasse
20 Hofgarten

MUNICH
MUNICH CITY WALK

first settled here: the monks (Mönchen). You'll spot this mini monk all over town, on everything from the city's coat of arms to souvenir shot glasses to ad campaigns (often holding not a book, but maybe a beer or a smartphone). The city symbol was originally depicted as a grown man, wearing a gold-lined black cloak and red shoes. By the 19th century, artists were representing him as a young boy, then a gender-neutral child, and, more recently, a young girl. These days, a teenage girl dressed as the Kindl kicks off the annual Oktoberfest by leading the opening parade on horseback, and then serves as the mascot throughout the festivities.

New Town Hall Tower Views: Take an elevator to the fourth floor (where you buy your ticket), then ride another elevator to the top of the New Town Hall tower for a commanding city view (€3, elevator located under glockenspiel; daily 10:00-19:00; Oct-April Mon-Fri 10:00-17:00, closed Sat-Sun).

The **golden statue** at the top of the column in the center of Marienplatz honors the square's namesake, the Virgin Mary. Sculpted in 1590, it was a rallying point in the religious wars of the Reformation. Back then, Munich was a bastion of southern-German Catholicism against the heresies of Martin Luther to the north. Notice how, at the four corners of the statue, cherubs fight the four great biblical enemies of civilization: the dragon of war, the lion of hunger, the rooster-headed monster of plague and disease, and the serpent. The serpent represents heresy—namely, Protestants. Bavaria is still Catholic country, and Protestants weren't allowed to worship openly here until about 1800.

To the right of the New Town Hall, the gray pointy building with the green spires is the **Old Town Hall** (Altes Rathaus). On its adjoining bell tower, find the city seal. It has the Münchner Kindl (symbolizing the first monks), a castle (representing the first fortifications), and a lion (represent-

ing the first ruler—Henry the Lion, who built them).

As you look around, keep in mind that the Allies bombed Marienplatz and much of Munich during World War II. Most of the buildings had to be rebuilt. The Old Town Hall looks newer now because it was destroyed by bombs and rebuilt after the war. The New Town Hall survived the bombs, and it served as the US military headquarters after the Americans occupied Munich in 1945.

Orientation Spin: Back on the ground, face the New Town Hall one more time and get oriented. Straight ahead is north. To the left is the pedestrian shopping street called Kaufingerstrasse, which leads to the old gate called Karlstor and the train station. To the right, the street leads to the Isartor gate and the Deutsches Museum. This east-west axis cuts through the historic core of Munich.

• *Turn around and notice the small street to the left leading a short block to St. Peter's Church, with its steeple poking up above a row of buildings.*

❷ St. Peter's Church

The oldest church in town, St. Peter's stands on the hill where Munich's original monks probably settled—perhaps as far back as the ninth century (though the city marks its official birthday as 1158). Today's church (from 1368) replaced the original monastery church.

St. Peter's ("Old Peter" to locals) is part of the soul of the city. There's even a popular song about it that goes, "Munich is not Munich without St. Peter's."

Cost and Hours: Church-free, tower climb-€3, Mon-Fri 9:00-18:30, Sat-Sun from 10:00.

Visiting the Church: On the outside of the church, notice the 16th- and 17th-century tombstones plastered onto the wall. Originally, people were buried in the holy ground around the church. But in the Napoleonic age, the cemeteries were dug up and relocated outside the city walls for

Old Town Hall

Climb the tower of St. Peter's Church for great views.

hygienic and space reasons. They kept a few tombstones here as a reminder.

Step inside. (If there's a Mass in progress, visitors are welcome, but stay in the back. If there's no Mass, feel free to explore.) Typical of so many Bavarian churches, it's whitewashed and light-filled, with highlights in pastel pinks and blues framed by gold curlicues. The ceiling painting opens up to the heavens, where Peter is crucified upside down.

Photos (on a pillar near the entrance) show how St. Peter's was badly damaged in World War II—the roof caved in, and the tower was demolished during an air raid. But the beloved church was rebuilt and restored, thanks to donations—half from the Augustiner brewery, the rest from private donors. (The accuracy of the restoration was possible thanks to Nazi catalog photos.) For decades after World War II, the bells played a popular tune that stopped just before the last note, reminding locals that the church still needed money to rebuild.

Explore further. The nave is lined with bronze statues of the apostles, and the altar shows a statue of St. Peter being adored by four Church fathers. The finely crafted, gray iron fences that line the nave were donated after World War II by the local blacksmiths of the national railway. The precious and fragile sandstone Gothic chapel altar (to the left of the main altar) survived the war only because it was buried in sandbags.

Find the second chapel from the back on the left side. Now there's something you don't see every day: a skeleton in a box. As the red Latin inscription says, this is St. Munditia. In the fourth century, she was beheaded by the Romans for her Christian faith. Munich has more relics of saints than any city outside Rome. That's because it was the pope's Catholic bastion against the rising tide of Protestantism in northern Europe during the Reformation. In 1675, St. Munditia's remains were given to Munich by the pope as thanks for the city's devoted service. It was also a vivid reminder to the faithful that those who die for the cause of the Roman Church go directly to heaven without waiting for Judgment Day.

The History of Munich

Born from Salt and Beer (1100-1500): Munich began in the 12th century, when Henry the Lion (Heinrich der Löwe) established a lucrative salt trade near a monastery of monks—München. After Henry's death, an ambitious merchant family, the Wittelsbachs, took over. By the 1400s, Munich's maypole-studded market bustled with trade in salt and beer, the twin-domed Frauenkirche drew pilgrims, and the Wittelsbachs made their home in the Residenz. When the various regions of Bavaria united in 1506, Munich (pop. 14,000) was the natural capital.

Religious Wars, Plagues, Decline (1500-1800): While Martin Luther and the Protestant Reformation raged in northern Germany, Munich became the ultra-Catholic heart of the Counter-Reformation, decorated in the ornate Baroque and Rococo style of its Italian Catholic allies. The religious wars and periodic plagues left the city weakened. While the rest of Europe modernized, Munich remained behind the times.

The Golden Age of Kings (1806-1886): When Napoleon invaded, the Wittelsbach dukes surrendered and were rewarded with a grander title: King of Bavaria. Munich boomed. **Maximilian I** (r. 1806-1825), a.k.a. Max Joseph, rebuilt in Neoclassical style—grand columned buildings connected by broad boulevards. **Ludwig I** (r. 1825-1848) turned Munich into a modern railroad hub, budding industrial city. His son **Maximilian II** (r. 1848-1864) continued Ludwig's modernization program. In 1864, 18-year-old **Ludwig II** (r. 1864-1886) became king. Ludwig didn't much like Munich, preferring to build castles in the Bavarian countryside.

• Leave St. Peter's out the door opposite the one you entered. Then, head to the right to the tower entrance. It's a long climb to the top of the **tower** (306 steps, no elevator)—but the view is dynamite. Try to be two flights from the top when the bells ring at the top of the hour. When your friends back home ask you about your trip, you'll say, "What?" Afterward, head downhill to join the busy commotion of the...

❸ Viktualienmarkt

The market (rated ▲▲, closed Sun) is a lively world of produce stands and budget eateries. Browse your way through the stalls and pavilions, as you make your way to the market's main landmark, the blue-and-white striped maypole. Early in

Viktualienmarkt

End of the Wittelsbachs (1886-1918): When Bavaria became part of the newly united Germany, Berlin overtook Munich as Germany's power center. Then World War I devastated Munich. After the war, mobs of poor, angry Münchners roamed the streets. In 1918, they drove the last Bavarian king out, ending 700 years of Wittelsbach rule.

Nazis, World War II, and Munich Bombed (1918-1945): In the power vacuum, a fringe group emerged—the Nazi party, headed by Adolf Hitler. Hitler rallied the Nazis in a Munich beer hall, leading a failed coup d'état known as the Beer Hall Putsch (1923). When the Nazis eventually took power in Berlin, they remembered their roots, dubbing Munich "Capital of the Movement." In World War II, nearly half the city was leveled by Allied air raids.

Munich Rebuilds (1945-Present): After the war, with generous American aid, Münchners rebuilt. Nazi authorities had created a photo archive of historic sights, which now came in handy. Munich chose to preserve the low-rise, medieval feel, but with a modern infrastructure. For the 1972 Olympic Games, they built a futuristic stadium, a sleek new subway system, and one of Europe's first pedestrian-only zones—Kaufingerstrasse. In 1990, when Germany reunited, Berlin once again became the country's focal point, relegating Munich to the role of sleepy Second City.

These days, Munich seems to be comfortable just being itself rather than trying to keep up with Berlin. Though rich and modern—home to BMW and Siemens, and a producer of software, books, movies, and the latest fashions—it remains safe, clean, and cultured. It's a university town, built on a human scale, and close to the beauties of nature.

the morning, you can still feel small-town Munich here. Remember, Munich has been a market town since its earliest days as a stop on the salt-trade crossroads. By the 1400s, the market bustled, most likely beneath a traditional maypole, just like you see today.

Besides salt, Munich gained a reputation for beer. By the 15th century, more than 30 breweries pumped out the golden liquid, brewed by monks, who were licensed to sell it. They stored their beer in cellars under courtyards kept cool by the shade of bushy chestnut trees—a tradition Munich's breweries still follow.

The market's centerpiece seems to be its **beer garden** (daily 10:00-22:00, weather permitting). Its picnic tables are filled with hungry and thirsty locals, all in the shade of the traditional chestnut trees. Shoppers often pause here for a late-morning snack of *Weisswurst*—white sausage—served with mustard, a pretzel, and a beer. Here, you can order just a half-liter—unlike some other beer gardens that only sell by the full liter. This is handy for shoppers who want just a quick sip. As is the tradition at all the city's beer gardens, some tables—those without tablecloths—are set aside for patrons who bring their own food; they're welcome here as long as they buy a drink. The Viktualienmarkt is ideal for a light meal (see page 88).

Now make your way to the towering **maypole.** Throughout Bavaria, colorfully

Viktualienmarkt's maypole

ornamented maypoles decorate town squares. Many are painted, like this one, in Bavaria's colors, white and blue. The decorations are festively replaced every year on the first of May. Traditionally, rival communities try to steal each other's maypole. Locals guard their new pole day and night as May Day approaches. Stolen poles are ransomed only with lots of beer for the clever thieves.

The decorations that line each side of the pole explain which merchants are doing business in the market. Munich's maypole gives prominence (on the bottom level) to a horse-drawn wagon bringing in beer barrels. And you can't have a kegger without coopers—find the merry barrel makers, the four cute guys dancing. Today, traditional barrel making is enjoying a comeback as top breweries like to have real wooden kegs.

The bottom of the pole celebrates the world's oldest food law. The German Beer Purity Law (*Reinheitsgebot*) of 1487 actually originated here in Munich. It stipulated that beer could consist only of three ingredients: barley, hops, and water. (Later they realized that a fourth ingredient, yeast, is always present in fermentation.) Why was beer so treasured? Back in the Middle Ages, it was considered liquid food.

From the maypole, take in the bustling scene around you. The market was modernized in the 1800s as the city grew. Old buildings were torn down, replaced with stalls and modern market halls. Now, in the 21st century, this traditional market (sitting on the city's most expensive real estate) survives thanks to a ban on fast-food chains and city laws that favor small-time merchants with low taxes. This keeps the market classy and authentic.

• *At the far end of the Viktualienmarkt, spot* **Café Frischhut** *with its colorful old-time sign hanging out front (at Prälat-Zistl-Strasse 8). This is Munich's favorite place to stop for a fresh* Schmalznudel—*a traditional fried-dough treat (best enjoyed warm, with a sprinkling of sugar).*

Continue straight to a modern glass-and-iron building.

The **Schrannenhalle,** an 1800s grain exchange, has been renovated into a high-end paradise for foodies, especially those seeking Italian edibles. Stroll through Eataly, past enticing bottles of olive oil. Pause to watch bakers tending to the day's bread, and make your way to the far end, where wine connoisseurs could detour downstairs for a vast wine collection (and a WC).

• *When you're ready to move on, exit the Schrannenhalle midway down on the right-hand side. You'll spill out into* **Sebastiansplatz,** *a small square lined with healthy eateries. Continue through Sebastiansplatz and veer left, where you'll see a cube-shaped building, the...*

❹ Ohel Jakob Synagogue

This modern synagogue anchors a revitalized Jewish quarter. In the 1930s, about 10,000 Jews lived in Munich, and the main synagogue stood near here. Then, in 1938,

Ohel Jakob Synagogue

Hitler demanded that the synagogue be torn down. By the end of World War II, Munich's Jewish community was gone. But thanks to Germany's acceptance of religious refugees from former Soviet states, the Jewish population has now reached its prewar size. The new synagogue was built in 2006. There's also a kindergarten and day school, playground, fine kosher restaurant (at #18), and bookstore. Notice the low-key but efficient security.

While the synagogue is shut tight to nonworshippers, its architecture is striking from the outside. Lower stones of travertine evoke the Wailing Wall in Jerusalem, while an upper section represents the tent that held important religious wares during the 40 years of wandering through the desert. The synagogue's door features the first 10 letters of the Hebrew alphabet, symbolizing the Ten Commandments.

The cube-shaped **Jewish History Museum** (behind the cube-shaped synagogue) is stark and windowless. While the museum's small permanent collection is disappointing, good temporary exhibits might justify the entry fee (€6; ticket gets you half-price admission to Munich City Museum, Nazi Documentation Center, and Lenbachhaus; Tue-Sun 10:00-18:00, closed Mon, St.-Jakobs-Platz 16, tel. 089/2339-6096, www.juedisches-museum-muenchen.de).

• *Facing the synagogue, on the same square, is the...*

❺ Munich City Museum (Münchner Stadtmuseum)

The highs and lows of Munich's history are covered in this surprisingly honest municipal museum (rated ▲). It covers the cultural upheavals of the early 1900s, Munich's role as the birthplace of the Nazis, and the city's renaissance during Germany's postwar "economic miracle." There's scant information posted in English, but an included audioguide can fill in the gaps.

• *You can stop and tour the museum now (see page 64). Otherwise, continue through the synagogue's square, past the fountain, across the street, and one block farther to the pedestrianized Sendlinger Strasse. Take a left and walk 100 yards until you see a fancy facade on your right (at #32), which marks the...*

❻ Asam Church (Asamkirche)

This tiny church (rated ▲) is a slice of heaven on earth—a gooey, drippy Baroque-concentrate masterpiece by Bavaria's top two Rococonuts, the Asam brothers. Just 30 feet wide, it was built in 1740 to fit within this row of homes. Originally, it was a private chapel where these two brother-architects could show off their work (on their own land, next to their home and business headquarters, to the left), but it's now a public place of worship.

Cost and Hours: Free, Sat-Thu 9:00-18:00, Fri from 13:00, tel. 089/2368-7989. The church is small, so visitors are asked not to enter during Mass.

Visiting the Church: This place of worship served as a promotional brochure to woo clients, and is packed with every architectural trick in the book. Imagine approaching the church not as a worshipper, but as a shopper representing your church's building committee. First stand outside: Hmmm, the look of those foundation stones really packs a punch. And the legs hanging over the portico... nice effect. Those starbursts on the door would be a hit back home, too.

Asam Church

Then step inside: I'll take a set of those over-the-top golden capitals, please. We'd also like to order the gilded garlands draping the church in jubilation, and the twin cupids capping the confessional. And how about some fancy stucco work, too? (Molded-and-painted plaster was clearly an Asam brothers specialty.) Check out the illusion of a dome painted on the flat ceiling—that'll save us lots of money. The yellow glass above the altar has the effect of the thin-sliced alabaster at St. Peter's in Rome, but it's within our budget! And, tapping the "marble" pilasters to determine that they are just painted fakes, we decide to take that, too. Crammed between two buildings, light inside this narrow church is limited, so there's a big, clear window in the back for maximum illumination—we'll order one to cut back on our electricity bill.

On the way out, say goodbye to the gilded grim reaper in the narthex (left side as you're leaving) as he cuts the thread of life—reminding all who visit of our mortality...and, by the way, that shrouds have no pockets.

• *Leaving the church, look to your right, noticing the Sendlinger Tor at the end of the street—part of the fortified town wall that circled Munich in the 14th century. Then turn left and walk straight up Sendlinger Strasse. Walk toward the Münchner Kindl, still capping the spire of the New Town Hall in the distance, and then up (pedestrian-only) Rosenstrasse, until you hit Marienplatz and the big, busy...*

❼ Kaufingerstrasse

This car-free street leads you through a great shopping district, past cheap department stores, carnivals of street entertainers, and good old-fashioned slicers and dicers. As far back as the 12th century, this was the town's main commercial street. Traders from Salzburg and Augsburg would enter the town through the fortified Karlstor. This street led past the Augustiner beer hall (opposite St. Michael's Church to this day), right to the main square and cathedral.

Up until the 1970s, the street was jammed with car traffic. Then, for the 1972 Olympics, it was turned into one of Europe's first pedestrian zones. At first, shopkeepers were afraid that would ruin business. Now it's Munich's living room. Nearly 9,000 shoppers pass through it each hour. Merchants nearby are begging for their streets to become traffic-free, too.

The 1972 Olympics transformed this part of Munich—the whole area around Marienplatz was pedestrianized and the transit system expanded. Since then, Munich has become one of the globe's greenest cities. Skyscrapers have been banished to the suburbs, and the nearby Frauenkirche is still the tallest building in the center.

• *Stroll a few blocks away from Marienplatz toward the Karlstor, until you arrive at the imposing church on the right.*

❽ St. Michael's Church (Michaelskirche)

This is one of the first great Renaissance buildings north of the Alps. The ornate facade, with its sloped roofline, was inspired by the Gesù Church in Rome—

St. Michael's Church

home of the Jesuit order. Jesuits saw themselves as the intellectual defenders of Catholicism. St. Michael's was built in the late 1500s—at the height of the Protestant Reformation—to serve as the northern outpost of the Jesuits. Appropriately, the facade features a statue of Michael fighting a Protestant demon.

Cost and Hours: Church-free, generally daily 8:00-19:00, until later on Sun and summer evenings; crypt-€2, Mon-Fri 9:30-16:30, Sat until 14:30, closed Sun; frequent concerts—check schedule posted outside; tel. 089/231-7060.

Visiting the Church: Inside, admire the ornate Baroque interior, topped with a barrel vault, the largest of its day. Stroll up the nave to the ornate pulpit, where Jesuit priests would hammer away at Reformation heresy. The church's acoustics are spectacular, and the choir—famous in Munich—sounds heavenly singing from the organ loft high in the rear.

The **crypt** (*Fürstengruft*, down the stairs to the right by the altar) contains 40 stark, somewhat forlorn tombs of Bavaria's ruling family, the Wittelsbachs.

The most ornate tomb (center of back wall, facing altar) holds the illustrious Ludwig II, known for his fairy-tale castle at Neuschwanstein. Ludwig didn't care much for Munich. He escaped to the Bavarian countryside where he spent his days building castles, listening to music, and dreaming about knights of old. His excesses earned him the nickname "Mad" King Ludwig. But of all the Wittelsbachs, it's his tomb that's decorated with flowers—placed here by romantics still mad about their "mad" king.

Also on the back wall is the tomb of Wilhelm V, who built this church, and Maximilian I, who saved Munich from Swedish invaders during the Thirty Years' War. Finally there's Otto, who went insane and was deposed in 1916, virtually bringing the Wittelsbachs' seven-century reign to an end.

• *Our next stop, the Frauenkirche, is a few*

hundred yards away. Backtrack a couple of blocks up Kaufingerstrasse to the wild boar statue, which marks the German Hunting and Fishing Museum. This place has outdoorsy regalia, kid-friendly exhibits, and the infamous Wolpertinger—a German "jackalope" created by very creative local taxidermists. At the boar statue, turn left on Augustinerstrasse, which leads to Munich's towering, twin-domed cathedral.

❾ Frauenkirche

These twin onion domes are the symbol of the city. They're unusual in that most Gothic churches have either pointed steeples or square towers. Some say Crusaders, inspired by the Dome of the Rock in Jerusalem, brought home the idea. Or it may be that, due to money problems, the towers weren't completed until Renaissance times, when domes were popular. Whatever the reason, the Frauenkirche's domes may be the inspiration for the characteristic domed church spires that mark villages all over Bavaria.

Cost and Hours: Free, generally open daily 7:00-20:30, tel. 089/290-0820.

Restorations: The church towers are

Frauenkirche

under restoration and may not be open for climbing during your visit.

Rick's Tip: *If the* **Frauenkirche** *towers are closed for renovation during your visit, you can enjoy great* **city views** *from* **New Town Hall** *(elevator) or the towers of* **St. Peter's Church** *(stairs only).*

Visiting the Church: The church was built in just 22 years, from 1466 to 1488. It's made of brick—easy to make locally, and cheaper and faster to build with than stone. Construction was partly funded with the sale of indulgences (which let sinners bypass purgatory on the way to heaven). It's dedicated to the Virgin—Our Lady *(Frau)*—and has been the city's cathedral since 1821.

Step inside, and remember that much of this church was destroyed during World War II. The towers survived, and the rest was rebuilt essentially from scratch.

Near the entrance is a big, black, ornate, tomb-like monument honoring Ludwig IV the Bavarian (1282-1347), who was elected Holy Roman Emperor—a big deal. The Frauenkirche was built a century later with the express purpose of honoring his memory. His monument was originally situated in front at the high altar, right near Christ. Those Wittelsbachs—always trying to be associated with God. This alliance was instilled in people through the prayers they were forced to recite: "Virgin Mary, mother of our duke, please protect us."

Nearby, a relief (over the back pew on the left) honors one of Munich's more recent citizens. Joseph Ratzinger was born in Bavaria in 1927, became archbishop of the Frauenkirche (1977-1982), then moved to the Vatican where he later served as Pope Benedict XVI (2005-2013).

Now walk slowly up the main aisle, enjoying stained glass right and left. This glass is obviously modern, having replaced the original glass that was shattered in World War II. Ahead is the high altar, under a huge hanging crucifix. Find the throne—

the ceremonial seat of the local bishop. From here, look up to the tops of the columns, and notice the tiny painted portraits. They're the craftsmen from five centuries ago who helped build the church.

Walk behind the altar to the apse, where the three tall windows still have their original 15th-century glass. To survive the bombs of 1944, each pane was lovingly removed and stored safely away.

• *Our next stop is on Promenadeplatz, just 400 yards north of here. Facing the altar, take the left side exit and walk straight 50 yards until you see a tiny but well-signed passageway (on the left) called the Aufhauser Passage. Follow it through a modern building, where you'll emerge at a little park called* **Promenadeplatz.** *Detour a few steps left into the park, where you'll find a colorful modern memorial. (If the passage is closed, circle around the block to the next stop.)*

🔟 *Michael Jackson Memorial*

When Michael Jackson was in town, he'd stay at the Hotel Bayerischer Hof, like many VIPs. Fans would gather in the park waiting for him to appear at his window. He'd sometimes oblige (but his infamous baby-dangling incident happened in Berlin, not here). When Jackson died in 2009, devotees created this memorial by taking over a statue of Renaissance composer Orlando di Lasso. They still visit daily, leave a memento, and keep it tidy.

• *Now exit the park at the end with the giant silver statue and turn left down Kardinal-Faulhaber-Strasse, lined with former 18th-century mansions that have since become offices and bank buildings. At #11, turn right and enter a modern shopping mall called the Fünf Höfe Passage. The place takes your basic shopping mall and gives it more class. It's divided into five connecting courtyards ("fünf Höfe"), spruced up with bubbling fountains, exotic plants, and a hanging garden.*

Emerging on a busy pedestrian street, turn right, and head down the street (noticing the Münchner Kindl again high above) to a big green square: Marienhof, with the most aristocratic grocery store in all of Germany.

⓫ Marienhof

This square, tucked behind the New Town Hall, was left as a green island after the 1945 bombings. For now, the square's all dug up while Munich builds an additional subway tunnel here. With virtually the entire underground system converging on nearby Marienplatz, this new tunnel will provide a huge relief to the city's congested subterranean infrastructure.

• *On the far side of Marienhof, the stately yellow building is...*

⓬ Dallmayr Delicatessen

When the king called out for dinner, he called Alois Dallmayr. This place became famous for its exotic and luxurious food items: tropical fruits, seafood, chocolates, fine wines, and coffee (there are meat and cheese counters, too). As you enter, read the black plaque with the royal seal by the door: *Königlich Bayerischer Hof-Lieferant* ("Deliverer for the King of Bavaria and his Court"). Catering to royal and aristocratic tastes (and budgets) since 1700, it's still the choice of Munich's old rich (closed Sun, www.dallmayr.com).

• *Leaving Dallmayr, turn right and then right again to continue along Hofgraben. Walk straight three blocks, gently downhill, to Platzl—"small square." (If you get turned around, ask any local to point you toward the Hofbräuhaus.)*

Marienhof

⓭ Platzl

As you stand here—admiring classic facades in the heart of medieval Munich—recall that everything around you was flattened in World War II. Here on Platzl, reconstruction happened in stages: From 1945 to 1950, they removed 12 million tons of bricks and replaced roofs to make buildings weather-tight. From 1950 to 1972, they redid the exteriors. From 1972 to 2000, they refurbished the interiors. Today, the rebuilt Platzl sports new—but old-looking—facades.

Officials estimate that hundreds of unexploded bombs still lie buried under Munich. As recently as 2012, a 550-pound bomb was found in Schwabing, a neighborhood just north of the old city center. They had to evacuate the neighborhood and detonate the bomb.

Today's Platzl hosts a lively mix of places to eat and drink—chains like Starbucks and Hard Rock Café alongside local spots like Schuhbecks Eissalon, a favorite for ice cream (Pfisterstrasse 11).

• *At the bottom of the square (#9), you can experience the venerable...*

⓮ Hofbräuhaus

The world's most famous beer hall (rated ▲▲) is a trip. Whether or not you slide your lederhosen on its polished benches, it's a great experience just to walk through the place in all its rowdy glory (with its own gift shop).

Cost and Hours: Free to enter, daily 9:00-23:30, live oompah music at lunch and dinner; tel. 089/2901-3610, www.hofbraeuhaus.de. For details on eating here, see page 83.

Visiting the Hofbräuhaus: Before going in, check out the huge arches at the entrance and the crown logo. The original brewery was built here in 1589. As the crown suggests, it was the Wittelsbachs' personal brewery, to make the "court brew" (*Hof Brau*). In 1880, the brewery moved out, and this 5,000-seat food-and-beer palace was built in its place.

Hofbräuhaus

After being bombed in World War II, the Hofbräuhaus was one of the first places to be rebuilt (German priorities).

Now, dive headlong into the sudsy Hofbräu mosh pit. Don't be shy. Everyone's drunk anyway. The atmosphere is thick with the sounds of oompah music, played here every night of the year.

You'll see locals stuffed into lederhosen and dirndls, giant gingerbread cookies that sport romantic messages, and kiosks selling postcards of the German (and apparently beer-drinking) ex-pope. Notice the quirky 1950s-style painted ceiling, with Bavarian colors, grapes, chestnuts, and fun "eat, drink, and be merry" themes. You'll see signs on some tables reading *Stammtisch,* meaning they're reserved for regulars, and their racks of old beer steins made of pottery and pewter. Beer halls like the Hofbräuhaus sell beer only by the liter mug, called a *Mass* (mahs). You can get it light *(helles)* or dark *(dunkles).* A slogan on the ceiling above the band reads: *Durst ist schlimmer als Heimweh*—"Thirst is worse than homesickness."

• *Leaving the Hofbräuhaus, turn right and walk two blocks, then turn left when you reach the street called...*

⓮ Maximilianstrasse

This broad east-west boulevard, lined with grand buildings and exclusive shops, introduces us to Munich's Golden Age of the 1800s. In that period, Bavaria was ruled by three important kings: Max

Joseph, Ludwig I, and Ludwig II. They transformed Munich from a cluster of medieval lanes to a modern city of spacious squares, Neoclassical monuments, and wide boulevards. At the east end of this boulevard is the palatial home of the Bavarian parliament.

The street was purposely designed for people and for shopping, not military parades. And to this day, Maximilianstrasse is busy with shoppers browsing Munich's most exclusive shops.

• *Maximilianstrasse leads to a big square—Max-Joseph-Platz.*

⓰ Max-Joseph-Platz

The square is fronted by two big buildings: the National Theater (with its columns) and the Residenz (with its intimidating stone facade).

The **Residenz,** the former "residence" of the royal Wittelsbach family, started as a crude castle (c. 1385). Over the centuries, it evolved into one of Europe's most opulent palaces (see "Sights," later).

The centerpiece of the square is a grand statue of **Maximilian I**—a.k.a. Max Joseph. In 1806, Max was the city's duke, serving in the long tradition of his Wittelsbach family... until Napoleon invaded and deposed the duke. But then Napoleon—eager to marry into the aristocracy—agreed to reinstate Max, with one condition: that his daughter marry Napoleon's stepson. Max Joseph agreed, and was quickly crowned not duke but king of Bavaria.

Max Joseph and his heirs ruled as constitutional monarchs. Now a king, Max Joseph was popular; he emancipated Protestants and Jews, revamped the Viktualienmarkt, and graced Munich with grand buildings like the **National Theater.** This Neoclassical building, opened in 1818, celebrated Bavaria's strong culture, deep roots, and legitimacy as a nation; four of Richard Wagner's operas were first performed here. It's now where the Bavarian State Opera and the Bavarian State Orchestra perform. (The Roman

Max-Joseph-Platz

numerals MCMLXIII in the frieze mark the year the theater reopened after WWII bombing restoration—1963.)
• *Leave Max-Joseph-Platz opposite where you entered, walking alongside the Residenz on Residenzstrasse for about 100 yards to the next grand square. But before you get to Odeonsplatz, pause at the first corner on the left and look down Viscardigasse at the gold-cobbled swoosh in the pavement.*

🕖 Viscardigasse

The cobbles in Viscardigasse recall one of Munich's most dramatic moments: It was 1923, and Munich was in chaos. World War I had left Germany in shambles. Angry mobs roamed the streets. Out of the fury rose a new and frightening movement—Adolf Hitler and the Nazi Party. On November 8, Hitler launched a coup, later known as the Beer Hall Putsch, to try to topple the German government. It started with a fiery speech by Hitler in a beer hall a few blocks from here (the beer hall no longer exists). The next day, Hitler and his mob of Nazis marched up Residenzstrasse. A block ahead, where Residenzstrasse spills into Odeonsplatz, stood a hundred government police. Shots were fired. Hitler was injured, and 16 Nazis were killed, along with four policemen. The coup was put down, and Hitler was sent to a prison outside Munich. During his nine months there, he wrote down his twisted ideas in his book *Mein Kampf.*

Ten years later, when Hitler finally

came to power, he made a memorial at Odeonsplatz to honor the "first martyrs of the Third Reich." Germans were required to raise their arms in a *Sieg Heil* salute as they entered the square. The only way to avoid the indignity of saluting Nazism was to turn left down Viscardigasse instead. That stream of shiny cobbles marks the detour taken by those brave dissenters.
• *But now that Hitler's odious memorial is long gone, you can continue to...*

🕗 Odeonsplatz

This square links Munich's illustrious past with the Munich of today. It was laid out by the Wittelsbach kings in the 1800s. They incorporated the much older (yellow) church that was already on the square, the Theatinerkirche. This church contains about half of the Wittelsbach tombs. The church's twin towers and 230-foot-high dome are classic Italian Baroque, reflecting Munich's strong Catholic bent in the 1600s.

Overlooking the square from the south is an arcaded loggia filled with statues. In the 1800s the Wittelsbachs commissioned this Hall of Heroes to honor Bavarian generals. It was modeled after the famous Renaissance loggia in Florence. Odeonsplatz was part of the Wittelsbachs' grand vision of modern urban planning.

At the far end of the square, several wide boulevards lead away from here. Look west (left) down 🕘 **Brienner Strasse** (watch out for bikes). In the distance, and just out of sight, a black obelisk commemorates the 30,000 Bavarians who marched with Napoleon to Moscow and never returned. Beyond the obelisk is the grand Königsplatz, or "King's Square," with its Neoclassical buildings. Back in the 1930s, Königsplatz was the center of the Nazi party. Today, the Nazi shadow has largely lifted from that square (only two buildings from that era remain) and Königsplatz is home to Munich's cluster of great art museums. A few miles beyond Königsplatz is the Wittelsbachs' impressive summer home, Nymphenburg Palace.

Odeonsplatz and Theatinerkirche

Now turn your attention 90 degrees to the right. The boulevard heading north from Odeonsplatz is **Ludwigstrasse.** It stretches a full mile, flanked by an impressive line of uniform 60-foot-tall buildings in the Neo-Gothic style. In the far distance is the city's Triumphal Arch, the Siegestor, capped with a figure of Bavaria, a goddess riding a lion-drawn chariot. The street is named for the great Wittelsbach builder-king Ludwig I, who truly made Munich into a grand capital. ("I won't rest," he famously swore, "until Munich looks like Athens.") Ludwigstrasse was used for big parades and processions, as it leads to that Roman-style arch.

Beyond the arch—and beyond what you can see—lie the suburbs of modern Munich, including the city's modern skyscrapers, Olympic Park, and the famous BMW headquarters.

Yes, Munich is a major metropolis, but you'd hardly know it by walking through its pleasant streets and parks.

• *We'll finish our walk in the pleasant Hofgarten. Its formal gate is to your right as you're facing up Ludwigstrasse. Step through the gate and enter the...*

⑳ *Hofgarten*

The elegant "garden of the royal court" is a delight. Built by the Wittelsbachs as their own private backyard to the Residenz palace, it's now open to everyone. Just inside the gate is an arcade decorated with murals commissioned by Ludwig I in the early 1800s. While faded, they still tell the glorious story of Bavaria from 1155 until 1688. The garden's 400-year-old centerpiece is a Renaissance-style temple with great acoustics. (There's often a musician performing here for tips.) It's decorated with the same shell decor as was popular inside the Residenz.

• *This walk is done. Where to go next? You're near the English Garden (just a few blocks away—see the map on page 36; people surf in the rapids created as the small river tumbles underground beneath the bridge east of Haus der Kunst), the Residenz complex, and the Odeonsplatz U-Bahn stop for points elsewhere.*

SIGHTS

Most of the top sights in the city center are covered on my self-guided walk. But there's much more to see in this city.

Rick's Tip: *If you're unsure about which of Munich's top two palaces to visit, the* **Residenz** *is more central and has the best interior, while* **Nymphenburg** *has the finest garden and outdoor views.*

▲▲The Residenz Complex

For 500 years, this was the palatial "residence" and seat of power of the ruling Wittelsbach family. It began (1385) as a crude castle with a moat around it. The main building was built from 1550 to 1650, and decorated in Rococo style during the 18th century. The final touch (under Ludwig I) was the grand south facade modeled after Florence's Pitti Palace. In March 1944, Allied air raids left the Residenz in shambles, so much of what we see today is a reconstruction.

The vast Residenz complex is divided into three sections: The **Residenz Museum** is a long hike through 90 lavishly decorated rooms. The **Residenz Treasury** shows off the Wittelsbach crown jewels. The **Cuvilliés Theater** is an ornate Rococo opera house. While each has its

own admission, I'd just get the combo-ticket and see them all.

Rick's Tip: *The Bavarian Palace Department offers a* **14-day ticket** *(called the* **Mehrtagesticket***) that covers admission to Munich's Residenz and Nymphenburg Palace complexes, as well as the Neuschwanstein and Linderhof castles in Bavaria. If you're planning to visit at least three of these sights within a two-week period, the pass will likely pay for itself (€24, €44 family/partner pass, purchase at participating sights or online at www.schloesser.bayern.de).*

Planning Your Time: Start your visit with the Residenz Treasury—small, manageable, and dazzling. Then hike through the sprawling palace called the Residenz Museum. The Cuvilliés Theater is a quick dollop of architectural whipped cream at the end. If you run out of time or energy, you can reenter with the same ticket on another day to visit anything you missed. The entrances on Max-Joseph-Platz and Residenzstrasse both lead to the ticket office, gift shop, and start of the treasury and Residenz Museum tours.

The Residenz—the "residence" of Bavaria's rulers

Cost and Hours: Residenz Museum-€7, Residenz Treasury-€7 (both include essential audioguides), Cuvilliés Theater-€3.50; €11 combo-ticket covers museum and treasury; €13 version covers all three; treasury and museum open daily 9:00-18:00, mid-Oct-mid-March 10:00-17:00; theater generally open Mon-Sat 14:00-18:00, Sun from 9:00, longer hours Aug-mid-Sept; last entry one hour before closing for all three sights, mandatory bag check, tel. 089/290-671, www.residenz-muenchen.de.

RESIDENZ TREASURY (SCHATZKAMMER)

The treasury shows off a thousand years of Wittelsbach crowns and knickknacks. You'll see the regalia used in Bavaria's coronation ceremonies, the revered sacred objects that gave the Wittelsbachs divine legitimacy, and miscellaneous wonders that dazzled their European relatives. It's the best treasury in Bavaria, with fine 13th- and 14th-century crowns and delicately carved ivory and glass.

Visiting the Treasury: In **Room 1,** the oldest jewels are 200 years older than Munich. Treasures of particular interest line the left wall. The gem-studded Crown of Kunigunde is associated with the saintly Bavarian queen, who was crowned Holy Roman Empress in 1014 by the pope in St. Peter's Basilica in Rome. The pearl-studded prayer book of Charles the Bald (Charlemagne's grandson) allowed the book's owner to claim royal roots dating all the way back to that first Holy Roman Emperor crowned in 800. The spiky Crown of an English Queen (c. 1370) is actually England's oldest crown, brought to Munich by an English princess who married a Wittelsbach duke. The angel and gilt-embellished Crown of Henry II (c. 1270-1280) dates from Munich's roots, when the town was emerging as a regional capital.

Along the right side of the room are religious objects such as reliquaries and portable altars. The tiny mobile altar allowed a Carolingian king to pack light in 890—and still have a little Mass while on the road. Many of the precious and very old objects in this room came from various prince-bishops' collections when their realms came under Bavarian rule in the Napoleonic era (c. 1800).

Room 3: Study the reliquary with St. George killing the dragon—sparkling with more than 2,000 precious stones. Get up close (it's OK to walk around the rope posts)...you can almost hear the dragon hissing. A gold-armored St. George, seated atop a ruby-studded ivory horse, tramples an emerald-green dragon. The golden box below contained the supposed relics of St. George, who was the patron saint of the Wittelsbachs. If you could lift the minuscule visor, you'd see that the carved ivory face of St. George is actually the Wittelsbach Duke Wilhelm V—the great champion of the Catholic Count-

Crown of Henry II

St. George reliquary

er-Reformation—slaying the dragon of Protestantism.

Room 4: The incredibly realistic carved ivory crucifixes from 1630 were done by local artist Georg Petel. Look at the flesh of Jesus' wrist pulling around the nails. In the center of the room is the intricate portable altarpiece (1573-74) of Duke Albrecht V, the Wittelsbach ruler who (as we'll see in the Residenz Museum) made a big mark on the Residenz.

Room 5: The freestanding glass case (#245) holds the impressive royal regalia of the 19th-century Wittelsbach kings—the crown, scepter, orb, and sword that were given to the king during the coronation ceremony. (The smaller pearl crown was for the queen.) They date from the early 1800s when Bavaria had been conquered by Napoleon. The Wittelsbachs struck a deal that allowed them to stay in power, under the elevated title of "king" (not just "duke" or "prince-elector" or "prince-archbishop"). These objects were made in France by the same craftsmen who created Napoleon's crown.

Rooms 6-10: The rest of the treasury has objects that are more beautiful than historic. Admire the dinnerware made of rock crystal (Room 6), stone (Room 7), and gold and enamel (Room 8). Room 9 has a silver-gilt-and-marble replica of Trajan's Column. Finally, explore the "Exotica" of Room 10, including an ancient green Olmec figure encased in a Baroque niche and a Chinese rhino-horn bowl with a teeny-tiny Neptune inside.

• *From the micro-detail of the treasury, it's time to visit the expansive Residenz Museum. Stop by the audioguide desk to have your wand reprogrammed for the museum, cross the hall, and enter the...*

RESIDENZ MUSEUM (RESIDENZMUSEUM)

Though called a "museum," what's really on display here are the 90 rooms of the Residenz itself: the palace's spectacular banquet and reception halls, and the Wittelsbachs' lavish private apartments.

The rooms are decorated with period (but generally not original) furniture: chandeliers, canopied beds, Louis XIV-style chairs, old clocks, tapestries, and dinnerware of porcelain and silver. It's the best place to glimpse the opulent lifestyle of Bavaria's late, great royal family.

(Whatever happened to the Wittelsbachs, the longest continuously ruling family in European history? They're still around, but they're no longer royalty, so most of them have real jobs now—you may well have passed one on the street.)

❍ **Self-Guided Tour:** The place is big. Follow the museum's prescribed route, using this section to hit the highlights and supplementing it with the audioguide. Grab a free museum floor plan as you enter to help locate specific room numbers mentioned here. Be flexible. The route can vary because rooms are occasionally closed off.

• *One of the first "rooms" you encounter (it's actually part of an outdoor courtyard) is the...*

❶ **Shell Grotto** (Room 6): This artificial grotto is made of volcanic tuff and covered completely in Bavarian freshwater shells. In its day, it was an exercise in man controlling nature—a celebration of the Renaissance humanism that flourished in the 1550s. Mercury—the pre-Christian god of trade and business—oversees the action. Check out the statue in the courtyard—in the Wittelsbachs' heyday, red wine would have flowed from the mermaid's breasts and dripped from Medusa's severed head.

• *Before moving on, note the door marked 00, leading to handy WCs. Now continue into the next room, the...*

❷ **Antiquarium** (Room 7): This long, low, arched hall stretches 220 feet end to end. It's the oldest room in the Residenz, built around 1550. The room was, and still is, a festival banquet hall. The ruler presided from the raised dais at the near end (warmed by the fireplace). Two hundred dignitaries can dine here, surrounded by

The Antiquarium, the palace's banquet hall

allegories of the goodness of just rule on the ceiling.

The hall is lined with busts of Roman emperors. In the mid-16th century, Europe's royal families (such as the Wittelsbachs) collected and displayed such busts, implying a connection between themselves and the enlightened ancient Roman rulers. There was such huge demand for these classical statues in the courts of Europe that many of the "ancient busts" were fakes cranked out by crooked Romans. Still, a third of the statuary you see here is original.

The small paintings around the room show 120 Bavarian villages as they looked in 1550. Even today, when a Bavarian historian wants a record of how his village once looked, he comes here. Notice the town of Dachau in 1550 (in the archway closest to the entrance door).

• *Follow the red arrows through a few more rooms, then up a stairway to the upper floor. Pause in the* **Black Hall** *(Room 13) to admire the head-spinning trompe l'oeil ceiling, which makes the nearly flat roof appear to be a much grander arched vault. From here, the prescribed route winds through a number of rooms surrounding a large courtyard.*

❸ **Upper Floor Apartments** (Rooms 14-45): In this series of rooms we get the first glimpse of the Residenz Museum's forte: chandeliered rooms decorated with ceiling paintings, stucco work, tapestries, parquet floors, and period furniture.

Rooms to the left of the Black Hall are the **Electoral Apartments** (Rooms 22-31), the private apartments of the monarch and his consort.

The door from the Black Hall that's opposite the staircase leads to the long **All Saints' Corridor** (Room 32), where you can glance into the adjoining All Saints' Chapel. This early 19th-century chapel, commissioned by Ludwig I, was severely damaged in World War II and didn't reopen until 2003.

From the All Saints' Corridor you can reach the **Charlotte Chambers/Court Garden Rooms,** a long row of impressive rooms across the courtyard from the Electoral Apartments, first used to house

Residenz Tour

Ground Floor

Odeonsplatz

↑ To Odeonsplatz Ⓤ

Imperial Courtyard

Apothecary Courtyard

ACCESS TO CUVILLIÉS THEATER

CUVILLIÉS THEATER ENTRANCE

CUVILLIÉS THEATER

Chapel Courtyard

COURT-CHAPEL

TOUR BEGINS ①

Fountain Courtyard

STAIRS FROM FIRST FLOOR

Grotto Courtyard

⑦

MUSEUM ENTRANCE

②

COURT CHURCH OF ALL SAINTS

ACCESS TO MUSEUM & TREASURY

RESIDENZ MUSEUM*

TICKETS

TOUR ENDS

HALLS OF THE NIBELUNGEN

TREASURY ENTRANCE

TREASURY

STAIRS UP TO FIRST FLOOR

ACCESS TO MUSEUM & TREASURY

Max-Joseph-Platz

↓ To Marienplatz

*Note: Residenz Museum is on two floors & extends over much of Residenz complex

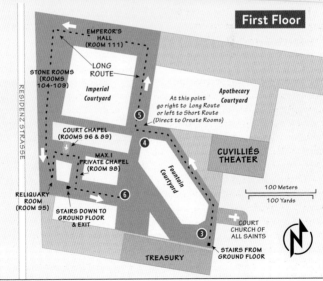

First Floor

EMPEROR'S HALL (ROOM 111)

LONG ROUTE

STONE ROOMS (ROOMS 104-109)

Imperial Courtyard

Apothecary Courtyard

At this point go right to Long Route or left to Short Route (Direct to Ornate Rooms)

⑤

COURT CHAPEL (ROOMS 96 & 89)

④

MAX. I PRIVATE CHAPEL (ROOM 98)

CUVILLIÉS THEATER

RELIQUARY ROOM (ROOM 95)

⑥

Fountain Courtyard

STAIRS DOWN TO GROUND FLOOR & EXIT

100 Meters

100 Yards

COURT CHURCH OF ALL SAINTS

③

STAIRS FROM GROUND FLOOR

TREASURY

Ⓝ

① Shell Grotto
② Antiquarium
③ Upper Floor Apartments
④ Room 45
⑤ "Long" Route
⑥ Ornate Rooms
⑦ Porcelain Cabinet & Ancestral Gallery

visiting rulers. Some of them later served as the private rooms of Princess Charlotte, Max Joseph's daughter.

• *Your visit eventually reaches a hallway—*

❹ *Room 45—where you have a choice: To the left is the "short" route that heads directly to the stunning Ornate Rooms (described later). But we'll take the "long" route to the right (starting in Room 47) that adds a dozen-plus rooms to your visit.*

❺ **The "Long" Route:** Walk through the lavish rooms that border the courtyard. The large **Emperor's Hall** (Room 111) was once the most important room for grand festivities; the **Stone Rooms** (104-109) are so-called for their colorful marble—both real and fake. Then come several small rooms, where the centerpiece painting on the ceiling is just blank black, as no copy of the original survived World War II.

The **Reliquary Room** (Room 95) harbors a collection of gruesome Christian relics (bones, skulls, and even several mummified hands) in ornate golden cases.

• *A few more steps brings you to the balcony of the...*

Court Chapel (Rooms 96/89): Dedicated to Mary, this late-Renaissance/ early-Baroque gem was the site of "Mad" King Ludwig's funeral after his mysterious murder—or suicide—in 1886. (He's buried in St. Michael's Church, described in my "Munich City Walk," earlier.) About 75 years earlier, in 1810, his grandfather and namesake (Ludwig I) was married here. After the wedding ceremony, carriages rolled his guests to a rollicking reception, which turned out to be such a hit that it became an annual tradition—Oktoberfest.

Ahead is the **Private Chapel of Maximilian I** (Room 98). Duke Maximilian I, the dominant Bavarian figure in the Thirty Years' War, built one of the most precious rooms in the palace. The miniature pipe organ (from about 1600) still works. The room is sumptuous, from the gold leaf ceiling and the fine altar with silver reliefs to the miniature dome and the walls made of *scagliola*—fake marble—a special mix of stucco. Note the post-Renaissance perspective tricks decorating the walls; they were popular in the 17th century.

• *Whichever route you take—long or short—you'll eventually reach a set of rooms known as the...*

❻ **Ornate Rooms** (Rooms 55-62): As the name implies, these are some of the

Every Residenz room is unique and ornate.

richest rooms in the palace. The Wittelsbachs were always trying to keep up with the Habsburgs, and this long string of ceremonial rooms—used for official business—was designed to impress. The decor and furniture are Rococo—over-the-top Baroque. The family art collection, now in the Alte Pinakothek, once decorated these walls.

The rooms were designed in the 1730s by François de Cuvilliés. The Belgian-born Cuvilliés first attracted notice as the clever court dwarf for the Bavarian ruler. He was sent to Paris to study art and returned to become the court architect. Besides the Residenz, he went on to also design the Cuvilliés Theater and Amalienburg at Nymphenburg Palace. Cuvilliés' style, featuring incredibly intricate stucco tracery twisted into unusual shapes, defined Bavarian Rococo. As you glide through this section of the palace, be sure to appreciate the gilded stucco ceilings above you.

The **Green Gallery** (Room 58)—named for its green silk damask wallpaper—was the ballroom. Imagine the parties they had here—aristocrats in powdered wigs, a string quartet playing Baroque tunes, a card game going on, while everyone admired the paintings on the walls or themselves reflected in the mirrors.

The **State Bedroom** (Room 60), though furnished with a canopy bed, wasn't an actual bedroom—it was just for show. Rulers invited their subjects to come at morning and evening to stand at the railing and watch their boss ceremonially rise from his slumber to symbolically start and end the working day.

Perhaps the most ornate of these Ornate Rooms is the **Cabinet of Mirrors** (Room 61) and the adjoining **Cabinet of Miniatures** (Room 62) from 1740. In the Cabinet of Mirrors, notice the fun visual effects of the mirrors around you—the corner mirrors make things go on forever. Then peek inside the coral red

room and imagine visiting the duke and having him take you here to ogle miniature copies of the most famous paintings of the day, composed with one-haired brushes.

• *After exploring the Ornate Rooms (and the many other elaborate rooms here on the upper floor), find the staircase (past Room 69) that heads back downstairs. On the ground floor, you emerge in the long Ancestral Gallery (Room 4). Before walking down it, detour to the right, into Room 5.*

❼ **Porcelain Cabinet** (Room 5) and **Ancestral Gallery** (Room 4): In the 18th century, the royal family bolstered their status with an in-house porcelain works: Nymphenburg porcelain. See how the mirrors enhance the porcelain vases, creating the effect of infinite pedestals. If this inspires you to acquire some pieces of your own, head to the Nymphenburg Porcelain Store at Odeonsplatz.

The Ancestral Gallery (Room 4) was built in the 1740s to display portraits of the Wittelsbachs. All official guests had to pass through here to meet the duke (and his 100 Wittelsbach relatives). The room's symbolism reinforced the Wittelsbachs' claims to being as powerful as the Habsburgs of Vienna.

Midway down the hall, find the family tree labeled (in Latin) "genealogy of an imperial family." The tree is shown being planted by Hercules, to boost their royal street cred. Opposite the tree are two notable portraits: Charlemagne, the first Holy Roman Emperor, and to his right, Louis IV (wearing the same crown), the first Wittelsbach H.R.E., crowned in 1328. For the next 500 years, this lineage was used to substantiate the family's claim to power as they competed with the Habsburgs. (After failing to sort out their differences through strategic weddings, the two families eventually went to war.)

Allied bombs took their toll on this hall. The central ceiling painting has been restored, but since there were no photos documenting the other two ceiling paintings, those spots remain empty. Looking carefully at the walls, you can see how each painting was hastily cut out of its frame. That's because—though most of Munich's museums were closed during World War II—the Residenz remained open to instill confidence in local people. It wasn't until 1944, when bombs were imminent, that the last-minute order was given to hide the paintings away.

Also on the ground floor are the **Halls of the Nibelungen** (*Nibelungensäle,* Rooms 74-79), which feature mythological scenes that were the basis of Wagner's *Der Ring des Nibelungen.* Wagner and "Mad" King Ludwig were friends and spent time hanging out here (c. 1864). The images in this hall could well have inspired Wagner to write his Ring and Ludwig to build his "fairy-tale castle," Neuschwanstein.

• *Your Residenz Museum tour is over. The doorway at the end of the hall leads back to the museum entrance. If you're visiting the Cuvilliés Theater, exit the museum and return to Residenzstrasse. Enter the Chapel Courtyard by passing between the green lions standing guard. Walk to the far end of the lane until you reach a fountain. Just above a doorway to the left you'll see a nondescript sign that says* Cuvilliés Theater.

CUVILLIÉS THEATER

In 1751, this was Germany's ultimate Rococo theater. Mozart conducted here several times. Designed by the same brilliant architect who did the Amalienburg, this theater is dazzling enough to send you back to the days of divine monarchs.

It's an intimate, horseshoe-shaped performance venue, seating fewer than 400. The four tiers of box seats were for the four classes of society: city burghers on bottom, royalty next up (in the most elaborate seats), and lesser courtiers in the two highest tiers. The ruler occupied the large Royal Box directly opposite the stage. "Mad" King Ludwig II occasionally bought out the entire theater to watch performances here by himself.

François Cuvilliés' interior is exquisite. Red, white, and gold hues dominate. Most of the decoration is painted wood, even parts that look like marble. Even the proscenium above the stage—seemingly draped with a red-velvet "curtain"—is actually made of carved wood. Also above the stage is an elaborate Wittelsbach coat of arms. The balconies seem to be supported by statues of the four seasons and are adorned with gold garlands. Cuvilliés achieved the Rococo ideal of giving theater-goers a multimedia experience—uniting the beauty of his creation with the beautiful performance on stage. It's still a working theater.

WWII bombs completely obliterated the old Cuvilliés Theater, which originally stood at a different location a short distance from here. Fortunately, much of the carved wooden interior had been removed from the walls and stored away for safekeeping. After the war, this entirely new building was built near the ruins of the old theater and paneled with the original decor.

Near the Residenz

▲MUNICH CITY MUSEUM (MÜNCHNER STADTMUSEUM)

The museum's permanent exhibit on Munich's history (called "Typically Munich!") is interesting, but it's an exhaustive and confusing maze, and there's no posted English information. Use the following mini tour for an overview, then supplement it with the audioguide and English booklet.

Cuvilliés Theater

Cost and Hours: €4, includes good audioguide, €7 includes temporary exhibits; ticket gets you half-price admission to Jewish History Museum, Nazi Documentation Center, and Lenbachhaus; Tue-Sun 10:00-18:00, closed Mon; St.-Jakobs-Platz 1, tel. 089/2332-2370, www.muenchner-stadtmuseum.de. The humorous Servus Heimat souvenir shop in the courtyard is worth a stop.

Eating: The museum's recommended Stadt Café is handy for a light meal.

Visiting the Museum: Start in the ticketing hall with the wooden model showing Munich today. Find the Frauenkirche, Isar River, New Town Hall, Residenz...and no skyscrapers. The city looks remarkably similar in scale to the model (in the next room) from 1570.

Ground Floor (Medieval): An imposing gray statue of Henry the Lion introduces us to the city's 12th-century founder. The eight statues of Morris dancers (1480) became a symbol of the vibrant market town (and the tradition continued with the New Town Hall glockenspiel's dancing coopers). On the rest of the ground floor, paintings, swords, and cherubs clad in armor capture more medieval ambience.

First Floor (1800s): The "New Munich" was created when the city was expanded beyond the old medieval walls (see the illuminated view of the city from 1761 in the "Canaletto-Blick" opposite the top of the stairs). The city was prosperous, as evidenced by the furniture and paintings on display. In the center of the room, find

big paintings ("Effigies") of the century's magnificent kings—Maximilian I, Maximilian II, and Ludwig I.

Second Floor (Munich 1900): As Munich approached its 700th birthday, it was becoming aware of itself as a major capital. The Münchner Kindl logo was born. It was a city of artists (Wagner operas, Lenbach portraits, Von Stuck soirées), *Jugendstil* furniture, beer, and a cosmopolitan outlook (see the "Kaiser Panorama," the big barrel-shaped 3-D peep show of Indian/Asian peoples). But after the destruction of World War I, Munich became a hotbed of discontent. The "revue" room shows the city's clash of ideas: communists, capitalists, Nazis, and the anarchic theater of comedian Karl Valentin and early works by playwright Bertolt Brecht. A nearby display gives some background on Munich's role as the birthplace of Nazism (thoroughly covered in the museum's National Socialism wing).

Third Floor (Puppetry and Fairground Art): Consider a trip to the third floor to see the puppetry exhibit (worthwhile and included with your ticket). The collection of objects from the 19th century onward highlights Germany's long tradition of puppetry. Fair and Oktoberfest items may attract children, but beware that horror-house displays may scare the daylights out of them.

Video Finish: End your visit back on the first floor with a kaleidoscope of video images capturing contemporary Munich—rock music, World Cup triumphs, beer gardens, and other things "typically Munich."

National Socialism Wing: This small but worthwhile exhibit (in a building across the courtyard) of photos and uniforms takes you chronologically through the Nazi years: the post-WWI struggles, Hitler's 1923 Beer Hall Putsch, his writing of *Mein Kampf,* the mass rallies in Königsplatz and Odeonsplatz, the Dachau concentration camp, the destruction rained on Munich in World War II, and postwar reconstruction.

Munich City Museum

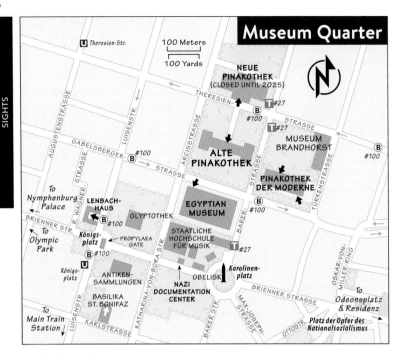

Museum Quarter (Kunstareal)

This quarter's impressive cluster of fine museums displays art from 3000 BC right up to the present. We'll focus on the Egyptian Museum, Alte Pinakothek, and Lenbachhaus. Most people don't come to Munich for the art, but this group makes a case for the city's world-class status.

Getting There: Handy tram #27 whisks you right to the Pinakothek stop from Karlsplatz (between the train station and Marienplatz). You can also take bus #100 from the train station, or walk 10 minutes from the Theresienstrasse or Königsplatz stops on the U-2 line.

▲▲ALTE PINAKOTHEK

The Alte Pinakothek ("Old Art Gallery," pronounced ALL-teh pee-nah-koh-TEHK) shows off a world-class collection of European masterpieces from the 14th to 19th century, starring the two tumultuous centuries (1450-1650) when Europe went from medieval to modern.

See paintings from the Italian Renaissance (Raphael, Leonardo, Botticelli, Titian) and the German Renaissance it inspired (Albrecht Dürer). Through the art displayed here, you can follow along as the Reformation of Martin Luther eventually split Europe into two subcultures—Protestant and Catholic—with their two distinct art styles (exemplified by Rembrandt and Rubens, respectively). You may also see some top-notch paintings (from 1800 to 1920, including Impressionism) belonging to the museum's younger sister across the street—the Neue Pinakothek—which is closed for renovations until 2025.

Cost and Hours: €7, €1 on Sun, covered by day pass and combo-ticket; Wed-Sun 10:00-18:00, Tue until 20:00, closed Mon; excellent audioguide (free, but €4.50 on Sun), pleasant Café Klenze; U-2: Theresienstrasse, tram #27, or bus #100; Barer Strasse 27, tel. 089/2380-5216, www.pinakothek.de/alte-pinakothek.

Visiting the Museum: All the paintings we'll see are on the upper floor, which is

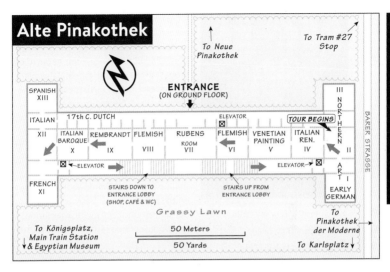

laid out like a barbell. Start at one fat end and work your way through the "handle" to the other end. From the ticket counter, head up the stairway to the left to reach the first rooms.

German Renaissance (Room II): Albrecht Altdorfer's *The Battle of Issus* (*Schlacht bei Issus*) shows a world at war. Masses of soldiers are swept along in the currents and tides of a battle completely beyond their control, their confused motion reflected in the swirling sky. Though the painting depicts Alexander the Great's history-changing victory over the Persians (find the Persian king Darius turning and fleeing), it could as easily have been Germany in the 1520s. Christians were fighting Muslims, peasants battled masters, and Catholics and Protestants were squaring off for a century of conflict. The armies melt into a huge landscape, leaving the impression that the battle goes on forever.

Albrecht Dürer's larger-than-life *Four Apostles* (*Johannes und Petrus* and *Paulus und Marcus*) are saints of a radical new religion: Martin Luther's Protestantism. Just as Luther challenged Church authority, Dürer—a friend of Luther's—strips these saints of any rich clothes, halos, or trappings of power and gives them down-to-earth human features: receding hairlines, wrinkles, and suspicious eyes. The inscription warns German rulers to follow the Bible rather than Catholic Church leaders. The figure of Mark—a Bible in one hand and a sword in the other—is a fitting symbol of the dangerous times.

Dürer's *Self-Portrait in Fur Coat* (*Selbstbildnis im Pelzrock*) looks like Jesus Christ but is actually 28-year-old Dürer himself, gazing out, with his right hand solemnly giving a blessing. This is the

Dürer, Self-Portrait in Fur Coat

A *Leonardo da Vinci,* Virgin and Child
B *Raphael,* Canigiani Holy Family
C *Rubens,* Rubens and Isabella Brant

ultimate image of humanism: the artist as an instrument of God's continued creation.

Italian Renaissance (Room IV): With the Italian Renaissance—the "rebirth" of interest in the art and learning of ancient Greece and Rome—artists captured the realism, three-dimensionality, and symmetry found in classical statues. Twenty-one-year-old Leonardo da Vinci's *Virgin and Child (Maria mit dem Kinde)* need no halos—they radiate purity. Mary is a solid pyramid of maternal love, flanked by Renaissance-arch windows that look out on the hazy distance. Baby Jesus reaches out to play innocently with a carnation, the blood-colored symbol of his eventual death.

Raphael's *Holy Family at the Canigiani House (Die hl. Familie aus dem Hause Canigiani)* takes Leonardo's pyramid form and runs with it. Father Joseph forms the peak, with his staff as the strong central axis. Mary and Jesus (on the right) form a pyramid-within-the-pyramid, as do Elizabeth and baby John the Baptist on the left.

In Botticelli's *Lamentation over Christ (Die Beweinung Christi),* the Renaissance "pyramid" implodes, as the weight of the dead Christ drags everyone down, and the tomb grins darkly behind them.

Venetian Painting (Room V): In Titian's *Christ Crowned with Thorns (Die Dornenkrönung),* a powerfully built Christ sits silently enduring torture by prison guards. The painting is by Venice's greatest Renaissance painter, but there's no symmetry, no pyramid form, and the brushwork is intentionally messy and Impressionistic. By the way, this is the first painting we've seen done on canvas rather than wood, as artists experimented with vegetable oil-based paints.

Rubens and Baroque (Room VII): Europe's religious wars split the Continent in two—Protestants in the northern countries, Catholics in the south. (Germany itself was divided, with Bavaria remaining Catholic.) The Baroque style, popular in Catholic countries, featured large canvases, bright colors, lots of flesh, rippling motion, wild emotions, grand themes... and pudgy winged babies, the sure sign of Baroque. This room holds several canvases by the great Flemish painter Peter Paul Rubens.

In Rubens' 300-square-foot *Great Last Judgment (Das Grosse Jüngste Gericht)*, Christ raises the righteous up to heaven (left side) and damns the sinners to hell (on the right). This swirling cycle of nudes was considered risqué and kept under wraps by the very monks who'd commissioned it.

Rubens and Isabella Brant in the Honeysuckle Bower shows the artist with his first wife, both of them the very picture of health, wealth, and success. They lean together unconsciously, as people in love will do, with their hands clasped in mutual affection. When his first wife died, 53-year-old Rubens found a replacement—16-year-old Hélène Fourment, shown in an adjacent painting (just to the left) in her wedding dress. You may recognize Hélène's face in other Rubens paintings.

The Rape of the Daughters of Leucippus (Der Raub der Töchter des Leukippos) has many of Rubens' most typical elements—fleshy, emotional, rippling motion; bright colors; and a classical subject. The legendary twins Castor and Pollux crash a wedding and steal the brides as their own. The chaos of flailing limbs and rearing horses is all held together in a subtle X-shaped composition. Like the weaving counterpoint in a Baroque fugue, Rubens balances opposites.

Rembrandt and Dutch (Room IX): From Holland, Rembrandt van Rijn's *Six Paintings from the Life of Christ* are a down-to-earth look at supernatural events. *The Holy Family (Die Heilige Familie)* is set in a carpenter's workshop (with tools on the wall). The canvases are dark brown, lit by strong light. The *Holy Family*'s light source is the Baby Jesus himself—literally the "light of the world." In the *Raising of the Cross (Kreuzaufrichtung)*, a man dressed in blue is looking on—a self-portrait of Rembrandt.

In the *Deposition (Kreuzabnahme)*, the light bounces off Christ's pale body onto his mother Mary, who has fainted in the shadows, showing how his death also hurts her. The drama is underplayed, with subdued emotions.

▲▲EGYPTIAN MUSEUM (STAATLICHES MUSEUM ÄGYPTISCHER KUNST)

To enjoy this museum, you don't need a strong interest in ancient Egypt (but you may have one by the time you leave). This modern space was custom-made to evoke the feeling of being deep in an ancient tomb, from the wide, easy-to-miss staircase outside that descends to the narrow entry, to the twisty interior rooms that grow narrower and more catacomb-like as you progress. The museum's clever design creates a low-stress visit (just follow the one-way route marked by brass arrows in the floor).

Cost and Hours: €7, €1 on Sun, Wed-Sun 10:00-18:00, Tue until 20:00, closed Mon, audioguide is usually free (€1 on Sun); U-2 or U-8 to Königsplatz, tram #27 to Karolinenplatz, or bus #100 to Pinakothek stop; 10-minute walk from main train station, Gabelsbergerstrasse 35, tel. 089/2892-7630, www.smaek.de.

▲▲LENBACHHAUS

Locals like to say, "Berlin had generals, Munich had artists." And that was particularly true in the decades before World War I. A bunch of art-school cronies got fed up with being told how and what to paint, and together, as the revolutionary "Blue Rider" *(Blaue Reiter)* group, they galloped toward a brand-new horizon—abstract art. In the Lenbachhaus' pleasant galleries you can witness the birth of Modernist nonrepresentational art, with paintings by Kandinsky, Klee, and Marc, then stroll the rest of the building's offerings (including the apartments of painter Franz von Lenbach).

Lenbachhaus

Cost and Hours: €10, includes well-done audioguide; ticket gets you half-price admission to Jewish History Museum, Nazi Documentation Center, and Munich City Museum (or use any of those tickets to get half-price admission here); Wed-Sun 10:00-18:00, Tue until 20:00, closed Mon; Luisentrasse 33, tel. 089/2333-2000, www.lenbachhaus.de.

Visiting the Museum: The collection includes three distinct sections: 19th century (conservative, colorful, optimistic); Blue Rider (emotional, inspired, modern); and Post-1945 (abstract). The Blue Rider revolution begins on the second floor, with seemingly innocuous paintings of the cute Bavarian town of Murnau. It was here in 1908 that two Munich couples—Wassily Kandinsky, Alexej Jawlensky, and their artist girlfriends—came for vacation. The four painted together, employing intense colors, thick paint, and bold black outlines. Over the next few years (c. 1911-1914), they'd gather together into a group of

Munich-based artists calling themselves the Blue Rider, which included Paul Klee and Franz Marc. They were all devoted to expressing spiritual truths by using intense colors and geometric shapes.

The Blue Rider School was blown apart by World War I: The artists who survived went on to pioneer abstract art. Kandinsky's "Improvisations" eventually became the art world's first purely abstract canvases. Soon his style spread everywhere. Jawlensky and Klee also went on to develop a simpler and more abstract style.

One floor down, in the "Art After 1945" section, you'll see big, empty canvases by the Abstract Expressionists who tried to "express" deep truths through "abstract" color and line alone. Finally, across the entry hall from the ticket desk and up one floor, enter the luxe villa of Franz von Lenbach, who made portraits of 19th-century notables. His paintings fill the walls of ornate rooms accentuated by fine 15th- to 19th-century furnishings.

▲▲NAZI DOCUMENTATION CENTER (NS-DOKUMENTATIONSZENTRUM MÜNCHEN)

This center—housed in a stark, light-filled, cube-shaped building—documents the rise and fall of Nazism with a focus on Munich's role and the reasons behind it, as this city, like the rest of Germany, is determined to learn from its 20th-century nightmare. While there are no actual artifacts here, the learning experience is moving and a worthwhile companion to the Dachau Concentration Camp Memorial.

Cost and Hours: €5 includes well-done and techie audioguide; ticket gets you half-price admission to Jewish History Museum, Munich City Museum, Villa Stuck, or Lenbachhaus—or use any of those tickets to get half-price admission here; Tue-Sun 10:00-19:00, closed Mon, U-2: Königsplatz, Brienner Strasse 34, tel. 089/2336-7001, www.ns-dokumentationszentrum-muenchen.de.

Visiting the Museum: The museum is arranged chronologically and begins on the top floor. (Take the elevator to avoid confusion.) The top floor covers the end of World War I and the beginning of Hitler's movement in Munich (1918-1933). It includes gripping biographies of the early opponents of the Nazi Party.

The third floor (covering 1933-1939) documents the establishment of the racially pure *Volksgemeinschaft* ("people's community") and the effect of Nazi domination on everyday life, including a timeline that illustrates the restrictions and ordinances that worsened Jewish isolation. Look out onto Königsplatz and envision Hitler's rise to power, which started right here. The second floor (1939-1945) covers the horrors of war, the Holocaust, and the "denazification" period after the end of Nazi rule. Find the video showing Munich in ruins immediately following the war and compare the footage to what you see today.

The first floor (after 1945) examines the faith people put in the Nazi regime and the difficulty in coming to terms with the past. The Learning Center, in the basement, encourages reflection, with a collection of books banned during Nazi rule and research stations where you can delve into topics of interest.

Near the River

▲ENGLISH GARDEN (ENGLISCHER GARTEN)

Munich's "Central Park," the largest urban park on the Continent, was laid out in 1789 by an American. More than 100,000 locals commune with nature here on sunny summer days (including lots of students from the nearby university). The park stretches three miles from the center, past the university and the trendy Schwabing quarter. For the best quick visit, take bus #100 or tram #18 to the Nationalmuseum/Haus der Kunst stop. Under the bridge, you'll see surfers. (The surf's always up here—even through the night; surfers bring their own lights.) Follow the path, to the right of the surfing spot, downstream until you reach the big lawn. The Chinese Tower beer garden is just beyond the tree-covered hill to the right. Follow the oompah music and walk to the hilltop temple, with a postcard view of the city on your way. Afterward, instead of retracing your steps, you can walk (or take bus #54 a couple of stops) to the Giselas-

English Garden

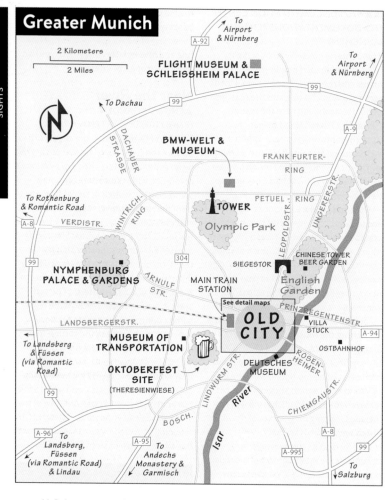

Greater Munich

2 Kilometers
2 Miles

To Airport & Nürnberg

A-92

To Airport & Nürnberg

**FLIGHT MUSEUM &
SCHLEISSHEIM PALACE**

99

A-9

To Dachau

99

DACHAUER STRASSE

**BMW-WELT &
MUSEUM**

FRANK FURTER-
RING

PETUEL - RING

UNGERERSTR.

To Rothenburg
& Romantic Road

A-8

VERDISTR.

WINTRICH-RING

TOWER

Olympic Park

LEOPOLDSTR.

99

304

ARNULF STR.

**NYMPHENBURG
PALACE & GARDENS**

SIEGESTOR

CHINESE TOWER
BEER GARDEN

**MAIN TRAIN
STATION**

*English
Garden*

PRINZREGENTENSTR.

LANDSBERGERSTR.

See detail maps

**OLD
CITY**

VILLA
STUCK

A-94

To Landsberg
& Füssen
(via Romantic
Road)

**MUSEUM OF
TRANSPORTATION**

LINDWURM STR.

**DEUTSCHES
MUSEUM**

ROSEN-HEIMER

OSTBAHNHOF

**OKTOBERFEST
SITE**
(THERESIENWIESE)

Isar River

CHIEMGAUSTR.

99

BOSCH.

A-96 To
Landsberg,
Füssen
(via Romantic Road)
& Lindau

A-95 To
Andechs
Monastery &
Garmisch

A-8

99

A-995

To
Salzburg

trasse U-Bahn station and return to town on the U-3 or U-6.

A rewarding respite from the city, the park is especially fun—and worth ▲▲—on a bike under the summer sun and on warm evenings (unfortunately, there are no bike-rental agencies in or near the park; to rent some wheels, see page 95). Caution: While local law requires sun worshippers to wear clothes on the tram, the park is sprinkled with buck-naked sunbathers—quite a shock to prudish Americans (they're the ones riding their bikes into the river and trees).

▲DEUTSCHES MUSEUM (MAIN BRANCH)

Germany's answer to our Smithsonian Institution, the Deutsches Museum traces the evolution of science and technology. Enjoy wandering through rooms of historic airplanes, spaceships, mining, the harnessing of wind and water power, hydraulics, musical instruments, printing, chemistry, computers, astronomy, and nanotechnology. The museum feels a bit dated, and not all the displays have English descriptions—but major renovations are under way. Though about a third of the collection may be closed during your visit, even those on roller skates will still need to be selective. Use my mini tour to get oriented.

Cost and Hours: €12, daily 9:00-17:00, English map available, several small cafés in the museum, tel. 089/217-9333, www.deutsches-museum.de.

Getting There: Take tram #17 to the Deutsches Museum stop. Or, take the S-Bahn or tram #18 to Isartor, then walk 300 yards over the river and turn right, following the signs. The entrance is near the far end of the building along the riverside.

Visiting the Museum: After buying your ticket, head inside and stop by the information desk to ask about the day's schedule of demonstrations (for example, electric power or glass-blowing). Pick up a floor plan (you'll get lost without it) and walk toward the vast high-ceilinged room dominated by a tall-masted ship.

Ground Floor: Get oriented and locate the handy elevator behind you—it's one of the few elevators in this labyrinthine building that goes to all six floors. Now, let's explore.

The exhibit on **marine navigation** is anchored by the 60-foot sailing ship *Maria.* Take the staircase down, where you can look inside her cut-away hull and imagine life below decks. Before heading back upstairs, find the bisected U1 submarine (on the wall farthest from the entrance)—the first German *U-Boot* (undersea boat), dating from 1906.

Now make your way to several technology exhibits—DNA and nanotechnology (downstairs). Children will enjoy the "Kinderreich" (past the cloakroom to the left as you enter) and the exciting twice-daily high-voltage demonstrations (ground floor) creating a five-foot bolt of lightning.

First Floor: The **historic aviation** collection occupies the center of the first floor. You'll see early attempts at flight—gliders, hot-air balloons, and a model of the airship pioneered by Ger-

many's Count Zeppelin. The highlight is a Wright Brothers double-decker airplane from 1909—six years after their famous first flight, when they began to manufacture multiple copies of their prototype. By World War I, airplanes were becoming a formidable force. The Fokker triplane was made famous by Germany's war ace the Red Baron (Manfred von Richthofen).

Second Floor: Gathered together near the main elevator, you'll find a replica of prehistoric **cave paintings** and daily **glass-blowing** demonstrations. Don't miss the flight simulator—a training device that is almost identical to flying a real airplane.

Third Floor: The third floor traces the history of **measurement,** including time (from a 16th-century sundial and an 18th-century clock to a scary Black Forest wall clock complete with grim reaper), weights, and geodesy (surveying and mapping). In the **computer** section, you go from the ancient abacus to a 1956 Univac computer—as big as a room, with a million components, costing a million dollars, and with less computing power than your smartphone.

Floors 4-6: The focus here is on **astronomy.** A light-show exhibit traces the evolution of the universe. The **planetarium** lecture is in German, but might be worthwhile if you love the stars. Finally, you emerge on the museum rooftop—the **"sundial garden"**—with great views. On a clear day, you can see the Alps.

▲▲Nymphenburg Palace Complex

For 200 years, this oasis of palaces and gardens was the Wittelsbach rulers' summer vacation home, a getaway from the sniping politics of court life in the city. Their kids could play, picnic, ride horses, and frolic in the ponds and gardens, while the adults played cards, listened to music, and sipped coffee on the veranda. It was at Nymphenburg that a seven-year-old Mozart gave a widely heralded concert, that 60-year-old Ludwig I courted the femme fatale Lola Montez, and that "Mad" King Ludwig II (Ludwig I's grandson) was born and baptized.

Today, Nymphenburg Palace and the surrounding one-square-mile park are a great place for a royal stroll or discreet picnic. Indoors, you can tour the Bavarian royal family's summer quarters and visit the Royal Stables Museum (carriages, sleighs, and porcelain). If you have time, check out playful extras such as a hunting lodge (Amalienburg), bathhouse (Badenburg), pagoda (Pagodenburg), and fake ruins (Magdalenenklause). The complex also houses a humble natural history museum and Baroque chapel. Allow at least three hours (including travel time) to see the palace complex at a leisurely pace.

Cost and Hours: Palace–€6; combo-ticket–€11.50 (€8.50 off-season) covers the palace, Royal Stables Museum, and outlying sights. All of these sights are open daily 9:00-18:00, mid-Oct-March 10:00-16:00—except for Amalienburg and the other small palaces in the park, which are closed in winter; park open daily 6:00-dusk and free to enter; audioguide–€3.50,

tel. 089/179-080, www.schloss-nymphenburg.de.

Getting There: The palace is three miles northwest of central Munich. Take tram #17 (direction: Amalienburgstrasse) from the train station or Karlsplatz. In 15 minutes you reach the Schloss Nymphenburg stop. From the bridge by the tram stop, you'll see the palace—a 10-minute walk away. The palace is a pleasant 30-minute bike ride from the main train station (either follow Arnulfstrasse all the way to Nymphenburg, or turn up Landshuter Allee—at Donersburgerbrücke—then follow Nymphenburger Strasse until you hit the canal that stretches to the palace). Be aware that biking in the palace grounds is not permitted.

Eating: A $$ café serves lunch and snacks in a winter garden or on a nice terrace, a five-minute walk behind and to the right of the palace (open year-round). More eating options are near the tram stop.

NYMPHENBURG PALACE
In 1662, after 10 years of trying, the Bavarian ruler Ferdinand Maria and his wife, Henriette Adelaide of Savoy, finally had a

Nymphenburg Palace

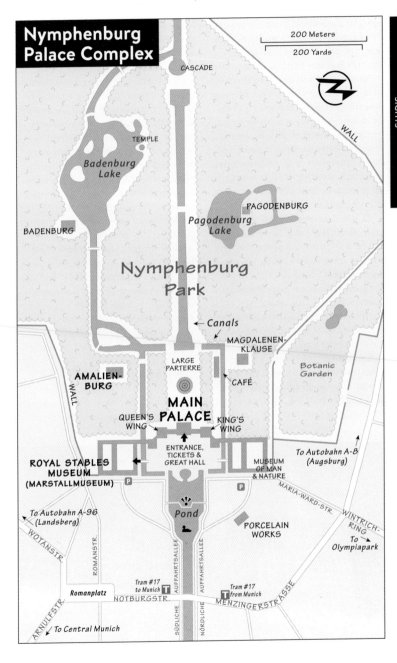

Nymphenburg Palace Complex

200 Meters
200 Yards

CASCADE

WALL

TEMPLE

Badenburg Lake

BADENBURG

PAGODENBURG

Pagodenburg Lake

Nymphenburg Park

← Canals

MAGDALENEN-KLAUSE

AMALIEN-BURG

WALL

LARGE PARTERRE

CAFÉ

Botanic Garden

MAIN PALACE

QUEEN'S WING

KING'S WING

ENTRANCE, TICKETS & GREAT HALL

ROYAL STABLES MUSEUM (MARSTALLMUSEUM)

MUSEUM OF MAN & NATURE

To Autobahn A-8 (Augsburg)

MARIA-WARD-STR.

WINTRICH-RING

To Autobahn A-96 (Landsberg)

WOTANSTR.

Pond

PORCELAIN WORKS

To Olympiapark

ROMANSTR.

AUFFAHRTSALLEE

SÜDLICHE AUFFAHRTSALLEE

NÖRDLICHE AUFFAHRTSALLEE

Tram #17 to Munich

Tram #17 from Munich

Romanplatz

NOTBURGSTR.

MENZINGERSTRASSE

ARNULFSTR.

← To Central Munich

son, Max Emanuel. In gratitude for a male heir, Ferdinand gave this land to his Italian wife, who proceeded to build an Italian-style Baroque palace as their summer residence. Their son expanded the palace to its current size. (Today's Wittelsbachs, who still refer to themselves as "princes" or "dukes," live in one wing of the palace.)

The palace interior, while interesting, is much less extensive than Munich's Residenz. The place is stingy on free information; you'll need the serviceable audioguide if you'd like more info than what I've provided below.

○ Self-Guided Tour: Your visit starts in the **Great Hall** (a.k.a. **Stone Hall**). As the central room of the palace, this light and airy space was the dining hall, site of big Wittelsbach family festivals. One of the grandest and best-preserved Rococo rooms in Bavaria (from about 1760), it sports elaborate stucco work and a ceiling fresco by Johann Baptist Zimmermann (of Wieskirche fame).

Zimmermann's fresco opens a sunroof to the heavens, where Greek gods cavort. In the sunny center, Apollo drives his chariot to bring the dawn, while bearded Zeus (astride an eagle) and pea-cock-carrying Juno look on. The rainbow symbolizes the peace brought by the enlightened Wittelsbachs. Around the borders of the painting, notice the fun optical illusions: For example, a painted dog holds a stucco bird in its mouth. The painting's natural setting and joie de vivre reflect the pastoral pleasures enjoyed here at the Wittelsbachs' summer home. At one end of the fresco (away from the windows) lounges a lovely maiden with flowers in her hair: It's Flora, the eponymous nymph who inspired this "nymph's castle"—Nymphenburg.

From here, two wings stretch to the left and right. They're mirror images of one another: antechamber, audience chamber, bedchamber, and private living quarters. Guests would arrive here in the Great Hall for an awe-inspiring first impression, then make their way through a series of (also-impressive) waiting rooms for their date with the Wittelsbach nobility.

• *The tour continues to the left (as you look out the big windows).*

North Wing (Rooms 2-9): Breeze quickly through this less interesting wing, filled with tapestries and Wittelsbach portraits (including curly-haired Max Eman-

The Great Hall has remained unchanged since 1758.

uel, who built this wing). Pause in the long corridor **(the North Gallery)** lined with paintings of various Wittelsbach palaces. The ones of Nymphenburg show the place around 1720, back when there was nothing but countryside between it and downtown (and gondolas plied the canals). Imagine the logistics when the royal family—with their entourage of 200—decided to move out to the summer palace.

• *Return to the Great Hall and enter the other wing.*

South Wing (Rooms 10-20): Pass through the gold-and-white Room 10 and turn right into the red-walled **South Apartment Antechamber.** The room calls up the exuberant time of Nymphenburg's founding couple, Ferdinand and Henriette. A portrait on the wall shows them posing together in their rich courtly dress. The large painting on the left depicts the family in a Greek myth: Henriette (as the moon goddess) leads her youngest son Joseph Clemens by the hand, while her first son Max Emanuel (as Hercules) receives the gift of a sword. On the right side of the room, Ferdinand is represented as Endymion, a mortal loved by the moon goddess.

After admiring the Queen's Bedroom and Chinese lacquer cabinet, head back down the long hall to **King Ludwig I's Gallery of Beauties.** The room is decorated top to bottom with portraits of 36 beautiful women (all painted by Joseph Stieler between 1826 and 1850). Ludwig I was a consummate girl-watcher.

Ludwig prided himself on his ability to appreciate beauty regardless of social rank. He enjoyed picking out the prettiest women from the general public and, with one of the most effective pickup lines of all time, inviting them to the palace for a portrait. Who could refuse? The portraits were on public display in the Residenz, and catapulted their subjects to stardom. The women range from commoners to princesses, but notice that they share one physical trait—Ludwig obviously preferred

brunettes. The portraits are done in the modest and slightly sentimental Biedermeier style popular in central Europe, as opposed to the more flamboyant Romanticism (so beloved of Ludwig's "mad" grandson) also thriving at that time.

Most of these portraits have rich stories behind them, none more than Lola Montez, the king's most notorious mistress, who led him to his downfall. The portrait shows her the year she met Ludwig (she was 29, he was 60), wearing the black-lace mantilla and red flowers of a Spanish dancer. Lola became his mistress, and he fawned over her in public, scandalizing Munich. The Münchners resented her spending their tax money and dominating their king. In 1848, as Europe was swept by a tide of revolution, the citizens rose up and forced Ludwig to abdicate.

Pass through the blue Audience Room (with elaborate curtain rods and mahogany furniture in the French-inspired Empire style) and into the (other) **Queen's Bedroom.** The room has much the same furniture it had on August 25, 1845, when Princess Marie gave birth to the future King Ludwig II. Little Ludwig (see his bust, next to brother Otto's) was greatly inspired by

Stieler, Lola Montez *(detail)*

Nymphenburg—riding horses in summer, taking sleigh rides in winter, reading poetry at Amalienburg. The love of nature and solitude he absorbed at Nymphenburg eventually led Ludwig to abandon Munich for his castles in the remote Bavarian countryside. By the way, note the mirror in this bedroom. Royal births were carefully witnessed, and the mirror allowed for a better view. While Ludwig's birth was well-documented, his death was shrouded in mystery (see page 167).

PALACE GROUNDS

The wooded grounds extend far back beyond the formal gardens and are popular with joggers and walkers. Find a bench for a low-profile picnic. The park is laced with canals and small lakes, where court guests once rode on Venetian-style gondolas.

ROYAL STABLES MUSEUM (MARSTALLMUSEUM)

These former stables (to the left of the main palace as you approach the complex) are full of gilded coaches that will make you think of Cinderella's journey to the king's ball. Upstairs, a porcelain exhibit shows off some of the famous Nymphenburg finery. If you don't want to visit the main palace, you can buy a €4.50 ticket just for this museum (no audioguide available).

Visiting the Museum: Wandering through the collection, you can trace the evolution of 300 years of coaches—getting lighter and with better suspension as they were harnessed to faster horses.

Royal Stables Museum

In the big entrance hall is a golden carriage drawn by eight fake white horses. In 1742, it carried Karl Albrecht Wittelsbach to Frankfurt to be crowned Holy Roman Emperor. As emperor, he got eight horses—kings got only six. The event is depicted in a frieze on the museum wall; Karl's carriage is #159.

Other objects bear witness to the good times of the relaxed Nymphenburg lifestyle and are a window into the pomp and circumstance surrounding the royals.

Next up are some over-the-top objects—sleighs, golden carriages, and (in the glass cases) harnesses—owned by Ludwig II. Ludwig's over-the-top coaches were Baroque. But this was 1870. The coaches, like the king, were in the wrong century.

Head upstairs to a collection of **Nymphenburg porcelain.** Historically, royal families such as the Wittelsbachs liked to have their own porcelain factories to make fit-for-a-king plates, vases, and so on. The Nymphenburg Palace porcelain works is still in operation (the factory store on Odeonsplatz is happy to see you). Find the large room with copies of 17th-century Old Masters' paintings from the Wittelsbach art collection (now at the Alte Pinakothek). Ludwig I had these paintings copied onto porcelain for safekeeping into the distant future. Take a close look—they're exquisite.

AMALIENBURG

Three hundred yards from Nymphenburg Palace, hiding in the park (head into the sculpted garden and veer to the left, following signs), you'll find a fine little Rococo hunting lodge, which takes just a few minutes to tour. In 1734, Prince-Elector Karl Albrecht had it built for his wife, Maria Amalia. Amalienburg was designed by François de Cuvilliés (of Residenz fame) and decorated by Johann Baptist Zimmermann. It's the most worthwhile of the four small "extra" palaces buried in the park that are included on the combo-ticket. The others are the Pagodenburg, a Chinese-inspired pavilion;

Amalienburg

Badenburg, an opulent bathing house and banquet hall; and the Magdalenenklause, a mini palace that looks like a ruin from the outside but has an elaborate altar and woody apartments inside.

Visiting Amalienburg: As you approach, circle around and notice the facade. Above the pink-and-white grand entryway, Diana, goddess of the chase, is surrounded by themes of the hunt and flanked by busts of satyrs. The queen would shoot from the perch atop the roof. Behind a wall in the garden, dogs would scare nonflying pheasants. When they jumped up in the air above the wall, the sporting queen—as if shooting skeet—would pick the birds off.

Tourists now enter this tiny getaway through the back door. Doghouses under gun cupboards fill the first room. In the fine yellow-and-silver bedroom, the bed is flanked by portraits of Karl Albrecht and Maria Amalia—decked out in hunting attire. She liked her dogs. The door under her portrait leads to stairs to the rooftop pheasant-shooting perch.

The mini Hall of Mirrors is a blue-and-silver commotion of Rococo nymphs designed by Cuvilliés. In the next room, paintings depict court festivities, formal hunting parties, and no-contest kills (where the animal is put at an impossible disadvantage—like shooting fish in a barrel). Finally, the sparse kitchen is decorated with Chinese-style drawings on Dutch tile.

Outside the Center
▲BMW-WELT AND MUSEUM

At the headquarters of BMW ("beh-em-VEH" to Germans), Beamer dreamers can visit two space-age buildings to learn more about this brand's storied heritage (worth ▲▲ to enthusiasts). The renowned *Autos* and *Motorräder* are beautifully displayed (perhaps even fetishized by car enthusiasts). This vast complex—built on the site of Munich's first airstrip and home to the BMW factory since 1920—has four components: the headquarters (in the building nicknamed "the Four Cylinders"—not open to the public), the factory (tourable with advance reservations), the showroom (called BMW-Welt—"BMW World"), and the BMW Museum.

Cost and Hours: Museum-€10; Tue-Sun 10:00-18:00, closed Mon; BMW-Welt showroom-free, building open daily until 24:00, exhibits staffed 9:00-18:00; tel. 089/125-016-001, www.bmw-welt.com.

Tours: English tours are offered of both the museum (€13, 1 hour, call or email ahead for times) and BMW-Welt (€7.50, 1 hour, Mon-Wed and Sat at 15:30). Factory tours must be booked at least two months in advance (€9, 2.5 hours, Mon-Fri only, ages 6 and up, reservations tel. 089/125-016-001, infowelt@bmw-welt.com).

Getting There: From the city center, ride the U-3 to Olympia-Zentrum. Follow *Ausgang* signs to BMW-Welt/BMW Museum. Leaving the station, climb the stairs and get oriented: Ahead is the BMW-Welt (showroom) entry, and the BMW Museum is marked by the gray "soup bowl." To reach the BMW Museum, head down Lerchenauer Strasse, staying parallel to the factory on your left, and cross at the stoplight just before the bridge.

Visiting BMW: The futuristic, bowl-shaped **museum** encloses a world of floating walkways linking exhibits highlighting BMW motorcycle and car design and technology through the years. The museum traces the Bavarian Motor

The futuristic BMW-Welt is a one-of-a-kind auto showroom.

Works' history since 1917, when the company began making airplane engines. Motorcycles came next, followed by the first BMW sedan in 1929. You'll see how design was celebrated here from the start. Exhibits showcase motorsports, roadsters, and luxury cars. Stand on an *E* for English to hear the chief designer talk about his favorite cars in the "treasury." And the 1956 BMW 507 is enough to rev almost anyone's engine.

After the museum, cross over the swoopy bridge to enter **BMW-Welt** on the first floor. The building itself—a cloud-shaped, glass-and-steel architectural masterpiece—is reason enough to visit. It's free and filled with exhibits designed to enthuse car lovers so they'll find a way to afford a Beemer. While the adjacent museum reviews the BMW past, BMW-Welt shows you the present and gives you a breathtaking look at the future. This is where customers come to pick up their new Beemers (stand on the sky bridge viewpoint to watch in envy), and where hopeful customers-to-be come to nurture their automotive dreams.

EXPERIENCES

Oktoberfest

The 1810 marriage reception of King Ludwig I was such a success that it turned into an annual bash. These days, Oktoberfest lasts just over two weeks, starting on a Saturday in September and usually ending on the first Sunday in October (www. oktoberfest.de). It's held at the Theresienwiese fairground south of the main train station, in a meadow known as the "Wies'n" (VEE-zen), where huge tents seat nearly 120,000 beer drinkers. The festivities kick off with an opening parade and then, for the next two weeks, it's a frenzy of drinking, dancing, music, and food. Total strangers stroll arm-in-arm down rows of picnic tables amid a carnival of beer, pretzels, and wurst, drawing visi-

tors from all over the globe. A million gallons of beer later, they roast the last ox.

If you'll be here during the festivities, it's best to reserve a room early. During the fair, the city functions even better than normal, but is admittedly more expensive and crowded. It's a good time to sightsee, even if beer-hall rowdiness isn't your cup of tea.

The enormous beer tents are often full, especially on weekends—if possible, avoid going on a Friday or Saturday night. For some cultural background, consider hiring a local guide or going with a group (Radius Tours, for example, offers a €140 tour that includes two beers, half a chicken, and guaranteed seating, Sun-Fri at 10:00, none on Sat, reserve ahead, www.radiustours.com; Size Matters Beer Tour runs options for €129-209 that include breakfast, lunch, four beers, and reserved seating, www.sizemattersbeertour.de).

In the city center, the humble **Beer and Oktoberfest Museum** (Bier- und Oktoberfestmuseum) offers a low-tech and underwhelming take on beer history (€4, Tue-Sat 13:00-18:00, closed Sun-Mon,

Sterneckerstrasse 2, tel. 089/2423-1607, www.bier-und-oktoberfestmuseum.de).

Rick's Tip: *Along with Oktoberfest, the Theresienwiese fairground also hosts a* **Spring Festival** *(Frühlingsfest, two weeks in late April-early May, www.fruehlingsfest-muenchen.de) and* **Tollwood,** *an artsy, multicultural event held twice a year—once in summer (late June-July) and in winter (alternative Christmas market, late Nov-Dec, www.tollwood.de).*

Shopping

While the whole city is great for shopping, the most glamorous area is around Marienplatz. It's fun to window shop, even if you have no plans to buy. Stroll from Marienplatz down the pedestrianized Weinstrasse (to the left as you face the New Town Hall). Look for **Fünf Höfe** on your left, a delightful indoor/outdoor mall filled with Germany's top shops (Mon-Fri 10:00-19:00, Sat until 18:00, closed Sun).

Bavarian Souvenirs: Servus Heimat's amusing shops are a good source for unusual gifts (City Museum store, between Munich City Museum and Stadt Café: daily 10:00-18:00, St.-Jakobs-Platz 1, tel. 089/2370-2380; also at Im Tal 20—between Marienplatz and the Isartor—and at Brunnstrasse 3—near Asam Church, Mon-Sat 10:00-19:00, closed Sun; www.servusheimat.com).

For that beer stein you promised your uncle, try the shops on the pedestrian zone by St. Michael's Church and the gift shops that surround the Hofbräuhaus.

Dirndls and Lederhosen: For fine-quality (and very expensive) traditional clothing (*Trachten*), head to the third floor of **Loden-Frey Verkaufshaus** (Mon-Sat 10:00-20:00, closed Sun, a block west of Marienplatz at Maffeistrasse 7, tel. 089/210-390, www.loden-frey.com). For less expensive (but still good quality) gear, visit **Angermaier Trachten**, near the Viktualienmarkt (Mon-Fri 10:00-19:00, Sat until 18:00, closed Sun; Rosental 10, tel. 089/2300-0199, www.trachten-angermaier.de).

Department Stores: Ludwig Beck, an upscale department store at Marienplatz, has been a local institution since 1861 (Mon-Sat 10:00-20:00, closed Sun). For more reasonable prices near Marienplatz, try **C&A** (cheap yet respected; sells only clothing) and **Galeria Kaufhof** (midrange; sells everything).

Nightlife

Here are a few nightlife alternatives to the beer-and-oompah scene. Ballet and opera fans can check the schedule at the **Bayerisch Staatsoper,** centrally located next door to the Residenz. Book at least two months ahead—seats range from reasonable to very pricey (Max-Joseph-Platz 2, tel. 089/2185-1920, www.bayerische.staatsoper.de). The **Hotel Bayerischerhof**'s posh nightclub has major jazz acts plus pop, soul, and disco (Promenadeplatz 2, tel. 089/212-0994, www.bayerischerhof.de). For familiar Broadway-style musicals (usually in German), try the **Deutsches Theatre,** located near the train station (Schwanthalerstrasse 13, tel. 089/5523-4444, www.deutsches-theater.de).

EATING

Munich's cuisine is traditionally seasoned with beer. In beer halls, beer gardens, or at the Viktualienmarkt, try the most typical meal in town: *Weisswurst* (white-colored veal sausage—peel off the skin before eating, often available only until noon) with *süsser Senf* (sweet mustard), a salty *Brezel* (pretzel), and *Weissbier* ("white" wheat beer). Another traditional favorite is *Obatzter,* a mix of soft cheeses, butter, paprika, and often garlic or onions that's spread on bread. *Brotzeit,* literally "bread time," gets you a wooden platter of cold cuts, cheese, and pickles and is a good option for a light dinner.

Beer Halls and Gardens

Nothing beats the Hofbräuhaus (the only beer hall in town where you'll find oompah music) for those in search of the boisterous, clichéd image of the beer hall. Locals prefer the innumerable beer gardens. On a warm day, when you're looking for the authentic outdoor beer-garden experience, your best options are the Augustiner

(near the train station), the small beer garden at the Viktualienmarkt (near Marienplatz), or the sea of tables in the English Garden (near the Chinese Tower).

Rick's Tip: *By law,* **any place serving beer** *must admit the public (whether or not they're customers) to* **use the WCs.**

Near Marienplatz

$$ The Hofbräuhaus (HOAF-broy-howz) is the world's most famous beer hall. While it's grotesquely touristy, it's a Munich must. You can drop by anytime for a large or light meal, or just for a drink. Except for *Weissbier*, the Hofbräuhaus sells beer only by the *Mass* (one-liter mug) after 18:00—and they claim to sell 10,000 of these liters every day. Choose from four zones: the rowdy main hall on the ground floor, a quieter courtyard under the stars, a dainty restaurant with mellow music the first floor up, or the giant festival hall under a big barrel vault on the top floor. Live oompah music plays at lunch and dinner in the main hall/restaurant (daily 9:00-23:30, 5-minute walk from Marienplatz at Platzl 9, tel. 089/2901-3610).

$$$ Haxnbauer, stark and old-school, is a hit with German tourists for one reason: the best pork knuckle in town (half *Schweinshaxe*-€19, slightly less if you just get some slices). It's clearly the place for what looks like a pork knee—notice the rotisserie window luring customers inside (daily 11:00-24:00, two blocks from Hofbräuhaus at Sparkassenstrasse 6, tel. 089/216-6540).

$$ Andechser am Dom sits at the rear of the twin-domed Frauenkirche on a breezy square, serving Andechs beer brewed by monks and great food to appreciative regulars. Münchners favor the dark beer (ask for *dunkles*), but I love the light (*helles*). The *Gourmetteller* is a great sampler of their specialties, but you can't go wrong with *Rostbratwurst* with kraut (daily 10:00-24:00, Weinstrasse 7a, reserve during peak times, tel. 089/2429-2920, www.andechser-am-dom.de).

$$ Nürnberger Bratwurst Glöckl am Dom, around the corner from Andechser am Dom, offers a more traditional, fiercely

Munich's Beer Scene

Beer is truly a people's drink—and the best is in Munich. The big question among connoisseurs is, "Which brew today?"

Huge liter beers (called *eine Mass* in German, or "a pitcher" in the US) cost about €8. You can order your beer *Helles* (light), *Dunkles* (dark), or ask for a *Weissbier* or *Weizen* ("white" or wheat-based beer—cloudy and sweet) or a *Radler* (half lemon soda, half beer).

Many beer halls have a cafeteria system. If two prices are listed, *Selbstbedienung* is for self-service (*Bitte bedienen Sie sich selbst* means "please serve yourself"), while *Bedienung* is for table service. At a large *Biergarten,* assemble your dream feast by visiting various counters, marked by type of food (*Bier* or *Bierschänke* for beer, *Bratwürste* for sausages, *Brotzeiten* for lighter fare served cold, and so on).

Look for these Munich specialties:

Fleischpfanzerl, a.k.a. *Fleischklösse* or *Frikadellen:* Meatballs

Hendl or *Brathähnchen:* Roasted chicken

Radi: Radish that's thinly spiral-cut and salted

Schweinrollbraten: Pork belly

Schweinshax'n, or just **Hax'n:** Pork knuckle

Steckerlfisch: A whole fish, usually mackerel, herbed and grilled on a stick

---

Bavarian evening. Dine outside under the trees or in the dark, medieval interior. Enjoy the tasty little *Nürnberger* sausages with kraut and shredded pancake for dessert (daily 10:00-24:00, Frauenplatz 9, tel. 089/291-9450).

$$$ Altes Hackerhaus is popular for its traditional *Bayerisch* (Bavarian) fare served with a slightly fancier feel in one of the oldest buildings in town. It offers a small courtyard and a fun forest of characteristic nooks. Naturally, Hacker-Pschorr beer is popular, especially the *Weisse* ("small appetite" menu available, daily 10:30-24:00, Sendlinger Strasse 14, tel. 089/260-5026).

$$$ Der Pschorr, an upscale beer hall occupying a former slaughterhouse, has a terrace overlooking the Viktualienmarkt and serves what many consider Munich's finest beer. With organic "slow food" including vegan and vegetarian options, this place mixes modern concepts with traditional dishes. The sound of the hammer tapping wooden kegs lets patrons know their beer is good and fresh (seasonal specials, daily 10:00-24:00, Viktualienmarkt 15, at end of Schrannenhalle, tel. 089/442-383-940).

$ Viktualien Beer Garden, at the center of the Viktualienmarkt, has about the best budget eating in town. It's just steps from Marienplatz (daily 10:00-22:00 in good weather). There's table service wherever you see a tablecloth; to picnic, choose a table without one—but you must buy a drink from the counter. Countless stalls surround the beer garden and sell wurst, sandwiches, produce, and more.

$$$ Spatenhaus is the opera-goers' classy beer hall, serving elegant food in a rustic, traditional setting since 1896—maybe it's not even right to call it a "beer hall." You can also eat outside, on the square facing the opera and palace. It's pricey, but you won't find better quality Bavarian cuisine. The upstairs restaurant is more formal—reservations recommended (daily 9:30-23:00, on Max-Joseph-Platz opposite opera, Residenzstrasse 12, tel. 089/290-7060, www.spatenhaus.de).

Near the Train Station
$$ Augustiner Beer Garden, a true under-the-leaves beer garden packed with Münchners, is a delight. In fact, most Münchners consider Augustiner the best beer garden in town—which may be why it has 6,000 seats. There's no music, it's away from the tourist hordes, and it serves up great beer, good traditional food, huge portions, reasonable prices, and perfect conviviality. The outdoor self-service (at the opposite end from the entrance) is best on a nice summer evening. Parents with kids can sit at tables adjoining a sizable playground. There's also indoor and outdoor seating at a more expensive **$$$** restaurant with table service by the entrance (daily 11:30-24:00, Arnulfstrasse 52, 3 loooong blocks from station going away from the center—or take tram #16/#17 one stop to Hopfenstrasse, tel. 089/594-393).

$$ Park Café Beer Garden is a nice hideaway in good weather, tucked inside the Alter Botanischer Garten, just north of the train station. Order Bavarian food from self-service counters (don't forget to reclaim your deposit at the counter for your plate and mug). The indoor **$$$** restaurant is a modern and cozy pricier option, and often features DJs or live music in the late evening (daily 11:00-24:00, beer garden open until 19:00 in nice weather, Sophienstrasse 7, tel. 089/5161-7980).

In the English Garden
$$ The Chinese Tower beer garden (*Chinesischer Turm Biergarten*), deep in the English Garden, is famed for outdoor ambience and a cheap meal; it's a great place for a balmy, relaxed evening. You're welcome to B.Y.O. food and grab a table, or buy from the cafeteria-style food stalls.

Chinese Tower beer garden

Don't bother to phone ahead—they have 6,000 seats. This is a fine opportunity to try a *Steckerlfisch*, sold at a separate kiosk. Take your blue token and your beer mug around back to redeem your refund (daily, long hours in good weather, usually live music, playground, tel. 089/383-8730; take tram #18 from main train station or Sendlinger Tor to Tivolistrasse, or U-3 or U-6 to Giselastrasse and then bus #54 or #154 two stops).

Restaurants
Man does not live by beer alone. Well, maybe some do. But for the rest of us, I recommend the following alternatives.

On and near Marienplatz
$$$ Glockenspiel Café is good for a coffee or a meal with a bird's-eye view down on the Marienplatz action—I'd come for the view more than the Italian food. Regardless of the weather, I grab a seat overlooking Marienplatz—but after 18:00, you must order dinner for view seating (Mon-Sat 9:00-24:00, Sun 10:00-19:00, ride elevator from Rosenstrasse entrance,

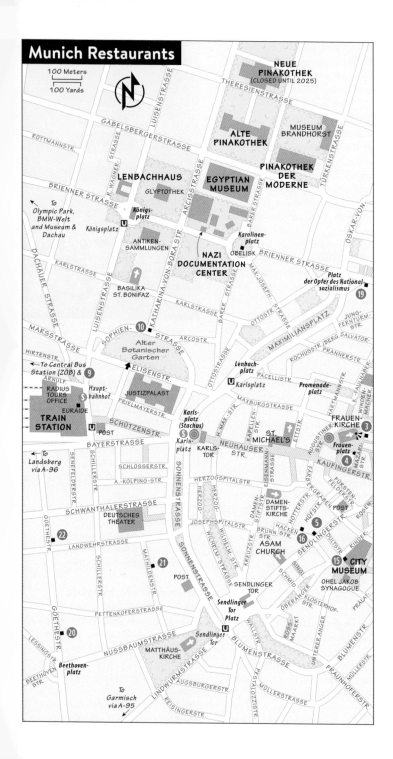

Munich Restaurants

100 Meters
100 Yards

NEUE PINAKOTHEK (CLOSED UNTIL 2025)

THERESIENSTRASSE

ROTTMANNSTR.

GABELSBERGERSTRASSE

LUISENSTRASSE

R. WAGNER-STR.

STRASSE

ALTE PINAKOTHEK

MUSEUM BRANDHORST

TÜRKENSTRASSE

BRIENNER STRASSE

LENBACHHAUS

GLYPTOTHEK

EGYPTIAN MUSEUM

PINAKOTHEK DER MODERNE

ARCISSTRASSE

BARER STRASSE

To Olympic Park, BMW-Welt and Museum & Dachau

Königs-platz

Königsplatz

ANTIKEN-SAMMLUNGEN

KATHARINA-VON-BORA STR.

NAZI DOCUMENTATION CENTER

Karolinen-platz

OBELISK

BRIENNER STRASSE

OSKAR-VON-

DACHAUER STRASSE

KARLSTRASSE

Platz der Opfer des National-sozialismus **19**

BASILIKA ST. BONIFAZ

MAX-JOSEPH-STRASSE

MAXIMILIANSPLATZ

JUNG-FERNTURM-STR.

MARSSTRASSE

LUISENSTRASSE

SOPHIEN-

KARLSTRASSE

ARCOSTR.

OTTOSTR.

SALVATOR-

ROCHUSSTR./BERG

PRANNERSTR.

HIRTENSTR.

STRASSE **10**

Alter Botanischer Garten

Lenbach-platz

PACELLISTR.

Promenade-platz

K.-FAULHABER-

HARTMANNSTR.

WINDEN-MACHER-

To Central Bus Station (ZOB) & **9**

ELISENSTR.

ARNULF

Karlsplatz

OTTOSTRASSE

MAXBURGSTRASSE

RADIUS TOURS OFFICE **S**

EURAIDE

Haupt-bahnhof

JUSTIZPALAST

PRIELMAYERSTR.

Karls-platz (Stachus) **S**

H. MAX. STR.

KAPELLEN-STR.

AUGUSTINER-

ETISTR.

FRAUEN-KIRCHE **3**

TRAIN STATION

POST

SCHÜTZENSTR.

Karls-platz

KARLS-TOR

NEUHAUSER-STR.

ST. MICHAEL'S

Frauen-platz **4**

MAZALL-

To Landsberg via A-96

BAYERSTRASSE

SENEFELDERSTR.

SCHILLERSTR.

SCHLOSSSTR.

A.-KOLPING-STR.

SONNENSTRASSE

HERZOGSPITALSTR.

EISENMANN-STRASSE

KAUFINGERSTR.

FARBERGRABEN

FÜRSTEN-FELDERSTR.

ROBEN-

SCHWANTHALERSTRASSE

DEUTSCHES THEATER

HERZOG-

DAMEN-STIFTSTR.

DAMEN-STIFTS-KIRCHE

HÖFESTR.

POST

GOETHESTR. **22**

LANDWEHRSTRASSE

MATHILDENSTR.

JOSEPHSPITALSTR.

WILHELM-STRASSE

KREUZSTR.

BRUNN-STR.

HACKEN-STR.

SENDLINGERSTR.

DÜLTSTR.

RINDER-

SINGL-

ASAM CHURCH **16**

SCHMID

SCHILLERSTR.

POST **21**

SONNENSTRASSE

5

15 CITY MUSEUM

OHEL JAKOB SYNAGOGUE

OBERANGER

KLOSTERHOF-STR.

PRÄLE-

BLUMENSTR.

PETTENKOFERSTRASSE

SENDLINGER TOR

WALLSTR.

KOBEL-

MARKT

UNTERER ANGER

GOETHESTR.

20

NUSSBAUMSTRASSE

Sendlinger Tor Platz

Sendlinger Tor

LINDWURMSTRASSE

MATTHÄUS-KIRCHE

AUGSBURGERSTR.

BLUMENSTRASSE

PISTALOZZISTR.

FRAUNHOFERSTR.

MÜLLERSTR.

LESSINGSTR.

BEETHOVEN-STR.

Beethoven-platz

To Garmisch via A-95

REISINGERSTR.

MÜLLERSTRASSE

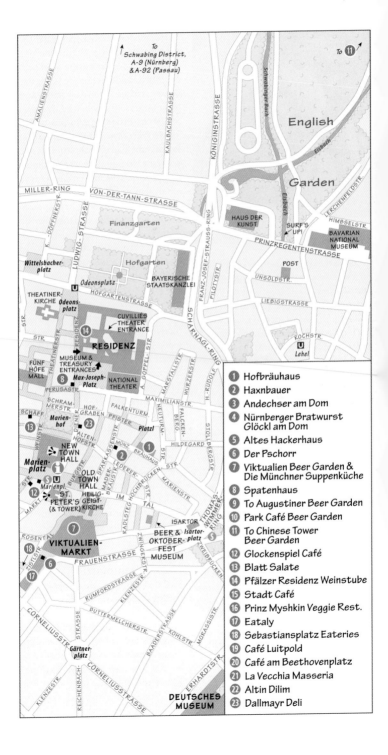

1. Hofbräuhaus
2. Haxnbauer
3. Andechser am Dom
4. Nürnberger Bratwurst Glöckl am Dom
5. Altes Hackerhaus
6. Der Pschorr
7. Viktualien Beer Garden & Die Münchner Suppenküche
8. Spatenhaus
9. To Augustiner Beer Garden
10. Park Café Beer Garden
11. To Chinese Tower Beer Garden
12. Glockenspiel Café
13. Blatt Salate
14. Pfälzer Residenz Weinstube
15. Stadt Café
16. Prinz Myshkin Veggie Rest.
17. Eataly
18. Sebastiansplatz Eateries
19. Café Luitpold
20. Café am Beethovenplatz
21. La Vecchia Masseria
22. Altin Dilim
23. Dallmayr Deli

opposite glockenspiel at Marienplatz 28, tel. 089/264-256).

$$ Blatt Salate is a self-serve salad bar on a side street between the Frauenkirche and the New Town Hall; it's a great little hideaway for a healthy, quick lunch (vegetarian and meat salads and soups, Mon-Sat 11:00-19:00, closed Sun, Schäfflerstrasse 7, tel. 089/2102-0281).

$$ Pfälzer Residenz Weinstube, a very traditional German dining hall actually in the Residenz complex, is dedicated to food and wine from the Rhineland (Palatine)—which was ruled by the Wittelsbach family. Serving small wine-friendly dishes and a big variety of German wines by the tiny glass, it's ideal for wine lovers needing a break from beer (daily 10:30-24:00, Residenzstrasse 1, tel. 089/225-628).

Around the Viktualienmarkt

$ Die Münchner Suppenküche ("Munich Soup Kitchen"), a soup tent at the Viktualienmarkt, is a fine place for a small, cozy sit-down lunch at picnic tables under a closed-in awning. The red sign lists the soups of the day—I go for the goulash or Bavarian potato soup (Mon-Sat 10:00-18:00, closed Sun, near corner of Reichenbachstrasse and Frauenstrasse, tel. 089/260-9599).

$$ Stadt Café is a lively café serving a selection of sandwiches, with a nice wine list and cakes. This informal, no-frills restaurant draws newspaper readers, stroller moms, and locals meeting for a drink after work. Dine in the quiet cobbled courtyard, inside, or outside facing the new synagogue (open daily 10:00-24:00, in same building as Munich City Museum, St.-Jakobs-Platz 1, tel. 089/266-949).

$$$ Prinz Myshkin Vegetarian Restaurant is an upscale vegetarian eatery in the old center. Don't miss the enticing appetizer selection on display as you enter (they do a fine €14 mixed-appetizer plate). They also have vegetarian sushi, pastas, Indian dishes, and their own baker, so they're proud of their sweets (lunch specials, seasonal menu, daily 11:00-late, Hackenstrasse 2, tel. 089/265-596).

$$ Eataly at Schrannenhalle, the former grain exchange just off Viktualienmarkt, is a sparkling, pricey food court full of Italian taste treats. It's a festival of food fun with great seating inside the old market hall and outside overlooking the square (café open Mon-Sat 8:00-20:00, Sun 10:00-19:00; restaurants open Mon-Sat 11:30-22:30, Sun until 21:30, Viktualienmarkt 15, tel. 089/248-817-711).

Eateries on Sebastiansplatz: Looking for a no-schnitzel-or-dumplings alternative? Sebastiansplatz is a long, pedestrianized square across from Eataly, between the Viktualienmarkt and the synagogue, lined with **$$ bistros** handy for a healthy and quick lunch. Options range from French to Italian to Asian to salads. You can eat out on the busy cobbled square or inside.

Near Odeonsplatz

$$ Café Luitpold is where Munich's high society comes to sip its coffee and nibble on exquisite cakes. The café is proudly home to the original *Luitpoldtorte* (sponge cake with layers of marzipan and buttercream, covered in dark chocolate). I prefer their strawberry-cream cake (Tue-Sat 8:00-23:00, Sun-Mon 9:00-19:00, Brienner Strasse 11, tel. 089/242-8750).

Near the Train Station

$$$ Café am Beethovenplatz feels like an old Vienna café with its inviting, woody interior and charming garden. While just a 10-minute walk from the station, it's in a leafy and quiet residential neighborhood. They serve a mix of Italian, Bavarian, and vegetarian fare, offer cheap lunch specials and homemade cakes, and have live music almost nightly (daily 9:00-24:00, at Mariandl Hotel, Goethestrasse 51, tel. 089/552-9100).

$$$ La Vecchia Masseria, between Sendlinger Tor and the train station hotels, serves Italian food in a cozy Tuscan farmhouse-style interior, or outside in a beautiful flowery courtyard. Pasta, pizzas, and seasonal, more expensive main courses are served. Can't decide which pasta to get? Ask for a *bis,* half-portions of two pastas (daily 11:30-23:30, garden dining until 21:30, reservations smart, Mathildenstrasse 3, tel. 089/550-9090, www.lavecchiamasseria.de).

$$ Altin Dilim, a cafeteria-style Turkish restaurant, is a standout among the many hole-in-the-wall Middle Eastern places in the ethnic area near the station. A handy pictorial menu helps you order (cheap *döner kebabs,* daily 6:00-24:00, Goethestrasse 17, tel. 089/9734-0869).

Picnics

For a truly elegant (and pricey) picnic, **Dallmayr's** is the place to shop. The crown in their emblem reflects that even the royal family assembled its picnics at this historic delicatessen. Put together a royal spread to munch in the nearby Hofgarten or visit the classy café that serves light meals on the first floor (Mon-Sat 9:30-19:00, closed Sun, behind New Town Hall, Dienerstrasse 14, tel. 089/213-5110).

Budget Picnic: To save money, buy at a **supermarket** (generally open Mon-Sat until 20:00, closed Sun. The ones in the basements of department stores are on the upscale side: **Galeria Kaufhof** stores at Marienplatz and Karlsplatz, or **Karstadt**

across from the train station. Cheaper stores include the **REWE** in the basement at Fünf Höfe (entrance is in Viscardihof), **Lidl** at Schwanthalerstrasse 31 (near train-station hotels), or **Yorma's** (several at the train station).

SLEEPING

I've listed accommodations in two main neighborhoods: within a few blocks of the central train station (Hauptbahnhof), and in the old center, between Marienplatz and Sendlinger Tor.

Near the Train Station

Good-value hotels cluster in the multicultural area immediately south of the station. To some this is a colorful neighborhood, for others it feels seedy after dark, but it's sketchy only for those in search of trouble.

$$$$ Hotel Deutsches Theater, filled with brass and marble, has 27 well-worn, three-star rooms. The back rooms face the courtyard of a neighboring theater—when there's a show, there can be some noise (breakfast extra, elevator, Landwehrstrasse 18, tel. 089/545-8525, www.hoteldeutschestheater.de, info@ hoteldeutschestheater.de).

$$$$ Hotel Uhland is a stately mansion that rents 29 rooms with modern bathrooms in a genteel residential neighborhood a slightly longer walk from the station than other places listed here (toward the Theresienwiese Oktoberfest grounds). It's been in the Hauzenberger and Reim families for 60 years (family rooms, some waterbeds, limited parking, Uhlandstrasse 1, tel. 089/543-350, www. hotel-uhland.de, info@hotel-uhland.de). From the station, take bus #58 (direction: Silberhornstrasse) to Georg-Hirth-Platz, or walk 15 minutes: Out the station's south exit, cross Bayerstrasse, take Paul-Heyse-Strasse three blocks to Georg-Hirth-Platz, then take a soft right on Uhlandstrasse.

$$$ Hotel Monaco is a delightful and

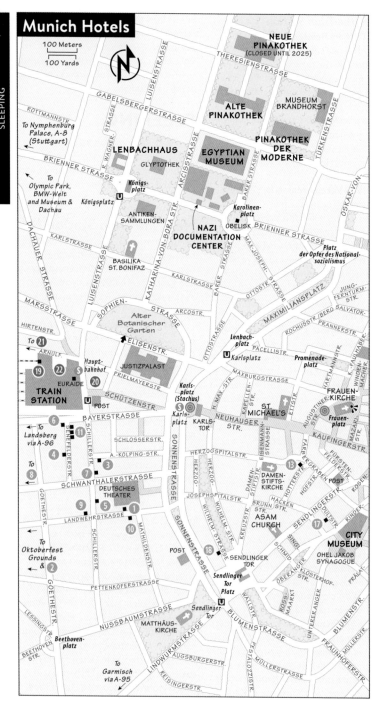

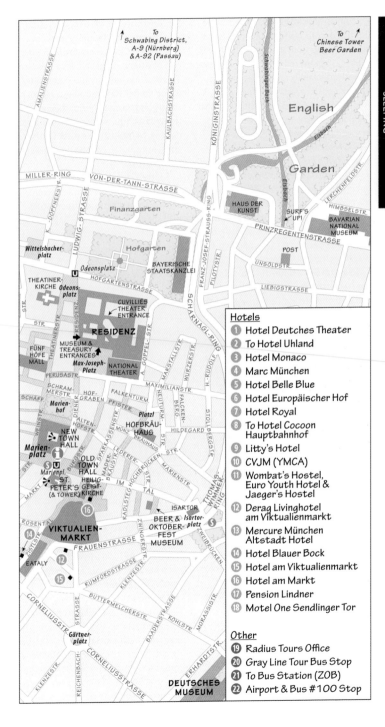

To Schwabing District,
A-9 (Nürnberg)
& A-92 (Passau)

To
Chinese Tower
Beer Garden

English

Garden

AMALIENSTRASSE
KAULBACHSTRASSE
KÖNIGINSTRASSE
Schwabinger Bach
LERCHENFELDSTR.

MILLER-RING
VON-DER-TANN-STRASSE
HIMBSELSTR.

Finanzgarten
HAUS DER
KUNST
SURF'S
UP!
BAVARIAN
NATIONAL
MUSEUM

K.-DÖPFNERSTR.
LUDWIG-STRASSE
PRINZREGENTENSTRASSE
Eisbach

Wittelsbacher-
platz
Hofgarten
FRANZ-JOSEF-STRAUSS-RING
PILOTYSTR.
POST
UNSOLDSTR.

Odeonsplatz
BAYERISCHE
STAATSKANZLEI
LIEBIGSTRASSE

THEATINER-
KIRCHE
Odeons-
platz
HOFGARTENSTRASSE

STR.
RESIDENZTR.
CUVILLIES
THEATER
ENTRANCE
SCHARNAGL-RING

RESIDENZ

STR.

FÜNF
HÖFE
MALL
MUSEUM &
TREASURY
ENTRANCES
Max-Joseph-
Platz
NATIONAL
THEATER
MARSTALLSTR.
MÜRZERSTR.
H.-RUDOLF

THEATINERSTR.
J.-DOPPEL-STR.

PERUSASTR.
SCHRAM-
MERSTR.
HOF-
GRABEN
FALKENTURM
MAXIMILIANSTR.
FALCKEN-
BERG

SCHÄFF-
Marien-
hof
DIENERSTR.
PFISTER
NEUTURM
HILDEGARD

Marien-
platz
NEW
TOWN
HALL
ALTEN-
HOFSTR.
SPARK-
ASSENSTR.
Platzl
HOFBRÄU-
HAUS

Marienpl.
OLD
TOWN
HALL
MADER-
BRÄUSTR.
LEDERER-
STR.
BRAUHAUS
STR.
THOMAS-
WIMMER-
RING

ST.
HEILIG-
PETER'S GEIST-
(& TOWER) KIRCHE
HOCHBRÜCKEN-STR.
IM
TAL
MARIENSTR.

MARKT
RADLSTEG
ISARTOR
Isartor-
platz

ROSENTAL
BEER &
OKTOBER-
FEST
MUSEUM

VIKTUALIEN-
MARKT
ZISTLSTR.
FRAUENSTRASSE
ZWINGERSTR.
ZWEIBRÜCKEN-

EATALY
RUMFORDSTRASSE
KLENZESTR.

BUTTERMELCHERSTR.
BAADERSTRASSE
KOHLSTR.
MORASSISTR.

CORNELIUSSTR.
STRASSE

Gärtner-
platz
CORNELIUSSTRASSE
ERHARDTSTR.

KLENZESTR.
REICHENBACH-STR.
DEUTSCHES
MUSEUM

Hotels

1 Hotel Deutches Theater
2 To Hotel Uhland
3 Hotel Monaco
4 Marc München
5 Hotel Belle Blue
6 Hotel Europäischer Hof
7 Hotel Royal
8 To Hotel Cocoon
Hauptbahnhof
9 Litty's Hotel
10 CVJM (YMCA)
11 Wombat's Hostel,
Euro Youth Hotel &
Jaeger's Hostel
12 Derag Livinghotel
am Viktualienmarkt
13 Mercure München
Altstadt Hotel
14 Hotel Blauer Bock
15 Hotel am Viktualienmarkt
16 Hotel am Markt
17 Pension Lindner
18 Motel One Sendlinger Tor

Other

19 Radius Tours Office
20 Gray Line Tour Bus Stop
21 To Bus Station (ZOB)
22 Airport & Bus #100 Stop

welcoming little hideaway, tucked inside three floors of a giant, nondescript building two blocks from the station (breakfast extra, cash preferred, cheaper rooms with shared bath, family rooms, pay parking nearby, Schillerstrasse 9, entrance on Adolf-Kolping-Strasse, reception on fifth floor, tel. 089/545-9940, www.hotel-monaco.de, info@hotel-monaco.de).

$$$ Marc München—polished, modern, and with 80 rooms—is a good option if you need a little more luxury than the other listings here and are willing to pay the price. It's just a half-block from the station, and has a refined lobby and classy breakfast spread (RS%, air-con, pay parking, Senefelderstrasse 12, tel. 089/559-820, www.hotel-marc.de, info@hotel-marc.de).

$$ Hotel Belle Blue, three blocks from the station, has 30 brightly colored rooms and air-conditioning. Run by Irmgard, this hotel has been in the family for 90 years and offers a good value. The breakfast is tops, and several stylish apartments with kitchenettes are perfect for families (elevator, pay parking, Schillerstrasse 21, tel. 089/550-6260, www.hotel-belleblue.de, info@hotel-belleblue.com).

$$ Hotel Europäischer Hof, across the street from the station, is a huge, impersonal hotel with 150 decent rooms. During cool weather, when you can keep the windows shut, the street-facing rooms are an acceptable option. The quieter, courtyard-facing rooms are more expensive and a lesser value (RS%, includes breakfast when you book directly, cheaper rooms with shared bath, elevator, pay parking, Bayerstrasse 31, tel. 089/551-510, www.heh.de, info@heh.de).

$$ Hotel Royal is one of the best values in the neighborhood (if you can ignore the strip joints flanking the entry). While a bit institutional, it's plenty comfortable and clean. Most importantly, it's energetically run by Pasha and Christiane. Each of its 40 rooms is sharp and bright (RS%, family rooms, comfort rooms on the quiet side cost extra—worth it in summer when you'll want the window open, elevator,

Schillerstrasse 11a, tel. 089/5998-8160, www.hotel-royal.de, info@hotel-royal.de).

$$ Hotel Cocoon Hauptbahnhof is part of a trendy chain but it's a good value. This location has a rustic countryside/alpine theme. Ride the elevator like a personal gondola up to one of their 103 rooms (breakfast extra, air-con, bike rental, pay parking, Mittererstrasse 9, tel. 089/5999-3905, www.hotel-cocoon.de, info@hotel-cocoon.de).

$ Litty's Hotel is a basic place offering 42 small rooms with little personality (breakfast extra, cheaper rooms with shared bath, elevator, pay parking, Landwehrstrasse 32c, tel. 089/5434-4211, www.littyshotel.de, info@littyshotel.de, Verena and Bernd Litty).

¢ The **CVJM** (YMCA), open to all ages, rents 87 beds in clean, slick, and simple rooms, each with its own bathroom. Doubles are head-to-head; triples are like doubles with a bunk over one of the beds (family rooms available, reserve at least 6 months ahead for Oktoberfest weekdays, a year ahead for Oktoberfest weekends; Landwehrstrasse 13, tel. 089/552-1410, www.cvjm-muenchen.org/hotel, hotel@cvjm-muenchen.org).

Hostels near the Station

The following hostels are casual and well-run, with friendly and creative management, and all cater expertly to the needs of young beer-drinking backpackers enjoying Munich on a shoestring. With 900 cheap dorm beds, this is a spirited street. Each place has a lively bar that rages until the wee hours. All have 24-hour receptions, none has a kitchen, but each offers a reasonably priced buffet breakfast.

¢ Wombat's Hostel, perhaps the most hip and colorful, rents cheap doubles and dorm beds, plus some private rooms. The dorms are fresh, modern, and contain bathrooms. The bright rooms facing the winter garden have huge windows (family room available, Senefelderstrasse 1, tel. 089/5998-9180, www.wombats-hostels.com/munich, office@wombats-munich.de).

¢ **Euro Youth Hotel** fills a rare pre-WWII building (includes breakfast for private rooms, bar with live music and game nights, Senefelderstrasse 5, tel. 089/5990-8811, www.euro-youth-hotel.de, info@euro-youth-hotel.de).

¢ **Jaeger's Hostel** has all the fun and efficiency you'd hope for in a hostel—plus the only air-conditioning on the street. Popular with backpackers and business travelers, this is the quietest hostel of the group (family rooms available, Senefelderstrasse 3, tel. 089/555-281, www.jaegershostel.de, office@jaegershostel.de).

In the Old Center

A few good deals remain in the area south of Marienplatz, going toward the Sendlinger Tor. This neighborhood feels more genteel and is convenient for sightseeing.

$$$$ **Derag Livinghotel am Viktualienmarkt** rents 83 rooms in two connected buildings. One is elegant and tech-savvy, with great views of the Viktualienmarkt. The other has stylish rooms with kitchenettes but no views. Both buildings share the same homey breakfast room (breakfast extra, complimentary minibar, air-con, elevator, laundry facilities, pay parking, entrance facing the market on Frauenstrasse 4, tel. 089/885-6560, www.deraghotels.de, res.vik@derag.de).

$$$$ **Mercure München Altstadt Hotel** is reliable, with all the modern comforts in its 80 pricey business-class rooms, and is well-located on a quiet street close to Marienplatz. It's a bit bland, but has fine service (family rooms, air-con, laundry service, a block south of the pedestrian zone at Hotterstrasse 4, tel. 089/232-590, www.mercure-muenchen-altstadt.de, h3709@accor.com).

$$$ **Hotel Blauer Bock,** formerly a dormitory for Benedictine monks, has been on the same corner near the Munich City Museum since 1841. Its 69 contemporary Bavarian rooms are classy, the breakfast is top-notch, and the location is great (family rooms, elevator, guest iPads at front desk, pay parking, Sebastiansplatz 9, tel. 089/231-780, www.hotelblauerbock.de, info@hotelblauerbock.de).

$$$ **Hotel am Viktualienmarkt** rents 26 rooms on a small side street a couple of blocks from the Viktualienmarkt. Everything is small but well-designed—including the elevator and three good-value, tiny single rooms (family rooms, apartment, Utzschneiderstrasse 14, tel. 089/231-1090, www.hotel-am-viktualienmarkt.de, reservierung@hotel-am-viktualienmarkt.de).

$$ **Hotel am Markt,** right next to the Viktualienmarkt, has 32 simple rooms with lots of wainscoting. Light sleepers may need earplugs—the neighboring church's bells ring hourly (skip expensive breakfast, elevator, Heiliggeiststrasse 6, tel. 089/225-014, www.hotel-am-markt.eu, service@hotel-am-markt.eu).

$$ **Pension Lindner** is clean and quiet, with nine pleasant, pastel-bouquet rooms off a bare stairway. Frau Marion Sinzinger offers a warm welcome and good buffet breakfasts (cheaper rooms with shared bath, tiny elevator, Dultstrasse 1, tel. 089/263-413, www.pension-lindner.com, info@pension-lindner.com).

$$ **Motel One Sendlinger Tor,** around the corner from the Sendlinger Tor tram and U-Bahn stop, is a posh-feeling, 241-room, inexpensive chain hotel in a fine location. The stylish, modern rooms are fairly tight and lack some basic amenities (phones, minibars), but otherwise are a good value—and tend to sell out a few weeks in advance. Streetside rooms on upper floors have great views for a little extra. When booking on their website, make sure to choose the Sendlinger Tor location (breakfast extra, air-con, guest iPad at front desk, pay parking, Herzog-Wilhelm-Strasse 28, tel. 089/5177-7250, www.motel-one.com, muenchen-sendlingertor@motel-one.com).

TRANSPORTATION

Getting Around Munich

Much of Munich is walkable. But given that the city is laced by many trams, buses, and subways, it's worth learning the system and considering getting a day pass. Public transit also makes it easy to access sights outside the historic core, such as Dachau or Nymphenburg Palace. Taxis are honest and professional, but expensive (about €12 between the Hauptbahnhof and Marienplatz) and generally unnecessary.

By Public Transit

Munich's transit system uses the same ticket for its subway/trains, buses, and trams. There are two types of trains: The U-Bahn, like a subway, and the S-Bahn, light rail that stops only at major stations. Transit lines are numbered (for example, S-3 or U-5). U-Bahn lines mainly run north-south, while S-Bahn lines are generally east-west. There are four concentric zones: Zone 1 (inner zone where you'll spend most of your time), Zone 2 (Dachau), Zone 3, and Zone 4 (airport).

Information: Pick up a transit map at the TI or station, use the journey planner at www.mvv-muenchen.de, or download the MVV app. You can also head straight to an **MVG customer service center** underground at the train station (open daily) and at Marienplatz (closed Sun); kiosks outside open long hours daily; tel. 0800-344-226-600, www.mvg.de.

TICKET OPTIONS

Transit tickets are sold at booths in the subway and at any ticket machine that has an MVG (blue machines) or DB (red machines) logo. Though operated by different companies, the machines work much the same way (and accept coins, bills, and credit cards).

A one-zone **regular ticket** (*Einzelfahrkarte*) costs €2.90 and is good for three hours in one direction, including changes and stops. For short rides (four stops max, only two of which can be on the subway lines), buy the €1.50 **short-stretch ticket** (*Kurzstrecke*), good for one ride. The €6.70 **all-day pass** (*Single-Tageskarte*) for Zone 1 is a great deal for a single traveler.

All-day small-group passes (*Partner-Tageskarte*) are an even better deal—they cover all public transportation for up to five adults (or up to two adults and six kids). A *Partner-Tageskarte* for Zone 1 costs €12.80. The **XXL** version, which includes Dachau, costs €16.10; and the **airport-city day ticket** (*Flughafen*) costs €24.30 and includes all four zones. These partner tickets are a real steal. The only catch is that you've got to stay together.

USING THE SYSTEM

To find the right platform, look for the name of the last station in the direction (*Richtung*) you want to travel. For example, *Richtung: Marienplatz* means that that particular subway, bus, or tram is traveling in the direction of Marienplatz. Know where you're going relative to Marienplatz, the Hauptbahnhof, and Ostbahnhof, as these are often referred to as end points.

You must stamp tickets with the date and time prior to using them (for an all-day or multiday pass, stamp it only the first time you use it; some tickets bought at a machine come prestamped). For the subway, punch your ticket in the blue machine *before* going down to the platform. For buses and trams, stamp your ticket once on board. Plainclothes ticket checkers enforce this honor system, rewarding freeloaders with stiff €60 fines.

USEFUL TRANSIT LINES

Several subway lines, trams, and buses are especially convenient for tourists. All the main S-Bahn lines (S-1 through S-8) run east-west along the main tourist axis between the Hauptbahnhof, Marienplatz, and the Ostbahnhof. For travel within the city center, just find the platform for

Arriving and Departing
By Plane

Munich's airport is an easy 40-minute ride on the S-1 or S-8 **subway** (both run every 20 minutes from 4:00 to after midnight). The S-8 is a bit quicker and easier; the S-1 line has two branches and some trains split—if you ride the S-1 to the airport, be certain your train is going to the *Flughafen* (airport). A single **airport ticket** costs €11.20, but the all-day pass (€12.80) is worth getting if you'll be making even one more public transport trip that day. The trip is free with a validated and dated rail pass.

The **Lufthansa airport bus** links the airport with the main train station (€10.50, €17 round-trip, 4/hour, 45 minutes, buses depart airport 6:30-22:30, depart train station 5:15-20:00, buy tickets on bus; from inside the station, exit near track 26 and look for yellow *Airport Bus* signs; www.airportbus-muenchen.de. Avoid taking a **taxi** from the airport—it's a long, expensive drive (roughly €65). Airport info: Tel. 089/97500, www.munich-airport.de.

By Train

For quick help at the main train station (München Hauptbahnhof), stop by the service counter in front of track 18. For better English and more patience, drop by the EurAide desk in the *Reisezentrum* (see page 35). Train info: www.bahn.com.

A complete renovation of Munich's main train station is in progress as the city builds a new S-Bahn tunnel (the locations of some services may change as construction progresses).

The Hauptbahnhof is a hive of activity, with a vast **shopping mall** stretching for blocks underground (open daily). Clean, high-tech, pay **WCs** are downstairs near tracks 11 and 26. Check out the bright and modern **food court** or the Dean & David kiosk opposite track 14. For prepared meals to bring on board, I shop at **Yorma's** (four branches: by track 26, by track 32, at street level next to the TI, and in Bahnhofplatz, the underground passage-

lines S-1 through S-8. One track (*Gleis*) will be headed east to the Ostbahnhof, the other west to the Hauptbahnhof. Hop on any train going your direction. The U-3 goes to the BMW sights, and the S-2 goes to Dachau. Bus #100 is useful for getting to the English Garden (from the train station) and to the Museum Quarter (from Odeonsplatz). Tram #17 goes to Nymphenburg Palace (from the train station and the Sendlinger Tor).

By Bike

Level, compact, and with plenty of bike paths, Munich feels made for those on two wheels. You can take your bike on the subway, but not during rush hour (Mon-Fri 6:00-9:00 & 16:00-18:00) and only if you buy a €2.60 bike day pass.

Rick's Tip: *The* **strip of pathway closest to the street is usually reserved for bikes.** *Signs painted on the sidewalk or blue-and-white street signs show which part of the sidewalk is designated for pedestrians and which is for cyclists.*

You can **rent bikes** quickly and easily from **Radius Tours** in the train station in front of track 32 (RS%—ask, daily 8:30-19:00, May-Aug until 20:00, closed Nov-March, tel. 089/543-487-7730, www.radiustours.com).

Munich Transportation

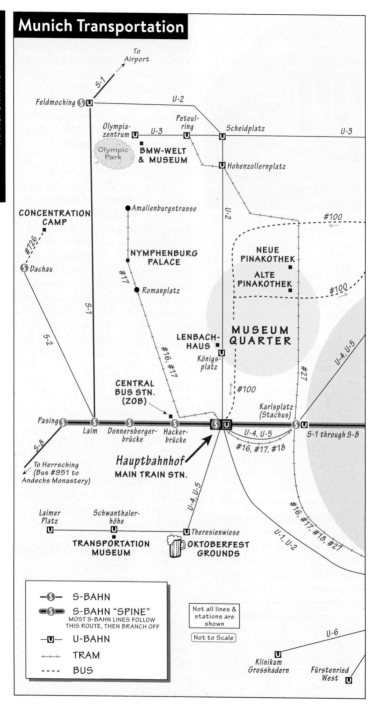

To Airport

S-1

Feldmoching Ⓢ Ⓤ

U-2

Olympia-zentrum Ⓤ

U-3

Peteul-ring Ⓤ

Scheidplatz Ⓤ

U-3

Olympic Park

BMW-WELT & MUSEUM

Hohenzollernplatz Ⓤ

● Amalienburgstrasse

CONCENTRATION CAMP

#726

NYMPHENBURG PALACE

#17

● Romanplatz

Ⓢ Dachau

S-1

S-2

#16, #17

NEUE PINAKOTHEK

ALTE PINAKOTHEK

#100

#100

U-2

LENBACH-HAUS

MUSEUM QUARTER

Königs-platz

#100

U-4, U-5

#27

CENTRAL BUS STN. (ZOB)

Pasing Ⓢ

Laim Ⓢ

Donnersberger-brücke Ⓢ

Hacker-brücke Ⓢ

Ⓢ Ⓤ

Karlsplatz (Stachus) Ⓤ

Ⓤ

S-1 through S-8

S-8

U-4, U-5

#16, #17, #18

To Herrsching
(Bus #951 to Andechs Monastery)

Hauptbahnhof
MAIN TRAIN STN.

U-4, U-5

Laimer Platz Ⓤ

Schwanthaler-höhe Ⓤ

Ⓤ Theresienwiese

#16, #17, #18, #27

U-1, U-2

TRANSPORTATION MUSEUM

🍺 OKTOBERFEST GROUNDS

—Ⓢ— S-BAHN

—Ⓢ—Ⓢ— S-BAHN "SPINE"
MOST S-BAHN LINES FOLLOW THIS ROUTE, THEN BRANCH OFF

—Ⓤ— U-BAHN

+++ TRAM

- - - - BUS

Not all lines & stations are shown

Not to Scale

U-6

Klinikum Grosshadern Ⓤ

Fürstenried West Ⓤ

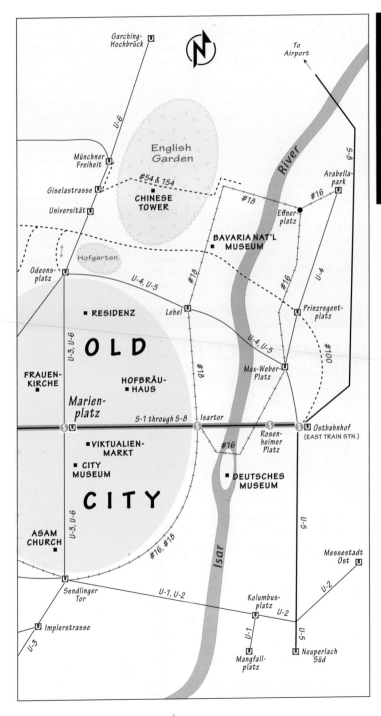

way). You'll find a city-run **TI** (out front of station and to the right) and **lockers** (opposite track 26 and near track 17). Up the escalators opposite track 22 are **car-rental agencies.**

Subway lines, trams, and buses connect the station to the rest of the city (though many of my recommended hotels are within walking distance of the station). If you get lost in the underground maze of subway corridors while you're trying to get to the train station, follow the signs for *DB* (Deutsche Bahn) to surface successfully. Watch out for the hallways with blue ticket-stamping machines in the middle—these lead to the subway, where you could be fined if you don't have a validated ticket.

From Munich to: Füssen (hourly, 2 hours, half with easy transfer in Buchloe; for a Neuschwanstein Castle day trip, leave as early as possible), **Oberammergau** (nearly hourly, 2 hours, transfer in Murnau), **Salzburg,** Austria (2/hour, 1.5 hours on fast train), **Cologne** (2/hour, 4.5 hours, some with transfer), **Würzburg** (1-2/hour, 2 hours), **Rothenburg** (hourly, 3.5 hours, 2-3 transfers), **Frankfurt** (hourly, 3.5 hours), **Dresden** (every 2 hours, 5 hours, transfer in Leipzig), **Hamburg** (hourly direct, 6.5 hours), **Berlin** (hourly, 4-5 hours).

By Bus

Munich's central bus station (ZOB) is by the Hackerbrücke S-Bahn station (from the train station, it's a short walk or one hop on the S-Bahn; www.muenchen-zob. de). The Romantic Road bus leaves from here (see page 214).

NEAR MUNICH

DACHAU CONCENTRATION CAMP MEMORIAL

Established in 1933, Dachau (Gedenkstätte Dachau) was the first Nazi concentration camp. In its 12 dismal years of operation, about 40,000 people died here. Today, it's an easily accessible camp for travelers, rated ▲▲▲, and an effective voice from our recent but grisly past, pleading, "Never again." A visit to Dachau is a powerful and valuable experience and, when approached thoughtfully, well worth the trouble.

Getting There

The camp is a 45-minute trip from downtown Munich. S-Bahn trains run directly from Munich to Dachau, where buses complete the rest of the journey. Munich-based tour companies also provide good value, combining transportation and a guided visit.

By S-Bahn and Bus: Take the S-2 (direction: Petershausen) from any of the central stops in Munich to Dachau (3/hour, 20-minute trip from Hauptbahnhof). At Dachau station, go down the stairs and out to the bus platforms; find the one marked *KZ-Gedenkstätte-Concentration Camp Memorial Sight.* Here, catch bus #726 and ride it seven minutes to the KZ-Gedenkstätte stop (3/hour). Be sure to note the return times back to the station.

The Munich XXL day pass covers the entire trip (€8.90/person, €16.10/partner ticket for up to 5 adults). If you've already invested in a three-day Munich transport pass, you can save a couple of euros by buying and stamping single tickets (€2.90/person each way) to cover the Dachau part of the trip.

By Guided Tour: Radius and Munich Walk tours are a great value for a guided visit. Allow roughly five hours total. It's smart to reserve the day before

Powerful art at the Memorial

(**Radius**—€28, RS%-select "student rate" when booking online; tel. 089/543-487-7740, www.radiustours.com; **Munich Walk**—€25, tel. 089/2423-1767, www.munichwalktours.de).

Orientation

Cost and Hours: Free, daily 9:00-17:00. Some areas of the camp may begin to close before 17:00. The museum discourages parents from bringing children under age 14.

The Town: The town of Dachau—quiet, tree-lined, and residential—is more pleasant than its unfortunate association with the camp on its outskirts, and it tries hard to encourage you to visit its old town and castle (www.dachau.de).

Visitors Center: Coming from the bus stop or parking lot, you'll first see the visitors center, outside the camp wall. It lacks exhibits, but does have a small cafeteria, a bookstore with English-language books, and a WC (more WCs inside the camp). At the information desk, pick up the English pamphlet, rent an audioguide (€4, cash only, leave ID; not essential), or sign up for a tour. Two different **guided walks** in English start from the visitors center (€3, daily at 11:00 and 13:00, 2.5 hours; limited to 30 people so show up early—especially in summer, 11:00 walk fills up first; call or visit website to confirm times, tel. 08131/669-970, www.kz-gedenkstaette-dachau.de).

⊙ Self-Guided Tour

You enter, like the inmates did, through the infamous **iron gate** that held the taunting slogan *Arbeit macht frei* ("Work makes you free"). Inside are the four key experiences: the museum, the bunker behind the museum, the restored barracks, and a pensive walk across the huge but now-empty camp to the memorials and crematorium at the far end.

Museum: Enter the museum, housed in a former camp maintenance building. Immediately to the right, check show times for the museum's powerful 22-minute documentary film (usually shown in English at 10:00, 11:30, 12:30. 14:00, and 15:00). The museum is organized

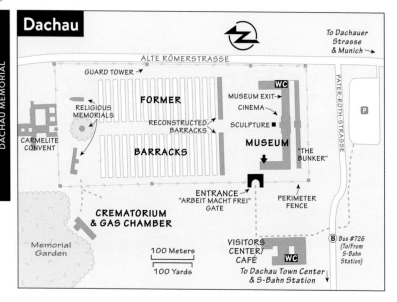

Dachau

ALTE RÖMERSTRASSE

To Dachauer Strasse & Munich →

GUARD TOWER →

FORMER

RELIGIOUS MEMORIALS

CARMELITE CONVENT

RECONSTRUCTED BARRACKS

BARRACKS

WC

MUSEUM EXIT →

CINEMA →

SCULPTURE ■

MUSEUM

↓

"THE BUNKER"

ENTRANCE
"ARBEIT MACHT FREI"
GATE

PERIMETER FENCE

PATER-ROTH-STRASSE

P

CREMATORIUM & GAS CHAMBER

Memorial Garden

100 Meters

100 Yards

VISITORS CENTER/ CAFÉ

WC

To Dachau Town Center & S-Bahn Station ↓

Ⓑ Bus #726 (To/From S-Bahn Station)

chronologically, everything is thoughtfully described in English, and touch-screens let you watch early newsreels.

Rooms 1-2 cover the founding of the camp and give an overview of the Nazi camp system. Some were concentration camps (like Dachau), and others were extermination camps, built with the express purpose of executing people on a mass scale. Photos and posters chronicle the rise of Hitler in the 1920s.

Rooms 3-7 are devoted to the early years of the camp. Besides political activists, prisoners included homosexuals, Jehovah's Witnesses, Roma, and Jews. The camp was run by the SS, the organization charged with Germany's internal security. Dachau was a work camp, where inmates were expected to pay for their "crimes" with slave labor. The camp was strictly regimented: a wake-up call at 4:00, an 11-hour workday, roll call at 5:15 and 19:00, lights out at 21:00. The work was hard, whether quarrying or hauling loads or constructing the very buildings you see today. The rations were meager, rule-breakers were punished severely, and all manner of torture took place here.

Rooms 8-15 document the war years and their immediate aftermath. Once the war began, conditions at Dachau deteriorated. The original camp had been designed to hold just under 3,000 inmates. In 1937 and 1938, the camp was expanded, with barracks intended to hold 6,000 prisoners. With the war, the prisoner population swelled, and the Nazis found other purposes for the camp. It was less a concentration camp for German dissidents and more a dumping ground for foreigners, POWs, and even 2,000 Catholic priests. From Dachau, Jewish prisoners were sent east to the gas chambers. Inmates were used as slave labor for the German war machine—many were shipped to nearby camps to make armaments. Prisoners were used as human guinea pigs for war-related medical experiments of human tolerance for air pressure, hypothermia, and biological agents like malaria; the photos of these victims may be the most painful to view.

As the Allies closed in on both fronts, Dachau was bursting with more than 30,000 prisoners jammed into its 34 barracks. In the winter of 1944-1945, disease

Memorials throughout Dachau remind visitors: Never Again.

broke out and food ran short. With coal for the crematorium running low, those who died were buried in mass graves outside the camp site. The Allies arrived on April 29. After 12 years of existence, Dachau was finally liberated.

Bunker: This was a cellblock for prominent "special prisoners," such as failed Hitler assassins, German religious leaders, and politicians who challenged Nazism. Most of the 136 cells are empty, but exhibits in a few of them (near the entrance) profile the inmates and the SS guards who worked at Dachau, and allow you to listen to some inmates' testimonies. Cell #2 was the interrogation room. Cell #9 was a "standing cell"—inmates were tortured here by being forced to stay on their feet for days at a time.

Barracks: Take a quick look inside to get an idea of what sleeping and living conditions were like in the camp. There were 34 barracks, each measuring about 10 yards by 100 yards. When the camp was at its fullest, there was only about one square yard of living space per inmate.

Religious Remembrance Sites: At the far end of the camp, there are now three places of meditation and worship (Jewish to your right, Catholic straight ahead, and Protestant to your left).

Camp Crematorium: A memorial garden surrounds the two camp crematorium buildings, which were used to burn the bodies of prisoners who had died or been killed. The newer, larger concrete crematorium was built to replace the smaller wooden one. One of its rooms is a **gas chamber,** which worked on the same principles as the much larger one at Auschwitz, and was originally disguised as a shower room (the fittings are gone now). It was never put to use at Dachau for mass murder, but survivors have testified that small groups were killed in it "experimentally." In the garden near the buildings is a Russian Orthodox shrine.

Salzburg

Just over the Austrian border, lively Salzburg is tantalizingly close to Munich (1.5 hours by fast train). Thanks to its charming Old Town, splendid gardens, Baroque churches, and one of Europe's largest intact medieval fortresses, the city feels made for tourism. Its huge annual music festival and constant concerts have made it a musical mecca. Salzburgers are forever smiling to the tunes of Mozart and *The Sound of Music*.

SALZBURG IN 1 DAY

While Salzburg's museums are mediocre, the town itself is a Baroque showpiece of cobbled streets and elegant buildings—simply a stroller's delight by day or floodlit night.

With one day, start with my Salzburg Old Town Walk, seeing sights (such as the cathedral) along the way. In the afternoon, choose what appeals to you most: Consider taking *The Sound of Music* tour;

you'll get a city overview, *S.O.M.* sights, and a fine drive by the lakes. Other good options (which could easily fill another day) are the Hohensalzburg Fortress, Salzburg Museum, Mozart's Birthplace, and outside of town, the Hellbrunn Palace with its trick fountains. You can also bike along the riverside paths and hike across the Mönchsberg.

If you have the time, spend at least two nights in Salzburg—nights are important for lingering in atmospheric beer gardens

The Mirabell Gardens are filled with Baroque statuary and fountains.

and attending concerts in Baroque halls and chapels. Seriously consider one of Salzburg's many evening musical events.

ORIENTATION

Salzburg, a city of 150,000 (Austria's fourth largest), is divided into old and new. The Old Town (Altstadt), between the Salzach River and Salzburg's Mönchsberg mountain, holds nearly all the charm and most of the tourists. The New Town (Neustadt), across the river, has the train station, a few sights and museums, and some good accommodations.

Rick's Tip: **Welcome to Austria**, *which uses the same* **euro currency** *as Germany, though* **postage stamps** *work only in the country where you buy them. To* **telephone** *from a German number to an Austrian one, dial 00-43 and then the number (omitting the initial zero). To call from an Austrian phone to a German one, dial 00-49 and then the number (again, omitting the initial zero).*

Tourist Information

Salzburg has two helpful TIs (main tel. 0662/889-870, www.salzburg.info): at the **train station** (9:00-18:00, until 19:00 in summer; tel. 0662/8898-7340) and on **Mozartplatz** in the old center (similar hours but closed Sun in winter, tel. 0662/8898-7330).

At either TI, you can pick up a free city-center map (or purchase a map with broader coverage if biking out of town), the free bus map (*Liniennetz*), and an events guide. Inside the Mozartplatz TI is the privately run Salzburg Ticket Service counter, where you can book concert tickets.

Sightseeing Pass: TIs sell the Salzburg Card, which covers all public transportation (including the Mönchsberg elevator and funicular to the fortress) and admission to all the city sights (including Hellbrunn Palace and a river cruise). The card can be a convenience and a money saver

if you'll be seeing lots of sights (€28/24 hours, €37/48 hours, cheaper off-season, www.salzburg.info). As Salzburg's major sights are pricey, busy sightseers can save plenty. Do the math on the places you want to see to evaluate whether the card makes financial sense.

Helpful Hints

Festivals: The Salzburg Festival runs each year from mid-July to the end of August (for more details on this and other big annual musical events, see page 135). In mid-September, St. Rupert's Fair (Ruperti-Kirtag) fills the sky with fireworks and Salzburg's Old Town with music and food stands (www.rupertikirtag.at). And from mid-November throughout Advent, Salzburg boasts a handful of Christmas markets—the biggest sprawling across Domplatz and Residenzplatz (www.christkindlmarkt.co.at), with smaller ones up at the fortress (mostly just Fri-Sun), on Mirabellplatz (daily), and elsewhere around town (www.weihnachtsmarkt-salzburg.at).

Laundry: Two launderettes are in the New Town near my recommended Linzer Gasse hotels: at Paris-Lodron-Strasse 16 and **Green and Clean** at Ignaz-Harrer-Strasse 32.

Tours

▲▲THE SOUND OF MUSIC TOURS

Salzburg is the joyful setting of *The Sound of Music*. The Broadway musical and 1965 movie tell the story of a stern captain who hires a governess for his unruly children and ends up marrying her. Though the movie took plenty of Hollywood liberties (see "*The Sound of Music:* Fact and Fiction" sidebar), it's based on the actual Von Trapp family who really did come from Salzburg. Maria really was a governess who became the captain's wife. They did sing in the Festival Hall, they did escape from the Nazis, and they ended up after the war in Vermont, where Maria passed away in 1987.

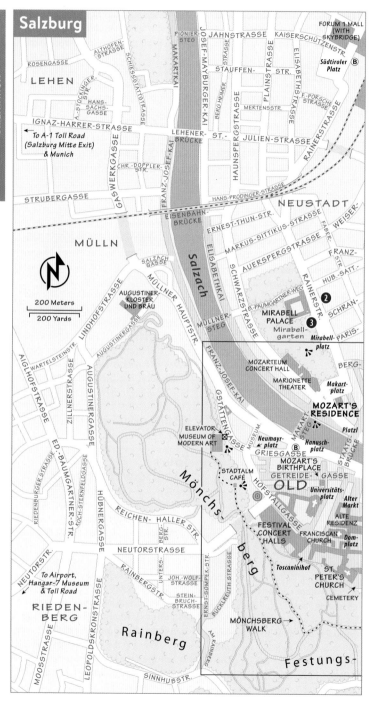

Salzburg

FORUM 1 MALL
(WITH
SKYBRIDGE)

PIONIER-
STEG

JAHNSTRASSE
KAISERSCHÜTZENSTR.

JOSEF-MAYBURGER-KAI
STAUFFEN-

Südtiroler
Platz (B)

ROSENGASSE

ALTHOFEN-
STRASSE

MAKARTKAI

BERGHEIMER

PLAINSTRASSE

STR.

ELISABETHSTRASSE

F.-PORSCHE-
STRASSE

LEHEN

A-STOCKER STR.

HANS-
SACHS-
GASSE

MERTENSSTR.

RAINERSTRASSE

IGNAZ-HARRER-STRASSE

SCHIESSSTATTSTRASSE

LEHENER-
BRÜCKE

ST.-
HAUNSPERGSTRASSE

JULIEN-STRASSE

To A-1 Toll Road
(Salzburg Mitte Exit)
& Munich

GASWERKGASSE

CHR.-DOPPLER-
STR.

FRANZ-JOSEF-KAI

HANS-PRODINGER-STRASSE

NEUSTADT

STRUBERGASSE

EISENBAHN-
BRÜCKE

ERNEST-THUN-STR.

MARKUS-SITTIKUS-STRASSE

WEISER-

MÜLLN

SALZACH
GASSE

Salzach

ELISABETHKAI

SCHWARZSTRASSE

AUERSPERGSTRASSE

RAINERSTR.

FABER-

FRANZ-
STR.

HUB.-SATT.-

N

AUGUSTINER-
KLOSTER
UND BRÄU

MÜLLNER HAUPTSTR.

MÜLLNER-
STEG

T.-B.-PAUMGARTNER-WEG

MIRABELL
PALACE

Mirabell-
garten

2

3

SCHRAN-

Mirabell-
platz

PARIS-

200 Meters

200 Yards

LINDHOFSTRASSE

AUGUSTINERGASSE

FRANZ-JOSEF-KAI

MOZARTEUM
CONCERT HALL

BERG-

Makart-
platz

WARTELSTEINSTR.

AIGLHOFSTRASSE

ZILLNERSTRASSE

GSTÄTTENGASSE

MARIONETTE
THEATER

MUSEUM

MOZART'S
RESIDENCE

Platzl

RIEDENBURGER STRASSE

ED.-BAUMGARTNER-STR.

AUGUSTINERGASSE

KOCH-STERNFELDGASSE

Mönchs-

ELEVATOR
MUSEUM OF
MODERN ART

MAKARTSTEG

Neumayr-
platz

Hanusch-
platz

(B)

GRIESGASSE

MOZART'S
BIRTHPLACE

STAATS-
BRÜCKE

HÜBNERGASSE

REICHEN-HALLER STR.

STADTALM
CAFÉ

berg

HOFSTALLGASSE

GETREIDE-GASSE

OLD

Universitäts-
platz

Alter
Markt

ALTE
RESIDENZ

NEUTORSTRASSE

UNTERS-BERG-STR.

FESTIVAL
CONCERT
HALLS

FRANCISCAN
CHURCH

Dom-
platz

NEUTORSTR.

To Airport,
Hangar-7 Museum
& Toll Road

RAINBERGSTR.

JOH.-WOLF-
STRASSE

ERNST-SOMPEK-STR.

BÜCKLREUTH STRASSE

Toscaninihof

ST.
PETER'S
CHURCH

RIEDEN-
BERG

MOOSSTRASSE

LEOPOLDSKRONSTRASSE

STEIN-
BRUCH-
STRASSE

AM RAINBERG

CEMETERY

Rainberg

MÖNCHSBERG
WALK

SINNHUBSTR.

Festungs-

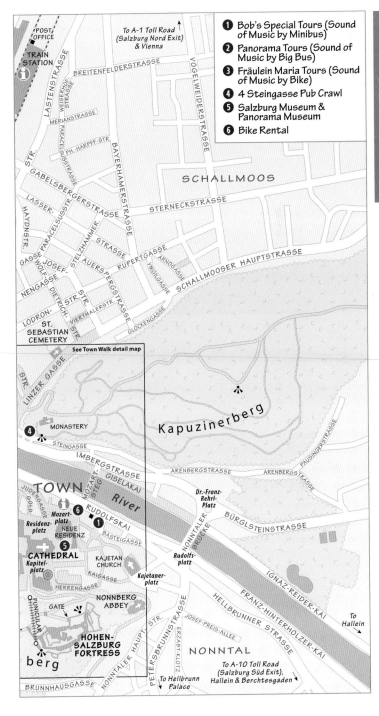

1 Bob's Special Tours (Sound of Music by Minibus)
2 Panorama Tours (Sound of Music by Big Bus)
3 Fräulein Maria Tours (Sound of Music by Bike)
4 4 Steingasse Pub Crawl
5 Salzburg Museum & Panorama Museum
6 Bike Rental

SALZBURG AT A GLANCE

▲▲▲**Salzburg Town Walk** Old town's best sights in a handy orientation walk. See page 112.

▲▲*Sound of Music* **Tours** Bus or bike through *S.O.M.* sights of Salzburg and surrounding countryside. See page 105.

▲▲**Salzburg Cathedral** Glorious, harmonious Baroque main church of Salzburg. **Hours:** Mon-Sat 8:00-19:00, Sun from 13:00; March-April, Oct, and Dec until 18:00; Jan-Feb and Nov until 17:00. See page 115.

▲▲**Getreidegasse** Picturesque old shopping lane with characteristic wrought-iron signs. See page 121.

▲▲**Salzburg Museum** Best place for city history. **Hours:** Tue-Sun 9:00-17:00, closed Mon. See page 123.

▲▲**Hohensalzburg Fortress** Imposing mountaintop castle, with small museums, commanding views, and concerts most evenings. **Hours:** Museums open daily 9:00-19:00, Oct-April 9:30-17:00. See page 125.

▲▲**Mozart's Birthplace** House where Mozart was born in 1756, featuring his instruments and other exhibits. **Hours:** Daily 9:00-17:30, July-Aug 8:30-19:00. See page 123.

▲▲**Hellbrunn Palace** Lavish palace on the outskirts of town featuring gardens with trick fountains. **Hours:** Daily 9:00-17:30, July-Aug until 21:00, March-April and Oct until 16:30, closed Nov-late March. See page 131.

▲**Mozart's Residence** Restored house where the composer lived. **Hours:** Daily 9:00-17:30, July-Aug 8:30-19:00. See page 130.

▲**Mirabell Gardens and Palace** Beautiful palace grounds and concert venue with fine views and *Sound of Music* memories. **Hours:** Free; gardens open until dusk, summer concerts in the park on Sun and Wed; palace open daily 8:00–18:00 and nightly during concerts. See page 130.

▲**Steingasse** Historic cobbled lane with trendy pubs in a tourist-free part of old Salzburg. See page 139.

The Sound of Music: Fact and Fiction

Rather than visit the real-life sights from the life of Maria von Trapp and family, most tourists want to see the places where Hollywood chose to film this fanciful story. Local guides are happy not to burst any *S.O.M.* pilgrim's bubble, but keep these points in mind:

"Edelweiss:" The song is not a cherished Austrian folk tune or national anthem. Like all the "Austrian" music in *S.O.M.*, it was composed for Broadway by Rodgers and Hammerstein.

Religious Calling: *S.O.M.* implies that Maria was devoutly religious throughout her life, but Maria's foster parents raised her as a socialist and atheist. Maria discovered her religious calling while studying to be a teacher. After completing school, she entered the convent as a novitiate.

Job Description: Maria's position was not as governess to all the children, but specifically as governess and teacher for the Captain's second-oldest daughter, also called Maria, who was bedridden with rheumatic fever.

Whistling: The Captain didn't run a tight domestic ship—but he did use a whistle to call his children—each kid was trained to respond to a certain pitch.

Name Changes: Though the Von Trapp family did have seven children, the show changed all their names and even their genders. As an adult, Rupert, the eldest child, responded to the often-asked question, "Which one are you?" with "I'm Liesl!" Maria and the Captain later had three more children together.

Escape: The family didn't escape by hiking to Switzerland (which is a five-hour drive away). Rather, they pretended to go on one of their frequent mountain hikes. With only the possessions in their backpacks, they "hiked" all the way to the station at the edge of their estate and took a train to Italy. The movie scene showing them climbing into Switzerland was filmed near Berchtesgaden, Ger-

Salzburg has a number of *Sound of Music* sights—mostly locations where the movie was shot, but also some places associated with the real Von Trapps:

Mirabell Gardens, with its arbor and Pegasus statue, where the kids in the movie sing "Do-Re-Mi."

Festival Hall, where the real-life Von Trapps performed, and where (in the movie) they sing "Edelweiss."

St. Peter's Cemetery, the inspiration for the scene where the family hides from Nazi guards (actually filmed on a Hollywood set).

Nonnberg Abbey, where the nuns sing "How Do You Solve a Problem like Maria?"

Leopoldskron Palace, which serves as the Von Trapps' lakeside home in the movie (although it wasn't their actual home).

Hellbrunn Palace gardens, now home to the famous gazebo where Liesl, the Von Trapp's oldest daughter, sings "I am sixteen going on seventeen."

There are many more sights—the horse pond, the wedding church in Mondsee, the fountain in Residenzplatz. Since they're scattered throughout greater Salzburg, taking a tour is the best way to see them efficiently.

I took a *S.O.M.* tour skeptically (as part of my research)—and enjoyed it. The bus tour version includes a quick general city tour, hits the *S.O.M.* spots, and shows you

many...home to Hitler's Eagle's Nest, and certainly not a smart place to flee to.

Family Home: The actual Von Trapp house exists...but it's not the one in the film. The mansion in the movie is actually two different buildings—one used for the front, the other for the back. The interiors were filmed on Hollywood sets. And the much-vaunted "Sixteen Going on Seventeen" gazebo you'll see at Hellbrunn Palace was built just for the movie, then moved twice to reach its current location.

Set Shots: For the film, Boris Levin designed a reproduction of the Nonnberg Abbey courtyard so faithful to the original (down to its cobblestones and stained-glass windows) that many still believe the cloister scenes were really shot at the abbey. And no matter what you hear in Salzburg, the graveyard scene (in which the Von Trapps hide from the Nazis) was also filmed on the Fox lot.

Swindled!: In 1956, a German film producer offered Maria $9,000 cash for the rights to her book. Because it was more money than the family had seen in all their years of singing, she accepted the deal. The agent claimed that German law forbids film companies from paying royalties to foreigners (Maria had by then become a US citizen). She agreed to the contract and unknowingly signed away all film rights to her story. Later, she discovered the agent had swindled the family—no such law existed.

Restitution: Rodgers, Hammerstein, and other producers gave the Von Trapps a percentage of the royalties, even though they weren't required to—but it was a fraction of what they otherwise would have earned. But Maria wasn't bitter. She said, "The great good the film and the play are doing to individual lives is far beyond money."

a lovely stretch of the Salzkammergut Lake District. Warning: Many think rolling through the Austrian countryside with 30 Americans singing "Doe, a deer..." is pretty schmaltzy. Austrians don't understand all the commotion (many have never seen the movie).

Taking a Tour: Two companies do S.O.M. tours by bus (Bob's and Panorama), while a third company does a bike version. It's best to reserve ahead. Note: Your hotel will be eager to call to reserve for you—to get their commission—but you won't get the discount I've negotiated.

Minibus Option: Most of **Bob's Special Tours** use an eight-seat minibus (and occasionally a 16-seat bus), promote a more laid-back feel, and waste less time loading and unloading. Online bookings close three days prior to the tour date—after that, email, call, or stop by the office to reserve (€55 for adults; RS%—student price with this book if you pay cash and book directly, €50 for kids 7-21 and students with ID, €45 for kids 6 and under—includes required car seat but must reserve in advance; daily at 9:00 and 14:00 year-round, tours leave from Bob's office along the river just east of Mozartplatz at Rudolfskai 38, tel. 0662/849-511, www.bobstours.com, office@bobstours.com). Nearly all of Bob's tours stop for a fun luge ride in Fuschl am See when the weather is dry (mountain bobsled—€5 extra, generally April-Oct, confirm beforehand).

Big Bus Option: Many travelers appreciate **Panorama Tours'** roomier buses, higher vantage point, and business-like feel (€45, RS%—€5 discount for *S.O.M.* tours if you pay in cash and book by phone or in person, daily at 9:15 and 14:00 year-round, tours leave from their kiosk at Mirabellplatz, book by calling 0662/874-029 or 0662/883-2110, www.panoramatours.com).

Fräulein Maria's Bicycle Tour: For some exercise—and much better access to the in-town sights, meet your guide (more likely a *herr* than a *fräulein*) at the Mirabell Gardens (at Mirabellplatz 4, 50 yards to the left of palace entry). The main attractions of the eight-mile pedal include the Mirabell Gardens, the horse pond, St. Peter's Cemetery, Nonnberg Abbey, Leopoldskron Palace, and, of course, the gazebo. The tour is very family-friendly, and there'll be lots of stops for goofy photo ops (€35 includes bike, €20 for kids 13-18, €15 for kids under 13, RS%—€2 discount with this book; daily April-Oct at 9:30, June-Aug also at 16:30, allow 3.5 hours, reservations required, mobile 0650-342-6297, www.mariasbicycletours.com).

WALKING TOURS

Any day of the week, you can take a one-hour, informative guided walk of the Old Town without a reservation—just show up at the TI on Mozartplatz at the tour time and pay the guide (€10, daily at 12:15 and 14:00, tel. 0662/8898-7330).

LOCAL GUIDES

Salzburg has many good guides, including **Sabine Rath** (€160/2 hours, €225/4 hours, €335/8 hours, mobile 0664-201-6492, www.tourguide-salzburg.com, info@tourguide-salzburg.com) and **Anna Stellnberger** (€150/2 hours, €220/4 hours, €320/8 hours, mobile 0664-787-5177, anna.stellnberger@aon.at). For a longer list, see www.salzburgguides.at.

SALZBURG TOWN WALK

I've linked the best sights in the Old Town into this handy self-guided orientation walk (rated ▲▲▲). Allow about 1.5 hours.

🎧 Download my free Salzburg Town Walk audio tour.

➋ Self-Guided Walk

• *Begin at the Mozartsteg, the wrought-iron, Art Nouveau pedestrian bridge over the Salzach River.*

❶ *Mozartsteg*

Get your bearings: Face the sprawling fortress atop the hill—it overlooks the Old Town. Behind you is the New Town, across the river.

Take in the charming, well-preserved, historic core of Salzburg's Old Town. The skyline bristles with Baroque steeples and green, copper domes. Salzburg has 38 Catholic churches, plus two Protestant churches and a synagogue. The biggest green dome is the cathedral, which we'll visit shortly. Overlooking it all is the castle called the Hohensalzburg Fortress. Far to the right of the fortress, find the Museum of Modern Art—a blocky modern building atop the hill. The castle-like structure behind it is a water reservoir.

The Salzach is called "salt river" not because it's salty, but because of the precious cargo it once carried. The salt mines of Hallein are just 12 miles upstream. For 2,000 years, barges carried salt from here to the wider world—to the Danube, the Black Sea, and on to the Mediterranean. As barges passed through, they had to pay a toll on their salt. The city was made great from the trading of salt (*Salz*) defended by a castle (*Burg*)—"Salz-burg."

• *Now let's plunge into Salzburg's Old Town. From the bridge, walk one block toward the hill-capping castle into the Old Town. Pass the traffic barriers (that keep this quiet town free of too much traffic) and turn right into a big square, called...*

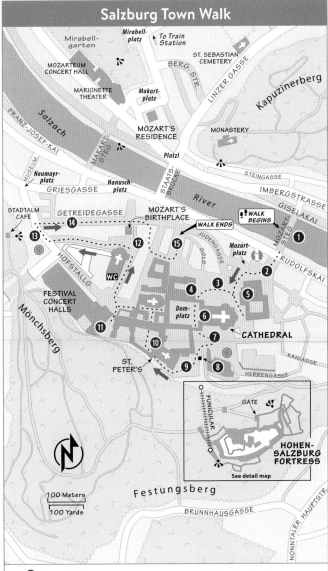

Salzburg Town Walk

1. Mozartsteg
2. Mozartplatz
3. Residenzplatz
4. Residenz
5. New Residenz & Glockenspiel
6. Salzburg Cathedral
7. Kapitelplatz
8. Waterwheel
9. St. Peter's Cemetery
10. St. Peter's Church
11. Toscaninihof
12. Universitätsplatz
13. Mönchsberg Cliff Face
14. Getreidegasse
15. Alter Markt

The Mozartsteg pedestrian bridge connects the New Town with the Old Town.

Mozartplatz

❷ Mozartplatz

All the tourists around you probably wouldn't be here if not for the man honored by this statue—Wolfgang Amadeus Mozart. The great composer spent most of his first 25 years (1756-1781) in Salzburg. He was born just a few blocks from here. He and his father both served Salzburg's rulers before Wolfgang went on to seek his fortune in Vienna. The statue (considered a poor likeness) was erected in 1842, just after the 50th anniversary of Mozart's death. The music festival of that year planted the seed for what would become the now world-renowned Salzburg Festival.

Mozart stands atop the spot where the first Salzburgers settled. Two thousand years ago, the Romans had a salt-trading town here called Juvavum. In the year 800, Salzburg—by then Christian and home to an important abbey—joined Charlemagne's Holy Roman Empire as an independent city. The Church of St. Michael (which has a yellow tower that overlooks the square) dates from that time. It's Salzburg's oldest, if not biggest, church.

• *Before moving on, note the TI (which also sells concert tickets). The entrance to the Salzburg Museum is across the square (described on page 123). Now walk toward the cathedral and into the big square with the huge fountain.*

❸ Residenzplatz

As Salzburg's governing center, this square has long been ringed with important buildings. The cathedral borders the south side. The Residenz—the former palace of Salzburg's rulers—is to the right (as you face the cathedral). To the left is the New Residenz, with its bell tower.

In the 1600s, this square got a makeover in the then-fashionable Italian Baroque style. The rebuilding started under energetic Prince-Archbishop Wolf Dietrich, who ruled from 1587 to 1612. Dietrich had been raised in Rome. He counted the Medicis as his cousins, and had grandiose Italian ambitions for Salzburg. Fortunately for him, the existing cathedral conveniently burned down in 1598. Dietrich set about rebuilding it as part of his grand vision to make Salzburg the "Rome of the North."

The fountain is as Italian as can be, an over-the-top version of Bernini's famous Triton Fountain in Rome. It shows Triton on top blowing his conch-shell horn. The water cascades down the basins and sprays playfully in the wind.

Notice that Salzburg's buildings are made from three distinctly different types of stone. Most common is the chunky gray conglomerate (like the cathedral's side walls) quarried from the nearby cliffs. There's also white marble (like the cathedral's towers and windows) and red marble (best seen in monuments inside buildings), both from the Alps.

You'll likely see horse buggies (Fiaker) congregating at this square; they charge €48 for a 25-minute trot around the Old Town.

• Turn your attention to the building on the right, the...

❹ Residenz

This was the palace of Salzburg's powerful ruler, the prince-archbishop—that is, a ruler with both the political powers of a prince and the religious authority of an archbishop. The ornate Baroque entrance attests to the connections these rulers had with Rome. You can step inside the Residenz courtyard to get a glimpse of the impressive digs (to see the fancy interior with state rooms and an impressive collection of paintings, you must buy a Dom-Quartier ticket).

Notice that the Residenz has a white-stone structure (called the Cathedral Terrace) connecting it with the cathedral. This skyway gave the prince-archbishops an easy commute to church and a chance to worship while avoiding the public.

• At the opposite end of Residenzplatz from the Residenz is the...

❺ New (Neue) Residenz

In the days of the prince-archbishops, this building hosted parties in its lavish rooms. These days, the New Residenz houses

Residenzplatz and the New Residenz

both the Salzburg Museum and the Panorama Museum (for details on the Salzburg Museum, see "Sights in Salzburg," later). It's also home to the Heimatwerk, a fine shop showing off local handicrafts like dirndls and locally made jelly.

The New Residenz bell tower has a famous **glockenspiel.** This 17th-century carillon has 35 bells (cast in Antwerp) and chimes daily at 7:00, 11:00, and 18:00. It also plays little tunes appropriate to the season. The mechanism is a big barrel with adjustable tabs that turns like a giant music box, pulling the right bells in the right rhythm. (Twice-weekly tours let you get up close to watch the glockenspiel action: €4, April-Oct Thu at 17:30 and Fri at 10:30, no tours Nov-March, buy ticket and meet for tour at Panorama Museum, no reservations needed—but get tickets at least a few minutes ahead, ask for English handout.)

Notice the tower's ornamental top: an upside-down heart in flames surrounds the solar system, representing how God loves all of creation.

Residenzplatz sets the tone for the whole town. From here, a series of interconnecting squares—like you'll see nowhere else—make a grand procession through the Old Town. Everywhere you go, you'll see similar Italian architecture. As you walk from square to square, notice how easily you slip from noisy and commercial to peaceful and reflective.

• Exit the square by walking under the prince-archbishop's skyway. You'll step into Domplatz (Cathedral Square). A good place to view the cathedral facade is from the far end of the square.

❻ Salzburg Cathedral (Salzburger Dom)

Salzburg's cathedral (rated ▲▲) was one of the first Italian Baroque buildings north of the Alps. The dome stands 230 feet high, and two domed towers flank the very Italian-esque entrance.

Salzburg Cathedral, where Mozart was baptized

The church was consecrated in 1628. Experts differ on what motivated the builders. As it dates from the years of Catholic-Protestant warfare, it may have been meant to emphasize Salzburg's commitment to the Roman Catholic cause. Or it may have represented a peaceful alternative to the religious strife. Regardless, Salzburg's archbishop was the top papal official north of the Alps, and the city was the pope's northern outpost. With its rich salt production, Salzburg had enough money to stay out of the conflict and earn the nickname "The Fortified Island of Peace."

Cost and Hours: Free, donation requested, Mon-Sat 8:00-19:00, Sun from 13:00; March-April, Oct, and Dec until 18:00; Jan-Feb and Nov until 17:00; www.salzburger-dom.at. If the Jedermann theater production is underway (July and Aug), you may need to enter through the back door.

Visiting the Cathedral: As you approach the church, pause at the **iron gates.** The dates on the doors are milestones in the church's history. In the year 774, the first church, built in Romanesque style, was consecrated by St. Virgil (see his statue), an Irish monk who became Salzburg's bishop. It was destroyed by fire in 1167, rebuilt, and then burned again in 1598. It was replaced in 1628 by the one you see today. The year 1959 marks the completion of repairs after a WWII bomb severely damaged the dome.

Because it was built in just 14 years (1614-1628), the church boasts an unusually harmonious Baroque architecture. And it's big—330 feet long, 230 feet tall—built with sturdy pillars and broad arches. When Pope John Paul II visited in 1998, some 5,000 people packed the place.

Inside, notice how you're drawn toward the light—closer to God. Imagine being part of a sacred procession, passing from the relatively dim entrance to the bright altar with its painting of Christ's resurrection, bathed in light from the dome overhead. The church never had stained glass, just clear windows to let light power the message.

Under the soaring dome, look up and admire the exceptional stucco work, by an artist from Milan. It's molded into elaborate garlands, angels, and picture frames, some of it brightly painted. You're surrounded by the tombs (and portraits) of 10 archbishops.

You're also surrounded by four organs. (Actually, five. Don't forget the biggest organ, over the entrance.) Mozart served as organist here for two years, and he composed several Masses still played today. Salzburg's prince-archbishops were great patrons of music, with a personal orchestra that played religious music in the cathedral and dinner music in the Residenz. The tradition of music continues today. Sunday Mass here can be a musical spectacle—all five organs playing, balconies filled with singers and musicians, creating glorious surround-sound. Think of the altar in Baroque terms, as the center of a stage, with sunrays serving as spotlights in this dramatic and sacred theater.

At the collection box by the back pew, black-and-white photos show the bomb damage of October 16, 1944, which left a gaping hole where the dome once was. In the first chapel on the left is a dark bronze baptismal font. It dates from 1320—a rare survivor from the medieval cathedral. In 1756, little Wolfgang Amadeus Mozart was baptized here. For the next 25 years, this would be his home church. Amadeus, by the way, means "beloved by God."

• *As you leave the cathedral, check out the concert and Mass schedules posted near the entrance. Exiting the cathedral, turn left, heading in the direction of the distant fortress on the hill. You'll soon reach a spacious square with a golden orb.*

❼ Kapitelplatz

The playful modern sculpture in the square shows a man atop a golden orb. Every year, a foundation commissions a different artist to create a new work of public art somewhere in the city; this one's from 2007. Kapitelplatz is a pleasant square—notice the giant chessboard that often draws a crowd.

Follow the orb-man's gaze up the hill to **Hohensalzburg Fortress.** (I think he's trying to decide whether to shell out for the funicular or save money by hiking up.) Construction of the fortress began in 1077. Over the centuries, the small castle grew into a mighty, whitewashed fortress—so impressive that no army even tried attacking for over 800 years. These days, you can tour the castle grounds, visit some interior rooms and museums, and enjoy incredible views. You can walk up (Festungsgasse leads up from Kapitelplatz—follow the lane straight up from the golden ball) or, for a few euros more, take the funicular (for details, see page 125). While the castle's earliest funicular dates back to the 1500s, when animals pulled cargo up its tracks, today's funicular is electric, from 1910.

Now walk across the square to the pond surrounded by a balustrade and adorned with a Trevi-fountain-like **statue of Neptune.** It looks fancy, but the pond was built as a horse bath, the 18th-century equivalent of a car wash. Notice the gold lettering above Neptune. It reads, "Leopold the Prince Built Me." But the artist added a clever twist. The inscription uses the letters "LLDVI," and so on. Those are also Roman numerals—add 'em up: L is 50, D is 500, and so on. It all adds up to 1732—the year the pond was built.

This square hosts many free events and

Fountain in Kapitelplatz

concerts (including videos of great Salzburg Festival performances on a jumbo screen).

• *With your back to the cathedral, leave the square, exiting through the gate in the far-right corner.*

❽ Waterwheel (Wasserrad)

The waterwheel is part of a clever, still-functioning canal system built in the 12th century to bring water to Salzburg from the foothills of the Alps, 10 miles away. When the stream reached Salzburg, it was divided into five smaller canals for the citizens' use. The rushing water was harnessed to waterwheels, which powered factories. There were more than 100 watermill-powered firms as late as the 19th century. Residents also used the water to fight fires and, once a week, to flush the streets clean. Hygienic Salzburg never suffered from a plague...it's probably the only major town in Austria with no plague monument.

This particular waterwheel (actually, it's a modern replacement) once ground grain into flour to make bread for the monks of St. Peter's Abbey. Nowadays, you can pop into the adjacent **bakery**—fragrant and traditional—and buy a fresh-baked roll for about a euro (closed Wed and Sun).

• *You've entered the borders of the former St. Peter's Abbey, a monastic complex of churches, courtyards, businesses (like the bakery), and a cemetery. Find the Katakomben sign and step through the wrought-iron gates into...*

❾ St. Peter's Cemetery (Petersfriedhof)

This collection of lovingly tended graves abuts the sheer rock face of the Mönchsberg (free, silence requested, daily 6:30-20:00, Oct-March until 18:00, www.stift-stpeter.at). Walk in about 50 yards past a well to a junction of lanes in the middle of the cemetery. (Stop at the round stone ball on the right—perfect for stretching that stiff back.) You're surrounded by three churches, each founded in the early Middle Ages atop a pagan Celtic holy site. The biggest church, St. Peter's, sticks its big Romanesque apse into the cemetery. Notice the fancy tombstones lining the church's wall.

The graves surrounding you are tended by descendants of the deceased. In Austria (and many other European countries), gravesites are rented, not owned. Rent bills are sent out every 10 years. If no one cares enough to make the payment, your tombstone is removed. Note the well you passed, used to fill the watering cans for the family members who keep these flowery graves so pretty.

The cemetery plays a role in *The Sound of Music*. The Captain and his large family were well known in Salzburg for their musical talents. But when Nazi Germany annexed Austria in 1938, the Von Trapps decided to flee so that the father would not be pressed into service again. In the movie, they hid here as they made their daring escape. The scene was actually

Waterwheel

St. Peter's Cemetery

filmed on a Hollywood set inspired by St. Peter's Cemetery.

Look up the cliff, which has a few buildings attached—called (not quite accurately) "catacombs." Legendary medieval hermit-monks are said to have lived in the hillside here. For a small fee, you can enter the *Katakomben* and climb lots of steps to see a few old caves, a chapel, and some fine city views (€2, daily 10:00-18:00, Oct-April until 17:00, visit takes 10 minutes, entrance at the base of the cliff, under the arcade).

Explore the arcade at the base of the cliff with its various burial chapels. Alcove #XXI has the tomb of the cathedral architect Santino Solari—forever facing his creation. At the catacombs entry (#LIV) are two interesting tombs marked by plaques on the floor. "Marianne" is Mozart's sister, nicknamed "Nannerl." As children, Mozart and his sister performed together on grand tours of Europe's palaces. Michael Haydn was the brother of Joseph Haydn. He succeeded Mozart as church cathedral organist.

• *Exit the cemetery through the green door at the opposite end. Just outside, you enter a large courtyard anchored by...*

❿ *St. Peter's Church (Stiftskirche St. Peter)*

You're standing at the birthplace of Christianity in Salzburg. St. Peter's Abbey—the monastery that surrounds this courtyard—was founded in 696, barely two centuries after the fall of Rome. The recommended Stiftskeller St. Peter restaurant in the courtyard (known these days for its Mozart Dinner Concert) brags that Charlemagne ate here in the year 803, making it (perhaps) the oldest restaurant in Europe. St. Peter's Church dates from 1147.

Cost and Hours: Free, daily 8:00-21:00, Nov-March until 19:00, www.stift-stpeter.at.

Visiting the Church: Enter the church, pausing in the atrium to admire the Romanesque **tympanum** (from 1250) over the inner doorway. Jesus sits on a rainbow,

flanked by Peter and Paul. Beneath them is a stylized Tree of Life, and overhead, a Latin inscription reading, "I am the door to life, and only through me can you find eternal life."

Enter the **nave.** The once purely Romanesque interior (you may find a few surviving bits of faded 13th-century frescoes) now lies hidden under a sugary Rococo finish. It's Salzburg's only Rococo interior—all whitewashed, with highlights of pastel green, gold, and red. If it feels Bavarian, it's because it was done by Bavarian artists. The ceiling paintings feature St. Peter receiving the keys from Christ (center painting), walking on water, and joining the angels in heaven.

The monastery was founded by **St. Rupert** (c. 650-718). Find his statue at the main altar—he's the second gold statue from the left. Rupert arrived as a Christian missionary in what was then a largely pagan land. He preached the gospel, reopened the Roman salt mines, and established the city. It was he who named it "Salzburg."

Rupert's tomb is midway up the right aisle. It's adorned with a painting of him praying for his city. Beneath him is a depiction of Salzburg circa 1750 (when this was painted): one bridge, salt ships sailing the river, and angels hoisting barrels of salt to heaven.

• *Exit the courtyard at the opposite side from where you entered, through the arch under the blue-and-yellow sundial. The passageway takes you past dorms still used for student monks. At the T-intersection (where you bump into the Franciscan Church), turn right for a quick detour to appreciate another view of Domplatz.*

The Baroque style was all about putting on a show, which is wonderfully illustrated by the **statue of Mary** (1771) that welcomes visitors in this square. As you approach her from the center of this lane, walking between the little brass rails in the cobblestones, keep an eye on the golden crown above and far behind Mary on the cathedral's facade. Just as you get to

St. Peter's Church

ters building stage sets or hear performers practicing for an upcoming show.

The Von Trapp family performed in the Festival Hall. In the movie, this backstage courtyard is where Captain von Trapp nervously waited before walking onstage to sing "Edelweiss." Then the family slipped away to begin their escape from the Nazis.

The Toscaninihof also has the entrance to the city's huge, 1,500-space, inside-the-mountain parking lot. It originated in 1944 as the Mönchsberg air raid shelter—an underground system that offered 18,000 locals refuge from WWII bombs. The stone stairway in the courtyard leads a few flights up to a panoramic view.

• *Return to Max-Reinhardt-Platz. Continue straight along the right side of the big church, passing popular sausage stands and a public WC, then enter...*

the middle arch, watch as she's crowned Queen of Heaven by the two angels on the church facade. Bravo!

• *Do a U-turn and head back down Franziskanergasse. Pass beneath the archway painted with a modern Lamentation scene (1926) to enter a square called Max-Reinhardt-Platz. Pause here to admire the line of impressive Salzburg Festival concert halls ahead of you. Then turn left, through a square archway, into a small square called...*

⓫ *Toscaninihof*

In this small courtyard, you get a peek at the back end of the large Festival Hall complex (on your right). The Festival Hall has three theaters and seats 5,000 people (see photo on the wall). It's very busy during the Salzburg Music Festival each summer. The festival was started in the austere 1920s, after World War I, and Salzburg couldn't afford a new concert hall, so they remodeled what were once the prince-archbishop's stables and riding school.

The tunnel you see to the left leads to the actual concert hall. It's generally closed, but you may be able to look through nearby doorways and see carpen-

⓬ *Universitätsplatz*

This square, home to the huge Baroque Kollegienkirche (University Church), also hosts Salzburg's liveliest open-air produce market (and a lot of touristy food stands). It generally runs mornings, Monday through Saturday. It's at its best early Saturday morning, when the farmers are in town. The fancy yellow facade overlooking the square marks the back end of Mozart's Birthplace, which we'll see shortly.

Find the fountain—it's about 50 yards past the church, on the right. As with public marketplaces elsewhere, it's for washing fruit and vegetables. This fountain—

Market stalls at Universitätsplatz

though modern in design—is still part of a medieval-era water system. The water plummets down a hole and on to the river. The sundial over the water hole shows both the time and the date.

• *Continue toward the end of the long, tapering square. Along the way, you'll pass several nicely arcaded medieval passageways (on the right), which lead to Salzburg's old main street, Getreidegasse. (Try weaving back and forth through some.) When you reach the traffic-control bollards, you're looking at the...*

⑬ Mönchsberg Cliff Face

Rising 1,600 feet above you is the Mönchsberg, Salzburg's mountain. Today you see the remains of an aborted attempt in the 1600s to cut through the Mönchsberg. It proved too big a job, and when new tunneling technology arrived, that project was abandoned. The stones cut did serve as a quarry for the city's 17th-century growth spurt—the bulk of the cathedral, for example, is built of this economical and local conglomerate stone.

Early one morning in 1669, a huge landslide killed more than 200 townspeople who lived close to where the elevator is now (to the right). Since then, the cliffs have been carefully checked each spring and fall. Even today, you might see crews on the cliff, monitoring its stability.

Walk to the base of the cliff, where you'll see what was the giant horse trough for the prince-archbishops' stables.

Paintings show the various breeds and temperaments of horses in the stable. Like Vienna, Salzburg had a passion for the equestrian arts.

• *Before turning right onto the long pedestrian street, take note of the elevator up the Mönchsberg, which leaves from the cliffside just ahead. Now turn right onto...*

⑭ Getreidegasse

Old Salzburg's colorful main drag, Getreidegasse (rated ▲▲) has been a center of trade since Roman times. Check out all the old wrought-iron signs that advertise what's sold inside. This was the Salzburg of prosperous medieval burghers (businessmen). These days it bustles with tourist trade. Dating mainly from the 15th century, the buildings are tall and narrow because this was prime real estate, and there was nowhere to build but up. Space was always tight, as the town was squeezed between the river and the mountain, and lots of land was set aside for the church. The architecture still looks much as it did in Mozart's day—though many of the buildings themselves are now inhabited by chain outlets.

Enjoy the traditional signs, and try to guess what they sold. There are signs advertising spirits, a bookmaker, and a horn indicating a place for the postal coach. A brewery has a star for the name of the beer, "Sternbräu." There's a window maker, a key maker, a pastry shop, a tailor, a pretzel maker, a pharmacy, a hat

Horse troughs at the base of Mönchsberg cliff

Getreidegasse is Salzburg's main shopping street.

maker, and...ye olde hamburger shoppe, McDonald's.

On the right at #39, **Sporer** pours homemade spirits (about €4/shot, Mon-Fri 9:30-19:00, Sat 8:30-17:00, closed Sun). This has been a family-run show for a century—fun-loving, proud, and English-speaking. *Nuss* is nut, *Marille* is apricot (typical of Austria), the *Kletzen* cocktail is like a super-thick Baileys with pear, and *Edle Brande* is the stronger schnapps. The many homemade firewaters are in jugs at the end of the bar.

After noticing building #39's old doorbells—one per floor—continue down Getreidegasse. On the left at #40, **Eisgrotte** serves good ice cream. Across from Eisgrotte, a tunnel leads to the recommended **Balkan Grill** (sign reads *Bosna Grill*), the local choice for the very best wurst in town. Down the tunnel at #28 (a blacksmith shop since the 1400s), **Herr Wieber**, an ironworker and locksmith, welcomes the curious. Next door, McDonald's is required to keep its arches Baroque and low-key.

At Getreidegasse #9, the knot of excited tourists marks the home of Salzburg's most famous resident. Mozart was born here in 1756. It was here that he composed most of his boy-genius works. Inside you see paintings of his family, letters, personal items (a lock of his hair, a clavichord he might have played), all trying to bring life to the Mozart story (see the description on facing page).

• *At Getreidegasse #3, turn right, into the passageway. You'll walk under a whale bone (likely symbolizing the wares of an exotic import shop) and reach the Old World time-capsule café called **Schatz Konditorei** (worth a stop for coffee and pastry). At Schatz Konditorei, turn left through the passage. When you reach Sigmund-Haffner-Gasse, glance to the left (for a nice view of the city hall tower), then turn right. Walk along Sigmund-Haffner-Gasse and take your first left to reach a square called...*

⓯ *Alter Markt*

This is Salzburg's old marketplace. Here you'll find a sausage stand and the venerable and recommended Café Tomaselli.

• *Our walk is over. If you're up for more sightseeing, most everything's a short walk from here. The Old Town has several museums, or*

Hofapotheke pharmacy at Alter Markt

you can head up to the Hohensalzburg Fortress. To visit sights across the river in the New Town, cross the pedestrian bridge nearby.

SIGHTS

In the Old Town
▲▲▲SALZBURG MUSEUM
This is your best look at Salzburg's history. As the building was once the prince-archbishop's New Residence, many exhibits are in the lavish rooms where Salzburg's rulers entertained.

Cost and Hours: €8.50, includes so-so audio/videoguide (ID required), Tue-Sun 9:00-17:00, closed Mon, on Residenzplatz, tel. 0662/620-8080, www.salzburgmuseum.at.

Visiting the Museum: The first floor and the *Kunsthalle* in the basement house temporary exhibits. But the centerpiece of the museum is the permanent **Salzburg Myth** exhibit on the second floor. You'll learn how the town's physical beauty—nestled among the Alps, near a river—attracted 19th-century Romantics who made it one of Europe's first tourist destinations, an "Alpine Arcadia."

After that prelude, several rooms address the glory days of the prince-archbishops (1500-1800), with displays housed in impressive ceremonial rooms. Portraits of the prince-archbishops (in Room 2.07) show them to be cultured men, with sensitive eyes and soft hands, and carrying books. But they were also powerful secular rulers of an independent state that extended far beyond today's Salzburg (see the map in Room 2.08).

Room 2.09 displays Daniel Miller's paintings of the city as seen from Kapuzinerberg and from Mönchsberg. Even though both paintings are from 1635, almost everything in them is still identifiable.

The heart of the exhibit is Room 2.11, the big, colorful hall where the Salzburg Diet (the legislature) met. The elaborate painted relief ceiling depicts heroic

Romans who sacrificed for their country. Spend some time here with the grab bag of interesting displays, including old guns, rock crystals, and coins. A portrait shows the prince-archbishop who sums up Salzburg's golden age—Wolf Dietrich von Raitenau (1559-1617). Here he is at age 28, having just assumed power. Educated, well-traveled, a military strategist, and fluent in several languages, Wolf Dietrich epitomized the kind of Renaissance man who could lead both church and state. He largely created the city we see today—the rebuilt cathedral, Residenz, Residenzplatz, and Mirabell Palace—done in the Italian Baroque style. Nearby exhibits flesh out the man and his associates, including the Italian architect Vincenzo Scamozzi.

▲▲MOZART'S BIRTHPLACE (GEBURTSHAUS)
In 1747, Leopold Mozart—a musician in the prince-archbishop's band—moved into this small rental unit with his new bride. Soon they had a baby girl (Nannerl), and in 1756, a little boy was born—Wolfgang Amadeus Mozart. It was here that Mozart learned to play piano and violin, and composed his first boy-genius works. Even after the family gained fame, touring Europe's palaces and becoming the toast of Salzburg, they continued living in this rather cramped apartment.

Today this is the most popular Mozart sight in town—for fans, it's almost a pilgrimage. Shuffling through with the crowds, you'll peruse three floors of rooms displaying paintings, letters, personal items, and lots of context, all bringing life to the Mozart story.

Both Mozart sights in Salzburg—the Birthplace and the Residence—are expensive and equally good. If I had to choose, I'd go with the Birthplace as the best overall introduction (though it's more crowded), and consider the Residence extra credit. If you're truly interested in Mozart and his times, buy the combo-ticket and see both.

Cost and Hours: €11, €18 combo-ticket with Mozart's Residence, daily 9:00-17:30, July-Aug 8:30-19:00, Getreidegasse 9, tel. 0662/844-313, www.mozarteum.at. Avoid shoulder-to-shoulder crowds by visiting right when it opens or late in the day.

Visiting Mozart's Birthplace: You'll begin on the top floor in the actual apartment—five small rooms, including the kitchen and the bedroom where Mozart was born. The rooms are bare of any furnishings. Instead, you see Mozart's "square piano," detailed biographies and portraits of the famous family, and some memorabilia: Mozart's childhood viola, some (possible) locks of his hair, buttons from his jacket, and a letter to his wife, whom he calls his "little rascal, pussy-pussy." Snippets of correspondence between Mozart's family members (beneath the portraits) are filled with warmth and humor, revealing their individual personalities.

The museum portion begins with an exhibition on Mozart's life after he left Salzburg for Vienna: He jams with Haydn and wows the Viennese with electrifying concerts and new compositions. Despite his fame, Mozart fell on hard times, and died young and in debt. But, as the museum shows, his legacy lived on. Using computers, you can hear his music while following along on his handwritten scores.

Downstairs, the Mozart und Oper room examines the operas he wrote (*Don Giovanni, The Magic Flute, The Marriage of Figaro*), with stage sets and video clips. The prize piece is an old clavichord on which Mozart supposedly composed his final work—the *Requiem,* which was played for his own funeral. (A predecessor of the more complicated piano, the clavichord's keys hit the strings with a simple teeter-totter motion that allows you to play very softly—ideal for composers living in tight apartment quarters.)

The lower-floor Wunderkind Mozart exhibit takes you on the road with the child prodigy, and gives a slice-of-life portrait of what it was like to live and travel in

Mozart's Salzburg

Salzburg was Mozart's home for the first 25 years of his brief, 35-year life. He was born on Getreidegasse and baptized in the cathedral. He played his first big concert, at age six, at the Residenz. He was the organist for the cathedral, conducted the prince-archbishop's orchestra, and dined at (what's now called) Café Tomaselli. It was from Salzburg that he gained Europe-wide fame, touring the continent with his talented performing family. At age 17, Mozart and his family moved into lavish digs at (today's) Mozart's Residence.

As his fame and ambitions grew, Mozart eventually left Salzburg to pursue his dreams in Vienna. His departure from Salzburg's royal court in 1781 is the stuff of legend. Mozart, full of himself, announced that he was quitting. The prince-archbishop essentially said, "You can't quit; you're fired!" and as Mozart walked out, he was literally kicked in the ass.

Mozart's Birthplace

the 1700s. The restful, oval-shaped listening room allows you to take a break from the crowds and be immersed in beautiful music and perfect acoustics.

Atop the Cliffs Above the Old Town

Atop the Mönchsberg, the mini mountain that rises behind the Old Town, is a tangle of paved walking paths with great views, a couple of cafés (one cheap, one expensive, both with million-dollar views), a modern art museum, a neighborhood of very fancy homes, and one major sight: Hohensalzburg Fortress (perched on the Festungsberg, the Mönchsberg's southern arm).

Getting There: To get up to the cliffs, you can **climb** up from the Augustiner Bräustübl beer hall/garden, Toscaninihof, or Festungsgasse (at the base of the fortress); take the Mönchsberg **elevator** on the west side of the Old Town (€2.30 one-way, €3.60 round-trip—can descend via funicular at Hohensalzburg Fortress, normally Tue-Sun 8:00-23:00, Mon until 19:00); or ride the **funicular** into the fortress complex (€6.50 up, €8 round-trip—or buy a fortress ticket that includes the funicular).

▲▲HOHENSALZBURG FORTRESS (FESTUNG)

Construction of Hohensalzburg Fortress was begun by Archbishop Gebhard of Salzburg as a show of the Catholic Church's power. Built on a rock (called Festungsberg) 1,600 feet above the Salzach River, the fortress was never really used. That was the idea. It was a good investment— so foreboding, nobody attacked the town for over 800 years. The city was never taken by force, but when Napoleon stopped by, Salzburg wisely surrendered. After a stint as a military barracks, the fortress was opened to the public in the 1860s by Habsburg Emperor Franz Josef. Today, it remains one of Europe's mightiest castles, dominating Salzburg's skyline and offering impressive views in both directions, cafés, and a handful of mediocre museums. It's a pleasant place to grab an ice-cream cone and wander the whitewashed maze of buildings while soaking up some medieval ambience.

Cost: The **"basic" ticket** (€12.20 by funicular, €9.40 by foot) covers most castle sights: a brief audioguide tour of a small historical exhibit and a tower-top view (signed as A); a variety of museums, including the modern Fortress Museum and the military-oriented Rainer Regiment museums (B); and the Marionette Exhibit. The **"all-inclusive" ticket** (€15.20 by funicular—cheaper online and before 10:00, €11.70 by foot) covers everything in the "basic" ticket plus the Regency Rooms (signed as C). Even with a "basic" ticket, you can pay €3.50 at the door to enter the Regency Rooms (worth seeing but skippable if your time is short).

Hours: The museums are open daily 9:00-19:00, Oct-April 9:30-17:00.

*Rick's Tip: Since the view is more exciting than the museums, **save money by visiting the fortress in the evening.** After the museums close, you can usually walk up (free) or ride the funicular (small fee). After a certain time (about 20:30 in summer, 17:30 off-season), you won't be able to enter on foot, but you can still exit (the door will lock behind you). Enjoy the scenery over dinner or a drink at the café, then walk or ride back down in the dark (the path is well lit).*

The mighty Hohensalzburg Fortress dominates the city's skyline.

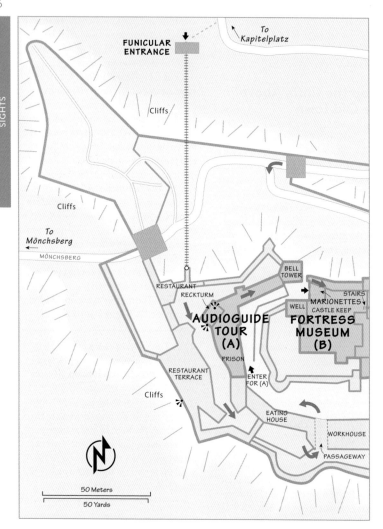

Information: Tel. 0662/8424-3011, www.salzburg-burgen.at.

Avoiding Crowds: Avoid waits for the funicular ascent with the Salzburg Card (which lets you skip to the head of the line) or by walking up. In summer, there can be long waits to start the audioguide tour (only 60 people are admitted at a time). To avoid ticket-line queues, buy your ticket online before you visit. To avoid crowds in general, visit early in the morning or late in the day.

Concerts: The fortress serves as a venue for evening concerts (the Festungskonzerte), which are held in the old banquet rooms on the upper floor of the palace museum. Concerts take place 300 nights a year and are a good way to see the fortress without crowds. For concert details, see page 134.

Eating: The $$ cafés to either side of the upper funicular station are a great place to linger while taking in the jaw-dropping view (daily 11:30-22:00,

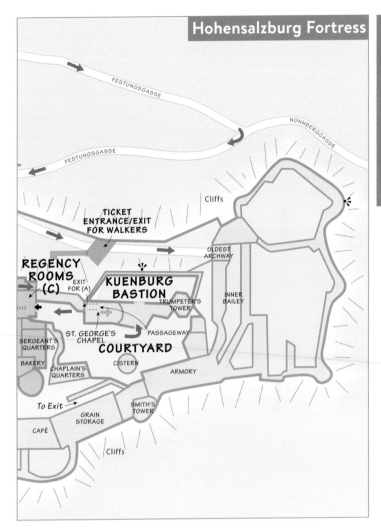

Hohensalzburg Fortress

food served until about 20:30, closed Jan-Feb).

○ Self-Guided Tour: The fortress is an eight-acre complex of some 50 buildings, with multiple courtyards and multiple rings of protective walls.

• At the top of the funicular, turn right, head to the panoramic terrace, and bask in the *view* toward the Alps. Continue up through the fortress gates—two defensive rings for double protection. Emerging into the light, go left (uphill) to find the entrance to the...

Audioguide Tour (A): The audioguide leads you through a few (mostly bare) rooms. The **Stable Block** highlights 17 prince-archbishops and displays models showing the fortress' growth, starting in 1460. The last model (1810) shows it at its peak. The fortress was never taken by force, but it did make a negotiated surrender with Napoleon, and never saw action again.

The tour then takes you to the base of the **prison tower,** with a room dedicated to the art of "enhanced interrogation" (to use American military jargon)—filled with tools of that gruesome trade. One of the most esteemed prisoners held here was Prince-Archbishop Wolf Dietrich, who lost favor with the pope, was captured by a Bavarian duke, and spent his last seven years in Hohensalzburg. It's a complicated story—basically, the pope counted on Salzburg to hold the line against the Protestants for several generations following the Reformation. Wolf Dietrich was a good Catholic, as were most Salzburgers. But the town's important businessmen and the region's salt miners were Protestant, and for Salzburg's financial good, Wolf Dietrich dealt with them in a tolerant and pragmatic way. Eventually the pope—who allowed zero tolerance for Protestants in those heady Counter-Reformation days—had Wolf Dietrich locked up and replaced.

Next, climb a spiral staircase to the top of one of the castle's towers, the **Reckturm.** Jockey your way to the railing at the upper platform and survey the scene. (If it's too crowded up here, you can enjoy nearly-as-good views from bigger terraces lower down.) To the north is the city. To the south are Salzburg's suburbs in a flat valley, from which rises the majestic 6,000-foot Untersberg massif of the Berchtesgaden Alps. To the east, you can look down into the castle complex to see the palace where the prince-archbishops lived. As you exit, at the end of the long battlement walkway, pause at the **"Salzburger Bull"**—a mechanical barrel organ used to wake the citizens every morning.
• Exit the tour into the...

Fortress Courtyard: The courtyard was the main square for the medieval fortress's 1,000-some residents, who could be self-sufficient when necessary. The square was ringed by the shops of craftsmen, blacksmiths, bakers, and so on. The well dipped into a rain-fed cistern. The church is dedicated to St. George, the protector of horses (logical for an army church) and decorated by fine red marble reliefs (1512). Behind the church is the

top of the old lift (still in use) that helped supply the fortress. Under the archway next to it are the steps that lead back into the city, or to the paths across the Mönchsberg.
• Just downhill from the chapel, find an opening in the wall that leads to a balcony with a view of Salzburg.

Kuenburg Bastion: Survey Salzburg from here and think about fortifying an important city by using nature. The fortress sits atop a ridgeline with sheer cliffs on three sides, giving it a huge defensive advantage. Meanwhile, the town of Salzburg sits between the natural defenses of the Salzach River and the ridge. (The ridgeline consists of the Mönchsberg, the cliffs to the left, and Festungsberg, the little mountain you're on.) The fortress itself has three concentric rings of defense: the original keep in the center (where the museums we're about to visit are located), the vast whitewashed walls (near you), and still more beefed-up fortifications (on the hillside below you, added against an expected Ottoman invasion). With all these defenses, the city only required a few more touches: The New Town across the river needed a bit of a wall arcing from the river to its hill. Back then, only one bridge crossed the Salzach into town, and it had a fortified gate. Cradled amid the security of its defenses—both natural and man-made—independent Salzburg thrived for nearly a thousand years.
• Back in the main courtyard, with the chapel on your right, head uphill through the stone gate and go straight ahead up the stairs. At the very top of the long staircase is the entrance to the...

Fortress Museum (Festungsmuseum, B): The first part of this extensive museum covers the history of the fortress (including models of how it was constructed) and military artifacts. Follow the one-way route, exploring the exhibits on this floor, then head one floor up.
• At this level, you have the chance to enter the Regency Rooms.

Marionette display at Hohensalzburg Fortress

Regency Rooms (C): These rooms are the most beautiful in the palace, with richly painted and gilded woodwork. You'll begin by viewing a fun seven-minute video presentation/puppet show setting the historical context for when the prince-archbishop built these rooms around the year 1500—the High Middle Ages. Then you'll see the Golden Hall, where evening concerts are held, and the Royal Apartment, consisting of two rooms—one with a colorfully painted tile stove in the corner, and the other featuring a toilet with a several-hundred-foot drop.

• *You'll loop right back to where you started. From here, you can proceed into...*

More Museums: The rest of this floor belongs to the **Rainer Regiments Museum,** dedicated to the Salzburg soldiers who fought mountain-to-mountain on the Italian front during World War I. Heading downstairs, you'll find the second part of the **Fortress Museum,** with a 16th-century kitchen, torture devices (including a chastity belt), a creatively displayed collection of pikes and swords, carved-wood furniture, and a fine collection of everyday decorative arts (dishes).

• *Exiting the museums and gift shop, turn left up the passage, head back down the long staircase, then hook a U-turn at the bottom to find the...*

Marionette Exhibit: Marionette shows are a Salzburg tradition (think of the "Lonely Goatherd" scene in *The Sound of Music*). Two fun rooms show off various puppets and scenery backdrops. Videos show glimpses of the Marionette Theater performances of Mozart classics (see page 134).

• *Our tour is over. To walk—either down to Salzburg or across the Mönchsberg—you can take any trail downhill.*

To reach the funicular, backtrack to the station between the two cafés. At the bottom of the lift, spend a minute or two at the fine little Alm River Canal Exhibit, which focuses on how the river powered the city before steam took over.

In the New Town, North of the River

The following sights are across the river from the Old Town. Cross the Makartsteg pedestrian bridge, walk two blocks inland, and take a left past the heroic statues into the Mirabell Gardens. From the gardens, it's a long block southeast to Makartplatz, where you'll find Mozart's residence.

▲MIRABELL GARDENS AND PALACE (MIRABELLGARTEN UND SCHLOSS)

These bubbly gardens, laid out in 1730 for the prince-archbishop, have been open to the public since 1850 (thanks to Emperor Franz Josef, who was rattled by the popular revolutions of 1848). The gardens are free and open until dusk. The palace is open daily and also hosts evening concerts. The statues and the arbor (far left) were featured in *The Sound of Music.*

Walk through the gardens toward the palace and find the statue of the horse (on the river side of the palace). Look back, enjoy the garden/cathedral/castle view, and imagine how the prince-archbishop must have reveled in a vista that reminded him of all his secular and religious power.

The rearing **Pegasus statue** is the site of a famous *Sound of Music* scene where the kids all danced before lining up on the stairs with Maria (30 yards farther along). The steps lead to a small mound in the park (made of rubble from a former theater).

Nearest the horse, stairs lead between two lions to a pair of tough gnomes welcoming you to Salzburg's **Dwarf Park.** Cross the elevated walk (noticing the city's fortified walls) to meet whimsical marble statues modeled after a dozen dwarfs who served in the court of the prince-archbishop in the 17th century.

There's plenty of **music** here, both in the park and in the palace. A brass band plays free park concerts (May-Aug Sun at 10:30 and Wed at 20:30). To properly enjoy the lavish Mirabell Palace—once the prince-archbishop's summer palace and now the seat of the mayor—get a ticket to a Schlosskonzerte (my favorite venue for a classical concert—see page 134).

▲MOZART'S RESIDENCE (WOHNHAUS)

In the fall of 1773, when Wolfgang was 17—and his family was flush with money from years of touring—the Mozarts moved here from their cramped apartment on Getreidegasse. Aimed toward the Mozart connoisseur, the exhibits feature original Mozart family instruments, and a good introductory video. The building itself, bombed in World War II, is a reconstruction.

Cost and Hours: €11 includes informative audioguide, €18 combo-ticket with Mozart's Birthplace, daily 9:00-17:30, July-Aug 8:30-19:00, Makartplatz 8, tel. 0662/8742-2740, www.mozarteum.at.

Visiting Mozart's Residence: The exhibit—seven rooms on one floor—starts in the main hall, which was used by the Mozarts to entertain Salzburg's high society. Consider spending time with the good introductory video in this room. Here, you can see Mozart's pianoforte from 1782, as well as his violin. The family portrait on the wall (from around 1780) shows Mozart

Mirabell Gardens and Palace

Mozart's Residence

with his sister Nannerl at the piano, their father on violin, and their mother—who'd died two years earlier in Paris.

Room 2 trumpets the successes the Mozart family enjoyed while living here: portraits of Salzburg bigwigs they hung out with, letters from Mozart bragging about his musical successes, and the publication of Leopold's treatise on playing violin.

Room 3 is dedicated to father Leopold—*Kapellmeister* of the prince—a member of the archbishop's orchestra, musician, and composer in his own right. Was Leopold a loving nurturer of young Wolfgang or an exploiting Svengali?

Room 4 stars "Nannerl" (Maria Anna), Mozart's sister, who was five years older. Though both were child prodigies, playing four-hand showpieces for Europe's crowned heads, Nannerl went on to lead a stable life as a wife and mother.

Room 5 boasts letters and music books from the nearby Mozarteum library. Rooms 6 describes the "cult of Mozart" and the use of his image in advertising, and Room 7 displays many portraits of Mozart (some authentic, some not), all a testament to his long legacy. By the time Mozart was 25, he'd grown tired of his father, this house, and Salzburg, and he went on to Vienna—to more triumphs, but ultimately, an early death at age 35 (likely due to an infection and fever).

▲ST. SEBASTIAN CEMETERY

Wander through this quiet oasis. Mozart is buried in Vienna, his mom's in Paris, and his sister is in Salzburg's Old Town (St. Peter's)—but Wolfgang's wife Constanze ("Constantia") and his father, Leopold, are buried here (from the black iron gate entrance on Linzer Gasse, walk 19 paces and look left). Continue straight past the Mozart tomb to the circular building that is Wolf Dietrich's mausoleum (English description at door). When Prince—Archbishop Wolf Dietrich had the cemetery moved from around the cathedral and put here, across the river, people didn't like it. To help popularize it, he had his own mau-

soleum built as its centerpiece. Continue straight past the Mozart tomb to the circular building that is Dietrich's mausoleum (English description at door).

Cost and Hours: Free, daily 9:00-18:00, Nov-March until 16:00, entry at Linzer Gasse 43 in summer; in winter go through the arch at #37 and around the building to the doorway under the blue seal.

Near Salzburg
▲▲HELLBRUNN PALACE AND GARDENS

In about 1610, Prince-Archbishop Markus Sittikus decided he needed a lavish palace with a vast and ornate garden purely for pleasure (I imagine after meditating on stewardship and Christ-like values). He built this summer palace and hunting lodge, and just loved inviting his VIP guests from throughout Europe to have some fun with his trick fountains. Today, Hellbrunn is a popular side trip. While the formal garden may be one of the oldest in Europe (with a gazebo made famous by *The Sound of Music*), it's nothing special. The real draws here are those amazing fountains and the surprisingly engaging exhibits inside the palace. Perhaps most of all, Hellbrunn provides an ideal excuse to get out of the city.

Cost and Hours: €12.50 ticket includes fountain tour and palace audioguide, daily 9:00-17:30, July-Aug until 21:00—but tours after 18:00 don't include the palace interior, April and Oct until 16:30, these

Hellbrunn Palace Garden

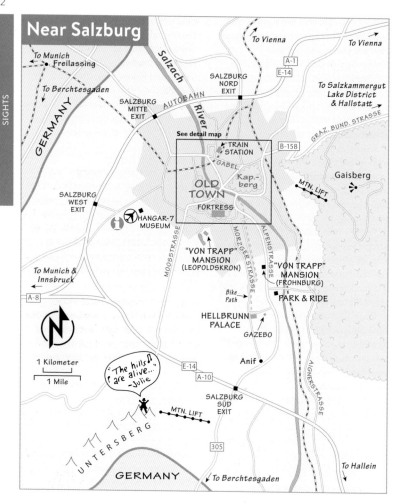

Near Salzburg

To Munich
Freilassing
To Berchtesgaden
GERMANY

Salzach River
AUTOBAHN

To Vienna
To Vienna

A-1
E-14

SALZBURG
NORD
EXIT

*To Salzkammergut
Lake District
& Hallstatt*

GRAZ. BUND. STRASSE

SALZBURG
MITTE
EXIT

See detail map

TRAIN
STATION

GABEL

B-158

Kap-
berg

Gaisberg

MTN. LIFT

OLD
TOWN

SALZBURG
WEST
EXIT

FORTRESS

HANGAR-7
MUSEUM

MOOSSTRASSE

MÖRZGER STRASSE

ALPENSTRASSE

"VON TRAPP"
MANSION
(LEOPOLDSKRON)

"VON TRAPP"
MANSION
(FROHNBURG)

PARK & RIDE

*To Munich &
Innsbruck*

A-8

*Bike
Path*

HELLBRUNN
PALACE

GAZEBO

1 Kilometer

1 Mile

N

"The hills
are alive..."
-Julie

E-14
A-10

Anif

SALZBURG
SÜD
EXIT

AIGNERSTRASSE

UNTERSBERG

MTN. LIFT

305

GERMANY

To Berchtesgaden

To Hallein

are last-tour times, closed Nov-March, tel. 0662/820-3720, www.hellbrunn.at.

Getting There: Hellbrunn is nearly four miles south of Salzburg. Take **bus** #25 from the train station or the Rathaus stop by the Staatsbrücke bridge, and get off at the Schloss Hellbrunn stop (2-3/hour, 20 minutes). Or, in good weather, the trip out to Hellbrunn is a delightful 30-minute **bike** excursion (see "Riverside or Meadow Bike Ride," later, and ask for a map when you rent your bike).

Visiting the Palace: Upon arrival, buy your **fountain tour** ticket and get a tour time (generally on the half-hour—if there's a wait until your fountain tour starts, you can see the palace first). The 40-minute English/German tours take you laughing and scrambling through a series of amazing 17th-century garden settings with lots of splashy fun and a guide who seems almost sadistic in the joy he has in soaking his group. (Hint: When you see a wet place, cover your camera or mobile device.)

After the fountain tour you're free to wander the delightful **garden** and see the **gazebo** made famous by the song "Sixteen

Going on Seventeen" from *The Sound of Music* (from the palace, head up the long, yellow-walled gravel road, then look right for *Sound-of-Music Pavilion* signs).

The **palace** was built in a style inspired by the Venetian architect Palladio, who was particularly popular around 1600, and it quickly became a cultural destination. This was the era when the aristocratic ritual was to go hunting in the morning (hence the wildlife-themed decor) and enjoy an opera in the evening. The first opera north of the Alps, imported from Italy, was performed here. The decor is Mannerist (between Renaissance and Baroque), with faux antiquities and lots of surprising moments—intentional irregularities were in vogue after the strict logic, balance, and Greek-inspired symmetry of the Renaissance. Today, those old rooms are filled with modern, creative exhibits that help put the palace into historical context: the emerging Age of Reason, when man was determined to conquer nature (such as harnessing hydropower to soak visiting VIPs).

▲▲RIVERSIDE OR MEADOW BIKE RIDE

The Salzach River has smooth, flat, and scenic bike lanes along each side (thanks to medieval tow paths—cargo boats would float downstream and be dragged back up by horses). On a sunny day, I can think of no more shout-worthy escape from the city. Rent a bike for an hour, pedal all the way up one side of the river to the outskirts, cross over, and pedal back. Even a quickie ride across town is a great Salzburg experience. In the evening, the riverbanks are a world of floodlit spires. For bike-rental information, see page 144.

For a longer trip, consider the pristine, meadow-filled farm-country four-mile ride path along Hellbrunner Allee to Hellbrunn Palace: From the middle of town, head along the river on Rudolfskai, with the river on your left and the fortress on your right. After passing the last bridge

at the edge of the Old Town (Nonntaler Brücke), cut inland along Petersbrunnstrasse until you reach the university and Akademiestrasse. Beyond it find the start of Freisaalweg, which becomes the delightful Hellbrunner Allee bike path... which parallels Morzgerstrasse and leads directly to the palace.

MUSIC

Music lovers come to Salzburg in late July and August for the Salzburg Festival, but you can enjoy concerts all year long. Pick up the events calendar brochure at the TI (free, bimonthly) or check www.salzburg. info (under "Events," click on "Classical Music"). I've never planned in advance, and I've enjoyed great concerts with every visit.

Rick's Tip: *Virtually all* **hotels make concert and bus tour recommendations based on their potential kickback,** *not what's best for you. If you book any event through your hotel, you're probably paying too much.* **Book direct.**

Daily Events

The following concerts are mostly geared to tourists and can have a crank-'em-out feel, but they still provide good value, especially outside festival times.

CONCERTS AT HOHENSALZBURG FORTRESS

Nearly nightly fortress concerts (Festungskonzerte) are held in the "prince's chamber" of the fortress atop the hill, featuring small chamber groups playing Mozart's greatest hits for beginners. The medieval-feeling chamber has windows overlooking the city, and the concert gives you a chance to enjoy the grand views and a stroll through the castle courtyard (€36-44, open seating after first six more expensive rows, funicular ride included if you come within an hour of the concert; at 20:00 or 20:30; doors open 30 minutes early, can combine with three-course dinner beforehand, reserve at tel. 0662/825-858 or via www.salzburghighlights.at, pick up tickets at the door).

CONCERTS AT THE MIRABELL PALACE

The nearly nightly palace concerts (Schlosskonzerte) are performed in a lavishly Baroque setting. They come with more sophisticated chamber music and better musicians than the fortress concerts...and Baroque music flying around a Baroque hall is a happy bird in the right cage (€32-38, open seating farther after first five pricier rows; RS%—10 percent discount, use code "RICK10"; usually at 20:00 but check flier for times, doors open one hour ahead, tel. 0662/828-695, www. salzburg-palace-concerts.com).

MOZART DINNER CONCERT

The elegant Stiftskeller St. Peter restaurant offers a traditional candlelit meal with Mozart's greatest hits performed by a string quintet and singers in historic costumes gavotting among the tables. In this elegant Baroque setting, tourists clap between movements and get three courses of food (from Mozart-era recipes) mixed with three 20-minute courses of crowd-pleasing music—structured much as such evenings were in Baroque-era times (€63, RS%—use code "RICK9" to receive €9 discount, music starts nightly at 19:30, arrive 30 minutes before that, dress is "smart casual," to reserve email office@skg.co.at or call 0662/828-695, www.mozart-dinner-concert-salzburg.com).

RESIDENZKONZERTE

On most afternoons, you can catch a 45-minute concert of 16th-century music ("from Baroque through Mozart") played on Renaissance instruments at the Residenz (€22, discount with Salzburg Card or DomQuartier ticket, daily at 15:00 and 17:00, tickets available 30 minutes before performances, mobile 0664-423-5645, www.agenturorpheus.at).

MARIONETTE THEATER

Spellbinding marionettes star in these operas performed to recorded music. A troupe of 10 puppeteers—actors themselves—brings to life the artfully created puppets at the end of their five-foot strings. The 180 performances a year alternate between *The Sound of Music* and various German-language operas (with handy superscripts in English). While the 300-plus-seat venue is forgettable, the art of the marionettes enchants adults and children alike (€20-37, kids-€15, June-Aug and Oct nearly nightly at 19:30 plus matinees on some days, fewer shows off-season, near Mozart's Residence at Schwarzstrasse 24, tel. 0662/872-406, www.marionetten.at).

Weekly Events

MOZART PIANO SONATAS (KLAVIERSONATEN)

These short (45-minute) and fairly inexpensive weekend concerts in St. Peter's Abbey are ideal for families (€22, €11 for kids, €55 for a family of four, almost every Fri and Sat at 19:00 year-round, in the abbey's Romanesque Hall—a.k.a. Romanischer Saal, enter from inner courtyard 20 yards left of St. Peter's Church, mobile 0664-423-5645, www.agenturorpheus.at).

FREE BRASS BAND CONCERTS
Traditional brass bands play in the Mirabell Gardens on Sundays and Wednesdays (May-Aug Sun at 10:30 and Wed at 20:30, may be canceled in bad weather).

MUSIC AT SUNDAY MASS
Each Sunday morning, three great churches offer a Mass, generally with glorious music. The **Salzburg Cathedral** is likely your best bet for fine music by which to worship. The 10:00 service generally features a Mass written by a well-known composer performed by choir, organist, or other musicians. The worship service is often followed at 11:30 by a free organ concert (music program at www.kirchen.net/dommusik). Nearby (just outside Domplatz, with the pointy green spire), the **Franciscan Church** is the locals' choice (at 9:00, www.franziskanerkirche-salzburg.at—click on "Programm"). **St. Peter's Church** sometimes has music (often at 10:15, www.stift-stpeter.at—click on "Kirchenmusik," then "Jahresprogramm").

Annual Festivals
SALZBURG FESTIVAL (SALZBURGER FESTSPIELE)
Each summer, from mid-July to the end of August, the city hosts its famous Salzburg Festival, founded in 1920 to employ Vienna's musicians in the summer. This fun and festive time is crowded—as many as 200,000 tickets are sold to festival events annually—but there are usually plenty of beds (except for a few August weekends). Events are pricey (€50-430) and take place primarily in three big halls: the Opera and Orchestra venues in the Festival House, and the Landestheater, where German-language plays are performed. The schedule is announced in November, tickets go on sale in January, and most seats are sold out by March. But many "go to the Salzburg Festival" by seeing smaller, nonfestival events that occur during the

same weeks. For these unofficial events, same-day tickets are normally available—ask at the TI for details. For specifics on the festival schedule and tickets, visit www.salzburgfestival.at.

Music lovers in town during the festival who don't have tickets (or money) can still enjoy **Festival Nights,** a free series of videos of previous years' festival performances, projected on a big screen on Kapitelplatz (behind the cathedral). It's a fun scene, with plenty of folding chairs and a food circus of temporary eateries. For info and schedules, go to www.salzburg.info and search for "Festival Nights."

Other Annual Music Festivals: Events include **Mozart Week** (January), the **Easter Music Festival**, and October's **Culture Days** and **Jazz & the City**.

EATING

In the Old Town
Restaurants
$$ **Gasthaus zum Wilder Mann** is a good bet in bad weather for traditional dishes. For a quick lunch, get the *Bauernschmaus*, a mountain of dumplings, kraut, and peasant's meats. Notice the century-old flood photos on the wall. While they have a few outdoor tables, the atmosphere is all indoors, and the menu is more geared to cold weather (kitchen open Mon-Sat 11:00-21:00, closed Sun, 2 minutes from Mozart's Birthplace, Getreidegasse 20

or Griesgasse 17, tel. 0662/841-787, www. wildermann.co.at; Robert, Kurt, and Reinhold).

$$ St. Paul Stubm Beer Garden is tucked away under the fortress with a decidedly untouristy atmosphere. The food is better than at beer halls, and a young, bohemian-chic clientele fills its two troll-like rooms and its idyllic tree-shaded garden. *Kasnock'n* is a tasty dish of *Spätzle* with cheese served in an iron pan—hearty enough for two. Reservations are smart (Mon-Sat 17:00-22:00, open later for drinks only, closed Sun, Herrengasse 16, tel. 0662/843-220, www.paul-stube.at, Bernard).

Rick's Tip: *On menus, look for a dessert called* **Salzburger Nockerl,** *a soufflé resembling mountain peaks, with a snowy dusting of powdered sugar. Sometimes served with raspberry sauce, this rich treat is designed to share.*

$$ Zirkelwirt serves Austrian standards (schnitzel, goulash, *Spätzle* with kraut) and big salads in an updated *Gasthaus* dining room and exotic plant-screened terrace. Just a block off Mozartplatz, it's a world away from the tourism of the Old Town (daily 11:30-22:00, Pfeifergasse 14, tel. 0662/842-796).

$$ Café Tomaselli (with its Kiosk annex and terrace seating diagonally across the way) has long been Salzburg's top place for lingering and people-watching. Tomaselli serves light meals and lots of drinks, keeps long hours, and has fine seating on the square, a view terrace upstairs, and indoor tables. Despite its fancy wood paneling, 19th-century portraits, and chandeliers, it's surprisingly low-key (Mon-Sat 7:00-19:00, Sun from 8:00, Aug until 21:00, Alter Markt 9, tel. 0662/844-488).

$$$$ Stiftskeller St. Peter has been in business for more than 1,000 years—it was mentioned in the biography of Charlemagne. These days it's classy and high-end touristy, serving uninspired traditional Austrian cuisine with indoor/outdoor seating (daily 11:30-22:00 or later, next to St. Peter's Church at foot of Mönchsberg, tel. 0662/841-268, www.stpeter.at). They host the recommended Mozart Dinner Concert described on page 134.

$$$$ Carpe Diem is a project by Red Bull tycoon Dietrich Mateschitz. Salzburg's beautiful people, fueled by Red Bull, present themselves here in the chic ground-floor **café** and trendy "lifestyle bar" (smoking allowed), which serves quality cocktails and fine finger food in cones (daily 8:30-23:00). Upstairs is an expensive, nonsmoking **restaurant** boasting a Michelin star (Mon-Sat 12:00-14:00 & 18:30-22:00, closed Sun; Getreidegasse 50, tel. 0662/848-800, www.carpediemfinestfingerfood.com).

Modern, Eclectic Cuisine in Kaiviertel

An oasis of contemporary, international restaurants and shops is tucked just behind the Salzburg Museum in the Kaiviertel quarter (around the intersection of Kaigasse and Chiemseegasse). Among the offerings are Polish, Irish, Vietnamese, and Mexican cuisine, as well as organic coffee. For cocktails, pizza, and snacks try **Stage Bar,** which hosts live music nightly (Tue-Sat 19:00-late, closed Sun-Mon, Chiemseegasse 3, mobile 0650-453-0547). Popular **Icezeit** serves ice cream in exotic flavors and has vegan options (Chiemseegasse 1).

On the Cliffs Above the Old Town

Riding the Mönchsberg elevator from the west end of the Old Town up to the clifftop deposits you near two very different eateries, but each has commanding city views.

$$$$ Mönchsberg 32 is a sleek, modern café/bar/restaurant overlooking Salzburg from the top of the Mönchsberg elevator. Even if you're not hiking anywhere, this makes for a great place to

enjoy a €5 coffee and the view. Or settle in for a pricey but high-quality meal (weekday lunch specials, Tue-Sun 9:00-24:00, closed Mon, popular breakfasts served until 12:00, buy a one-way elevator ticket—they give customers a free pass to descend, tel. 0662/841-000, www.m32.at).

$$ Stadtalm Café sits high above the Old Town on the edge of the cliff, with good traditional food and great views. Nearby are the remnants of the old city wall. If hiking across the Mönchsberg, make this a stop (cliff-side garden seating or cozy-mountain-hut indoor seating, generally Mon-Sat 11:30-23:00 or later, Sun until 18:00; closes earlier off-season, 5 minutes from top of Mönchsberg elevator, also reachable by stairs from Toscaninihof, Mönchsberg 19C, tel. 0662/841-729, Peter).

Rick's Tip: Austria has been slow to embrace the smoke-free movement. By law, big restaurants must offer smoke-free zones (and smoking zones, if they choose). Smaller places choose to be either smoking or nonsmoking, indicated by stickers on the door: red for smoking, or green for nonsmoking.

Eating Cheaply in the Old Town

$ Fisch Krieg Restaurant, on the river where the fishermen used to sell their catch, is a great value, serving fast, fresh, and inexpensive fish. Get your fishwich to go, or order from the affordable eat-in menu to enjoy the casual dining room—where trees grow through the ceiling—and the great riverside seating (Mon-Fri 8:30-18:30, Sat until 13:00, closed Sun, Hanuschplatz 4, tel. 0662/843-732).

$ Café Toskana is the university lunch canteen, very basic but fast and cheap—with drab indoor seating and a great courtyard for good weather. Choose between two daily soup and main-course specials (vegetarian options available, open Mon-Fri but also Sat in summer, closed Sun, generally 8:30-17:00, hot meals served 11:30-13:30 only, behind the Residenz, in the courtyard opposite Sigmund-Haffner-Gasse 16, tel. 0662/8044-6909).

$ Sausage stands (*Würstelstände*) serve the town's favorite "fast food." The best stands (like those on Universitätsplatz) use the same boiling water all day, which gives the weenies more flavor.
$ Balkan Grill has been a Salzburg insti-

tution since 1950, selling just one type of spicy sausage—*Bosna*—with your choice of toppings (choose one of the numbered options; takeout only, steady and sturdy local crowd, Mon-Sat 11:00-19:00, Sun 14:00-19:00, hours vary with demand, Jan-Feb closed Sun, hiding down the tunnel at Getreidegasse 33 across from Eisgrotte).

Picnics: Picnickers will appreciate the well-stocked **Billa supermarket** at Griesgasse 19a, across from the Hanuschplatz bus stop (Mon-Fri 7:40-20:00, Sat until 18:00, Sun 11:00-15:00).

Rick's Tip: Popular **farmers markets** *pop up Monday through Saturday at Universitätsplatz in the Old Town, and on Thursdays around the Andräkirche in the New Town. On summer weekends, a string of craft booths with fun goodies for sale stretches along the river.*

Away from the Center

$$ Augustiner Bräustübl, a huge 1,000-seat beer garden within a monk-run brewery in the Kloster Mülln, is rustic and raw. When it's cool outside, enjoy a historic indoor setting in any of several beer-sloshed and smoke-stained halls (one of which is still for smokers). On busy nights, it's like a Munich beer hall with no music but the volume turned up. On balmy evenings, it's like a Renoir painting outdoors under chestnut trees—but with beer breath and cigarette smoke. Local students mix with tourists eating hearty slabs of grilled meat with their fingers, while children frolic on the playground kegs. For your beer: Pick up a half-liter or full-liter mug, pay the lady (*Schank* means self-serve price, *Bedienung* is the price with waiter service), wash your mug, give Mr. Keg your receipt and empty mug, and you will be made happy. Waiters only bring beer; for food, go up the stairs, grab a tray, and assemble your meal from the deli counters (or, as long as you buy a drink, you can bring in a picnic—many do).

Classic pretzels from the bakery and spiraled, salty radishes make great beer even better. Locals agree that the hot food here is not as good as the beer. Stick with the freshly cooked meat dishes: I made the mistake of choosing schnitzel, which was reheated in the microwave. For dessert—after a visit to the strudel kiosk—enjoy the incomparable floodlit view of old Salzburg from the nearby Müllnersteg pedestrian bridge and a riverside stroll home (daily 15:00-23:00, Augustinergasse 4, tel. 0662/431-246).

Getting There: It's about a 15-minute walk along the river (with the river on your right) from the Old Town side of the Staatsbrücke bridge. After passing the Müllnersteg pedestrian bridge, just after Café am Kai, follow the stairs up to a busy street, and cross it. From here, either continue up more stairs into the trees and around the small church (for a scenic approach to the monastery), or stick to the sidewalk as it curves around to Augustinergasse. Either way, your goal is the huge yellow building. Don't be fooled by second-rate gardens serving the same beer nearby. You can also take a bus from Hanuschplatz (#4, #7, #21, #24, #27, or #28) two stops to the Landeskrankenhaus stop, right in front of the beer garden. Or you can walk down from Mönchsberg (follow signs for *Mülln*).

Rick's Tip: Visit the **strudel kiosk at Augustiner Bräustübl** *and enjoy your dessert alongside the incomparable floodlit* **views from the nearby Müllnersteg pedestrian bridge.**

North of the River
Restaurants near Linzer Gasse Hotels

$$ Spicy Spices is a trippy vegetarian-Indian restaurant where Suresh Syal (a.k.a. "Mr. Spicy") serves tasty curry and rice, samosas, organic salads, soups, and fresh juices. It's a *namaste* kind of place where everything's organic, and most items are vegan (Mon-Fri 11:00-21:00, Sat 11:30-21:00, closed Sun, Wolf-Dietrich-Strasse 1, tel. 0662/870-712).

$$ **Biergarten die Weisse,** close to the hotels on Rupertgasse and away from the tourists, is a longtime hit with the natives. If a beer hall can be happening, this one—modern yet with antlers—is it. Their famously good beer is made right there; favorites include fizzy wheat beer (Die Weisse Original) as well as seasonal beers (ask what's on offer). Enjoy the beer with their good, cheap, traditional food in the great garden setting or in the wide variety of indoor rooms—sports bar, young and noisy, or older and more elegant (Mon-Sat 10:00-24:00, closed Sun, Rupertgasse 10, bus #2 to Bayerhamerstrasse or #4 to Grillparzerstrasse, tel. 0662/872-246).

$$ **Café Bazar** overlooks the river between the Mirabell Gardens and the Staatsbrücke bridge. Its interior is as close as you'll get to a Vienna coffee house in Salzburg. While service is hit-or-miss, their outdoor terrace is a venerable spot for a classy drink with an Old Town and castle view (Mon-Sat 7:30-19:30, Sun 9:00-18:00, July-Aug daily until 23:00 or later, Schwarz-strasse 3, tel. 0662/874-278).

Steingasse Pub Crawl

For a fun post-concert activity, drop in on a couple of atmospheric bars at the Linzer Gasse end of Steingasse. These dark bars, filled with well-dressed Salzburgers lazily smoking cigarettes and talking philosophy as laid-back tunes play, are all within about 100 yards of each other (all open until the wee hours). Most don't serve food, but $ **Reyna,** a convenient four-table pizzeria and *döner kebab* shop (at #3), stays open late.

Pepe Cocktail Bar, with Mexican decor and Latin music, serves cocktails and nachos (Wed-Sat 19:00 until late, closed Sun-Tue, live DJs on Sat, Steingasse 3, tel. 0662/873-662).

Saiten Sprung wins the "Best Atmosphere" award. The door is kept closed to keep out the crude and rowdy. Just ring the bell and enter its hellish interior—lots of stone and red decor, with mountains of melted wax beneath age-old candlesticks and an ambience of classic '70s and '80s music. Stelios, who speaks English with Greek charm, serves cocktails and fine wine, though no food (Tue-Sat 21:00-late, closed Sun-Mon except in Dec, Steingasse 11, tel. 0662/881-377).

Fridrich, two doors down, is an intimate little place under an 11th-century vault, with lots of mirrors and a silver ceiling fan. Bernd Fridrich is famous for his martinis and passionate about Austrian wines, and has a tattered collection of vinyl that keeps the 1970s alive. Their Yolanda cocktail (grapefruit and vodka) is a favorite. He and his partner Ferdinand serve little dishes designed to complement the focus on socializing and drinking, though their €16 "little bit of everything dish" can be a meal for two (Thu-Tue from 18:00, closed Wed except during festivals and Dec, Steingasse 15, tel. 0662/876-218).

SLEEPING

Peak season is May through October, with rates rising significantly during the summer music festival, during the four Advent weeks leading up to Christmas (when street markets are at full blast), and around Easter. Many of my Salzburg listings will let you skip breakfast to save about €10 per person—if you don't need a big breakfast, ask about this option. Remember, to call an Austrian number from a German one, dial 00-43 and then the number (minus the initial zero).

In the New Town, North of the River
Near Linzer Gasse

These listings cluster around Linzer Gasse, a lively pedestrian shopping street

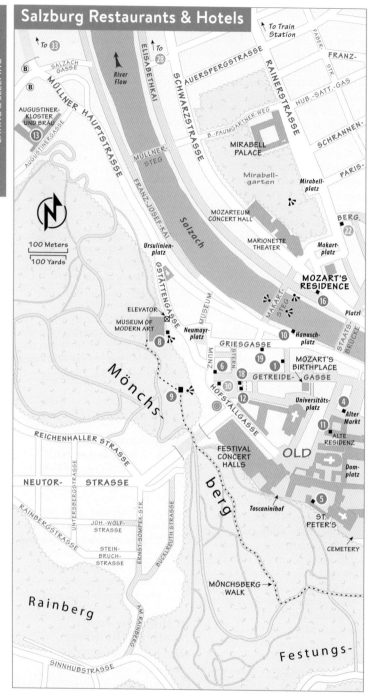

Salzburg Restaurants & Hotels

To Train Station

FRANZ-

FABER-STR.

To ③③

Ⓑ

SALZACH GASSE

ELISABETHKAI

AUERSPERGSTRASSE

RAINERSTRASSE

HUB.-SATT.-GAS.

SCHRANNEN-

To ②⑧

River Flow

Ⓑ

MÜLLNER HAUPTSTRASSE

SCHWARZSTRASSE

B.-PAUMGARTNER-WEG

MIRABELL PALACE

PARIS-

AUGUSTINER-KLOSTER UND BRÄU

⑬

AUGUSTINERGASSE

Mirabell-garten

Mirabell-platz

MÜLLNER-STEG

MOZARTEUM CONCERT HALL

BERG.

②②

FRANZ-JOSEF-KAI

N

100 Meters
100 Yards

Salzach

MARIONETTE THEATER

Makart-platz

Ursulinien-platz

MOZART'S RESIDENCE

GSTÄTTENGASSE

MAKART-STEG

⑯

Platzl

ELEVATOR

MUSEUM OF MODERN ART

MUSEUM

Neumayr-platz

⑩ Hanusch-platz

STAATS-BRÜCKE

⑧

GRIESGASSE

Mönchs-

MÜNZ-

STERN-

⑲ ①

MOZART'S BIRTHPLACE

⑥

⑱

GETREIDE-GASSE

HOFSTALLGASSE

⑤⓪

Universitäts-platz

④

⑨

⑫

Alter Markt

⑪

ALTE RESIDENCE

REICHENHALLER STRASSE

berg

FESTIVAL CONCERT HALLS

OLD

Dom-platz

NEUTOR-STRASSE

UNTERSBERGSTRASSE

JOH.-WOLF-STRASSE

ERNST-SOMPEK-STR.

BÜCKLRUTH STRASSE

Toscaninihof

⑤

ST. PETER'S

RAINBERGSTRASSE

STEIN-BRUCH-STRASSE

CEMETERY

Rainberg

AM RAINBERG

MÖNCHSBERG WALK

SINNHUBSTRASSE

Festungs-

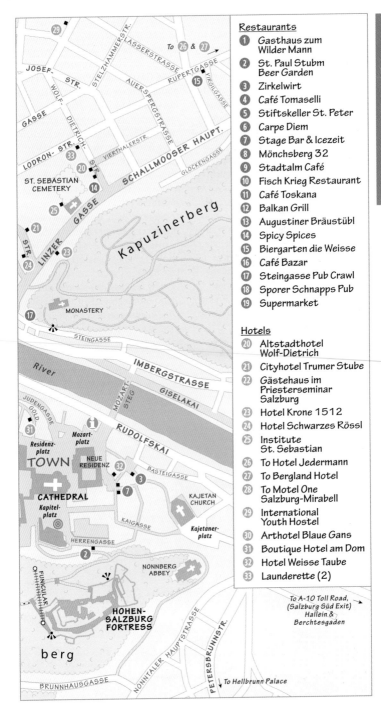

Restaurants

1. Gasthaus zum Wilder Mann
2. St. Paul Stubm Beer Garden
3. Zirkelwirt
4. Café Tomaselli
5. Stiftskeller St. Peter
6. Carpe Diem
7. Stage Bar & Icezeit
8. Mönchsberg 32
9. Stadtalm Café
10. Fisch Krieg Restaurant
11. Café Toskana
12. Balkan Grill
13. Augustiner Bräustübl
14. Spicy Spices
15. Biergarten die Weisse
16. Café Bazar
17. Steingasse Pub Crawl
18. Sporer Schnapps Pub
19. Supermarket

Hotels

20. Altstadthotel Wolf-Dietrich
21. Cityhotel Trumer Stube
22. Gästehaus im Priesterseminar Salzburg
23. Hotel Krone 1512
24. Hotel Schwarzes Rössl
25. Institute St. Sebastian
26. To Hotel Jedermann
27. To Bergland Hotel
28. To Motel One Salzburg-Mirabell
29. International Youth Hostel
30. Arthotel Blaue Gans
31. Boutique Hotel am Dom
32. Hotel Weisse Taube
33. Launderette (2)

a 15-minute walk or quick bus ride from the train station and a 10-minute walk to the Old Town. If you're coming from the Old Town, cross the main bridge (Staatsbrücke), and Linzer Gasse is straight ahead. If driving, exit the highway at Salzburg-Nord, follow Vogelweiderstrasse straight to its end, and turn right. Parking is easy at the nearby Mirabell-Congress garage (€18/day, your hotel may be able to get you a €1-2 discount, Mirabellplatz).

$$$$ Altstadthotel Wolf-Dietrich, around the corner from Linzer Gasse on pedestrian-only Wolf-Dietrich-Strasse, has 40 tastefully plush rooms (10 overlook St. Sebastian Cemetery; some are in an annex across the street). Prices include a huge breakfast spread (RS%, family rooms, nonsmoking, elevator, annex rooms have air-con, pool with loaner swimsuits, sauna, Wolf-Dietrich-Strasse 7, tel. 0662/871-275, www.salzburg-hotel.at, office@wolf-dietrich.at).

$$ Cityhotel Trumer Stube, well-located three blocks from the river just off Linzer Gasse, is a cozy, well-run, welcoming home base with 20 comfortable and attractive rooms (family rooms, in-room smartphones for free calls and navigation during your stay, nonsmoking, elevator, look for the flower boxes at Bergstrasse 6, tel. 0662/874-776, www.trumer-stube.at, info@trumer-stube.at, Vivienne).

$$ Gästehaus im Priesterseminar Salzburg occupies part of the Salzburg Seminary, where two floors have been turned into a comfortable, superbly located hotel with 60 high-ceilinged rooms. Each room has a Bible and a cross (and no TV), but guests are not required to be in a contemplative frame of mind. There's also a little guests' chapel, which looks down into the big church where Mozart used to play the organ. This is a rare place that doesn't charge extra during the Salzburg Festival—but for those dates you have to book by phone or email (family rooms, bike rental, elevator, communal kitchen, laundry facilities, reception closes at 20:00—arrange ahead if arriving later; Dreifaltigkeitsgasse 14, tel. 0662/8774-9510, www.gaestehaus-priesterseminar-salzburg.at, gaestehaus@priesterseminar.kirchen.net).

$$ Hotel Krone 1512, about five blocks from the river, offers 23 decent, simply furnished rooms in a building that dates to medieval times. Back-facing rooms

are quieter than the streetside ones (earplugs smart as nearby church bells ring from 7:00-22:00). Cheapskates can save by requesting the nearly window-less "student" double. Stay awhile in their pleasant cliffside garden (RS%, email reservation for discount, higher discounts if paying cash, family rooms, elevator, Linzer Gasse 48, tel. 0662/872-300, www. krone1512.at, hotel@krone1512.at, run by Ukrainian-Austrian-Canadian Niko).

$$ Hotel **Schwarzes Rössl** is a university dorm that becomes a student-run hotel for the months of July, August, and September. The location couldn't be handier, and its 56 rooms, while a bit spartan, are comfortable (family rooms, cheaper rooms with shared bath, no breakfast, just off Linzer Gasse at Priesterhausgasse 6, July-Sept tel. 0662/874-426, otherwise tel. 1401-7655, www.academiahotels.at, salzburg@academiahotels.at).

$ **Institute St. Sebastian** is in a somewhat sterile but clean historic building next to St. Sebastian Cemetery. From October through June, it houses students and rents 60 beds for travelers. From July through September, the students are gone, and they rent all 118 beds (including 20 twin rooms) to travelers. The building has spacious public areas, a roof garden, a piano, and some of the best rooms and dorm beds in town for the money. The immaculate doubles come with modern baths and head-to-toe twin beds (family rooms, cheaper rooms with shared bath, nonsmoking, elevator, self-service laundry, pay parking—request when you reserve; reception closes at 18:00; Linzer Gasse 41—enter through arch at #37, tel. 0662/871-386, www.st-sebastian-salzburg.at, office@st-sebastian-salzburg.at). Students like the ¢ dorms.

On Rupertgasse

These two well-run hotels are about five blocks farther from the river on Rupertgasse—a breeze for drivers, but with more

street noise than the places on Linzer Gasse. They're good values if you don't mind being a 15- to 20-minute walk or quick bus ride from the Old Town or paying extra for breakfast. From the station, take bus #2 to the Bayerhammerstrasse stop; from Hanuschplatz, take #4 to Grillparzerstrasse.

$$ **Hotel Jedermann** is tastefully quirky and stylishly minimalist, with an artsy painted-concrete ambience (look for the owner's street-art mural), a backyard garden, and 30 rooms (family rooms, nonsmoking, elevator, pay parking, Rupertgasse 25, tel. 0662/873-2410, www.hotel-jedermann.com, office@hotel-jedermann.com, Herr und Frau Gmachl).

$$ **Bergland Hotel** is charming, classy, and a great value, renting 18 comfortable rooms with an oddly stylish leather-wicker-beach theme (breakfast extra, elevator, free parking if you book direct, Rupertgasse 15, tel. 0662/872-318, www.berglandhotel.at, office@berglandhotel.at, Kuhn family).

Near the Train Station

$ **Motel One Salzburg-Mirabell** is an inexpensive chain hotel right along the river. Its 119 cookie-cutter rooms are small, but the staff is helpful, the decor is fun, and the lounge is inviting. It's six blocks (or a two-stop bus ride) from the train station, and a 15-minute riverside walk or short bus ride from the Old Town (breakfast extra, elevator, pay parking, Elisabethkai 58, bus #1 or #2 from platform D at station to St.-Julien-Strasse—use underpass to cross road safely, tel. 0662/885-200, www.motel-one.com, salzburg-mirabell@motel-one.com).

¢ **International Youth Hostel**, a.k.a. the "Yo-Ho," is a youthful, easygoing backpacker haven with cheap meals, lockers, a lively bar, and showings of *The Sound of Music* every evening at 20:00 (nonguests are welcome) with a pre-show happy hour at the bar. They welcome guests of any age—if you don't mind the noisy atmosphere (private rooms available, family rooms, breakfast extra, no curfew, laundry facilities, 6 blocks from station toward Linzer Gasse and 6 blocks from river at Paracelsusstrasse 9, tel. 0662/879-649, www.yoho.at, yoho@ yoho.at).

In the Old Town

These pricier hotels are nicely located in the heart of the Old Town. Although cars are restricted in this area, your hotel will give you instructions for driving in to unload and for parking.

$$$$ Arthotel Blaue Gans, at the start of Getreidegasse, comes with class and polish. Its 35 spacious and bright rooms mix minimalist modernity with old beams and bare wood. While pricey, it's worth considering if you can score a deal (family rooms, air-con, elevator, Getreidegasse 41, tel. 0662/842-491, www.blauegans.at, office@blauegans.at).

$$$ Boutique Hotel am Dom, on the narrow Goldgasse pedestrian street, offers 15 chic, upscale, boldly decorated (read: borderline gaudy) rooms, some with original wood-beam ceilings (family rooms, air-con, elevator, Goldgasse 17, tel. 0662/842-765, www.hotelamdom.at, office@hotelamdom.at).

$$$ Hotel Weisse Taube has 31 rooms—some straightforward and comfortable, some modern and chic—all in a quiet, 14th-century building with a cozy breakfast room. It's well located about a block off Mozartplatz (RS%, family rooms, elevator, tel. 0662/842-404, Kaigasse 9, www.weisse-taube.at, hotel@weissetaube.at).

TRANSPORTATION

Getting Around Salzburg
By Bus

Most Salzburg sights I list are within the *Kernzone* (core zone) of the city's extensive bus system. I've listed prices for buying tickets from the driver; you'll pay less

if you buy them ahead at a *Tabak/Trafik* shop or streetside ticket machine (found at tram stops at major hubs—such as the main train station). Note that "09/17" tickets are sold only at ticket machines or *Tabak/Trafik* shops.

These are your options: €2.60 basic single-ride ticket (*Einzelfahrt*, at a machine, select *Stundenkarte*); €1.30 ticket for 1-2 stops in a single direction (*Kurzstrecke*); €1.50 "09/17" ticket (valid Mon-Sat 9:00-17:00, not valid Sun or holidays); €5.70 24-hour ticket (*24-Stundenkarte*).

Remember to validate your ticket by inserting it in the machine on board.

Get oriented using the free bus map (*Liniennetz*), available at the TI. Many lines converge at Hanuschplatz, on the Old Town side of the river, between the Makartsteg and Staatsbrücke bridges. To get from the Old Town to the train station, catch bus #1 from the inland side of Hanuschplatz. From the other side of the river, find the Makartplatz/Theatergasse stop and catch bus #1, #3, #5, or #6. Busy stops like Hanuschplatz and Mirabellplatz have several bus shelters; look for your bus number.

For more information, visit www.svv-info.at, call 0662/632-900 (answered 24/7), or visit the Obus transit info office downstairs from bus platform C in front of the train station (Mon-Fri 6:00-18:00, Sat 7:00-15:00, closed Sun).

By Bike

Salzburg is great fun for cyclists. **A'Velo Radladen** rents bikes in the Old Town, just outside the TI on Mozartplatz (€12/4 hours, €18/24 hours, more for electric or mountain bikes, RS%—10 percent off with this book; daily 9:30-18:00, possibly later in summer, shorter hours off-season and in bad weather; passport number for security deposit, mobile 0676-435-5950, run by George). Some of my recommended hotels and pensions also rent or loan bikes to guests.

Arriving and Departing
By Plane
Salzburg's airport is easily reached by regular city buses #2, #10, and #27 (code: SZG, tel. 0662/85800, www.salzburg-airport.com).

By Train
The Salzburg station has tourist information, luggage lockers, a pay WC (by platform 5), and a handy Spar supermarket (generally 7:30-18:00, closed Sun). Ticket counters and ticket machines for both the Austrian and German railways are off the main hall. To find the TI, follow the green-and-white information signs (the blue-and-white ones lead to a railway "InfoPoint"). Next to the train station is Forum 1, a sizable shopping mall.

Getting downtown from the station is a snap. Simply step outside, find bus **platform C** (labeled *Zentrum-Altstadt*), and buy a ticket from the machine. Buses #1, #3, #5, #6 and #25 all do the same route into the city center before diverging. For most sights and Old Town hotels, get off just after the bridge (either Rathaus or Hanuschplatz, depending on the bus). For my recommended New Town hotels, get off at Makartplatz, just before the bridge.

A **taxi** from the station to most hotels is about €8.

To **walk** downtown (15 minutes), turn left as you leave the station, and walk straight down Rainerstrasse, which leads under the tracks past Mirabellplatz, turning into Dreifaltigkeitsgasse. From here, you can turn left onto Linzer Gasse for many of my recommended New Town hotels, or cross the river to the Old Town.

TRAIN CONNECTIONS
By train, Salzburg is the first stop over the German-Austrian border. This means that if Salzburg is your only stop in Austria, and you're using a rail pass that covers Germany (including the Regional Day Ticket for Bavaria) but not Austria, you don't have to pay extra or add Austria to your pass to get here. Deutsche Bahn (German Railway) ticket machines at the Salzburg train station make it easy to buy tickets to German destinations. Austrian train info: Tel. 051-717 (to get an operator, dial 2, then 2), from German phone call 00-43-51-717, www.oebb.at.

From Salzburg by Train to: Füssen (roughly hourly, 4 hours on fast trains, 5 hours on slow trains—included with Regional Day Ticket for Bavaria, change in Munich and sometimes in Kaufbeuren or Buchloe), **Nürnberg** (hourly with change in Munich, 3 hours), **Munich** (2/hour, 1.5 hours on fast trains, 2 hours on slower trains—included with Regional Day Ticket for Bavaria), **Frankfurt** (4/day direct, 6 hours). German train info: www.bahn.com.

By Car
Mozart never drove in Salzburg's Old Town, and neither should you. The best place to park is the **park-and-ride** lot at the Alpensiedlung bus stop, near the Salzburg Süd autobahn exit. Coming on A-8 from Munich, cross the border into Austria. Take A-10 toward Hallein, and then take the next exit (Salzburg Süd) in the direction of Anif. Stay on the Alpenstrasse (road 150) for about 2.5 miles, following *P+R* signs, to arrive at the park-and-ride (€5/24 hours). From the parking lot, catch bus #3 or #8 into town. Alternatively, groups of up to five people can buy a combo-ticket from the parking lot attendant, which includes the 24-hour parking fee and a 24-hour transit pass for the whole group (€14, group must stay together).

If you don't want to park-and-ride, head to the easiest, cheapest, most central parking lot: the 1,500-car Altstadtgarage, in the tunnel under the Mönchsberg (€18/day, note your slot number and in which of the twin lots you've parked). Your hotel may provide discounted parking passes. If staying in Salzburg's New Town, park at the Mirabell-Congress garage on Mirabellplatz.

Bavarian Alps

In this picturesque corner of the Alps bordering Germany and Austria, you'll find a timeless land of fairy-tale castles, painted houses, and locals who still dress in dirndls and lederhosen. They even yodel when they're happy.

You can tour "Mad" King Ludwig II's ornate Neuschwanstein Castle, stop by the Wieskirche, a lavishly decorated Baroque church that puts the faithful in a heavenly mood, and browse through Oberammergau, Germany's woodcarving capital. A cozy castle (Linderhof) and a sky-high viewpoint (the Zugspitze) round out Bavaria's top attractions.

The region is best traveled by car, and the sights can be seen within an easy 60-mile loop. Even if you're doing the rest of your trip by train, consider renting a car in Füssen or Munich for your time here.

The best home base is Füssen, near the region's biggest attraction, the "King's Castles" (Neuschwanstein and Hohenschwangau). It's also the easiest option for train travelers, offering frequent connections with Munich and beyond.

Drivers could also consider cute, little, touristy Oberammergau as a home base. World-famous for its once-per-decade Passion Play, it's much sleepier the other nine years.

You could do this region as a day trip from Munich by blitzing the top sights on a bus tour or coming independently by train to see just the King's Castles. But many travelers enjoy the magic of settling into this lovely green, hilly region.

BAVARIAN ALPS IN 2 DAYS

Reserve ahead for Neuschwanstein and Hohenschwangau to avoid wasting your time in line.

By Car: On the first day, visit Neuschwanstein and Hohenschwangau. Then choose among the sights that cluster nearby: the Tegelberg cable car, Tegelberg luge, Royal Crystal Baths, or a stroll in Füssen.

On the second day, drive a loop that includes the rugged Zugspitze, Oberammergau, and Linderhof Castle. You could fit in the glorious Wieskirche on either day, or when you're departing (or arriving in) the region.

Note that the first day's activities could be done by public transit; you could put off renting a car until the morning of the second day.

Without a Car: Using Füssen as a base, you can bus, bike, or taxi to Neuschwanstein, Hohenschwangau, and the Tegelberg cable car and luge. Fill out the day by exploring Füssen.

For the second day, I'd suggest taking a bus tour or hiring a driver guide to take you to other sights in the area. Otherwise, you could day-trip by bus to the Wieskirche or Oberammergau.

FÜSSEN

Dramatically situated under a renovated castle on the lively Lech River, Füssen (FEW-sehn) has been a strategic stop since ancient times. Its main street was once part of the Via Claudia Augusta, the Roman road across the Alps. Going north, early travelers could follow the Lech River downstream to the Danube and then cross over to the Main and Rhine valleys—a route now known to modern travelers as the "Romantic Road." Today, while Füssen is overrun by tourists in the summer, few venture to the back streets...

which is where you'll find the real charm. Apart from my self-guided walk and the Füssen Heritage Museum, there's little to do here—but it's a fine base for visiting the King's Castles and other surrounding attractions.

Orientation

Füssen's roughly circular old town huddles around its castle and monastery, along the Lech River. The train station, TI, and many shops are at the north end of town, and my recommended hotels and eateries are within easy walking distance. Roads spin off in all directions (to Neuschwanstein, to Austria, and to numerous lakes). Halfway between Füssen and the German border (as you drive, or a nice woodsy walk from town) is Lech Falls, a thunderous waterfall (with a handy WC).

Tourist Information: The TI is in the center of town (July-mid-Sept Mon-Fri 9:00-18:00, Sat 9:30-13:30, Sun until 12:30; off-season Mon-Fri 9:00-17:00, Sat 9:30-13:30, closed Sun; 3 blocks from station at Kaiser-Maximilian-Platz 1, tel. 08362/93850, www.fuessen.de).

Bike Rental: Ski Sport Luggi outfits sightseers with good bikes and tips (Mon-Fri 9:00-12:00 & 14:00-18:00, Sat until

The charming riverside town of Füssen

BAVARIAN ALPS AT A GLANCE

Near Füssen

▲▲▲**Neuschwanstein Castle** The ultimate fairy-tale castle, dreamed up by "Mad" King Ludwig. **Hours:** Ticket center open daily 7:30-17:00, mid-Oct-March 8:30-15:30. The first tour of the day departs at 9:00 (10:00 in off-season); the last tour departs at 17:00 (15:30 in off-season). See page 169.

▲▲▲**Hohenschwangau Castle** King Ludwig's boyhood home, a less famous but more historic castle than nearby Neuschwanstein. **Hours:** Same hours as Neuschwanstein. See page 168.

▲▲**Mary's Bridge** Pedestrian bridge overlooking Neuschwanstein, offering the best view of the castle. See page 171.

▲**Royal Crystal Baths** A pool/sauna complex outside Füssen, made for relaxing. **Hours:** Daily 9:00-22:00, Fri-Sat until 23:00; nude swimming everywhere Tue and Fri after 19:00. See page 160.

▲**Pöllat Gorge** An uncrowded hiking trail down from Neuschwanstein, a pleasant alternative to the road. **Hours:** Closed in winter. See page 172.

▲**Tegelberg Cable Car** A scenic ride to the mountain's 5,500-foot summit, popular with view-seekers and paragliders. **Hours:** First ascent daily at 9:00; last descent at 17:00, mid-Dec-March at 16:00, closed Nov-mid-Dec. See page 172.

▲**Tegelberg Luge** A fun summer luge course, next to the cable car's valley station. **Hours:** Typically April-Sept 10:00-17:00 depending on weather. See page 173.

Beyond Füssen

▲▲**Wieskirche** Germany's greatest Rococo-style church with a divinely decorated interior. **Hours:** Daily 8:00-20:00, Nov-March until 17:00; interior closed to sightseers during services: Sun 8:00-13:00; Tue, Wed, and Sat 10:00-12:00; and Fri 17:00-20:00. See page 174.

▲▲**Linderhof Castle** Exquisite, likeable mini-Versailles, another creation of "Mad" King Ludwig. **Hours:** Daily 9:00-18:00, mid-Oct-March 10:00-16:30 (outlying buildings closed mid-Oct-mid-April). See page 180.

▲▲**Zugspitze** Germany's tallest mountain at 9,700 feet, accessible by lifts or cogwheel train, with summit restaurants, shops, telescopes, and on a clear day, far-reaching views. **Hours:** Cable car departs at least every 30 minutes; daily 8:30-16:45. See page 182.

▲**Oberammergau** Adorable town well-known for woodcarving, frescoed buildings, and the Passion Play that it puts on every decade. See page 175.

Bavarian Alps

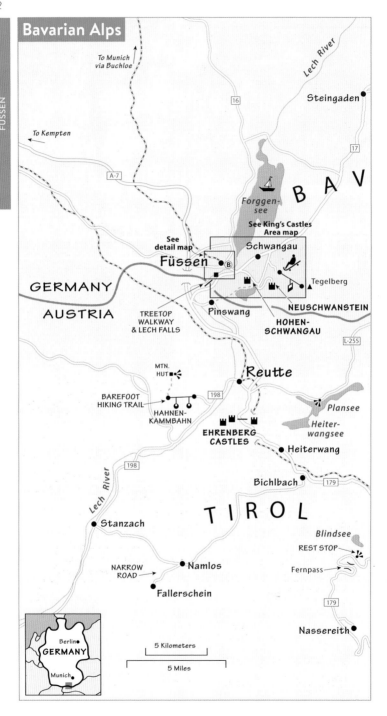

To Munich
via Buchloe

To Kempten

Lech River

Steingaden

16

17

A-7

B A V

Forggen-
see

See King's Castles
Area map

Schwangau

See
detail map

Füssen ®

Tegelberg

GERMANY

NEUSCHWANSTEIN

AUSTRIA

Pinswang

HOHEN-
SCHWANGAU

TREETOP
WALKWAY
& LECH FALLS

L-255

MTN.
HUT

Reutte

Plansee

BAREFOOT
HIKING TRAIL

198

Heiter-
wangsee

HAHNEN-
KAMMBAHN

EHRENBERG
CASTLES

Heiterwang

198

Bichlbach

179

Lech River

T I R O L

Stanzach

Blindsee

REST STOP

NARROW
ROAD

Namlos

Fernpass

Fallerschein

179

GERMANY

Berlin

Munich

Nassereith

5 Kilometers

5 Miles

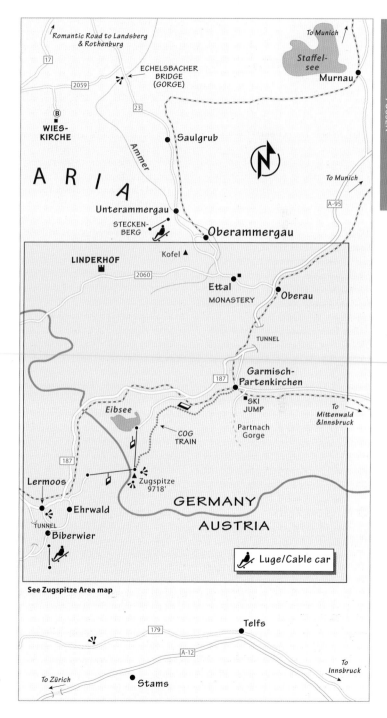

Romantic Road to Landsberg & Rothenburg

17

2059

ECHELSBACHER BRIDGE (GORGE)

23

To Munich

Staffel-see

Murnau

B
WIES-KIRCHE

Saulgrub

A R I A

Ammer

Unterammergau

STECKEN-BERG

Oberammergau

To Munich

A-95

LINDERHOF

Kofel ▲

2060

Ettal

MONASTERY

Oberau

TUNNEL

Garmisch-Partenkirchen

187

Eibsee

COG TRAIN

SKI JUMP

To Mittenwald & Innsbruck

Partnach Gorge

187

Lermoos

▲ Zugspitze 9718'

GERMANY

AUSTRIA

Ehrwald

TUNNEL

Biberwier

Luge/Cable car

See Zugspitze Area map

Telfs

179

A-12

To Zürich

To Innsbruck

Stams

13:00, Sun until 12:00 or by reservation; shorter hours off-season, call ahead to reserve, ID required, Luitpoldstrasse 11, tel. 08362/505-9155, mobile 0151-2700-0930, www.ski-sport-luggi.de).

Taxi: Call 08362/6222 for taxi service to Neuschwanstein Castle (€11), Tegelberg cable car (€14), and other places.

Car Rental: Hertz Rental Car is an easy taxi ride from the center (Mon-Fri 8:00-12:00 & 14:00-18:00, Sat 8:00-12:00, Sun and holidays by appointment, Füssener Strasse 112, tel. 08362/986-580, www.hertz.de).

Tours

Local Guide: Silvia Skelac, an American born to German parents, offers tours, hikes, and walks, and can drive you to far-flung sights (€80/half-day, up to 4 people, Austrian mobile 0664-978-7488, info@crossroads-services.com).

Bus Tour: House LA's full-day tour of Neuschwanstein, Hohenschwangau, Linderhof, and Oberammergau from Füssen can be a time-efficient option for those without a car (€90/person—price includes Neuschwanstein and Linderhof admission but not Hohenschwangau, mobile 0170-624-8610, www.fussen-info.com). They also offer private, half-day, and bike tours; book at least two days in advance; tours depart from House LA at 9:00—see listing in "Sleeping," later.

❷ Füssen Walk

For most, Füssen is just a home base for visiting Ludwig's famous castles. But the town has a rich history and hides some evocative corners. This 45-minute stroll is designed to get you out of the cutesy old cobbled core where most tourists spend their time. Throughout the town, "City Tour" information plaques explain points of interest in English (in more detail than I've provided).

• *Begin at the square in front of the TI, three blocks from the train station.*

Kaiser-Maximilian-Platz: The entertaining "Seven Stones" fountain on this square, by sculptor Christian Tobin, was built in 1995 to celebrate Füssen's 700th birthday. The stones symbolize community, groups of people gathering, conviviality...each is different, with "heads" nodding and talking. It's granite on granite. The moving heads are not connected and nod only with waterpower. It's frozen in winter but is a popular and splashy play zone for kids on hot summer days.

• *Walk along the pedestrian street toward the glass building. To your right, you'll soon see...*

Hotel Hirsch and Medieval Towers: Recent renovations have restored some of the original Art Nouveau flavor to Hotel Hirsch, which opened in 1904. In those days, aristocratic tourists came here to appreciate the castles and natural wonders of the Alps. Across the busy street stands one of two surviving towers from Füssen's medieval town wall (c. 1502), and next to it is a passageway into the old town.

• *Cross the street and walk 50 yards farther to another tower. You'll see an information plaque and an archway where a small street called Klosterstrasse emerges through a surviving piece of the old town wall. Step through the smaller pedestrian archway, walk along Klosterstrasse for a few yards, and turn left through the gate into the...*

Historic Cemetery of St. Sebastian (Alter Friedhof): This peaceful oasis of Füssen history, established in the 16th century, fills a corner between the town wall and the Franciscan monastery. It's technically full, and only members of great and venerable Füssen families (who already own plots here) can join those who are buried (free, daily 8:00-19:00, off-season until 17:00).

Immediately inside the gate and on the right is the tomb of Domenico Quaglio, who, in 1835, painted the Romantic scenes decorating the walls of Hohenschwangau Castle. Across the cemetery, on the old city wall (beyond the church), is the World War I memorial, listing all the names of men from this small town killed in that devastating conflict (along

Walking in Füssen's old town

with each one's rank and place of death). A bit to the right, also along the old wall, is a statue of the hand of God holding a fetus—a place to remember babies who died before being born. And in the corner, farther to the right, is a gated area with the simple wooden crosses of Franciscans who lived just over the wall in the monastery. Strolling the rest of the grounds, note the fine tomb art from many ages collected here, and the loving care this community gives its cemetery.

• *Exit on the far side, just past the dead Franciscans. Turn left just outside the gate and cross the street to the viewpoint.*

Town View from Franciscan Monastery (Franziskanerkloster): Enjoy a fine view over the medieval town with an alpine backdrop. In the distance, you'll see the Church of St. Magnus and High Castle (the former summer residence of the Bishops of Augsburg), where this walk ends. The tall, skinny smokestack (c. 1886) is a reminder that when Ludwig built Neuschwanstein the textile industry (linen and flax) was very big here. Retrace your steps and follow the wall of the Franciscan Monastery, which still has big responsibilities but only a handful of monks in residence.

• *Go around the corner and down the stairway. At the bottom, turn left through the medieval "Bleachers' Gate" (marked 5½, under the mural of St. George slaying the dragon) to the...*

Lech Riverbank: This low end of town, the flood zone, was the home of those whose work depended on the river— bleachers, rafters, and fishermen. In its heyday, the Lech River was an expressway to Augsburg (about 70 miles to the north). Around the year 1500, the rafters established the first professional guild in Füssen. Cargo from Italy passed here en route to big German cities farther north. Rafters would assemble rafts and pile them high with wine, olive oil, and other goods—or with people needing a lift. If the water was high, they could float all the way to Augsburg in as little as one day. There they'd disassemble their raft and sell off the lumber along with the goods they'd carried, then make their way home to raft again. Today you'll see no modern-day rafters here, as there's a hydroelectric plant just downstream.

• *Walk upstream a bit, appreciating the river's milky color, and turn right to head inland immediately after crossing under the bridge.*

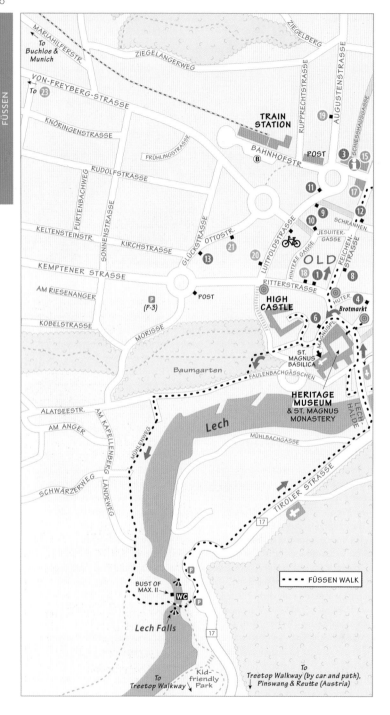

To Buchloe & Munich
MARIAHILFERSTR.

VON-FREYBERG-STRASSE

To 23

ZIEGELANGERWEG

ZIEGELBERG

KNÖRINGENSTRASSE

FRÜHLINGSTRASSE

RUDOLFSTRASSE

FURTENBACHWEG

SONNENSTRASSE

KELTENSTEINSTR.

KIRCHSTRASSE

OTTOSTR.

GLÜCKSTRASSE

KEMPTENER STRASSE

AM RIESENANGER

KOBELSTRASSE

MORISSE

Baumgarten

ALATSEESTR.

AM ANGER

AM KAPELLENBERG

MÜHLWEG

SCHWÄRZERWEG

LANDEWEG

RUPPRECHTSTRASSE

AUGUSTENSTRASSE

TRAIN STATION

BAHNHOFSTR.

POST

19

3

15

SCHIESSHAUSGASSE

11

17

9

10

12

SCHRANNEN

LUITPOLDSTRASSE

HINTERE GASSE

JESUITER-GASSE

21

20

13

18

1

OLD

8

REICHEN-STRASSE

RITTERSTRASSE

POST
(P-3)

HIGH CASTLE

6

MAGNUSPL.

HUTER

4

Brotmarkt

ST. MAGNUS BASILICA

FAULENBACHGÄSSCHEN

Lech

MÜHLBACHGASSE

HERITAGE MUSEUM
& ST. MAGNUS MONASTERY

LECH-HALDE

TIROLER STRASSE

17

P

BUST OF MAX. II

WC

P

Lech Falls

17

To Treetop Walkway

Kid-friendly Park

To Treetop Walkway (by car and path),
Pinswang & Reutte (Austria)

• • • • FÜSSEN WALK

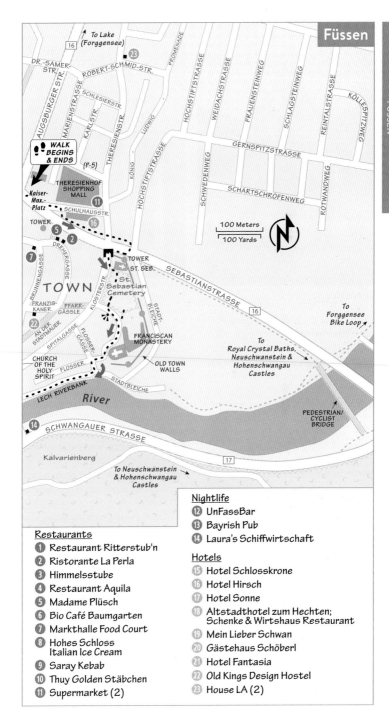

Füssen

To Lake
(Forggensee)

16

DR.-SAMER-
STR.

ROBERT-SCHMID-STR.

AUGSBURGER STR.

MARIENSTRASSE

SCHLESIERSTR.

KARLSTR.

THERESIENSTR.

KÖNIG

LUDWIG

HOCHSTIFTSTRASSE

PROMENADE

HOCHSTIFTSTRASSE

WEIDACHSTRASSE

FRAUENSTEINWEG

SCHWEDENWEG

SCHLAGSTEINWEG

REINTALSTRASSE

KÖLLESPITZWEG

GERNSPITZSTRASSE

SCHARTSCHROFENWEG

ROTWANDWEG

WALK
BEGINS
& ENDS   (P-5)

Kaiser-
Max.-
Platz

THERESIENHOF
SHOPPING
MALL

SCHULHAUSSTR.

TOWER

TOWN

DREIERGASSE

BRUNNENGASSE

FRANZIS-
KANER.

PFARR-
GÄSSLE

AN DER
STADTMAUER

SPITALGASSE

KLOSTERSTR.

FLOSSERGASSE

FLOSSER.

STADTBLEICHE

TOWER
ST. SEB.

St.
Sebastian
Cemetery

STADT
BLEICHE

SEBASTIANSTRASSE

16

To
Forggensee
Bike Loop

FRANCISCAN
MONASTERY

OLD TOWN
WALLS

CHURCH
OF THE
HOLY
SPIRIT

LECH RIVERBANK

River

SCHWANGAUER STRASSE

Kalvarienberg

To Neuschwanstein
& Hohenschwangau
Castles

To
Royal Crystal Baths,
Neuschwanstein &
Hohenschwangau
Castles

PEDESTRIAN/
CYCLIST
BRIDGE

17

100 Meters
100 Yards

Restaurants

1. Restaurant Ritterstub'n
2. Ristorante La Perla
3. Himmelsstube
4. Restaurant Aquila
5. Madame Plüsch
6. Bio Café Baumgarten
7. Markthalle Food Court
8. Hohes Schloss
   Italian Ice Cream
9. Saray Kebab
10. Thuy Golden Stäbchen
11. Supermarket (2)

Nightlife

12. UnFassBar
13. Bayrish Pub
14. Laura's Schiffwirtschaft

Hotels

15. Hotel Schlosskrone
16. Hotel Hirsch
17. Hotel Sonne
18. Altstadthotel zum Hechten;
    Schenke & Wirtshaus Restaurant
19. Mein Lieber Schwan
20. Gästehaus Schöberl
21. Hotel Fantasia
22. Old Kings Design Hostel
23. House LA (2)

Church of the Holy Spirit

Füssen Heritage Museum

Church of the Holy Spirit, Bread Market, and Lutemakers: Climbing uphill, you pass the colorful Church of the Holy Spirit (Heilig-Geist-Spitalkirche) on the right. As this was the church of the rafters, their patron, St. Christopher (with the Baby Jesus on his shoulder), is prominent on the facade. Today it's the church of Füssen's old folks' home (it's adjacent—notice the easy-access skyway).

Farther up the hill on the right is Bread Market Square (Brotmarkt), with a fountain honoring a famous 16th-century lutemaking family, the Tieffenbruckers. In its day, Füssen (surrounded by forests) was a huge center of violin- and lutemaking, with about 200 workshops. Today only three survive.

• *Backtrack and go through the archway into the courtyard of the former...*

St. Magnus Monastery (Kloster St. Mang): From 1717 until secularization in 1802, this Benedictine monastery was the power center of town. Today the courtyard is popular for concerts, and the building houses the City Hall and the Füssen Heritage Museum.

Füssen Heritage Museum: This is Füssen's one must-see sight (€6, €7 com-bo-ticket includes High Castle painting gallery and tower; Tue-Sun 11:00-17:00, closed Mon; shorter hours and closed Mon-Thu Nov-March; tel. 08362/903-146, www.museum.fuessen.de).

Pick up the loaner English translations and follow the signs to the St. Anna Chapel, with its famous *Dance of Death*. This was painted shortly after a plague devastated the community in 1590. It shows 20 social classes, each dancing with the Grim Reaper—starting with the pope and the emperor. The words above say, essentially, "You can say yes or you can say no, but you must ultimately dance with death."

Upstairs, exhibits illustrate Füssen's important trades: ropemaking, rafting, and violin- and lutemaking (with a complete workshop)—but the building itself outshines these creaky displays. Among the exquisitely decorated Baroque rooms are an ornate imperial ballroom and a two-tiered oval library displaying cupid statues and frescoes dating from 1719, with an opening to the refectory below.

• *Leaving the courtyard, hook left around the old monastery and go slightly uphill to the square tower. This marks...*

Bavarian Craftsmanship

The scenes you'll see painted on the sides of houses in Bavaria are called *Lüftlmalerei*. The term came from the name of the house ("Zum Lüftl") owned by a man from Oberammergau who pioneered the practice in the 18th century. As the paintings became popular during the Counter-Reformation Baroque age, themes tended to involve Christian symbols, saints, and stories (such as scenes from the life of Jesus), to reinforce the Catholic Church's authority in the region. Some scenes also depicted an important historical event that took place in that house or town.

Especially in the northern part of this region, you'll see *Facwerkhäuser*—half-timbered houses. A timber frame outlines the wall, which was traditionally filled in with a mixture of wicker and clay. These are most often found inside fortified cities that were once strong and semi-independent (such as Rothenberg). Farther south, you'll see sturdy, white-walled masonry houses with woodwork on the upper stories and an overhanging roof. The interiors of many Bavarian homes and hotels have elaborate wooden paneling and furniture, often beautifully carved or made from special sweet-smelling wood.

St. Magnus Basilica (Basilika St. Mang): St. Mang is Füssen's favorite saint. In the eighth century, he worked miracles all over the area with his holy rod. For centuries, pilgrims came to this medieval basilica from far and wide to enjoy art depicting the great works of St. Magnus. Then, in the 18th century, the basilica got a Baroque facelift. Above the altar dangles a glass cross containing the saint's relics (including that holy stick). At the rear of the church is a chapel bright with primary colors that honors a much more modern saint—Franz Seelos (1819-1867), the local boy who went to America (Pittsburgh and New Orleans) and lived such a righteous life that in 2000 he was beatified by Pope John Paul II.

• *From the church, find the grassy knolls and the trail ahead of you, and walk uphill toward the castle entrance.*

High Castle (Hohes Schloss): This castle, long the summer residence of the Bishop of Augsburg, houses a painting gallery (the upper floor is labeled in English) and a tower with a view over the town and lake (€6, €7 combo-ticket includes Füssen Heritage Museum, same hours as museum). The courtyard (with handy WCs under the sundial, just before the tower climb) is worth even a few minutes to admire the striking perspective tricks painted onto its flat walls.

• *Exit the castle wall, and follow the call of the Lech River through the ivy-covered archway to the right into the Baumgarten. It's a 15-minute walk from here to the falls.*

Baumgarten and Lech Falls: As you explore the castle garden, notice the impressive walls that kept the High Castle safe from pesky invaders. Wander toward the Lech River and follow the signs (away from town and into a quaint neighborhood) that point you toward Lech Falls—it's just beyond the tall, skinny smokestack you saw earlier.

Cross the bridge to enjoy a bit of impressive natural beauty tucked away just outside town. Some say that the name

"Füssen" is derived from the Latin word for gorge. Royals and tourists alike have enjoyed this gorge for centuries. Imagine "Mad" King Ludwig coming here with his family to enjoy a special tea arranged on top of the gorge. High above looms a bust of his father (Maximilian II); down below, the interesting rock formations bulge and twist above the roaring water.

• The Treetop Walkway (described later) is just a 10-minute walk ahead on Tiroler Strasse. Otherwise, from here you can walk downhill to return to town, enjoying a backside view of St. Magnus Monastery where it borders the Lech River. Take a left at the bridge and head back uphill to find the city's main drag (once the Roman Via Claudia and now Reichenstrasse), which leads from a grand statue of St. Magnus past lots of shops, cafés, and strolling people to Kaiser-Maximilian-Platz and the TI...where you began.

Experiences

These places lie within a mile or two of Füssen, and can be reached by car, bike, or foot. See the "King's Castles Area" map for locations.

▲ROYAL CRYSTAL BATHS (KÖNIGLICHE KRISTALL-THERME)

This pool/sauna complex just outside Füssen is the perfect way to relax on a rainy day or to cool off on a hot one. The main part of the complex (downstairs), called the Therme, contains two heated indoor pools and a café; outside you'll find a shallow kiddie pool, a lap pool, a heated Kristallbad with massage jets and a whirlpool, and a salty mineral bath. The extensive saunas upstairs are well worth the few extra euros, if you're OK with nudity. (Swimsuits are required in the downstairs pools but verboten in the upstairs saunas.) Pool and sauna rules are posted in German, but don't worry—just follow the locals' lead.

To enter the baths, first choose the length of your visit and your focus (big outdoor pool only, all ground-floor pools but not the saunas, or the whole enchilada—a flier explains all the prices in English). You'll get a wristband and a credit card-sized ticket with a bar code. Insert that ticket into the entry gate, note your entry time, and keep your ticket—you'll need it to get out. Enter through the changing stalls—where you'll change into your bathing suit (use the clever lever at knee level to lock the door). Then choose a storage locker (€1 coin deposit). When it's time to leave, reinsert your ticket in the gate—if you've gone over the time limit, feed extra euros into the machine.

Cost and Hours: Baths only-€14.50/2 hours, €19/4 hours, €24/all day; saunas-about €6 extra, they rent towels and robes and sell swimsuits; daily 9:00-22:00, Fri-Sat until 23:00; nude swimming everywhere Tue and Fri after 19:00; tel. 08362/819-630, www.kristalltherme-schwangau.de.

Getting There: From Füssen, drive, bike, or walk across the river, turn left toward Schwangau, and then, about a mile later, turn left at signs for Kristall-Therme. It's at Am Ehberg 16.

TREETOP WALKWAY (BAUMKRONENWEG ZIEGELWIES)

This elevated wooden "treetop path" lets you stroll for a third of a mile, high in the trees on a graceful yet sturdy suspension-bridge-like structure 60 feet in the air. The walkway crosses the Austria-Germany border and offers views of the surrounding mountains and the "wild" alpine Lech River, which can be a smooth glacier-blue mirror one day and a muddy torrent the next. Located east of Füssen, just past Lech Falls on the road to Reutte, the walkway can be accessed at either end. The Austrian end (closer to Reutte) has a large parking lot and a tiny ticket booth. At the German end (closer to Füssen) there is a nature center and café, and parking is scarce. Stairs (kids can take the slide) lead down to a riverside trail that loops about a mile through a kid-friendly park, with a log raft to cross a little creek, a wonky little bridge, and a sandy stream great for wading. Those with more energy to burn can try the slightly longer mountain loop, accessed by a tunnel under the road.

Cost and Hours: €5, free for kids 15 and under, daily 10:00-17:00, April and Nov until 16:00, closed Dec-March and in bad weather, Tiroler Strasse 10, tel. 08362/938-7550, www.baumkronenweg.eu.

Eating

$$ Restaurant Ritterstub'n offers delicious, reasonably priced German grub plus salads, veggie plates, and a fun kids' menu. They have three eating zones: modern decor in front, traditional Bavarian in back, and a courtyard (cheap lunch specials, €19 three-course fixed-price dinners, Tue-Sun 11:30-14:00 & 17:30-21:30, closed Mon, Ritterstrasse 4, tel. 08362/7759).

$$ Schenke & Wirtshaus (inside Altstadthotel zum Hechten) dishes up hearty, traditional Bavarian dishes from goulash to pork knuckle in a classic interior. Their specialty is pike (*Hecht*) pulled from the Lech River, served with a tasty fresh-herb sauce (daily 11:00-21:00, Ritterstrasse 6, tel. 08362/91600).

$$$ Ristorante La Perla is an Italian restaurant with a classic rosy interior, streetside tables, and a hidden courtyard (cheaper pizzas and pastas, daily 11:00-22:00, Nov-Jan closed 14:30-17:30 and all day Mon, Drehergasse 44, tel. 08362/7155).

$$$ The **Himmelsstube**, right on Füssen's main traffic circle, offers a weekday lunch buffet and live Bavarian zither music most Fridays and Saturdays during dinner. Choose between a traditional dining room and a pastel winter garden (daily 11:30-14:30 & 18:00-22:00, Prinzregentenplatz 2, tel. 08362/930-180).

$$ Restaurant Aquila serves modern German and Italian-influenced dishes and serious salads in a simple indoor setting, but I prefer the outdoor tables on delightful Brotmarkt square (Wed-Mon 11:30-21:00, closed Tue, reservations smart, Brotmarkt 9, tel. 08362/6253, www.aquila-fuessen.de).

$$$ Madame Plüsch, old-school and elegant, serves tasty Bavarian dishes (fish, pork, beef, and veggie options), prepared and seasoned with care. Dine in a cozy interior or at tables on the square (Thu-Mon 11:30-15:00 & 17:00-23:00, Wed 17:00-23:00, closed Tue, reservations recommended, Drehergasse 48, tel. 08362/938-0949, www.madame-pluesch.de).

$ Bio Café Baumgarten is a tiny healthy oasis near the St. Magnus Basilica tower, with tables inside and out on the square. Its organic fare includes breakfast, smoothies, salads, and sweet and savory crêpes, plus homemade cakes (daily 9:00-18:00, Magnusplatz 6, tel. 08362/989-9750).

Food Court: The fun **$ Markthalle** offers a wide selection of reasonably priced, wurst-free food. Located in a former warehouse from 1483, it's now home to a fishmonger, deli counters, a fruit stand, a bakery, and a wine bar. Buy

your food from one of the vendors, park yourself at any one of the tables, then look up and admire the Renaissance ceiling (Mon-Fri 8:00-18:30, Sat until 15:00, closed Sun, corner of Schrannengasse and Brunnengasse).

Gelato: Hohes Schloss Italian Ice Cream is a popular *gelateria* on the main drag with a huge menu of decadent sundaes and an inviting people-watching perch (Reichenstrasse 14).

Cheap Eats: $ Saray Kebab is the town's favorite Middle Eastern take-away joint (Mon-Sat 11:00-23:00, closed Sun, Luitpoldstrasse 1, tel. 08362/2847).

$ Thuy Golden Stäbchen serves a mix of Vietnamese, Chinese, and Thai food on a deserted back street with outdoor tables and a castle view (Tue-Sun 10:00-22:00, closed Mon, Hinteregasse 29, tel. 08362/939-7714).

Picnic Supplies: Bakeries and butcher shops (*Metzger*) abound and frequently have ready-made sandwiches. For groceries, try the discount **Netto** supermarket, at the roundabout across from Hotel Schlosskrone, or the midrange **REWE** in the Theresienhof shopping complex (both supermarkets open Mon-Sat 7:00-20:00, closed Sun).

Nightlife: At the **UnFassBar,** on Füssen's main drag, locals crowd at streetside tables or inside the cozy interior for drinks and small bites (Wed-Sat 10:00-22:00, closed Sun-Tue, Reichenstrasse 32, tel. 08362/929-6688). **Bayrish Pub** is popular for soccer viewing, live music, and conviviality (Tue-Fri 17:30-late, Sat from 14:30, closed Sun-Mon, Otto-strasse 7, tel. 08362/930-7444). **Laura's Schiffwirtschaft,** just across the river, attracts a younger crowd with live music, a foosball table, and basic bar food (Wed-Sat 17:00-24:00, closed Sun-Tue, tel. 08362/924-3370).

Sleeping

My recommended accommodations are within a few handy blocks of the train sta-

tion and the town center. Parking is easy, and some hotels also have their own lot or garage. Many hotels give a 5-10 percent discount for two-night stays—always ask—and prices drop by 10-20 percent off-season. Competition is fierce, so shop around.

Rick's Tip: *Ask your hotelier for a* **Füssen Card,** *which gives you* **free use of public transit** *in the immediate region (including the bus to Neuschwanstein), as well as* **discounts** *at major attractions. You may be asked for a small deposit.*

Big Hotels in the Center of Town

$$$ Hotel Schlosskrone is formal, with 62 rooms in two wings and all the amenities you need to pamper yourself after a long castle visit. It also runs two restaurants and a fine pastry shop (some rooms with balconies, family rooms, air-con, elevator, free sauna and fitness center, spa, playroom, pay parking, Prinzregentenplatz 2, tel. 08362/930-180, www.schlosskrone.de, rezeption@schlosskrone.de).

$$$ Hotel Hirsch is a well-maintained, family-run, 71-room, old-style hotel that takes pride in tradition. Most of their standard rooms are cozy with modern bathrooms, and their rooms with historical and landscape themes are a fun splurge (family rooms, elevator, nice rooftop terrace, free parking, Kaiser-Maximilian-Platz 7, tel. 08362/93980, www.hotelfuessen.de, info@hotelhirsch.de).

$$$ Hotel Sonne takes pride in its decorating (some would say overdecorating). From eclectic to classic, its 50 rooms are a convenient home base for a night or two (some rooms with balconies, family rooms, air-con in some rooms, elevator, free laundry machine, free sauna and fitness center, pay parking, kitty-corner from TI at Prinzregentenplatz 1, on GPS you may need to enter Reichenstrasse 37, tel. 08362/9080, www.hotel-sonne.de, info@hotel-sonne.de).

Midpriced Hotels and Pensions

$$ Altstadthotel zum Hechten offers 35 rooms (some with balconies) in a friendly, family-run hotel with bright, comfortable rooms and a borderline-kitschy breakfast room. It's a good value, with a few fun extras including a travel-resource/game room, borrowable hiking gear, and a recommended restaurant (two buildings, family rooms, elevator, pay parking, situated right under Füssen Castle in the old-town pedestrian zone at Ritterstrasse 6, on GPS you may need to enter Hinteregasse 2, tel. 08362/91600, www.hotel-hechten.com, info@hotel-hechten.com).

$$ Mein Lieber Schwan, a block from the train station, offers four superbly outfitted apartments, each with a double bed, sofa bed, kitchen, and antique furnishings (cash or PayPal only, no breakfast, free parking, laundry facilities, garden, Augustenstrasse 3, tel. 08362/509-980, www.meinlieberschwan.de, fewo@meinlieberschwan.de).

$ Gästehaus Schöberl rents six bright and spacious rooms just off the main drag. One room is in the owners' house, and the rest are in the building next door (cash only, family room, free parking, closed in Nov, Luitpoldstrasse 14—check-in at #16 around back, tel. 08362/922-411, www.schoeberl-fuessen.de, info@schoeberl-fuessen.de).

$ Hotel Fantasia has 16 trendy rooms adorned with violet paint and lots of pictures of King Ludwig that might make the nuns who once lived here blush (breakfast extra, family rooms, pay parking, peaceful garden, trampoline, Ottostrasse 1, tel. 08362/9080, www.hotel-fantasia.de, info@hotel-fantasia.de).

Budget Beds

¢ Old Kings Design Hostel shoehorns two dorm rooms and three private doubles into an old townhouse that doesn't resemble a typical hostel. While the quarters are tight (all rooms share bathrooms), the central location, creative decor, and reasonable prices are enticing (bike rental, reception open daily 7:00-11:00 & 16:00-21:00, buried deep in the pedestrian zone at Franziskanergasse 2, tel. 08362/883-4090, www.oldkingshostel.com, info@oldkingshostel.com).

¢ House LA has two branches. The backpacker house has 11 basic, clean dorm rooms at rock-bottom prices about a 10-minute walk from the station (private room available, free parking, Wachsbleiche 2). A second building has five family apartments with kitchen and bath (RS%, breakfast extra, free parking, 6-minute walk back along tracks from station to von Freybergstrasse 26; contact info for both: tel. 08362/607-366, mobile 0170-624-8610, www.housela.de, info@housela.de). Both locations rent bikes and have laundry facilities.

Transportation
Arriving and Departing

BY CAR

Füssen is known for its traffic jams, and you can't drive into the old town. The most convenient lots (follow signs) are the underground P-5 (near the TI) and the aboveground P-3 (off Kemptener Strasse).

BY TRAIN

The train station is three blocks from the center of town and the TI. Buses to Neuschwanstein and elsewhere leave from a parking lot next to the station.

From Füssen to: Munich (hourly trains, 2 hours, half with easy transfer in Buchloe); **Salzburg** (roughly hourly, 4 hours on fast trains, 5 hours on slow trains—included with Regional Day Ticket for Bavaria, transfer in Munich and sometimes in Kaufbeuren or Buchloe); **Rothenburg ob der Tauber** (hourly trains, 5-6 hours, look for connections with only 3 transfers—often in Augsburg, Treuchtlingen, and Steinach); **Frankfurt** (hourly trains, 5-6 hours, 1-2 changes). Train info: www.bahn.com.

BY BUS

Bus schedules from Füssen can be very confusing. The website www.bahn.com is good for figuring out your options for a particular day and route. The DB Navigator app is also useful for planning your journey.

From Füssen to: Neuschwanstein (bus #73 or #78, departs from train station, most continue to Tegelberg cable car station after castles, at least hourly, 10 minutes, €2.30 one way, buses #9606 and #9651 also make the trip); **Wieskirche** (bus #73, #9606, or #9651; 2-6 buses/day, 45-60 minutes); **Oberammergau** (bus #9606, 1-3/day, 1.5 hours, bus sometimes starts as #73 and changes number to #9606 en route—confirm with driver that bus is bound for Oberammergau); **Zugspitze** (possible as day trip via bus #74 to Reutte, then train to Ehrwald for Austrian ascent or Garmisch, allow up to 3.5 hours total to reach the top).

THE KING'S CASTLES

Two miles from Füssen, you'll find the otherworldly "King's Castles" of Neuschwanstein and Hohenschwangau. With fairy-tale turrets in a fairy-tale alpine setting built by a fairy-tale king, these castles are understandably a huge hit. The older Hohenschwangau, King Ludwig's boyhood home, is less famous but more historic. The more dramatic Neuschwanstein, which inspired Walt Disney, is the one everyone visits. I recommend visiting both and hiking above Neuschwanstein to Mary's Bridge. Reservations are a magic wand that smooths out your visit.

Getting There

If arriving by **car,** note that road signs in the region refer to the sight as *Königsschlösser.* There's plenty of parking (all lots-€6). The first lots require more walking. The most convenient lot, by the lake (#4, *Parkplatz am Alpsee*), is up the small road past the souvenir shops and ticket center.

From **Füssen,** those without cars can catch **bus** #73 or #78 (at least hourly, generally departs Füssen's train station at :05 past the hour, extra buses often run when crowded, €2.30 each way, 10 minutes; a few departures of #9606 and #9651 also make this trip). A Regional Day Ticket for Bavaria (see Rick's Tip on page 166) or the Füssen Card available from your hotel (see Rick's Tip on page 162) let you ride for free.

You can also take a **taxi** (€11 one-way), ride a rental **bike** (3 level miles), or—if you're in a pinch—**walk** (less than an hour). The bus drops you at the tourist office (note return times so you aren't stuck waiting); it's a one-minute walk from there to the ticket office. When returning, note that buses #73 and #78 pointing left (with your back to the TI) are headed to Füssen, while the same numbers pointing right are going elsewhere.

For a day-long **bus tour** from Füssen that includes Neuschwanstein and other regional sights, see the **House LA** listing on page 154.

Orientation

Cost: Timed-entry tickets for Neuschwanstein and Hohenschwangau cost €13 apiece. A "Königsticket" combo-ticket for both castles costs €25—the Bavarian Palace Department's 14-day ticket may be a better deal if you're only touring Neuschwanstein but seeing other Bavarian sights (see Rick's Tip on this page). Children under age 18 (accompanied by an adult) get in free.

---

*Rick's Tip: The Bavarian Palace Department offers a 14-day ticket (the Mehrtagesticket) that covers admission to Neuschwanstein (but not Hohenschwangau) and Linderhof, as well as sights in Munich and beyond (€24). Don't confuse the **Mehrtagesticket** pass with the **pointless combination ticket** for "Mad" Ludwig's castles, which costs about the same but covers only three castles—Neuschwanstein, Linderhof, and Herrencheimsee (farther east and not covered in this book).*

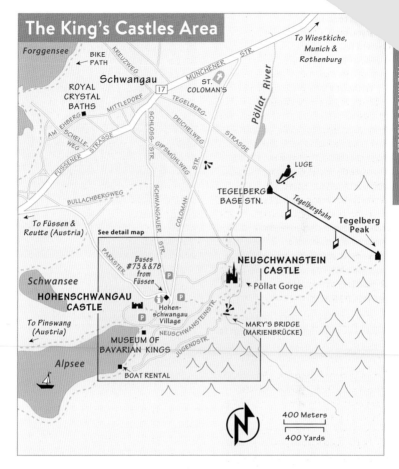

The King's Castles Area

Hours and Entry Times: The ticket center, located at street level between the two castles, is open daily (7:30-17:00, mid-Oct-March 8:30-15:30). The first castle tour of the day departs at 9:00 (10:00 in off-season); the last tour departs at 17:00 (15:30 in off-season).

Tickets, whether reserved in advance or bought on the spot, come with admission times. If you miss your appointed tour time, you can't get in. To tour both castles, you must do Hohenschwangau first (logical, since this gives a better introduction to King Ludwig's short life). You'll get two entry times: Hohenschwangau and then, two hours later, Neuschwanstein.

Information: Tel. 08362/930-830, www.hohenschwangau.de.

Reservations: Reserve ahead, particularly for holidays and weekends during peak season (June-Oct—especially July-Aug) when slots can book up several days in advance. Reservations cost €1.80 per person per castle and must be made online at least two days in advance (no later than 15:00 local time, www.hohenschwangau.de). With enough notice, a few hotels can book tickets for you. You must pick up reserved tickets an hour before your appointed entry time, as it takes a while to get up to the castles. Show up late and they may have given

ne else (but will likely
ew reservation). If you
s in advance that you're
d can call the office (tel.
,0), they'll likely rebook you.

a Reservation: A percentage
of cash... kets are set aside for in-person
purchase, so if reservations for your day of
choice are sold out online, you can still get
a ticket if you arrive early; arrive by 11:00 to
beat the crowd. During August, the busiest month, tickets for English tours can
run out by around noon.

Arrival: Make the **ticket center** your
first stop. If you have a reservation, stand in
the short line for picking up tickets. If you
don't have a reservation...welcome to the
very long line. Arrive by 7:30 in summer,
and you'll likely be touring around 9:00.

---

*Rick's Tip: Rather than buy point-to-point
train tickets,* **day-trippers from Munich
should buy the Regional Day Ticket for
Bavaria,** *which covers buses and slower
regional trains, including the bus between
Füssen and the castles, at a low price (€25/
day for the first person plus €6 for each
additional person). The only catch is that on
weekdays, the pass isn't valid before 9:00.*

Getting Up to the Castles: From the
ticket booth, Hohenschwangau is an easy
10-minute **walk** up the paved path past
the bus parking (for a quicker ascent,
zigzag up to the big yellow castle using
the ramp/stairs behind Hotel Müller).
Neuschwanstein is a moderately steep,
30-minute hike in the other direction
(also well signed—the most direct and
least steep approach begins across the
street from the ticket center).

A **shuttle bus** departs about every 20
minutes from the parking lot just below
Hohenschwangau and drops you off near
Mary's Bridge (Marienbrücke), leaving you
a steep, 10-minute downhill walk to the
castle—so be sure to see the view from
Mary's Bridge *before* hiking down (€2.50
uphill, €1.50 downhill, €3 round-trip).

Horse-drawn carriages, which leave
from in front of Hotel Müller, are slower
than walking and stop below Neuschwanstein, leaving you a five-minute
uphill hike (€6 up, €3 down). Carriages
also run to Hohenschwangau (€4.50 up,
€2 down).

Be warned that both buses and carriages can have long lines at peak times—
especially if it's raining. You might wait
up to 45 minutes, making it slower than
walking. If you're cutting it close to your
appointed time, you may need to hoof
it. Note that buses don't run in snowy or
icy conditions, which can happen even in
spring.

With time, here's the most economical and least strenuous plan: Ride the bus
to Mary's Bridge for the view, hike down
to Neuschwanstein, and then catch the
horse carriage from below the castle down
to the parking lot (round-trip cost: €5.50).
If you're on a tight schedule, consider taking the bus back down, as carriages can be
unpredictable.

Entry Procedure: At each castle,
tourists jumble in the courtyard, waiting
for their ticket number to light up on the
board. When it does, power through the
mob and go to the turnstile. Warning: You
must use your ticket while your number is

"Mad" King Ludwig (1845-1886)

Tragic Ludwig II (a.k.a. "Mad" King Ludwig) ruled Bavaria for 22 years until his death in 1886 at age 40. Bavaria was weak. Ludwig's political options were to "rule" either as a pawn of Prussia or a pawn of Austria. Rather than deal with politics in Bavaria's capital, Munich, Ludwig frittered away his time at his family's hunting palace, Hohenschwangau. He spent much of his adult life constructing his fanciful Neuschwanstein Castle—like a kid builds a tree house—on a neighboring hill upon the scant ruins of a medieval castle. Here and in his other projects (such as Linderhof Castle), even

as he strove to evoke medieval grandeur, he embraced the state-of-the-art technology of the Industrial Age in which he lived. Neuschwanstein had electricity, running water, and a telephone (but no Wi-Fi).

Ludwig was a true romantic. His best friends were artists, poets, and composers such as Richard Wagner. His palaces are wallpapered with misty medieval themes—especially those from Wagnerian operas.

Although Ludwig spent 17 years building Neuschwanstein, he lived in it only 172 days. Soon after he moved in (and before his vision for the castle was completed), Ludwig was declared mentally unfit to rule Bavaria and taken away. Two days after this eviction, Ludwig was found dead in a lake. To this day, people debate whether the king was murdered or committed suicide.

still on the board. If you space out, you'll miss your entry window.

Renovations: Neuschwanstein is undergoing restoration work, so you may encounter scaffolding, and some furnishings may have protective coverings when you visit (photos in rooms show the space without the coverings).

Services: A TI, bus stop, ATM, pay WC, lockers, and post machine cluster around the main intersection a couple hundred yards before you get to the ticket office (TI open daily April-Oct 10:00-17:30, Nov-March Sat-Sun until 16:00, closed Mon-Fri, tel. 08362/81980, www.schwangau.de). While the tiny bathrooms inside the castles themselves are free, you'll pay to use the WCs elsewhere.

Eating: I prefer to bring a packed lunch. The park by the Alpsee (the nearby lake) is ideal for a picnic, although you're not allowed to sit on the grass—only on the benches (or eat out on the lake in one of the old-fashioned rowboats (rented by the hour in summer). The restaurants in the "village" at the foot of Neuschwanstein are mediocre and over-priced. You can find decent German fare at the snack stand across from the TI or next to Hotel Alpenstuben (between the TI and ticket center). Up near Neuschwanstein itself (near the horse carriage drop-off) is a cluster of overpriced eateries, and inside the castle is a café with remarkable views, solid sustenance, and unremarkable coffee.

The Castles

The two castles complement each other perfectly. But if you have to choose one, Neuschwanstein's wow factor—inside and out—is undeniable.

▲▲▲HOHENSCHWANGAU CASTLE

Standing quietly below Neuschwanstein, the big, yellow Hohenschwangau Castle is where Ludwig spent his summers as a young boy. Originally built in the 12th century, it was ruined by Napoleon. Ludwig's father, King Maximilian II, rebuilt it in 1830. Hohenschwangau (hoh-en-SHVAHN-gow, loosely translated as "High Swanland") was used by the royal family as a summer hunting lodge until 1912. The Wittelsbach family (which ruled Bavaria for nearly seven centuries) still owns the place (and lived in the annex—today's shop—until the 1970s).

The interior decor (mostly Neo-Gothic, like the castle itself) is harmonious, cohesive, and original—all done in 1835, with paintings inspired by Romantic themes. As you tour the castle, imagine how the paintings must have inspired young Ludwig. For 17 years, he lived here at his dad's place and followed the construction of his dream castle across the way—you'll see the telescope still set up and directed at Neuschwanstein.

Visiting the Castle: The excellent 30-minute tour gives a better glimpse of Ludwig's life than the more visited and famous Neuschwanstein Castle tour. Tours here are smaller (35 people rather than 60) and more relaxed. You'll explore rooms on two floors—the queen's rooms, and then, upstairs, the king's. (Conveniently, their bedrooms were connected by a secret passage.) You'll see photos and busts of Ludwig and his little brother, Otto; some Turkish-style flourishes (to please the king, who had been impressed after a visit to the Orient); countless swans—try to find them (honoring the Knights of Schwangau, whose legacy the Wittelsbachs inherited); over-the-top gifts the Wittelsbachs received from their adoring subjects; and paintings of VIGs (very important Germans, including Martin Luther—who may or may not have visited here—and an infant Charlemagne).

One of the most impressive rooms is

Hohenschwangau Castle

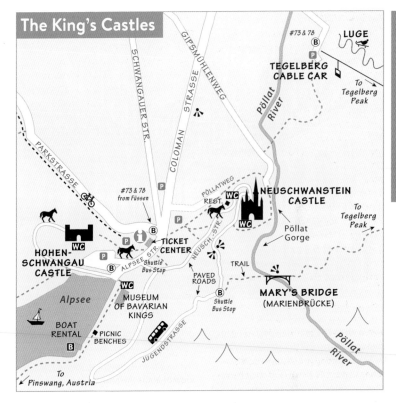

The King's Castles

the Banquet Hall (also known as the Hall of Heroes); one vivid wall mural depicts a savage, yet bloodless, fifth-century barbarian battle. Just as the castle itself had running water and electricity despite its historic appearance (both were installed in the 1900s under King Luitpold, Ludwig's uncle), its Romantic decor presents a sanitized version of the medieval past, glossing over inconvenient details. You'll also see Ludwig's bedroom, which he inherited from his father. He kept most of the decor (including the nude nymphs frolicking over his bed) but painted the ceiling black and installed transparent stars that could be lit from the floor above to create the illusion of a night sky.

After the tour is over, wind through the castle gardens and imagine Ludwig frolicking here with his sights set on the hill far in the distance.

▲▲▲NEUSCHWANSTEIN CASTLE

Imagine "Mad" King Ludwig as a boy, climbing the hills above his dad's castle, Hohenschwangau, dreaming up the ultimate fairy-tale castle. Inheriting the throne at the young age of 18, he had the power to make his dream concrete and stucco. Neuschwanstein (noy-SHVAHN-shtine, roughly "New Swanstone") was designed first by a theater-set designer...then by an architect. While it was built upon the ruins of an old castle and looks medieval, Neuschwanstein is modern iron-and-brick construction with a sandstone veneer— only about as old as the Eiffel Tower. It feels like something you'd see at a home show for 19th-century royalty. Built from 1869 to 1886, it's the epitome of the Romanticism popular in 19th-century Europe. Construction stopped with Ludwig's death (only a third of the interior was finished), and

Banquet Hall

within six weeks, tourists were paying to go through it.

During World War II, the castle took on a sinister role. The Nazis used Neuschwanstein as one of their primary secret storehouses for stolen art. After the war, Allied authorities spent a year sorting through and redistributing the art, which filled 49 rail cars from this one location alone. It was the only time the unfinished rooms were put to use.

Visiting the Castle: Today, guides herd groups of 60 through the castle, giving an interesting—yet often unenthusiastic and rushed—30-minute tour. (While you're waiting for your tour time to pop up on the board, climb the stairs to the upper courtyard to see more of the exterior, which isn't covered on your tour.) Once inside, you'll go up and down more than 300 steps, visiting 15 lavish rooms with their original furnishings and fanciful wall paintings—mostly based on Wagnerian opera themes. While renovations are under way, furnishings may be covered up, but the opulence of the building itself

delivers plenty of drama.

Rick's Tip: *In the morning, your initial* **view of Neuschwanstein** *may be hazy and disappointing. Later in the day, the sun drops down into the pasture, lighting up Neuschwanstein magnificently. Regardless of the time of day, the* **best accessible view is from Mary's Bridge,** *an easy 10-minute hike from the castle.*

Ludwig's extravagant throne room, modeled in a Neo-Byzantine style to emphasize his royal status, celebrates six valiant Christian kings (whose mantle Ludwig clearly believed he had donned) under a huge gilded-bronze, crown-like chandelier. The exquisite two-million-stone mosaic floor is a visual encyclopedia of animals and plants. While you're standing on a replica, original segments ring the perimeter. The most memorable stop may be the king's gilded-lily bedroom, with his elaborately carved canopy bed (with a forest of Gothic church spires on top), washstand (filled with water piped in

Storybook Neuschwanstein Castle

from the Alps), and personal chapel. After passing through Ludwig's living room and a faux grotto, you'll climb to the fourth floor for the grand finale: the Singers' Hall, an ornately decorated space filled with murals depicting the story of Parzival, the legendary medieval knight with whom Ludwig identified.

After the tour, weave through the crowded gift shop and past the WCs and café to see the 13-minute video (runs continuously, English subtitles). This uses historical drawings and modern digital modeling to tell the story of how the castle was built, and illustrates all the unfinished parts of Ludwig's vision (more prickly towers, a central chapel, a fancy view terrace, an ornate bathhouse, and more). Finally, you'll see a digital model of Falkenstein—a whimsical, over-the-top, never-built castle that makes Neuschwanstein look stubby. Falkenstein occupied Ludwig's fantasies the year he died.

Then head downstairs to the kitchen (state-of-the-art for this high-tech king in its day), where you'll see a room lined with fascinating drawings of the castle plans (described in English), as well as a large castle model.

Sights near the Castles

▲▲MARY'S BRIDGE (MARIENBRÜCKE)

Before or after the Neuschwanstein tour, climb up to Mary's Bridge (named for Ludwig's mom) to marvel at Ludwig's castle, just as Ludwig did. Jockey with a United Nations of tourists for the best angle—there's usually a line just to get onto the structure. This bridge was quite an engineering accomplishment 100 years ago. (Access to the bridge is closed in bad winter weather, but many travelers walk around the barriers to get there—at their own risk, of course.)

For an even more glorious castle view, the frisky can hike even higher: After crossing the bridge, you'll see very rough, steep, unofficial trails crisscrossing the hillside on your left. If you're willing to ignore the *Lebensgefahr* (risk of death) signs, you can scamper up to the bluff just over the bridge.

Mary's Bridge straddles the Pöllat Gorge.

The trail connecting Neuschwanstein to Mary's Bridge is also scenic, with views back on Neuschwanstein's facade in one direction, and classic views of Hohenschwangau—perched on its little hill between lakes, with cut-glass peaks on the horizon—in the other.

▲PÖLLAT GORGE (PÖLLATSCHLUCHT)

If it's open, the river gorge that slices into the rock just behind Neuschwanstein's lofty perch is a more interesting and scenic—and less crowded—alternative to shuffling back down the main road. While it takes an extra 15 minutes or so, it's well worth it. You'll find the trailhead just above the Neuschwanstein exit, on the path toward Mary's Bridge (look for *Pöllatschlucht* signs; trail closed in winter and sometimes impassable due to rockslides).

You'll begin by walking down a steep, well-maintained set of concrete stairs, with Germany's finest castle looming through the trees. Then you'll pop out along the river, passing a little beach (with neatly stacked stones) offering a view up at the grand waterfall that gushes beneath Mary's Bridge. From here, follow the river

as it goes over several smaller waterfalls—and stroll for a while along steel walkways and railings that make this slippery area safer. After passing an old wooden channel used to harness the power of all that water, you'll hit level ground; turn left and walk through a pleasantly untouristy residential settlement back toward the TI.

▲TEGELBERG CABLE CAR (TEGELBERGBAHN)

Just north of Neuschwanstein is a fun play zone around the mighty Tegelberg cable car, a scenic ride to the mountain's 5,500-foot summit. At the top on a clear day, you get great views of the Alps and Bavaria and the vicarious thrill of watching hang gliders and paragliders leap into airborne ecstasy. Weather permitting, scores of adventurous Germans line up and leap from the launch ramp at the top of the lift. With someone leaving every two or three minutes, it's great for spectators. Thrill seekers with exceptional social skills may talk themselves into a tandem ride with a paraglider. From the top of Tegelberg, it's a steep and demanding 2.5-hour hike down to Ludwig's castle. (Avoid the treacherous trail directly below the cable car.) Around

Luge Lesson

Taking a wild ride on a summer luge (pronounced "loozh") is a quintessential alpine experience. In German, it's called a *Sommerrodelbahn* ("summer toboggan run"). To try one of Europe's great accessible thrills, take the lift up to the top of a mountain, grab a wheeled sled-like go-cart, and scream back down the mountainside on a banked course. Then take the lift back up and start all over again.

Luge courses are highly weather dependent and can close at the slightest hint of rain. If the weather's questionable, call ahead to confirm that your preferred luge is open. Stainless steel courses are more likely than concrete ones to stay open in drizzly weather.

Operating the sled is simple: Push the stick forward to go faster, pull back to apply brakes. Even a novice can go very, very fast. Most are cautious on their first run, speed demons on their second...and bruised and bloody on their third. To avoid a bumper-to-bumper traffic jam, let the person in front of you get as far ahead as possible before you start. You'll emerge from the course with a wind-blown hairdo and a smile-creased face.

For a luge and alpine coaster options near Oberammergau, see page 178.

the cable car's valley station, you'll find a playground, a cheery eatery, the stubby remains of an ancient Roman villa, and a summer luge ride.

Cost and Hours: €20.60 round-trip, €13.30 one-way; first ascent daily at 9:00; last descent at 17:00, mid-Dec-March at 16:00, closed Nov-mid-Dec; 4/hour, 5-minute ride to the top, in bad weather call first to confirm, tel. 08362/98360, www.tegelbergbahn.de.

Getting There: From the castles, most #73 and #78 buses from Füssen continue to the Tegelbergbahn valley station (5-minute ride). It's a 30-minute walk or 10-minute bike ride from the castles.

▲TEGELBERG LUGE

Next to the cable car's valley station is a summer luge course (*Sommerrodelbahn*). A summer luge is like a bobsled on wheels. This course's stainless steel track is heated, so it's often dry and open even when drizzly weather shuts down the concrete luges. A funky cable system pulls riders (in their sleds) to the top without a ski lift.

Cost and Hours: €3.90/ride, shareable 6-ride card-€16.30; hours typically

Tegelberg Gondola

Zipping downhill on a luge

April-Sept daily 10:00-17:00 depending on weather; call first to confirm, waits can be long in good weather, no children under age 3, ages 3-8 may ride with an adult, tel. 08362/98360, www.tegelbergbahn.de.

WIESKIRCHE

Germany's greatest Rococo-style church, this "Church in the Meadow"—worth ▲▲—looks as brilliant now as the day it floated down from heaven. Overripe with decoration but bright and bursting with beauty, this church is a divine droplet, a curly curlicue, the final flowering of the Baroque movement.

Getting There

By **car,** the Wieskirche is a 30-minute drive north of Neuschwanstein or Füssen. Head north, turn right at Steingaden, and follow the brown signs to pay parking. With careful attention to schedules, you can day-trip here from Füssen by **bus** (#73, #9606, or #9651; 2-6/day, 45-60 minutes), but it's a long round-trip for a church that most see in 10-15 minutes.

Orientation

Cost and Hours: Donation requested, daily 8:00-20:00, Nov-March until 17:00. The interior is closed to sightseers during services: Sun 8:00-13:00; Tue, Wed, and Sat 10:00-12:00; and Fri 17:00-20:00.

Information: Tel. 08862/932-930, www.wieskirche.de.

Services: Trinket shops, snack stands (one sells freshly made doughnuts—look for *Wieskücherl* sign), and a WC clog the parking area in front of the church.

◑ Visiting the Church

This pilgrimage church is built around the much-venerated statue of a scourged (or whipped) Christ, which supposedly wept in 1738. The carving—too graphic to be accepted by that generation's Church—was the focus of worship in a peasant's barn. Miraculously, it shed tears—empa-

thizing with all those who suffer. Pilgrims came from all around. A tiny and humble chapel was built to house the statue in 1739. (You can see it where the lane to the church leaves the parking lot.) Bigger and bigger crowds came. Two of Bavaria's top Rococo architects, the Zimmermann brothers (Johann Baptist and Dominikus), were commissioned to build the Wieskirche that stands here today.

Follow the theological sweep from the altar to the ceiling: Jesus whipped, chained, and then killed (notice the pelican above the altar—recalling a pre-Christian story of a bird that opened its breast to feed its young with its own blood); the painting of Baby Jesus posed as if on the cross; the golden sacrificial lamb; and finally, high on the ceiling, the resurrected Christ before the Last Judgment. This is the most positive depiction of the Last Judgment around. Jesus, rather than sitting on the throne to judge, rides high on a rainbow—a symbol of forgiveness—giving any sinner the feeling that there is still time to repent, with plenty of mercy on hand. In the back, above the pipe organ, notice the closed door to paradise, and at the opposite end (above the main altar), the empty throne—waiting for Judgment Day.

Above the doors flanking the altar are murky glass cases with 18th-century handkerchiefs. People wept, came here, were healed, and no longer needed their hankies. Walk through either of these doors and up an aisle flanking the high altar to see

Wieskirche, the "Church in the Meadow"

The Wieskirche's decor is Rococo to the max.

votives—requests and thanks to God (for happy, healthy babies, and healing for sick loved ones). Notice how the kneelers are positioned so that worshippers can meditate on scenes of biblical miracles painted high on the ceiling and visible through the ornate scalloped frames. A priest here once told me that faith, architecture, light, and music all combine to create the harmony of the Wieskirche.

Rick's Tip: *If you'd like* **to attend a church service,** *look for the* **Gottesdienst schedule.** *In every small German town in the very Catholic south, when you pass the big town church, look for a sign that says* Heilige Messe. *This is the schedule for holy Mass, usually on Saturday (Sa.) or Sunday (So.).*

Two paintings flank the door at the rear of the church. The one on the right shows the ceremonial parade in 1749 when the white-clad monks of Steingaden carried the carved statue of Christ from the tiny church to its new big one. The second painting (on the left), from 1757, is a votive from one of the Zimmermann brothers, the artists and architects who built this church. He is giving thanks for the successful construction of the new church.

If you can't visit the Wieskirche, visit one of the other churches that came out of the same heavenly spray can: Munich's Asam Church, Würzburg's Hofkirche Chapel (at the Residenz), and, on a lesser scale, Füssen's St. Magnus Basilica.

OBERAMMERGAU

Exploited to the hilt by the tourist trade, Oberammergau wears too much makeup. During its famous Passion Play (every 10 years, in 2020, 2030, etc.), the crush is unbearable—and the prices at the hotels and restaurants can be as well. The village has about 1,200 beds for the 5,000 playgoers coming daily. But the rest of the time, Oberammergau—while hardly "undiscovered"—is a pleasant, and at times even sleepy, Bavarian village.

If you're passing through, Oberammergau is a ▲ sight—worth a wander among the half-timbered, frescoed *Lüftlmalerei* houses (ask at the TI for a map). For drivers partial to villages, it makes a cozy home base. Train travelers would do better to stay in well-connected Füssen.

Orientation

This village of about 5,000 feels even smaller, thanks to its remote location. The downtown core, huddled around the onion-domed church, is compact and invites strolling; all of my recommended sights, hotels, and restaurants are within about a 10-minute walk of each other. While the town's name sounds like a mouthful, it's based on the name of the local river (the Ammer) and means, roughly, "Upper Ammerland."

Tourist Information: The helpful, well-organized TI provides English information on area hikes and will store your bags for free during opening hours (Mon-Fri 9:00-18:00, Sat-Sun until 13:00; closed Sun mid-Sept-mid-June, also closed Sat Nov-Dec; Eugen-Papst-Strasse 9A, tel. 08822/922-740, www.oberammergau.de).

Hotel Card: Travelers staying in the Oberammergau area are entitled to a Gäste-Karte—be sure to ask your hotel for one. The TI has a sheet explaining the card's benefits, such as free travel on mountain lifts and local buses (including Garmisch, Linderhof, and Füssen) and free admission to the Oberammergau Museum, Passion Play Theater, and WellenBerg swimming pool.

Sights

▲LOCAL ARTS AND CRAFTS

The town's best sight is its woodcarving shops (*Holzschnitzerei*). Browse through these small art galleries filled with very expensive whittled works. The beautifully frescoed **Pilatus House** at Ludwig-Thoma-Strasse 10 has an open workshop where you can watch woodcarvers and painters at work on summer afternoons (free, late May-mid-Oct Tue-Sun 13:00-17:00, closed Mon and off-season, open weekends in Dec, tel. 08822/949-511). Upstairs in the Pilatus House is a small exhibit of "reverse glass" paintings (*verre églomisé*) that's worth a quick glance.

Woodcarving in Oberammergau

The Ammergau region is relatively poor, with no appreciable industry and no agriculture, save for some dairy farming. What they *do* have is wood. Carving religious and secular themes became a lucrative way for the locals to make some money, especially when confined to the house during the long, cold winter. Carvers from Oberammergau peddled their wares across Europe, carrying them on their backs (on distinctive wooden backpack-racks called *Kraxe*) as far away as Rome.

Today, the Oberammergau Carving School (founded in 1887) is a famous institution that takes only 20 students per year out of 450 applicants. Their graduates do important restoration work throughout Europe.

▲OBERAMMERGAU MUSEUM

This museum showcases local woodcarving, with good English explanations. The ground floor has a small exhibit of nativity scenes (*Krippe*—mostly made of wood, but some of paper or wax). In the back, find the small theater, where you can watch an interesting film in English about the 2010 Passion Play. Upstairs is a much more extensive collection of the wood carvings that helped put Oberammergau on the map, including a room of old woodcarving tools, plus a small exhibit on Roman archaeological finds in the region. Your ticket also lets you into the lobby of the Passion Play Theater, described next.

Cost and Hours: €3.50; €6 combo-ticket includes museum and theater lobby; Easter-Oct and Dec-mid-Jan Tue-Sun 10:00-17:00, closed Mon and off-season; Dorfstrasse 8, tel. 08822/94136, www.oberammergaumuseum.de.

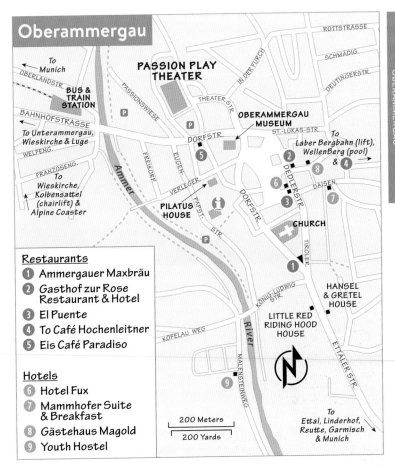

Oberammergau

PASSION PLAY THEATER

BUS & TRAIN STATION

OBERAMMERGAU MUSEUM

To Laber Bergbahn (lift), WellenBerg (pool)

PILATUS HOUSE

CHURCH

HANSEL & GRETEL HOUSE

LITTLE RED RIDING HOOD HOUSE

To Munich

To Unterammergau, Wieskirche & Luge

To Wieskirche, Kolbensattel (chairlift) & Alpine Coaster

To Ettal, Linderhof, Reutte, Garmisch & Munich

200 Meters
200 Yards

Restaurants

1 Ammergauer Maxbräu
2 Gasthof zur Rose Restaurant & Hotel
3 El Puente
4 To Café Hochenleitner
5 Eis Café Paradiso

Hotels

6 Hotel Fux
7 Mammhofer Suite & Breakfast
8 Gästehaus Magold
9 Youth Hostel

BAVARIAN ALPS
OBERAMMERGAU

PASSION PLAY THEATER (FESTSPIELHAUS)

Back in 1633, in the midst of the bloody Thirty Years' War and with horrifying plagues devastating entire cities, the people of Oberammergau promised God that if they were spared from extinction, they'd "perform a play depicting the suffering, death, and resurrection of our Lord Jesus Christ" every decade thereafter. The town survived, and as it heads into its 42nd decade, the people of Oberammergau are still making good on the deal. For 100 days every 10 years, about half of the town's population (a cast of 2,000) are involved in the production of this extravagant five-hour Passion Play—telling the story of Jesus' entry into Jerusalem, the Crucifixion, and the Resurrection.

If you're not visiting during the Passion Play performances, you'll have to settle for reading the book, seeing Nicodemus tool around town in his VW, or taking a quick look at the theater, a block from the center of town.

Visiting the Theater: The theater lobby hosts a modest exhibit on the history of the performances. A long wall of photographs of past performers shows the many generations of Oberammergauers who have participated in this tradition. Climb the stairs and peek into

The Passion Play has been performed in Oberammergau every decade since 1634.

the theater itself, which has an unusual indoor/outdoor design and a real-life alpine backdrop.

To learn more, take a 45-minute guided tour of the theater, organized by the museum (€3.50, €6 combo-ticket with Oberammergau Museum, €8 with guided tour; tours run Easter-Oct only, Tue-Sun at 11:00 in English, additional tour times in German; theater open same hours as museum, tel. 08822/94136, www.oberammergaumuseum.de; for Passion Play info, see www.passionsspieleoberammergau.de).

Near Oberammergau

These attractions are a long walk from town but easy to reach by car or bike.

MOUNTAIN LIFTS, LUGES, AND MORE

Laber Bergbahn, a gondola that lifts you up to fine views, is at the east end of town. For an easy hike, take the lift up and walk down in about 2.5 hours (www.laberbergbahn.de).

Kolbensattel, across town to the west, is a family-friendly park with a chairlift, a mountain playground, a high-ropes course, and a speedy 1.5-mile-long **Alpine**

Coaster (similar to a luge, closed off-season; €7.50 each for chairlift or coaster, €11.50 coaster combo-ticket with lift, €26 combo-ticket for coaster, ropes course, and lift, daily April-Nov 10:00-17:00 in good weather, tel. 08822/4760, www.kolbensattel.de).

WELLENBERG SWIMMING POOL

Near the Laber Bergbahn lift and a 25-minute walk from town is this sprawling complex of indoor and outdoor pools and saunas (€8/3 hours, €12/day, €4.50 extra for sauna, daily 10:00-21:00, Himmelreich 52, tel. 08822/92360, www.wellenberg-oberammergau.de).

SOMMERRODELBAHN STECKENBERG

The next town over, Unterammergau, hosts a stainless-steel summer luge track with double seats and two sticks—one for each hand; be careful of your elbows. Unlike other luges, children under age three are allowed, and you only pay one fare when a parent and child ride together.

Cost and Hours: €3.50/ride, €15/6 rides; May-late Oct Mon-Fri 13:00-17:00, Sat-Sun 10:00-18:00, closed off-season and when wet; Liftweg 1 in Unterammergau, tel. 08822/4027, www.steckenberg.de.

Eating

$$$ Ammergauer Maxbräu, in the Hotel Maximilian on the edge of downtown, serves high-quality, thoughtfully presented Bavarian fare with a modern, international twist. The rustic-yet-mod interior—with big copper vats where they brew their own beer—is cozy on a rainy day. And in nice weather, locals fill the beer garden out front (daily 11:00-22:00, right behind the church, Ettaler Strasse 5, tel. 08822/948-740).

$$ Gasthof zur Rose, a couple of blocks off the main drag, serves reasonably priced Bavarian food in its dining room and at a few outdoor tables (Tue-Sun 11:30-14:00 & 17:30-21:00, closed Mon, Dedlerstrasse 9, tel. 08822/4706).

$$ El Puente may vex Mexican-food purists, but it's the most hopping place in town, with margaritas and cocktails attracting young locals and tourists alike. Come not for the burritos and enchiladas but for the bustling energy (pricier steaks, Mon-Sat 18:00-23:30, closed Sun, Daisenbergerstrasse 3, tel. 08822/945-777).

$ Café Hochenleitner, just a few minutes from the center, is quiet with nice outdoor seating and run by a family whose young son is winning awards for his creative confections (Tue-Sun 12:00-18:00, closed Mon, Faistenmantlgasse 7, tel. 08822/1312).

Dessert: Eis Café Paradiso serves up good gelato along the main street. In nice weather, Germans sunbathe with their big €5 sundaes on the generous patio out front (daily 9:00-23:00 in summer, Dorfstrasse 4, tel. 08822/6279).

Sleeping

Accommodations in Oberammergau tend to be affordable (compared to Füssen) and friendly. All offer free parking. I've ranked these based on summer prices (generally May-Oct).

$$ Hotel Fux—quiet, romantic, and well run—rents 10 large rooms and six apartments decorated in the Bavarian *Landhaus* style (free sauna, indoor playground, Mannagasse 2a, tel. 08822/93093, www.hotel-in-oberammergau.de, info@firmafux.de).

$$ Mammhofer Suite & Breakfast offers nine contemporary-Bavarian rooms (mostly suites and most with views) in a quiet, residential neighborhood just across the street from the town center (Daisenbergerstrasse 10, tel. 08822/923-753, www.mammhofer.com, stay@mammhofer.com).

$ Gasthof zur Rose is big and centrally located, with 19 mostly small but comfortable rooms. At the reception desk, look at the several decades' worth of photos showing the family performing in the Passion Play (family rooms, Dedlerstrasse 9, tel. 08822/4706, www.rose-oberammergau.de, info@rose-oberammergau.de).

$ Gästehaus Magold, homey and family-friendly, has three bright and spacious rooms and two apartments—twice as nice as the cheap hotel rooms in town, and for much less (cash only, immediately behind Gasthof zur Rose at Kleppergasse 1, tel. 08822/4340, www.gaestehaus-magold.de, info@gaestehaus-magold.de).

¢ Oberammergau Youth Hostel, on the river, is just a short walk from the center (family rooms, reception open 8:00-10:00 & 17:00-19:00, closed mid-Nov-Dec, Malensteinweg 10, tel. 08822/4114, www.oberammergau.jugendherberge.de, oberammergau@jugendherberge.de).

Transportation
Arriving and Departing
BY CAR
Drivers can get to Oberammergau from Füssen or Munich in about an hour. There are two exits from the main road into Oberammergau—at the north and south ends. Either way, make your way to the free lot between the TI and the river.

Rick's Tip: If you're driving between the Wieskirche and Oberammergau, you'll cross **Echelsbacher Brücke,** *a bridge arching 230 feet over the Pöllat Gorge.* **Thoughtful drivers let their passengers walk across** *to enjoy the views, then meet them at the other side. Any kayakers below?*

BY TRAIN OR BUS

Arrival in Oberammergau: The town's train station is a short walk from the center: Turn left, cross the bridge, and you're already downtown. **Trains** run from Munich to Oberammergau (nearly hourly, 2 hours, change in Murnau). From Füssen, you can take the **bus** (#9606, 1-3/day, 1.5 hours, bus may start as #73 and change to #9606 en route—confirm with driver that bus is going to Oberammergau).

From Oberammergau to: Linderhof Castle (bus #9622, 5-6/day Mon-Fri, 4/day Sat-Sun, 30 minutes); **Hohenschwangau** (for Neuschwanstein) and **Füssen** (bus #9606, 3-4/day, 1.5 hours, some transfer or change number to #73 at Echelsbacher Brücke), **Garmisch** (bus #9606, nearly hourly, better frequency in morning, 40 minutes; possible by train with transfer in Murnau, 1.5 hours; from Garmisch, you can ascend the **Zugspitze**), **Munich** (nearly hourly trains, 2 hours, change in Murnau). Train info: www.bahn.com.

LINDERHOF CASTLE

This homiest of "Mad" King Ludwig's castles is a small, comfortably exquisite mini Versailles—good enough for a minor god, and worth ▲▲. Set in the woods 15 minutes from Oberammergau and surrounded by fountains and sculpted, Italian-style gardens, it's the only palace I've toured that actually had me feeling envious.

Getting There

Without a car, getting to (and back from) Linderhof is a royal headache, unless you're staying in Oberammergau. Buses from Oberammergau take 30 minutes (#9622, 5-6/day Mon-Fri, 4/day Sat-Sun). If you're driving, pay to park near the ticket office.

Orientation

Cost: €8.50, €7.50 in winter

Hours: Daily 9:00-18:00, mid-Oct-March 10:00-16:30. Outlying buildings are closed mid-Oct-mid-April.

Information: Tel. 08822/92030, www.linderhof.de.

Crowd-Beating Tips: July and August crowds can mean an hour's wait between when you buy your ticket and when you start your tour. It's most crowded in the late morning. During this period, you're wise to arrive after 15:00. Any other time of year, your wait to tour the palace should be brief. If you do wind up with time to kill, consider it a blessing—the gardens are fun to explore, and some of the smaller buildings can be seen quickly while you're waiting for your appointment.

Sightseeing Tips and Procedure: The complex sits isolated in natural splendor. Plan for lots of walking and a two-hour stop to fully enjoy this royal park. Bring rain gear in iffy weather. Your ticket comes with an entry time to tour the palace, which is a 10-minute walk from the ticket office. At the palace entrance, wait in line at the turnstile listed on your ticket (A through D) to take the required 30-minute English tour. Afterward, explore the rest of the park (grotto closed through 2021) and the other royal buildings dotting the king's playground if you like. You can eat lunch at a **$$** café across from the ticket office.

➋ Visiting the Castle

Background: The main attraction here is the **palace** itself. While Neuschwanstein is Neo-Gothic—romanticizing the medieval glory days of Bavaria—Linderhof is

Linderhof is the smallest of King Ludwig II's castles.

Baroque and Rococo, the frilly, overly ornamented styles more associated with Louis XIV, the "Sun King" of France. And, while Neuschwanstein is full of swans, here you'll see fleur-de-lis (the symbol of French royalty) and multiple portraits of Louis XIV, Louis XV, Madame Pompadour, and other pre-Revolutionary French elites. Though they lived a century apart, Ludwig and Louis were spiritual contemporaries: Both clung to the notion of absolute monarchy, despite the realities of the changing world around them. Capping the palace roofline is one of Ludwig's favorite symbols: Atlas, with the weight of the world literally on his shoulders. Oh, those poor, overburdened, misunderstood absolute monarchs!

Ludwig was king for 22 of his 40 years. He lived much of his last eight years here—the only one of his castles that was finished in his lifetime. Frustrated by the limits of being a "constitutional monarch," he retreated to Linderhof, inhabiting a private fantasy world where extravagant castles glorified his otherwise weakened kingship. You'll notice that the castle is small—designed for a single occupant.

Ludwig, who never married or had children, lived here as a royal hermit.

Inside the Castle: The castle tour includes 10 rooms on the upper floor. (The downstairs, where the servants lived and worked, now houses the gift shop.) You'll see room after room exquisitely carved with Rococo curlicues, wrapped in gold leaf. Up above, the ceiling paintings have 3-D legs sticking out of the frame. Clearly inspired by Versailles, Linderhof even has its own (much smaller) hall of mirrors—decorated with over a hundred Nymphenburg porcelain vases and a priceless ivory chandelier. The bedroom features an oversized crystal chandelier, delicate Meissen porcelain flowers framing the mirrors, and a (literally) king-size bed—a two-story canopy affair draped in blue velvet. Perhaps the most poignant sight, a sad commentary on Ludwig's tragically solitary lifestyle, is his dinner table—preset with dishes and food—which could rise from the kitchen below into his dining room so he could eat alone. (Examine the incredibly delicate flowers in the Meissen porcelain centerpiece.)

Grotto at Linderhof

Kiosk. With over-the-top decor seemingly designed by a sultan's decorator on acid, these allowed Ludwig to "travel" to exotic lands without leaving the comfort of Bavaria. (The Moorish Kiosk is more interesting; look for its gilded dome in the woods beyond the grotto.) At the far edge of the property is **Hunding's Hut,** inspired by Wagner's *The Valkyrie*—a rustic-cottage stage-set with a fake ash tree inside it. And closer to the entrance—along the path between the ticket booth and the palace—is the **King's Cottage,** used for special exhibitions (often with an extra charge).

Castle Grounds: The palace is flanked on both sides with grand, terraced **fountains** (peopled by gleaming golden gods) that erupt at the top and bottom of each hour. If you're waiting for your palace tour to begin, hike up to the top of the terrace for a fine view.

Ludwig's **grotto,** behind the palace, is currently undergoing restoration work. Inspired by Wagner's *Tannhäuser* opera, this artificial cave (300 feet long and 70 feet tall) is actually a performance space. Its rocky walls are made of cement poured over an iron frame. (While Ludwig exalted the distant past, he took full advantage of then-cutting-edge technology to bring his fantasies to life.) The grotto provided a private theater for the reclusive king to enjoy his beloved Wagnerian operas—he was usually the sole member of the audience. The grotto features a waterfall, fake stalactites, and a swan boat floating on an artificial lake (which could be heated for swimming). Brick ovens hidden in the walls could be used to heat the huge space. The first electricity in Bavaria was generated here, to change the colors of the stage lights and to power Ludwig's fountain and wave machine.

Several other smaller buildings are scattered around the grounds; look for posted maps and directional signs to track them down. Most interesting are the **Moroccan House** and **Moorish**

ZUGSPITZE

The tallest point in Germany, worth ▲▲ in clear weather, is also a border crossing. Lifts from both Austria and Germany meet at the 9,700-foot summit of the Zugspitze (TSOOG-shpit-seh). You can straddle the border between two great nations while enjoying an incredible view. Restaurants, shops, and telescopes await you at the summit.

Summiting the Zugspitze
German Approach
There are several ways to ascend from this side, but they all cost the same (€56 round-trip, less in winter, tel. 08821/7970, www.zugspitze.de).

If relying on **public transit,** first head to Garmisch (for details on getting there from Füssen, see page 164; from Oberammergau, see page 180). From there, ride a train to Eibsee (30 minutes, hourly departures daily 8:15-14:15), at which point you have a choice. You can walk across the parking lot and zip up to the top in a cable car (10 minutes, daily 8:30-16:45, departs at least every 30 minutes; in busy times departs every 10 minutes, but since each car fits only 35, you may have to wait to board). Or you can transfer to a cogwheel train (45 minutes to the top, departs hourly—coordinated with Garmisch train;

once up top, transfer from the train to a short cable car for the quick, 3-minute ascent to the summit).

Drivers can go straight to Eibsee (about 10 minutes beyond Garmisch—head through town following signs for *Fernpass/Reutte,* and watch for the Zugspitze turnoff on the left); once there, you have the same cable car vs. cog railway choice described above. (Even though they're not taking the train from Garmisch, drivers pay the same—€56 round-trip, plus another €4 for parking.)

You can choose how you want to go up and down at the spur of the moment: both ways by cable car, both by cog train, or mix and match. Although the train ride takes longer, many travelers enjoy the more involved cog railway experience—at least one way. The disadvantage of the train is that more than half of the trip is through dark tunnels deep in the mountains; aside from a few fleeting glimpses of the Eibsee sparkling below, it's not very scenic.

Arriving **at the top,** you'll want to head up to the third floor (elevators recommended, given the high altitude)—follow signs for *Gipfel* (summit).

To get back down to Eibsee, keep in mind that the last cable car departs the summit at 16:45, and the last cogwheel train at 16:30. On busy days, you may have to **reserve a return time** once you reach the top—if it's crowded, look for signs and prebook your return to avoid getting stuck up top longer than you want. In general, allow plenty of time for afternoon descents: If bad weather hits in the late afternoon, cable cars can be delayed at the summit, causing tourists to miss their train connection from Eibsee back to Garmisch.

Austrian Approach

The Tiroler Zugspitzbahn ascent is less crowded and cheaper than the Bavarian one. Make your way to the village of Ehrwald (drivers follow signs for *Tiroler Zugspitzbahn;* free parking). Departing from above Ehrwald, a lift zips you to the top in 10 minutes (€45 round-trip, departures in each direction at :00, :20, and :40 past the hour, daily 8:40-16:40 except closed during bad weather May-June and Oct-Nov, last ascent at 16:00, Austrian tel. 05673/2309, www.zugspitze.at).

⊙ Self-Guided Tour

Whether you've ascended from the Austrian or German side, you're high enough now to enjoy a little tour of the summit. The two terraces—Bavarian and Tirolean—are connected by a narrow walkway, which was the border station before Germany and Austria opened their borders. The Austrian (Tirolean) side was higher until the Germans blew its top off in World War II to make a flak tower, so let's start there.

Tirolean Terrace: Before you stretches the Zugspitzplatt glacier. Is it melting? A reflector once stood here to slow it from shrinking during summer months. Many ski lifts fan out here, as if reaching for a ridge that defines the border between Germany and Austria. The circular metal building is the top of the cog railway line that the Germans cut through the mountains in 1931. Just above that, find a small square building—the *Hochzeitskapelle* (wedding chapel) consecrated in 1981 by Cardinal Joseph Ratzinger (a.k.a. the retired Pope Benedict XVI).

Both Germany and Austria use this rocky pinnacle for communication purposes. The

The cable car to the Zugspitze

LINDERHOF

Kofel ▲

Zugspitze Area

2060

Ettal
MONASTERY

Oberau

To Reutte
and Füssen

TUNNEL

Garmisch-
Partenkirchen

187

Eibsee

COG
TRAIN

SKI
JUMP

To →
Mittenwald
&Innsbruck

Partnach
Gorge

187

Lermoos

Zugspitze
9,718'

GERMANY

Ehrwald

AUSTRIA

TUNNEL Biberwier

5 Kilometers

5 Miles

Luge/Cable car

square box on the Tirolean Terrace provides the Innsbruck airport with air traffic control, and a tower nearby is for the German *Katastrophenfunk* (civil defense network).

This highest point in Germany (there are many higher points in Austria) was first climbed in 1820. The Austrians built a cable car that nearly reached the summit in 1926. (You can see it just over the ridge on the Austrian side—look for the ghostly, abandoned concrete station.) In 1964, the final leg, a new lift, was built connecting that 1926 station to the actual summit, where you stand now. Before then, people needed to hike the last 650 feet to the top. Today's lift carries half a million people up to the Zugspitze every year. The Austrian station, which is much nicer than the German station, has a fine little museum—free with Austrian ticket, €4 if you came up from Germany—that

shows three interesting videos (6-minute 3-D mountain show, 30-minute making-of-the-lift documentary, and 45-minute look at the nature, sport, and culture of the region).

Looking up the valley from the Tirolean Terrace, you can see the towns of Ehrwald and Lermoos in the distance, and the valley that leads to Reutte. Looking farther clockwise, you'll see the Eibsee below. Hell's Valley, stretching to the right of the Eibsee, seems to merit its name.

Bavarian Terrace: The narrow passage connecting the two terraces used to be a big deal—you'd show your passport here at the little blue house and shift from Austrian schillings to German marks. Notice the regional pride here: no German or Austrian national banners, but regional ones instead—*Freistaat Bayern* (Bavaria) and *Land Tirol*.

The Zugspitze is Germany's highest mountain.

The German side features a golden cross marking the summit...the highest point in Germany. A priest and his friends hauled it up in 1851. The historic original was shot up by American soldiers using it for target practice in the late 1940s, so what you see today is a modern replacement. In the summer, it's easy to "summit" the Zugspitze, as there are steps and handholds all the way to the top. Or you can just stay behind and feed the birds. The yellow-beaked ravens get chummy with those who share a little pretzel or bread. Below the terrace, notice the restaurant that claims—irrefutably—to be the "highest *Biergarten* in Deutschland."

The oldest building up here is the first mountaineers' hut, built in 1897 and entwined with mighty cables that cinch it down. In 1985, observers clocked 200-mph winds up here—those cables were necessary. Step inside the restaurant to enjoy museum-like photos and paintings on the wall (including a look at the team who hiked up with the golden cross in 1851).

Near the waiting area for the cable cars and cogwheel train is a little museum (in German only) that's worth a look if you have some time to kill before heading back down. If you're going down on the German side, remember you must choose between the cable car (look for the *Eibsee* signs) or cog railway (look for *Talfahrt/ Descent,* with a picture of a train; you'll board a smaller cable car for the quick trip to the train station).

Rothenburg
& the
Romantic Road

The Romantic Road takes you through Bavaria's medieval heartland, a route strewn with picturesque villages, farmhouses, onion-domed churches, Baroque palaces, and walled cities. The route, which runs from Würzburg to Füssen, is the most scenic way to connect Frankfurt with Munich. No trains run along the full length of the Romantic Road, but Rothenburg (ROH-tehn-burg), the most interesting town along the way, is easy to reach by rail. Drivers can either zero in on Rothenburg or meander from town to town on the way. For nondrivers, a tour bus travels a portion of the Romantic Road several days a week in summer.

Countless travelers have searched for the elusive "untouristy Rothenburg." There are many contenders (such as Michelstadt, Miltenberg, Bamberg, Bad Windsheim, and Dinkelsbühl), but none holds a candle to the king of medieval German cuteness. Even with crowds, overpriced souvenirs, and, yes, even *Schneeballen,* Rothenburg is best. Save time and mileage and be satisfied with the winner.

ROTHENBURG & THE ROMANTIC ROAD IN 2 DAYS

I'd spend one full day in Rothenburg this way: Start with my self-guided town walk, including a visit to St. Jakob's Church (for the carved altarpiece) and the Rothenburg Museum (historic artifacts). Spend the afternoon visiting the Medieval Crime and Punishment Museum and taking my "Schmiedgasse-Spitalgasse Shopping Stroll," followed by a walk on the wall (from Spitaltor to Klingentor).

Cap your day with the entertaining Night Watchman's Tour at 20:00. Locals love "die blaue Stunde" (the blue hour)—the time just before dark when city lamps and the sky hold hands. Be sure to be out enjoying the magic of the city at this time.

Other evening options include beer-garden fun (at Gasthof Rödertor) if the weather's good, or the English Conversation Club (at Altfränkische Weinstube am Klosterhof) if it's Wednesday.

With extra time in Rothenburg, spread out your sightseeing and add the Old Town Historic Walk (offered by the TI), the Town Hall Tower climb, and the German Christmas Museum.

If you're driving, take in the top Romantic Road highlights en route, devoting a half-day to the sights on your way to Rothenburg and another half-day after leaving it.

ROTHENBURG OB DER TAUBER

In the Middle Ages, when Berlin and Munich were just wide spots on the road, Rothenburg ob der Tauber was a "free imperial city" beholden only to the Holy Roman Emperor. From 1150 to 1400, because of its strategic location on the trade routes, along with the abundant resources of its surrounding farmlands, Rothenburg thrived, with a whopping population of 6,000. But the Thirty Years' War and a plague that followed did the town in. With no money to fix up its antiquated, severely leaning buildings, the town was left to languish in this state. Today, it's the country's best-preserved medieval walled town, enjoying tremendous tourist popularity without losing its charm.

Rick's Tip: *Germany has several towns named Rothenburg.* **Make sure you're going to Rothenburg ob der Tauber** *(not "ob der" any other river). People really do sometimes drive or ride the train to the wrong Rothenburg by accident.*

Rothenburg's great trade these days is tourism: Two-thirds of the 2,500 people who live within its walls are employed to serve you. While roughly 2 million people visit each year, most come only on day trips. Rothenburg is yours after dark, when the groups vacate and the town's floodlit cobbles wring some romance out of any travel partner.

ORIENTATION

Think of the town map as a human head. Its nose—the castle garden—sticks out to the left, and the skinny lower part forms a neck, with the youth hostel and a recommended hotel being the Adam's apple. The town is a delight on foot. No sights or hotels are more than a 15-minute walk from the train station or each other.

Most of the buildings you'll see were in place by 1400. The city was born around its long-gone castle fortress—built in 1142, destroyed in 1356—which was located where the castle garden is now. You can see the shadow of the first town wall, which defines the oldest part of Rothenburg, in its contemporary street plan.

Picturesque Rothenburg ob der Tauber

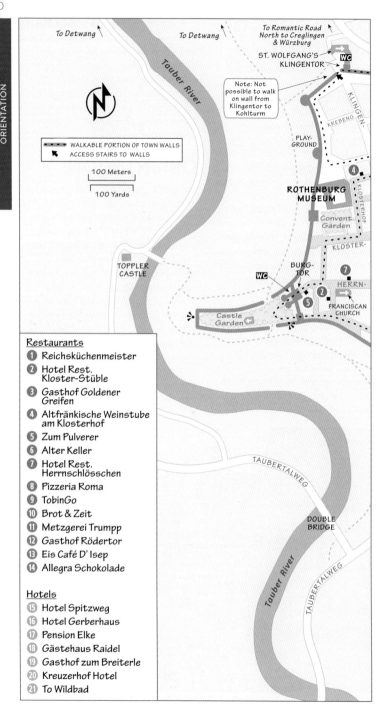

To Detwang

To Detwang

To Romantic Road
North to Creglingen
& Würzburg

ST. WOLFGANG'S
KLINGENTOR

WC

Tauber River

KLINGEN-

KREBENG-

Note: Not
possible to walk
on wall from
Klingentor to
Kohlturm

PLAY-
GROUND

▰▰▰▰ WALKABLE PORTION OF TOWN WALLS
↖ ACCESS STAIRS TO WALLS

100 Meters

100 Yards

KLOSTERHOF

**ROTHENBURG
MUSEUM**

Convent
Garden

KLOSTER-

TOPPLER
CASTLE

BURG-
TOR

WC

HERRN-

FRANCISCAN
CHURCH

Castle
Garden

TAUBERTALWEG

Restaurants

❶ Reichsküchenmeister

❷ Hotel Rest.
Kloster-Stüble

❸ Gasthof Goldener
Greifen

❹ Altfränkische Weinstube
am Klosterhof

❺ Zum Pulverer

❻ Alter Keller

❼ Hotel Rest.
Herrnschlösschen

❽ Pizzeria Roma

❾ TobinGo

❿ Brot & Zeit

⓫ Metzgerei Trumpp

⓬ Gasthof Rödertor

⓭ Eis Café D' Isep

⓮ Allegra Schokolade

Hotels

⓯ Hotel Spitzweg

⓰ Hotel Gerberhaus

⓱ Pension Elke

⓲ Gästehaus Raidel

⓳ Gasthof zum Breiterle

⓴ Kreuzerhof Hotel

㉑ To Wildbad

DOUBLE
BRIDGE

Tauber River

TAUBERTALWEG

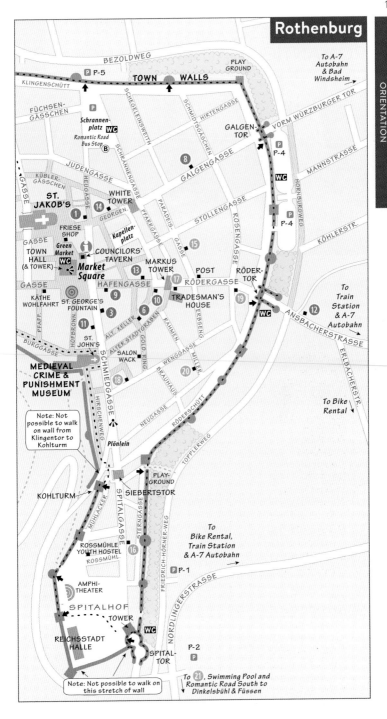

BEZOLDWEG

KLINGENSCHÜTT

P-5

TOWN WALLS

PLAY GROUND

To A-7 Autobahn & Bad Windsheim

FÜCHSEN-GÄSSCHEN

SCHEGELEINSWETH

SCHMIDSGÄSSCHEN

HIRTENGASSE

VORM WÜRZBURGER TOR

Schrannen-platz WC

Romantic Road Bus Stop B

JUDENGASSE

HEDGASSE

SCHRANNENGASSE

PFARRGASSE

PARADEIS GASSE

GALGENGASSE

GALGEN-TOR

P-4

WC

MANNSTRASSE

HORNBURGWEG

KÜBLER-GÄSSCHEN

GASSE

ST. JAKOB'S

14

WHITE TOWER

GEORGEN...

STOLLENGASSE

ROSENGASSE

P-4

KÖHLERSTR.

1

FRIESE SHOP

Kapellen-platz

GASSE

Green Market

COUNCILORS' TAVERN

TOWN HALL (& TOWER) WC

Market Square

MARKUS TOWER

15

POST

RÖDER-TOR

To Train Station & A-7 Autobahn

GASSE

KÄTHE WOHLFAHRT

HAFENGASSE

13

17

RÖDERGASSE

19

ANSBACHERSTRASSE

12

PFAFF...

HOFBRONN.

ST. GEORGE'S FOUNTAIN

9

3

6

10

TRADESMAN'S HOUSE

WC

ERBSENG

11

BURGGASSE

ST. JOHN'S

ALT. KELLER

ALTER STADTGRABEN

GOLD. RING

KAHMEN

RÖMEN

MILLER

ERLBACHERSTR.

MEDIEVAL CRIME & PUNISHMENT MUSEUM

SCHMIEDGASSE

SALON WACK

BRAUHAUS

20

WEINGASSE

To Bike Rental

Note: Not possible to walk on wall from Klingentor to Kohlturm

HIRSCHENWEG

18

NEUGASSE

RÖDERSCHÜTT

TÖPPLERWEG

Plönlein

PLAY-GROUND

KOHLTURM

MÜHLACKER

SPITALGASSE

SIEBERTSTOR

STERNGASSE

FRIEDRICH-HÖRNER-WEG

To Bike Rental, Train Station & A-7 Autobahn

ROSSMÜHLE YOUTH HOSTEL

ROSSMÜHL.

16

P-1

AMPHI-THEATER

NORDLINGERSTRASSE

P-2

SPITALHOF

TOWER

WC

REICHSSTADT HALLE

SPITAL-TOR

Note: Not possible to walk on this stretch of wall

To 21, Swimming Pool and Romantic Road South to Dinkelsbühl & Füssen

Rothenburg

▲▲▲**Rothenburg Town Walk** A self-guided loop, starting and ending on Market Square, covering the town's top sights. See page 196.

▲▲**Night Watchman's Tour** Germany's best hour of medieval wonder, led by an amusing, medieval-garbed guide. **Hours:** Mid-March-Dec nightly at 20:00. See page 194.

▲▲**St. Jakob's Church** Home to Tilman Riemenschneider's breathtaking, wood-carved Altar of the Holy Blood. **Hours:** Daily April-Oct 9:00-17:00, Dec 10:00-16:45, off-season 10:00-12:00 & 14:00-16:00, on Sun wait to enter until services end at 10:45. See page 199.

▲▲**Rothenburg Museum** An artifact-filled sweep through Rothenburg's history. **Hours:** Daily 9:30-17:30, Nov-March 13:00-16:00. See page 201.

▲▲**Schmiedgasse-Spitalgasse Shopping Stroll** A fun look at crafts and family-run shops, on a (mostly) picturesque street running between Market Square and the town's most impressive tower, Spitaltor. See page 204.

▲▲**Walk the Wall** A strollable wall encircling the town, providing great views and a good orientation to Rothenburg. **Hours:** Always open and walkable. See page 205.

▲▲**Medieval Crime and Punishment Museum** Specializing in everything connected to medieval justice, this exhibit is a cut above the tacky torture museums around Europe. **Hours:** Daily 10:00-18:00, Nov and Jan-Feb 14:00-16:00, Dec and March 13:00-16:00. See page 206.

▲**Old Town Historic Walk** Covers the serious side of Rothenburg's history and the town's architecture. **Hours:** Easter-Oct and Dec daily at 14:00. See page 196.

▲**Historical Town Hall Vaults** An insightful look at Rothenburg during the Catholics-vs.-Protestants Thirty Years' War. **Hours:** Daily 9:30-17:30, shorter hours Nov-April, closed Jan, weekends only Feb. See page 198.

▲**Town Hall Tower** Rothenburg's tallest perch, with a commanding view. **Hours:** Daily in season 9:30-12:30 & 13:00-17:00. See page 206.

▲**German Christmas Museum** Tells the interesting history of Christmas decorations. **Hours:** Daily 10:00-17:30, shorter and irregular hours Jan-March. See page 207.

Along the Romantic Road

▲▲**Wieskirche** Lovely Baroque-Rococo church set in a meadow. See page 174 of the Bavarian Alps chapter.

▲**Creglingen's Herrgottskirche** Church featuring Riemenschneider's greatest carved altarpiece. See page 214.

▲**Weikersheim** Picturesque town with an impressive palace, Baroque gardens, and a quaint town square. See page 214.

▲**Dinkelsbühl** A town like Rothenburg's little sister, cute enough to merit a short stop. See page 216.

▲**Nördlingen** Workaday town with one of the best walls in Germany and a crater left by an ancient meteor. See page 216.

Two gates from this wall still survive: the Markus Tower and the White Tower. The richest and biggest houses were in this central part. The commoners built higgledy-piggledy (read: picturesque) houses farther from the center but still inside the present walls.

Although Rothenburg is technically in Bavaria, the region around the town is called—and strongly identifies itself as—"Franken," one of Germany's many medieval dukedoms ("Franconia" in English).

Rick's Tip: *A* **fun pictorial town map,** *which also helpfully indicates some walking paths in the countryside beyond the town walls, is available for free with this book at the* **Friese shop** *(see page 208).*

Tourist Information: The TI is on Market Square (May-Oct and Dec Mon-Fri 9:00-18:00, Sat-Sun 10:00-17:00; off-season Mon-Fri until 17:00, Sat until 13:00, closed Sun; Marktplatz 2, tel. 09861/404-800, www.rothenburg.de/tourismus, run by Jörg Christöphler). The free city map comes with a walking guide to the town.

The *Events* booklet covers the basics in English. They offer a variety of themed tours; ask when you arrive or check their website in advance.

Bike Rental: A ride through the nearby countryside is enjoyable on nice days (get route suggestions from rental shop). **Rad & Tat** rents bikes for €14 for a 24-hour day (otherwise €10/6 hours, electric bike-€28/day; Mon-Fri 9:00-18:00, Sat until 13:00, closed Sun; Bensenstrasse 17, tel. 09861/87984, www.mietraeder.de). To reach it, leave the old town toward the train station, take a right on Erlbacher Strasse, cross the tracks, and look across the street from the Lidl supermarket.

Taxi: For a taxi, call 09861/2000 or 09861/7227.

TOURS

▲▲NIGHT WATCHMAN'S TOUR

This tour is flat-out the most entertaining hour of medieval wonder anywhere in Germany and the best evening activity in town. The Night Watchman (a.k.a. Hans-Georg Baumgartner) jokes like a medieval John Cleese as he lights his lamp and takes tourists on his rounds, telling

Rothenburg's Night Watchman

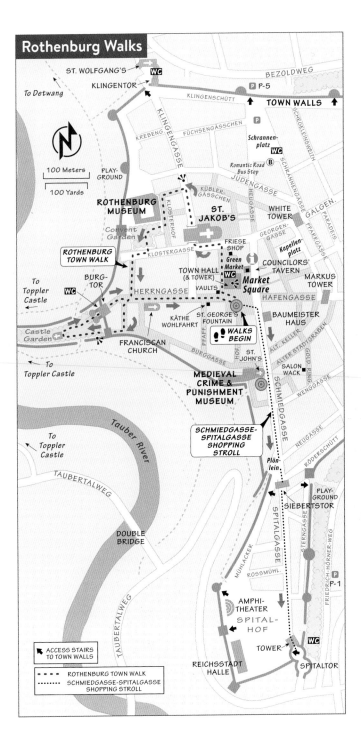

Rothenburg Walks

ST. WOLFGANG'S · WC
KLINGENTOR
To Detwang
BEZOLDWEG
P P-5
KLINGENSCHÜTT
TOWN WALLS

KREBENG · KLINGENGASSE · FÜCHSENGÄSSCHEN
SCHEGELEINSWEITH

P

Schrannen-
platz · WC
Romantic Road
Bus Stop · B

100 Meters
100 Yards

PLAY-
GROUND
KÜBLER-
GÄSSCHEN · JUDENGASSE
SCHRANNENGASSE · HEUGASSE · WHITE
TOWER · GALGEN · PARADEIS

ROTHENBURG
MUSEUM · ST.
JAKOB'S

Convent
Garden
KLOSTERHOF
GEORGEN-
GASSE · Kapellen-
platz · PFARRGASSE

ROTHENBURG
TOWN WALK · KLOSTERGASSE
FRIESE
SHOP · COUNCILORS'
TAVERN · MARKUS
TOWER

To
Toppler
Castle · BURG-
TOR · WC · Green
Market · Market
Square · TOWN HALL
(& TOWER) · WC
HERRNGASSE · VAULTS · HAFENGASSE

Castle
Garden · KÄTHE
WOHLFAHRT · ST. GEORGE'S
FOUNTAIN · WALKS
BEGIN · BAUMEISTER
HAUS

To
Toppler Castle · FRANCISCAN
CHURCH · BURGGASSE · ST.
JOHN'S · SALON
WACK · ALT. KELLER · ALTER STADTGRABEN · GOLDGASSE · WENGGASSE

MEDIEVAL
CRIME &
PUNISHMENT
MUSEUM · SCHMIEDGASSE

Tauber River

To
Toppler
Castle · SCHMIEDGASSE-
SPITALGASSE
SHOPPING
STROLL · NEUGASSE · RÖDERSCHÜTT

TAUBERTALWEG · Plön-
lein · PLAY-
GROUND
SIEBERTSTOR

DOUBLE
BRIDGE · SPITALGASSE · STERNGASSE · FRIEDRICH-HÖRNER-WEG · P P-1

TAUBERTALWEG · MÜHLACKER · ROSSMÜHL.
AMPHI-
THEATER
SPITAL-
HOF

ACCESS STAIRS
TO TOWN WALLS
ROTHENBURG TOWN WALK
SCHMIEDGASSE-SPITALGASSE
SHOPPING STROLL · REICHSSTADT
HALLE · TOWER · WC · SPITALTOR

slice-of-gritty-life tales of medieval Rothenburg (€8, teens–€4, free for kids 12 and under, mid-March-Dec nightly at 20:00, in English, meet at Market Square, www.nightwatchman.de).

▲OLD TOWN HISTORIC WALK

The TI offers engaging 1.5-hour guided walking tours in English (€8, Easter-Oct and Dec daily at 14:00, departs from Market Square). Just show up and pay the guide directly—there's always room. Take this tour for the serious side of Rothenburg's history, and to make sense of the town's architecture; you won't get as much of that on the fun—and completely different—Night Watchman's Tour. Taking both tours is a smart way to round out your overall Rothenburg experience.

LOCAL GUIDES

A local historian can really bring the ramparts alive. Reserve a guide by emailing the TI (info@rothenburg.de; more info at www.tourismus.rothenburg.de—look under "Guided Tours"; €75/1.5 hours, €95/2 hours). I've had good experiences with **Martin Kamphans** (tel. 09861/7941, www.stadtfuehrungen-rothenburg.de, kamphans@posteo.de) and **Daniel Weber** (to get rates listed above ask for Rick Steves discount, mobile 0795-8311, www.toot-tours.com, mail@toot-tours.com).

ROTHENBURG WALKS

❺ Town Walk

This self-guided loop, worth ▲▲▲, weaves the town's top sights together, takes about an hour without stops, and starts and ends on Market Square. (Note that this is roughly the same route followed by city guides on their daily Old Town Historic Walk, described earlier.)

🎧 Download my free Rothenburg Town Walk audio tour.

• *Start the walk on Market Square.*

Market Square Spin-Tour

Stand in front of the fountain at the bottom of Market Square and spin 360 degrees clockwise, starting with the Town Hall tower. Now do it again, this time more slowly to take in some details:

Town Hall and Tower: Rothenburg's tallest spire is the Town Hall tower (Rathausturm). At 200 feet, it stands atop the old Town Hall, a white, Gothic, 13th-century building. Notice the tourists enjoying the best view in town from the black top of the tower (see "Sights" for details on climbing the tower). After a fire in 1501 burned down part of the original building, a new Town Hall was built alongside what survived of the old one (fronting the square). This half of the rebuilt complex is in the Renaissance style from 1570. The double eagles you see decorating many buildings here are a repeated reminder that this was a "free imperial city" belonging directly to the (Habsburg) Holy Roman Emperor, a designation that came with benefits.

Meistertrunk Show: At the top of Market Square stands the proud Councilors' Tavern (clock tower from 1466). In its day, the city council—the rich guys who ran the town government—drank here. Today, it's the **TI** and the focus of most tourists' attention when the little doors on either side of the clock flip open and the wooden figures (from 1910) do their thing. Be on Market Square at the top of any hour (between 10:00 and 22:00) for the ritual gathering of the tourists to see the less-than-breathtaking reenactment of the Meistertrunk ("Master Draught") story:

In 1631, in the middle of the Thirty Years' War, the Catholic army took this Protestant town and was about to do its rape, pillage, and plunder thing. As was the etiquette, the mayor had to give the conquering general a welcoming drink. The general enjoyed a huge tankard of local wine. Feeling really good, he told the mayor, "Hey, if you can drink this entire three-liter tankard of wine in one gulp,

Rothenburg's Town Hall and Tower

I'll spare your town." The mayor amazed everyone by drinking the entire thing, and Rothenburg was saved. (While this is a nice story, it was dreamed up in the late 1800s for a theatrical play designed—effectively—to promote a romantic image of the town. In actuality, if Rothenburg was spared, it had likely bribed its way out of the jam.) The city was occupied and ransacked several times in the Thirty Years' War, and it never recovered—which is why it's such a well-preserved time capsule today.

Bottom of Market Square: As this was the most prestigious address in town, it's ringed by big homes with big carriage gates. One of the finest is just downhill from the bottom end of the square—the **Baumeister** ("master builder") **Haus,** where the man who designed and built the Town Hall lived. It features a famous Renaissance facade with statues of the seven virtues and the seven vices. The statues are copies; the originals are in the Rothenburg Museum (described later). While "Gluttony" is easy to find, see if you can figure out what his companions represent.

Behind you, take in the big 17th-century **St. George's fountain.** Its long metal gutters could slide to deposit the water into villagers' buckets. It's part of Rothenburg's ingenious water system: Built on a rock, the town had one real source above, which was plumbed to serve a series of fountains; water flowed from high to low through Rothenburg. Its many fountains had practical functions beyond providing drinking water—some were stocked with fish on market days and during times of siege, and their water was useful for fighting fire. Because of its plentiful water supply—and its policy of requiring relatively wide lanes as fire breaks—the town never burned entirely, as so many neighboring villages did.

Two fine half-timbered buildings behind the fountain show the old-time lofts with warehouse doors and pulleys on top for hoisting. All over town, lofts like these were filled with grain. A year's supply was required by the city so it could survive any siege. The building behind the fountain is an art gallery showing off work by members of the local artists' association. To the right is Marien Apotheke, an old-time pharmacy mixing old and new in typical Rothenburg style.

The broad street running under the

Herrngasse

Town Hall tower is **Herrngasse.** The town originated with its castle fortress (built in 1142 but now long gone; a lovely garden now fills that space). Herrngasse connected the castle to Market Square. The last leg of this circular walking tour will take you from the castle garden up Herrngasse and back here.

For now, walk a few steps down Herrngasse and stop by the arch under the Town Hall tower (between the new and old town halls). On the wall to the left of the gate are the town's measuring rods—a reminder that medieval Germany was made of 300 independent little countries, many with their own weights and measures. Merchants and shoppers knew that these were the local standards: the rod (4.3 yards), the *Schuh* ("shoe," roughly a foot), and the *Ell* (from elbow to fingertip—four inches longer than mine...climb up and try it). The protruding cornerstone you're standing on is one of many all over town—intended to protect buildings from careening horse carts. In German, going recklessly fast is called "scratching the cornerstone."

• *Careen around that stone and under the arch to find the...*

Historical Town Hall Vaults

The vaults (Historiengewölbe, worth ▲) house an eclectic and grade-schoolish little museum that gives a waxy but interesting look at Rothenburg during the Catholics-vs.-Protestants Thirty Years' War. Popping in here can help prep your imagination to filter out the tourists and picture ye olde Rothenburg along the rest of this walk. With helpful English descriptions, it offers a look at "the fateful year 1631," a replica of the mythical Meistertrunk tankard, an alchemist's workshop, and a dungeon—used as a bomb shelter during World War II—complete with three dank cells and some torture lore.

Cost and Hours: €3.50, daily 9:30-17:30, shorter hours Nov-April, closed Jan, weekends only Feb, tel. 09861/86751, www.meistertrunk.de.

• *Leaving the museum, turn left (past a venerable and much-sketched-and-photographed door) and find a posted copy of a centuries-old map showing the territory of Rothenburg.*

Map of Rothenburg City Territory

In 1537 Rothenburg actually ruled a little country—one of about 300 petty dukedoms like this that made up what is today's Germany. The territory spanned a 12-by-12-mile area, encompassing 180 villages—a good example of the fragmentation of feudal Germany. While not to scale (Rothenburg is actually less than a mile wide), the map is fun to study. In the 1380s, Mayor Toppler purchased much of this territory. In 1562 the city sold off some of its land to neighboring dukes, which gave it the money for all the fine Renaissance buildings that embellish the town to this day.

• *Continue through the courtyard and into a square called...*

Green Market (Grüner Markt)

Once a produce market, this parking lot fills with Christmas stands during December. Notice the clay-tile roofs. These "beaver tail" tiles became standard after thatched roofs were outlawed to prevent fires. Today, all the town's roofs are made of these. The little fences stop heaps of snow from falling off the roof and onto people below. A free public WC is on your left, and the recommended Friese gift shop (see "Shopping," later) is on your right.

• *Continue straight ahead to St. Jakob's Church. Study the exterior first, then pay to go inside.*

St. Jakob's Church (St. Jakobskirche)

Rothenburg's main church, worth ▲▲ is home to Tilman Riemenschneider's breathtaking, wood-carved *Altar of the Holy Blood*.

Cost and Hours: €2.50, daily April-Oct 9:00-17:00, Dec 10:00-16:45, off-season 10:00-12:00 & 14:00-16:00, on Sun wait to enter until services end at 10:45.

Tours and Information: A free, helpful English info sheet is available. Guided tours in English run on Sat at 15:30 (April-Oct) for no extra charge. Or get the worthwhile audioguide (€2, 45 minutes) for a handful of important stops in the church.

Visiting the Church: Start by viewing the exterior. Then, enter the church, where you'll see the main nave first, then climb above the pipe organ (in the back) to finish with the famous carved altar.

Exterior: Outside the church, under the little roof at the base of the tower, you'll see 14th-century statues (mostly original) showing Jesus praying at Gethsemane, a common feature of Gothic churches. The sculptor is anonymous—in the Gothic age (pre-Albrecht Dürer), artists were nameless craftspeople working only for the glory of God. Five yards to the left (on the wall), notice the nub of a sandstone statue—a rare original, looking pretty bad after 500 years of weather and, more recently, pollution. Most original statues are now in the city museum. The better-preserved statues you see on the church are copies. Also outside the church is a bronze model of the city. Look closely to appreciate the detail, including descriptions in braille.

Before entering, notice how the church was extended to the west and actually built over the street. The newer chapel was built to accommodate pilgrims and to contain the sumptuous Riemenschneider carved altarpiece.

If it's your wedding day, take the first entrance—marked by a very fertile Eve and, around the corner, Adam showing off an impressive six-pack. Otherwise, head toward the church's second (downhill) door. Before going inside, notice the modern statue at the base of the stairs. This is **St. James** (a.k.a. Sankt Jakob in German, Santiago in Spanish, and Saint-Jacques in French). You can tell this important saint by his big, floppy hat, his walking stick, the gourd on his hip (used by pilgrims to carry water), and—most importantly—the scallop shell in his hand. St. James' remains are entombed in the grand cathedral of Santiago de Compostela, in the northwestern corner of Spain. The medieval pilgrimage route called the Camino de

Map of Old Rothenburg

St. Jakob's Church

Santiago passed through here on its way to that distant corner of Europe. Pilgrims would wear the scallop shell as a symbol of their destination (where that type of marine life was abundant). To this day, the word for "scallop" in many languages carries the name of this saint: *Jakobsmuschel* in German, *coquille Saint-Jacques* in French, and so on.

Inside the Church: Built in the 14th century, this church has been Lutheran since 1544. The interior was "purified" by Romantics in the 19th century—cleaned of everything Baroque or not original and refitted in the Neo-Gothic style. (For example, the baptismal font—in the middle of the choir—and the pulpit above the second pew *look* Gothic but are actually Neo-Gothic.) The stained-glass windows behind the altar, which are most colorful in the morning light, are originals from the 1330s. Admiring this church, consider what it says about the priorities of a town of just a few thousand people, who decided to use their collective wealth to build such a place. The size of a church is a good indication of the town's wealth when it was built. Medallions and portraits of Rothenburg's leading families and church leaders line the walls above the choir in the front of the church.

The **main altar,** from 1466, is by Friedrich Herlin. Below Christ are statues of six saints—including St. James (a.k.a. Jakob), with the telltale shell on his floppy hat. Study the painted panels—ever see Peter with spectacles (below the carved saints)? Go around the back of the altarpiece to look at the doors. In the upper left, you'll see a painting of Rothenburg's Market Square in the 15th century, looking much like it does today, with the exception of the full-Gothic Town Hall (as it was before the big fire of 1501). Notice Christ's face on the white "veil of Veronica" (center of back side, bottom edge). It follows you as you walk from side to side—this must have given the faithful the religious heebie-jee-bies four centuries ago.

The **Tabernacle of the Holy Eucharist** (just left of the main altar—on your right as you walk back around) is a century older. It stored the wine and bread used for Holy Communion. Before the Reformation this was a Roman Catholic church, which meant that the bread and wine were considered to be the actual body and blood of Jesus (and therefore needed a worthy repository). Notice the unusual Trinity: The Father and Son are bridged by a dove, which represents the Holy Spirit. Stepping back, you can see that Jesus is standing on a skull—clearly "overcoming death."

Now, as pilgrims did centuries ago, climb the stairs at the back of the church that lead up behind the pipe organ to a loft-like chapel. Here you'll find the artistic highlight of Rothenburg and perhaps the most wonderful wood carving in all of Germany: the glorious 500-year-old, 35-foot-high **Altar of the Holy Blood.** Tilman Riemenschneider, the Michelangelo of German woodcarvers, carved this from 1499 to 1504 (at the same time Michelangelo was working on his own masterpieces). The altarpiece was designed to hold a rock-crystal capsule—set in the cross you see high above—that contains a precious scrap of tablecloth stained in the shape of a cross by a drop of communion wine considered to be the actual blood of Christ.

The altar is a realistic commotion, showing that Riemenschneider—a High

Altar of the Holy Blood

Gothic artist—was ahead of his time. Below, in the scene of the Last Supper, Jesus gives Judas a piece of bread, marking him as the traitor, while John lays his head on Christ's lap. Judas, with his big bag of cash, could be removed from the scene (illustrated by photos on the wall nearby), as was the tradition for the four days leading up to Easter.

Everything is portrayed exactly as described in the Bible. In the relief panel on the left, Jesus enters the walled city of Jerusalem. Notice the exacting attention to detail—down to the nails on the horseshoe. In the relief panel on the right, Jesus prays in the Garden of Gethsemane.

Take a moment to simply linger over the lovingly executed details: the curly locks of the apostles' hair and beards, and the folds of their garments; the delicate vines intertwining above their heads; Jesus' expression, at once tender and accusing.

• *After leaving the church, walk around the corner to the right and under the chapel (built over the road). Go two blocks down Klingengasse and stop at the corner of the street called Klosterhof. Looking farther ahead of you down Klingengasse, you see the...*

Klingentor

This cliff tower was Rothenburg's water reservoir. From 1595 until 1910, a 900-liter (240-gallon) copper tank high in the tower provided clean spring water—pumped up by river power—to the privileged. To the right of the Klingentor is a good stretch of wall rampart to walk. To the left, the wall is low and simple, lacking a rampart because it guards only a cliff.

Now find the shell decorating a building on the street corner next to you. That's once again the symbol of St. James, indicating that this building is associated with the church.

• *Turn left down Klosterhof, passing the shell and, on your right, the colorful, recommended Altfränkische Weinstube am Klosterhof pub. As you approach the next stop, notice the lazy Susan embedded in the wall*

(to the right of the museum door), which allowed cloistered nuns to give food to the poor without being seen.

Rothenburg Museum

You'll get a vivid and artifact-filled sweep through Rothenburg's history at this excellent ▲▲ museum, housed in a former Dominican convent. The highlight for many is the painted glass mug said to have prompted the myth of the Meistertrunk.

Cost and Hours: €6; daily 9:30-17:30, Nov-March generally 13:00-16:00; pick up English info sheet at entrance, Klosterhof 5, tel. 09861/939-043, www.reichsstadtmuseum.rothenburg.de.

Visiting the Museum: As you follow the *Rundgang/Tour* signs to the left, watch for these highlights:

Immediately inside, a glass case displays the 1616 Prince Elector's colorful glass tankard (which inspired the famous legend of the Meistertrunk) and a set of golden Rothenburg coins. Down the hall, find a modern city model and trace the city's growth, its walls expanding like rings on a big tree. Before going upstairs, you'll see medieval and Renaissance sculptures, including original sandstone statues from St. Jakob's Church and original statues that once decorated the Baumeister Haus near Market Square. Upstairs in the nuns' dormitory are craftsmen's signs that once hung outside shops (see if you can guess the craft before reading the museum's

Rothenburg Museum

label), ornate locks, tools for various professions, and a collection of armor and weapons. You'll then go through two levels of rooms showcasing old furniture, housewares, and the Baroque statues that decorated the organ loft in St. Jakob's Church from 1669 until the 19th century, when they were cleared out to achieve "Gothic purity." Take time to enjoy the several rooms and shop fronts outfitted as they would have been centuries ago.

The painting gallery is lined with Romantic paintings of Rothenburg, which served as the first tourist promotion and depict the city as it appeared in centuries past. Look for the large, gloomy work by Englishman Arthur Wasse (labeled *"Es spukt"*)—does that door look familiar?

Back downstairs near where you entered, circle left around the cloister to see a 14th-century convent kitchen (*Klosterküche*) with a working model of a lazy Susan (the kind that nuns used to share food with the poor outside the convent) and a massive chimney (step inside and look up). Continue around to an exhibit of Jewish culture in Rothenburg through the ages (*Judaika*), then see the grand finale (in the *Konventsaal*), the *Rothenburger Passion*. This 12-panel series of paintings showing scenes leading up to Christ's Crucifixion—originally intended for the town's Franciscan church (which we'll pass later)—dates from 1492.

• *Leaving the museum, go around to the right and into the Convent Garden (when locked at night, continue straight to the T-intersection and turn right).*

Convent Garden

This spot is a peaceful place to work on your tan...or mix a poisoned potion. Monks and nuns—who were responsible for concocting herbal cures in the olden days, finding disinfectants, and coming up with ways to disguise the taste of rotten food—often tended herb gardens. Smell (but don't pick) the *Pfefferminze* (peppermint), *Heidewacholder* (juniper/gin), *Rosmarin*

Convent Garden

(rosemary), *Lavandel* (lavender), and the tallest plant, *Hopfen* (hops...monks were the great medieval brewers). Don't smell the plants that are poisonous (potency indicated by the number of crosses). Appreciate the setting, taking in the fine architecture and expansive garden—all within the city walls, where land was at such a premium. It's a reminder of the power of the pre-Reformation Church.

• *Exit opposite from where you entered, angling left through the nuns' garden, leaving via an arch along the far wall. Then turn right and go downhill to the...*

Town Wall

This part of the wall takes advantage of the natural fortification provided by the cliff (view through bars, look to far right) and is therefore much shorter than the ramparts.

• *Angle left along the wall. Cross the big street (Herrngasse, with the Burgtor tower on your right—which we'll enter from outside soon) and continue downhill on Burggasse until you hit another section of the town wall. Turn right, go through a small tower gate, and park yourself at the town's finest viewpoint.*

Castle Garden Viewpoint

From here enjoy a fine view of fortified Rothenburg. You're looking at the Spitaltor end of town (with the most interesting gate and the former hospital). After this walk, you can continue with my "Schmiedgasse-Spitalgasse Shopping Stroll," which leads from Market Square down to this end of town, known as Plönlein, and then enter the city walls and walk the ramparts 180 degrees to the Klingentor tower (which we saw earlier, in the distance just after St. Jakob's Church). The droopy-eyed building at the far end of town (today's youth hostel) was the horse mill—which provided grinding power when the water mill in the valley below was not working (during drought or siege). Stretching below you is the fine parklike land around the Tauber River, nicknamed the "Tauber Riviera."

• Now explore deeper into the park.

Castle Garden and the Burgtor Gate

The park (Burggarten) before you was a castle fortress until it was destroyed in the 14th century. The chapel (50 yards straight into the park, on the left) is the only surviving bit of the original castle. In front of the chapel is a memorial to local Jews killed in a 1298 slaughter. A few steps beyond that is a flowery trellis that provides a fine picnic spot. If you walk all the way out to the garden's far end, you'll find another great viewpoint.

When you're ready to leave the park, approach the Burgtor, the ornate fortified gate flanked by twin stubby towers, and imagine being locked out in the year 1400. (There's a WC on the left.) The tall tower behind the gate was accessed by a wooden drawbridge—see the chain slits above the inner gate, and between them the "pitch" mask with holes designed to allow defenders to pour boiling Nutella on attackers. High above is the town coat of arms: a red (roten) castle (Burg).

As you go through the gate, study the big wooden door with the tiny "eye of the needle" door cut into it. If you were trying to enter town after curfew, you could have bribed the guard to let you through this door, which was small enough to keep out any fully armed attackers. Note also the square hole on the right and imagine the massive timber that once barricaded the gate.

• Now climb up the big street, Herrngasse, as you return to your starting point.

Herrngasse

Many towns have a Herrngasse, where the richest patricians and merchants (the Herren) lived. Predictably, it's your best chance to see the town's finest old mansions. Strolling back to Market Square, you'll pass, on the right, the **Franciscan Church** (from 1285—the oldest in town). Across the street, the mint-green house at #18 is the biggest patrician house on this main drag. The front door was big enough to allow a carriage to drive through it; a human-sized door cut into it was used by those on foot. The gift shop at #11 (Hornburghaus, on the right) offers a chance to poke into one of these big landowners' homes and appreciate their structure: living quarters in front above carriage-sized doors, courtyard out back functioning as a garage, stables, warehouse, servants' quarters, and a private well.

Farther up, also on the right, is Hotel Eisenhut, Rothenburg's fanciest hotel and worth a peek inside. Finally, passing the Käthe Wohlfahrt Christmas headquarters/shop (described under "Shopping," later), you'll be back at Market Square, where you started this walk.

• From here, you can continue walking by following my "Schmiedgasse-Spitalgasse Shopping Stroll," next. This stroll ends at the city gate called Spitaltor, a good access point for a walk on the town walls.

Burgtor Gate

❍ Schmiedgasse-Spitalgasse Shopping Stroll

After doing the basic town walk and visiting the town's three essential interior sights (Rothenburg Museum, Medieval Crime and Punishment Museum, and St. Jakob's Church), your next priority might be Rothenburg's shops and its town wall. This fun walk, worth ▲▲, goes from Market Square in a straight line south (past the best selection of characteristic family-run shops) to the city's most impressive fortification (Spitaltor).

Standing on Market Square, with your back to the TI, you'll see a street sloping downward toward the south end of town. That's where you're headed. This street changes names as you walk, from **Obere Schmiedgasse** (upper blacksmith street) to **Spitalgasse** (hospital street), and runs directly to the **Spitaltor** tower and gate. From Spitaltor you can access the town wall and walk the ramparts 180 degrees around the city to the Klingentor tower.

As you stroll down this delightful lane, pop in and explore shops along this cultural and historical scavenger hunt. I've provided the street number and "left" or "right" to indicate the side of the street (see the "Rothenburg Walks" map).

The facade of the fine Renaissance **Baumeister Haus** at #3 (left) celebrates a secular morality, with statues representing the seven virtues and the seven vices.

At #5 (left), **Gasthof Goldener Greifen** was once the home of the illustrious Mayor Toppler (d. 1408). By the looks of its door (right of the main entrance), the mayor must have had an impressive wine cellar. Note the fine hanging sign of a gilded griffin. Business signs in a mostly illiterate medieval world needed to be easy for all to read. The entire street is ornamented with fun signs like this one. Nearby, a pretzel marks the bakery, and the crossed swords advertise the weaponmaker.

Shops on both sides of the street at #7 display examples of *Schneeballen* gone wild. These "snowballs," once a humble way to bake extra flour into a simple treat, are now iced and dolled up a million ways.

Waffenkammer, at #9 (left), is "the weapons chamber," where Johannes Wittmann works hard to make a wonderland in which young-at-heart tourists can shop for (and try out) medieval weapons, armor, and clothing. Fun photo ops abound, especially downstairs (ask about Rick Steves discount).

At #18 (right), **Metzgerei Trumpp,** a top-end butcher, is a carnivore's heaven. Check out the endless wurst offerings in the window—a reminder that in the unrefrigerated Middle Ages meat needed to be smoked or salted. Locals who love bacon opt for fat slices of pork with crackling skins. At the next corner, with **Burggasse,** find the Catholic St. John's Church. The Medieval Crime and Punishment Museum (just down the lane to the right) marks the site of Rothenburg's first town wall.

The **Jutta Korn** shop, on the right at #4, showcases the work of a local artisan who has designed her own jewelry here for more than 30 years. At #6 (right), **Leyk** sells "lighthouses" made in town, many modeled after local buildings. The **Kleiderey,** an offbeat clothing store at #7 (left), is run by Tina, the Night Watchman's wife. The clothing is inspired by their southeast Asian travels.

At #13 (left), look opposite to find a narrow lane **(Ander Eich)** that leads to a little viewpoint in the town wall. Overlooking the "Tauber Riviera," it's a popular romantic perch in the evening.

At #17 (left), the **Lebe Gesund Vegetarian** shop is all about healthy living. This charming little place (run by tasty-sample-dealing Universalist Christians who like to think of Jesus as a vegan) seems designed to offer forgiveness to those who loved the butcher's shop but are ready to repent.

The **Käthe Wohlfahrt** shop at #19 (left) is one of the six Wohlfahrt stores around town, all owned by a local family and selling German clichés with gusto. Also on the left, at #21, the **An Ra** shop is where Annett Perner designs and sells her flowery clothes. (There's more of An Ra across the street at #26.) Annett was behind a recent initiative, called "Hand-made in Rothenburg," that formed a coalition between 10 local business owners who make everything from chocolate to jewelry to ceramics—an example of the special bond of Rothenburg's town members.

At #29 (left), **Glocke Weinladen am Plönlein** is an inviting shop of wine glasses and related accessories. The **Gasthof Glocke,** next door, with its wine-barrel-sized cellar door just waiting for some action, is a respected restaurant and home to the town's last vintner—a wonderful place to try local wines. The picturesque corner immediately to your right is dubbed **Plönlein,** named for the carpenter's plumb line—a string that dangles exactly straight down when anchored by a plumb (a lead weight). The line helps carpenters build things straight, but of course, here, nothing is made "to plumb." If this scene feels nostalgic, that's because Rothenburg was the inspiration for the village in the 1940 Disney animated film *Pinocchio.*

Walk a few more yards and look far up the lane **(Neugasse)** to the left. You'll see some cute pastel buildings with uniform windows and rooflines—clues that the buildings were rebuilt after WWII

bombings. Straight ahead, the **Siebertstor Tower** marks the next layer of expansion to the town wall. Continue through the tower. The former tannery is now a pub featuring **Landwehr Bräu,** the local brew.

Farther along, at #14 (right), **Antiq & Trödel,** which smells like an antique shop should, is fun to browse through.

Still farther down, on the left at #25, **Hotel-Café Gerberhaus** is a fine stop for a coffee and cake, with a delicate dining room and a peaceful courtyard hiding out back under the town wall.

From here, the town runs out of energy. This is Spitalhof—the former Hospital Quarter—with some nice architecture and the town's retirement home. Continue a few blocks to Spitaltor, the gate with the tall tower marking the end of town (and a good place to begin a ramparts ramble).

Outside the fortified gate is the ditch that kept artillery at a distance (most medieval moats were dry like this one; water and alligators were mostly added by Hollywood). Standing outside the wall, ponder this sight as if approaching the city 400 years ago. The wealth of a city was shown by its walls and towers. (Stone was costly—in fact, the German saying for "filthy rich" is "stone rich.")

Circle around to the right. Look up at the formidable tower. The guardhouse atop it, one of several in the wall, was manned 24/7. Above the entry gate, notice the emblem: Angels bless the double eagle of the Holy Roman Emperor, which blesses the town (symbolized by the two red towers).

◑ Walk the Wall

Just longer than a mile and a half around, providing great views and a good orientation, this walk can be done by those under six feet tall in less than an hour. Much of the walk is covered and is a great option in the rain. Photographers will stay very busy, especially before breakfast or at sunset, when the lighting is best and the crowds

The city ramparts

are gone. You can enter or exit the ramparts at nearly every tower.

While the ramparts circle the city, some stretches aren't walkable per se: Along much of the western side of town, you can't walk atop the wall, but you can walk alongside it and peek over or through it for great views outward from street level. Refer to my "Rothenburg Walks" map, earlier, to see which portions of the wall are walkable.

If you want to make a full town circuit, Spitaltor—at the south end of town, with the best fortifications—is a good starting place. From here it's a counterclockwise walk along the eastern and northern ramparts. After exiting at Klingentor you can follow the wall for a bit, but you'll have to cut away from the wall when you hit the Rothenburg Museum and again near the Medieval Crime and Punishment Museum. At the Kohlturm tower, at the southern end of town, you can climb the stairs and walk atop the remaining stretch of wall to the Spitalhof quarter, where you'll need to exit again. Spitaltor, where you started, is just a *Schneeball's* toss away.

The TI has installed a helpful series of English-language plaques at about 20 stops along the route. The names you see along the way belong to people who donated money to rebuild the wall after World War II, and those who've more recently donated for the maintenance of Rothenburg's heritage.

SIGHTS

Note that a number of sights (including St. Jakob's Church and the Rothenburg Museum) have already been covered in the Rothenburg Town Walk.

On and Near Market Square

▲TOWN HALL TOWER

From Market Square you can see tourists on the crow's nest capping the Town Hall's tower. For a commanding view from the town's tallest perch, climb the steps of the tower. It's a rigorous but interesting 214-step climb that gets narrow and steep near the top—watch your head. Be here during the first or last hour of the day to avoid day-tripping crowds.

Cost and Hours: €2.50, pay at top, daily in season 9:30-12:30 & 13:00-17:00, enter from the grand steps overlooking Market Square.

▲▲MEDIEVAL CRIME AND PUNISHMENT MUSEUM (MITTELALTERLICHES KRIMINALMUSEUM)

Specializing in everything connected to medieval criminal justice, this exhibit (well described in English) is a cut above all the tacky torture museums around Europe. Nearly everything on display here is an actual medieval artifact. In addition to ogling spiked chairs, thumbscrews, and shame masks, you'll learn about medieval police and criminal law. The museum is more eclectic than its name and includes exhibits on general history, superstition, witchcraft, biblical art, and so on. The museum is undergoing renovations in 2019, which may affect some areas. A thoughtfully curated **Luther and the Witches** exhibit, created for the 500th anniversary of the Protestant Reformation, should still be on display when you visit.

Cost and Hours: €7, includes Luther exhibit; daily 10:00-18:00, Nov and Jan-

suggested that the person had acted pig-gishly. The infamous "iron maiden" started out as more of a "shame barrel"; the internal spikes were added to play up popular lore when it went on display for 18th-century tourists. For more serious offenses, criminals were branded—so that even if they left town, they'd take that shame with them for the rest of their lives. When all else failed, those in charge could always turn to the executioner's sword.

To safely capture potential witches, lawmen used a device resembling a metal collar—with spikes pointing in—that was easy to get into but nearly impossible to escape. A neck violin—like a portable version of a stock—kept the accused under control. The chastity belts were used to ensure a wife's loyalty and/or to protect women from rape, then a commonplace crime.

The exit routes you through a courtyard garden to a **last building** with temporary exhibits and a café. If you must buy a *Schneeball*, consider doing it here. A recent blind taste test among the town's tour guides deemed these the best.

Feb 14:00-16:00, Dec and March 13:00-16:00; last entry 45 minutes before closing, fun cards and posters, Burggasse 3-5, tel. 09861/5359, www.kriminalmuseum.eu.

Visiting the Museum: It's a one-way route—just follow the yellow arrows. Keep an eye out for several well-done interactive media stations that provide extra background on the museum's highlights.

From the entrance, head downstairs to the **cellar** to see some enhanced-interrogation devices. Torture was common in the Middle Ages—not to punish, but to extract a confession (medieval "justice" required a confession). Just the sight of these tools was often enough to make an innocent man confess. You'll see the rack, "stretching ladder," thumb screws, spiked leg screws, and other items that would make Dick Cheney proud. Medieval torturers also employed a waterboarding-like technique—but here, the special ingredient was holy water.

Upstairs, on the **first and second floors,** the walls are lined with various legal documents of the age, while the dusty glass cases show off law-enforcement tools—many of them quite creative. Shame was a big tool back then. The town could publicly humiliate those who ran afoul of the law by tying them to a pillory in the main square and covering their faces in an iron mask of shame. Fanciful mask decorations indicated the crime: Chicken feathers meant promiscuity, horns indicated that a man's wife slept around (i.e., cuckold), and a snout

▲**GERMAN CHRISTMAS MUSEUM (DEUTSCHES WEIHNACHTSMUSEUM)**
This excellent museum, in a Disney-esque space upstairs in the giant Käthe Wohlfahrt Christmas Village shop, tells the history of Christmas decorations. There's a unique and thoughtfully described collection of tree stands, mini trees sent in boxes to WWI soldiers at the front, early Advent calendars, old-time Christmas cards, and a look at the evolution of Father Christmas as well as tree decorations through the ages. The museum is not just a ploy to get shoppers to spend more money but a serious collection managed by professional curator Felicitas Höptner.

Cost and Hours: €4 most of the year, €2.50 low-season rate available to my readers year-round with this book; daily 10:00-17:30, shorter and irregular hours Jan-March; Herrngasse 1, tel. 09861/409-365, www.christmasmuseum.com.

EXPERIENCES

Shopping

Rothenburg is one of Germany's best shopping towns. Lovely prints, carvings, wine glasses, Christmas-tree ornaments, and beer steins are popular. Rödergasse is the old town's everyday shopping street. There's also a modern shopping center across the street from the train station.

To find local artisans, pick up the *Handmade in Rothenburg* pamphlet at the TI or visit the group's website (www.rothenburg-handmade.com).

For an appealing string of family-run shops, follow my "Schmiedgasse-Spitalgasse Shopping Stroll" (described earlier, under "Rothenburg Walks"). Below are two shops not on that walk:

KÄTHE WOHLFAHRT CHRISTMAS HEADQUARTERS

Rothenburg is the headquarters of the Käthe Wohlfahrt Christmas trinkets empire, which has spread across the half-timbered reaches of Europe. Rothenburg has six Wohlfahrts. Tourists flock to the two biggest, just below Market Square (Herrngasse 1 and 2). Start with the **Christmas Village** (Weihnachtsdorf) at Herrngasse 1. This Christmas wonderland is filled with enough twinkling lights (196,000—mostly LEDs) to require a special electrical hookup. You're greeted by instant Christmas mood music and tourists hungrily filling little woven shopping baskets with goodies (items handmade in Germany are the most expensive). With this book, you'll get 10 percent off official wooden KW products (look for the *Käthes Original* tag; must show book to receive discount).

Let the spinning, flocked tree whisk you in, and pause at the wall of Steiff stuffed animals. Then head downstairs to find the sprawling "made in Germany" section, surrounding a slowly spinning 15-foot tree decorated with a thousand glass balls. The fascinating **Christmas Museum** upstairs is described earlier, under "Sights." The

smaller shop (across the street at Herrngasse 2) specializes in finely crafted wooden ornaments. Käthe opened her first storefront here in Rothenburg in 1977. The company is now run by her son Harald (Christmas Village open Mon-Sat 9:00-18:00, Sun from 10:00 beginning in late April; shorter hours at other locations).

FRIESE SHOP

Cuckoo with friendliness, trinkets, and reasonably priced souvenirs, the Friese shop has been open for more than 90 years—and they've been welcoming my readers for more than 30. They give shoppers with this book tremendous service: a 10 percent discount off all items and a free pictorial map. Run for many years by Anneliese Friese, it's now lovingly run by her son, Bernie. They let tired travelers leave their bags in the back room for free (Mon-Sat 9:00-17:00, Sun from 10:00, 20 steps off Market Square at Grüner Markt 8—around the corner from TI and across from free public WC, tel. 09861/7166).

Festivals

For one weekend each spring (during Pentecost), beer gardens spill out into the street and Rothenburgers dress up in medieval costumes to celebrate Mayor Nusch's **Meistertrunk** victory (www.meistertrunk.de). The **Reichsstadt festival** every September celebrates Rothenburg's history, and the town's **Weindorf festival** celebrates its wine (mid-Aug). Check the TI website for specifics.

In winter, Rothenburg is quiet except for its **Christmas Market** in December, when the entire town cranks up the medieval cuteness with concerts and costumes, shops with schnapps, stalls filling squares, hot spiced wine, and mobs of ear-muffed Germans. Try to avoid Saturdays and Sundays, when big-city day-trippers really clog the grog.

EATING

My recommendations are all within a five-minute walk of Market Square. While all survive on tourism, many still feel like local hangouts. Your choices are typical German or ethnic. You'll see regional Franconian (*fränkische*) specialties advertised, such as the German ravioli called *Maultaschen* and Franconian bratwurst (similar to other brats, but a bit more coarsely ground, with less fat, and liberally seasoned with marjoram). Many restaurants take a midafternoon break and stop serving lunch at 14:00; dinner may end as early as 20:00.

Traditional German Restaurants

$$$ Reichsküchenmeister's interior is like any forgettable big-hotel restaurant's, but on a balmy evening, its pleasant tree-shaded terrace overlooking St. Jakob's Church and reliably good dishes are hard to beat, including the *Flammkuchen*—southern German flatbread

(daily 11:30-22:30, reservations smart, Kirchplatz 8, tel. 09861/9700, www.hotel-reichskuechenmeister-rothenburg.de).

$$$ Hotel Restaurant Kloster-Stüble, on a small street off Herrngasse near the castle garden, is a classy place for delicious and beautifully presented traditional cuisine, including homemade *Maultaschen* (German ravioli). Choose from their shaded terrace, sleek-and-stony modern dining room, or woody traditional dining room (daily 18:00-20:30, Sat-Sun also 12:00-14:30, Heringsbronnengasse 5, tel. 09861/938-890).

$$ Gasthof Goldener Greifen, in a historic building with a peaceful garden out back, is just off the main square. The Klingler family serves quality Franconian food at a good price...and with a smile. The wood is ancient and polished from generations of happy use, and the ambience is practical rather than posh (affordable kids' meals, Wed-Mon 11:30-21:00, closed Tue, Obere Schmiedgasse 5, tel. 09861/2281, Ursula).

English Conversation Club

Rick's Tip: *For a rare chance to* **meet the locals,** *bring your favorite slang and tongue-twisters to the* **English Conversation Club** *at* **Altfränkische Weinstube am Klosterhof.** *Hermann the German and his sidekick Wolfgang are regulars. A big table is reserved from 18:30 on Wednesday evenings. Consider arriving early for dinner, or after 21:00, when the beer starts to sink in and everyone speaks that second language more easily.*

$$ Altfränkische Weinstube am Klosterhof seems designed for gnomes to celebrate their anniversaries. At this very dark pub, classically candlelit in a 650-year-old building, Mario whips up gourmet pub grub (hot food served Wed-Mon 18:00-21:30, closed Tue, off Klingengasse at Klosterhof 7, tel. 09861/6404).

$$ Zum Pulverer ("The Powderer") is a very traditional *Weinstube* (wine bar) just inside the Burgtor gate that serves a menu of affordable and well-executed regional fare, some with modern flourishes. The interior is a cozy wood-hewn place that oozes history, with chairs carved in the shape of past senators of Rothenburg (daily 17:00-23:00 except Sat-Sun from 12:00, closed Tue, Herrengasse 31, tel. 09861/976-182).

$$ Alter Keller is a modest, tourist-friendly restaurant with an extremely characteristic interior and outdoor tables on a peaceful square just a couple blocks off Market Square. The menu has German classics at reasonable prices—*Spätzle,* schnitzel, and roasts—as well as steak (Wed-Sun 11:30-15:00 & 17:30-21:00, closed Mon-Tue, Alter Keller 8, tel. 09861/2268, Markus and Miriam).

Non-Franconian Fare

$$$$ Hotel Restaurant Herrnschlösschen offers a small menu of international and seasonal dishes. There's always a serious vegetarian option and a €50 fixed-price meal with wine pairing. It's perhaps the most elegant dining in town, whether in the classy dining hall or in the shaded Baroque garden out back. Reservations are a must (Herrngasse 20, tel. 09861/873-890, Ulrika, www.hotel-rothenburg.de).

$$ Pizzeria Roma is the locals' favorite for Italian. The Magrini family moved here from Tuscany in 1968, and they've been cooking pasta for Rothenburg ever since (Thu-Tue 11:30-23:00, closed Wed and mid-Aug-mid-Sept, Galgengasse 19, tel. 09861/4540, Riccardo).

$ TobinGo, just off Market Square, serves cheap and tasty Turkish food to eat in or take away. Their *döner kebab* must be the best €4.20 hot meal in Rothenburg. For about €1 more, try a less-bready *dürüm döner*—same ingredients but in a warm tortilla (daily 10:00-22:00, Hafengasse 2).

Sandwiches and Snacks

$ Brot & Zeit (a pun on *Brotzeit,* "bread time," the German term for snacking), conveniently located a block off Market Square, is like a German bakery dressed up as a Starbucks. In a bright, modern atmosphere just inside the super-picturesque Markus Tower gate, they sell take-away coffee, sandwiches, and a few hot dishes, making it a good one-stop shop (Mon-Sat 6:00-18:30, Sun 7:30-18:00, Hafengasse 24, tel. 09861/936-8701).

Bakery and Butcher Sandwiches: While any bakery in town can sell you a sandwich for a couple of euros, I like to pop into **$ Metzgerei Trumpp,** a high-quality butcher shop serving up cheap and tasty sausages on a bun with kraut to go (Mon-Fri 7:30-18:00, Sat until 16:00, usually closed Sun, a block off Market Square at Schmiedgasse 18).

Beer Garden

$$ Gasthof Rödertor, just outside the wall through the Rödertor, runs a backyard *Biergarten* that's popular with locals. It's great for a rowdy crowd looking for classic beer garden fare and good beer. Try a plate of *Schupfnudeln*—potato noodles with sauerkraut and bacon (May-Sept Tue-Sat

17:30-22:00, Sun until 21:00, closed Mon and in bad weather, table service only—no ordering at counter, Ansbacher Strasse 7, look for wooden gate, tel. 09861/2022). If the *Biergarten* is closed, their indoor restaurant, with a more extensive menu, is a good value (Tue-Sun 11:30-14:00 & 17:30-21:00, closed Mon).

Dessert

Eis Café D'Isep, with a pleasant "Venetian minimalist" interior, has been making gelato in Rothenburg since 1960, using family recipes that span four generations. Their sidewalk tables are great for lazy people-watching (daily 10:00-22:00, closed early Oct-mid-Feb, one block off Market Square at Hafengasse 17, run by Paolo and Paola D'Isep and son Enrico).

The **Allegra Schokolade** chocolate shop is run by delightful Alex, a pastry chef-turned-chocolatier who trained in Switzerland. He makes artisan chocolates with local ingredients and can arrange group workshops (Tue-Sat 10:00-18:00, Sun from 11:00, closed Mon; workshops from €10, minimum 4 people, 1.5 hours, arrange in advance; Georgengasse 9, tel. 9861/688-0293, www.allegra-schokolade. de, info@allegra-schokolade.de).

Rothenburg's **bakeries** (*Bäckereien*) offer succulent pastries, pies, and cakes... but skip the bad-tasting *Rothenburger Schneeballen.* Unworthy of the heavy promotion they receive, *Schneeballen* are bland pie crusts crumpled into a ball and dusted with powdered sugar or frosted with sticky-sweet glop. There's little reason to waste your appetite on a *Schneeball* when you can enjoy a curvy *Mandelhörnchen* (almond crescent cookie), a triangular *Nussecke* ("nut corner"), a round *Florentiner* cookie, a couple of fresh *Krapfen* (like jelly doughnuts), or a soft, warm German pretzel.

SLEEPING

Rothenburg is crowded with visitors, but most are day-trippers. Except for the rare Saturday night and during festivals (see page 400), finding a room is easy. Competition keeps quality high. If you want to splurge, you'll snare the best value by paying extra for the biggest and best rooms at the hotels I recommend. In the off-season (Nov and Jan-March), hoteliers may be willing to discount.

Train travelers save steps by staying in the Rödertor area (east end of town). Hotels and guesthouses will sometimes pick up tired heavy-packers at the station. If you're driving, call ahead to get directions and parking tips. Save some energy to climb the stairs: Only one of my recommended hotels (Wildbad) has an elevator.

Keep your key when out late. As Rothenburg's hotels are small and mostly family-run, they often lock up early (at about 22:00) and take one day a week off, so you'll need to let yourself in at those times.

In the Old Town

$$$$ Hotel Herrnschlösschen prides itself on being the smallest (8 rooms) and most exclusive hotel in Rothenburg. If you're looking for a splurge, this 1,000-year-old building has a beautiful Baroque garden and every amenity you'd ever want (including a sauna), but you'll pay for them (Herrngasse 20, tel. 09861/873-890, www.herrnschloesschen. de, info@herrnschloesschen.de).

$$$ Gasthof Goldener Greifen, once Mayor Toppler's home, is a big, traditional, 650-year-old place with 14 spacious rooms and all the comforts. It's run by a helpful family staff and creaks with rustic splendor (family rooms, free loaner bikes for guests, free and easy parking, half a block downhill from Market Square at Obere Schmiedgasse 5, tel. 09861/2281, www.gasthof-greifen-rothenburg.de, info@gasthof-greifen-rothenburg.de; Brigitte, daughter Ursula, and Klingler family). The family also runs a good restaurant, serving meals in the back garden or dining room.

$$ Hotel Kloster-Stüble, deep in the old town near the castle garden, is one of my classiest listings. Twenty-one rooms, plus two apartments, each with its own special touches, fill two medieval buildings connected by a modern atrium (family rooms, just off Herrngasse at Heringsbronnengasse 5, tel. 09861/938-890, www.klosterstueble.de, hotel@klosterstueble.de, energetic Erika).

$$ Hotel Spitzweg is a rustic-yet-elegant 1536 mansion (never bombed or burned) with 10 big rooms, new bathrooms, open beams, and endearing hand-painted antique furniture. It's run by gentle Herr Hocher, whom I suspect is the former Wizard of Oz—now retired and in a very good mood (apartment, inviting old-fashioned breakfast room, free but limited parking, Paradeisgasse 2, tel. 09861/94290, www.hotel-spitzweg.de, info@hotel-spitzweg.de).

$$ Hotel Gerberhaus mixes modern comforts into 20 bright and airy rooms—some with four-poster *Himmel* beds—that maintain a sense of half-timbered elegance. Enjoy the pleasant garden in back and the delightful breakfast buffet. It's just inside the town wall, a five-minute walk to the main square (family rooms, apartment, pay parking, pay laundry, Spitalgasse 25, tel. 09861/94900, www.gerberhaus.rothenburg.de, info@hotelgerberhaus.com, Inge).

$$ Hotel Altfränkische Weinstube am Klosterhof is *the* place for well-heeled bohemians. Mario and Hanne rent eight cozy rooms above their dark and evocative pub in a 650-year-old building. It's an upscale *Lord of the Rings* atmosphere, with modern plumbing, open-beam ceilings, and some canopied four-poster beds (off Klingengasse at Klosterhof 7, tel. 09861/6404, www.altfraenkische.de, altfraenkische-weinstube@web.de). Their pub is a candlelit classic—and a favorite with locals, serving hot food to Hobbits

(see listing earlier, under "Eating").

$ Pension Elke, run by spry Erich Endress and his son Klaus, rents 12 comfy rooms above the family grocery store. Guests who jog are welcome to join Klaus on his half-hour run around the city every evening at 19:30 (RS%, cheaper rooms with shared bath, cash only; reception in grocery store until 19:00, otherwise go around back and ring bell at top of stairs; near Markus Tower at Rödergasse 6, tel. 09861/2331, www.pension-elke-rothenburg.de, info@pension-elke-rothenburg.de).

$ Gästehaus Raidel rents eight rooms in a 500-year-old house filled with furniture all handmade by friendly, soft-spoken Norry Raidel. The ramshackle ambience makes me want to sing the *Addams Family* theme song, but the place has a rare, time-passed family charm. Norry, who plays in a Dixieland band, invented a fascinating hybrid saxophone/trombone called the Norryphone...and loves to jam (family rooms, cash only, pleasant terrace with small garden, Wenggasse 3, tel. 09861/3115, Norry asks you to use the reservations form at www.romanticroad.com/raidel).

$ Gasthof zum Breiterle offers 23 comfortable rooms with wooden accents above their spacious breakfast room near the Rödertor. Because the inn sits on a busy street, light sleepers may want to request a room not facing Wenggasse (apartment, reception in restaurant, pay parking, Rödergasse 30, tel. 09861/6730, www.breiterle.de, info@breiterle.de, Mike and Nicole).

$ Kreuzerhof Hotel offers 11 decent rooms surrounding a courtyard on a quiet side street near the Rödertor (family rooms, pay parking in courtyard, Millergasse 2, tel. 09861/3424, www.kreuzerhof.eu, info@kreuzerhof.eu, Heike and Walter Maltz).

Outside the Wall

$$ Wildbad provides a tranquil escape on the edge of the Tauber River. Offering 58 stylish rooms, this historic building occupies the site of a former 10th-century spa. The vast park surrounding the hotel, replete with walking trails, offers free summer concerts and Sunday *Kaffee und Kuchen* on the terrace. There's even a covered *Kegeln* lane where you can rent 19th-century wooden pins and try your hand at ninepin bowling. An elevator covers the first seven floors, but you'll have to walk to the eighth, where there's a tiny chapel and library (family rooms, free parking, Taubertalweg 42, tel. 09861/9770, www.wildbad.de, info@wildbad.de). While it's walkable to town, those arriving by train can take a taxi for around €7.

TRANSPORTATION

Arriving and Departing

BY TRAIN

Arriving in Rothenburg: It's a 10-minute walk from the station to Rothenburg's Market Square (following the brown *Altstadt* signs, exit left from station, walk a block down Bahnhofstrasse, turn right on Ansbacher Strasse, and head straight into the Middle Ages). Taxis wait at the station (€10 to any hotel). Day-trippers can leave luggage in lockers on the platform. Free WCs are behind the Speedy snack bar on track 1.

The Rothenburg station has ticket machines for fare and schedule information and ticket sales. For extra help, visit the combined ticket office/travel agency in the station (€1-3 surcharge for most tickets, Mon-Fri 10:00-18:00, Sat 9:00-13:00, closed Sun, tel. 09861/7711). The station at Steinach is entirely unstaffed but has ticket machines. Train info: www.bahn.com.

Getting to/from Rothenburg via Steinach: If you take the train to or from Rothenburg, you'll transfer at Steinach. A tiny branch train line shuttles back and forth hourly between Steinach and Rothenburg (15 minutes, generally departs Steinach at :35 and Rothenburg at :06). Train connections in Steinach are usually quick and efficient (trains to and from Rothenburg generally use track 5; use the

conveyor belts to haul your bags smartly up and down the stairs).

Note that the last train from Steinach to Rothenburg departs at about 22:30. But all is not lost if you arrive in Steinach after the last train: A subsidized taxi service runs to Rothenburg (cheaper for the government than running an almost-empty train). To use this handy service, called AST (*Anrufsammeltaxi*), make an appointment with a participating taxi service (call 09861/2000 or 09861/7227) at least an hour in advance (2 hours ahead is better), and they'll drive you from Steinach to Rothenburg for the cost of train fare (€4.70/person) rather than the regular €30 taxi fare.

From Rothenburg (via Steinach) by Train to: Würzburg (hourly, 70 minutes), **Nürnberg** (hourly, 1.5 hours, change in Ansbach), **Munich** (hourly, 3.5 hours, 2-3 changes), **Füssen** (hourly, 5 hours, often with changes in Treuchtlingen and Augsburg), **Frankfurt** (hourly, 3 hours, change in Würzburg), **Frankfurt Airport** (hourly, 3.5 hours, change in Würzburg), **Berlin** (hourly, 5.5 hours, 3 changes).

BY CAR

Driving and parking rules in Rothenburg change constantly—ask your hotelier for advice. In general, you're allowed to drive into the old town to get to your hotel. Otherwise, driving within the old walled center is discouraged. Some hotels offer private parking (either free or paid). To keep things simple, park in one of the lots—numbered P-1 through P-5—that line the outside of the town walls (€5/day, buy ticket from *Parkscheinautomat* machines and display, 5- to 10-minute walk to Market Square).

Driving from Frankfurt Airport: The three-hour autobahn drive from **Frankfurt Airport** to Rothenburg is something even a jet-lagged zombie can handle. It's a 75-mile straight shot to Würzburg on the A-3 autobahn; just follow the blue autobahn signs toward *Würzburg*. Then turn south on A-7 and take the *Rothenburg o.d.T.* exit (#108).

NEAR ROTHENBURG

The Romantic Road

The countryside between Frankfurt and Munich is Germany's medieval heartland. Walls and towers ring half-timbered towns, flowers spill over the windowsills of well-kept houses, and glockenspiels dance from town halls. Many travelers bypass these small towns by fast train or autobahn. But, especially if you're driving, consider an extra day or two to take in the slow pace of small-town German life.

Getting There

BY CAR

Wander through quaint hills and rolling villages along the 220-mile scenic driving route called the Romantic Road (*Romantische Strasse,* www.romantischestrasse. de), stopping wherever the cows look friendly or a town fountain beckons. If your goal is to meander and explore, skip the GPS, get a good map, and follow the brown *Romantische Strasse* signs. If you're driving north of Rothenburg, good stops are Creglingen and Weikersheim. Driving south of Rothenburg (whether heading toward it or leaving it), stop at the Wieskirche and the towns of Nördlingen and Dinkelsbühl.

BY BUS

The Romantic Road bus runs Wednesday and Sunday from April through October, with a third departure on Saturday from mid-May to early September. One bus goes north to south (Frankfurt to Munich), and another follows the reverse route south to north (Munich to Frankfurt). Check the full timetable at www. romantischestrasse.de (choose "Bus & Train," then "Romantic Road Bus").

North of Rothenburg

CREGLINGEN

While Creglingen itself isn't worth much fuss (www.creglingen.de), two quick and rewarding sights sit across the road from each other a mile south of town.

The peaceful 14th-century **Herrgottskirche Church,** worth ▲, is graced with Tilman Riemenschneider's greatest carved altarpiece, completed sometime between 1505 and 1510, and nearly 30 feet high—tall enough that its tip pokes up between the rafters. The church's other, colorful (non-Riemenschneider) altars are also worth a peek (www. herrgottskirche.de).

The **Fingerhut Museum,** showing off thimbles (literally, "finger hats"), is far more interesting than it sounds. You'll step from case to case to squint at the collection, which numbers about 4,000 (but still fits in a single room) and comes from all over the world; some pieces are centuries old (www. fingerhutmuseum.de).

▲WEIKERSHEIM

This picturesquely set town, nestled between hills, has a charming little main square offering easy access to a fine park and an impressive palace.

The palace at Weikersheim has fine gardens.

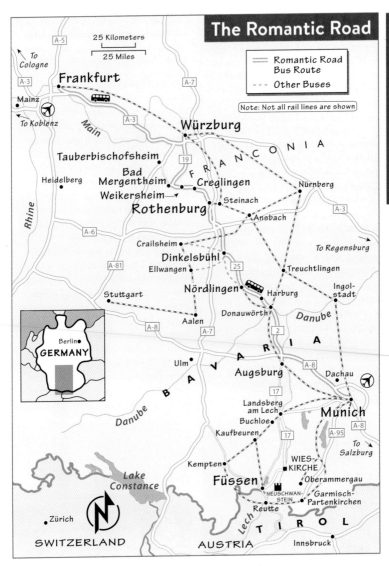

The Romantic Road

Romantic Road Bus Route

--- Other Buses

Note: Not all rail lines are shown

25 Kilometers
25 Miles

To Cologne

Frankfurt

Mainz

To Koblenz

Main

Rhine

Würzburg

Tauberbischofsheim

Bad Mergentheim

Heidelberg

Weikersheim →

Rothenburg

Creglingen

Steinach

F R A N C O N I A

Nürnberg

Ansbach

Crailsheim

Dinkelsbühl

Ellwangen

Stuttgart

Aalen

Nördlingen

Harburg

Donauwörth

Treuchtlingen

Ingol-stadt

To Regensburg

Danube

GERMANY

Berlin

Ulm

Augsburg

Dachau

B A V A R I A

Danube

Landsberg am Lech

Buchloe

Kaufbeuren

Munich

To Salzburg

Kempten

Lake Constance

Zürich

SWITZERLAND

WIES-KIRCHE

Füssen

NEUSCHWAN-STEIN

Reutte

Oberammergau

Garmisch-Partenkirchen

T I R O L

AUSTRIA

Innsbruck

Lech

Weikersheim's **palace** (Schloss Weikersheim), across a moat-turned-park from the main square, was built in the late 16th century as the Renaissance country estate of a local count. With its bucolic location and glowing sandstone texture, it gives off a *Downton Abbey* vibe. The palace interior is only viewable by a guided tour in German (www.schloss-weikersheim.de)—skip the tour and instead focus on exploring the palace's fine Baroque **gardens.**

If you have time after your garden visit, Weikersheim's pleasant **town square** and cobbled old town are worth exploring. The **city park** (*Stadtpark*, enter off town square) is a fine picnic spot, and from it you can peer over the hedge into the palace gardens.

South of Rothenburg

▲DINKELSBÜHL

Rothenburg's little sister is cute enough to merit a short stop. A moat, towers, gates, and a beautifully preserved medieval wall surround this town. Park at one of the free lots outside the town walls, which are well signed from the main road.

To orient yourself, head for the tower of **St. Georg's Cathedral,** at the center of town. This 15th-century church has a surprisingly light, airy interior and fine carved altarpieces. On good-weather summer weekends, you can climb to the top of the tower.

Outside the church, follow signs around the corner (to the **TI** (www.dinkelsbuehl.de), which doubles as the ticket office for the fine **City History Museum** (Haus der Geschichte) in the same building.

Sleeping in Dinkelsbühl: Dinkelsbühl has a good selection of hotels. Options include: $$$ Hezelhof Hotel (modern rooms in an old shell at Segringer Strasse 7, www.hezelhof.com), $$$ Weisses Ross ("White Horse," attached to a historic restaurant at Steingasse 12, www.hotel-weisses-ross.de), and Dinkelsbühl's unique ¢ youth hostel (in a medieval granary at Koppengasse 10, www.dinkelsbuehl.jugendherberge.de).

▲NÖRDLINGEN

Nördlingen is a real workaday town that has one of the best city walls in Germany, not to mention a surprising geological history. For centuries, Nördlingen's residents puzzled over the local terrain, a flattish plain called the Ries, which rises to a low circular ridge that surrounds the town in the distance. In the 1960s, geologists figured out that Nördlingen lies in the middle of an impact crater blasted out 15 million years ago by a meteor.

Park in one of the big, free lots at the Delninger Tor and the Baldinger Tor, then head into the center of town by zeroing in on the tower of **St. Georg's Church.** The rickety 350-step climb up the church tower rewards you with the very best view of the city walls and crater. With more time, walk all the way around on the top of the **town wall,** which is even better preserved than Rothenburg's or Dinkelsbühl's. It's more than a mile and a half long, has 16 towers and 5 gates, and

Dinkelsbühl

St. Georg's Church dominates Nördlingen.

offers great views of backyards and garden furniture.

Sleeping in Nördlingen: Several small hotels surrounding St. Georg's Church offer mediocre but reasonably priced rooms. Try **$$ Hotel Altreuter** (over an inviting bakery/café at Marktplatz 11, www. hotel-altreuter.de).

▲▲*Wieskirche*

Germany's most glorious Baroque-Rococo church is beautifully restored and set in a sweet meadow. For a full description, see the Bavarian Alps chapter.

BEST OF THE REST

Würzburg

Historic, midsized Würzburg (VEWRTS-boorg) is worth a stop to see its stately prince-bishop's Residenz and the palace's sculpted gardens. Surrounded by vineyards and filled with atmospheric *Wein-stuben* (wine bars), this tourist-friendly town is easy to navigate. Today, 25,000 of its 130,000 residents are students—making Würzburg feel young and very alive.

Holy Roman Emperor Frederick Barbarossa came here in the 12th century to get the bishop's OK to divorce his wife. The bishop said "No problem," and the emperor thanked him by giving him secular rule of the entire region of Franco-nia. From then on, the bishop was also a prince. He answered only to the Holy Roman Emperor and built the palace that still dominates the town.

Day Plan

Würzburg has a few hours' worth of sightseeing. Begin by touring the Residenz palace. With more time, cross the bridge and hike up to the hilltop Marienberg Fortress. If you're overnighting here, be sure to stroll the bridge at sunset, when you can join the friendly local crowd that gathers there in good weather.

Bustling Würzburg is easy to navigate.

Orientation

Würzburg's old town core huddles along the bank of the Main (pronounced "mine") River. The tourists' Würzburg is bookended by the opulent Residenz and the hill-capping Marienberg Fortress across the river. You can walk from the Residenz to the river (below the fortress) in about 15 minutes; the train station is a 15-minute walk to the north.

Tourist Information: Würzburg's helpful TI is on Market Square (closed Sun off-season, www.wuerzburg.de).

Getting There

Würzburg enjoys frequent, well-connected train service, including Rothenburg (hourly, 70 minutes) and Nürnberg (2-3/hour, 1 hour). From the station, **trams** #1, #3, and #5 go into town; the Dom stop is close to Market Square and the TI.

To **walk** toward town, cross over the busy Röntgenring and head up the shop-lined Kaiserstrasse. **Drivers** entering Würzburg can follow signs to the *Residenz* and parking in the vast cobbled square that faces the palace.

Rick's Tip: *For a quick 40-minute loop through town (with English headphone commentary), consider the* **tourist train** *(€9, leaves at the top of the hour in front of the Residenz, www.city-tour.info).*

Sights

▲▲RESIDENZ PALACE

In the early 18th century, Würzburg's powerful prince-bishop decided to relocate from his hilltop residence at Marienberg, across the river, into new digs down in the city. His opulent, custom-built, 360-room palace and its associated sights—the chapel (Hofkirche; worth ▲▲) and garden—are the main tourist attractions of today's Würzburg. This Franconian Versailles features grand rooms, 3-D art, and a massive fresco by Giovanni Battista Tiepolo.

Cost and Hours: Palace-€7.50, includes guided tour, daily April-Oct 9:00-18:00, Nov-March 10:00-16:30; chapel-free, same hours as palace; gardens-free, daily until dusk, www.residenz-wuerzburg.de.

Generations of Würzburg prince-bishops lived at the Residenz Palace.

Sightseeing Strategies and Tours: A guided tour is included with your ticket and covers the main rooms along with the otherwise inaccessible South Wing (45-60 minutes; English tours daily at 11:00 and 15:00, April-Oct also at 13:30 and 16:30). To see everything worthwhile, follow my self-guided tour, then jump onto any German tour heading into the South Wing.

⊙ SELF-GUIDED TOUR

• *Begin at the entrance.*

Vestibule and Garden Hall: This indoor area functioned as a grand circular driveway, exclusively for special occasions—just right for six-horse carriages to drop off their guests at the base of the stairs.

• *Now picture yourself dressed up in your fanciest imaginary finery...and ascend the stairs.*

Grand Staircase: The elegant stairway comes with low steps, enabling high-class ladies to glide up gracefully. Hold your lady's hand high and get into the ascending rhythm.

• *As you reach the top of the stairs, look up at the...*

Tiepolo Fresco: In 1752, the Venetian master Giovanni Battista Tiepolo was instructed to make a grand fresco illustrating the greatness of Europe, Würzburg, and the prince-bishop. And he did—completing the world's largest fresco (more than 7,000 square feet) in only 13 months.

The ceiling celebrates the esteemed prince-bishop, seen in the medallion wrapped with a red, ermine-trimmed cape. The ceiling features Apollo (in the sunburst) and a host of Greek gods, all paying homage to the P-B. Ringing the room are the four continents, each symbolized by a woman on an animal and pointing to the prince-bishop. Walk the perimeter of the room to study and enjoy the symbolism of each continent one by one: **America** on an alligator, **Africa** on a camel, **Asia** riding an elephant, and **Europe** on a bull.

White Hall: This "white" hall—a Rococo-stucco fantasy—is actually gray to provide better contrast with the colorful rooms on either side. The stucco decorations (particularly in the corners) have an armor-and-weapons theme, as this marked the entrance to the prince-bishop's private apartments—which had to be carefully guarded.

• *From the White Hall, continue to your left, following signs for Rundgang/Circuit.*

Imperial Hall: Enjoy the artistic ensemble of this fine room in its entirety and feel its liveliness. This glorious hall—which was smartly restored—is the ultimate example of Baroque: harmony, symmetry, illusion, and the bizarre.

The room features three scenes: On the ceiling, find Father Main amusing himself with a nymph. On the wall to the right as you enter, the bishop presides over the marriage of a happy Emperor Friedrich Barbarossa. The bishop's power is demonstrated through his oversized fingers (giving the benediction) and through the details of his miter (tall hat), which displays his coat of arms. On the left wall is the payoff: Barbarossa, now the Holy Roman Emperor, gives the bishop Franconia and the secular title of prince.

• *If you're not already on a guided tour, keep a lookout for any group headed from here into the South Wing—if you see one, join it. Otherwise, continue with me into the...*

North Wing (Northern Imperial Apartments): This string of lavish rooms—evolving from fancy Baroque to fancier Rococo—was used for the prince-bishop's VIP guests. It's a straight shot to the **Green Lacquered Room** in the far corner, named for its silver-leaf walls, painted green. The Escher-esque inlaid floor was painstakingly restored after WWII bombings.

Keep going through a few more small rooms, then step out into the **hallway** to see photos of the building's destruction in the 1945 firebombing of Würzburg and its subsequent restoration. While about three-quarters of the Residenz was destroyed during World War II, the most

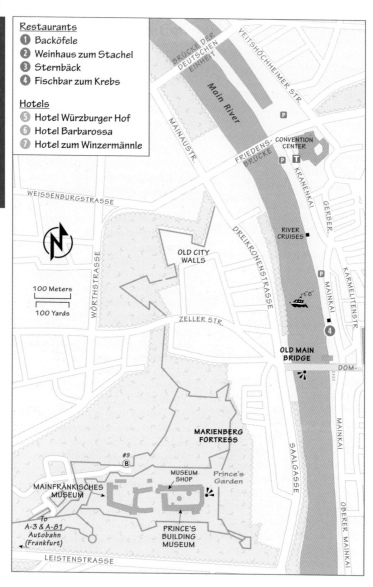

Restaurants
1. Backöfele
2. Weinhaus zum Stachel
3. Sternbäck
4. Fischbar zum Krebs

Hotels
5. Hotel Würzburger Hof
6. Hotel Barbarossa
7. Hotel zum Winzermännle

precious parts—the first rooms on this tour, including the Tiepolo frescoes—were unscathed. A temporary roof saved the palace from total ruin, but it was not until the late 1970s that it was returned to more or less its original condition.

• *If you haven't yet joined a tour but want to see the South Wing, find your way back to the Imperial Hall and wait until a group comes along. Then tag along for about 15 minutes as you stroll the...*

South Wing (By Tour Only): The dark and woody South Wing feels more masculine than the North Wing. You'll first come to the waiting room (antechamber), the audience chamber/throne room (with

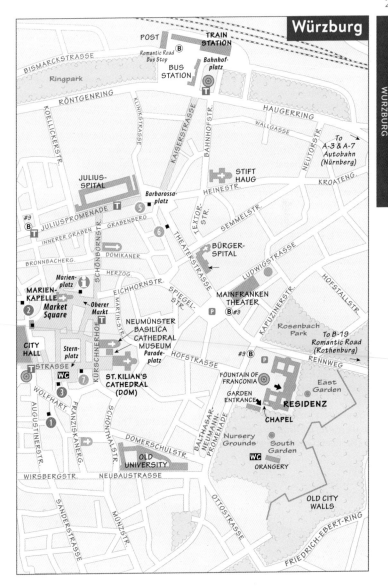

BISMARCKSTRASSE
POST
TRAIN STATION
Romantic Road Bus Stop
BUS STATION
Bahnhof-platz
Ringpark
RÖNTGENRING
HAUGERRING
WALLGASSE
To A-3 & A-7 Autobahn (Nürnberg)
KOELLICKERSTR.
KLINIKSTRASSE
KAISERSTRASSE
BAHNHOFSTR.
NEUTORSTR.
KROATENG.
JULIUS-SPITAL
Barbarossa-platz
STIFT HAUG
HEINESTR.
KROATENG.
#9
JULIUSPROMENADE
GRABENBERG
TEXTOR-STR.
SEMMELSTR.
LUDWIGSTRASSE
HOFSTALLSTR.
INNERER GRABEN
SCHÖNBORNSTR.
DOMIKANER
BÜRGER-SPITAL
BRONNBACHERG.
HERZOG.
Marien-platz
EICHHORNSTR.
SPIEGEL-STR.
THEATERSTRASSE
MAINFRANKEN THEATER
#9
Rosenbach Park
To B-19 Romantic Road (Rothenburg)
MARIEN-KAPELLE
Market Square
Oberer Markt
MARTIN-STR.
NEUMÜNSTER BASILICA CATHEDRAL MUSEUM
Parade-platz
HOFSTRASSE
RENNWEG
CITY HALL
Stern-platz
STRASSE
KÜRSCHNERHOF
ST. KILIAN'S CATHEDRAL (DOM)
#9
FOUNTAIN OF FRANCONIA
East Garden
WC
WOLFHART
AUGUSTINERSTR.
FRANZISKANERG.
SCHÖNTALSTR.
GARDEN ENTRANCE
BALTHASAR-NEUMANN-PROMENADE
RESIDENZ
CHAPEL
DOMERSCHULSTR.
Nursery Grounds
South Garden
WC
ORANGERY
OLD UNIVERSITY
WIRSBERGSTR.
NEUBAUSTRASSE
SANDERSTRASSE
MÜNZSTR.
OTTOSTRASSE
OLD CITY WALLS
FRIEDRICH-EBERT-RING

circa-1700 Belgian tapestries showing scenes from the life of Alexander the Great), and the Venetian Room (which was a bedroom; note the three tapestries, made around 1740 in Würzburg).

The 18th-century **Mirror Cabinet** was where the prince-bishop showed off his amazing wealth. It features six lavish pounds of gold leaf, lots of Asian influence, and allegories of the four continents in the corners (all restored after World War II).

The **Art Gallery** room is next, with portraits of different prince-bishops who ruled until the early 1800s, when Napoleon said, "Enough of this nonsense" and secularized politics in places like Franconia.

• *Finish your tour of the Residenz at the Court Chapel. To get there, head back down the stairs, past the ticket office and through the locker room. Follow signs to the southern wing of the big complex. An arch leads left into a courtyard, from which a humble door leads toward the ornate chapel. Follow signs to Court Chapel/Hofkirche.*

▲▲**Court Chapel** (Hofkirche): This sumptuous chapel was for the exclusive use of the prince-bishop and his court. The decor and design are textbook Baroque. Architect Johann Balthasar Neumann challenge was to bring in light and create symmetry. He did it with mirrors and hidden windows. All the gold is real—if paper-thin—gold leaf. The columns are "manufactured marble," which isn't marble at all but marbled plaster, half-inch veneer. You can tell if a "marble" column is real or fake by resting your hand on it. If it warms up, it's not marble.

The faded painting in the dome high above the altar shows three guys in gold robes losing their heads. The two side paintings are by the great fresco artist Tiepolo.

• *To reach the garden, enter through the gate at the right of the Residenz building.*

Residenz Garden: One of Germany's finest Baroque gardens is a delightful park cradling the palace. The South Garden, just inside the gate, features statues of Greek gods; carefully trimmed, remarkably conical, 18th-century yew trees; and an orangery (at the far back). The nursery grounds (to the right) is like a wild park. The East Garden, directly behind the palace around to the left, is grand—à la Versailles—using terraces to create the illusion of spaciousness.

MARIENBERG FORTRESS (FESTUNG MARIENBERG)

This 13th-century fortified retreat was the original residence of Würzburg's prince-bishops before the opulent Residenz was built. After being stormed by the Swedish army during the 17th-century Thirty Years' War, the fortress was expanded in Baroque style.

Cost and Hours: Grounds and Prince's Garden-free, daily 9:00-17:30 except Mon until 16:00, closed Nov-March, tel. 0931/355-1750, www.schloesser.bayern.de.

Tours and Information: On weekends from April to October, a 45-minute English-language tour brings the fortress to life (€3.50, Sat-Sun at 15:00).

Getting There: To walk there, cross the Old Main Bridge and follow small *Festung Marienberg* signs to the right uphill for a

Sunset in Würzburg

heart-thumping 20 minutes. Or take infrequent bus #9 (direction: Festung) to the last stop (Schönborntor) and walk through the tunnel to enter the fortress. Taxis wait near the Old Main Bridge (€10 to fortress).

Visiting the Fortress: The **fortress grounds** provide fine city views and a good place for a picnic. You can wander freely through the fortress courtyards and peek into the original tower stronghold and the round church, where carved relief monuments to former bishops decorate the stone floor. For the best views of the town, go through the archway off the inner courtyard (next to church entrance) into the **Prince's Garden**—look for the *Fürstengarten* sign.

The fortress houses two museums: The **Mainfränkisches Museum** highlights the work of Tilman Riemenschneider, Germany's top woodcarver, and the **Prince's Building Museum** (Fürstenbaumuseum) shows off relics of the prince-bishops and the history of Würzburg (small admission fee, both closed Mon).

Eating

$$$ Backöfele is a fun hole-in-the-wall offering a rustic menu (reservations smart, Ursulinergasse 2, www.backoefele. de). **$$$ Weinhaus zum Stachel** is an elegant setting for gourmet Franconian meals (closed Mon, reservations smart, Gressengasse 1, www.weinhaus-stachel. de). **$$ Sternbäck** is an inviting *Kneipe* (pub) with rickety tables and cheap eats (Sternplatz 4). **$ Fischbar zum Krebs** is a fun-loving little fish-and-chips boat tied up near the Old Main Bridge (closed in bad weather and Nov-April).

Sleeping

$$$ Hotel Würzburger Hof has large, Baroque rooms (Barbarossaplatz 2, www. hotel-wuerzburgerhof.de), while **$$ Hotel Barbarossa** has a more modern sensibility (RS%, Theaterstrasse 2, www. hotelbarbarossa-wuerzburg.de). **$$ Hotel zum Winzermännle** is simple but tasteful (Domstrasse 32, www.winzermaennle.de).

BEST OF THE REST

Nürnberg

Nürnberg ("Nuremberg" in English), Bavaria's second city, is known for its glorious medieval architecture, important Germanic history museum, haunting Nazi past, and Germany's biggest Christmas market.

Nürnberg's large Imperial Castle marked it as a stronghold of the Holy Roman Empire. Today, though Nürnberg has a half-million residents, the charming Old Town—with its red-sandstone Gothic buildings—makes visitors feel like they are in a far smaller city. Nürnberg's downtown is lively and inviting day and night.

Day Plan

Stroll from the train station through the Old Town up to the castle, stopping at sights of interest along the way (including the outstanding Germanic National Museum). Then visit the Nazi Documentation Center and Rally Grounds (easy to reach on public transit). Nearly all of the city's museums are closed on Monday.

Orientation

Nürnberg's Old Town is surrounded by a three-mile-long wall and moat, with a ring road beyond that. At the southeast corner of the ring is the train station; across the street, just inside the ring, is the medieval Königstor gate. The former Nazi Rally Grounds are southeast of the center.

Tourist Information: Nürnberg's TI is in a modern building just opposite the Königstor gate (daily, Königstrasse 93, tel. 0911/233-6132, www.tourismus. nuernberg.de).

Nürnberg's Old Town

Getting There

Direct trains run frequently from **Würz-burg** and **Munich** (2-3/hour, 1 hour); there are hourly departures from **Rothenburg** (1.5 hours). To reach the **Königstor** (the medieval city's southern gate) from the station, follow signs for *Ausgang/City* down the escalator, then signs to *Altstadt* in the underpass. When you emerge, the TI is on your right and the Königstor tower is on your left.

To go directly from the station by tram to the **Nazi Documentation Center** and the **former Nazi Rally Grounds,** follow pink *Tram* signs in the underpass and head up the escalators to the stop in front of the Postbank Center. Get your ticket from the red vending machine (marked *VAG Fahrausweise,* near the stairwell for the U-Bahn) and catch tram #9 (direction: Doku-Zentrum).

Drivers will find a handful of well-signed public garages located within the city walls.

Sights

▲▲ST. LAWRENCE CHURCH (LORENZKIRCHE)

This once-Catholic, now-Protestant church is a massive house of worship. The interior wasn't completely furnished until more than a century after the church was built—just in time for the Reformation. Most of the decorations inside were donated by wealthy Nürnbergers trying to cut down on their time in purgatory. Through the centuries, this art survived three separate threats: the iconoclasm of the Reformation, the whitewashing of the Baroque age, and the bombing of World War II.

While Nürnberg was the first "free imperial city" to break with the Catholic Church and become Lutheran, locals didn't go wild in tearing down the rich, Mary-oriented decor of their fine churches. Suspended over the altar, the sculptural **Annunciation** is by Veit Stoss, a Nürnberg citizen and one of Central Europe's best woodcarvers.

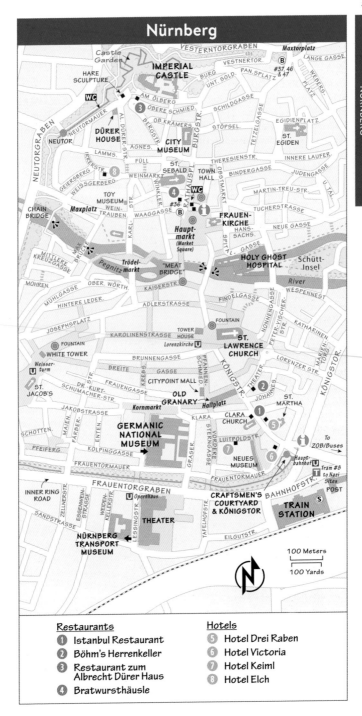

Nürnberg

Restaurants

1. Istanbul Restaurant
2. Böhm's Herrenkeller
3. Restaurant zum Albrecht Dürer Haus
4. Bratwursthäusle

Hotels

5. Hotel Drei Raben
6. Hotel Victoria
7. Hotel Keiml
8. Hotel Elch

Cost and Hours: €2 donation requested, Mon-Sat 9:00-17:00, Sun 13:00-16:00, www.lorenzkirche.de.

▲▲HAUPTMARKT (MAIN MARKET SQUARE)

When Nürnberg began booming in the 13th century, it consisted of two distinct walled towns separated by the river. As the towns grew, they merged and the middle wall came down. This square, built by Holy Roman Emperor Charles IV, became the center of the newly united city. The most powerful man in Europe in his time, Charles oversees the square from a perch high on the facade of the Frauenkirche, the church on the square.

Year-round, the Hauptmarkt is lively every day but Sunday with fruit, flower, and souvenir stands. For a few weeks before Christmas, it hosts Germany's largest Christmas market.

Opposite the Frauenkirche, the pointy gold **Beautiful Fountain** (Schöner Brunnen) is packed with allegorical meaning representing everything from the earthly arts (such as philosophy, music, and astronomy) to the electors of the Holy Roman Emperor and the prophets.

Connoisseurs of sausage and bread will want to take a short side-trip from here: Head a block down Waaggasse (the street leading left, away from the Beautiful Fountain) and take a quick left on Winklerstrasse to find the recommended **Schwarz Bakery** one block down.

▲IMPERIAL CASTLE (KAISERBURG)

In the Middle Ages, Holy Roman Emperors stayed here when they were in town, and the imperial regalia, including the imperial cross, imperial sword, and crown, were stored here from 1424 until 1796.

Cost and Hours: €5.50 for castle only, €3.50 for Deep Well and Sinwell Tower, €7 combo-ticket, €2 audioguide, daily 9:00-18:00, Oct-March 10:00-16:00, tel. 0911/244-6590, www.kaiserburg-nuernberg.de.

Visiting the Castle: For a no-way-to-get-lost, one-way route, just follow the *Rundgang* signs.

The **Lower Hall** is empty of furniture because, in the 12th century, the imperial court was mobile. Royal roadies would arrive and set things up before the emperor got there. Through the door at the end of the hall, find the **Romanesque church**—one of few buildings that wasn't destroyed during World War II. It has a triple-decker design: lower nobility on the lower floor, upper nobility above that, and the emperor

Hauptmarkt

worshipping from the topmost balcony.

The **Upper Hall** (also called the Imperial Hall) is most interesting, with interactive screens and artifacts that show what the heck the Holy Roman Empire actually was. Then comes a series of creaky-floored **former living quarters,** with painted ceilings (many dismantled and stored in bunkers during the war—they're that precious), and a copy of the imperial crown (the original is in Vienna). The final exhibit is on **old weapons.**

There are other interesting parts of the complex. The **Deep Well** is indeed deep—165 feet. Visits are simple, fun, and only possible with a guide (10-minute English tours leave on the hour and half-hour; separate or combo-ticket required). You'll see water poured way, waaay down—into an incredible hole dug in the 14th century.

A climb up the **Sinwell Tower** offers only a higher city view and lots of exercise—113 steps. For an easy alternative, walk out around the round tower to enjoy a commanding **city view** from the rampart just behind it. Then find your way to the fine **castle garden** (*Burggarten*). Wrapped around the back of the castle, the garden offers great views of the town's 16th-century fortifications and former moat.

Albrecht Dürer House

▲ALBRECHT DÜRER HOUSE

Nürnberg's most famous resident lived in this house for the last 20 years of his life. Albrecht Dürer (1471-1528), a contemporary of Michelangelo, studied in Venice and brought the Renaissance to stodgy medieval Germany. As a painter of exquisite detail, Dürer attracted royal patrons such as Emperors Maximilian I, Charles V, and King Christian II of Denmark, but he gained his steady income and international fame from the "mass production" of his prints.

Nothing in the museum is original (except the house itself, which survived WWII bombs). But the museum does a fine job of capturing the way Dürer actually lived, and it includes a replica of the workshop, with a working printing press, where he painted and printed his woodcuts and metal engravings.

Cost and Hours: €6 includes audioguide; Mon-Wed and Fri 10:00-17:00, Thu until 20:00, Sat-Sun until 18:00, closed Mon Oct-June; ask about daily art demonstrations, Albrecht-Dürer-Strasse 39, tel. 0911/231-2568, www.museums.nuremberg.de.

▲▲▲GERMANIC NATIONAL MUSEUM (GERMANISCHES NATIONALMUSEUM)

This sprawling, sweeping museum is dedicated to the cultural history of the German-speaking world. It occupies an interconnected maze of buildings, old and new, in the southern part of the Old Town.

Cost and Hours: €8, free Wed after 18:00; open Tue-Sun 10:00-18:00, Wed until 21:00, closed Mon; worthwhile audioguide-€2 (ID required), check website for occasional English tours, two blocks west of Königstrasse at Kartäusergasse 1, enter through the modern glass lobby in middle of street, tel. 0911/13310, www.gnm.de.

Visiting the Museum: The museum's star attraction is its **German art collection**. You'll find Albrecht Dürer's meticulously detailed paintings, Lucas Cranach the Younger's polyptych *Heart-Shaped Winged Altarpiece*, and works by wood-carver Tilman Riemenschneider.

Another highlight is the oldest surviving **globe** in the world, crafted by Nürnberg's own Martin Behaim (1492). For those interested in the Reformation, there's a wonderful Martin Luther section.

▲▲NÜRNBERG TRANSPORT MUSEUM

Just outside the city walls, within the mighty Nürnberg Transport Museum building, are the Deutsche Bahn's German Railway (DB) Museum and the Communications Museum. As you'll end up weaving in and out of both museums—and your ticket includes both—think of them as one sight. Exhibits tell the story of the German railroad system with a focus on how it influenced the nation's history. Don't miss "Mad" King Ludwig's crown-topped *Salonwagen*—practically a palace on wheels, complete with a rolling veranda.

Cost and Hours: €6, €5 with any same-day transit ticket, free with valid rail pass; Tue-Fri 9:00-17:00, Sat-Sun 10:00-18:00, closed Mon; Lessingstrasse 6; DB Museum tel. 0800-326-87386, www.dbmuseum.de.

Nazi Sites

The sprawling complex containing the Nazi Documentation Center and Rally Grounds is wrapped around a lake called Dutzendteich, southeast of the Old Town. Take tram #8 from the train station (direction: Doku-Zentrum, 10-minute trip) or bus #36 from the Hauptmarkt on Waaggasse. Both options go about every 10 minutes.

▲▲▲NAZI DOCUMENTATION CENTER (DOKUMENTATIONSZENTRUM)

Visitors to Europe's Nazi and Holocaust sites inevitably ask the same question: How could this happen? This superb museum does its best to provide an answer. It meticulously traces the evolution of the National Socialist movement, focusing on how it both energized and terrified the German people. Special attention is paid to Nürnberg's role in the Nazi movement, including the construction and use of the Rally Grounds, where Hitler's largest demonstrations took place.

Cost and Hours: €6, includes essential audioguide, Mon-Fri 9:00-18:00, Sat-Sun from 10:00, last entry at 17:00, Bayernstrasse 110, tel. 0911/231-7538, www.museen.nuernberg.de.

▲RALLY GROUNDS (REICHSPARTEITAGSGELÄNDE)

The Rally Grounds occupy four square miles behind the museum. Albert Speer designed this immense complex of buildings for the Nazi rallies. Not many of Hitler's ambitious plans were completed, but you can visit the courtyard of the Congress Hall, Zeppelin Field (where Hitler addressed his followers), and a few other remains. The easiest way to see them is to follow the circular route around the lake that's shown on the "Nazi Documentation Center & Rally Grounds" map and on the museum's free bilingual area plan (*Geländeplan*).

Figure a 1.5-hour round-trip from the Documentation Center for the full circuit. If you have less time, just look into the courtyard of the Congress Hall from the perch at the end of your museum visit and then walk the short way around the lake directly to Zeppelin Field and back.

Eating

$$$ Istanbul Restaurant is a local favorite for Turkish food (Königstrasse 60).

Nazi Documentation Center

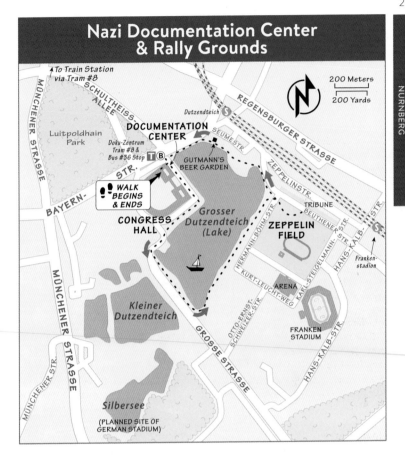

Nazi Documentation Center & Rally Grounds

$$$ **Böhm's Herrenkeller** serves classic Franconian standards at good prices (closed Sun, Theatergasse 9). At $$ **Restaurant zum Albrecht Dürer Haus,** the menu is updated Franconian (closed Mon, Obere Schmiedgasse 58). $ **Bratwursthäusle** is a high-energy place serving the best bratwurst in town—all made in-house (closed Sun, Rathausplatz 1).

Rick's Tip: *Nürnberg is famous for its* **pinkie-sized bratwurst,** *the "Nürnberger." All over town, signs read 3 im Weckle (or im Weggle), meaning "three Nürnberger bratwurst in a blankie." It's a good snack for about €3.*

Sleeping
$$$ **Hotel Drei Raben** is an artsy and fun splurge (Königstrasse 63, www.hoteldreiraben.de). $$ **Hotel Victoria** offers new-feeling rooms behind its historic 1896 facade (Königstrasse 80, www.hotelvictoria.de). $ **Hotel Keiml** rents bright if worn rooms (RS%, Luitpoldstrasse 7, www.hotel-keiml.de). $$$ **Hotel Elch,** the oldest hotel in town, is buried deep in the Old Town (Irrerstrasse 9, www.hotel-elch.com).

Rhine Valley

The Rhine Valley is storybook Germany, a fairy-tale world of legends and "robber-baron" castles. Cruise the most turret-studded stretch of the romantic Rhine as you listen for the song of the treacherous Loreley. For hands-on thrills, climb through the Rhineland's greatest castle, Rheinfels, above the town of St. Goar. Castle connoisseurs enjoy the fine interiors of Marksburg Castle near Koblenz and Burg Eltz on the Mosel River.

Spend your nights in a castle-crowned village, either Bacharach or St. Goar. They're 10 miles apart, connected by milk-run trains, riverboats, and a riverside bike path. Bacharach is a more interesting town, but St. Goar has the famous Rheinfels Castle.

Marvel at the Rhine's ever-changing parade. Ever since Roman times, when this was the empire's northern boundary, the Rhine has been one of the world's busiest shipping rivers. Traveling along the river today, you'll see a steady flow of barges with 1,000- to 2,000-ton loads. Cars, buses, and trains rush along highways and tracks lining both banks as cruiseboats glide by, making it easy to get around.

If possible, visit the Rhine between April and October, when it's at its touristic best. In winter, some sights close, along with some hotels and restaurants, and only one riverboat runs.

THE RHINE VALLEY IN 1 OR 2 DAYS

With one day and two nights, stay in Bacharach. Cruise the best and most scenic stretch of the river (the hour from Bacharach to St. Goar), and tour Rheinfels Castle. Enjoy dinner in Bacharach, and maybe a wine tasting, too.

For a busier day, take a longer cruise, following all or part of my Rhine Blitz Tour. For example, you could cruise from Bacharach to Braubach (to tour Marksburg Castle), before returning by train to Bacharach.

With a second day, visit Burg Eltz on the Mosel as a day trip. Or bike or hike along the Rhine. This is a fun place to relax and explore.

If you're traveling by car, park it at your hotel, cruise the Rhine by boat, and visit Burg Eltz and/or Cologne on your drive in or out.

RHINE VALLEY AT A GLANCE

On the Rhine

▲▲▲**Rhine Blitz Tour** One of Europe's great joys—touring the Rhine River by boat, train, bike, or car. See page 234.

▲▲▲**Rheinfels Castle** The best opportunity to explore a ruined castle on the river. **Hours:** Daily 9:00-18:00, Nov-mid-March possibly Sat-Sun only 11:00-17:00 (call ahead). See page 256.

▲▲**Marksburg Castle in Braubach** The best-preserved medieval castle on the Rhine. **Hours:** Daily 10:00-17:00, Nov-mid-March 11:00-16:00, last tour departs one hour before closing. See page 262.

Near the Rhine Valley

▲▲▲**Burg Eltz, on the Mosel** My favorite castle in Europe, set deep in a forest, with a rare furnished interior—take the required guided tour. **Hours:** Daily from 9:30, last tour departs at 17:30, closed Nov-March. See page 266.

▲▲▲**Cologne Cathedral** Germany's most exciting church, with a massive facade, vast interior, tower climb, and an easy-to-visit location next to the train station. **Hours:** Mon-Sat 9:30-11:30 & 12:30-16:30, Sun 12:30-16:30, closed to sightseers during services. See page 270.

Rhine Overview

Düsseldorf

Rhine

Cologne

UNROMANTIC RHINE

Bonn

Aachen

Remagen

BEST OF THE RHINE
See detail map

BELG.

BURG ELTZ

Koblenz

St. Goar

Cochem

Beilstein

Oberwesel

Bingen

Wies-baden

Frankfurt

Main R.

Frankfurt

Mosel R.

Bacharach

Mainz

LUX.

Trier

Hahn

Lux. City

GERMANY

Neckar R.

Heidelberg

Rhine

50 Kilometers
50 Miles

FRANCE

Berlin
GERMANY

N

Rick's Tip: *Rhine Valley* **guesthouses and hotels often have similar names.** *When reserving, double-check that you're contacting the one in your planned destination.*

RHINE BLITZ TOUR

One of Europe's great train thrills is zipping along the Rhine enjoying this self-guided blitz tour, worth ▲▲▲. For short distances, cruising is best because it's slower. A cruise going upstream (heading south, toward Bingen) takes longer than the same cruise going downstream (north, toward Koblenz). If you want to draw out

a short cruise, go upstream (for instance, from St. Goar to Bacharach).

To cover long distances (e.g., Koblenz to Bingen), consider the train. Or take the boat one way and the train back. See page 241 for specifics on traveling the Rhine.

➲ Self-Guided Tour

This quick and easy tour (you can cut in anywhere) skips most of the syrupy myths filling normal Rhine guides. You can follow along on a train, boat, bike, or car. By train or boat, sit on the left (river) side going south from Koblenz.

You'll notice large black-and-white kilometer markers along the riverbank. I erected these years ago to make this tour

Castles of the Rhine

Many of the castles of the Rhine were "robber-baron" castles, put there by petty rulers (there were 300 independent little countries in medieval Germany) to levy tolls on passing river traffic. A robber baron would put his castle on, or even in, the river. Then, often with the help of chains and a tower on the opposite bank, he'd stop each ship and get his toll. There were 10 customs stops in the 60-mile stretch between Mainz and Koblenz alone.

Some castles were built to control and protect settlements, and others were the residences of kings. As times changed, so did the lifestyles of the rich and feudal. Many castles were abandoned for more comfortable mansions in the towns.

Most Rhine castles date from the 11th, 12th, and 13th centuries. When the pope successfully asserted his power over the German emperor in 1076, local princes ran wild over the rule of their emperor. The castles saw military action in the 1300s and 1400s, as emperors began reasserting their control over Germany's many silly kingdoms.

The castles were also involved in the Reformation wars, in which Europe's Catholic and Protestant dynasties fought it out using a fragmented Germany as their battleground. The Thirty Years' War (1618-1648) devastated Germany. The outcome: Each ruler got the freedom to decide if his people would be Catholic or Protestant, and one-third of Germans died. (Production of Gummi Bears ceased entirely.)

The French—who feared a strong Germany and felt the Rhine was the logical border between them and Germany—destroyed most of the castles as a preventive measure (Louis XIV in the 1680s, the Revolutionary army in the 1790s, and Napoleon in 1806). Many were rebuilt in the Neo-Gothic style in the Romantic Age—the late 1800s—and today are enjoyed as restaurants, hotels, hostels, and museums.

easier to follow. They tell the distance from the Rhine Falls, where the Rhine leaves Switzerland and becomes navigable. (Today, river-barge pilots also use these markers to navigate.)

We're tackling just 36 miles (58 km) of the 820-mile-long (1,320-km) Rhine. This "Best of the Rhine" tour starts at Koblenz and heads upstream to Bingen. If you're going the other direction, it still works. Just hold the book upside-down.

🎧 Download my free Best of the Rhine audio tour—it works in either direction.

Koblenz to Bingen

Many of these sights are described in greater detail later in this chapter.

Little Bacharach's dock and boat ramp

Km 590—Koblenz: This Rhine blitz starts with Romantic Rhine thrills, at Koblenz. Koblenz isn't terribly attractive (it was hit hard in World War II), but its place at the historic Deutsches Eck ("German Corner")—the tip of land where the Mosel River joins the Rhine—gives it a certain patriotic charm. A cable car links the Deutsches Eck with the yellow Ehrenbreitstein Fortress across the river.

Km 586—Lahneck Castle: Above the modern autobahn bridge over the Lahn River, this castle *(Burg)* was built in 1240 to defend local silver mines. The castle was ruined by the French in 1688 and rebuilt in the 1850s in Neo-Gothic style. Burg Lahneck faces another Romantic rebuild, the yellow Schloss Stolzenfels (€5, out of view above the train, Tue-Sun 10:00-18:00, closed Mon, Sat-Sun only and shorter hours off-season, closed Dec-Jan, a 10-minute climb from tiny parking lot, www.schloss-stolzenfels.de). Note that a *Burg* is a defensive fortress, while a *Schloss* is mainly a showy palace.

Km 580—Marksburg Castle: This castle stands bold and white—restored to look like most Rhine castles once did, with their slate stonework covered with stucco to look as if made from a richer stone. You'll spot Marksburg with the three modern smokestacks behind it (these vent Europe's biggest car-battery recycling plant just up the valley), just before the town of Spay. This is the best-looking of all the Rhine

castles and the only surviving medieval castle on the Rhine. Because of its commanding position, it was never attacked in the Middle Ages (though it was captured by the US Army in March 1945). It's now a museum with a medieval interior second only to the Mosel Valley's Burg Eltz.

Km 570—Boppard: Once a Roman town, Boppard has some impressive remains of fourth-century walls. Look for the Roman towers and the substantial chunk of Roman wall near the train station, just above the main square.

If you visit Boppard, head to the fascinating Church of St. Severus below the main square. Find the carved Romanesque crazies at the doorway. Inside, to the right of the entrance, you'll see Christian symbols from Roman times. Also notice the painted arches and vaults (originally, most Romanesque churches were painted this way). Down by the river, look for the high-water *(Hochwasser)* marks on the arches from various flood years. You'll find these flood marks throughout the Rhine and Mosel valleys.

Km 567—Sterrenberg Castle and Liebenstein Castle: These neighboring castles, across from the town of Bad Salzig, are known as the "Hostile Brothers." Notice how they're isolated from each other by a low-slung wall. The wall was built to improve defenses from both castles, but this is the *romantic* Rhine so there has to be a legend: Take one wall between

Boppard

Maus Castle

castles, add two greedy and jealous brothers and a fair maiden, and create your own legend. **$$$ Burg Liebenstein** is now a fun, friendly, and reasonably affordable family-run hotel (9 rooms, giant king-and-the-family room, easy parking, tel. 06773/251, www.castle-liebenstein.com, info@burg-liebenstein.de, Nickenig family).

Km 559—Maus Castle: The Maus (mouse) got its name because the next castle was owned by the Katzenelnbogen family. (*Katz* means "cat.") In the 1300s, it was considered a state-of-the-art fortification...until 1806, when Napoleon Bonaparte had it blown apart with then-state-of-the-art explosives. It was rebuilt true to its original plans in about 1900. Today, Burg Maus is open for concerts, weddings, and guided tours in German (20-minute walk up, weekends only, reservations required, tel. 06771/2303, www.burg-maus.de).

St. Goar to Bacharach: The Best of the Rhine

Km 557—St. Goar and Rheinfels Castle: Cross to the other side of the train. The pleasant town of St. Goar was named for a sixth-century hometown monk. It originated in Celtic times as a place where sailors would stop, catch their breath, send home a postcard, and give thanks after surviving the seductive and treacherous Loreley crossing. St. Goar is worth a stop to explore its mighty Rheinfels Castle.

Km 556—Katz Castle: Burg Katz (Katzenelnbogen) faces St. Goar from across the river. Together, Burg Katz (built in 1371) and Rheinfels Castle had a clear view up and down the river, effectively controlling traffic (there was absolutely no duty-free shopping on the medieval Rhine). Katz got Napoleoned in 1806 and rebuilt in about 1900.

About Km 555: A statue of the Loreley, the beautiful-but-deadly nymph, combs her hair at the end of a long spit—built to give barges protection from vicious ice floes that until recent years raged down the river in the winter. The actual Loreley, a landmark cliff, is just ahead.

Km 554—The Loreley: Steep a big slate rock in centuries of legend and it becomes a tourist attraction—the ultimate Rhinestone. The Loreley (name painted near shoreline), rising 450 feet over the narrowest and deepest point of the Rhine, has long been important. It was a holy site in pre-Roman days. The fine echoes here—thought to be

The scenic cliffs of the Rhine, steeped in history

The Rhine River Trade and Barge-Watching

The Rhine is great for barge-watching. There's a constant parade of action, and each boat is different. Since ancient times, this has been a highway for trade. Today, Europe's biggest port (Rotterdam) waits at the mouth of the river.

Barge workers are almost a subculture. Many own their own ships. The captain lives in the stern, with his family. The family car is often parked on the stern. Workers live in the bow.

The flag of the boat's home country flies in the stern (Dutch—horizontal red, white, and blue; Belgian—vertical black, yellow, and red; Swiss—white cross on a red field; German—horizontal black, red, and yellow; French—vertical red, white, and blue). Logically, imports go upstream (Japanese cars, coal, and oil) and exports go downstream (German cars, chemicals, and pharmaceuticals). A clever captain ships goods in each direction. Recently, giant Dutch container ships (which transport five times the cargo) have been driving many of the traditional barges out of business, presenting the German economy with another challenge.

Going downstream, tugs can push a floating train of up to five barges at once, but upstream, as the slope gets steeper (and the stream gradient gets higher), they can push only one at a time. Before modern shipping, horses dragged boats upstream. From 1873 to 1900, workers laid a chain from Bonn to Bingen, and boats with cogwheels and steam engines hoisted themselves upstream. Today, 265 million tons travel each year along the 530 miles from Basel on the German-Swiss border to the Dutch city of Rotterdam on the Atlantic.

Riverside navigational aids are vital. Boats pass on the right unless they clearly signal otherwise with a large blue sign. Since ships heading downstream can't stop or maneuver as freely, boats heading upstream are expected to do the tricky do-si-do work. Cameras monitor traffic all along and relay warnings of oncoming ships by posting large triangular signals before narrow and troublesome bends in the river. Each triangle tells whether there's a ship in that sector. When the bottom side of a triangle is lit, that sector is empty. When the left side is lit, an oncoming ship is in that sector.

ghostly voices—fertilized legend-tellers' imaginations.

Because of the reefs just upstream (at km 552), many ships never made it to St. Goar. Sailors (after days on the river) blamed their misfortune on a *wunderbare Fräulein*, whose long, blond hair almost covered her body. Heinrich Heine's *Song of Loreley* tells the story of a count sending his men to kill or capture this siren after

she distracted his horny son, who forgot to watch where he was sailing and drowned. When the soldiers cornered the nymph in her cave, she called her father (Father Rhine) for help. Huge waves, the likes of which you'll never see today, rose from the river and carried Loreley to safety. And she has never been seen since.

But alas, when the moon shines brightly and the tour buses are parked, a soft, playful Rhine whine can still be heard from the Loreley. As you pass, listen carefully ("Sailors...sailors...over my bounding mane"). Today a visitors center keeps the story alive; if you visit you can hike to the top of the cliff.

Km 552—The Seven Maidens: Killer reefs, marked by red-and-green buoys, are called the "Seven Maidens." OK, one more goofy legend: The prince of Schönburg Castle (über Oberwesel—described next) had seven spoiled daughters who always dumped men because of their shortcomings. Fed up, he invited seven of his knights to the castle and demanded that his daughters each choose one to marry. But they complained that each man had too big a nose, was too fat, too stupid, and so on. The rude and teasing girls escaped into a riverboat. Just downstream, God turned them into the seven rocks that form this reef. While this story probably isn't entirely true, there was a lesson in it for medieval children: Don't be hard-hearted.

Km 550—Oberwesel: Cross to the other side of the train. The town of Oberwesel, topped by the commanding Schönburg Castle (now a hotel), boasts some of the best medieval wall and tower remains on the Rhine.

Notice how many of the train tunnels along here have entrances designed like medieval turrets—they were actually built in the Romantic 19th century. OK, back to the riverside.

Km 547—Gutenfels Castle and Pfalz Castle, the Classic Rhine View: Burg Gutenfels (now a privately owned hotel) and the shipshape Pfalz Castle (built in the river in the 1300s) worked effectively to tax medieval river traffic. The town of Kaub grew rich as Pfalz raised its chains when boats came, and lowered them only when the merchants had paid their duty. Those who didn't pay spent time touring its prison, on a raft at the bottom of its well. In 1504, a pope called for the destruction of Pfalz, but the locals withstood a six-week siege, and the castle still

Pfalz Castle (left) and Gutenfels Castle (on hillside)

stands. Notice the overhanging outhouse (tiny white room between two wooden ones). Pfalz (also known as Pfalzgrafenstein) is tourable but bare and dull (€2.50 ferry from Kaub, €3 entry, Tue-Sun 10:00-18:00, closed Mon; shorter hours in March; Nov and Jan-Feb Sat-Sun only, closed Dec; last entry one hour before closing, mobile 0172-262-2800, www.burg-pfalzgrafenstein.de).

In Kaub, on the riverfront directly below the castles, a green statue (near the waving flags) honors the German general Gebhard von Blücher. He was Napoleon's nemesis. In 1813, as Napoleon fought his way back to Paris after his disastrous Russian campaign, he stopped at Mainz—hoping to fend off the Germans and Russians pursuing him by controlling that strategic bridge. Blücher tricked Napoleon. By building the first major pontoon bridge of its kind here at the Pfalz Castle, he crossed the Rhine and outflanked the French. Two years later, Blücher and Wellington teamed up to defeat Napoleon once and for all at Waterloo.

Immediately opposite Kaub (where the ferry lands, marked by blue roadside flags) is a gaping hole in the mountainside. This marks the last working slate mine on the Rhine.

Km 544—"The Raft Busters": Just before Bacharach, at the top of the island, buoys mark a gang of rocks notorious for busting up rafts. The Black Forest, upstream from here, was once poor, and wood was its best export. Black Foresters would ride log booms down the Rhine to the Ruhr (where their timber fortified coal-mine shafts) or to Holland (where logs were sold to shipbuilders). If they could navigate the sweeping bend just before Bacharach and then survive these "raft busters," they'd come home reckless and horny—the German folkloric equivalent of American cowboys after payday.

Km 543—Bacharach and Stahleck Castle: Cross to the other side of the train. The town of Bacharach is a great stop. Some of the Rhine's best wine is from this town, whose name likely derives from "altar to Bacchus" (the Roman god of wine). Local vintners brag that the medieval Pope Pius II ordered Bacharach wine by the cartload. Perched above the town, the 13th-century Burg Stahleck is now a hostel. Return to the riverside.

Km 541—Lorch: This stub of a castle is barely visible from the road. The hillside vineyards once blanketed four times as much land as they do today, but modern economics have driven most of them out of business. The vineyards that do survive require government subsidies. Notice the small car ferry, one of several along the bridgeless stretch between Mainz and Koblenz.

Km 538—Sooneck Castle: Cross back to the other side of the train. Built in the 11th century, this castle was twice destroyed by people sick and tired of robber barons.

Km 534—Reichenstein Castle and **Km 533—Rheinstein Castle:** Stay on the other side of the train to see two of the first castles to be rebuilt in the Romantic era. Both are privately owned, tourable, and connected by a pleasant trail. Go back to the river side.

Km 530—Ehrenfels Castle: Opposite Bingerbrück and the Bingen station, you'll see the ghostly Ehrenfels Castle (clobbered by the Swedes in 1636 and by the French in 1689). Since it had no view of the river traffic to the north, the owner built the cute little *Mäuseturm* (mouse tower) on an island (the yellow tower you'll see near the train station today). Rebuilt in the 1800s in Neo-Gothic style, it's now used as a Rhine navigation signal station.

Km 528—Niederwald Monument: Across from the Bingen station on a

Stahleck Castle

Sooneck Castle

Ehrenfels Castle, with its little "mouse tower" on the river

Rhein in Flammen

During the annual "Rhine in Flames" festival, spectacular displays of fireworks take place along the most scenic stretches of the Rhine, while beautifully illuminated ships ply the river, offering up-close views of the fireworks above. Held on five separate days between May and September, the festival rotates between several Rhine towns. Traditional wine festivals and other local celebrations are often timed to coincide with the Rhein in Flammen (www.rhein-in-flammen.com).

hilltop is the 120-foot-high Niederwald monument, a memorial built with 32 tons of bronze in 1877 to commemorate "the re-establishment of the German Empire." A lift takes tourists to this statue from the famous and extremely touristy wine town of Rüdesheim.

From here, the Romantic Rhine becomes the industrial Rhine, and our tour is over.

Transportation
Getting Around the Rhine

The Rhine flows north from Switzerland to Holland, but the scenic stretch from Mainz to Koblenz hoards all the touristic charm. Studded with the crenellated cream of Germany's castles, it bustles with boats, trains, and highway traffic. Have fun exploring with a mix of big steamers, tiny ferries (*Fähre*), trains, and bikes.

BY BOAT

While some travelers do the whole Mainz-Koblenz trip by boat (5.5 hours downstream, 8.5 hours up), I'd just focus on the most scenic hour—from Bacharach to St. Goar. Sit on the boat's top deck with your handy Rhine map-guide (or the

kilometer-keyed tour in this chapter) and enjoy the parade of castles, towns, boats, and vineyards.

Two boat companies take travelers along this stretch of the Rhine. Boats run daily in both directions from early April through October, with only one boat running off-season.

Most travelers sail on the bigger, more expensive, and romantic **Köln-Düsseldorfer (K-D) Line** (recommended Bacharach-St. Goar trip: €14.80 one-way, €16.80 round-trip, bikes-€2.80/day; discounts: up to 30 percent if over 60, 20 percent with connecting train ticket, 20 percent with rail passes and does not count as a flexipass day; tel. 06741/1634 in St. Goar, tel. 06743/1322 in Bacharach, www.k-d.com). I've included an abridged K-D cruise schedule in this chapter. Complete, up-to-date schedules are posted at any Rhineland station, hotel, TI, and www.k-d.com. (Confirm times at your hotel the night before.) Purchase tickets at the dock up to five minutes before departure. The boat is never full. Romantics will enjoy the old-time paddle-wheeler *Goethe,* which sails each direction once a day (noted on schedule, confirm time locally).

K-D Line Rhine Cruise Schedule

This schedule is approximate; check www.k-d.com for the latest. Boats run from early April through October (usually 5/day, but 3-4/day in early April and most of Oct). From November through March, one boat runs daily for groups, but you can tag along if they know you're coming—call the boat directly (tel. 0172/1360-335) or the main office in Cologne (tel. 0221/2088-318).

Koblenz	Boppard	St. Goar	Bacharach
—	9:00	10:20	11:30
*9:00	*11:00	*12:20	*13:30
—	13:00	14:20	15:30
—	14:00	15:20	16:30
14:00	16:00	17:20	18:30
13:10	11:50	10:55	10:15
—	12:50	11:55	11:15
—	13:50	12:55	12:15
18:10	16:50	15:55	15:15
*20:10	*18:50	*17:55	*17:15

These sailings are generally on the 1913 paddle-wheeler Goethe.

The smaller **Bingen-Rüdesheimer Line** is slightly cheaper than the K-D, doesn't offer any rail pass deals, and makes three trips in each direction daily from mid-March through October (Bacharach-St. Goar: €13.40 one-way, €15.40 round-trip, bikes-€2/day, buy tickets at ticket booth or on boat, ticket booth opens just before boat departs, 30 percent discount if over 60; departs Bacharach at 10:10, 12:00, and 15:15; departs St. Goar at 11:00, 14:00, and 16:15; tel. 06721/308-0810, www.bingen-ruedesheimer.de).

BY CAR

Drivers have these options: 1) skip the boat; 2) take a round-trip cruise from St. Goar or Bacharach; 3) draw pretzels and let the loser drive, prepare the picnic, and meet the boat; 4) rent a bike, bring it on the boat, and bike back; or 5) take the boat one-way and return to your car by train. When exploring by car, don't hesitate to pop onto one of the many little ferries that shuttle across the bridge-less-around-here river.

BY FERRY

As there are no bridges between Koblenz and Mainz, you'll see car-and-passenger ferries (usually family-run for generations) about every three miles. Bingen-Rüdesheim, Lorch-Niederheimbach, Engelsburg-Kaub, and St. Goar-St. Goarshausen are some of the most useful routes (times vary; St. Goar-St. Goarshausen ferry departs each side every 20 minutes daily until 22:30, less frequently Sun; one-way fares: adult-€1.80, car and driver-€4.50, pay on boat; www.faehreloreley.de). For a fun little jaunt, take a quick round-trip with some time to explore the other side.

BY BIKE

Biking is a great way to explore the valley. You can bike either side of the Rhine, but for a designated bike path, stay on

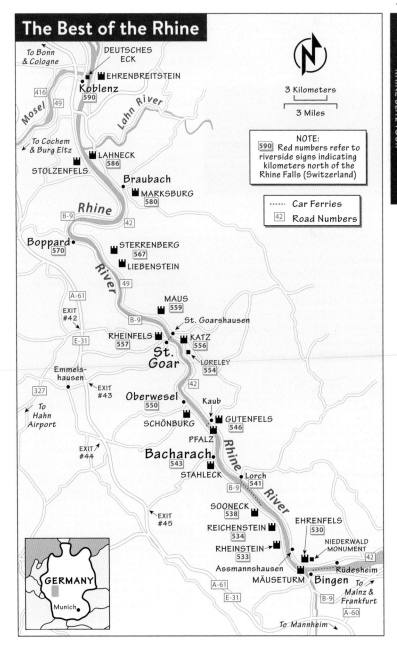

The Best of the Rhine

To Bonn & Cologne

DEUTSCHES ECK
EHRENBREITSTEIN
Koblenz
590
416
49
Mosel

Lahn River

To Cochem & Burg Eltz
STOLZENFELS
LAHNECK
586

Braubach
MARKSBURG
580

Rhine
B-9
42

Boppard
570

River

STERRENBERG
567
LIEBENSTEIN

49

A-61
EXIT #42
E-31

MAUS
559
St. Goarshausen
B-9
RHEINFELS
557
KATZ
556
St. Goar
LORELEY
554

Emmels-hausen
EXIT #43
327
To Hahn Airport

42

Oberwesel
550
Kaub
SCHÖNBURG
GUTENFELS
546
PFALZ

EXIT #44
Bacharach
543
STAHLECK
Lorch
B-9
541

River

EXIT #45
SOONECK
538
REICHENSTEIN
534
EHRENFELS
530
RHEINSTEIN
533
NIEDERWALD MONUMENT
42
Assmannshausen
MÄUSETURM
Rüdesheim
Bingen
To Mainz & Frankfurt
A-61
E-31
B-9
A-60

GERMANY
Munich

To Mannheim

3 Kilometers
3 Miles

NOTE:
590 Red numbers refer to riverside signs indicating kilometers north of the Rhine Falls (Switzerland)

······ Car Ferries
42 Road Numbers

Riesling wine grapes blanket the Rhine's hillsides.

the west side, where a 35-mile path runs between Koblenz and Bingen. The eight-mile stretch between St. Goar and Bacharach is smooth and scenic, but mostly along the highway. The bit from Bacharach to Bingen hugs the riverside and is car-free. Some hotels have bikes for guests; Hotel an der Fähre in St. Goar also rents to the public (reserve in advance).

Consider biking one-way and taking the bike back on the riverboat, or designing a circular trip using the fun and frequent shuttle ferries. A good target is Kaub (where a tiny boat shuttles sightseers to the better-from-a-distance castle on the island) or Rheinstein Castle.

BY TRAIN

Hourly milk-run trains hit every town along the Rhine (Bacharach-St. Goar in both directions about :50 after the hour, 10 minutes; Mainz-Bacharach, 40 minutes; Mainz-Koblenz, 1 hour). Express trains speed past the small towns, taking only 50 minutes nonstop between Mainz and Koblenz. Tiny stations are unstaffed—buy tickets at machines. Though generally user-friendly, some ticket machines only take exact change; others may not accept US credit cards. When buying a ticket, follow the instructions carefully. The ticket machine may give you the choice of validating your ticket for that day or a day in the near future—but only for some destinations (if you're not given this option, your ticket will automatically be validated for the day of purchase).

The **Rheinland-Pfalz-Ticket** day pass covers travel on milk-run trains to anywhere in this chapter, plus the Mosel Valley. It can save heaps of money, particularly on longer day trips or for groups (1 person-€24, up to 4 additional people-€5/ each, buy at station ticket machines—may need to select Rhineland-Palatinate, good after 9:00 Mon-Fri and all day Sat-Sun, valid on trains labeled *RB, RE,* and *MRB*). For a day trip between Bacharach and Burg Eltz (normally €35 round-trip), even one person saves with a Rheinland-Pfalz-Ticket, and a group of five adults saves €130—look for travel partners at breakfast.

BACHARACH

Once prosperous from the wine and wood trade, charming Bacharach (BAHKH-ah-rahkh, with a guttural *kh* sound) is now just a pleasant half-timbered village of 2,000 people working hard to keep its tourists happy. Businesses that have been "in the family" for eons are dealing with succession challenges, as the allure of big-city jobs and a more cosmopolitan life lure away the town's younger generation. But Bacharach retains its time-capsule quaintness.

Orientation

Bacharach cuddles, long and narrow, along the Rhine. The village is easily strollable—you can walk from one end of town to the other along its main drag, Oberstrasse, in about 10 minutes. Bacharach widens at its stream, where more houses trickle up its small valley (along Blücherstrasse) away from the Rhine. The hillsides above town are occupied by vineyards, scant remains of the former town walls, and a castle-turned-hostel.

Tourist Information: The bright and well-stocked TI, on the main street a block-and-a-half from the train station, will store bags and bikes for day-trippers (April-Oct Mon-Fri 9:00-17:00, Sat-Sun 10:00-15:00; Nov-March Mon-Fri 9:00-13:00, closed Sat-Sun; from the train station, exit right and walk down the main street with the castle high on your left—the TI will be on your right at Oberstrasse 10; tel. 06743/919-303, www.bacharach. de or www.rhein-nahe-touristik.de, Herr Kuhn and his team).

Rick's Tip: *Although more places are accepting credit cards,* **come prepared to pay cash** *for most things in the Rhine Valley.*

Bike Rental: Some hotels loan bikes to guests. For bike rental in town, head to **Rent-a-Bike Weber** (€10/day, Koblenzer Strasse 35, tel. 06743-1898, mobile 0175-168073, heidi100450@aol.com).

Parking: It's simple to park along the highway next to the train tracks or, better, in the big public lot by the boat dock (€4 from 9:00 to 18:00, pay with coins at *Park-*

scheinautomat, display ticket on dash, free overnight).

Local Guides: Thomas Gundlach happily gives 1.5-hour town walks to individuals or small groups for €35. History buffs will enjoy his "war tour," which focuses on the town's survival from 1864 through World War II. He also offers 4- to 10-hour hiking or biking tours for the more ambitious (mobile 0179-353-6004, thomas_gundlach@gmx.de). Also good is **Birgit Wessels** (€45/1.5-hour walk, tel. 06743/937-514, wessels.birgit@t-online. de). The **TI** offers 1.5-hour tours in English with various themes, including a night tour (prices vary, gather a group).

◗ Bacharach Town Walk

• *Start this self-guided walk at the Köln-Düsseldorfer ferry dock (next to a fine picnic park).*

   Riverfront: View the town from the parking lot—a modern landfill. The Rhine used to lap against Bacharach's town wall, just over the present-day highway. Every few years the river floods, covering the highway with several feet of water. Flat

Classic and quaint Bacharach

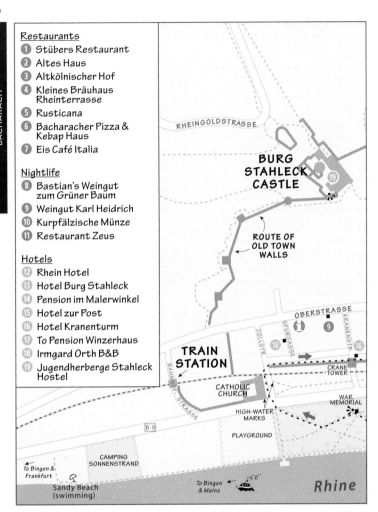

Restaurants
1 Stübers Restaurant
2 Altes Haus
3 Altkölnischer Hof
4 Kleines Bräuhaus
  Rheinterrasse
5 Rusticana
6 Bacharacher Pizza &
  Kebap Haus
7 Eis Café Italia

Nightlife
8 Bastian's Weingut
  zum Grüner Baum
9 Weingut Karl Heidrich
10 Kurpfälzische Münze
11 Restaurant Zeus

Hotels
12 Rhein Hotel
13 Hotel Burg Stahleck
14 Pension im Malerwinkel
15 Hotel zur Post
16 Hotel Kranenturm
17 To Pension Winzerhaus
18 Irmgard Orth B&B
19 Jugendherberge Stahleck
  Hostel

RHEINGOLDSTRASSE

BURG
STAHLECK
CASTLE

ROUTE OF
OLD TOWN
WALLS

OBERSTRASSE

KRANENSTR.

SPURGASSE

ZOLLSTR.

TRAIN
STATION

BAHNHOF-STRASSE

CRANE
TOWER

WAR
MEMORIAL

CATHOLIC
CHURCH

HIGH-WATER
MARKS

B-9

PLAYGROUND

CAMPING
SONNENSTRAND

To Bingen &
Frankfurt

Sandy Beach
(swimming)

To Bingen
& Mainz

Rhine

land like this is rare in the Rhine Valley, where towns are often shaped like the letter "T," stretching thin along the riverfront and up a crease in the hills beyond.

Reefs farther upstream forced boats to unload upriver and reload here. Consequently, in the Middle Ages, Bacharach was the biggest wine-trading town on the Rhine. A riverfront crane hoisted huge kegs of prestigious "Bacharach" wine (which, in practice, was from anywhere in the region). Today, the economy is based on tourism.

Look above town. The **castle** on the hill is now a hostel. Two of the town's original 16 towers are visible from here (up to five if you look really hard). The bluff on the right, with the yellow flag, is the **Heinrich Heine Viewpoint** (the end-point of a popular hike). Old-timers remember when, rather than the flag marking the town as a World Heritage site, a swastika sculpture 30 feet wide and tall stood there. Realizing that it could be an enticing target for Allied planes in the last months of World War II, locals tore it down even before Hitler fell.

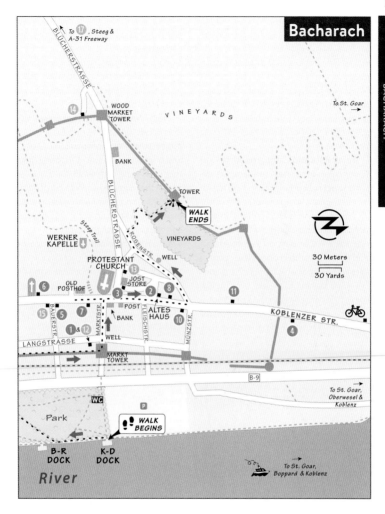

Bacharach

Nearby, a stone column in the park describes the Bingen to Koblenz stretch of the Rhine gorge.

• *Before entering the town, walk upstream through the...*

Riverside Park: The park was originally laid out in 1910 in the English style: Notice how the trees were planted to frame fine town views, highlighting the most picturesque bits of architecture. Erected in 2016, a Picasso-esque sculpture by Bacharach artist Liesel Metten—of three figures sharing a bottle of wine (a Riesling, perhaps?)—celebrates three men who brought fame to the area through poetry and prose: Victor Hugo, Clemens Brentano, and Heinrich Heine.

The dark, sad-looking monument—its "eternal" flame long snuffed out—is a **war memorial.** The German psyche is permanently scarred by war memories. Today, many Germans would rather avoid monuments like this, which recall the dark periods before Germany became a nation of pacifists. The military Maltese cross—flanked by classic German helmets—has a

W at its center, for Kaiser Wilhelm. On the opposite side, each panel honors sons of Bacharach who died for the Kaiser: in 1864 against Denmark, in 1866 against Austria, in 1870 against France, in 1914 during World War I. Review the family names below: You may later recognize them on today's restaurants and hotels.

• *Look upstream from here to see (in the distance) the...*

Trailer Park and Campground: In Germany, trailer vacationers and campers are two distinct subcultures. Folks who travel in motorhomes, like many retirees in the US, are a nomadic bunch, cruising around the countryside and paying a few euros a night to park. Campers, on the other hand, tend to set up camp in one place—complete with comfortable lounge chairs and TVs—and stay put for weeks, even months. They often come back to the same spot year after year, treating it like their own private estate. These camping devotees have made a science out of relaxing. Tourists are welcome to pop in for a drink or meal at the campground café.

• *Continue to where the park meets the playground, and then cross the highway to the fortified riverside wall of the Catholic church, decorated with...*

High-Water Marks: These recall various floods. Before the 1910 reclamation project, the river extended out to here, and boats would tie up at mooring rings that used to be in this wall.

• *From the church, go under the 1858 train tracks (and past more high-water marks) and hook right up the stairs at the yellow floodwater yardstick to reach the town wall. Atop the wall, turn left and walk under the long arcade. After 30 yards, on your left, notice a...*

Well: Rebuilt as it appeared in the 17th century, this is one of seven such wells that brought water to the townsfolk until 1900. Each neighborhood's well also provided a social gathering place and the

High-water marks indicate the heights reached by floodwaters.

A facsimile of a 17th-century well

communal laundry. Walk 50 yards past the well along the wall to an alcove in the medieval tower with a view of the war memorial in the park. You're under the crane tower (Kranenturm). After barrels of wine were moved overland from Bingen, avoiding dangerous stretches of river, the precious cargo could be lowered by cranes from here into ships to continue more safely down the river. The Rhine has long been a major shipping route through Germany. In modern times, it's a bottleneck in Germany's train system. The train company gives hotels and residents along the tracks money for soundproof windows.

• Continue walking along the town wall. Pass the recommended Rhein Hotel just before the...

Markt Tower: This marks one of the town's 15 original 14th-century gates and is a reminder that in that century there was a big wine market here.

• Descend the stairs closest to the Rhein Hotel, pass another well, and follow Marktstrasse away from the river toward the town center, the two-tone church, and the town's...

Main Intersection: From here, Bacharach's main street (Oberstrasse) goes right to the half-timbered red-and-white Altes Haus (which we'll visit later) and left 400 yards to the train station. Spin around to enjoy the higgledy-piggledy building styles. The town has a case of the doldrums: The younger generation is moving to the big cities and many long-established family businesses have no one to take over for their aging owners. In the winter the town is particularly dead.

• To the left (south) of the church, a golden horn hangs over the old...

Posthof: Throughout Europe, the postal horn is the symbol of the postal service. In olden days, when the postman blew this, traffic stopped and the mail sped through. This post station dates from 1724, when stagecoaches ran from Cologne to Frankfurt and would change horses here, Pony Express-style. Notice the cornerstones at the Posthof entrance, protecting the venerable building from

reckless carriage wheels. If it's open, inside the old oak doors (on the left) is the actual door to the post office that served Bacharach for 200 years. Find the mark on the wall labeled Rheinhöhe 30/1-4/2 1850. This recalls a historic flood caused by an ice jam at the Loreley just downstream. Notice also the fascist eagle in the alcove on the right (from 1936; a swastika once filled its center). The courtyard was once a carriage house and inn that accommodated Bacharach's first VIP visitors.

Two hundred years ago, Bacharach's main drag was the only road along the Rhine. Napoleon widened it to fit his cannon wagons. The steps alongside the church lead to the ruins of the 15th-century Werner Chapel and the castle.

• Return to the church, passing the recommended Italian ice-cream café (Eis Café Italia), where friendly Mimo serves his special invention: Riesling wine-flavored gelato.

Protestant Church: Inside the church (daily 10:00-18:00, closed Nov-March), you'll find grotesque capitals, brightly painted in medieval style, and a mix of round Romanesque and pointed Gothic arches. The church was fancier before the Reformation wars, when it (and the region) was Catholic. Bacharach lies on the religious border of Germany and, like the country as a whole, is split between Catholics and Protestants. To the left of the altar, some medieval (pre-Reformation) frescoes survive where an older Romanesque arch was cut by a pointed Gothic one.

Altes Haus is the oldest dwelling (1368) in Bacharach.

If you're considering bombing the town, take note: A blue-and-white plaque just outside the church's door warns that, according to the Hague Convention, this historic building shouldn't be targeted in times of war.

• *Continue down Oberstrasse to the...*

Altes Haus: Dating from 1389, this is the oldest house in town. Notice the 14th-century building style—the first floor is made of stone, while upper floors are half-timbered (in the ornate style common in the Rhine Valley). Some of its windows still look medieval, with small, flattened circles as panes, pieced together with molten lead (like medieval stained glass in churches). Frau Weber welcomes visitors to enjoy the fascinating ground floor of the recommended Altes Haus restaurant, with its evocative old photos and etchings (consider eating here later).

• *Keep going down Oberstrasse to the...*

Old Mint (Münze): The old mint is marked by a crude coin in its sign. As a practicality, any great trading town needed coinage, and since 1356, Bacha-

rach minted theirs here. Now, it's a restaurant and bar, **Kurpfälzische Münze,** with occasional live music. Across from the mint, the recommended **Bastian** family's wine garden is another lively place in the evening. Above you in the vineyards stands a lonely white-and-red tower— your final destination.

• *At the next street, look right and see the mint tower, painted in the medieval style, and then turn left. Wander 30 yards up Rosenstrasse to the* **well.** *Notice the sundial and the wall painting of 1632 Bacharach with its walls intact. Study the fine slate roof over the well: The town's roof tiles were quarried and split right here in the Rhineland. Continue another 30 yards up Rosenstrasse to find the tiny-stepped lane on the right leading up into the vineyard and to the...*

Tall Tower: The slate steps lead to a small path through the vineyard that deposits you at a viewpoint atop the stubby remains of the medieval wall and a tower. The town's towers jutted out from the wall and had only three sides, with the "open" side facing the town. Towers were covered with stucco to make them look more impressive, as if they were made of a finer white stone. If this tower's open, hike up to climb the stairs for the best view. (The top floor has been closed to give nesting falcons some privacy.)

Romantic Rhine View: Looking south, a grand medieval town spreads before you. For 300 years (1300-1600), Bacharach was big (population 4,000), rich, and politically powerful.

From this perch, you can see the ruins of a 15th-century chapel and six surviving **city towers.** Visually trace the wall to the Stahleck Castle. The castle was actually the capital of Germany for a couple of years in the 1200s. When Holy Roman Emperor Frederick Barbarossa went away to fight the Crusades, he left his brother (who lived here) in charge of his vast realm. Bacharach was home to one of the seven electors who voted for the Holy Roman Emperor in 1275. To protect their own power, these prince electors did their best to choose the weakest guy on the ballot. The elector from Bacharach helped select a two-bit prince named Rudolf von Habsburg (from a no-name castle in Switzerland). However, the underestimated Rudolf brutally silenced the robber barons along the Rhine and established the mightiest dynasty in European history. His family line, the Habsburgs, ruled much of Central and Eastern Europe from Vienna until 1918.

Plagues, fires, and the Thirty Years' War (1618-1648) finally did in Bacharach. The town has slumbered for several centuries. Today, the castle houses commoners—40,000 overnights annually by hostelers.

In the mid-19th century, painters such as J. M. W. Turner and writers such as Victor Hugo were charmed by the Rhineland's romantic mix of past glory, present poverty, and rich legend. They put this part of the Rhine on the old Grand Tour map as the "Romantic Rhine." Hugo pondered the chapel ruins that you see

under the castle: In his 1842 travel book, *Excursions Along the Banks of the Rhine,* he wrote, "No doors, no roof or windows, a magnificent skeleton puts its silhouette against the sky. Above it, the ivy-covered castle ruins provide a fitting crown. This is Bacharach, land of fairy tales, covered with legends and sagas." If you're enjoying the Romantic Rhine, thank Victor Hugo and company.

• *Our walk is done. To get back into town, just retrace your steps. Or, to extend this walk, take the level path away from the river that leads along the once-mighty wall up the valley to the next tower, the...*

Wood Market Tower: Timber was gathered here in Bacharach and lashed together into vast log booms known as "Holland rafts" (as big as a soccer field) that were floated downstream. Two weeks later the lumber would reach Amsterdam, where it was in high demand as foundation posts for buildings and for the great Dutch shipbuilders. Notice the four stones above the arch on the uphill side of the tower—these guided the gate as it was hoisted up and down.

• *From here, cross the street and go downhill into the parking lot. Pass the recommended* **Pension im Malerwinkel** *on your right, being careful not to damage the old arch with your head. Follow the creek past a delightful little series of half-timbered homes and cheery gardens known as* **"Painters' Corner"** *(Malerwinkel). Resist looking into some weirdo's peep show (on the right) and continue downhill back to the village center.*

Experiences
Wine Tasting
Bacharach is proud of its wine. Two places in town offer an inexpensive tasting alongside light plates of food.

At **$$ Bastian's Weingut zum Grüner Baum,** pay €29.50 for a wine carousel of 12 glasses—nine different white wines, two reds, and one lonely rosé—and a basket of bread. Spin the Lazy Susan, share a common cup, and discuss the taste.

The Bastian family insists: "After each wine, you must talk to each other" (daily 12:00-22:00, Nov-Dec closed Mon-Wed, closed Jan-Feb, just past Altes Haus, tel. 06743/1208).

$$ **Weingut Karl Heidrich** is a fun family-run wine shop and *Stube* in the town center, where Markus and daughters Magdalena and Katharina proudly share their family's centuries-old wine tradition, explaining its fine points. They offer a variety of €14.50 carousels with six wines, English descriptions, and bread—ideal for the more sophisticated wine taster—plus light meals and a meat-and-cheese plate (Thu-Mon 12:00-22:00, kitchen closes at 21:00, closed Tue-Wed and Nov-mid-April, Oberstrasse 16, will ship to the US, tel. 06743/93060, info@weingut-karl-heidrich.de).

Rick's Tip: *Bacharach goes to bed early, so if you're looking for* **nightlife,** *head to one of the* **wine-tasting places.** *Or try* **Kurpfälzische Münze,** *which often hosts live music.* **Restaurant Zeus** *has outdoor seating that adds a spark to the town center after dark (daily 17:30-24:00, Koblenzer Strasse 11, tel. 06743/909-7171). The hilltop youth hostel,* **Jugendherberge Stahleck,** *serves cheap wine with priceless views until late in summer.*

Shopping

The **Jost** German gift store, across the main square from the church, carries most everything a souvenir shopper could want—from beer steins to cuckoo clocks—and can ship purchases to the US (RS% with €10 minimum purchase: 10 percent with cash, 5 percent with credit card; open daily 9:00-18:00, closed Nov-Feb; Blücher-strasse 4, tel. 06743/909-7214).

Walk Along the Old Town Walls

A steep and rocky but clearly marked walking path follows the remains of

Bacharach's old town walls and makes for a good hour's workout. There are benches along the way where you can pause and take in views of the Rhine and Bacharach's slate roofs. The TI has maps that show the entire route. The path starts near the train station, climbs up to the hostel in what was Stahleck Castle (serves lunch from 12:00-13:30), descends into the side valley, and then continues up the other side to the tower in the vineyards before returning to town. To start the walk at the train station, find the house at Oberstrasse 2 and climb up the stairway to its left. Then follow the *Stadtmauer-Rundweg* signs. Good bilingual signposts tell the history of each of the towers along the wall—some are intact, one is a private residence, and others are now only stubs.

Eating

Restaurants

Bacharach has several reasonably priced, atmospheric restaurants offering fine indoor and outdoor dining. Most places don't take credit cards.

The recommended Rhein Hotel's $$$ **Stübers Restaurant** is Bacharach's best top-end choice. Andreas Stüber, his family's sixth-generation chef, creates regional plates prepared with a slow-food ethic. Consider the William Turner pâté starter plate, named after the British painter who liked Bacharach. Book in advance for the special Tuesday slow-food menu (discount for hotel guests, always good vegetarian and vegan options, daily 17:00-21:30 plus Sun 11:30-14:15, closed mid-Dec-Feb, call or email to reserve on weekends or for an outdoor table when balmy, family-friendly with a play area, Langstrasse 50, tel. 06743/1243, info@rhein-hotel-bacharach.de). Their Posten Riesling is well worth the splurge and pairs well with both the food and the atmosphere.

$$$ **Altes Haus,** the oldest building in town (see "Bacharach Town Walk," earlier), serves classic German dishes with

Bacharach's most romantic atmosphere. Find the cozy dining room with photos of the opera singer who sang about Bacharach, adding to its fame (Thu-Tue 12:00-14:30 & 18:00-21:30, Mon dinner only, limited menu and closes at 18:00 on weekends, closed Wed and Dec-Easter, dead center by the Protestant church, tel. 06743/1209).

$$$ Altkölnischer Hof is a family-run place with outdoor seating right on the main square, serving Rhine specialties that burst with flavor. This restored 18th-century banquet hall feels sophisticated inside, with high ceilings and oil paintings depicting the building's history. Reserve an outdoor table for a more relaxed meal, especially on weekends when locals pack the place (Tue-Sun 12:00-14:30 & 17:30-21:00, closed Mon and Nov-Easter, Blücherstrasse 2, tel. 06743/947-780, www.altkoelnischer-hof.de).

Casual Options

$$ Kleines Brauhaus Rheinterrasse is a funky microbrewery serving hearty meals, fresh-baked bread, and homemade beer under a 1958 circus carousel that overlooks the town and river. For a sweet finish, try the "beer-liquor," which tastes like Christmas (Tue-Sun 13:00-22:00, closed Mon, at the downstream end of town, Koblenzer Strasse 14, tel. 06743/919-179). The little flea market in the attached shed seems to fit right in.

$$ Rusticana, draped in greenery, is an inviting place serving homestyle German food and apple strudel that locals swear by. Sit on the delightful patio or at cozy tables inside (daily 11:00-20:00, credit cards accepted, Oberstrasse 40, tel. 06743/1741).

$ Bacharacher Pizza and Kebap Haus, on the main drag, is the town favorite for *döner kebabs*, cheap pizzas, and salads (daily 11:00-22:00, Oberstrasse 43, tel. 06743/3127).

Gelato: Right on the main street, **Eis Café Italia** is known for its refreshing, not-too-sweet Riesling-flavored gelato (no tastes offered, homemade, Waldmeister flavor is made with forest herbs—top secret, daily 13:00-19:00, closed mid-Oct-March, Oberstrasse 48).

Sleeping

The only listings with parking are Pension im Malerwinkel and Pension Winzerhaus. For the others, you can drive in to unload your bags and then park in the public lot (see "Orientation," earlier). If you'll arrive after 20:00, let your hotel know in advance (many hotels with restaurants stay open late, but none have 24-hour reception desks).

$$ Rhein Hotel, overlooking the river with 14 spacious and comfortable rooms, is classy, well-run, and decorated with modern flair. This place has been in the Stüber family for six generations and is decorated with works of art by the current owner's siblings. The large family room downstairs is über stylish, while the quaint "hiker room" on the top floor features terrific views of both the town and river. You can sip local wines in the renovated room where owner Andreas was born (river- and train-side rooms come with quadruple-paned windows and air-con, in-room sauna, packages available including big three-course dinner, ask about "picnic bags" when you check in, free loaner bikes, directly inland from the K-D boat dock at Langstrasse 50, tel. 06743/1243, www.rhein-hotel-bacharach.de, info@rhein-hotel-bacharach.de). Their recommended Stübers Restaurant is considered the best in town.

$$ Hotel Burg Stahleck, above a cozy café in the town center, rents five big, bright rooms, more chic than shabby. Birgit treats guests to homemade cakes at breakfast (family rooms, view room, free parking, cheaper rooms in guesthouse around the corner, Blücherstrasse 6, tel. 06743/1388, www.urlaub-bacharach.de, info@urlaub-bacharach.de).

$ Pension im Malerwinkel sits like a grand gingerbread house that straddles the town wall in a quiet little neighborhood so charming it's called "Painters' Corner" (Malerwinkel). The Vollmer family's super-quiet 20-room place is a short stroll from the town center. Here guests can sit in a picturesque garden on a brook and enjoy views of the vineyards (cash only, family rooms, elevator, no train noise, bike rentals, easy parking; from Oberstrasse, turn left at the church, walkers can follow the path to the left just before the town gate but drivers must pass through the gate to find the hotel parking lot, Blücherstrasse 41; tel. 06743/1239, www.im-malerwinkel.de, pension@im-malerwinkel.de, Armin and Daniela).

$ Hotel zur Post, refreshingly clean and quiet, is conveniently located right in the town center with no train noise. Its 12 rooms are a good value. Run by friendly and efficient Ute, the hotel offers more solid comfort than old-fashioned character, though the lovely wood-paneled breakfast room has a rustic feel (family room, Oberstrasse 38, tel. 06743/1277, www.hotel-zur-post-bacharach.de, h.zurpost@t-online.de).

$ Hotel Kranenturm, part of the medieval town wall, has 16 rooms with rustic castle ambience and Privatzimmer funkiness right downtown. The rooms in its former Kranenturm (crane tower) have the best views. While just 15 feet from the train tracks, a combination of medieval sturdiness and triple-paned windows makes the riverside rooms sleepable (RS%, family rooms, Rhine views come with train noise—earplugs on request, back rooms are quieter, closed Jan-Feb, Langstrasse 30, tel. 06743/1308, mobile 0176-8056-3863, www.kranenturm.com, hotel.kranenturm@gmail.com).

$ Pension Winzerhaus, a 10-room place run by friendly Sybille and Stefan, is just outside the town walls, directly under the vineyards. The rooms are simple, clean, and modern, and parking is a breeze (cash only, family room, laundry service, parking, nondrivers may be able to arrange a pickup at the train station—

ask in advance, Blücherstrasse 60, tel. 06743/1294, www.pension-winzerhaus.de, winzerhaus@gmx.de).

¢ Irmgard Orth B&B rents three bright rooms, two of which share a small bathroom on the hall. Charming Irmgard speaks almost no English, but is exuberantly cheery and serves homemade honey with breakfast (cash only, Spurgasse 2, tel. 06743/1553—speak slowly; she prefers email: orth.irmgard@gmail.com).

Transportation
Arriving and Departing
BY TRAIN

Milk-run trains stop at Rhine towns each hour starting as early as 6:00, connecting at Mainz and Koblenz to trains farther afield. Trains between St. Goar and Bacharach depart at about :50 after the hour in each direction (buy tickets from the machine in the unstaffed stations, carry cash since some machines won't accept US credit cards).

The durations listed below are calculated from Bacharach; for St. Goar, the difference is only 10 minutes. From Bacharach (or St. Goar), to go anywhere distant, you'll need to change trains in Koblenz for points north, or in Mainz for points south. Milk-run connections to these towns depart hourly, at about :50 past the hour for northbound trains, and at about :05 past the hour for southbound trains (with a few more on the half hour). Train info: www.bahn.com.

From Bacharach by Train to: St. Goar (hourly, 10 minutes), **Moselkern** near Burg Eltz (hourly, 1.5 hours, change in Koblenz), **Cologne** (hourly, 2 hours with change in Koblenz, 2.5 hours direct), **Frankfurt Airport** (hourly, 1 hour, change in Mainz or Bingen), **Frankfurt** (hourly, 1.5 hours, change in Mainz or Bingen), **Rothenburg ob der Tauber** (every 2 hours, 4.5 hours, 3-4 changes), **Munich** (hourly, 5 hours, 2 changes), **Berlin** (every 2 hours with a transfer in Frankfurt, 5.5 hours; more with 2-3 changes).

BY CAR

This region, with its small towns, can make an easygoing first (or last) stop in Germany. If you're using Frankfurt Airport, here are some tips.

Frankfurt Airport to the Rhine: Driving from Frankfurt to the Rhine or Mosel takes about an hour (follow blue autobahn signs from airport—major cities are signposted).

The Rhine to Frankfurt: From St. Goar or Bacharach, follow the river to Bingen, then autobahn signs to *Mainz*, then *Frankfurt*. From there, head for the airport (*Flughafen*) or downtown (signs to *Messe*, then *Hauptbahnhof*, to find the parking under Frankfurt's main train station).

ST. GOAR

St. Goar (sahnkt gwahr) is a classic Rhine tourist town. Its hulk of a castle overlooks a half-timbered shopping street and leafy riverside park, busy with sightseeing ships and contented strollers. Rheinfels Castle, once the mightiest on the river, is the single best Rhineland ruin to explore. While the town of St. Goar itself is less interesting than Bacharach, be sure to explore beyond the shops: Thoughtful little plac-

ards scattered around town explain factoids (in English) about each street, lane, and square. St. Goar also makes a good base for hiking or biking the region. A tiny car ferry will shuttle you back and forth across the busy Rhine from here.

Orientation

St. Goar is dominated by its mighty castle, Rheinfels. The village—basically a wide spot in the road at the foot of Rheinfels' hill—isn't much more than a few hotels and restaurants. From the riverboat docks, the main drag—Heerstrasse, a dull pedestrian mall without history—cuts through town before ending at the road up to the castle.

Tourist Information: The helpful St. Goar TI, which stores bags for free, is on the main pedestrian street (Mon-Fri 9:00-13:00 & 14:00-18:00, Sat-Sun 10:00-13:00; shorter hours and closed Sat-Sun off-season; from train station, go downhill around church and turn left after the recommended Hotel Am Markt, Heerstrasse 127; tel. 06741/383, www.st-goar.de).

Bike Rental: Call ahead to reserve a bike at Hotel an der Fähre, which rents wheels to the public (€10/day, pickup after 10:00, Heerstrasse 47, tel. 06741/980-577).

St. Goar on the Rhine

Parking: A free lot is at the downstream end of town, by the harbor. For on-street parking by the K-D boat dock and recommended hotels, get a ticket from the machine (Parkscheinautomat) and put it on the dashboard (€4/day, daily 9:00-18:00, coins only, free overnight). Make sure you press the button for a day ticket.

Sights

▲▲▲RHEINFELS CASTLE (BURG RHEINFELS)

Perched proudly atop the hill above St. Goar, the ruins of this once mightiest of Rhine River castles still exude a hint of menace. Built in the 13th century, Rheinfels ruled the river for more than 500 years. The castle you see today, though impressive and evocative sight to visit, is but a shadow of its former sprawling self.

Cost and Hours: €5, family card-€10, daily 9:00-18:00, Nov-mid-March possibly Sat-Sun only 11:00-17:00 (call ahead), last entry one hour before closing—weather permitting.

Information: Tel. 06741/7753, in winter 06741/383, www.st-goar.de.

Tours: Due to a multiyear restoration, parts of the castle grounds can only be seen with a guided tour. Tours are run in both German and English but determined on the day by who shows up; to arrange an English tour for a group, call 1-2 days in advance.

Services: A handy WC is immediately across from the ticket booth (men take note of the guillotine urinals—stand back when you pull to flush). There are also WCs in the hotel across from the entrance.

Rick's Tip: *To explore* the castle tunnels at Rheinfels, bring a flashlight—*or buy one at the ticket office. For real medieval atmosphere, they also sell candles with matches.*

Getting to the Castle: A **taxi** up from town costs €5 (tel. 06741/7011). Or take the shuttle bus (€2 one-way, generally April-Oct daily 10:55-16:55, departs roughly every 30 minutes or when full). The shuttle departs from the Catholic church just past the top end of the pedestrian street. **Parking** at the castle costs €1/hour, cash only.

Rheinfels' inner courtyard

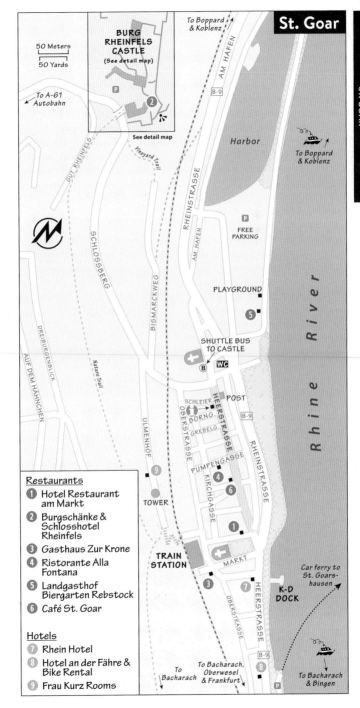

St. Goar

To Boppard & Koblenz

BURG RHEINFELS CASTLE
(See detail map)

50 Meters
50 Yards

To A-61 Autobahn

AM HAFEN

B-9

See detail map

Vineyard Trail

Harbor

To Boppard & Koblenz

GUT RHEINFELS

RHEINSTRASSE

AM HAFEN

SCHLOSSBERG

FREE PARKING

BISMARCKWEG

DREIBURGENBLICK

PLAYGROUND

Rhine River

AUF DEM HÄHNCHEN

Nature Trail

5

SHUTTLE BUS TO CASTLE

B WC

SCHLEIER POST
OBERSTRASSE
BORNG.
GREBELG.
B-9

ULMENHOF

PUMPENGASSE

KIRCHGASSE

HEERSTRASSE

RHEINSTRASSE

9

4

6

1

TOWER

TRAIN STATION

MARKT

Car ferry to St. Goars-hausen

3

7

K-D DOCK

HEERSTRASSE

OBERSTRASSE

To Bacharach

To Bacharach, Oberwesel & Frankfurt

B-9

8

To Bacharach & Bingen

Restaurants

1 Hotel Restaurant am Markt

2 Burgschänke & Schlosshotel Rheinfels

3 Gasthaus Zur Krone

4 Ristorante Alla Fontana

5 Landgasthof Biergarten Rebstock

6 Café St. Goar

Hotels

7 Rhein Hotel

8 Hotel an der Fähre & Bike Rental

9 Frau Kurz Rooms

To **walk** up to the castle, simply follow the main road up through the railroad underpass at the top end of the pedestrian street (5 minutes). But it's more fun to **hike** the nature trail: Start at the St. Goar train station. Take the underpass under the tracks at the north end of the station, climb the steep stairs uphill, turn right (following *Burg Rheinfels* signs), and keep straight along the path just above the old city wall. Small red-and-white signs show the way, taking you to the castle in 15 minutes.

Background: Burg Rheinfels *was* huge—for five centuries, it was the biggest castle on the Rhine. Built in 1245 to guard a toll station, it soon earned the nickname "the unconquerable fortress." In the 1400s, the castle was thickened to withstand cannon fire. Rheinfels became a thriving cultural center and, in the 1520s, was visited by the artist Albrecht Dürer and the religious reformer Ulrich Zwingli. It saw lots of action in the Thirty Years' War (1618-1648), and later became the strongest and most modern fortress in the Holy Roman Empire. It withstood a siege of 28,000 French troops in 1692. But eventually the castle surrendered to the French without a fight, and in 1797, the French Revolutionary army destroyed it. For years, the ruined castle was used as a source of building stone, and today—while still mighty—it's only a small fraction of its original size.

➲ Self-Guided Tour: We'll start at the museum, then circulate through the courtyards, up to the highest lookout point, finishing in a big cellar. To walk around the fortified ramparts, and to access the dark tunnels that require a flashlight, you'll need to book a tour (see earlier). If it's damp, be careful of slippery stones.

Pick up the free map and use its commentary to navigate the red signposts through the castle. My self-guided tour route is similar to the one marked on the castle map. That map, the one in this book, and this tour all use the same numbering system. (I've skipped a couple stops—just walk on by signs for ❷ *Darmstädter Bau* and ❺ *Stables.*)

• *Buy your ticket and walk through the castle's clock tower, labeled ❶ Uhrturm. Continue straight, passing a couple points of interest (which we'll visit later), until you get to the ❸ museum.*

Museum and Castle Model: The pleasant museum is located in the only finished room of the castle. It features a sweeping history exhibit with good English descriptions and Romantic Age etchings that give a sense of the place as it was in the 19th century (daily 10:00-12:30 & 13:00-17:30, closed Nov-mid-March).

The seven-foot-tall carved stone immediately to the right inside the door (marked *Flammensäule*)—a tombstone from a nearby Celtic grave—is from 400 years before Christ. There were people here long before the Romans...and this castle.

The massive fortification was the only Rhineland castle to withstand Louis XIV's assault during the 17th century. At the far left end of the room is a model reconstruction of the castle, showing how much bigger it was before French Revolutionary troops destroyed it in the 18th century. Find where you are. (Hint: Look for the tall tower.) This was the living quarters of the original castle, which was only the smallest ring of buildings around the tiny central courtyard (13th century). The ramparts were added in the 14th century. By 1650, the fortress was largely complete. Since its destruction by the French in the late 18th century, it's had no military value. While no WWII bombs were wasted on this ruin, it served St. Goar as a stone quarry for generations. The basement of the museum shows the castle pharmacy and an exhibit of Rhine-region odds and ends, including tools, an 1830 loom, and photos of icebreaking on the Rhine. While once routine, icebreaking hasn't been necessary here since 1963.

St. Goar's Rheinfels Castle

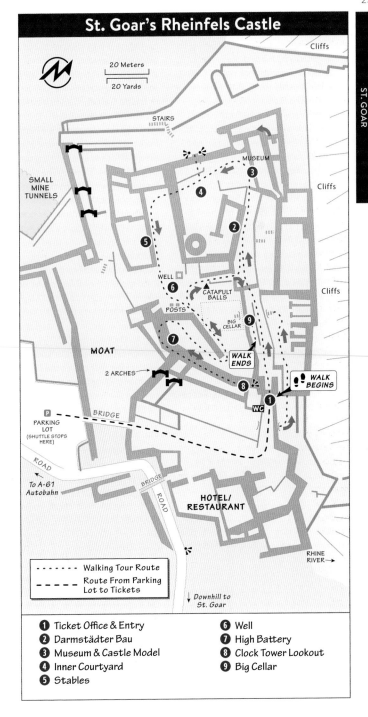

Cliffs

20 Meters
20 Yards

STAIRS

MUSEUM

3

SMALL
MINE
TUNNELS

4

2

5

WELL

6

CATAPULT
BALLS

9

POSTS

BIG
CELLAR

7

WALK
ENDS

MOAT

WALK
BEGINS

2 ARCHES

8

1

WC

P
PARKING
LOT
(SHUTTLE STOPS
HERE)

BRIDGE

ROAD

To A-61
Autobahn

BRIDGE

ROAD

HOTEL/
RESTAURANT

RHINE
RIVER →

Cliffs

Cliffs

Cliffs

·········· Walking Tour Route

— — — Route From Parking
Lot to Tickets

↓ Downhill to
St. Goar

1 Ticket Office & Entry
2 Darmstädter Bau
3 Museum & Castle Model
4 Inner Courtyard
5 Stables

6 Well
7 High Battery
8 Clock Tower Lookout
9 Big Cellar

• *Exit the museum and walk 20 yards directly out, slightly uphill and halfway into the castle courtyard. At the first opening on the right, step up for a peek out at the...*

Corner of Castle: Look right. That's the original castle tower. A three-story, half-timbered building originally rose beyond the tower's stone fortification. The two stone tongues near the top supported the toilet. (Insert your own joke here.) Lean and look left.

Thoop...You're Dead: Notice the smartly placed crossbow slits. While you're lying there, notice the stonework. The little round holes were for the scaffolds they used as they built up, which indicate that this stonework is original.

• *Pick yourself up and walk back into the inner courtyard,* ❹ *Innenhof.*

Medieval Castle Courtyard: Five hundred years ago, the entire castle encircled this courtyard. The place was self-sufficient and ready for a siege, with a bakery, pharmacy, herb garden, brewery, well (top of yard), and livestock. During peacetime, 300-600 people lived here; during a siege, there would be as many as 4,000. The walls were plastered and painted white. Bits of the original 13th-century plaster survive.

• *Continue through the courtyard under the* Erste Schildmauer *(first shield wall) sign, turn left, and walk straight toward the two old wooden upright posts. Find the pyramid of stone catapult balls on your left just before you reach the posts.*

Castle Garden: Catapult balls like these were too expensive not to recycle—they'd be retrieved after any battle. Across from the balls is a well ❻ *Brunnen*)—essential for any castle during the age of sieges. Look in. Thirsty? The old posts are for the ceremonial baptizing of new members of the local trading league. While this guild goes back centuries, it's now a social club that fills this court with a huge wine party every year on the third weekend of September.

• *Climb uphill to the castle's highest point by walking along the cobbled path (look for the* To the Tower *sign) up past the high battery* ❼ *Hohe Batterie) to the castle's best viewpoint—up where the German flag waves (signed* ❽ Uhrturm*).*

Highest Castle Tower Lookout: Enjoy a great view of the river, the castle, and the forest. Remember, the fortress once covered five times the land it does today. Notice how the other castles (across the river) don't poke above the top of the Rhine canyon. That would make them easy for invading armies to see.

From this perch, survey the Rhine Valley, cut out of slate over millions of years by the river. The slate absorbs the heat of the sun, making the grapes grown here well-suited for wine. Today the slate is mined to provide roofing. Imagine St. Goar himself settling here 1,500 years ago, establishing a place where sailors—thankful to have survived the treacherous Loreley—would stop and pray. Imagine the frozen river of years past, when the ice would break up and boats would huddle in man-made harbors like the one below for protection. Consider the history of trade on this busy river—from the days when castles levied tolls on ships, to the days when boats would be hauled upstream with the help of riverside towpaths, to the 21st century when 300 ships a day move their cargo past St. Goar. And imagine this castle before the French destroyed it... when it was the mightiest structure on the river, filled with people and inspiring awe among all who passed.

• *Return to the catapult balls, walk downhill and through the tunnel, and pause to look back up and see the original 13th-century core of the castle. Now go right toward the entrance, first veering down to see the...*

Big Cellar: This **9** *Grosser Keller* was a big pantry. When the castle was smaller, this was the original moat—you can see the rough lower parts of the wall. The original floor was 13 feet deeper. The draw-bridge rested upon the stone nubs on the left. When the castle expanded, the moat became this cellar. Halfway up the walls on the entrance side of the room, square holes mark spots where timbers made a storage loft, perhaps filled with grain. In the back, an arch leads to the wine cellar (probably blocked off) where finer wine was kept. Part of a soldier's pay was wine...table wine. This wine was kept in a single 180,000-liter stone barrel (that's 47,550 gallons), which generally lasted about 18 months.

The count owned the surrounding farmland. Farmers got to keep 20 percent of their production. Later, in more liberal feudal times, the nobility let them keep 40 percent. Today, the German government leaves the workers with 60 percent...and provides a few more services.

• *You're free. Climb out, turn right, and leave. For coffee on a terrace with a great view, visit Schlosshotel Rheinfels, opposite the entrance.*

Shopping

The Montag family runs two shops (one specializes in steins and the other in cuckoo clocks), both at the base of the castle hill road. The stein shop under Hotel Montag has Rhine guides and fine steins. The other shop boasts "the largest free-hanging cuckoo clock in the world"

(RS%—10 percent discount, €10 mini-mum purchase; both locations open daily 9:00-18:00, shorter hours Nov-April). They'll ship your souvenirs home—or give you a VAT form to claim your tax refund at the airport if you're carrying your items with you. A couple of other souvenir shops are across from the K-D boat dock.

Eating

$$ Hotel Restaurant am Markt serves tasty traditional meals with plenty of game and fish (specialties include marinated roast beef and homemade cheesecake) at fair prices with good atmosphere and ser-vice. Choose cozy indoor seating, or dine outside with a river and castle view (daily 9:00-21:00, closed Nov-Feb, Markt 1, tel. 06741/1689).

$$$ Burgschänke is easy to miss on the ground floor of Schlosshotel Rhe-infels (the hotel across from the castle entrance—enter through the souvenir shop). It offers the only reasonably priced lunches up at Rheinfels Castle, is fami-ly-friendly, and has a Rhine view from its fabulous outdoor terrace (*Flammkuchen* and regional dishes, Sun-Thu 11:00-21:00, Fri-Sat until 21:30, tel. 06741/802-806).

The **$$$$ Schlosshotel Rheinfels** dining room is your Rhine splurge, with an incredible indoor view terrace in an elegant, dressy setting. Call to reserve for weekends or if you want a window table (daily 7:00-11:00, 12:00-14:00 & 18:00-21:00, tel. 06741/8020, www.schloss-rheinfels.de).

$$ Gasthaus Zur Krone is the local choice for traditional German food in a restaurant off the main drag. There's no river view, but it's cozy and offers some outdoor seating on weekends (Thu-Tue 11:00-14:30 & 18:00-21:00, closed Wed, cash only, next to the train station and church at Oberstrasse 38, tel. 06741/1515).

$$ Ristorante Alla Fontana, tucked away on a back lane and busy with locals, serves the best Italian food in town at great prices in a lovely dining room or on a leafy patio (Tue-Sun 11:30-14:00 & 17:30-21:30, closed Mon, cash only, dinner reservations smart, Pumpengasse 5, 06741/96117).

$$ Landgasthof Biergarten Rebstock is hidden on the far end of town on the banks of the Rhine. They serve schnitzel and plenty of beer and wine. A nice playground and minigolf course on either side keeps the kids busy (April-Oct long hours daily—weather permitting, Am Hafen 1, tel. 06741/980-0337).

$ Café St. Goar is the perfect spot for a quick lunch or *Kaffee und Kuchen*. They sell open-face sandwiches, strudel, tiny cookies, and a variety of cakes to satisfy any appetite. Grab something for a picnic or enjoy seating on the pedestrian-only street out front (Mon-Sat 9:00-18:00, Sun from 10:00, Heerstrasse 95, tel. 06741/1635).

Sleeping

$ Hotel am Markt, run by Herr and Frau Marx, is a decent value with modern comforts. It features 15 rustic rooms in the main building (think antlers with a pastel flair), 10 classier rooms right next door, and a good restaurant. It's a stone's throw from the boat dock and train station (family rooms, some rooms with river view, two apartments also available, closed Nov-Feb, pay parking, Markt 1, tel. 06741/1689, http://hotel-sankt-goar.de, dashotel@t-online.de).

$ Rhein Hotel, on the other side of the church from Hotel am Markt and run with enthusiasm by young and energetic

Gil Velich, has 10 bright and stylish rooms in a spacious building (some rooms with river view and balconies, family rooms, pay laundry, closed mid-Nov-March, Heerstrasse 71, tel. 06741/981-240, www.rheinhotel-st-goar.de, info@rheinhotel-st-goar.de).

$ Hotel an der Fähre is a simple place on the busy road at the end of town, immediately across from the ferry dock. It rents 12 cheap and colorful rooms (cash only, some view rooms, cheapest rooms with shared bath, street noise but double-glazed windows, parking, closed Nov-Feb, Heerstrasse 47, tel. 06741/980-577, www.hotel-stgoar.de, info@hotel-stgoar.de, friendly Alessya). They also offer rental bikes by reservation.

$ Frau Kurz has been housing my readers since 1988 in St. Goar's best B&B, renting three delightful rooms (sharing 2.5 bathrooms) with a breakfast terrace with castle views, a garden, and homemade marmalade (cash only, free and easy parking, ask about apartment with kitchen, Ulmenhof 11, tel. 06741/459, www.gaestehaus-kurz.de, fewo-kurz@kabelmail.de). If you're not driving, it's a steep five-minute hike from the train station: Exit left from the station, take an immediate left under the tracks, and go partway up the zigzag stairs, turning right through an archway onto Ulmenhof; #11 is just past the tower.

MARKSBURG CASTLE IN BRAUBACH

Medieval invaders decided to give ▲▲ Marksburg a miss, thanks to its formidable defenses. This best-preserved castle on the Rhine can be toured only with a guide on a 50-minute tour. In summer, tours in English normally run daily at 13:00 and 16:00. Otherwise, you can join a German tour (3/hour in summer, hourly in winter) that's almost as good—there are no explanations in English in the castle itself, but your ticket includes an English hand-out. It's an awesome castle, and between the handout and my commentary below, you'll feel fully informed, so don't worry about being on time for the English tours.

Orientation

Cost and Hours: €7, family card-€16, daily 10:00-17:00, Nov-mid-March 11:00-16:00, last tour departs one hour before closing, tel. 02627/206, www.marksburg.de.

Getting There: Marksburg caps a hill above the village of Braubach, on the east bank of the Rhine. By **train,** it's a 10-min-ute trip from Koblenz to Braubach (1-2/hour); from Bacharach or St. Goar, it can take up to two hours, depending on the length of the layover in Koblenz. The train is quicker than the **boat** (downstream from Bacharach to Braubach-2 hours, upstream return-3.5 hours; €30.40 one-way, €36.40 round-trip). Consider taking the downstream boat to Braubach, and the train back. If traveling with luggage, store it in the convenient lockers in the underground passage at the Koblenz train station (Braubach has no enclosed sta-tion—just platforms—and no lockers).

Once you reach Braubach, **walk** into the old town (follow *Altstadt* signs—com-ing out of tunnel from train platforms, it's to your right); then follow the *Zur Burg* signs to the path up to the castle. Allow 25 minutes for the climb up. Scarce **taxis** charge at least €10 from the train plat-forms to the castle. A green **tourist train** circles up to the castle, but there's no fixed schedule (Easter-mid-Oct Tue-Sun, no trains Mon or off-season, €3 one-way, €5 round-trip, leaves from Barbaras-trasse, confirm departure times by calling 06773/587, www.ruckes-reisen.de). Even if you take the tourist train, you'll still have to climb the last five minutes up to the castle from its parking lot.

● Visiting the Castle

Your guided tour starts inside the castle's first gate.

Inside the First Gate: While the dra-matic castles lining the Rhine are generally Romantic rebuilds, Marksburg is the real McCoy—nearly all original construction. It's littered with bits of its medieval past, like the big stone ball that was swung on a

Marksburg Castle was built originally as a fortress, not a royal residence.

rope to be used as a battering ram. Ahead, notice how the inner gate—originally tall enough for knights on horseback to gallop through—was made smaller to deter enemies on horseback. Climb the Knights' Stairway, carved out of slate, and pass under the murder hole—handy for pouring boiling pitch on invaders. (Germans still say someone with bad luck "has pitch on his head.")

Coats of Arms: Colorful coats of arms line the wall just inside the gate. These are from the noble families who have owned the castle since 1283. In that year, financial troubles drove the first family to sell to the powerful and wealthy Katzenelnbogen family (who made the castle into what you see today). When Napoleon took this region in 1803, an Austrian family who sided with the French got the keys. When Prussia took the region in 1866, control passed to a friend of the Prussians who had a passion for medieval things—typical of this Romantic period. Then it was sold to the German Castles Association in 1900. Its offices are in the main palace at the top of the stairs.

Romanesque Palace: White outlines mark where the larger original windows were located, before they were replaced by easier-to-defend smaller ones. On the far right, a bit of the original plaster survives. Slate, which is vulnerable to the elements, needs to be covered—in this case, by plaster. Because this is a protected historic building, restorers can use only the traditional plaster methods...but no one knows how to make plaster that works as well as the 800-year-old surviving bits.

Cannons: The oldest cannon here— from 1500—was back-loaded. This was advantageous because many cartridges could be preloaded. But since the seal was leaky, it wasn't very powerful. The bigger, more modern cannons—from 1640— were one piece and therefore airtight, but had to be front-loaded. They could easily hit targets across the river from here. Stone balls were rough, so they let

the explosive force leak out. The best cannonballs were stones covered in smooth lead—airtight and therefore more powerful and more accurate.

Gothic Garden: Walking along an outer wall, you'll see 160 plants from the Middle Ages—used for cooking, medicine, and witchcraft. *Schierling* (hemlock, in the first corner) is the same poison that killed Socrates.

Inland Rampart: This most vulnerable part of the castle had a triangular construction to better deflect attacks. Notice the factory in the valley. In the 14th century, this was a lead, copper, and silver mine. Today's factory—Europe's largest car-battery recycling plant—uses the old mine shafts as vents (see the three modern smokestacks).

Wine Cellar: Since Roman times, wine has been the traditional Rhineland drink. Because castle water was impure, wine— less alcoholic than today's beer—was the way knights got their fluids. The pitchers on the wall were their daily allotment. The bellows were part of the barrel's filtering system. Stairs lead to the...

Gothic Hall: This hall is set up as a kitchen, with an oven designed to roast an ox whole. The arms holding the pots have notches to control the heat. To this day, when Germans want someone to hurry up, they say, "give it one tooth more." Medieval windows were made of thin sheets of translucent alabaster or animal skins. A nearby wall is peeled away to show the wattle-and-daub construction (sticks, straw, clay, mud, then plaster) of a castle's inner walls. The iron plate to the left of the next door enabled servants to stoke the heater without being seen by the noble family.

Bedroom: This was the only heated room in the castle. The canopy kept in heat and kept out critters. In medieval times, it was impolite for a lady to argue with her lord in public. She would wait for him in bed to give him what Germans still call "a curtain lecture." The deep window seat caught maximum light for needlework and reading. Women would sit here and chat (or "spin a yarn") while working the spinning wheel.

Hall of the Knights: This was the dining hall. The long table is an unattached plank. After each course, servants could replace it with another pre-set plank. Even today, when a meal is over and Germans are ready for the action to begin, they say, "Let's lift up the table." The action back then consisted of traveling minstrels who sang and told of news gleaned from their travels.

Notice the outhouse—made of wood—hanging over thin air. When not in use, its door was locked from the outside (the castle side) to prevent any invaders from entering this weak point in the castle's defenses.

Chapel: This chapel is still painted in Gothic style with the castle's namesake, St. Mark, and his lion. Even the chapel was designed with defense in mind. The small doorway kept out heavily armed attackers. The staircase spirals clockwise, favoring the sword-wielding defender (assuming he was right-handed).

Linen Room: About the year 1800, the castle—with diminished military value—housed disabled soldiers. They'd earn a little extra money working raw flax into linen.

Two Thousand Years of Armor: Follow the evolution of armor since Celtic times. Because helmets covered the entire head, soldiers identified themselves as friendly by tipping their visor up with their right hand. This evolved into the military salute that is still used around the world today. Armor and the close-range weapons along the back were made obsolete by the invention of the rifle. Armor was replaced with breastplates—pointed (like the castle itself) to deflect enemy fire. This design was used as late as the start of World War I. A medieval lady's armor hangs over the door. While popular fiction has men locking up their women before heading off to battle, chastity belts were actually used by women as protection against rape when traveling.

The Keep: This served as an observation tower, a dungeon (with a 22-square-foot cell in the bottom), and a place of last refuge. When all was nearly lost, the defenders would bundle into the keep and burn the wooden bridge, hoping to outwait their enemies.

Horse Stable: The stable shows off bits of medieval crime and punishment. Cheaters were attached to stones or pillories. Shame masks punished gossip-mongers. A mask with a heavy ball had its victim crawling around with his nose in the mud. The handcuffs with a neck hole were for the transport of prisoners. The pictures on the wall show various medieval capital punishments. Many times the accused was simply taken into a torture dungeon to see all these tools, and, guilty or not, confessions spilled out of him. On that cheery note, your tour is over.

NEAR THE RHINE VALLEY

While you're in the region, two stops worth considering are Burg Eltz, a beautiful castle on the Mosel River, and the city of Cologne, with its knockout cathedral. If you're using public transit, Burg Eltz makes a fine day trip from the Rhine, but Cologne (2 hours by train) works better as a stop en route to or from the Rhine.

Burg Eltz

My favorite castle in all of Europe—worth ▲▲▲—lurks in a mysterious forest. It's been left intact for 700 years and is decorated and furnished throughout much as it was 500 years ago. Thanks to smart diplomacy, clever marriages, and lots of luck, Burg Eltz (pronounced "boorg elts") was never destroyed. It's been in the Eltz family for 850 years.

Day Plan

Drivers can figure on a half-day to storm the castle. Day-trippers from the Rhine should allow all day (including the scenic 1.5-hour walk up the Elz Valley to the castle).

Getting There

The pleasant 1.5-hour **walk** from the nearest train station, in the little village of Moselkern, is not only easy, it's the most fun and scenic way to visit the castle. Alternatively, you can take a **taxi** (or, on summer weekends only, the **bus**) to the castle from the village of Karden (see "By Bus from the Treis-Karden Station," below).

Hiking to the Castle from Moselkern: You can do the hike in 75 minutes at a steady clip, but allow an extra 20 minutes or so to enjoy the scenery. The overall elevation gain from the river to the castle is less than 400 feet (you can reach Moselkern from towns on the Rhine, including Cologne and Bacharach).

To find the path up to the castle, turn right from the station along Oberstrasse and continue to the village church. Just past the church, turn right through the underpass. On your left is the Elzbach stream, which you'll follow all the way up to the castle. Just before the road crosses the stream on a stone bridge, take either the footpath (stay right) or the bridge—they join up again later.

When the road ends at the parking lot of the Hotel Ringelsteiner Mühle, stay to the right of the hotel and continue upstream along the easy-to-follow trail, which starts out paved but soon changes to dirt. From here, it's another 45 minutes through the forest to the castle.

By Bus from the Treis-Karden Station: From May through October on Saturdays and Sundays only, bus #330 runs to Burg Eltz from the Treis-Karden railway station (4/day, 40 minutes; check schedule with bus operator at tel. 02671/8976, or at www.burg-eltz.de).

By Taxi: You can taxi to the castle from **Moselkern** (€28 one-way, taxi tel. 02672/1407) or **Karden** (€30 one-way, taxi tel. 02672/1407). If you're planning to taxi from Moselkern, call ahead and ask the taxi to meet your train at Moselkern station. Consider taxiing up to Burg Eltz and then enjoying the hike downhill back to the train station in Moselkern.

By Car: Cars (and taxis) park in a lot near, but not quite at, Burg Eltz. From the lot, hike 15 minutes downhill to the castle or wait (10 minutes at most) for the red castle shuttle bus (€2 each way).

Drive/Hike Combo: If you're driving but would enjoy walking part of the path up to the castle, drive to Moselkern, follow the *Burg Eltz* signs up the Elz Valley, park at Hotel Ringelsteiner Mühle (buy ticket from machine), and hike about 45 minutes up the trail to the castle.

Orientation

Cost and Hours: €10 castle entry includes required guided tour and treasury, daily

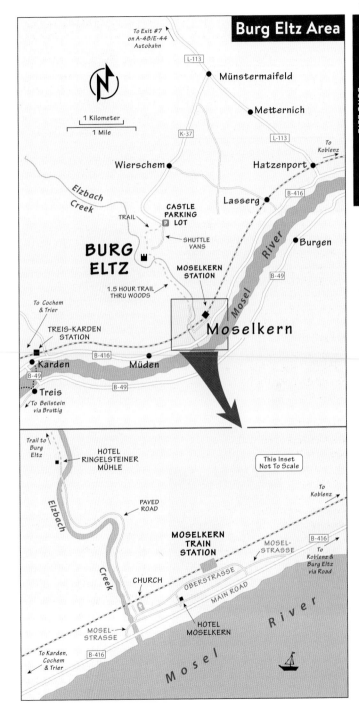

from 9:30, last tour departs at 17:30, closed Nov-March. Tel. 02672/950-500, www.burg-eltz.de.

Rick's Tip: Bring cash! *The castle (including the parking lot and café) doesn't accept credit cards (unless you spend at least €30 at the ticket desk), and there's no ATM.*

Eating: The $ castle café serves lunch, with soups and bratwurst-and-fries cuisine.

➲ Visiting the Castle

The first record of a *Burg* (castle) on the Elz is from 1157. By about 1490, the castle looked like it does today, with the homes of three big landlord families gathered around a tiny courtyard within one formidable fortification. Today, the excellent tour winds you through two of those homes, while the third is still the residence of the castellan (the man who maintains the castle). This is where members of the **Eltz family** stay when they're not at one of their other feudal holdings.

Burg Eltz

It was a comfortable castle for its day: 80 rooms made cozy by 40 fireplaces and wall-hanging tapestries. Many of its 20 toilets were automatically flushed by a rain drain. The delightful **chapel** is on a lower floor. Even though "no one should live above God," this chapel's placement was acceptable because it filled a bay window, which flooded the delicate Gothic space with light. The three families met—working out common problems as if sharing a condo complex—in the large "conference room." A carved jester and a rose look down on the big table, reminding those who gathered that they were free to discuss anything ("fool's freedom"—jesters could say anything to the king), but nothing discussed could leave the room (the "rose of silence"). In the **bedroom,** have fun with the suggestive decor: the jousting relief carved into the canopy, and the fertile and phallic figures hiding in the lusty green wall paintings.

Near the exit, the **treasury** fills the four higgledy-piggledy floors of a cellar with the precious, eccentric, and historic mementos of this family that once helped elect the Holy Roman Emperor.

Cologne

Cologne (Köln—pronounced "kurln"—in German) is an urban hot tub that keeps the Rhine churning. It's home to Germany's greatest Gothic cathedral, one of the country's best collections of Roman artifacts, a world-class art museum, and a healthy dose of German urban playfulness.

During World War II, bombs destroyed 95 percent of Cologne. But with the end of the war, the city immediately began putting itself back together. Today, it's a bustling commercial and cultural center that still respects its rich past.

Day Plan

Cologne couldn't be easier to visit—its important sights cluster within two blocks of the TI and train station. With a couple

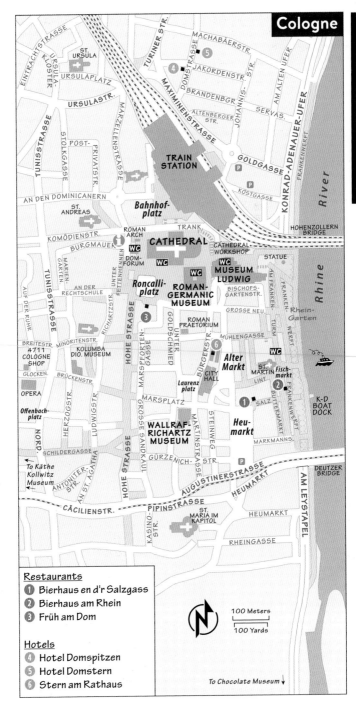

Cologne

TRAIN STATION

Bahnhofplatz

CATHEDRAL

MUSEUM LUDWIG

Roncalliplatz

ROMAN-GERMANIC MUSEUM

ROMAN PRAETORIUM

Alter Markt

Laurenz platz

CITY HALL

ST. MARTIN

Fischmarkt

WALLRAF-RICHARTZ MUSEUM

Heumarkt

K-D BOAT DOCK

ST. URSULA

ST. ANDREAS

KOLUMBA DIO. MUSEUM

4711 COLOGNE SHOP

OPERA

Offenbachplatz

← To Käthe Kollwitz Museum

ST. MARIA IM KAPITOL

ROMAN ARCH

DOM-FORUM

CATHEDRAL WORKSHOP

STATUE

Rhein-Garten

HOHENZOLLERN BRIDGE

DEUTZER BRIDGE

River

Rhine

To Chocolate Museum ↓

100 Meters
100 Yards

N

Restaurants
1. Bierhaus en d'r Salzgass
2. Bierhaus am Rhein
3. Früh am Dom

Hotels
4. Hotel Domspitzen
5. Hotel Domstern
6. Stern am Rathaus

of hours, you can toss your bag in a station locker, zip through the cathedral, and make it back to the station for your train. More time allows you to delve into a few of the city's fine museums and take in an old-time beer pub.

Orientation

For visitors, the area that matters is right around the train station and cathedral. Here you'll find most sights, the TI, and plenty of eateries and services.

Tourist Information: Cologne's energetic TI is opposite the cathedral entrance (daily, Kardinal-Höffner-Platz 1, tel. 0221/346-430, www.koelntourismus.de).

Rick's Tip: *The* **cathedral is off-limits to sightseers during services,** *which are more frequent on Sundays—check the current schedule at the TI or the cathedral's Domforum information office.*

Getting There

Fast trains run at least hourly from Frankfurt (1.5 hours), Bacharach/St. Goar (2-2.5 hours), Würzburg (2.5 hours), and points beyond. Exiting the front of the station (the end near track 1), you'll find yourself smack-dab in the shadow of the cathedral. Up the steps and to the right is the cathedral's main entrance (TI across street).

Drivers should follow signs to Zentrum, then continue to the huge Parkhaus am Dom garage under the cathedral or to the lot outside the garage.

Sights

▲▲▲COLOGNE CATHEDRAL (DOM)

The Gothic *Dom*—Germany's most exciting church—looms immediately up from the train station in one of the country's starkest juxtaposition of the modern and the medieval. The church is so big and so important that it has its own information office, the Domforum, in a separate building across the street.

Cost and Hours: Free, Mon-Sat 9:30-11:30 & 12:30-16:30, Sun 12:30-16:30; closed to tourists during services—confirm times at Domforum office or at www.koelner-dom.de.

Tours: The one-hour English-only tours are reliably excellent (€8, Mon-Sat at 10:30 and 14:30, Sun at 14:30, meet inside front door of Dom).

Cologne's great Gothic cathedral

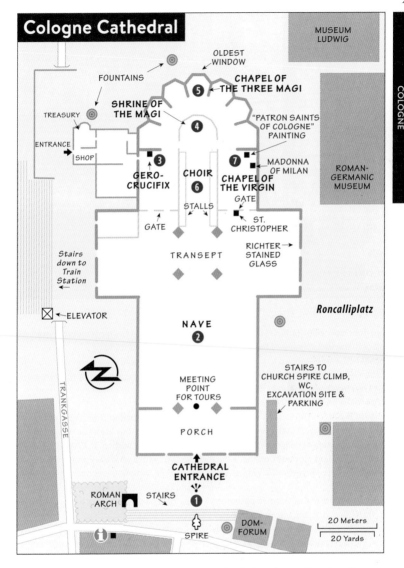

Cologne Cathedral

MUSEUM LUDWIG

OLDEST WINDOW

FOUNTAINS

CHAPEL OF THE THREE MAGI
❺

SHRINE OF THE MAGI

TREASURY

ENTRANCE ➤

SHOP

❹

"PATRON SAINTS OF COLOGNE" PAINTING

ROMAN-GERMANIC MUSEUM

❸

GERO-CRUCIFIX

CHOIR
❻

❼

MADONNA OF MILAN

CHAPEL OF THE VIRGIN

GATE

STALLS

GATE

ST. CHRISTOPHER

RICHTER → STAINED GLASS

Stairs down to Train Station

TRANSEPT

Roncalliplatz

⊠ ←ELEVATOR

NAVE
❷

TRANKGASSE

MEETING POINT FOR TOURS

STAIRS TO CHURCH SPIRE CLIMB, WC, EXCAVATION SITE & PARKING

PORCH

CATHEDRAL ENTRANCE
❶

ROMAN ARCH

STAIRS

SPIRE

DOM-FORUM

20 Meters

20 Yards

● **Self-Guided Tour:** If you don't take the guided tour, follow this seven-stop walk (note that stops 3-7 are closed off during confession Sat 14:00-18:00, and any time services are underway).

❶ **Cathedral Exterior:** The cathedral—the most ambitious Gothic building project north of France in the 13th century—was stalled in the Middle Ages and

not finished until 1880. Even though most of it was built in the 19th century, it's still technically a Gothic church (not "Neo-Gothic") because it was finished according to its original plans.

• *Step inside the church. Grab a pew in the center of the nave.*

❷ **Nave:** If you feel small, that's because you're supposed to. The

Stained-glass window depicting the Adoration of the Magi

140-foot-tall ceiling reminds us of our place in the vast scheme of things. Lots of stained glass—enough to cover three football fields—fills the church with light.

The church was begun in 1248. The choir—the lofty area from the center altar to the far end ahead of you—was inaugurated in 1322. Later, during the tumultuous wars of religious reformation, Catholic pilgrims stopped coming. This dried up funds, and eventually construction stopped.

But with the rise of German patriotism in the early 1800s, the movers and shakers behind German unity paid for the speedy completion of this gloriously Gothic German church.

The glass windows at the east end of the church (in the chapels and high above) are medieval. The glass surrounding you in the nave is not as old, but it's precious nevertheless. The glass on the left is early Renaissance.

While 95 percent of Cologne was destroyed by WWII bombs, the cathedral held up fairly well. It was hit by 15 bombs, but the skeletal Gothic structure flexed, and it remained standing.

• *Leave the nave to the left and step through the gate at the far end (beside the transept), into the oldest part of the church. Ahead of you on the left is the...*

❸ **Gero-Crucifix:** The Chapel of the Cross features the oldest surviving monumental crucifix north of the Alps. Carved in the 970s with a sensitivity 300 years ahead of its time, it shows Jesus not suffering and not triumphant—but with eyes closed... dead. He paid the price for our sins. It's great art and powerful theology in one.

• *Continue to the front end of the church, stopping to look at the big golden reliquary in the glass case behind the high altar.*

❹ **Shrine of the Magi:** Cologne's acquisition of the bones of the Three Kings in the 12th century put it on the pilgrimage map. This reliquary, made in about 1200 of gilded silver, jewels, and enamel, is the biggest and most splendid I've seen. On the long sides, Old Testament prophets line the bottom, and 12 New Testament apostles—with a

Gero-Crucifix

wingless angel in the center—line the top. The front looks like three stacked coffins, showing scenes of Christ's flagellation, Crucifixion, and Resurrection.

• *Opposite the shrine, at the far-east end of the church, is the...*

❺ Chapel of the Three Magi: The center chapel, at the church's far end, is the oldest. It also features the church's oldest window (center, from 1265). Later glass windows (which you saw lining the nave) were made from panes of clear glass that were painted and glazed. This medieval window, however, is actually colored glass, which is assembled like a mosaic. It was very expensive. The size was limited to what pilgrim donations could support. Notice the plain, budget design higher up.

• *Peek into the center zone between the high altar and the carved wooden central stalls. (You can't usually get inside, unless you take the tour.)*

❻ Choir: The choir is surrounded by 13th- and 14th-century art with carved oak stalls, frescoed walls, statues painted as they would have been, and original stained glass high above. Study the fanciful oak carvings.

• *The nearby chapel holds one of the most precious paintings of the important Gothic School of Cologne.*

❼ Chapel of the Virgin: The Patron Saints of Cologne was painted around 1440, probably by Stefan Lochner. Notice the photographic realism and believable depth. There are literally dozens of identifiable herbs in the grassy foreground.

Overlooking the same chapel (between the windows), the delicate **Madonna of Milan** sculpture (1290), associated with miracles, was a focus of pilgrims for centuries. The reclining medieval knight in the cage at the back of the chapel (just before the gate) is a wealthy but childless patron who donated his entire county to the cathedral.

Before leaving, look back above the tomb with the cage to find the statue of St. Christopher (with Jesus on his shoulder and the pilgrim's staff). He's facing the original south transept entry to the church. Since 1470, pilgrims and travelers have looked up at him and taken solace in the hope that their patron saint is looking out for them.

▲▲ROMAN-GERMANIC MUSEUM (RÖMISCH-GERMANISCHES MUSEUM)

One of Germany's top Roman museums offers minimal English information among its elegant and fascinating display of Roman glassware, jewelry, and mosaics. All these pieces are evidence of Cologne's status as an important site of civilization long before the cathedral was ever imagined. Temporary exhibits are on the ground floor. Upstairs, you'll see an original, reassembled arched gate to the Roman city with the Roman initials for the town, CCAA, still legible, and incredible glassware that Roman Cologne was famous for producing. The museum's main attraction is an in-situ Roman-mosaic floor, which you can see from the street for free through a large window.

Cost and Hours: €6.50; Tue-Sun 10:00-17:00, first Thu of month until 22:00, closed Mon; Roncalliplatz 4, tel. 0221/2212-4438, www.roemisch-germanisches-museum.de.

▲▲MUSEUM LUDWIG

This museum—in a slick and modern building—offers a stimulating trip through the art of the last century, including American Pop and post-WWII art. The collection includes works by the great German Expressionists Max Beckmann, Otto Dix, and Ernst Ludwig Kirchner as well as Picasso works spanning the artist's entire career.

Cost and Hours: €12; Tue-Sun 10:00-18:00, first Thu of month until 22:00, closed Mon; Heinrich-Böll-Platz, tel. 0221/2212-6165, www.museum-ludwig.de.

▲▲WALLRAF-RICHARTZ MUSEUM

Housed in a cinderblock of a building near the City Hall, this minimalist museum—Cologne's oldest—features a world-class collection of old masters, from medieval to northern Baroque and Impressionist. You'll see the best collection anywhere of Gothic School of Cologne paintings (1300-1550) as well as German, Dutch, Flemish, and French works by masters such as Dürer, Rubens, Rembrandt, Vincent Van Gogh, Renoir, Monet, Munch, and Cézanne.

Cost and Hours: €8-13 depending on special exhibits; Tue-Sun 10:00-18:00, first and third Thu until 22:00, closed Mon; on Obenmarspforten, tel. 0221/2212-1119, www.wallraf.museum.

KÄTHE KOLLWITZ MUSEUM

This museum contains the largest collection of the artist's powerful Expressionist art, welling from her experiences living in Berlin during the tumultuous first half of the 20th century.

Cost and Hours: €5; Tue-Fri 10:00-18:00, Sat-Sun from 11:00, closed Mon; Neumarkt 18, tel. 0221/227-2899, www.kollwitz.de.

Eating

The area around Alter Markt, a square a few blocks from the cathedral, is home to dozens of beer halls, most with both outdoor and indoor seating. Wander from Alter Markt through Heumarkt (an adjacent square) and down Salzgasse to Frankenwerft (along the river) to catch the flavor. **$$$ Bierhaus en d'r Salzgass** is where locals have been coming for beer since the 19th century (Salzgasse 5). The nearby **$$$ Bierhaus am Rhein** has the same menu, plus views of the Rhine (Frankenwerft 27). **$$ Früh am Dom** offers three floors of traditional German drinking and dining options (Am Hof 12).

Sleeping

These options are an easy roll from the train station with your luggage: **$$ Hotel Domspitzen** is a good value (Domstrasse 23, www.hotel-domspitzen.de); **$ Hotel Domstern** is fresh and pleasant (Domstrasse 26, www.hotel-domstern.de); and **$$ Stern am Rathaus** has a quiet location near City Hall (Bürgerstrasse 6, www.stern-am-rathaus.com).

BEST OF THE REST

Baden-Baden

Baden-Baden was the playground of Europe's high-rolling elite around 150 years ago. Royalty and aristocracy came from all corners of the continent to take the *Kur*—a soak in the curative mineral waters—and enjoy the world's top casino. Wrought-iron balconies on handsome 19th-century apartment buildings give Baden-Baden an elegant, almost Parisian feel.

With its appealing combination of Edenism and hedonism, the town remains popular today, attracting a middle-class crowd of European tourists in search of a slower pulse.

Day Plan

Baden-Baden is made for strolling...with a poodle. Feel yourself relax and settle in to the slow pace. Your essential experience is going to the baths; you can choose between the traditional Roman-Irish Bath or the modern Baths of Caracalla or try both. For an overview of the pleasant town, take my self-guided walk through Baden-Baden.

Orientation

Baden-Baden is a long, skinny town, strung over several miles along the narrow valley of the Oosbach River. The train station is at one end of the valley, three miles from downtown; the Lichtentaler Abbey marks the other end of the valley. The casino and town center are about halfway between.

Tourist Information: Baden-Baden's TI is in the Kurhaus (daily, 10:00–18:00, tel. 07221/275-200, www.baden-baden.de). For information about tickets to the theater, opera, orchestra, and musicals, visit www.tickets-baden-baden.de.

Getting There

Fast trains running hourly connect Baden-Baden with **Munich** (4 hours), **Frankfurt** (2 hours), and **Bacharach** (3 hours). To get from the station to downtown in 15 minutes, catch frequent bus #201 (€2.50, buy ticket from driver or machines). A taxi to the center costs about €20.

By car, follow blue *Therme* signs to the baths neighborhood; you'll find big garages in the town center.

Soothing Baden-Baden is the epitome of European spa towns.

➲ Baden-Baden Walk

This self-guided walk starts at the casino, loops through the Old Town to both of the famous baths, and ends back at the river.

• *Start on the steps of the...*

Casino: The impressive building called the Kurhaus is wrapped around a grand casino. Designed to resemble Versailles, it still looks the same as when it was built in the 1850s. You can tour it in the morning, then return to gamble away the afternoon and evening.

• *Leaving the casino, walk about 100 yards to the left, past the five 19th-century gas lampposts (still lit by hand each night) to the...*

Trinkhalle: Beyond the trees is the old Trinkhalle—with a long entrance hall decorated with nymphs and romantic legends. This grand corridor was designed for 19th-century needs: drinking the spa water while promenading out of the sun and rain. It's now home to the TI, a café, and a ticket agency. Wander around its fancy portico, studying the romantic circa-1850 paintings that spa-goers a century ago could easily relate to. For a sample of the warm spring water, go inside and look for the tap at the central column.

• *From the Trinkhalle, walk down the steps, tip your hat to Kaiser Wilhelm, and cross the mighty Oosbach River. Walk one block inland, then go left on the pedestrian Lange Strasse past fine shops. At the Hotel zum Hirsch, take a hard right, and climb up Hirschstrasse until you hit a big church.*

Catholic Church and Marktplatz: Baden-Baden's Catholic church looks over the marketplace that has marked the center of town since Roman times. Inside you'll see a fine crucifix, carved from a single stone in the 15th century. The front part of the church is lined with tombs and memorials to local big shots (counts and margraves) from the 16th to the 18th century. The fanciest memorial, filling most of the right wall, is Baroque and honors a local military figure who helped defend Europe against the Turks in the 17th century.

• *Now we'll explore the area around Baden-Baden's claim to fame.*

Baths Area: Walk to the back of the church, and head down the cobbled lane behind the Roman-Irish Bath complex. Because the soil is spa-warmed, a garden of lush Mediterranean vegetation stretches left from here up towards the castle. At the end (top of stairs), enjoy the **viewpoint**.

Take the steps down to the water spigot that taps the underground spring called the **Fettquelle** ("rich water source"). It's 105 degrees—as hot as a spa open to the public can legally be. Older locals remember being sent here to fetch hot water for their father's shave.

• *Beyond the Fettquelle spigot, take the stairs down into the parking level (signposted Römische Badruinen) into the small tunnel to find the...*

Ancient Spa Museum: This ancient bath, now in ruins, was built for Roman soldiers. It's just one room—most of which you can see through the big windows. As it was only for soldiers, this spa is just a simple terra-cotta structure with hollow walls and elevated floors to let the heat circulate.

• *Walking past the museum, you hit daylight, jog left, hook right around an outdoor café, then head down the pedestrian shopping lane called...*

Gernsbacher Strasse: Walking down Gernsbacher Strasse, consider the 2,000-year heritage of guests who have been housed, fed, and watered here at the spa. Fyodor Dostoyevsky, Mark Twain, Johannes Brahms, and Russian princes all called this neighborhood home in its 19th-century heyday. Germany's oldest tennis and golf clubs were created here (for the English community) in the 19th century.

In the late 20th century, Germany's healthcare system was very, very good for Baden-Baden. The government provided lavishly for spa treatment for its tired citizens. Times have changed, and now doctors must make the case to insurance companies that their patients are more than tired...they must actually be sick to have their visit subsidized by taxpayers.

• *After two blocks, you hit Sonnenplatz. Hang a left, then a right, and continue down...*

Sophienstrasse: This street enjoys the reliable shade of a long row of tall chestnut trees. In the 1870s, when it was lined exclusively by hotels, this was the town's aristocratic promenade.

• *Sophienstrasse leads directly to Leopoldsplatz, Baden-Baden's main square.*

Leopoldsplatz: Until 1985, this square was a busy traffic hub, with 30,000 cars muscling through it each day. Now a 1.5-mile-long tunnel takes the east-west traffic under the city, and the peace and quiet you'd expect in a spa town has returned.

• *From here the casino is ahead and to your right. A stroll to the left—down Lichtentaler Allee—takes you out to Lichtentaler Abbey.*

Sights

Baden-Baden's top sights—two much-loved but very different baths—stand side by side in a park at the top of the Old Town.

▲▲▲ROMAN-IRISH BATH (FRIEDRICHSBAD)

The highlight of most visits to Baden-Baden is a sober 17-step ritual called the Roman-Irish Bath. This bathhouse pampered the rich and famous in its elegant surroundings when it opened in 1877. Today, this steamy world of marble, brass columns, tropical tiles, herons, lily pads, and graceful nudity welcomes gawky tourists as well as locals.

Cost and Hours: €25/3 hours, €12 more gets you a soap-and-brush massage, another €12 for final crème massage; daily 9:00-22:00, last entry 2 hours before closing; no kids under age 14, Römerplatz 1, tel. 07221/275-920, www.friedrichsbad.eu.

Dress Code: Everyone in these baths is always nude (even prudish American tourists). On Mondays, Thursdays, and Saturdays, men and women use separate and nearly identical facilities—but the sexes can mingle briefly in the pool under the grand dome in the center of the complex (yes, everyone's nude there, too). Shy bathers should avoid Tuesdays, Wednesdays, Fridays, Sundays, and holidays, when all the rooms are mixed gender—including

A trip to the Roman-Irish Bath is a 17-step spa experience.

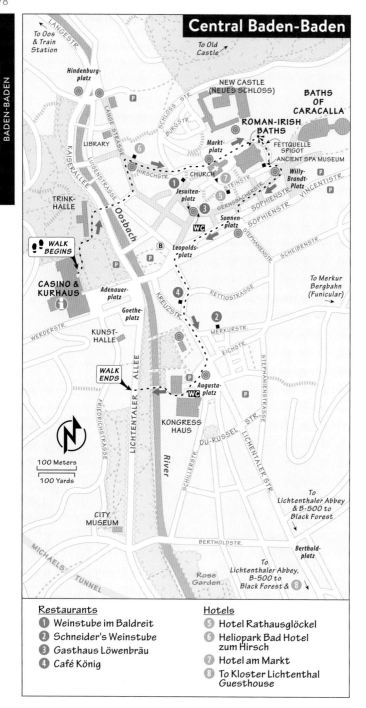

Central Baden-Baden

LANGESTR

To Oos
& Train
Station

To Old
Castle

Hindenburg-
platz

NEW CASTLE
(NEUES SCHLOSS)

BATHS
OF
CARACALLA

SCHLOSS STR

BURGSTR

ROMAN-IRISH
BATHS

LIBRARY

LANGE STRASSE

Markt-
platz

FETTQUELLE
SPIGOT
ANCIENT SPA MUSEUM

HIRSCHSTR.

CHURCH

STEINSTR.

Willy-
Brandt-
Platz

KAISERALLEE

LUISENSTRASSE

Jesuiten-
platz

GERNSBACHERSTR.

VINCENTISTR.

SOPHIENSTR.

TRINK-
HALLE

Oosbach

WC

Sonnen-
platz

SOPHIENSTR.

STEPHANIENSTR.

SCHEIBENSTR.

WALK
BEGINS

B

Leopolds-
platz

CASINO &
KURHAUS

Adenauer-
platz

To Merkur
Bergbahn
(Funicular)

KREUZSTR.

RETTIGSTRASSE

Goethe-
platz

WERDERSTR.

KUNST-
HALLE

MERKURSTR.

EICHSTR.

STEPHANIENSTR.

WALK
ENDS

LICHTENTALER ALLEE

WC

Augusta-
platz

FRIEDRICHSTRASSE

KONGRESS
HAUS

DU-RUSSEL STR.

LICHTENTALER STR.

N

100 Meters
100 Yards

River

SCHILLERSTR.

To
Lichtenthaler Abbey
& B-500 to
Black Forest

CITY
MUSEUM

BERTHOLDSTR.

Berthold-
platz

MICHAELS-

TUNNEL

Rose
Garden

To
Lichtenthaler Abbey,
B-500 to
Black Forest &

Restaurants

1 Weinstube im Baldreit
2 Schneider's Weinstube
3 Gasthaus Löwenbräu
4 Café König

Hotels

5 Hotel Rathausglöckel
6 Heliopark Bad Hotel
   zum Hirsch
7 Hotel am Markt
8 To Kloster Lichtenthal
   Guesthouse

the steam and massage rooms.

Procedure: You'll pay, get a wristband, and activate it as you enter. Choose a locker (where you'll find your bed-sheet-like towel), and change in a changing cabin. Lock your locker by pressing on the button with your wristband. Remember your locker number; for security, it's not indicated on your wristband. Inside the baths, the complex routine is written (in English) on the walls with recommended times—simply follow the room numbers from 1 to 17. Instructions are repeated everywhere. And English-speaking attendants are there when necessary.

For the first couple of stops only, you use plastic slippers and a towel for hygienic reasons and because the slats are too hot to sit on directly. You'll start by taking a shower. Grab a towel and put on plastic slippers before hitting the warm-air bath for 15 minutes and the hot-air bath for 5. Shower again. If you paid extra, take the rough and slippery soap-brush massage—which may finish with a good Teutonic spank for the gents and a gentler tap-tap for the ladies. Play Gumby in the shower; lounge under sunbeams in one of several thermal steam baths; and glide like a swan under a divine dome in the mixed-gender royal pool. Don't skip the invigorating cold plunge, then dry off with warmed towels.

If you prepaid for the eight-minute crème massage, now's the time. Then you'll be wrapped like a baby to lie on a bed for 30 minutes, thinking prenatal thoughts, in the mellow, yellow, silent room. At the end, there's a reading room with refreshing drinks, chaise lounges, and magazines. You don't appreciate how clean you are after this experience until you put your dirty socks back on (bring a clean pair).

All you need is money. Hair dryers are available, and clocks are prominently displayed throughout. If you wear glasses, consider leaving them in your locker (it's more relaxing without them). Otherwise, you'll find trays throughout for you to park your specs.

Afterward, before going downstairs, sip just a little of the terrible but "magic" hot water (*Thermalwasser*) from the elegant fountain (locals ignore the "no drinking water" sign), and stroll down the broad royal stairway, feeling, as they say, five years younger—or at least, after all that sweating, a pound or two lighter.

▲▲BATHS OF CARACALLA (CARACALLA THERME)

For a more modern experience, spend a few hours at the Baths of Caracalla, a huge palace of water, steam, and relaxed people. More like a mini water park, and with bathers clothed, this is a fun and accessible experience and is recommended for those who'd prefer less nudity (sauna-goers upstairs, however, are nude).

Cost and Hours: €15/1.5 hours, €16/2 hours, €19/3 hours, €23 buys the whole day, a few euros more for the sauna, discounts with hotel guest card (*Kurkarte*); massages and other spa treatments available; daily 8:00-22:00, last entry 1.5 hours before closing, no kids under age 7, kids 7-14 must be with parents; tel. 07221/275-940, www.caracalla.de.

Procedure: At this bath, you need to bring a towel (or rent one for €6) and a swimsuit (for sale in shop).

Find a locker, change clothes, strap the band around your wrist, and go play. Your wristband gets you into another poolside locker if you want to lock up your glasses. You won't need your wallet inside, but if you get something to eat or drink, you'll pay on exit (it's recorded on your wristband). Bring your towel to the pool. The baths are an indoor/outdoor wonderland of steamy pools, waterfalls, neck showers, hot tubs, hot springs, cold pools, lounge chairs, saunas, a wellness lounge/massage area, a cafeteria, and a bar. After taking a few laps around the fake river, you can join some kinky Germans for water spankings. Then join the gang in the central cauldron. The steamy "inhalation" room seems like purgatory's waiting room, with a misty

Baden-Baden's casino

minimum of visibility, filled with strange, silently aging bodies.

Nudity is limited to the sauna zone upstairs. The grand spiral staircase leads to a naked world of saunas, tanning lights, cold plunges, and sunbathing outside on lounge chairs. At the top of the stairs everyone stows their suit in a cubbyhole and wanders around with their towel (some are modest and wrapped; others just run around buck naked). There are three eucalyptus-scented saunas of varying temperatures (80, 90, and 95 degrees) and two saunas in outdoor log cabins (with mesmerizing robotic steam-makers). Follow the instructions on the wall. Towels are required, not for modesty but to separate your body from the wood benches. The highlight is the arctic bucket in the shower room. Pull the chain. Rarely will you ever feel so good.

▲▲CASINO AND KURHAUS

Baden-Baden's grand casino occupies a classy building called the Kurhaus, built in the 1850s. Inspired by the Palace of Versailles, it's filled with rooms honoring French royalty who never actually set foot in the place. But many other French people did. Gambling was illegal in 19th-century France...just over the border.

You can visit the casino on a guided tour in the mornings, when it's closed to gamblers, but it is most interesting to see in action. (While gambling starts at 14:00, there's a much better scene and energy later in the evening.) Lean against a gilded statue and listen to the graceful reshuffling of personal fortunes. Do some imaginary gambling or buy a few chips at the window near the entrance (an ATM is downstairs). The Russian novelist Fyodor Dostoyevsky came here, lost his fortune in these very rooms, and wrote a book about it: *The Gambler*.

The casino has a pricey restaurant (with a lovely garden), and the Equipage cocktail bar has live music and hanky-panky most nights (from 21:00 until late, closed Mon).

Cost and Hours: €5 entry, free with voucher from guided tour (described below; open daily 14:00 until very late; no athletic shoes, no sandals or short sleeves for men, coat and collared shirt required for men and ties are encouraged—nice

Lichtentaler Allee invites strollers.

jeans OK; passport required, under 21 not admitted; tel. 07221/30240, www.casino-baden-baden.de.

Tours: The casino gives 40-minute German tours every morning (€7; April-Oct at 9:30, 10:15, 11:00, and 11:45; Nov-March at 10:00, 10:45, and 11:30; grab the succinct yellow English information sheet, some guides might add short English summaries if asked; tel. 07221/30240). Even peasants wearing T-shirts, shorts, and sandals, with cameras and kids in tow, are welcome on tours. Tour-takers (21 and up) receive a voucher for free entry during regular gambling hours.

▲▲**STROLLING LICHTENTALER ALLEE**
Imagine yourself dressed as a 19th-century aristocrat as you promenade down elegant Lichtentaler Allee, a pleasant, picnic-perfect 1.5-mile-long lane that runs along the babbling brick-lined Oosbach River, past old mansions and under hardy oaks and exotic trees (street-lit all night).

By the tennis courts (gear rentable), cross the footbridge into the free Art Nouveau **Rose Garden** (Gönneranlage). The promenade leads all the way to the historic

Lichtentaler Abbey, an active Cistercian convent founded in 1245 (free, open daily but café closed Mon). You can either walk round-trip, or walk one way and take city bus #201 back (runs every 10 minutes along the main street, parallel to the promenade, on the other side of the river).

▲**FUNICULAR TO THE SUMMIT OF MERKUR**
This delightful trip to a hilltop overlooking Baden-Baden is easy and quick. Catch bus #204 or #205 from the city center (departing 2/hour from Leopoldsplatz) and ride 11 minutes to the end of the line at the base of the Merkur funicular (*Bergbahn*). Take the ear-popping funicular to the 2,000-foot summit.

At the top, you can enjoy a meal or drink (restaurant open until 18:00 or later) or explore some hiking trails. And, if the weather's good (with winds from the south or west), you can watch paragliders leaping into ecstasy.

Cost and Hours: €2 each way, departs frequently, daily 10:00-22:00, ticket office closes at 18:00.

Eating

$$$ **Weinstube im Baldreit** serves near-gourmet regional dishes—reservations are smart (closed Sun-Mon, Küferstrasse 3, tel. 07221/23136). At the convivial $$$$ **Schneider's Weinstube**, game and meat are the specialty, though there is always a good vegetarian dish (closed Sun, Merkurstrasse 3). $$ **Gasthaus Löwenbräu** slings good beer and basic schnitzel fare under a vine-covered trellis (Gernsbacher Strasse 9). $ **Café König** is *the* place for an elegant cup of coffee and a slice of Black Forest cake (Lichtentaler Strasse 12).

Sleeping

$$$ **Hotel Rathausglöckel** is one of the town's most inviting hotels (RS%, Steinstrasse 7, www.rathausgloeckel.de).

$$$ **Heliopark Bad Hotel zum Hirsch** is wonderfully located in the middle of the pedestrian zone (Hirschstrasse 1, www.heliopark-hirsch.de). $$ **Hotel am Markt** is peaceful and central (Marktplatz 18, www.hotel-am-markt-baden.de). $ **Kloster Lichtenthal Guesthouse** lets you be a part of the cloistered world of a Cistercian abbey (Hauptstrasse 40, www.abtei-lichtenthal.de).

Rick's Tip: *All Baden-Baden hotels and pensions are required to charge an additional €3.80 per person, per night* "spa tax." *This comes with a* "guest card" *(Kurkarte), offering small discounts on tourist admissions around town, including the casino and the Caracalla Spa.*

BEST OF THE REST

Frankfurt

Frankfurt, while low on Old World charm, offers a good look at today's no-nonsense, modern Germany. There's so much more to this country than castles and old cobbled squares.

Ever since the early Middle Ages, people have gathered here to trade. Frankfurt is a pragmatic city, and its decisions are famously based on what's good for business. Cosmopolitan Frankfurt—nicknamed "Bankfurt"—is a business hub of the united Europe and home to the European Central Bank. Fueled in part by the entrepreneurial spirit of its immigrant communities, Frankfurt is a unique and entertaining city.

Day Plan

You might fly into or out of Frankfurt—a major transit hub—or at least pass through. The city's main sights can be enjoyed in a half-day by using the train station as a springboard. At a minimum,

ride up to the top of the Main Tower for commanding city views and wander through the pedestrian zone to the Old Town area (Römerberg). My self-guided walk provides a framework for your explorations.

Orientation

Frankfurt perches on the banks of the Main River. The convention center *(Messe)* and the red light district are near the train station. Just to the east is the skyscraper banking district and the shopping and pedestrian area. Beyond that is what remains of Frankfurt's Old Town, around Römerberg, the city's central market square.

Tourist Information: The handiest TI is just inside the **train station**'s main entrance (daily, tel. 069/212-38800, www.frankfurt-tourismus.de). Another TI is on **Römerberg square.**

Getting There

Frankfurt is well connected by train to

Frankfurt's iconic main train station

all of Germany including: **Rothenburg** (hourly, 3 hours), **Würzburg** (1-2/hour, 70 minutes), **Nürnberg** (1-2/hour, 2 hours), **Munich** (hourly, 3.5 hours), **Baden-Baden** (hourly, 1.5-2 hours, direct or transfer in Karlsruhe), **Bacharach** (hourly, 1.5-2 hours, transfer in Mainz or Bingen), **Cologne** (hourly, 1-1.5 hours), **Berlin** (at least hourly, 4 hours), **Hamburg** (hourly, 4 hours). Frankfurt's main station is a 20-minute walk from the convention center *(Messe)*, or a three-minute subway ride or 20-minute walk from Römerberg.

The **airport,** which has its own train station, is just a 12-minute train ride from the city center. **Drivers** should follow signs for *Frankfurt,* then *Messe,* and finally *Hauptbahnhof* (train station), with its underground garage.

● Frankfurt Walk

This self-guided sightseeing walk, worth ▲▲, shows you the new Frankfurt and the old, as well as its hard edges and softer side.
• *Start at the main train station (Haupt-bahnhof).*

Train Station: Frankfurt has Germany's busiest train station: 350,000 travelers make their way to 24 platforms to catch 1,800 trains every day. Hop a train and you can be in either Paris or Berlin in around four hours.

Position yourself on the traffic island directly opposite the station's front door, and look back at the building's Neo-Renaissance facade—a style popular with Industrial Revolution-era architects. High above, a statue of Atlas carries the world—but only with some heavy-duty help: Green copper figures representing steam power and electricity pitch in.
• *With your back to the station, look down...*

Kaiserstrasse: This grand 19th-century boulevard features appropriately elegant facades that were designed to dress up the approach to what was a fine new station. Towering above and beyond the 100-year-old buildings are the skyscrapers of Frankfurt's banking district.

Sex and Drugs Detour: This walk continues to the banking district, but if you're game, take this adults-only detour. One block down Kaiserstrasse, jog left on Moselstrasse and walk a block to the corner of Taunusstrasse. This is where the city contains and controls its sex-and-drug scene. To the right, Taunusstrasse is lined half with brothels and half with

Frankfurt

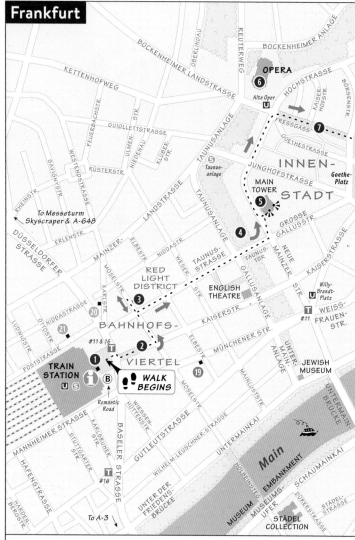

Walk

1. Train Station
2. Kaiserstrasse
3. Sex & Drugs Detour
4. Banking District
5. Main Tower
6. Opera House
7. Fressgass'
8. Hauptwache
9. Zeil
10. Kleinmarkthalle
11. St. Paul's Church
12. Römerberg
13. St. Bartholomew's Cathedral
14. Altstadt
15. Eiserner Steg Bridge

Restaurants

16. Weinstube im Römer
17. Cafébar im Kunstverein
18. Kleinmarkthalle Eateries
19. Merkez Kebab Haus

Hotels

20. Hotel Concorde
21. Hotel Hamburger Hof
22. Hotel Neue Kräme
23. Hotel Zentrum

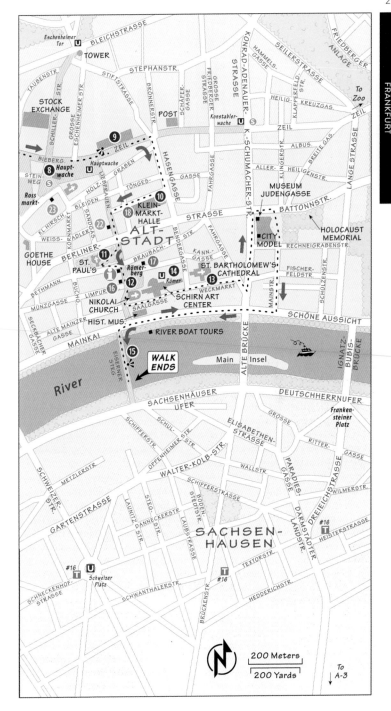

Eschenheimer Tor

BLEICHSTRASSE

TOWER

STEPHANSTR.

TAUBENSTR.

STIFTSTRASSE

STOCK EXCHANGE

SCHILLERSTR.

GROSSE ESCHENHEIMER STR.

BRÖNNERSTR.

SCHÄFERGASSE

POST

KONRAD-ADENAUER-STRASSE

GROSSE FRIEDBERGER STRASSE

HAMMELSGASSE

SEILERSTRASSE

FRIEDBERGER ANLAGE

To Zoo

HEILIG-KREUZGAS.

KLAPPERFELD STR.

Konstablerwache

ZEIL

ALBUS

BREITE GAS.

LANGE STRASSE

9

ZEIL

8 Hauptwache

Hauptwache

STEINWEG

Ross markt-

BIEBERGASSE

GRABEN

HOLZGRABEN

LIEBFRAUEN

TÖNGES-GASSE

HASENGASSE

FAHRGASSE

ALLER-

KLINGERSTR.

HEILIGENSTR.

MUSEUM JUDENGASSE

BATTONNSTR.

HOLOCAUST MEMORIAL

23

KL. HIRSCH

WEISS-

KORNMARKT

KORDLERSTR.

SYONS

BLEIDENSTR.

22

10

18 KLEIN-MARKT-HALLE

ALT-STADT

STRASSE

BENDERGASSE

FAHRGASSE

K.-SCHUMACHER-STR.

CITY MODEL

RECHNEIGRABENSTR.

FISCHER-FELDSTR.

SCHOLZENSTR.

GOETHE HOUSE

BERLINERSTR.

11

ST. PAUL'S

BRAUBACH

Römerberg

17

14

Römer

KANN-GASSE

ST. BARTHOLOMEW'S CATHEDRAL

13

MAINSTR.

BETHMANN-

PUDIG

12

16 LIMPUR-

SAALGASSE

WECKMARKT

SCHIRN ART CENTER

SCHÖNE AUSSICHT

MÜNZGASSE

ALTE MAINZER GASSE

SECKBÄCHER GASSE

NIKOLAI CHURCH

HIST. MUS.

MAINKAI

■ RIVER BOAT TOURS

EISERNER STEG

15

WALK ENDS

Main Insel

ALTE BRÜCKE

IGNATZ-BUBIS-BRÜCKE

DEUTSCHHERRNUFER

River

SACHSENHÄUSER UFER

GROSSE

Frankensteiner Platz

SCHIFFERSTR.

SCHUL-

OPPENHEIMER STR.

ELISABETHEN-STRASSE

RITTER-

GASSE

PARADIESGASSE

DARMSTÄDTER LANDSTR.

DREIEICHSTRASSE

WILMERSTR.

SCHWEIZERSTR.

METZLERSTR.

WALTER-KOLB-STR.

WALLSTR.

SCHIFFERSTRASSE

#16

HEISTERSTRASSE

GARTENSTRASSE

LAUNITZ STR.

DANNECKERSTR.

STEG-

BODEN-STEDTSTR.

LAUBESTRASSE

BRÜCKENSTR.

SACHSEN-HAUSEN

TEXTORSTR.

#16

HEDDERICHSTR.

#16

Schweizer Platz

SCHNECKENHOF STRASSE

SCHWANTHALERSTR.

N

200 Meters

200 Yards

To A-3

Cosmopolitan Frankfurt

bank towers. And across Taunusstrasse and farther down Moselstrasse is a heroin-maintenance clinic, known here as a "drug-consumption room."

• *If you're skipping the sex-and-drugs detour, walk straight down Kaiserstrasse for four blocks and cross the street to the park.*

Banking District: Find the statue of the poet Schiller (a Romantic and friend of Goethe), on your left. This park is part of a greenbelt that encircles the old center and marks the site of Frankfurt's medieval moat and fortifications, and it's the center of Frankfurt's banking district (worth ▲). The post-WWII Marshall Plan was administered from here—requiring fancy money-handling. And the mighty deutsche mark was born in a 1930s-era building facing the park (in the third building, a low Art Deco mansion, now a Deutsche Bundesbank headquarters, on the left of the square as you entered). After World War II, Germany's economy was in chaos. In 1948, the US gave it a complete currency transfer—like a blood transfusion—literally printing up the new deutsche marks and shipping them across the Atlantic to inject them from here directly into the German economy.

Beyond the statue of Schiller stand the twin towers of the Deutsche Bank (not to be confused with the DB—Deutsche Bahn—tower to your left). This country's #1 bank, its assets are greater than the annual budget of the German government. If money makes the world go round, the decisions that spin Germany are made in Frankfurt.

Make a 360-degree spin and survey all the bank towers. Notice the striking architecture. By law, no German worker can be kept out of natural light for more than four hours, so work environments are filled with windows. And, as you can see, Germans like their skyscrapers with windows that open.

• *Find the skyscraper with the red-and-white candy cane on top. That's your destination—the Main Tower. To reach it, continue straight along Taunustor a block, then turn left on Neue Mainzer Strasse and look for the tower symbol on the doors on the right.*

Main Tower: Finished in 2000, this ▲▲ tower houses the Helaba Bank and offers the best (and only public) open-air viewpoint from the top of a Frankfurt skyscraper. A 55-second, ear-popping elevator ride to the 54th floor (watch the meter on the wall as you ascend) and then 50 stairs take you to the rooftop, 650 feet above the city (€7.50, Sun-Thu 10:00-21:00, Fri-Sat until 23:00; closes earlier off-season and during bad weather; enter at Neue Mainzer Strasse 52, between Taunustor and Junghofstrasse, www.maintower.de).

• *Exit right from the Main Tower and continue walking along Neue Mainzer Strasse (crossing Junghofstrasse) for a couple of blocks, to where you see a large square open to your left. Across the square is the...*

Opera House (Alte Oper): Finished in 1880, Frankfurt's opera house celebrated German high culture and the newly created nation. Mozart and Goethe flank the entrance, reminders that this is a house of both music and theater.

• *Facing the opera, turn right down Frankfurt's famous...*

Fressgass': The official names for this pedestrian street are Grosse Bockenheimer Strasse and Kalbächer Gasse... but everyone in Frankfurt calls it the Fressgass', roughly "Feeding Street." It's packed gable-to-gable with eateries and shoulder-to-shoulder with workers wolfing cheap sandwiches, plates of Asian food, and more. It also offers great people-watching. Join in if you're hungry—or

A one-man bratwurst *stand*

wait for more eating options in a couple of blocks.

• *Fressgass' leads to a square called Rathenauplatz, but it's known as Goethe Platz for its central statue. Cross the square and continue straight—the pedestrian street is now called Biebergasse—another block to the...*

Hauptwache: The small, red-and-white building—which has given its name to the square (and the subway station below it)—was built in 1730 to house the Frankfurt city militia. Now it's a café. The square, entirely closed to traffic, is one of the city's hubs.

• *Straight ahead of you is a boulevard called the...*

Zeil: This tree-lined pedestrian drag is Frankfurt's main shopping street. Crowds swirl through the Galeria Kaufhof department store, the Zeil Galerie, and the MyZeil shopping center (the one with the glassy hole in its wall) along the left side of the street.

• *Continue down Zeil a block to the fountain at the next intersection. Turn right on Hasengasse. After about two blocks, find the low-key green entrance to Kleinmarkthalle on the right.*

Kleinmarkthalle: This delightful, old-school market was saved from developers by local outcry, and to this day it's a neighborhood favorite. Explore and sample your way through the ground floor. It's an adventure in fine eating (with a line of simple eateries upstairs, too).

• *Exit the Kleinmarkthalle opposite where you entered. Angle right, and climb five steps into a square (Leibfrauenberg) with a red-brick fountain and the 14th-century Church of Our Lady (rebuilt after World War II). On the far side is Lebkuchen-Schmidt, a fun shop selling traditional gingerbread, a local favorite. Turn left and head downhill on Neue Kräme, then cross Berliner Strasse to Paulsplatz.*

St. Paul's Church (Paulskirche): To your right, the former church dominating the square (worth ▲) is known as the "cradle of German democracy." It

Römerberg, Frankfurt's medieval-style market square

was here, during the political upheaval of 1848, that the first freely elected National Assembly met and the first German Constitution was drafted, paving the way for a united Germany in 1871. Following its destruction by Allied bombs in 1944, the church became the first historic building in the city to be rebuilt. Displays inside tell the story of 1848 (free, daily 10:00-17:00).

• *Walk across the square, cross the next street and tram tracks, and enter what's left of Frankfurt's Old Town.*

Römerberg: Frankfurt's market square (worth ▲) was the birthplace of the city. This is the site of the first trade fairs (12th century), bank (1405), and stock exchange (1585). Now, crowds of tourists convene here. Römerberg's central statue is the goddess of justice without her customary blindfold. She oversees the Town Hall, which itself oversees trade. The Town Hall (*Römer*) houses the *Kaisersaal,* or Imperial Hall, where Holy Roman Emperors celebrated their coronations. The cute row of half-timbered homes (rebuilt in 1983) opposite the *Römer* is typical of Frankfurt's quaint old center before the square was destroyed in World War II. The Gothic red-and-

white Old Nikolai Church (Alte Nikolaikirche, with fine stained glass) dates from the 13th century and was restored after the war.

• *Turn left past the Old Nikolai Church and walk through the courtyard of the Schirn Art Center to the big red...*

St. Bartholomew's Cathedral (Kaiserdom): Holy Roman Emperors were elected at this Catholic church starting in 1152 and crowned here between 1562 and 1792.

Enter on the side opposite the river (free, www.dom-frankfurt.de). Frescoes from the 15th century survive (flanking the high altar and ringing the choir). They show 27 scenes from the life of St. Bartholomew. The Electors Chapel (to the right of the altar) is where the electors convened to choose the Holy Roman Emperor in the Middle Ages.

Before the WWII bombs fell, everything of value that could be moved was taken from the church. The delightful sandstone Chapel of Sleeping Mary (to the left of the high altar), carved and painted in the 15th century, was too big to move—so it was fortified with sandbags.

• *Exit the cathedral where you entered and turn left, passing the red-and-white, half-timbered, gold-trimmed house that marks the start of the...*

Altstadt ("New Old Town"): This "new" development (officially called the DomRömer Quarter)—70 years in the making—is a reconstruction of the half-timbered Old Town destroyed during World War II. Notice the buildings' eclectic mix of colors and styles, some with slate roofs, others with red sandstone facades, and others with doors made from 300-year-old oak. This mix of new and old architecture is a microcosm of today's Frankfurt.

Before the war, this was a lively center of pubs, small businesses, and workshops. While today's Altstadt feels a bit saccharin, the city hopes this mix of reconstructed and new buildings will return the square to something close to its former character.

• *Returning to the cathedral, you can turn left on Weckmarkt and continue a couple of blocks to visit the* **Jewish Holocaust Memorial,** *and/or the* **Frankfurt City Model** *(both free). Or head down to the river, turn right, and walk along the pleasant riverfront park to the next bridge. Head out to its center.*

Eiserner Steg Bridge: This iron bridge, the city's second oldest, dates to 1869. (The oldest is just upstream: the Alte Brücke, a fifth-century crossing.) From the middle of the bridge, survey the skyline and enjoy the lively scene along the riverbanks of Frankfurt.

• *For a quick return to your starting point at the main train station (Hauptbahnhof), walk back to Römerberg and take the U-Bahn or board tram #11 or #12.*

Rick's Tip: *The cobbled Sachsenhausen neighborhood is the place to find characteristic* **Apfelwein** (apple wine) **pubs.** *Cross the river on the pedestrian-only Eiserner Steg bridge, and head to one of these woodsy, rustic spots, open late daily:* **Dauth-Schneider** *(Neuer Wall 5) ,* **Atschel** *(Wallstrasse 7), or* **Fichtekränzi** *(evenings only, Wallstrasse 5).*

Eating

On Römerberg, the classic **$$ Weinstube im Römer** serves good schnitzel (closed Mon, Römerberg 19). **$$ Cafébar im Kunstverein,** a few steps off the square, is a fine value and hosts more locals than tourists (cash only, Markt 44).

The **$ Kleinmarkthalle** is one of the most charming and inviting indoor market halls you'll find anywhere in Germany, and a great place for a simple lunch (closed Sun). Near the station, **$$ Merkez Kebab Haus** is the best place for Turkish food (Münchener Strasse 33).

Sleeping

Near the train station, consider **$$ Hotel Concorde,** in a restored 1890s building (Karlstrasse 9, www.hotelconcorde.com) or **$$ Hotel Hamburger Hof,** in a quiet and safe-feeling location (Poststrasse 10, www.hamburgerhof.com). **$$ Hotel Neue Kräme** is a quiet little oasis just steps from Römerberg (Neue Kräme 23, www.hotel-neuekraeme.de). You'll find **$$ Hotel Zentrum** hidden in a great location near the Hauptwache (Rossmarkt 7, www.hotel-zentrum.de).

Berlin

Berlin is a city of leafy boulevards, grand Neoclassical buildings, world-class art, glitzy shopping arcades, and funky graffitied neighborhoods with gourmet street food. It's big and bombastic—the showcase city of kings and kaisers, of the Führer and 21st-century commerce.

Berlin is still largely defined by its WWII years, and the Cold War. The East-West division was set in stone in 1961, when the East German government surrounded West Berlin with the Berlin Wall. Since the fall of the Wall in 1989, Berlin has been a constant construction zone. Standing on ripped-up streets and under a canopy of cranes, visitors have witnessed the city's reunification and rebirth. Today Berlin is a world capital once again.

In the city's top-notch museums, you can walk through an enormous Babylonian gate amid rough-and-tumble ancient statuary, fondle a chunk of the Berlin Wall, and peruse canvases by Dürer and Rembrandt. A series of thought-provoking memorials confront Germany's difficult past. And some of the best history exhibits anywhere—covering everything from Prussian princes to Nazi atrocities to life under communism—can turn even those who claim to hate history into armchair experts.

Berlin is simply a pleasurable place—captivating, lively, fun-loving, and easy on the budget. Grab a drink from a sidewalk vendor, find a bench along the river, watch the sun set over a skyline of domes and cranes...and simply bask in Berlin.

BERLIN IN 3 DAYS

Day 1: Begin your day getting oriented to this huge city. For a quick and relaxing once-over-lightly tour, jump on one of the many hop-on, hop-off buses that make orientation loops through the city.

Then take Part 1 of my self-guided "Berlin City Walk," starting at the Reichstag (reservations and passport required to climb its dome), going through the Brandenburg Gate, and down the boulevard, Unter den Linden. Visit the charming Gendarmenmarkt square. Then tour the German History Museum.

On any evening: Any of these neighborhoods (all near each other) are worth exploring: Hackescher Markt, the old Jewish quarter, and Prenzlauer Berg. Take in live music or cabaret. Linger at a beer garden or stroll the banks of the Spree River. Or even continue your sightseeing—a number of sights stay open late, including the Reichstag and its view dome.

Day 2: Start your morning at Bebelplatz with Part 2 of my "Berlin City Walk." Along the way, visit any museum that interests you on Museum Island or nearby: Pergamon, Neues, Old National Gallery, or the DDR.

In the afternoon, catch a one-hour boat tour (or pedal a rented bike) along the parklike banks of the Spree River. Explore the Hackescher Markt's shops and nearby Hackesche Höfe (connected shopping courtyards), and stay into the evening.

Day 3: Tour the sights of the Third Reich and Cold War: the Topography of Terror exhibit and Museum of the Wall at Checkpoint Charlie. The Jewish Museum Berlin is also nearby.

In the afternoon, visit the Gemäldegalerie art museum.

Head to Prenzlauer Berg to visit the Berlin Wall Memorial, then stay for the café and nightlife scene.

ORIENTATION

Berlin is huge and spread out—a series of colorful neighborhoods, with broad boulevards, pleasant parks, long blocks, and low five-story buildings.

Historic Core: Berlin's 1.5-mile sightseeing axis runs west-to-east along **Unter den Linden** boulevard. At the western edge, you'll find the **Reichstag** (parliament), the

historic **Brandenburg Gate,** and poignant memorials. It runs past the grand squares of Gendarmenmarkt and Bebelplatz before ending at **Museum Island**—home to the Pergamon, Neues, German History, and DDR museums, among others.

Northern Berlin: The trendy **old Jewish quarter,** near the Hackescher Markt transit hub, has eateries, shopping, and Jewish history. Farther out is the even hipper **Prenzlauer Berg,** with recommended hotels, restaurants, and shopping. Also in this zone are the **Berlin Wall Memorial**—the best place in town to learn more about the Wall—and the **Hauptbahnhof** (main train station).

Southern Berlin: South of Unter den Linden, **fascism and Cold War sights** dominate, anchored by Checkpoint Charlie (former Wall crossing point) and the Topography of Terror (documenting Nazi atrocities). The Jewish Museum Berlin is also here.

Eastern Berlin: East of Museum Island, Unter den Linden changes its name to Karl-Liebknecht-Strasse and leads to **Alexanderplatz**—formerly the hub of communist East Berlin, still marinated in brutal architecture, and marked by its impossible-to-miss TV Tower.

The Brandenburg Gate—historic and grand

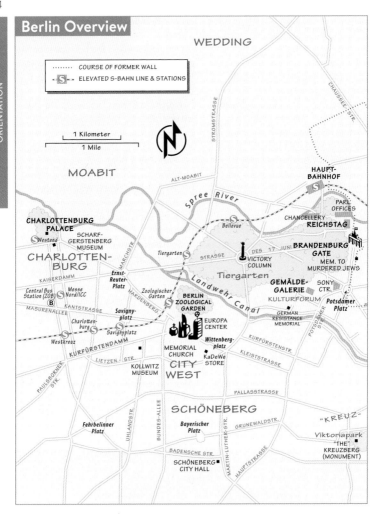

Berlin Overview

- ········· COURSE OF FORMER WALL
- --S-- ELEVATED S-BAHN LINE & STATIONS

1 Kilometer

1 Mile

WEDDING

MOABIT

ALT-MOABIT

STROMSTRASSE

CHAUSSEE-STR.

HAUPT-BAHNHOF

Spree River

PARL. OFFICES

CHARLOTTENBURG PALACE

Westend

SCHARF-GERSTENBERG MUSEUM

CHARLOTTEN-BURG

KAISERDAMM

MARCHSTR.

Bellevue

Tiergarten

STRASSE

DES 17 JUNI

VICTORY COLUMN

Tiergarten

CHANCELLERY

REICHSTAG

BRANDENBURG GATE

MEM. TO MURDERED JEWS

Landwehr Canal

GEMÄLDE-GALERIE

SONY CTR.

Ernst-Reuter-Platz

Central Bus Station (ZOB)

Messe Nord/ICC

(B)

MASURENALLEE

HARDENBERG

Zoologischer Garten

Savigny-platz

BERLIN ZOOLOGICAL GARDEN

KULTURFORUM

GERMAN RESISTANCE MEMORIAL

Potsdamer Platz

POTSDAMER STR.

KANTSTRASSE

Charlotten-burg

Savignyplatz

EUROPA CENTER

Westkreuz

KURFÜRSTENDAMM

LIETZEN STR.

KOLLWITZ MUSEUM

MEMORIAL CHURCH

Wittenberg-platz

KaDeWe STORE

KURFÜRSTENSTR.

KLEISTSTRASSE

PAULSBORNER STR.

CITY WEST

PALLASSTRASSE

UHLANDSTR.

BUNDES-ALLEE

SCHÖNEBERG

MARTIN-LUTHER-STR.

GRUNEWALDSTR.

"KREUZ-

Fehrbelliner Platz

Bayerischer Platz

Viktoriapark

"THE" KREUZBERG (MONUMENT)

BADENSCHE STR.

SCHÖNEBERG CITY HALL

HAUPTSTRASSE

Rick's Tip: *What Americans called* **"East Germany"** *was technically the German Democratic Republic—the Deutsche Demokratische Republik, or* **DDR** *(pronounced day-day-AIR). You'll still see those initials around what was once East Germany. The name for what was "West Germany"—the Federal Republic of Germany (Bundesrepublik Deutschland, or* **BRD**)—*is now the name shared by all of Germany.*

Western Berlin: Just west of the Brandenburg Gate is Berlin's huge central park, **Tiergarten.** South of the gate, **Potsdamer Platz** is home to Berlin's 21st-century glitz, with skyscrapers and shopping plazas. Down the street, the **Kulturforum** is a cluster of museums, including the impressive Gemäldegalerie (starring Rembrandt, Dürer, and others).

Tourist Information

Berlin's TIs are for-profit agencies that are only marginally helpful (tel. 030/250-025,

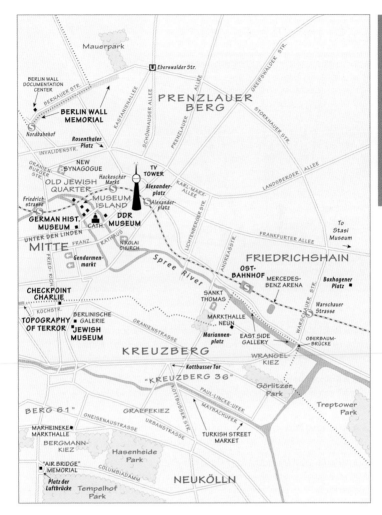

www.visitberlin.de). You'll find one at the **Hauptbahnhof** (daily 8:00-21:00, by main entrance on Europaplatz), and "info box" kiosks at the **Brandenburg Gate** (daily 9:30-19:00, Nov-March until 18:00) and **Tegel Airport** (daily 8:00-21:00).

Sightseeing Passes

The €29 **Museum Pass Berlin** is best for serious museumgoers—it covers nearly all the city sights for three consecutive days (see details at www.visitberlin.de). It gets you into more than 35 museums,

including the national museums and most of the recommended biggies. Covered sights include the Museum Island museums, German History Museum, and the Gemäldegalerie. Buy it at any participating museum or a TI. The pass generally lets you skip the line and go directly into the museum—except at the Pergamon and Neues, where you should prebook a time slot on their websites.

The €18 **Museum Island Pass** (not sold at TIs; see www.smb.museum) covers all sights on Museum Island and is a fine value

BERLIN AT A GLANCE

▲▲▲**Reichstag** Germany's historic parliament building, topped with a striking modern dome you can climb (reservations required). **Hours:** Daily 8:00-24:00. See page 313.

▲▲▲**Brandenburg Gate** One of Berlin's most famous landmarks, a massive columned gateway, at the former border of East and West. See page 315.

▲▲▲**German History Museum** The ultimate swing through Germany's tumultuous story. **Hours:** Daily 10:00-18:00. See page 322.

▲▲▲**Berlin Wall Memorial** Museums with videos and displays, several outdoor exhibits, and lone surviving stretch of an intact Wall section. **Hours:** Museums open Tue-Sun 10:00-18:00, closed Mon; outdoor areas accessible daily 24 hours. See page 324.

▲▲**Memorial to the Murdered Jews of Europe** Holocaust memorial with almost 3,000 symbolic pillars, plus an exhibition about Hitler's Jewish victims. **Hours:** Memorial always open; information center Tue-Sun 10:00-20:00, Oct-March until 19:00, closed Mon year-round. See page 315.

▲▲**Unter den Linden** Leafy boulevard in the heart of former East Berlin, lined with some of the city's top sights. See page 315.

▲▲**Memorials near the Reichstag** Tributes to Nazi victims, including Jews, Roma, homosexuals, and opposing politicians. See page 314.

▲▲**Pergamon Museum** World-class museum of classical antiquities on Museum Island (Pergamon Altar closed through 2025). **Hours:** Daily 10:00-18:00, Thu until 20:00. See page 318.

▲▲**Neues Museum** Egyptian antiquities collection and proud home of the exquisite 3,000-year-old bust of Queen Nefertiti. **Hours:** Daily 10:00-18:00, Thu until 20:00. See page 320.

▲▲**Old National Gallery** German paintings, mostly from the Romantic Age. **Hours:** Tue-Sun 10:00-18:00, Thu until 20:00, closed Mon. See page 321.

▲▲**DDR Museum** Quirky collection of communist-era artifacts. **Hours:** Daily 10:00-20:00, Sat until 22:00. See page 323.

▲▲**Courtyards** (Höfe) Interconnected courtyards with shops, eateries, and museums, best explored in the old Jewish quarter. See page 323.

▲▲**Prenzlauer Berg** Lively, colorful neighborhood with hip cafés, restaurants, boutiques, and street life. See page 324.

▲▲**Topography of Terror** Chilling exhibit documenting the Nazi perpetrators, built on the site of the former Gestapo/SS headquarters. **Hours:** Daily 10:00-20:00. See page 331.

▲▲**Gemäldegalerie** Germany's top collection of 13th- through 18th-century European paintings, featuring Holbein, Dürer, Cranach, Van der Weyden, Rubens, Hals, Rembrandt, Vermeer, Raphael, and more. **Hours:** Tue-Fri 10:00-18:00, Thu until 20:00, Sat-Sun 11:00-18:00, closed Mon. See page 333.

▲**Museum of the Wall at Checkpoint Charlie** Stories of brave Cold War escapes, near the site of the famous former East-West border checkpoint; the surrounding street scene is almost as interesting. **Hours:** Daily 9:00-22:00. See page 329.

(though for just €11 more, the three-day Museum Pass Berlin described above gives you triple the days and many more entries).

TIs sell the **WelcomeCard,** a transportation pass that includes discounts for many sights; it's a good value if you'll be using public transit frequently (see page 350).

Helpful Hints

Closures: Many museums are closed on Monday, including the Berlin Wall Memorial Visitors Center and Documentation Center, and the Gemäldegalerie, but many also stay open late on Thursdays.

Laundry: You'll find several self-service launderettes near my recommended hotels (generally daily 6:00-22:00). In Prenzlauer Berg, try **Eco-Express Waschsalon** (Danziger Strasse 7) or **Schnell & Sauber Waschcenter** (Oderberger Strasse 1). In the old Jewish quarter, there are two launderettes around the corner from Rosenthaler Platz: **Waschsalon 115** (Wi-Fi, Torstrasse 115) and **Eco-Express Waschsalon** (Torstrasse 109).

Tours

▲▲HOP-ON, HOP-OFF BUSES

Several companies offer a circuit of the city with unlimited, all-day hop-on, hop-off privileges for around €25. Buses make about a dozen stops at the city's major tourist spots (Museum Island, Brandenburg Gate, and so on). Look for brochures in your hotel lobby or at the TI, or check the websites for **CitySightseeing Berlin,** a.k.a. Berlin City Tour (www.berlin-city-tour.de) and **City Circle Sightseeing,** a.k.a.

BEX (www.berlinerstadtrundfahrten.de). Try to catch a bus with a live guide, not recorded narration (buses generally run daily 10:00-18:00, 4/hour, last departure from all stops around 16:00, 2-hour loop; Nov-March 2/hour, last departure 15:00).

▲▲SPREE RIVER CRUISES

Several boat companies offer €15 trips up and down the river in one relaxing hour. Boats leave from docks clustered near the bridge behind the Berlin Cathedral (just off Unter den Linden, near the DDR Museum). For better views, go for a two-story boat with open-deck seating. I enjoyed the Historical Sightseeing Cruise from **Stern und Kreisschiffahrt** (departures on the half-hour, mid-March-Nov daily 10:30-17:30, leaves from Nikolaiviertel Dock—cross bridge from Berlin Cathedral toward Alexanderplatz and look right; RS%—show this book for free English audioguide, otherwise €2; tel. 030/536-3600, www.sternundkreis.de).

▲▲▲WALKING TOURS

Berlin's fascinating and complex history can be challenging to appreciate on your own, but a good Berlin tour guide and walking tour makes the city's dynamic story come to life. Germany has no regulations controlling who can give city tours, so guide quality is hit-or-miss. To improve your odds of landing a great guide, try one of my recommendations. Most tours cost about €12-15 and last 3-4 hours.

Original Berlin Walks' "Discover Berlin" walk offers a solid overview with a smart itinerary in four hours (daily, RS%—

€2 less with this book). Tours depart from opposite the Hackescher Markt S-Bahn station (tel. 030/301-9194, www.berlinwalks.de).

Insider Tour runs the full gamut of itineraries, as well as a day trip to Dresden. Their tours meet in front of the McDonald's outside the Zoologischer Garten S-Bahn station and outside the AM to PM Bar at the Hackescher Markt S-Bahn station (tel. 030/692-3149, www.insidertour.com).

Rick's Tip: *Supposedly* **"free" tours are advertised all over town.** *English-speaking students deliver a memorized script and expect to be "tipped in paper" (€5 minimum per person is encouraged). While the guides can be highly entertaining, when it comes to walking tours, you get what you pay for.*

LOCAL GUIDES
Most licensed guides charge €65/hour or €200-300/day. Guides can get booked up—especially in summer—so reserve ahead. I've personally worked with and can strongly recommend archaeologist **Nick Jackson** (mobile 0171-537-8768, www.jacksonsberlintours.com).

Lee Evans (makes 20th-century Germany a thriller, mobile 0176-6335-5565, lee.evans@berlin.de); **Torben Brown** (a walking Berlin encyclopedia, mobile 0176-5004-2572, www.berlinperspectives.com); and **Holger Zimmer** (a cultural connoisseur and public radio journalist, mobile 0163-345-4427, explore@berlin.de).

BERLIN CITY WALK

Trace Germany's turbulent 20th-century history on this two-mile self-guided walk, worth ▲▲▲. We'll start in front of the Reichstag, pass through the Brandenburg Gate, walk down Unter den Linden, and finish on Alexanderplatz, near the TV Tower. If you have just one day in Berlin, or want a good orientation to the city, simply

follow this walk (allow 2-3 hours at a brisk pace, not counting museum visits). If you have more time and want to use this walk as a spine for your sightseeing, entering sights and museums as you go, consider doing Part 1 and Part 2 on different days.

Part 1 goes from the Reichstag and partway down Unter den Linden, with stops at the Brandenburg Gate, Memorial to the Murdered Jews of Europe, and Friedrichstrasse, the glitzy shopping street. Part 2 continues down Unter den Linden, from Bebelplatz to Alexanderplatz, visiting Museum Island and the Spree River, the Berlin Cathedral, and the iconic TV Tower.

Tours: ∩ Download my free Berlin City Walk audio tour.

⊙ Self-Guided Walk
Part 1: The Reichstag to Unter den Linden
• *Start in Platz der Republik and take in your surroundings. Dominating this park is a giant domed building.*

❶ REICHSTAG
The Reichstag is the heart of Germany's government. It's where the Bundestag—the lower house of parliament—meets to govern the nation (similar to the US House of Representatives).

When the building was inaugurated in 1895, Germany was still a kingdom. Back then, the real center of power was a mile east of here, at the royal palace. But after the emperor was deposed in World War I, the German Republic was proclaimed. Meanwhile, the storm of National Socialism was growing—the Nazis. Soon the Reichstag had dozens of duly elected National Socialists, and Adolf Hitler seized power. In 1933, the Reichstag building nearly burned down. Many believe that Hitler planned the fire as an excuse to frame the communists and grab power for himself.

With Hitler as Führer and real democracy a thing of the past, the Reichstag was

The Reichstag is the symbolic heart of German democracy.

hardly used. But it remained a powerful symbol and was a prime target for Allied bombers during World War II. As the war wound down and Soviet troops advanced on the city, it was here at the Reichstag that 1,500 German troops made their last stand. After the war, Berlin was divided and the Berlin Wall ran right behind the Reichstag. The building fell into disuse, and the West German capital was moved from Berlin to the remote city of Bonn.

After the Berlin Wall fell, the Reichstag again became the focus of the new nation. It was renovated by British architect Norman Foster, who added the glass dome. In 1999, the new Reichstag reopened, and the parliament reconvened. To many Germans, the proud resurrection of their Reichstag symbolizes the end of a terrible chapter in their country's history.

Look now at the Reichstag's modern **dome.** The cupola rises 155 feet above the ground. Inside the dome, a cone of 360 mirrors reflects natural light into the legislative chamber below, and an opening at the top allows air to circulate. Lit from inside after dark, it gives Berlin a memorable nightlight. If you make a reservation to visit the interior, you can climb the spiral ramp all the way to the top of the dome for a grand city view (for details on visiting, see the Reichstag listing under "Sights," later).

Facing the Reichstag, do a 360-degree spin to find some other big landmarks. To the left of the Reichstag, at the Bundestag U-Bahn stop, the long, partly transparent building houses parliamentary offices. Beyond that, in the distance, is the tower of the huge main train station, the Hauptbahnhof (marked *DB* for Deutsche Bahn, the German rail company). Farther left is the mammoth, white, concrete-and-glass Chancellery (nicknamed "the Washing Machine"). This is the office of Germany's most powerful person, the chancellor. To remind the chancellor who he or she works for, Germany's Reichstag (housing the parliament) is about six feet taller than the Chancellery.

• *Approach the Reichstag, turn right, walk nearly to the street, and find a small memorial next to the shipping container-like entrance buildings. It's a row of slate stones sticking out of the ground—it looks like a bike rack. This is the...*

❷ MEMORIAL TO POLITICIANS WHO OPPOSED HITLER

These 96 slabs honor the 96 Reichstag members who spoke out against Adolf Hitler and the rising tide of fascism. When Hitler became chancellor, these critics were persecuted and murdered. On each slab, you'll see a name and political party—most are KPD (Communists) and SPD (Social Democrats)—and the date and location of death (*KZ* denotes those who died in concentration camps).

• *Walk east, along the right side of the Reichstag, on busy Scheidemannstrasse, toward the rear of the building. At the intersection at the back of the Reichstag, turn right and cross the street to a humble row of white crosses that predate the fall of the wall.*

❸ BERLIN WALL VICTIMS MEMORIAL

The Berlin Wall once stood right here, running north-south down what is now busy Ebertstrasse, dividing the city in two. The row of white crosses commemorates a few of the many brave East Berliners who died trying to cross the Wall to freedom. (For more on the Wall, see page 330.) The last person killed was 20-year-old Chris Gueffroy. He died nine months before the Wall fell, shot through the heart just a few steps away from here.

Several other memorials dedicated to groups targeted by the Nazis (from Sinti/Roma to homosexuals) are in the vicinity.

For details and where to find them, see page 314.

• *Continue south down Ebertstrasse toward the Brandenburg Gate, tracing the former course of the Berlin Wall. A thin strip of memorial bricks embedded in the street pavement indicates where it once stood. Ebertstrasse spills into a busy intersection dominated by the imposing Brandenburg Gate. To take in this scene, cross the Berlin Wall bricks to the piazza in front of the...*

❹ BRANDENBURG GATE

This massive classical-looking monument is the grandest—and last survivor—of the 14 original gates in Berlin's old city wall. (This one led to the neighboring city of Brandenburg.) The majestic four-horse chariot on top is driven by the Goddess of Peace. When Napoleon conquered Prussia in 1806, he took this statue to the Louvre in Paris. Then, after the Prussians defeated Napoleon, they got it back (in 1813)...and the Goddess of Peace was renamed the "Goddess of Victory."

The gate straddles the major east-west axis of the city. The western segment—behind you—stretches four miles, running through Tiergarten Park to the Olympic Stadium. To the east—on the other side of the gate—the street is called Unter den Linden. That's where we're headed.

Historically, the Brandenburg Gate was just another of this city's many stately Prussian landmarks. But in our lifetime, it

Memorial to Politicans Who Opposed Hitler

Berlin Wall Victims Memorial

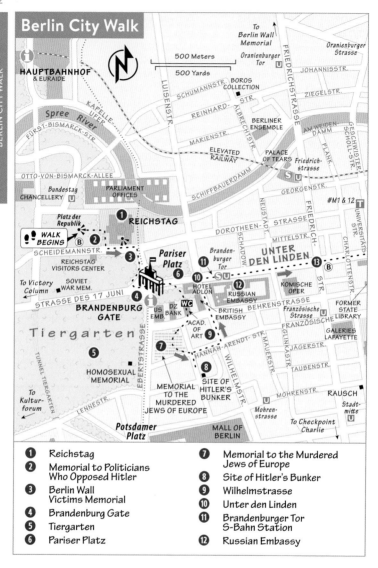

Berlin City Walk

500 Meters
500 Yards

1 Reichstag
2 Memorial to Politicians Who Opposed Hitler
3 Berlin Wall Victims Memorial
4 Brandenburg Gate
5 Tiergarten
6 Pariser Platz
7 Memorial to the Murdered Jews of Europe
8 Site of Hitler's Bunker
9 Wilhelmstrasse
10 Unter den Linden
11 Brandenburger Tor S-Bahn Station
12 Russian Embassy

became *the* symbol of Berlin—of its Cold War division and its reunification. That's because, from 1961 to 1989, the gate was stranded in the no-man's land between East and West. For an entire generation, scores of German families were divided—some on this side of the Wall, some on the other. This landmark stood tantalizingly close to both East and West...but was off-limits to all.

By the 1980s, the once-mighty Soviet empire was slowly crumbling from within. Finally, on November 9, 1989, the East German government opened the border. The world rejoiced at the sight of happy Berliners standing atop the Wall. They chipped away at it with hammers, passed beers to their long-lost cousins on the other side, and adorned the Bran-

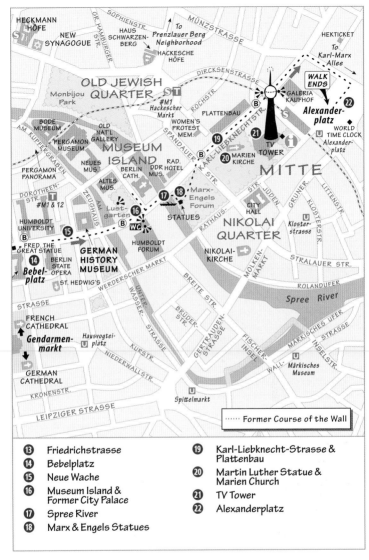

13	Friedrichstrasse	**19**	Karl-Liebknecht-Strasse & Plattenbau
14	Bebelplatz	**20**	Martin Luther Statue & Marien Church
15	Neue Wache		
16	Museum Island & Former City Palace	**21**	TV Tower
17	Spree River	**22**	Alexanderplatz
18	Marx & Engels Statues		

denburg Gate with flowers like a parade float.

• *Turn 180 degrees and take in the vast, green expanse of the park called...*

❺ TIERGARTEN

Look down the long boulevard (Strasse des 17. Juni) that bisects the 500-acre park called Tiergarten ("Animal Garden"). The boulevard's name comes from the 17th of June, 1953, when brave East Germans rose up against their communist leaders. The rebellion was crushed, and East Berliners had to wait another 36 years for the freedom to walk through the Brandenburg Gate. In the distance is the 220-foot **Victory Column,** topped with a golden statue that commemorates the three big military victories that established Prussia as a world power in the late 1800s—over France, Denmark, and Austria—and kicked off Berlin's golden age.

• *Walk through the Brandenburg Gate, entering what for years was forbidden territory. Just past the gate, there's a small TI on the right, and on the left is the Room of Silence, dedicated to meditation. As you cross through this historic but long forbidden gate, you enter a grand square known as...*

❻ PARISER PLATZ

Pariser Platz marks the start of Unter den Linden, the broad boulevard that stretches before you. "Parisian Square" was so named after the Prussians defeated France and Napoleon in 1813. The square was once filled with important government buildings, but all were bombed to smithereens in World War II. For decades, it was an unrecognizable, deserted no-man's-land, cut off from both East and West by the Wall. But now it's rebuilt, and the banks and hotels that were here before the bombing have reclaimed their original places, with a few modern additions. And the winners of World War II—the US, France, Great Britain, and Russia—continue to enjoy this prime real estate: Their embassies are all on or near this square.

The **US Embassy** (on the right as you come through the gate) reopened here in its original location on July 4, 2008. To the left of the US Embassy is the **DZ Bank Building,** built as a conference center in 2001 by Canadian-American architect Frank Gehry (its low-profile exterior was designed so as not to draw attention away from the Brandenburg Gate). To get your fix of wild and colorful Gehry, step into the building's lobby. The undulating interior is like a big, slithery fish.

Two doors past the bank is the ritzy **Hotel Adlon.** Over the years, this place has hosted celebrities and VIPs from Charlie Chaplin to Albert Einstein. And yes, this was where pop star Michael Jackson shocked millions by dangling his infant son over the railing (from the second balcony up).

• *The most direct route to our next stop is by cutting through the **Academy of Arts** (Akademie der Künst) building—it's between Hotel Adlon and the DZ Bank, at Pariser Platz 4. (If the Academy of Arts is closed, loop to the left around the Hotel Adlon to Behrenstrasse.)*

Enter the glassy Academy of Arts (WC in basement) and head toward the back. Just past the ground-floor café (an oasis of calm) is the former office of Albert Speer, Hitler's architect. Continue on, passing Speer's favorite statue, Prometheus (from around 1900). This is the kind of art that turned on Hitler: a strong, soldierly, vital man, defending the homeland.

• *As you exit out the back of the building, veer right on Behrenstrasse and cross the street. You'll wind up at our next stop, a sprawling field of stubby concrete pillars.*

❼ MEMORIAL TO THE MURDERED JEWS OF EUROPE

This memorial consists of 2,711 coffin-shaped pillars covering an entire city block. More than 160,000 Jewish people lived in Berlin when Hitler took power. Tens of thousands fled, and many more were arrested, sent to nearby Sachsenhausen concentration camp and eventually murdered. The memorial remembers them and the other six million Jews who were killed by the Nazis during World War II. Completed in 2005 by the Jewish-American architect Peter Eisenman, this was the first formal, German government-sponsored Holocaust memorial. Using the word "murdered" in the title was intentional, and a big deal. Germany, as a nation, was admitting to a crime.

Inside the **information center** (in the far-left corner), exhibits trace the rise of Nazism and tell the victims' stories (for details on visiting the information center, see page 315).

• *At the far-left corner, a little beyond the information center, you eventually emerge*

Memorial to the Murdered Jews of Europe

on the street corner. Our next stop is about a block farther. Carefully jaywalk across Hannah-Arendt-Strasse and continue straight (south) down Gertrud-Kolmar-Strasse. On the left side of the street, you'll reach a rough parking lot. At the far end of the lot is an information plaque labeled Führerbunker. *This marks the...*

❽ SITE OF HITLER'S BUNKER

You're standing atop the buried remains of the *Führerbunker*. In early 1945, as Allied armies advanced on Berlin and Nazi Germany lay in ruins, Hitler and his staff retreated to this bunker complex behind the former Reich Chancellery. He stayed here for two months.

It was here, on April 30, 1945—as the Soviet army tightened its noose on the Nazi capital—that Hitler and Eva Braun, his wife of less than 48 hours, committed suicide. A week later, the war in Europe was over. The information board here explains the rest of the story. Though the site of Hitler's bunker is part of history, there really isn't much to see here. And

that's on purpose. No one wants to turn Hitler's final stronghold into a tourist attraction.

• *Backtrack up Gertrud-Kolmar-Strasse, and turn right on Hannah-Arendt-Strasse. Take your first left (at the traffic light) on...*

❾ WILHELMSTRASSE

This street was the traditional center of the German power, beginning back when Germany first became a nation in the 19th century. It was lined with stately palaces housing foreign embassies and government offices. This was the home of the Reich Chancellery, where the nation's chief executive presided. When the Nazis took control, this street was where Hitler waved to his adoring fans, and where Joseph Goebbels had his Ministry of Propaganda.

During World War II, Wilhelmstrasse was the nerve center of the German war command. From here, Hitler directed the war and ordered the Blitz (the air raids that destroyed much of London). As the war turned to the Allies' side, Wilhelmstrasse and the neighborhood around it were heavily bombed. Most of the stately palaces were destroyed, and virtually nothing historic survives today.

• *The pedestrianized part of the street is home to the* **British Embassy.** *The fun purple color of its wall represents the colors of the Union Jack mixed together. Wilhelmstrasse spills out onto Berlin's main artery, the tree-lined Unter den Linden, next to the Hotel Adlon.*

⓾ UNTER DEN LINDEN

This boulevard, worth ▲▲, is the heart of imperial Germany. During Berlin's Golden Age in the late 1800s, this was one of Europe's grand boulevards—the Champs-Elysées of Berlin, a city of nearly two million people. It was lined with linden trees, so as you promenaded down, you'd be walking *"unter den Linden."* The street got its start in the 15th century as a way to connect the royal palace (a half-mile down the road, at the end of this walk) with the king's hunting grounds (today's Tiergarten Park). Over the centuries, aristocrats moved into this area so their palaces could be close to their king's.

Many of the grandest landmarks we'll pass along here are thanks to Frederick the Great, who ruled from 1740 to 1786, and put his kingdom (Prussia) and his capital (Berlin) on the map. After World War II, this part of Berlin fell under Soviet influence, and Unter den Linden was the main street of communist East Berlin.

• *Turn your attention to the subway stop in front of the Hotel Adlon (labeled Brandenburger Tor). We'll enter the station and reemerge a block or so farther down the boulevard.*

⓫ BRANDENBURGER TOR S-BAHN STATION

For a time-travel experience back to DDR days, head down the stairs into this station (no ticket necessary). Keep to the right as you descend (toward the S-Bahn, not the U-Bahn) to the subway tracks. As you walk along the platform about 200 yards, survey the historic black-and-white photos on the walls and feel the 1950s vibe of the station.

For decades, the Brandenburger Tor S-Bahn station was unused—one of Berlin's "ghost stations." There's the original 1930s green tilework on the walls, and harsh fluorescent lighting. Some old signs (on the central kiosks) still have *Unter den Linden* (the original name of this stop) written in old Gothic lettering. During the Cold War, the zigzag line dividing East and West Berlin meant that some existing train lines crossed the border underground. To make a little hard Western cash, the East German government allowed a few trains to cut under East Berlin (without stopping) on their way between Western destinations. For 28 years, as Western trains slowly passed through, passengers saw only East German guards...and lots of cobwebs. Then, in 1989, within days of the fall of the Wall, these stations were reopened.

Unter den Linden

Brandenburger Tor ghost subway station

• At the far end of the platform, ascend the escalator, bear right, and head up the stairs to exit. You'll emerge on the right side of Unter den Linden. Belly up to the bars and look in at the...

⑫ RUSSIAN EMBASSY

Built from the ashes of World War II, this imposing building made it clear to East Berliners who was now in charge: the Soviet Union. It was the first big postwar building project in East Berlin, built in the powerful, simplified Neoclassical style that Stalin liked. After the fall of the Soviet Union in 1991, this building became the Russian Embassy, flying the white, blue, and red flag. Find the hammer-and-sickle motif decorating the window frames—a reminder of the days when Russia was part of the USSR.

• Keep walking down the boulevard for two blocks. You'll pass blocks of dull banks, tacky trinket shops, and a few high-end boutiques, eventually reaching cultural buildings—the university, the opera, and so on. That's intentional: The Prussian kings wanted to have culture closer to their palace. Pause when you reach the intersection with...

⑬ FRIEDRICHSTRASSE

You're standing at perhaps the most central crossroads in Berlin—named for, you guessed it, Frederick the Great. Before World War II, Friedrichstrasse was the heart of cultural Berlin. In the Roaring Twenties, it was home to anything-goes nightlife and cabarets where entertainers like Marlene Dietrich, Bertolt Brecht, and Josephine Baker performed. And since the fall of the Wall, it's become home to supersized department stores and big-time hotels.

Consider popping into the grand **Galeries Lafayette** department store (two blocks down to your right). Inside, you can ogle a huge glass-domed atrium—a miniature version of the Reichstag cupola. There's a WC and a handy designer food court in the basement—which you can see below the cupola viewpoint. Note:

If you were to continue down Friedrichstrasse from here, you'd wind up at **Checkpoint Charlie** in about 10 minutes.

• We've reached the end of Part 1. This is a good place to take a break, if you'd like, and tackle Part 2 another time. But if you're up for ambling on, head down Unter den Linden a few more blocks, past the large equestrian statue of Frederick the Great. Frederick is pointing east, toward the epicenter of Prussian imperial power, where his royal palace once stood. We're now entering the stretch of Unter den Linden that best represents Frederick's legacy.

Turn right into Bebelplatz.

Part 2: Bebelplatz to Alexanderplatz

• Head to the center of the square, and find the square of glass window set into the pavement. We'll begin with some history and a spin tour, then consider the memorial below our feet.

⑭ BEBELPLATZ: SQUARE OF THE BOOKS

Frederick the Great built this square to show off Prussian ideals: education, the arts, improvement of the individual, and a tolerance for different groups—provided they were committed to the betterment of society. This square was the cultural center of Frederick's capital. In many ways, it still is. Spin counterclockwise to take in the cultural sights, some of which date back to Frederick's time.

Start by looking across Unter den Linden. That's **Humboldt University,** one of Europe's greatest. Continue panning left. Fronting Bebelplatz is the **former state library**—which was funded by Frederick the Great. After the library was damaged in World War II, communist authorities decided to rebuild it in the original style...but only because Lenin studied here during much of his exile from Russia. The square's far end is marked by one of Berlin's swankiest lodgings—**Hotel de Rome,** housed in a historic bank building.

A plaque and memorial on Bebelplatz mark the site of a Nazi book burning.

Their trendy rooftop bar is a treat in good weather.

Next, the green-domed structure is **St. Hedwig's Church** (nicknamed the "Upside-Down Teacup"). It stands as a symbol of Frederick the Great's religious and cultural tolerance. The pragmatic king wanted to encourage the integration of Catholic Silesians into Protestant Prussia.

Up next is the **Berlin State Opera** (*Staatsoper*)—originally established in Frederick the Great's time. Frederick believed that the arts were essential to having a well-rounded populace. He moved the opera house from inside the castle to this showcase square.

Look down through the glass window in the pavement at what appears to be a room of empty bookshelves. This **book-burning memorial** commemorates a notorious event that took place here during the Nazi years. It was on this square in 1933 that staff and students from the university built a bonfire. Into the flames they threw 20,000 newly forbidden books—authored by the likes of Einstein, Hemingway, Freud, and T.S. Eliot. Overseeing it all was the Nazi propaganda minister, Joseph Goebbels. Hitler purposely chose this square—built by Frederick the Great to embody culture and enlightenment—to symbolically demonstrate that the era of tolerance and openness was over.

• *Leave Bebelplatz toward Unter den Linden, cross to the university side, and continue heading east down Unter den Linden. You'll pass in front of Humboldt University's main gate. Immediately in front of the gate, embedded in the cobbles, notice the row of square, bronze plaques—each one bearing the name of a university student who was executed by the Nazis. You'll see similar* **Stolpersteine** *("stumbling stones") all over Berlin. Just beyond the university on the left, head for a building that looks like a Greek temple set in a small park filled with chestnut trees.*

⑮ NEUE WACHE

The "New Guardhouse" was built in 1816 as just that—a fancy barracks for the bodyguards assigned to the Hohenzollern palace just ahead (it's the Neoclassical building across the street, with four tall columns marking the doorway). Over the years, the Neue Wache has been transformed into a memorial for fallen warriors.

Memorial at the Neue Wache

In 1993, the austere interior was fitted with the statue we see today—a replica of *Mother with Her Dead Son*, by Käthe Kollwitz, a Berlin artist who lived through both world wars. It marks the tombs of Germany's unknown soldier and an unknown concentration camp victim. The memorial, open to the sky, incorporates the elements—sunshine, rain, snow—falling on this modern-day pietà.

• *Continue down Unter den Linden, passing by the pink yet formidable Zeughaus (early 1700s), the oldest building on the boulevard. Built in the Baroque style as the royal arsenal, it later became a military museum, and today houses the excellent* **German History Museum** *(see page 322). When you reach the bridge, cross the Spree and step onto Museum Island.*

⑯ MUSEUM ISLAND AND FORMER CITY PALACE

This island, sitting in the middle of the Spree River, is Berlin's historic birthplace. As the city grew, the island remained the site of the ruler's castle and residence. At its peak under Prussian rulers (1701-1918), it was a splendid and sprawling Baroque palace called the Stadtschloss, topped at one end with a dome (as you see on the right side of Unter den Linden). The palace was gutted in a 1945 air raid in the last days of World War II. In 1950, the East Germans erected in its place the Palace of the Republic—a massive, blocky parliament building. In the early 21st century, that communist building was demolished, and for years this entire city block was just a big grassy park.

Now, at great expense, Germany has rebuilt a palace on the site, creating the **Humboldt Forum,** a huge public space for business, a celebration of diverse cultures, and a place of higher education. The open "piazza" courtyard inside helps give it a community feel. This "palace for all" (which may be open by 2020) complements the cultural offerings on Museum Island, rounding out what this central place brings to Berlin.

• *Now, turn your attention to the left side of Unter den Linden. There's a spacious garden, bordered on two sides by impressive buildings.*

MUSEUM ISLAND SIGHTS

For 300 years, the **Lustgarten** has flip-flopped between being a military parade

The elegant Berlin Cathedral (flanked by the DDR-era TV Tower)

ground and a people-friendly park. In the Nazi era, Hitler enjoyed giving speeches from the top of the museum steps over-looking this square. At the far end of the Lustgarten stand grandiose museum buildings that represent the can-do Ger-man spirit of the 1800s, when city leaders envisioned the island as an oasis of cul-ture and learning. Today, these impres-sive buildings host five grand museums: the **Altes Museum** (classical antiquities), **Neues Museum** (Egyptian, prehistoric, and classical antiquities), **Pergamon Museum** (classical antiquities), **Old National Gallery** (German Romantic painting), and **Bode Museum** (Byzantine art and mosaics).

Dominating the island is the towering, green-domed **Berlin Cathedral** (Berliner Dom). This is only a century old, built during the reign of Kaiser Wilhelm II—who led Europe into World War I. The Wilhelmian style is over the top: a garish mix of Neoclassical, Neo-Baroque, and Neo-Renaissance, with rippling stucco and gold-tiled mosaics. The church is at its most impressive from the outside.

• *Continue down Unter den Linden past the cathedral, and pause on the bridge over the Spree. Look left, past the cathedral.*

⓱ SPREE RIVER

The Spree River is people-friendly and welcoming. A parklike promenade leads all the way from here to the Haupt-bahnhof. Along it, you'll find impromptu "beachside" beer gardens with imported sand, barbecues in pocket parks, and lots of locals walking their dogs, taking a lazy bike ride, or jogging. Spree River boat tours depart from near here (for details, see page 298).

• *From here you could return to Museum Island to see the sights there or backtrack to the German History Museum. But we'll continue toward the TV Tower and Alex-anderplatz (where this walk ends). Cross the bridge and find the statues of Marx and Engels, at the river-end of the big park. Note that as the boulevard crosses the river, Unter den Linden becomes Karl-Liebknecht-Strasse.*

⓲ STATUES OF KARL MARX AND FRIEDRICH ENGELS

These statues of the founders of com-munism mark the Marx-Engels-Forum,

Spree River sightseeing boats

a park dedicated in 1986 by the East German government. During the heady days before the Berlin Wall and the Iron Curtain fell, a half-million Berliners gathered here to call for freedom and an end to the economic and social experiment preached by these two philosophers.

• *From here, with your back to the river, angle through the park veering left, in the direction of the TV Tower. As you emerge from the park and hit Spandauer Strasse, look right to see the red-brick* **city hall,** *where Berlin's mayor has an office. It was built after the revolutions of 1848 and was arguably the first democratic building in the city. At the intersection, a cute DDR-era Ampelmännchen ("little traffic-light man") street light will tell you to stop or walk.*

Cross Spandauer Strasse. To your left is...

⓳ KARL-LIEBKNECHT-STRASSE AND *PLATTENBAU*

This street is named for a founder of Germany's communist party: Karl Liebknecht. As you continue walking toward the TV Tower, notice the uniformity of the high-rise concrete buildings lining the boulevard to your left. These are *Plattenbau* ("panel buildings"). While the DDR gov-

ernment maintained a few token historic landmarks (like the Rotes Rathaus), their real architectural forte was prefabricated, high-capacity, low-aesthetics housing.

But residents prided themselves on creating cozy and welcoming little nests inside, and being invited to dinner at one of these apartments showed you the stark contrast between cold, paranoid public life and colorful, gregarious private life.

• *Head for the old church up on the right.*

⓴ MARTIN LUTHER STATUE AND MARIEN CHURCH

Approaching the church, you see a bold statue of **Martin Luther.** Marien Church, like the rest of Europe, was Roman Catholic until about 500 years ago when this solitary German monk rocked European history by kicking off the Protestant Reformation.

The **Marien Church,** with its prominent steeple, dates from 1270. Just inside the church, an artist's rendering helps you follow the interesting but very faded old "Dance of Death" mural that wraps around the narthex (dating from before Luther). In true Protestant style, the interior is dominated by the pulpit (for Protestants, it's all about the word of God) and the pipe organ (Luther said, "When you sing, you pray double").

• *Across the street and a half-block down is another Berlin memorial that's worth a detour—the **Women's Protest Memorial**. It commemorates a courageous—and unusually successful—protest by the Gentile wives of Jewish men who were arrested by the Nazis. Remarkably, these brave women actually won the freedom of their husbands.*

Otherwise, gaze up at the 1,200-foot-tall...

❹ TV TOWER (FERNSEHTURM)

The communist regime is long gone, but it left this enduring legacy. The TV Tower—built in 1969 to celebrate the 20th anniversary of communist East Germany—was meant to show the power of the atheistic state at a time when DDR leaders were removing crosses from the country's church domes and spires. But when the sun hit the tower, the reflected light created a huge, bright cross on the mirrored ball. Cynics called it "The Pope's Revenge." East Berliners joked that if the TV tower fell over, they'd have an elevator to freedom in the West. (For a steep price you can ride to the top for a grand view.)

• *Return to the church side of the boulevard and continue walking east down Karl-Liebknecht-Strasse, passing the TV Tower on your right. You'll cross under a railway overpass, then walk alongside a mall called Galeria Kaufhof. Just past the mall, turn right onto a broad pedestrian street. It leads through a low tunnel and into a big square...*

❺ ALEXANDERPLATZ

Alexanderplatz was built in 1805, during the Prussian Golden Age. Because this was a gateway for trade to Eastern Europe, it was named for a Russian czar, Alexander. In the Industrial Age, it became a transportation hub. In the roaring 1920s, it was a center of cabaret nightlife to rival Friedrichstrasse. And under the DDR, it was transformed into a commercial center. This was the pride and joy of East Berlin shoppers. And then, on November 4, 1989, more than a half-million East Berliners gathered on Alexanderplatz to demand their freedom; a week later, the Berlin Wall was history.

Stand just beyond the first U-Bahn station entrance and take a clockwise spin-tour—starting with Galeria Kaufhof, to the right of the TV Tower. In communist times, the Kaufhof department store was the ultimate shopping mecca... which wasn't saying much. In front is an abstract-sculpture fountain ringed with a colorful base that attracts sitters. Next, the tall, glassy skyscraper is a DDR-era hotel, now called the Park Inn. Continuing clockwise past the Saturn electronics store and the colorful Kandinsky-esque Alexa building, notice the once-futuristic **World Time Clock,** a nostalgic favorite installed in 1969 that remains a popular meeting point.

• *From here, you can hike back a bit to catch the Spree riverboat tour, visit Museum Island or the German History Museum, or venture*

The TV Tower punctuates Berlin's skyline.

*into the colorful Prenzlauer Berg neighbor-
hood. Or you can take bus #100 or #200
back along Karl-Liebknecht-Strasse and on
to Unter den Linden.*

SIGHTS

Reichstag and
Brandenburg Gate Area

Much of Berlin's sightseeing is concen-
trated in this area, which is covered in
more detail in my "Berlin City Walk" (earlier; also available as a free 🎧 audio tour).

▲▲▲REICHSTAG

Germany's historic parliament building—
completed in 1894, burned in 1933, sad
and lonely in a no-man's-land throughout the Cold War, and finally rebuilt and
topped with a glittering glass cupola in
1999—is a symbol of a proudly reunited
nation. Visit here to spiral up the remarkable dome and gaze across Berlin's roof-
tops, and to watch today's parliament
in action. Because of security concerns,
you'll need a reservation and your passport to enter.

Cost and Hours: Free, reservations
required—see below, daily 8:00-24:00,
last entry at 22:00, metal detectors, no big
luggage allowed, Platz der Republik 1; S- or
U-Bahn: Friedrichstrasse, Brandenburger
Tor, or Bundestag.

Information: Tel. 030/2273-2152, www.
bundestag.de.

Advance Tickets: You must make a
free reservation. It's easy to do online, but
book early—spots often fill up several days
in advance. Go to www.bundestag.de,
and from the "Visit the Bundestag" menu,
select "Online registration." You have two
choices: "Visit to the dome" includes a
good audioguide and is plenty for most; or,
the 90-minute guided tour provides more
in-depth information. You'll be sent an
email link to a website where you'll enter
details for each person in your party. A final
email will contain your reservation (with a

The Reichstag's original facade

letter you must print out or download to
your mobile device).

Another option is to have lunch or
dinner at the pricey rooftop restaurant,
$$$$ Käfer Dachgarten (daily 12:00-16:30
& 18:30-24:00, last access at 22:00, reserve
well in advance at tel. 030/2262-9933 or
www.feinkost-kaefer.de/berlin).

Getting In: Report 15 minutes before
your appointed time to the tempo-
rary-looking entrance facility in front of
the Reichstag, and be ready to show your
passport and confirmation letter. After
passing through a security check, you'll
wait with other visitors for a guard to take
you to the Reichstag entrance.

Visiting the Reichstag: The open,
airy **lobby** towers 100 feet high, with
65-foot-tall colors of the German flag.
See-through glass doors show the central
legislative chamber. The message: There
will be no secrets in this government.
Look inside. Spreading his wings behind
the podium is a stylized German eagle,
the *Bundestagsadler* (affectionately nicknamed the "Fat Hen"), representing the
Bundestag (each branch of government
has its own symbolic eagle). Notice the
doors marked *Ja* (Yes), *Nein* (No), and
Enthalten (Abstain)...an homage to the
Bundestag's traditional "sheep jump" way
of counting votes by exiting the chamber through the corresponding door. (For
critical votes, however, they vote with
electronic cards.)

Germany's Bundestag (comparable
to the US House of Representatives)

Inside the Reichstag's glass dome

meets here. Its 631 members are elected to four-year terms. They in turn elect the chancellor. Unlike America's two-party system, Germany has a handful of significant parties, so they must form coalitions to govern effectively. Bundestag members have offices in the building to the left of the Reichstag.

Ride the elevator to the base of the **glass dome** (where you'll pick up the *Berlin Panorama* flier and your audioguide). The dome is 80 feet high, 130 feet across, and weighs a quarter of a million pounds. It uses about 33,000 square feet of glass, or nearly enough to cover a football field.

Study the photos and read the circle of captions (around the base of the central funnel) telling the Reichstag story. Then study the surrounding architecture: a broken collage of new on old, torn between antiquity and modernity, like Germany's history. Notice the dome's giant and unobtrusive sunscreen that moves as necessary with the sun. Peer down through the skylight to look over the shoulders of the elected representatives at work. For Germans, the best view from here is down—

keeping a close eye on their government.

Walking up the ramp, you'll spiral past 360-degree views of the city, including the Tiergarten, the "green lungs of Berlin"; the Teufelsberg ("Devil's Hill"; famous during the Cold War as a powerful ear of the West—notice the telecommunications tower on top); Potsdamer Platz; the Brandenburg Gate; Frank Gehry's fish-like roof of the DZ Bank building; the Memorial to the Murdered Jews of Europe; the former East Berlin, with a forest of 300-foot-tall skyscrapers in the works; Berlin's huge main train station; and the blocky, postmodern Chancellery, the federal government's headquarters (the audioguide explains what you're seeing as you walk).

▲▲MEMORIALS NEAR THE REICHSTAG
The area immediately surrounding the Reichstag is rich with memorials. Within a few steps, you'll find monuments to politicians who opposed Hitler and victims of the Berlin Wall (both described earlier, on the "Berlin City Walk").

In the park just behind the Berlin Wall Victims Memorial is the **Monument to** the Murdered Sinti and Roma of Europe, an opaque glass wall, with a timeline in English and German, commemorating the roughly 500,000 Holocaust victims who identified as "Sinti" and "Roma" —the main tribes and politically correct terms for the group often called "Gypsies."

Also in the park (toward the Victory Column) is the **Soviet War Memorial.** It honors the Soviet army soldiers who died in the bitter battle for Berlin, which brought World War II to a decisive conclusion.

Across the street from the Memorial to the Murdered Jews of Europe, tucked into a corner of the park, is the **Memorial to the Homosexuals Persecuted Under the National Socialist Regime.** Access it from the Jewish memorial's southwest corner, across Ebertstrasse from Hannah-Arendt-Strasse. Through a small window, you can watch a film loop of same-sex couples kissing—a reminder that life and love are precious.

▲▲▲BRANDENBURG GATE

The icon of Berlin, this majestic gateway has seen more than its share of history. Armies from Napoleon to Hitler have marched under its gilded statues, and for more than 25 years, it sat forlorn in the Berlin Wall's death strip. Today it's a symbol of Berlin's rejuvenated capital.

Just inside (east of) the Brandenburg gate is the tidy "Parisian Square"—Pariser Platz. This prime real estate is ringed by governmental buildings, banks, historic plush hotels, the Academy of Arts, and the heavily fortified US Embassy.

▲▲MEMORIAL TO THE MURDERED JEWS OF EUROPE (DENKMAL FÜR DIE ERMORDETEN JUDEN EUROPAS)

This labyrinth of 2,711 irregularly shaped pillars memorializes the six million Jewish people who were executed by the Nazis. Loaded with symbolism, it's designed to encourage a pensive moment in the heart of a big city. Inside the **information center** (far-left corner), exhibits trace the rise of Nazism and how it led to World War II. Six portraits, representing the six million Jewish victims, put a human face on the numbers, as do diaries, letters, and final farewells penned by Holocaust victims. You'll learn about 15 Jewish families from very different backgrounds, who all met the same fate. A continually running soundtrack recites victims' names. To read them all aloud would take more than six and a half years.

Cost and Hours: Memorial—free and always open; information center—free, open Tue-Sun 10:00-20:00, Oct-March until 19:00, closed Mon year-round, last entry 45 minutes before closing, security screening at entry, audioguide-€3; S-Bahn: Brandenburger Tor or Potsdamer Platz, tel. 030/2639-4336, www.stiftung-denkmal.de.

Unter Den Linden

▲▲STROLLING UNTER DEN LINDEN

Berlin's main boulevard—"Under the Linden Trees"—has been the city's artery since the 15th century. Today, it's a well-tended place to stroll. This main drag and its sights are covered in my "Berlin City Walk" earlier (and also available as a free 🎧 audio tour).

GENDARMENMARKT

Berlin's finest square sits two blocks south of Unter den Linden (and one block south of Bebelplatz). The square, like its name ("Square of the Gens d'Armes," Frederick the Great's French guard), is a hybrid of Prussia and France. The square is bookended by two matching churches: the **German Cathedral** (with a free exhibit on the German parliamentary system) and the **French Cathedral** (dedicated to the French Huguenots who found refuge in Prussia). Gendarmenmarkt's centerpiece is the Concert Hall (Konzerthaus), commissioned by Frederick the Great and built by his favorite architect, Karl Friedrich Schinkel. In summer, Gendarmenmarkt hosts outdoor cafés, *Biergartens,* and occasional outdoor concerts.

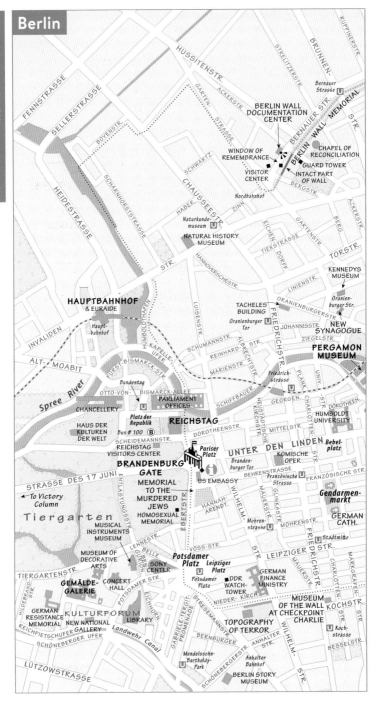

Berlin

HUSSITENSTR

STRELITZERSTR.

BRUNNEN

RUPPINERSTR.

FENNSTRASSE

SELLERSTRASSE

BOYENSTR.

SCHWARTZ

GARTEN STRASSE

ACKERSTR.

Bernauer
Strasse U

BERLIN WALL
DOCUMENTATION
CENTER

BERLIN WALL MEMORIAL

STR.

CHAPEL OF
RECONCILIATION

WINDOW OF
REMEMBRANCE

GUARD TOWER

VISITOR
CENTER

INTACT PART
OF WALL

HEIDESTRASSE

SCHARNHORSTSTRASSE

CHAUSSEESTR.

BERGSTR.

HABER

ZINN

Nordbahnhof

Naturkunde-
museum U

NATURAL HISTORY
MUSEUM

EICHEN DORFF

BERG

GARTENSTR.

ACKERST.

TIEKSTRASSE

TORSTR.

STR.

KENNEDYS
MUSEUM

HANNOVERSCHESTR.

LINIENSTR.

Oranien-
burger Str.

HAUPTBAHNHOF
& EURAIDE

Haupt-
bahnhof

HUMBOLDTHAFEN

KAPELLE-
UFER

LUISENSTR.

SCHUMANNSTR.

ORANIENBURGERSTR.

TACHELES
BUILDING

FRIEDRICHSTR

JOHANNISSTR.

NEW
SYNAGOGUE

INVALIDEN

Oranienburger
Tor

ZIEGELSTR.

PERGAMON
MUSEUM

ALT - MOABIT

FÜRST-BISMARCK-STR

REINHARD STR.

ALBRECHTSTR.

MARIENSTR.

Friedrich-
strasse

PLANK

UNIV.

STR.

Spree River

Bundestag

OTTO-VON-
BISMARCK-ALLEE

CHANCELLERY

U

PARLIAMENT
OFFICES

SCHIFFBAUER

NEUSTÄDTISCHE
KIRCHSTR.

GEORGEN.

CHARLOTTEN.

STR.

DOROTHEEN

HUMBOLDT
UNIVERSITY

Platz der
Republik

REICHSTAG

DOROTHEENSTR.

MITTELSTR.

Bebel-
platz

HAUS DER
KULTUREN
DER WELT

Bus # 100 B

SCHEIDEMANNSTR.

REICHSTAG
VISITORS CENTER

Pariser
Platz

UNTER DEN LINDEN

KOMISCHE
OPER

STR.

BRANDENBURG
GATE

Branden-
burger Tor

BEHRENSTRASSE

Französische U
Strasse

FRANZÖSISCHE STR

To Victory
Column

STRASSE DES 17 JUNI

MEMORIAL
TO THE
MURDERED
JEWS

US EMBASSY

ENTLASTUNGSSTR.

EBERSTR.

HANNAH-
ARENDT-

WILHELM-

MAUERSTR.

GLINKASTR.

Gendarmen-
markt

Tiergarten

HOMOSEXUAL
MEMORIAL

Mohren-
strasse U

MOHRENSTR.

GERMAN
CATH.

MUSICAL
INSTRUMENTS
MUSEUM

LENNÉSTR.

VOSS-STR.

LEIPZIGER

STR.

Städtmitte U

FRIEDRICHSTR.

MUSEUM OF
DECORATIVE
ARTS

BELLE-
GÜRTEL

SONY
CENTER

Potsdamer
Platz

Leipziger
Platz

LEIPZIGER STR.

MAUERSTR.

CHARLOTTEN-

MARKGRAFEN-

TIERGARTENSTR.

GEMÄLDE-
GALERIE

CONCERT
HALL

POTSDAMER STR.

U
Potsdamer
Platz

DDR
WATCH-
TOWER

GERMAN
FINANCE
MINISTRY

KOCHSTR.

HILDEBRAND-
STR.

GERMAN
RESISTANCE
MEMORIAL

KULTURFORUM

NEW NATIONAL
GALLERY

EICHHORN

LIBRARY

GABRIELE-TERGIT-
PROMENADE

STRESEMANNSTR.

NIEDER- KIRCH.

MUSEUM
OF THE WALL
AT CHECKPOINT
CHARLIE

WILHELM-

U Koch-
strasse

BESSELSTR.

REICHPIETSCHUFER

SCHÖNEBERGER UFER

Landwehr Canal

BERNBURGER

TOPOGRAPHY
OF TERROR

LÜTZOWSTRASSE

Mendelssohn-
Bartholdy-
Park

Anhalter
Bahnhof

SCHÖNEBERGERSTR.

ANHALTER-
STR.

STR.

BERLIN STORY
MUSEUM

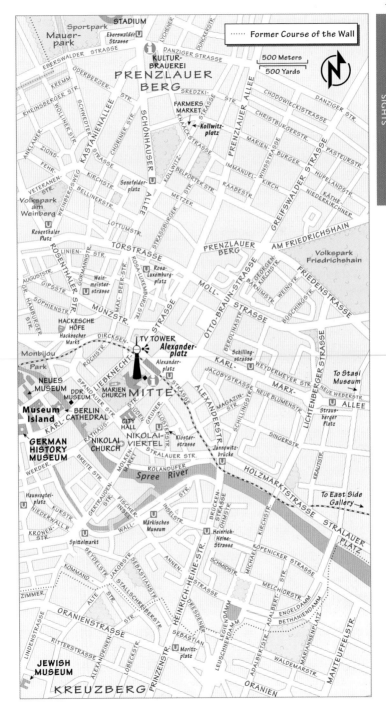

······ Former Course of the Wall

STADIUM
Sportpark
Mauer-
park
Eberswalder
Strasse
EBERSWALDER STRASSE
DANZIGER STRASSE
KULTUR-
BRAUEREI
PRENZLAUER
BERG
SREDZKI-
FARMERS
MARKET
Kollwitz-
platz
500 Meters
500 Yards
N
ODERBERGER STR.
KREMM-
RHEINSBERGER STR.
WOLLINER STR.
SCHWEDTER STR.
KASTANIENALLEE
CHORINER STR.
SCHÖNHAUSER ALLEE
KNAACKSTRASSE
KOLLWITZ-STR.
PRENZLAUER ALLEE
CHODOWIECKISTRASSE
DANZIGER STR.
CHRISTBURGERSTR.
MARIEN- BURGER STR.
PASTEURSTR.
ANKLAMER STR.
ZIONS-
FEHR.
VETERANEN-
Volkspark
am
Weinberg
U
Rosenthaler
Platz
WEINBERGSWEG
BELLINERSTR.
KIRCHSTR.
Senefelder-
platz
U
LOTTUMSTR.
BELFORTER STR.
METZER
STRASSBURGER STR.
IMMANUEL-
KIRCH
RAABESTR.
WINSSTR.
GREIFSWALDER STRASSE
HUFELANDSTR.
NIEDERKIRCHNER.
KÄTHE-
NIEDERKIRCHNER.
LINIEN-
STR.
TORSTRASSE
PRENZLAUER
BERG
AM FRIEDRICHSHAIN
Volkspark
Friedrichshain
ROSENTHALER STR.
GORMANNSTR.
Wein-
meister-
strasse
Rosa-
Luxemburg-
platz
MAX- BEER- STR.
ROSA-LUXEMBURG-STRASSE
MOLL-
STRASSE
OTTO-BRAUN-STRASSE
GEORGEN-
KIRCHSTR.
BARNIMSTR.
WEINSTR.
BÜSCHINGSTR.
FRIEDENSTRASSE
AUGUSTSTR.
GIPSSTR.
GR. HAMBURGER STR.
SOPHIENSTR.
MÜNZSTR.
HACKESCHE
HÖFE
Hackescher
Markt
DIRCKSEN-
ROCHSTR.
SPANDAUER STR.
LIEBKNECHT-
TV TOWER
Alexander-
platz
Alexander-
platz
KARL-
Schilling-
strasse
WEYDEMEYER STR.
LICHTENBERGER STRASSE
NEUE WEBERSTR.
To Stasi
Museum
U
ALLEE
Monbijou
Park
NEUES
MUSEUM
DDR
MUSEUM
MARIEN
CHURCH
MITTE
STRASSE
GRUNER-
KLOSTERSTR.
ALEXANDERSTR.
MARX-
JACOBYSTRASSE
SCHILLINGSTR.
MAGAZIN-
STR.
NEUE BLUMENSTR.
SINGERSTR.
Strauss-
berger
Platz
Museum
Island
BERLIN
CATHEDRAL
KARL-
CITY
HALL
NIKOLAI-
VIERTEL
Kloster-
strasse
GERMAN
HISTORY
MUSEUM
RATHAUS-
NIKOLAI
CHURCH
MOLKEN-
MARKT
STRALAUER STR.
ROLANDUFER
Jannowitz-
brücke
KRAUTSTR.
BREITE STR.
WERDER-
Spree River
HOLZMARKTSTRASSE
To East Side
Gallery
Hausvogtei-
platz
U
KURSTR.
NIEDERWALL-R.
GEERTRAUDEN-STR.
FISCHER-
INSELSTR.
STR.
BRÜCKEN-
STRASSE
OHMSTR.
KÖPENICKER STRASSE
STRALAUER
PLATZ
KRONEN-
STR.
Spittelmarkt
U
WALL-
Märkisches
Museum
U
Heinrich-
Heine-
Strasse
MICHAEL-
KIRCHSTR.
MELCHIORSTR.
ZIMMER-
KOMMAND-
SEYDELSTR.
STALLSCHREIBERSTR.
JAKOBSTR.
SEBASTIANSTR.
ALTE
STR.
ANNEN-
HEINRICH-HEINE-STR.
DRESDENER STR.
SCHMIDSTR.
LINDENSTRASSE
ORANIENSTRASSE
RITTERSTRASSE
STR.
ALEXANDRINEN-STR.
LÜBECKER STR.
PRINZENSTR.
SEBASTIAN
U
Moritz-
platz
LEUSCHNERDAMM
LEGIENDAMM
ADALBERTSTR.
ADALBERTSTR.
ENGELDAMM
BETHANIENDAMM
MARIANNENPLATZ
WALDEMARSTR.
MANTEUFFELSTR.
JEWISH
MUSEUM
KREUZBERG
ORANIEN

Museum Island Area

Filling a spit of land in the middle of the Spree River, Museum Island has perhaps Berlin's highest concentration of serious sightseeing. The island's centerpiece is the grassy square called Lustgarten, ringed by five museums and the hulking Berlin Cathedral. Also, two recommended museums flank the island: the German History Museum across the river to the west, and the DDR Museum across the river to the east.

Note that three Museum Island landmarks—the **Lustgarten, Berlin Cathedral,** and **Humboldt Forum**—are described earlier in my "Berlin City Walk"; see page 309.

Museum Island (Museumsinsel)

Five of Berlin's top museums—featuring art and artifacts from around the world—are just a few steps apart on Museum Island. I highlight the top three: Pergamon, Neues, and Old National Gallery.

Cost and Hours: Each museum has a separate admission (€10-12, includes audioguide). If you're visiting at least two museums here, get the €18 Museum Island Pass (which covers all 5; also consider the €29 Museum Pass Berlin—see page 295). The museums are open 10:00-18:00 (Thu until 20:00). The Pergamon and Neues are open daily; the Old National Gallery is closed Mon.

Information: Tel. 030/266-424-242, www.smb.museum.

Advance Tickets Recommended: To skip ticket-buying lines, purchase a timed ticket for the Pergamon or Neues Museum in advance at the museum website. If you have a Museum Island Pass or Museum Pass Berlin, you can book a free timed-entry reservation. The Pergamon is most crowded in the morning, on weekends, and when it rains; Thursday evenings are the least crowded.

Getting There: The island is a 10-minute walk from the Hackescher Markt or Friedrichstrasse S-Bahn stations. Trams #M1 and #12 connect to Prenzlauer Berg. Buses #100 and #200 run along Unter den Linden, stopping near the museums at the Lustgarten stop.

▲▲PERGAMON MUSEUM (PERGAMONMUSEUM)

This world-class museum contains Berlin's Collection of Classical Antiquities (Antikensammlung)—full-sized buildings from the most illustrious civilizations of the ancient world. Its namesake and highlight—the gigantic Pergamon Altar—is under renovation and off-limits to visitors until 2025. But there's still plenty to see: the massive Babylonian Processional Way and Ishtar Gate (slathered with glazed blue tiles, from the sixth century BC); the full-sized market gate from the ancient Roman settlement of Miletus (first century BC); and, treasures from the Islamic world.

Visiting the Museum: The superb audioguide (included) helps broaden your experience. From the entry hall, head up to floor 1 and all the way back to 575 BC and Mesopotamia.

Processional Way and Ishtar Gate:

Ishtar Gate

Market Gate of Miletus

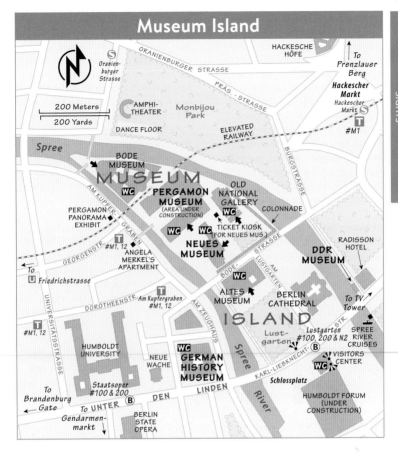

Museum Island

The ruler Nebuchadnezzar II made sure that all who approached his city got a grand first impression. His massive blue Ishtar Gate stands 46 feet tall and 100 feet wide. This was the grandest of Babylon's gates, one of eight in the 11-mile wall that encompassed this city of 200,000. The Gate was one of the original Seven Wonders of the World. All the pieces in this hall—the Gate, Processional Way, and Throne Room panels—are made of decorative brick, glazed and fired in the ancient Egyptian faience technique. Decorations like the lions, which project outward from the surface, were carved or molded before the painted glaze went on.

The museum's Babylonian treasures are meticulous reconstructions. A Berlin archaeologist discovered the ruins in modern-day Iraq in 1900. What was recovered was little more than piles of shattered shards of brick. It's since been augmented with modern tilework and pieced together like a 2,500-year-old Babylonian jigsaw puzzle. (You could peek into Room 6—if it's open—to see a model of Babylon.)

Market Gate of Miletus: You've flashed forward 700 years to ancient Miletus—the wealthy, cosmopolitan, Roman-ruled, and Greek-speaking city on the southwest coast of Asia Minor (modern Turkey). Dominating this room is the huge Market Gate of Miletus. This served as the entrance to the town's agora, or marketplace. Traders from across the Mediterranean and Middle East passed through the three arched doorways into a football-field-sized courtyard surrounded by arcades.

Miletus was destroyed by an earthquake centuries ago and the gate was painstakingly reconstructed here in Berlin. This room also displays an exquisite mosaic floor of colored stone and glass from the dining room of a Roman villa in Miletus, c. AD 200, and features the mythical Greek musician Orpheus.

Islamic Treasures: Head up to **floor 2,** which is dedicated to the **Museum of Islamic Art.** It demonstrates how—after Rome fell and Europe was mired in medievalism—the Islamic world carried the torch of civilization. The impressive Aleppo Room is illustrated with motifs from Christian, Arabic, Persian, and Jewish traditions.

What About the Pergamon Altar? During the museum's restoration, a special exhibit called *Pergamonmuseum-Das Panorama* is in a pavilion on Am Kupfergraben (directly across from Museum Island). The main attraction is a huge, wraparound panorama painting of the city of Pergamon in AD 129. Some of the original sculpture from the altar, the largest piece of the altar frieze, and digital 3D models help visitors fill in the details (€19 combo-ticket with Pergamon Museum, €6 with Museum Island Pass or Museum Pass Berlin, open same hours as the museum).

▲▲NEUES (NEW) MUSEUM

This beautiful museum, featuring objects from the prehistoric world, contains three collections. Most visitors focus on the Egyptian Collection, with the stunning bust of Queen Nefertiti. But it's also worth a walk through the Museum of Prehistory and Early History and the Collection of Classical Antiquities (artifacts from ancient Troy). Everything is well-described in English (fine audioguide included with admission; for more on the museum, see www.neues-museum.de).

Visiting the Museum: The Neues Museum ticket desk is across the courtyard from the entrance. Ticket in hand, enter and pick up the floor plan. The main reason to visit is to enjoy one of the great thrills in art appreciation—gazing into the still young and beautiful face of Queen Nefertiti. If you're in a pinch for time, make a beeline to her (floor 2, far corner of Egyptian Collection in Room 210).

To tour the whole collection, start at the top (floor 3), the **prehistory section.** The entire floor is filled with Stone Age, Ice Age, and Bronze Age items. You'll see early human remains, tools, spearheads, and pottery.

The most interesting item on this floor (in corner of Room 305)—the tall, conehead-like **Golden Hat,** made of paper-thin gold leaf—was likely worn by the priest of a sun cult popular among the Celtic people of central Europe around 1,000 BC. Admire the incredible workmanship of these prehistoric people. The

Neues Museum   *Queen Nefertiti*

hat, 30 inches tall, was hammered from a pound of gold into a single sheet of gold leaf less than a millimeter thick.

On floor 2, in a room all her own (Room 210), is the 3,000-year-old bust of **Queen Nefertiti,** wife of Akhenaton—the most famous piece of Egyptian art in Europe. Nefertiti has all the right beauty marks: long slender neck, perfect lips, almond eyes, symmetrical eyebrows, pronounced cheekbones, and a perfect spray-on tan. And yet, despite her seemingly perfect beauty, Nefertiti has a touch of humanity. Notice the fine wrinkles around the eyes—these only enhance her beauty. She has a slight Mona Lisa smile, pursed at the corners.

The bust never left its studio, but served as a master model for all other portraits of the queen. (That's probably why the artist didn't bother putting the quartz inlay in the left eye.) Stare at her long enough, and you may get the sensation that she's winking at you.

▲▲OLD NATIONAL GALLERY (ALTE NATIONALGALERIE)

Of Berlin's many top-notch art collections, this is the best for *German* art—mostly paintings from the 19th century, the era in which "German culture" first came to mean something. For a concise visit, focus on the Romantic German paintings (top floor), where Caspar David Friedrich's hauntingly beautiful canvases offer an insightful glimpse into German landscapes...and the German psyche. With more time, peruse the French and German Impressionists and German Realists on the first and second floors.

Visiting the Museum: Start on the third floor and work your way down.

Casa Bartholdy Murals (Room 3.02): These frescoes tell the biblical story of Joseph. They were done by idealistic artists of the artistic brotherhood called the Nazarenes. It was the early 1800s, and the German people were searching for their unique national identity. In art, the Nazarenes were seeking a purer form of expression that was uniquely German.

This almost religious fervor would inspire the next generation of German artists—the Romantics.

Karl Friedrich Schinkel (Room 3.05): Schinkel is best known as the Neoclassical architect who remade Berlin in the 1820s. But as a painter, Gothic cathedrals and castles dominate his scenes. Where puny humans do appear, they are dwarfed by the landscape and buildings. Scenes are lit by a dramatic, eerie light, as though the world is charged from within by the power of God. Welcome to Romanticism.

Caspar David Friedrich (Room 3.06): The greatest German artist of the Romantic era was Caspar David Friedrich (1774-1840). A quick glance around this room gives you a sense of Friedrich's subjects: craggy mountains, twisted trees, ominous clouds, burning sunsets, and lone figures in the gloom. The few people he painted are tiny and solitary, pondering the vastness of their surroundings.

Biedermeier Style (Rooms 3.08-3.13): These rooms feature paintings in the so-called Biedermeier style (c. 1815-1848). Biedermeier landscapes are pretty, not dramatic. The style is soft-focus, hypersensitive, super-sweet, and sentimental. The poor are happy, the middle class are happy, and the world they inhabit is perfectly lit.

French Impressionists (Room 2.03): Unlike the carefully composed, turbulent, and highly symbolic paintings of the German Romantics, these scenes appear like simple unposed "snapshots" of everyday life. Pan the room to see Renoir's pink-cheeked girls, Degas' working girls, Cézanne's fruit bowls, and Gauguin's Tahitian girls.

Rest of the Museum: In Room 2.14 are two well-known **portraits by Franz von Lenbach** of world-changing Germans: Otto von Bismarck (Germany's first prime minister) and the composer Richard Wagner.

Near Museum Island

The German History Museum is on Unter den Linden, immediately west of

Museum Island; and the DDR Museum is (fittingly) just east of Museum Island, on the riverbank facing the back of the Berlin Cathedral.

▲▲▲GERMAN HISTORY MUSEUM (DEUTSCHES HISTORISCHES MUSEUM)

This impressive museum offers the best look at German history under one roof, anywhere. The permanent collection packs 9,000 artifacts into two huge rectangular floors of the old arsenal building. You'll stroll through insightfully described historical objects, paintings, photographs, and models—all intermingled with multimedia stations. The 20th-century section—on the ground floor—is far better than any of the many price-gouging historical Nazi or Cold War "museums" all over town. A thoughtful visit here provides valuable context for your explorations of Berlin (and Germany).

Cost and Hours: €8, covered by Museum Pass Berlin, daily 10:00-18:00, worthwhile €3 audioguide, Unter den Linden 2.

Information: Tel. 030/2030-4751, www.dhm.de.

Getting There: It's at Unter den Linden 2. Buses #100, #200, and #TXL stop right in front (Staatsoper stop). By tram, the Am Kupfergraben stop (for trams #M1 and #12) is a block behind the museum. The nearest S-Bahn stops are Friedrichstrasse and Hackescher Markt, each about a 10-minute walk away.

Visiting the Museum: As you tour the collection, stay on track by locating the museum's historic chapters (pillars along the way marked with a date span) then browse the exhibits nearby.

First Floor (500-1918): This floor weaves its way through the centuries, with exhibits on early cultures, the Middle Ages, the Reformation, the Thirty Years' War, and the German Empire.

Several rooms are dedicated to the German monk Martin Luther, who in the 16th century shocked Europe with new and radical ideas, sparking the Protestant Reformation. You'll find a number of Luther artifacts, including the Edict of Worms (next to the portrait of Charles V), where Charles V condemned the Protestant heretic, and a Bible translated by Luther into everyday German.

Frederick the Great made Prussia (an area of northern Germany) a European power and Berlin a cultural capital. Science flourished (see scientific instruments) as did music (see early keyboards and a picture of the Mozart family). In the 1800s, Prussia took over Germany's destiny when Wilhelm I and his shrewd prime minister, Otto von Bismarck (see their busts), forged Germany's principalities and dukedoms together. In 1871, the German people united, and they waved an eagle flag (on display) of a new nation: Germany.

Ground Floor (20th Century): World War I pit Germany against France, England, and others. Photos show the grim reality of a war fought from defensive trenches, while posters (and a poignant woodcut by Berlin artist Käthe Kollwitz)

Exhibits at the German History Museum are comprehensive and thought-provoking.

capture the bitter and cynical mood that descended over Germany.

Europe's victors dealt harshly with Germany, sowing enormous resentment. In 1933, the Nazis took control of Germany under Adolf Hitler, who appealed to Germans' sense of national and ethnic pride. Hitler made plans to turn Berlin into "Welthaupstadt Germania," the "world capital" of his far-reaching Third Reich. The centerpiece would be the impossibly huge domed Volkshalle—950 feet high and able to accommodate 180,000 people. It would squat over the Spree River, just north of the Reichstag.

Exhibits document the atrocities at Hitler's concentration camps, including registration photos of prisoners and a model of a crematorium at Auschwitz (in Nazi-occupied Poland), which were designed to exterminate Jews. By the end of the war, more than 60 million were dead, including 6 million Jews and 6 million non-Jewish Germans.

After losing the war, Berlin and Germany were divided between the Soviet-leaning East and the US-leaning West. Exhibits juxtapose slices of life in the two Germanys. By the 1980s, the Soviet empire was cracking, and in 1989 the Berlin Wall began crumbling.

For architecture buffs, the big attraction is the modern annex behind the history museum, designed by American architect I. M. Pei, who is famous for his glass pyramid at Paris' Louvre. (To get there, cross through the courtyard, admiring the Pei glass canopy overhead.) This annex complements the museum with temporary exhibits. A striking glassed-in spiral staircase unites four floors with surprising views and lots of light.

▲▲DDR MUSEUM

This museum has a knack for helping outsiders understand life in communist East Germany (the *Deutsche Demokratische Republik,* or DDR). It's well-stocked with kitschy everyday items from the DDR period, plus photos, video clips, and concise English explanations. You can crawl

through a Trabant car (known as a "Trabi"; take it for a virtual test drive) and pick up some DDR-era black humor ("East Germany had 39 newspapers, four radio stations, two TV channels...and one opinion"). The highlight is a tourable reconstructed communist-era home.

Cost and Hours: €8.50, buy online in advance to avoid waiting in a long line at the entrance; daily 10:00-20:00, Sat until 22:00; just across the Spree from Museum Island at Karl-Liebknecht-Strasse 1, tel. 030/847-123-731, www.ddr-museum.de.

Old Jewish Quarter

Immediately northeast of the Spree River is the old Jewish quarter which, in addition to being packed with intriguing shops and fun eateries, is one of the most important areas for Berlin's historic Jewish community—offering insights into a culture that thrived here until the 1940s.

▲▲COURTYARDS *(HÖFE)*

The old Jewish quarter is a particularly handy place to explore Berlin's unique *Höfe*—interconnected courtyards that burrow through city blocks, today often filled with trendy shops and eateries. Two starkly different examples are nearly next door, and just steps from the Hackescher Markt transit hub: the upscale, *Jugendstil* Hackesche Höfe (Rosenthaler Strasse 40), with eye-pleasing architectural flourishes and upscale shops; and the funky Haus Schwarzenberg (Rosenthaler Strasse 39), with a museum honoring Otto Weidt—a Berliner who defied the Nazis and saved many lived by employing blind and deaf Jews in his workshop.

NEW SYNAGOGUE (NEUE SYNAGOGUE)

Marked by its beautiful golden dome, this large, mid-19th-century synagogue is now a museum memorializing the Berlin Jewish community that was decimated by the Nazis. Berlin was long the center of German Jewry and this small but moving exhibit (with good English descriptions) tells the

New Synagogue

story of this community through the centuries. You'll enter through a low-profile door in the modern building to the right of the synagogue facade and go through very tight security. A cutaway model shows the entire synagogue that once housed 3,200 worshippers. The upper floor personalizes the Nazi terror with individual stories.

Cost and Hours: €7; Sun-Fri 10:00-18:00, closed Sat; audioguide-€3, Oranienburger Strasse 28, S-Bahn: Oranienburger Strasse, tel. 030/8802-8300, www.centrumjudaicum.de.

▲**PALACE OF TEARS (*TRÄNENPALAST*) AT FRIEDRICHSTRASSE STATION**
Just south of the old Jewish quarter (cross the river on Friedrichstrasse at Weidendammer Brücke and bear right) stands this impactful Cold War site. The Friedrichstrasse train station was one of the few places where Westerners were allowed to cross into East Berlin. And when crossing back into the free world, this was where they'd take leave of their East German loved ones. The scene of so many sad farewells, it earned the nickname *"Tränenpalast"* (palace of tears). The boxy structure that was once attached to the station is now a museum

about everyday life in a divided Germany, with a fascinating peek into the paranoid border-control world of the DDR.

Cost and Hours: Free, includes excellent audioguide, Tue-Fri 9:00-19:00, Sat-Sun 10:00-18:00, closed Mon, on the river side of the Friedrichstrasse station—look for the building with large glass windows and blue trim, Reichstagufer 17, tel. 030/4677-7790, www.hdg.de/traenenpalast.

Berlin Wall Memorial near Prenzlauer Berg

The thriving Prenzlauer Berg district, worth ▲▲, offers an ideal opportunity to see a corner of today's "real Berlin," just beyond the core tourist zone but still easily accessible. Prenzlauer Berg (PRENTS-low-er behrk) was largely untouched by WWII bombs, fell into disrepair during DDR days, and has since been completely rejuvenated. Prenzlauer Berg is also a great place to sleep, eat, shop, and enjoy nightlife.

▲▲▲**BERLIN WALL MEMORIAL (GEDENKSTÄTTE BERLINER MAUER)**
This is Berlin's most substantial and educational sight relating to its gone-but-not-forgotten Wall. As you visit the park, you'll

Fragments of the Berlin Wall in the memorial area

learn about how the Wall went up, the brutal methods used to keep Easterners in, and the stories of brave people who risked everything to be free.

Exhibits line up along several blocks of Bernauer Strasse, stretching more than a mile northeast from the Nordbahnhof S-Bahn station (one of the DDR's "ghost stations") to Schwedter Strasse and the Mauerpark. For a targeted visit, focus on the engaging sights clustered near the Nordbahnhof: two museums (the Visitors Center and the Documentation Center)—with films, photos, and harrowing personal stories; various open-air exhibits and memorials; original Wall fragments; and observation tower views into the only preserved, complete stretch of the Wall system (with "death strip").

Cost and Hours: Free; outdoor areas accessible daily 24 hours; Visitors Center and Documentation Center both open Tue-Sun 10:00-18:00, closed Mon, memorial chapel closes at 17:00; on Bernauer Strasse at #119 (Visitors Center) and #111 (Documentation Center).

Information: Tel. 030/4679-86666, www.berliner-mauer-gedenkstaette.de.

Getting There: Take the S-Bahn (line S1, S2, or S25) to Nordbahnhof. Exit by following signs for *Bernauer Strasse*—you'll pop out at the memorial. You can also get there on tram #12 or #M10 (from near Prenzlauer Berg hotels).

Overview: Begin at the Nordbahnhof and pick up an informational pamphlet from the Visitors Center. Head up Bernauer Strasse, visit the exhibits and memorials, then ride home from the Bernauer Strasse U-Bahn station. For a longer visit, walk several more blocks to the Mauerpark. The entire stretch is lined with informational posts and larger-than-life images from the Wall on the sides of buildings.

➔ SELF-GUIDED WALK

• *Start your visit at the...*

❶ **Visitors Center** (Bezucherzentrum): Check the next showtimes for the two 15-minute introductory films in English. The film titled **The Berlin Wall** covers the four-decade history of the Wall. The other film—**Walled In!**—features a 3-D re-creation of the former death strip, helping you visualize what it is you're about to walk through.

• *Exit the Visitors Center, cross Bernauer Strasse, and enter the Memorial park. Find the rusty rectangular monument with a 3-D map.*

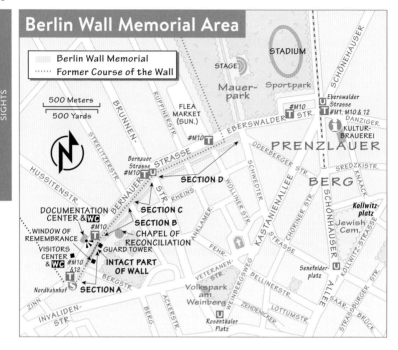

Berlin Wall Memorial Area

Berlin Wall Memorial
Former Course of the Wall

500 Meters
500 Yards

STADIUM

STAGE

Mauer-park

Sportpark

FLEA MARKET (SUN.)

#M10

EBERSWALDER

#M10 STR.

Eberswalder Strasse
#M1, M10 & 12

DANZIGER

KULTUR-BRAUEREI

ODERBERGER STR.

PRENZLAUER

Bernauer Strasse #M10

BERNAUER STRASSE

SECTION D

SCHWEDTER

WOLLINER STR.

SREDZKISTR.

BERG

KNAACK

RHEINS.

HUSSITENSTR.

DOCUMENTATION CENTER & WC

SECTION C

SECTION B

CHAPEL OF RECONCILIATION

#M10

ANKLAMER

FEHR.

KASTANIENALLEE

CHORINER STR.

SCHÖNHAUSER

Kollwitz-platz

Jewish Cem.

WINDOW OF REMEMBRANCE

VISITORS CENTER & WC

GUARD TOWER

#M10 #12

INTACT PART OF WALL

VETERANEN-STR.

WEINBERGSWEG

BELLINERSTR.

STRASSE

ALLEE

KOLLWITZSTRASSE

Senefelder-platz

Nordbahnhof

SECTION A

BERGSTR.

ZINN

INVALIDEN-STR.

ACKERSTR.

BERG

Volkspark am Weinberg

ZEHDENICKER

WEINBERG

Rosenthaler Platz

LOTTUMSTR.

STRASS-BURGER STR.

❷ 3-D Map of the Former Neighborhood: The map shows what this neighborhood looked like back in the Wall's heyday. Fifty years ago, you'd be right at the division between East and West Berlin—in the narrow strip between two sets of walls. One of those walls is still standing—there it is, stretching along Bernauer Strasse. As you gaze down the long park, West Berlin would be to your left (on the north side of Bernauer Strasse), and East Berlin to your right.

Now find the Nordbahnhof, across the street on your left. While the Wall stood, the Nordbahnhof station straddled both East and West—one of the "ghost stations" of Cold War Berlin (inside the station, photos compare 1989 with 2009).
• Stroll along the path through this first section of the park ("Section A"). Along the way are small sights, remembrances, and exhibits. As you stroll, you're walking through the...

❸ "Death Strip" (Section A): Today's grassy park, with a pleasant path through

it, was once the notorious "death strip" (Todesstreifen). If someone was trying to escape from the East, they'd have to scale one wall (a smaller one, to your right), cross this narrow strip of land, and climb the main Wall (to your left, along Bernauer Strasse). The death strip was an obstacle course of barbed wire, tire-spike strips to stop cars, and other diabolical devices. Armed guards looked down from watchtowers, with orders to shoot to kill.
• About midway through this section of the park, find the freestanding rusted-iron wall filled with photos.

❹ Window of Remembrance: Find Otfried Reck, just 17 years old (eighth from the left, top row). On November 27, 1962, he and a friend pried open a ventilation shaft at the boarded-up Nordbahnhof, and descended to the tracks, where they hoped to flag down a passing westbound train. The police discovered them, and Reck was shot in the back.

Continue walking through Section A.

You're now walking along the original, pre-served asphalt patrol path.

• *Now, walk across the grass and find a place to get a good close-up look at...*

❺ The Wall: The Wall here is typical of the whole system: about 12 feet tall, made of concrete and rebar, and capped by a rounded pipe that made it tough for escapees to get a grip. This was part of a 96-mile-long Wall that encircled West Berlin, making it an island of democracy in communist East Germany. The West Berlin side of the Wall was typically covered with colorful graffiti by free-spirited West Berliners.

• *Now, exit the park through the hole in the Wall, turn right along Bernauer Strasse, and make your way a short distance to the cross-walk. Across Bernauer Strasse is a modern gray building at #119 (labeled* Gedenkstätte Berliner Mauer). *This is the...*

❻ Documentation Center (Doku-mentationszentrum Berliner Mauer): This excellent museum is geared to a new generation of Berliners who can hardly imagine their hometown split so brutally in two. The two floors of exhibits have photos and displays to explain the logis-tics of the city's division and its effects. Listen to the riveting personal accounts of escapees—and of the border guards armed with machine guns and tasked with stopping them.

On the second floor, be sure to watch the poignant seven-minute film, ***Peace-ful Revolution.*** The video highlights the power of the people and traces the events that led to the Wall's collapse. From this floor, stairs lead to the rooftop **Tower** (*Turm*) where you're rewarded with a view. You can look across Bernauer Strasse and down at Berlin's last preserved stretch of the death strip with an original guard tower. More than 100 sentry towers like this one kept a close eye on the Wall.

• *Exit and continue on. Cross Bernauer Strasse (where it intersects with Acker-strasse) and enter the next section of the Memorial park.*

❼ Escapes from Border-Strip Build-ings (Section B): Ahead, you'll see a group of information panels. The panels tell the story of what happened here: On August 13, 1961, the East German government officially closed the border. People began fleeing to the parts of Berlin controlled by other European powers.

Over the next few months, the border hardened. Ackerstrasse was closed as East German soldiers laid down rows of barbed wire. People were suddenly separated from their West Berlin neighbors just across the street. During this brief window of time (summer of '61 to early '62), there were many escape attempts.

• *Keep going up the path through Section B, to the round building up ahead.*

❽ Chapel of Reconciliation (Kapelle der Versöhnung): This modern chapel stands on the site of the old Church of Reconciliation. Built in 1894, the old church served the neighborhood par-ish. When the Wall went up, the church found itself stranded in the death strip. It

Intact part of the Wall

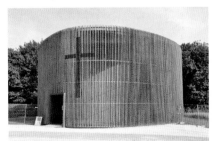

Chapel of Reconciliation

became famous in the West as a symbol of how the godless commies had driven out religion. The church was finally blown up by the East Germans in 1985.

After the Wall came down, this chapel was built. The carved wooden altarpiece inside was saved from the original structure. The chapel hosts daily prayer services for the victims of the Wall.

• *Continue past the chapel into the second portion of Section B.*

Tunnels and More: Walk uphill then bear left to a large open-air display under a canopy (amid the ruins of a destroyed Bernauer Strasse home). Photos, info boards, and press-the-button audio clips explain what it was like to live here, so close to the front line of the Cold War. Head back up to the main path, turn left, and continue. You'll pass two parallel rows of metal slabs, labeled *Fluchttunnel 1964*. This marks the route of the most famous tunnel of all: ❾ **Tunnel 57** (named after the 57 people who escaped through it).

• *The main part of our walk is done. To experience more of the Memorial, you could continue through more open-air exhibits.* **Section C** *focuses on the building of the Wall.* **Section D**—*nearly as long as the first three sections combined—covers everyday life in the shadow of the Berlin Wall.*

If you're ready to leave, the Bernauer Strasse U-Bahn station is just a block farther up Bernauer Strasse. Or you can backtrack to the Nordbahnhof. And tram #M10 follows Bernauer Strasse all the way to Eberswalder Strasse, in the heart of Prenzlauer Berg.

Fascism and Cold War Sites near Checkpoint Charlie

▲CHECKPOINT CHARLIE

Famous as the place where many visiting Westerners crossed into East Berlin during the Cold War, the original Checkpoint Charlie is long gone. But today a reconstructed guard station—with big posters of American and Soviet guards,

Checkpoint Charlie

and a chilling "You are leaving the American sector" sign—attracts curious tourists for a photo op. Nothing here is original (except for the nearby museum—described next), and the whole area feels like a Cold War theme park, with kitschy communist-themed attractions, hucksters, and sleazy vendors who charge through the nose for a DDR stamp in your passport. The replica checkpoint is free to view and always open (but you'll pay to take photos with the "guards").

For nearly three decades (1961-1989), this was a border crossing between East and West Berlin. It became known worldwide and stood as a symbol of the Cold War itself. The name "Charlie" came about because it was the third checkpoint in a series. Checkpoint A (Alpha) was at the East-West German border. Checkpoint B (Bravo) was where people left East Germany and entered the Allied sector of Berlin. And this was Checkpoint C (Charlie), on the border between the US-occupied neighborhood and the Soviet zone. Checkpoint Charlie was a humble shack for document-checking GIs. It sat on a traffic island in the middle of Friedrichstrasse, fortified with a few piles of sandbags.

Today you see a **mock-up**, with a guard station, sandbags, and a US flag. Larger-than-life posters show an American soldier facing east and a young Soviet soldier facing west—look at these portraits and consider the decades of armed standoffs here.

329

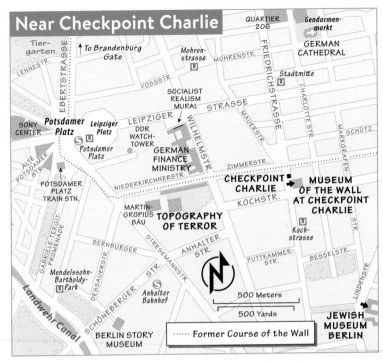

Near Checkpoint Charlie

QUARTIER 206

Gendarmen-markt

GERMAN CATHEDRAL

Tier-garten

↑ To Brandenburg Gate

Mohren-strasse

MOHRENSTR.

Stadtmitte

VOSSSTR.

SOCIALIST REALISM MURAL

STRASSE

SONY CENTER

Potsdamer Platz

Leipziger Platz

LEIPZIGER

Potsdamer Platz

DDR WATCH-TOWER

GERMAN FINANCE MINISTRY

SCHÜTZ

POTSDAMER PLATZ TRAIN STN.

NIEDERKIRCHNERSTR.

ZIMMERSTR.

CHECKPOINT CHARLIE

KOCHSTR.

MUSEUM OF THE WALL AT CHECKPOINT CHARLIE

MARTIN-GROPIUS BAU

TOPOGRAPHY OF TERROR

Koch-strasse

BERNBURGER

STRESEMANNSTR.

ANHALTER STR.

PUTTKAMMER-STR.

BESSELSTR.

Mendelssohn-Bartholdy-Park

Anhalter Bahnhof

500 Meters

500 Yards

JEWISH MUSEUM BERLIN

BERLIN STORY MUSEUM

······ Former Course of the Wall

BERLIN SIGHTS

▲MUSEUM OF THE WALL AT CHECKPOINT CHARLIE (MAUERMUSEUM HAUS AM CHECKPOINT CHARLIE)

This ragtag but riveting celebration of the many ways desperate East Germans managed to slip through the Wall to freedom has stood here since 1963... taunting DDR authorities. Today East Germany and its Wall are long gone, but the museum is still going strong. Some of the displays have yellowed, the place is cramped and confusing, and the ticket price is way too high, but the museum retains a special sense of history. Visiting here, you'll learn about the creation of the Wall and the many escape attempts (including several of the actual items used by clever escapees). If you're pressed for time, visit after dinner, when most other museums are closed. Compared to the soberly academic official Berlin Wall Memorial near the Nord-

Museum of the Wall at Checkpoint Charlie

The Berlin Wall (and Its Fall)

The East German government erected the 96-mile-long Wall almost overnight in 1961. It was intended to stop the outward flow of people from the communist East to the capitalist West: Three million souls had leaked out between 1949 and 1961.

The Wall *(Mauer)* was actually two walls, with a no-man's-land between them. During the 28 years it stood, there were 5,043 documented successful escapes (565 of these were East German guards). At least 138 people died or were killed at the Wall while trying to escape.

As a tangible symbol for the Cold War, the Berlin Wall got a lot of attention from politicians. Two of the 20th century's most repeated presidential quotes were uttered within earshot of the Wall. In 1963, President John F. Kennedy professed American solidarity with the struggling people of Berlin: *"Ich bin ein Berliner."* In 1987, with the winds of change already blowing westward from Moscow, President Ronald Reagan issued an ultimatum to his Soviet counterpart: "Mr. Gorbachev, tear down this wall."

The actual fall of the Wall had less to do with presidential proclamations than with the obvious failings of the Soviet system, a general thawing in Moscow, the brave civil disobedience of ordinary citizens behind the Wall—and a bureaucratic snafu.

By November 1989, change was in the air. Hungary had already opened its borders to the West that summer, making it impossible for East German authorities to keep people in. Anti-regime protests swept nearby Leipzig, attracting hundreds of thousands of supporters. A rally in East Berlin's Alexanderplatz on November 4—with a half-million protesters chanting, *"Wir wollen raus!"* (We want out!)—persuaded the East German politburo to begin gradually relaxing travel restrictions.

The DDR intended to crack the door to the West, but an unknowing spokesman inadvertently threw it wide open. In back-room meetings early on November 9, officials decided they would allow a few more Easterners to cross into the West. The politburo members then left town for a long weekend. The announcement of the decision was left to Günter Schabowski, who knew only what was on a piece of paper handed to him moments before a routine press conference. At 18:54, Schabowski read the statement on live TV, with little emotion: "exit via border crossings...possible for every citizen." Reporters, unable to believe what they were hearing, prodded him about when the borders would open. Schabowski shrugged and offered his best guess: *"Ab sofort, unverzüglich."* ("Immediately, without delay.")

Schabowski's words spread like wildfire. East Berliners showed up at Wall checkpoints, demanding that border guards let them pass. Finally, around 23:30, a border guard at the Bornholmer Strasse crossing decided to open the gates. Easterners flooded into the West, embracing their long-separated cousins, unable to believe their good fortune. Once open, the Wall could never be closed again. After that wild night, Berlin faced a fitful transition to reunification. Two cities—and countries—became one at a staggering pace.

bahnhof, this museum has more personality, buoyed by a still-defiant spirit.

Cost and Hours: €14.50, daily 9:00-22:00, last entry one hour before closing, audioguide-€5, U6 to Kochstrasse or U2 to Stadtmitte, Friedrichstrasse 43, tel. 030/253-7250, www.mauermuseum.de.

▲▲TOPOGRAPHY OF TERROR (TOPOGRAPHIE DES TERRORS)

A rare undeveloped patch of land in central Berlin, right next to a surviving stretch of Wall, was once the nerve center for the Gestapo and the SS—the most despicable elements of the Nazi government. Today this site hosts a modern documentation center, along with an outdoor exhibit in the Gestapo headquarters' excavated foundations. While there isn't much in the way of original artifacts, the exhibit does a good job of telling this powerful story, in the place where it happened. The information is a bit dense, but WWII historians (even armchair ones) find it fascinating.

Cost and Hours: Free, includes audioguide, daily 10:00-20:00, outdoor exhibit closes at dusk and closed entirely Dec-Jan, Niederkirchnerstrasse 8, U-Bahn: Potsdamer Platz or Kochstrasse, S-Bahn: Anhalter Bahnhof or Potsdamer Platz.

Information: Tel. 030/254-5090, www.topographie.de.

Visiting the Museum: Start in the lobby and study a **model** of the neighborhood showing the home of the German government at the outbreak of World War II. (We're standing at #20.) Back in the 1930s and '40s, this was just one of many governmental office buildings along Wilhelmstrasse. Seeing this sprawling bureaucratic quarter gives you a sense of how much mundane paperwork was involved in administering Hitler's reign of terror in an efficient, rational way. In the small theater nearby, the six-minute film provides context for the exhibit (and can be shown in English upon request).

The **ground floor** houses the permanent collection. Stepping in, you begin a chronological journey (with a timeline of events, old photographs, documents, and newspaper clippings) through the evolution of Nazism, the reign of terror, the start of World War II, and the Holocaust.

The displays illustrate how Hitler,

Some exhibits at the Topography of Terror are incorporated into a surviving stretch of the Berlin Wall.

Himmler, and their team expertly manipulated the German people to build a broadly supported "dictatorship of consent." You'll learn about the Gestapo and SS *(Schutzstaffel)*, and their brutal methods—including their chillingly systematic implementation of the Holocaust.

Some images here are indelible. Gleeful SS soldiers, stationed at Auschwitz, yuk it up on a retreat in the countryside (as their helpless prisoners were being gassed and burned a few miles away). Graphic images show executions—by hanging, firing squad, and so on.

The exhibits end with the conclusion of the war in 1945. While the Nazi leadership was captured and prosecuted at the Nürnberg trials, the majority of midlevel bureaucrats who routinely facilitated genocide with the flick of a pen...were never brought to justice.

With more time, use the audioguide and posted signs to explore the grounds surrounding the blocky building. Around the corner (to the right facing the museum entrance) are the scant remains of the **House Prison** outlined in cement. The building was equipped with dungeons, where the Gestapo detained and tortured prisoners.

Nearby: Immediately next door is an unusually long surviving stretch of the Berlin Wall. A block beyond that is the looming, fascist-style former Air Ministry for Hitler's Luftwaffe (air force), today the German Finance Ministry, though still adorned with cheery 1950s communist propaganda. A short walk away is a surviving DDR watchtower.

▲JEWISH MUSEUM BERLIN
(JÜDISCHES MUSEUM BERLIN)
Combining a remarkable building with a thoughtful permanent exhibit, this is the most educational Jewish-themed sight in Berlin. Designed by American architect Daniel Libeskind (the master planner for the redeveloped World Trade Center in New York), the zinc-walled building has a zigzag shape pierced by voids symbolic of the irreplaceable cultural loss caused by the Holocaust.

Enter the 18th-century Baroque building next door to reach three memorial spaces. Follow the **Axis of Exile**—lined with the names of cities where the Jew-

The Jewish Museum's fractured facade suggests the dislocation of the Holocaust.

ish diaspora settled—to a disorienting slanted garden with 49 pillars. Next, the **Axis of Holocaust**—lined with names of concentration camps and artifacts from Jews imprisoned and murdered by the Nazis—leads to an eerily empty tower shut off from the outside world. Finally, the **Axis of Continuity** takes you to stairs and the main exhibit (if the extensive renovation has been completed).

Cost and Hours: €8, daily 10:00-20:00, closed on Jewish holidays; tight security includes bag check and metal detectors; tel. 030/2599-3300, www.jmberlin.de.

Getting There: Take the U1/U6 to Hallesches Tor, find the exit marked *Jüdisches Museum,* exit straight ahead, then turn right onto Franz-Klühs-Strasse at the first corner. The museum is a five-minute walk ahead on your left, at Lindenstrasse 9.

Eating: The museum's **$$** restaurant offers good Jewish-style meals, albeit not kosher.

Kulturforum Complex

The Kulturforum, off the southeast corner of Tiergarten park, hosts Berlin's concert hall and several sprawling museums, but only the Gemäldegalerie is a must for art lovers.

▲▲GEMÄLDEGALERIE

This "Painting Gallery" is one of Germany's top collections of great works by European masters. The Gemäldegalerie shows off fine works from the 13th through 18th century. While there's no one famous piece of art, you'll get an enticing taste of just about all the big names. In the North Wing are painters from Germany (Albrecht Dürer, Hans Holbein, Lucas Cranach), the Low Countries (Jan van Eyck, Pieter Brueghel, Peter Paul Rubens, Anthony van Dyck, Frans Hals, Johannes Vermeer), Britain (Thomas Gainsborough), France (Antoine Watteau), and an impressive hall of Rembrandts. The South Wing is the terrain of Italian greats, including Giotto,

Botticelli, Titian, Raphael, and Caravaggio.

Cost and Hours: €10, includes audioguide; Tue-Fri 10:00-18:00, Thu until 20:00, Sat-Sun 11:00-18:00, closed Mon; clever little loaner stools, great salad bar in cafeteria upstairs, Matthäikirchplatz 4.

Information: Tel. 030/266-424-242, www.smb.museum.

Getting There: Ride the S-Bahn or U-Bahn to Potsdamer Platz, then walk along Potsdamer Platz.

Visiting the Museum: When you buy your ticket, pick up the current museum map for help locating specific paintings (artwork locations may change). Northern Art is on one side (where we'll begin) and Italian art is on the other (where we'll end). Note that inner rooms have Roman numerals (I, II, III), while adjacent outer rooms use Arabic numerals (1, 2, 3). We'll work counterclockwise (and roughly chronologically) through the collection.

Hans Holbein the Younger, 1497-1543 (Room 1): Holbein's portrait *Merchant Georg Gisze* (*Der Kaufmann Georg Gisze,* 1532) depicts a wealthy 34-year-old German businessman. His black beret and immaculate clothes mark him as a suc-

Holbein the Younger, The Merchant Georg Gisze

A *Van der Weyden,* Portrait of a Woman

B *Rubens,* Jesus Giving Peter the Keys to Heaven

C *Rembrandt,* Self-Portrait with a Velvet Beret

D *Vermeer,* The Glass of Wine

cessful dealer in cloth. Around him are the tools of his trade—logbooks, business letters with wax seals, signet rings, scales, and coins. Typical of detail-rich Northern European art, the canvas is bursting with highly symbolic tidbits. The clock (on the table, inside the small gold canister) reminds the viewer that time passes and worldly success fades. The unbalanced scales suggest that wealth is fleeting. Those negative symbols are counterbalanced by the carnations and herbs in the vase, representing Gisze's upcoming marriage.

Albrecht Dürer, 1471-1528 (Room 2): In 1494, the young Dürer traveled from Germany to Italy, where he soaked up the technique and spirit of the burgeoning Renaissance movement. In his portrait *Hieronymus Holzschuher* (1526), Dürer captured the personality of a white-bearded friend from Nürnberg, right down to the sly twinkle in his sidelong glance. Dürer does not gloss over the 57-year-old's unflattering features like the wrinkles or receding hairline (with the clever comb-over).

Lucas Cranach the Elder, 1472-1553 (Room III): Cranach's *Fountain of Youth* (*Der Jungbrunnen,* 1546) depicts the perennial human pursuit of eternal youth. Ladies flock to bathe in the swimming pool of youth. They arrive (on the left) as old women—by wagon, on horseback, carried by men, even in a wheelbarrow. They strip and enter with sagging breasts, frolic awhile in the pool, rinse and repeat, then emerge (on the right) young again. Newly nubile, the women go into a tent to dress up, snog with noblemen in the bushes (right foreground), dance merrily beneath the trees, and dine grandly beneath a landscape of mountains and towers.

Rogier van der Weyden, 1400-1464 (Room IV): Dutch painters were early adopters of oil paint, and Van der Weyden was a virtuoso of the new medium. In *Portrait of a Young Woman* (*Bildnis einer jungen Frau,* 1440-1445), the subject wears a typical winged bonnet, addressing the viewer directly with her fetching blue eyes. In the same room is a remarkable, rare trio of three-panel altarpieces by Van der Weyden showing the life of the Virgin Mary, the life of John the Baptist, and the story of the Nativity. Savor the fine details in each panel.

Peter Paul Rubens, 1577-1640 (Room VIII): We've fast-forwarded a hundred years, and it's apparent how much the Protestant Reformation changed the tenor of Northern European art. Rubens' paintings represent the Catholic response, the Counter-Reformation. You'll see huge, brightly-colored canvases of Mary, alongside angels, bishops, and venerated saints (like the arrow-pierced martyr, St. Sebastian). This exuberant Baroque style trumpeted the greatness of the Catholic Church.

You'll also catch glimpses of Rubens' second wife, Helene Fourment, in mythological scenes such as *Andromeda* (1638). Helene, the amply-figured nymph with a sweetly smiling face, came to define the phrase "Ruben-esque."

Frans Hals, c. 1582-1666 (Room 13): Hals' *Portrait of Catharina Hooft with Her Nurse* (*Bildnis der Catharina Hooft mit ihrer Amme*, 1619-1620) presents a startlingly self-possessed baby (the newest member of a wealthy merchant family), dressed in the lacy, jeweled finery of a queen and clutching a golden rattle. At the other end of the social spectrum is Hals' *Malle Babbe* (1633-1635). The subject, a notorious barfly nicknamed "Crazy" Babbe, was well known in Hals' hometown. Hals captures her hefting her pewter beer stein and turning to laugh at a joke. The messy brushstrokes that define her collar and cap are as wild and lively as her over-the-top personality.

Rembrandt van Rijn, 1606-1669 (Room X): The ultimate Dutch master, Rembrandt was propelled to fame in his lifetime by his powers of perception and invention. Browse Room X and the adjoining galleries to get a taste of the range of Rembrandt's work. There are storytelling scenes, taut with pulse-racing emotion (*The Rape of Persephone*, 1631, Room 16). There are Bible scenes (*Samson and Delilah*, 1628-1629, Room 16; *Samson Threatens His Father-in-Law*, 1635, Room X).

And there are expressive portraits. In Room X, a *Self-Portrait* (1634) shows Rembrandt wearing a beret. The 28-year-old genius was already famous. He soon married the beautiful Saskia (*Portrait of Saskia*, 1643, Room 16), and seemed to have it all. But then Saskia died, Rembrandt declared bankruptcy, and his painting style went out of fashion...all of which contributed to his brooding, dark canvases.

Johannes Vermeer, 1632-1675 (Room 18): Vermeer was a master at conveying a complicated story through a deceptively simple scene with a few significant details. *Young Woman with a Pearl Necklace* (1664) is classic Vermeer. He lets us glimpse an intimate, unguarded moment in the life of an everyday woman. She wears a beautiful yellow coat with an ermine fur lining, ribbons in her hair, and pearl earrings. Vermeer tells us a bit about the woman with objects on the table: her comb, make-up brush, and water bowl.

Caravaggio, 1573–1610 (Room XIV): In the year 1600, living in Rome, Caravaggio burst onto the scene with a new and shocking art style. Even religious and allegorical subjects got his uncompromising, gritty, ultrarealistic treatment. In Caravaggio's *Amor Vincit Omnia* (1601-1602), "Love Conquers All." Cupid stands victorious over all the vain accomplishments of ambitious men: Military triumphs (symbolized by the fallen armor), Art (the discarded musical instruments), Literature (paper and pen), Science (a globe), Grand Architecture (compass and square), and Power (the crown). Cupid—a young, naked boy—mocks those grown-up ambitions. He laughs derisively and splays his genitals over the fallen symbols.

Now turn your attention to a painting in Room XIV by a different artist—**Giovanni Baglione**'s *Sacred and Profane Love* (1602-1603). Baglione was hired by a conservative cardinal to paint a moralizing response to Caravaggio. Here, the main figure is a more upright incarnation of love—Sacred Love—embodied by a radiant angel. He corners his rascally counterpart, the cowering and "Profane" little Cupid (lower right).

EXPERIENCES

Shopping

One big draw is **communist kitsch.** Gift shops at museums (such as the DDR Museum or Museum of the Wall at Checkpoint Charlie) sell a variety of "East Berlin" paraphernalia. Maybe *the* top communist-kitsch souvenir is anything with the image of the **Ampelmännchen** (traffic-light man), the DDR-era crossing-guard symbol that's become Berlin's unofficial mascot. The best selection is at the local chain of Ampelmann shops; the flagship store—with a hunk of Berlin Wall autographed by David Hasselhoff (no joke)—is along Unter den Linden at #35 (at the corner with Friedrichstrasse).

Flea Markets (Flohmarkt)

Virtually every Berlin neighborhood hosts a regular flea market. In **Prenzlauer Berg,** the Sunday rummage market in the **Mauerpark** isn't just about buying and selling—it's an excuse for a big, weekly, community-wide party. You'll find lots of inventive snack stalls and, in the afternoon, karaoke in the park's amphitheater (Sun 10:00-18:00, U2: Eberswalder Strasse, www.flohmarktimmauerpark.de). On Sundays there's also a lively "junk market" (*Trödelmarkt*) several blocks south on **Arkonaplatz** (10:00-16:00, U8: Bernauer Strasse or a 10-minute walk from Mauerpark). **Hackescher Markt** hosts a twice-weekly market with an odd variety of produce, clothes, trinkets, jewelry, hats, and food stalls; less funky than the best Berlin markets, it's conveniently located (Thu 9:00-18:00, Sat from 10:00). One of Berlin's largest flea markets is right next to the Tiergarten park on **Strasse des 17 Juni,** with great antiques, more than 200 stalls, collector-savvy merchants, and fun German fast-food stands (Sat-Sun 10:00-17:00, S-Bahn: Tiergarten, www.berlinertroedelmarkt.com).

Hackesche Höfe

This delightfully restored old series of eight interlocking shopping courtyards sits in the heart of the old Jewish quarter. It's a convenient place to window-shop for everything from locally made porcelain to fashion (typically open Mon-Sat from 10:00 or 11:00 until 19:00, closed Sun, Rosenthaler Strasse 40, www.hackesche-hoefe.com).

Chocolate Shops on Gendarmenmarkt

This delightful square has two very different chocolate shops: one bourgeois, the other proletarian.

Rausch claims to be Europe's biggest chocolate store and proudly displays its sweet delights—250 kinds—on a 55-foot-long buffet. Upstairs is an elegant café with fine views (Mon-Sat 10:00-20:00, Sun from 11:00, corner of Mohrenstrasse at Charlottenstrasse 60, tel. 030/757-882-440). If you're a choco-populist, head to the Volkswagen of candy, **Rittersport Bunte Schokowelt**—the flagship store of Rittersport. This is basically Germany's answer to the M&M's store (daily 10:00-19:00, Französische Strasse 24, tel. 030/200-950-810).

Big, Glitzy Department Stores

Unter den Linden is lined with some high-end shops, but for a wider selection, head a few blocks south. The French department store **Galeries Lafayette** has several floors of high-end goods under a glass dome (top-quality basement food court; Mon-Sat 10:00-20:00, closed Sun, Französische Strasse 23). Several blocks west is the massive, state-of-the-art **Mall of Berlin,** with 270 shops surrounding a cavernous glass-covered passageway (Mon-Sat 10:00-21:00, closed Sun, Vossstrasse 35, www.mallofberlin.de). Nearby, **Potsdamer Platz** and **Sony Center** have additional shops.

Nightlife

Berlin is a happening place for nightlife—whether it's clubs, pubs, jazz, cabaret, concerts, or even sightseeing.

For good **live music** listings, see www.askhelmut.com or shell out a few euros for a Berlin magazine (sold at kiosks): *Zitty* (www.zitty.de) and *Tip* (www.tip-berlin.de) are the top guides to alternative culture (mostly in German); *Exberliner Magazine* is colorfully written in English (www.exberliner.com).

Berlin's ticket clearinghouse, **Hek-ticket,** offers advance tickets and deeply discounted last-minute tickets (daily after 14:00, up to half off, ticket prices usually €10-40). Call or go online (tel. 030/230-9930, www.hekticket.de), or visit their booth near Alexanderplatz (cash only) to see what's on the push list for that evening (Mon-Fri 10:30-19:00, closed Sat-Sun, Alexanderstrasse 1).

Rick's Tip: *Stretch your sightseeing day into the night. These museums are* **open late** *every day:* **Reichstag** *(last entry at 22:00),* **Museum of the Wall at Checkpoint Charlie** *(until 22:00), and* **Topography of Terror** *(until 20:00).* **Museum Island** *museums are open until 20:00 on Thursdays. Outdoor monuments such as the* **Berlin Wall Memorial** *and the* **Memorial to the Murdered Jews of Europe** *are safe and well-lit late into the night, even though their visitor centers close earlier.*

Jazz

Berlin has a lively jazz scene (for schedules, see www.jazzclubsinberlin.com). Near the TV Tower, **B-Flat Acoustic**

Festivals keep Berlin lively year-round.

Music and Jazz Club has live shows and jam sessions (from free to €15, nightly from 21:00, in Alexanderplatz at Dircksenstrasse 40, tel. 030/283-3123, www.b-flat-berlin.de).

Theater

Berliner Ensemble—made famous under the direction of Bertolt Brecht—stages a dozen or so productions ranging from classic to contemporary in the majestic Theater am Schiffbauerdamm, across from the Friedrichstrasse Bahnhof (€12-50, generally daily at 19:30 or 20:00, box office open Mon-Sat 10:00-18:30, Bertolt-Brecht-Platz 1, tel. 030/2840-8155, www.berliner-ensemble.de).

Live Music

Berlin has a staggering array of smaller music venues. Here are two: **Frannz Club,** in Prenzlauer Berg's Kulturbrauerei, attracts talented rock and alternative bands (www.frannz.com). **Aufsturz,** the recommended pub in the old Jewish quarter, hosts jazz and other music (www.aufsturz.de).

Big concerts are often held at **Olympic** Stadium, **Mercedes-Benz Arena** in Friedrichshain, the **Spandau Citadel,** and the outdoor **Waldbühne** ("Forest Stage").

Al Fresco Summer Fun

Berlin's emerging **beach bar** scene—where people grab a drink along the Spree riverfront and watch the excursion boats go by—is a great way to wind down from a day of sightseeing. The classic spot is the **Strandbar Mitte** in **Monbijoupark,** with a breezy and scenic setting overlooking the Bode Museum on Museum Island.

EATING

Near Museum Island

$$ Deponie No. 3 is a rustic if touristy Berlin *Kneipe* (pub). Garden seating in the back is nice but comes with the noise of the S-Bahn passing directly above. The bar interior is cozy and woody with several inviting spaces. They serve basic salads, traditional Berlin dishes, and hearty daily specials (daily 10:00-24:00, S-Bahn arch #187 at Georgenstrasse 5, tel. 030/2016-5740).

Berliner Street Food

Sausage stands are everywhere. You may even see portable human hot-dog stands—cooks in clever harnesses that let them grill and sell hot dogs from under an umbrella.

Most sausage stands specialize in **Currywurst,** created in Berlin after World War II when a fast-food cook got her hands on some curry and Worcestershire sauce from British troops stationed here. It's basically a grilled pork sausage smothered with curry sauce. *Currywurst* comes either *mit Darm* (with casing) or *ohne Darm* (without casing). If the casing is left on to grill, it gives the sausage a smokier flavor. (*Berliner Art*—"Berlin-style"—means that the sausage is boiled *ohne Darm,* then grilled.) Either way, the grilled sausage is then chopped into small pieces or cut in half (East Berlin style) and topped with sauce. While some places simply use ketchup and sprinkle on some curry powder, real *Currywurst* joints use a proper *Currysauce:* tomato paste, Worcestershire sauce, and curry. With your wurst comes either a toothpick or small wooden fork; you'll usually get a plate of fries as well.

The other big Berlin street food is fast Turkish and Middle Eastern food. Schwarma and falafel joints are cheap and tasty. And the kebab—either **döner kebab** (Turkish-style skewered meat slow-roasted and served in pita bread) or the vegetarian alternative, **Gemüse kebab** (with lots of veggies, and sometimes falafel)—is a quick way to fill up for a couple euros.

$$ Brauhaus Lemke, near the TV Tower, is a big, lively beer hall (still in its 1970s DDR shell) that makes its own brews and offers Berliner specialties and Bavarian dishes. They have decent salads and serve a six-beer sampler board (daily 12:00-24:00, across from the TV Tower and tucked a bit back from the street at Karl-Liebknecht-Strasse 13, tel. 030/3087-8989).

Near Gendarmenmarkt

South of Unter den Linden, Gendarmenmarkt, with its twin churches, is a delightful place for an al fresco meal.

$$$$ Lutter & Wegner Restaurant is respected for its Austrian cuisine (*Schnitzel* and *Sauerbraten*). It's dressy, with fun sidewalk seating or a dark and elegant interior. Weekday €9 lunch specials are an affordable way to sample their cooking (daily 12:00-24:00, Charlottenstrasse 56, tel. 030/202-9515, www.l-w-berlin.de).

$ Dom Curry, behind the German Cathedral, is a *Currywurst* stand that works for a quick bite out on the square (daily 12:00-20:00).

$$ Galeries Lafayette Food Circus is a French festival of fun eateries in the basement of the landmark department store. You'll find sandwiches, savory crêpes, quiches, sushi bar, *les macarons,* and so on (Mon-Sat 10:00-20:00, closed Sun, Friedrichstrasse 76, U6: Französische Strasse, tel. 030/209-480).

Prenzlauer Berg

$ Prater Biergarten is Berlin's oldest beer garden. It's mellow, shaded, and super-cheap—with a family-friendly outdoor area, including a playground (no table service, order food at one counter, beer at the other). Prater's rustic indoor restaurant (more expensive, with table service) serves well-executed German classics (restaurant open Mon-Sat 18:00-24:00,

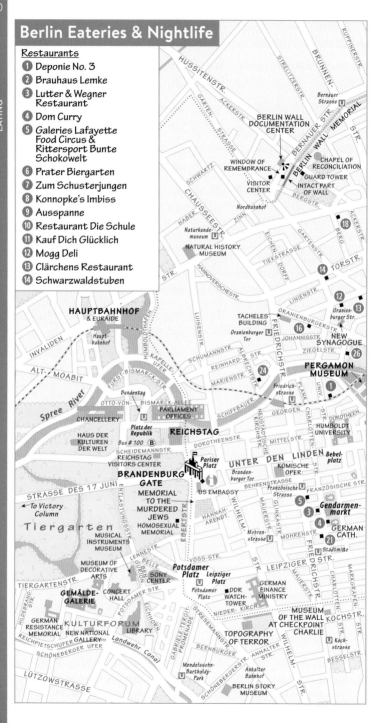

Berlin Eateries & Nightlife

Restaurants

1. Deponie No. 3
2. Brauhaus Lemke
3. Lutter & Wegner Restaurant
4. Dom Curry
5. Galeries Lafayette Food Circus & Rittersport Bunte Schokowelt
6. Prater Biergarten
7. Zum Schusterjungen
8. Konnopke's Imbiss
9. Ausspanne
10. Restaurant Die Schule
11. Kauf Dich Glücklich
12. Mogg Deli
13. Clärchens Restaurant
14. Schwarzwaldstuben

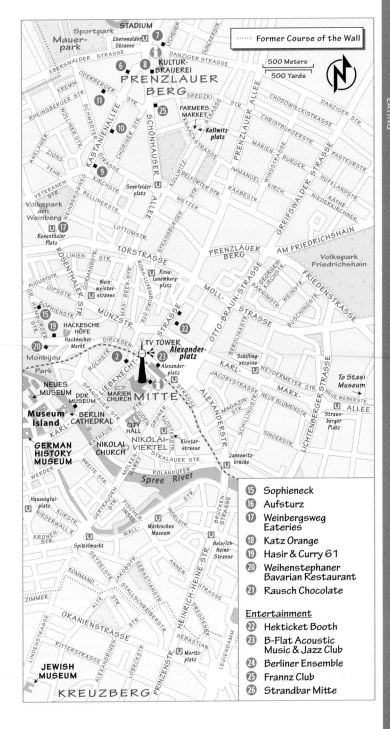

..... Former Course of the Wall

500 Meters

500 Yards

STADIUM
Mauer-park
Sportpark
Eberswalder Strasse 7
KULTUR-BRAUEREI 6 8
PRENZLAUER BERG
FARMERS MARKET 25
Kollwitz-platz
11
10
9
Senefelder-platz
Volkspark am Wainberg
Rosenthaler Platz 17
TORSTRASSE
PRENZLAUER BERG
AM FRIEDRICHSHAIN
Volkspark Friedrichshain
Rosa-Luxemburg-platz
Wein-meister-strasse
HACKESCHE HÖFE 15
19
Hackescher Markt
Monbijou Park 20
MÜNZSTR.
22
TV TOWER
2 23
Alexander-platz
Alexander-platz
Schilling-strasse
KARL-MARX-ALLEE
To Stasi Museum
Strauss-berger Platz
NEUES MUSEUM
DDR MUSEUM
MARIEN CHURCH
MITTE
Museum Island
BERLIN CATHEDRAL
CITY HALL
NIKOLAI-VIERTEL
Kloster-strasse
GERMAN HISTORY MUSEUM
RATHAUS
NIKOLAI CHURCH
Spree River
Jannowitz-brücke
Hausvogtei-platz
Märkisches Museum
Heinrich-Heine-Strasse
Spittelmarkt
ORANIENSTRASSE
JEWISH MUSEUM
KREUZBERG
Moritz-platz

15 Sophieneck
16 Aufsturz
17 Weinbergsweg Eateries
18 Katz Orange
19 Hasir & Curry 61
20 Weihenstephaner Bavarian Restaurant
21 Rausch Chocolate

Entertainment
22 Hekticket Booth
23 B-Flat Acoustic Music & Jazz Club
24 Berliner Ensemble
25 Frannz Club
26 Strandbar Mitte

Sun from 12:00; beer garden open daily in good weather 12:00-24:00, closed in winter; Kastanienallee 7, tel. 030/448-5688).

$$ Zum Schusterjungen ("The Cobbler's Apprentice") is a classic, German-with-attitude eatery that retains its circa-1986 DDR decor. Famous for its filling meals (including schnitzel and pork knuckle), it's a no-frills place with quality ingredients and a strong local following (small 40-seat dining hall plus outdoor tables, daily 12:00-24:00, corner of Lychener Strasse and Danziger Strasse 9, tel. 030/442-7654).

$ Konnopke's Imbiss, a super-cheap German-style sausage stand with a small section of covered picnic tables underneath the ever-rumbling U2 train tracks, has been a Berlin institution since 1930. Loyal Berliners say Konnopke's cooks up some of the city's best *Currywurst;* they also serve a wide variety of other wurst specialties (Tue-Sat 10:00-20:00, Sun 12:00-18:00, closed Mon; Schönhauser Allee 44A—underneath elevated train tracks where Kastanienallee dead-ends, tel. 030/442-7765).

$$$ Ausspanne looks like a traditional, uninspired hotel restaurant. But the small, always fresh menu boldly elevates German classics with surprising flourishes—such as a puff of habanero foam with duck breast and red cabbage (daily 17:00-22:00, in recommended Hotel Kastanienhof at Kastanienallee 65, tel. 030/4430-5199).

$$$ Restaurant Die Schule is a dressy, modern eatery where you can sample €3 tapas-style plates of old-fashioned German food. They have several varieties of *Flammkuchen* (German pizza—a flatbread dish from the French borderlands) and seasonal main dishes (daily 11:00-22:00, Kastanienallee 82, tel. 030/780-089-550).

Kauf Dich Glücklich serves an enticing array of sweet Belgian waffles and homemade ice cream in an inviting candy-sprinkled, bohemian lounge and a garden-like front terrace on a great street (or get your dessert to go, daily 10:00-23:00, Oderberger Strasse 44, tel. 030/4862-3292).

Old Jewish Quarter

Most of these places are a reasonable walk from Unter den Linden and within 10 minutes of the Hackescher Markt S-Bahn station.

$$ Mogg Deli is a foodie favorite, serving a short but thoughtful menu of soups, salads, and sandwiches. They're known for their home-cured pastrami, especially their monster, designed-to-be-shared Reuben (Mon-Sat 11:00-22:00, Sun until 20:00; inside the huge red-brick former Jewish girls school at Auguststrasse 11, tel. 030/330-060-770).

$$ Clärchens Restaurant fills the courtyard in front of Clärchens Ballhaus (a classic old Berlin ballroom) with twinkle lights, ramshackle furniture, and a bohemian-chic atmosphere—especially nice on a balmy evening. They serve German and Italian dishes, including brats, pizza, and homemade cakes. You can also eat in the dance hall or in a garden out back. After 21:00, the DJ cranks up the music in the ground floor dance hall (daily 12:00-22:00, Auguststrasse 24, tel. 030/282-9295).

$$$ Schwarzwaldstuben is a Black Forest-themed pub—which explains the antlers and cuckoo clocks. It's friendly, with good service, food, and prices. If they're full, you can eat at the long bar (daily 12:00-23:00, Tucholskystrasse 48, tel. 030/2809-8084).

$$ Sophieneck upholds its *Kneipe* roots as the neighborhood's ersatz living room, serving hearty Berliner specialties like *Buletten* and *Eisbein* on a breezy corner to a happy mix of locals and tourists (daily 12:00-22:30, Grosse Hamburger Strasse 37, tel. 030/283-4065).

$$ Aufsturz is a lively pub that's more for serious drinkers than serious eaters. It has a huge selection of beer and whisky and dishes up traditional Berliner pub grub to a young crowd (daily 12:00-24:00, Oranienburger Strasse 67, tel. 030/2804-7407).

Rosenthaler Platz Area

This busy neighborhood sits roughly between the old Jewish quarter and Prenzlauer Berg, near the U8: Rosenthaler Platz station and on the tram #M1 line.

Eclectic Eats on Weinbergsweg: Don't miss the first block of Weinbergsweg, the tram track-lined lane that heads north to Prenzlauer Berg. In just one block, you'll find cafés, bakeries, superfoods and organic juice, *Gemüse kebab, döner kebab,* an Italian deli, Mexican street food, Russian, Korean barbecue, a French bistro, Chinese dumplings, and gelato.

$$$$ Katz Orange is a mecca for foodies and feels regal from the moment you enter its intimate courtyard. It's surprisingly affordable and known for its "candy on the bone" slow-cooked meat (daily 18:00-23:00, reservations recommended, Bergstrasse 22, tel. 030/9832-08430, www.katzorange.com).

Hackescher Markt Area

$$$ Hasir is a popular, somewhat stuffy opportunity to splurge on Turkish and Anatolian specialties amid candles and hardwood floors. While a bit past its prime and with hit-or-miss service, Hasir enjoys a handy location (large and split-table portions, daily 16:00-24:00, a block from the Hackescher Markt S-Bahn station at Oranienburger Strasse 4, tel. 030/2804-1616).

$$ Weihenstephaner Bavarian Restaurant serves traditional Bavarian food in an atmospheric cellar, on an inner courtyard, or on a busy people-watching terrace facing the delightful Hackescher Markt square; and, of course, it has excellent beer (daily 11:00-24:00, Neue Promenade 5 at Hackescher Markt, tel. 030/8471-0760).

$ Curry 61 serves, for many, the best *Currywurst* in Berlin; vegetarians and vegans appreciate good options, too. Eat in or grab a €5 meal to eat on a bench at the fine Monbijoupark across the street (daily, long hours, Oranienburger Strasse 6).

SLEEPING

Prenzlauer Berg

My favorite Berlin neighborhood to call home, Prenzlauer Berg offers easy transit connections to sightseeing; diverse eateries, coffeehouses, and nightspots; and a welcoming personality (think of all that graffiti as just some people's way of saying they care).

The area's transit hub is the Eberswalder Strasse U-Bahn station (U2 line). Trams #M1 and #12 run up and down Kastanienallee, connecting to the Rosenthaler Platz U-Bahn (#M1 continues all the way to the Hackescher Markt S-Bahn station).

$$$ Hotel Jurine is a pleasant and well-run 53-room business-style hotel on a peaceful street. If you want calm atmosphere, your own peaceful back garden, and a very friendly staff, this is my choice (mention Rick Steves when you book for a free upgraded room, breakfast extra, elevator, pay parking—reserve ahead, Schwedter Strasse 15, 5-minute walk to #M1: Zionskirchplatz or U2: Senefelderplatz, tel. 030/443-2990, www.hotel-jurine.de, mail@hotel-jurine.de).

$$$ Hotel Oderberger has 70 modern rooms filling part of a Neo-Renaissance bathhouse complex (originally opened in 1902, renovated in 2016). From the reception, you can peek into the elegant old swimming pool area. It's a fine choice, with its understated elegance, historic aura, and good location, tucked away on a quiet side street near the most happening stretch of Kastanienallee (elevator, guest discount for swimming pool, Oderberger Strasse 57, tel. 030/780-089-760, www.hotel-oderberger.de, info@hotel-oderberger.berlin).

$$ Myer's Hotel rents 50 comfortable rooms decorated with lots of bold colors. Located on a tranquil, tree-lined street, you'll find it hard to believe you're in the heart of a capital city. The gorgeous public spaces, including an art-filled patio

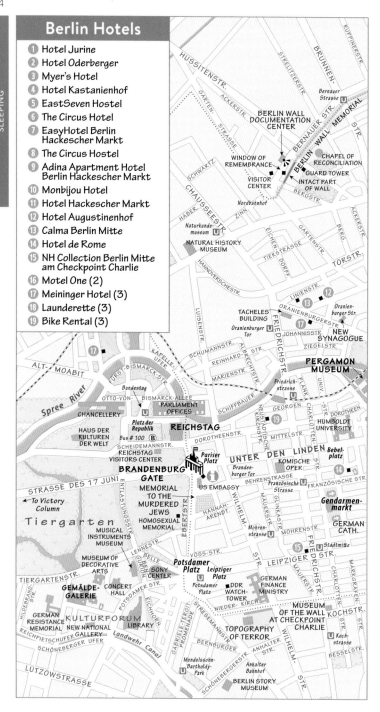

Berlin Hotels

① Hotel Jurine

② Hotel Oderberger

③ Myer's Hotel

④ Hotel Kastanienhof

⑤ EastSeven Hostel

⑥ The Circus Hotel

⑦ EasyHotel Berlin Hackescher Markt

⑧ The Circus Hostel

⑨ Adina Apartment Hotel Berlin Hackescher Markt

⑩ Monbijou Hotel

⑪ Hotel Hackescher Markt

⑫ Hotel Augustinenhof

⑬ Calma Berlin Mitte

⑭ Hotel de Rome

⑮ NH Collection Berlin Mitte am Checkpoint Charlie

⑯ Motel One (2)

⑰ Meininger Hotel (3)

⑱ Launderette (3)

⑲ Bike Rental (3)

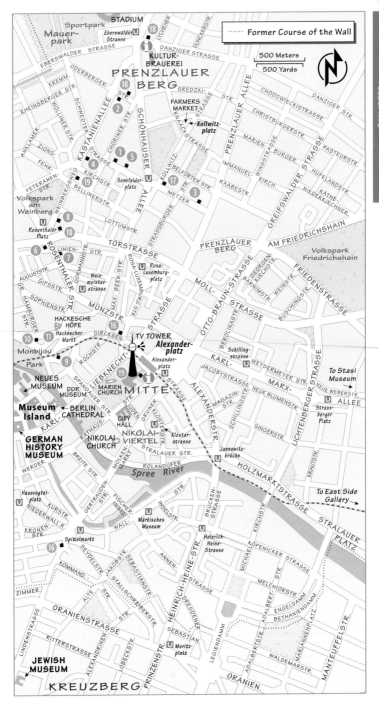

Former Course of the Wall

500 Meters
500 Yards

STADIUM
Sportpark
Mauer-
park
Eberswalder
Strasse

EBERSWALDER STRASSE

KULTUR-
BRAUEREI

PRENZLAUER
BERG

DANZIGER STRASSE

SREDZKI-
STR.

CHODOWIECKISTRASSE

DANZIGER STR.

CHRISTBURGERSTRASSE

FARMERS
MARKET

Kollwitz-
platz

KNAACKSTRASSE

MARIEN-
STRASSE

PASTEURSTR.

KREMM

ODERBERGER

RHEINSBERGER STR.

WÖLLINER STR.

SCHWEDTER

KASTANIENALLEE

CHORINER

SCHÖNHAUSER ALLEE

BURGER

IMMANUEL-
KIRCH

WINSSTRASSE

GREIFSWALDER STRASSE

HUFELANDSTR.

KÄTHE-
NIEDERKIRCHNER

ANKLAMER

ZIONS-

FEHR-

KASTANIEN-
STRASSE

KOLLWITZ-

Senefelder-
platz

BELFORTER STR.

RAABESTR.

VETERANEN-
STR.

KIRCHSTR.

METZER

Volkspark
am
Weinberg

WEINBERGSWEG

BELLINERSTR.

LOTTUMSTR.

PRENZLAUER
BERG

AM FRIEDRICHSHAIN

Rosenthaler
Platz

TORSTRASSE

Volkspark
Friedrichshain

LINIEN-
STR.

GORMANNSTR.

ROSA-LUXEMBURG-STRASSE

Rosa-
Luxemburg-
platz

OTTO-BRAUN-STRASSE

BEROLINASTR.

GEORGEN-
STR.

BARNIMSTR.

WEINSTR.

FRIEDENSTRASSE

BÜSCHINGSTR.

AUGUSTSTR.

GIPSSTR.

SOPHIENSTR.

Wein-
meister-
strasse

MÜNZSTR.

MAX-BEER-STR.

MOLL-

STRASSE

GR. HAMBURGER STR.

HACKESCHE
HÖFE

Hackescher
Markt

DIRCKSEN-

TV TOWER

Alexander-
platz

KARL-

Schilling-
strasse

WEYDEMEYER STR.

MARX-

LICHTENBERGER STRASSE

To Stasi
Museum

Monbijou
Park

ROCHSTR.

LIEBKNECHT

SPANDAUER STR.

Alexander-
platz

JACOBYSTRASSE

NEUE BLUMENSTR.

SCHILLINGSTR.

NEUE WEBERSTR.

ALLEE

NEUES
MUSEUM

DDR
MUSEUM

MARIEN-
CHURCH

MITTE

ALEXANDERSTR.

Straus-
berger
Platz

Museum
Island

BERLIN
CATHEDRAL

KARL-

CITY
HALL

GRUNER-

KLOSTERSTR.

MAGAZIN-

SINGERSTR.

GERMAN
HISTORY
MUSEUM

RATHAUS-

NIKOLAI
CHURCH

NIKOLAI-
VIERTEL

Kloster-
strasse

MOLKEN-
MARKT

STRALAUER STR.

Jannowitz-
brücke

HOLZMARKTSTRASSE

WERDER-

BREITE STR.

ROLANDUFER

Spree River

STR.

To East Side
Gallery

Hausvogtei-
platz

KURSTR.

NIEDERWALL-

GERTRAUDEN-

FISCHER-

INSELSTR.

BRÜCKEN-
STRASSE

KIRCHSTR.

KRAUTSTR.

STRALAUER
PLATZ

KRONEN-
STR.

Spittelmarkt

WALL-

Märkisches
Museum

SEYDELSTR.

JACOBYSTR.

SEBASTIANSTR.

Heinrich-
Heine-
Strasse

MICHAEL

KÖPENICKER STRASSE

MELCHIORSTR.

ZIMMER-

KOMMAND-

ALTE STR.

STALLSCHREIBERSTR.

DRESDENER

ENGELDAMM

BETHANIENDAMM

LINDENSTRASSE

ORANIENSTRASSE

RITTERSTRASSE

ALEXANDRINEN-

LÜBECKSTR.

PRINZENSTR.

SEBASTIAN

HEINRICH-HEINE-STR.

Moritz-
platz

LEGIENDAMM

ADALBERTSTR.

MARIANNENPLATZ

MANTEUFFELSTR.

JEWISH
MUSEUM

KREUZBERG

ORANIEN-

WALDEMARSTR.

and garden, host frequent cultural events (air-con, elevator, sauna, Metzer Strasse 26—midway between U2: Senefelderplatz and #M2 tram: Prenzlauer Allee/Metzer Strasse, #M2 goes to/from Alexanderplatz, tel. 030/440-140, www.myershotel.de, info@myershotel.de).

$$ Hotel Kastanienhof feels like a traditional small-town German hotel. It's on the #M1 tram line, with easy access to the Prenzlauer Berg bustle (so ask for a quiet room in the back). Its 44 rooms come with helpful service (breakfast extra, deluxe top-floor rooms offer air-con and/or balcony, elevator, wheelchair-accessible room, pay parking, 20 yards from #M1: Zionskirchplatz at Kastanienallee 65, tel. 030/443-050, www.kastanienhof.berlin, info@kastanienhof.berlin).

¢ EastSeven Hostel rents 100 of the best cheap beds in Prenzlauer Berg. Modern and conscientiously run, it offers all the hostel services plus an inviting lounge, guest kitchen, backyard terrace, and bike rental. Children are welcome (private rooms available, no curfew, 100 yards from U2: Senefelderplatz at Schwedter Strasse 7, tel. 030/9362-2240, www.eastseven.de, info@eastseven.de).

Old Jewish Quarter

The old Jewish quarter is closer to the historic core than Prenzlauer Berg but feels less residential, and the hotels here are bigger and less personable.

Near Rosenthaler Platz

Though bustling and congested, Rosenthaler Platz makes a good base for getting around the city thanks to its U-Bahn (U8: Rosenthaler Platz) and tram service (#M1 and #M8).

$$ The Circus Hotel is fun, entirely comfortable, and a great value. The achingly hip lobby has a café serving delicious (optional) breakfasts, and the 60 rooms are straightforward and colorful. As the hotel overlooks a busy intersection, ask for a quieter back room (breakfast extra, elevator, Rosenthaler Strasse 1, tel. 030/2000-3939, www.circus-berlin.de, info@circus-berlin.de). The Circus also offers spacious, modern **$$$ apartments** within the hotel and two blocks away at Choriner Strasse 84.

$ EasyHotel Berlin Hackescher Markt is part of an unapologetically cheap, Europe-wide chain where you pay for exactly what you use—nothing more, nothing less. The 125 orange-and-gray rooms are very small, basic, and feel popped out of a plastic mold (no breakfast, elevator, call to request a quieter back room after booking online, Rosenthaler Strasse 69, tel. 030/4000-6550, www.easyhotel-berlin.de, enquiries@berlinhm.easyhotel.com).

¢ The Circus Hostel is a brightly colored, well-run place with 250 beds, and a trendy lounge and microbrewery. It has typical hostel dorms as well as some hotel-like private rooms; for a few big steps up in comfort, consider the Circus Hotel, listed earlier (no curfew, elevator, Weinbergsweg 1A, tel. 030/2000-3939, www.circus-berlin.de, info@circus-berlin.de).

By Hackescher Markt

Lively Hackescher Markt is brimming with people, eateries, and on some days, an open-air market. It has an S-Bahn station and is connected to Prenzlauer Berg by tram #M1.

$$$ Adina Apartment Hotel Berlin Hackescher Markt has 134 studio and one-bedroom apartments with kitchenettes, though breakfast is available for an extra fee (air-con, elevator, pay parking, An der Spandauer Brücke 11, tel. 030/209-6980, www.adinahotels.com, berlinhm@adina.eu).

$$$ Monbijou Hotel's 101 rooms are small, but they make up for it with pleasing public spaces, a postcard-worthy rooftop terrace (with views of the cathedral and TV Tower), and a flair for design—from antique furnishings to plenty of natural light (breakfast extra, family rooms, air-con, elevator, pay parking, Monbijouplatz 1, tel. 030/6162-0300, www.monbijouhotel. com, info@monbijouhotel.com).

$$ Hotel Hackescher Markt, with 32 rooms, offers an inviting lounge and modern decor without being predictable or pretentious (breakfast extra, family rooms, elevator, Grosse Präsidentenstrasse 8, tel. 030/280 030, www.hotel-hackescher-markt.com, reservierung@hotel-hackescher-markt.com).

On or near Auguststrasse

These good-value hotels are between the Oranienburger Strasse S-Bahn (S1/S2) and Oranienburger Tor U-Bahn (U6), and tram #M1 is nearby.

$$ Hotel Augustinenhof has 66 spacious rooms, nice woody floors, and firm beds. Rooms in front overlook the courtyard of the old Imperial Post Office, rooms in back are a bit quieter, and some rooms have older, thin windows (breakfast extra, elevator, Auguststrasse 82, tel. 030/3088-6710, www.hotel-augustinenhof.de, augustinenhof@albrechtshof-hotels.de).

$$ Calma Berlin Mitte, part of a small local chain, is a good budget bet. Its 46 straightforward but comfortable, modern rooms are tucked away on a tranquil courtyard, just steps from the lively Oranienburger Strasse scene (breakfast extra, elevator, Linienstrasse 139, tel. 030/9153-9333, www.lindemannhotels.de, calma@lindemannhotels.de).

Other Sleeping Options

$$$$ Hotel de Rome, holding court on Frederick the Great's showpiece Bebelplatz and facing Unter den Linden, is *the* Berlin splurge, with 108 rooms and all the luxurious little extras. If money is no object, this is a tempting choice for your Berlin address (air-con, elevator, Behrenstrasse 37, tel. 030/460-6090, www.roccofortehotels.com, info.derome@roccofortehotels.com).

$$$ NH Collection Berlin Mitte am Checkpoint Charlie is an elegant chain hotel on a busy street a short walk from Gendarmenmarkt, with nearly 400 fresh, interchangeable rooms at reasonable rates (air-con, elevator, Leipziger Strasse 106, U2: Stadtmitte, tel. 030/203-760, www.nh-hotels.com, nhcollectionberlinmitte@nh-hotels.com).

$ Motel One has multiple locations across Berlin; all have the same aqua-and-brown decor and posh-feeling but small rooms. Two convenient locations are between Hackescher Markt and Alexanderplatz (Dircksenstrasse 36, tel. 030/2005-4080, berlin-hackeschermarkt@motel-one.com) and a few blocks east of Gendarmenmarkt (Leipziger Strasse 50, U2: Spittelmarkt, tel. 030/2014-3630, berlin-spittelmarkt@motel-one.com).

Meininger is a Europe-wide budget-hotel chain with several locations in Berlin. With both ¢ cheap dorm beds and $$ comfortable, hotelesque private rooms, Meininger is basic but lively, modern, and generally a solid budget option, even for nonhostelers. They have three well-located branches: in Prenzlauer Berg ("Alexanderplatz" branch, actually at Schönhauser Allee 19 on Senefelderplatz); in the old Jewish quarter (Mitte "Humboldthaus" branch, next to the recommended Aufsturz pub at Oranienburger Strasse 67); and near the Hauptbahnhof at Ella-Trebe-Strasse 9 (all locations have elevator and 24-hour reception, pay parking at some, tel. 030/666-36100, www.meininger-hostels.com, welcome@meininger-hostels.com).

TRANSPORTATION

Getting Around Berlin
By Public Transit

Berlin's transit system uses the same ticket for its buses, trams (*Strassenbahn*), and trains. There are two types of trains: The U-Bahn—like a subway, making lots of short hops around town—is run by transit

Berlin Public Transportation

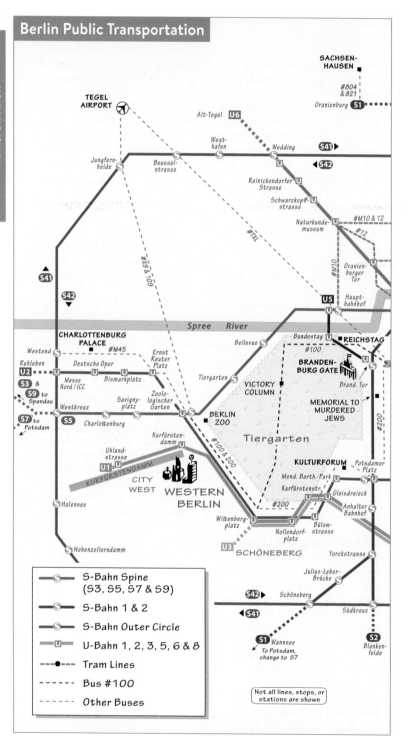

SACHSEN-
HAUSEN

#804
& 821

Oranienburg **S1**

TEGEL
AIRPORT

Alt-Tegel **U6**

West-
hafen   Wedding   **S41** ▶

◀ **S42**

Jungfern-
heide   Beussel-
strasse

Reinickendorfer
Strasse

Schwarzkopf-
strasse

Naturkunde-   #M10 & 12
museum

#12

S41 ▲   #TXL

Oranien-
burger
Tor

S42 ▼   #M10   Hauptbahnhof

U5

Spree   River

CHARLOTTENBURG
PALACE   #M45

Bellevue **S**   Bundestag   **REICHSTAG**

#100   BRANDEN-
BURG GATE

Westend **S**

Ruhleben   Ernst
Reuter
Platz   Tiergarten   Brand. Tor

Deutsche Oper

U2   Bismarkplatz

Messe   VICTORY
Nord / ICC   COLUMN   MEMORIAL TO
MURDERED
JEWS

S3 &
S9 to
Spandau   Savigny-
platz   Zoo-
logischer
Garten

Westkreuz   Tiergarten   #200

S7 to
Potsdam   **S5**   Charlottenburg   BERLIN
ZOO

Kurfürsten-   KULTURFORUM   Potsdamer
damm **U**   Platz

Uhland-   #100 & 200   Mend. Barth-Park
strasse

U1   KURFÜRSTENDAMM   CITY   Kurfürstenstr.   Gleisdreieck
WEST   Anhalter
WESTERN   #200   Bahnhof
BERLIN

S Halensee   Wittenberg-   Bülow-
platz **U**   strasse

Nollendorf-
platz

U3   SCHÖNEBERG   Yorckstrasse

S Hohenzollerndamm

Julius-Leber-
Brücke **S**

─── **S** S-Bahn Spine
(S3, S5, S7 & S9)

─── **S** S-Bahn 1 & 2   **S42** ▶   Schöneberg **S**   Südkreuz

─── **S** S-Bahn Outer Circle   ◀ **S41**

─── **U** U-Bahn 1, 2, 3, 5, 6 & 8   **S1** Wannsee   **S2**
To Potsdam,
─•─ Tram Lines   change to S7   Blanken-
felde

───── Bus #100

───── Other Buses   Not all lines, stops, or
stations are shown

Not to Scale

U8 Wittenau
Rosenthal Nord
Schillerstr.
Pankow U2
S2 Bernau
#M1
Pasedagplatz
#12
Gesund-brunnen
Bornholmer Strasse
U Vinetastr.
U Schön-hauser Allee
#M1
Prenzlauer Allee
Greifswalder Str.
NORTHERN BERLIN
Voltastr.
Humboldt-hain
Mauer-park
BERLIN WALL MEM.
Eberswalder Strasse
#M1 & 12
PRENZLAUER BERG
#M10
Nord-bahnhof
#M10
Bernauer Strasse
#12
Senefelder-platz
Landsberger Allee
Oranien-burger Strasse
#M1
Rosenthaler Platz
Weinmeister-strasse
Rosa-Luxemburg-Strasse
Storkower Str.
#M1 & M12
Friedrich-strasse
OLD JEWISH QUARTER
Hackescher Markt
DDR MUSEUM
EASTERN BERLIN
S42
S41
Am Kupfer-graben
PERGAMON MUSEUM
DOM
#100 UNTER DEN LINDEN
MUSEUM ISLAND
Alexanderplatz
Samariterstr.
Frankfurter Allee
U5
CENTRAL BERLIN
#200 & TXL
Klosterstrasse
Jannowitzbrücke
Frankfurter Tor
Franzősische Strasse
GENDARMEN-MARKT
Märkisches Museum
Ost-bahnhof
FRIEDRICHS-HAIN
to Ahrens-felde
S7
Spittelmarkt
Heinrich-Heine-Strasse
Warschauer Strasse
Ostkreuz
S5
to Strausberg Nord
SOUTHERN BERLIN
Mohren-strasse
Stadtmitte
Hausvogtei-platz
Schlesisches Tor
U1 U3
Spree River
S3
to Erkner
TOPOGRAPHY OF TERROR
CHECKPOINT CHARLIE
Moritzplatz
#165 & 265
Kochstrasse
KREUZBERG
Görlitzer Bahnhof
Treptower Park
Treptower Park
Halleschesn Tor
JEWISH MUSEUM
Prinzen-strasse
Kottbusser Tor
Möckernbrücke
Mehringdamm
Herkomer-strasse
Platz der Luftbrücke
Tempelhof Field
Hermann-strasse
Neukölln
S42
Sonnenallee
Paradestr.
S41
U8
Tempelhof
SCHÖNEFELD AIRPORT
S9
U6 Alt-Mariendorf

Note: Express trains RB & RE run along the "S-Bahn Spine" stopping at Hauptbahnhof and other select destinations

authority BVG; the S-Bahn, a fast light rail that stops only at major stations, is operated by Deutsche Bahn. For all types of transit, there are three lettered zones: A, B, and C. Most of your sightseeing will be in zones A and B (in the city proper).

Timetables, prices, and trip planning are available on two helpful websites: BVG (www.bvg.de) or VBB (www.vbb. de). Both offer handy, free apps with on-the-go trip routing for U-Bahn, S-Bahn, tram, and bus connections.

TICKET OPTIONS

The €2.80 **basic single** ticket (*Einzelfahrschein*) covers two hours of travel in one direction. It's easy to make this ticket stretch to cover several rides...if they're in the same direction.

The €1.70 **short-ride** ticket (*Kurzstrecke Fahrschein*) covers a single ride of up to six bus/tram stops or three subway stations (one transfer allowed on subway). You can save on short-ride tickets by buying them in groups of four (€5.60).

The €9 **four-trip** ticket (*4-Fahrten-Karte*) is the same as four basic single tickets at a small discount.

The **day pass** (*Tageskarte*) is good until 3:00 the morning after you buy it (€7 for zones AB, €7.70 for zones ABC). For longer stays, consider a seven-day pass (*Sieben-Tage-Karte;* €30 for zones AB, €37.50 for zones ABC), or the WelcomeCard (described below). The *Kleingruppenkarte* lets groups of up to five travel all day (€19.90 for zones AB, €20.80 for zones ABC).

If you plan to cover a lot of ground using public transportation during a two- or three-day visit, the **WelcomeCard** is usually the best deal (available at TIs and U-Bahn/S-Bahn ticket machines; www.visitberlin.de/welcomecard). It covers all public transportation and gives up to 50 percent discounts off lots of minor and a few major museums, sightseeing tours (including 25 percent off the recommended Original Berlin Walks and Insider Tour), and music and theater events. The

Berlin-only card covers transit zones AB (€19.90/48 hours, €28.90/72 hours).

Buying Tickets: You can buy U-Bahn/S-Bahn tickets from machines at stations (coins and bills accepted). Tickets are also sold at BVG pavilions at train stations and at the TI, from machines onboard trams (coins only), and on buses from drivers, who give change. Select the zone and type of ticket you want, then pay. Most travelers want the AB ticket—either single or all-day ticket. Note that "adult" (*Erwachsener*) means anyone 14 or older.

Boarding Transit: As you board the bus or tram or enter the subway, validate your ticket in a clock machine (or risk a €60 fine; with a pass, stamp it only the first time you ride). Tickets are checked periodically, often by plainclothes inspectors. You may be asked to show your ticket when boarding the bus. Note that not all tram stops (marked by a sign with a green *H* in a gold circle) have designated platforms on raised sidewalks.

By Taxi and Uber

Cabs are easy to flag down, and taxi stands are common. A typical ride within town costs around €10, and a crosstown trip will run about €20.

Tariff 1 is for a *Kurzstrecke* ticket (short-stretch ride). This ticket can save you several euros for any ride of less than two kilometers (about a mile). To get this rate, you must flag down the cab on the street—not at a taxi stand—and ask for the *Kurzstrecke* rate as soon as you hop in. Confidently say *"Kurzstrecke, bitte"* (KOORTS-shtreh-keh, BIT-teh); your driver will grumble and flip the meter to a fixed €5 rate (for a ride that would otherwise cost €8). All other rides are **tariff 2** (€3.90 drop plus €2/km for the first seven kilometers, then €1.50/km after that). If possible, use cash: Credit card payment comes with a surcharge.

Uber works in Berlin like it does in the US (but rates are tied to taxi fares, so you don't really save any money).

By Bike

Flat Berlin is a very bike-friendly city, but be careful—motorists don't brake for bicyclists (and bicyclists don't brake for pedestrians). Fortunately, many roads and sidewalks have special red-painted bike lanes. Don't ride on the regular sidewalk—it's *verboten* (though locals do it all the time).

Fat Tire Bikes rents good bikes at the base of the TV Tower near Alexanderplatz (€14/day, cheaper for 2 or more days, trekking bikes available, free luggage storage, daily 9:30-20:00, shorter hours off-season, tel. 030/2404-7991, www.berlinbikerental.com).

Take a Bike—near the Friedrichstrasse S-Bahn station—is owned by a knowledgeable Dutch-German with a huge inventory (3-gear bikes: €8/4 hours, €12.50/day, €19/2 days, slightly cheaper for longer rentals, more for better bikes, includes helmets, daily 9:30-19:00, Nov-March closed Tue-Thu, Neustädtische Kirchstrasse 8, tel. 030/2065-4730, www.takeabike.de). To find it, leave the S-Bahn station via the Friedrichstrasse exit, turn right, go through a triangle-shaped square, and hang a left on Neustädtische Kirchstrasse.

Bike Rental Berlin is a good option in Prenzlauer Berg (€10/day, helmets-€1, kids' bikes and child seats available, daily 10:00-18:00, often closed off-season—call ahead, Kastanienallee 55, tel. 030/7153-3020, http://bike-rental-berlin.de).

Simple **Rent a Bike** stands outside Berlin shops, restaurants, and hotels charge €12/day (no maps, no helmets); I prefer the full-service rental shops listed earlier.

Arriving and Departing

By Plane

The state-of-the-art **Willy Brandt Berlin-Brandenburg International Airport** (airport code: BER), 11 miles south of central Berlin, has been under construction since 2006 and may go into service in late 2020. When it finally does open, the airport should be connected to the city center by fast and frequent Airport Express trains. **Tegel Airport** (airport code: TXL), four miles northwest of the center, serves as Berlin's "main airport" until Willy Brandt opens. To reach the city center, hop on **bus #TXL**, which stops at the Hauptbahnhof and then heads to Alexanderplatz.

Most flights from the east and many discount airlines arrive at **Schönefeld Airport** (airport code: SXF), 11 miles south of downtown. From the arrivals hall, it's a three-minute walk to the train station, where you can catch a regional express train into the city. Airport Express RE and RB trains go directly to Ostbahnhof, Alexanderplatz, Friedrichstrasse, and Hauptbahnhof (€3.40, 2/hour, direction: Nauen or Dessau, covered by ABC transit ticket). A taxi to the city center costs about €45.

By Train

Virtually all long-distance trains pass through the **Berlin Hauptbahnhof** ("Berlin Hbf" on schedules)—a massive temple of railroad travel in the heart of the city. This mostly underground train station is where the national train system meets Berlin's S-Bahn.

Services: On the main floor (EG), you'll find the **TI** and the **"Rail & Fresh WC"** facility (public pay toilets, near the food court). Up one level (OG1) are the Deutsche Bahn *Reisezentrum* information center, a 24-hour **pharmacy,** and **lockers** (directly under track 14). **Car rental** offices are down one level (UG1), near platforms 7-8.

Rick's Tip: EurAide *is an American-run* **information desk** *with answers to your questions about train travel around Europe. It's located at counter 12 inside the Deutsche Bahn* **Reisezentrum** *information center on the Hauptbahnhof's first upper level (OG1). This is a good place to make fast-train and couchette reservations (closed Jan-Feb and Sat-Sun year-round; www.euraide.com).*

Getting into Town: Taxis and buses wait outside the station on the Washingtonplatz side, but the S-Bahn is probably your best bet for connecting to most hotels. It's simple: S-Bahn trains are on tracks 15 and 16 at the top of the station (level OG2). Trains on track 15 go east, stopping at Friedrichstrasse, Hackescher Markt, Alexanderplatz, and Ostbahnhof; trains on track 16 go west, toward Zoologischer Garten and beyond.

To reach most hotels in the **Prenzlauer Berg** neighborhood, it's fastest to take any train on track 15 two stops to Hackescher Markt. Once there, follow signs to *Hackescher Markt* down the stairs, then exit to Spandauer Strasse and cross the tracks to the tram stop. Here you'll catch tram #M1 north (direction: Schillerstrasse).

From Berlin by Train to: Dresden (direct every 2 hours, 2 hours), **Hamburg** (1-2/hour, 2 hours), **Frankfurt** (at least hourly, 4 hours), **Bacharach** (every 2 hours with transfer in Frankfurt, 5.5 hours), **Würzburg** (hourly, 4 hours, transfer points vary), **Rothenburg** (hourly, 5.5 hours, 3 changes), **Nürnberg** (hourly, 3.5 hours), **Munich** (hourly, 4-5 hours), **Cologne** (hourly, 4.5 hours, night train possible).

By Bus

The city's bus station, **ZOB** (Zentraler Omnibusbahnhof), is in Charlottenburg (Masurenallee 4, U2: Kaiserdamm or S41/S42: Messe Nord, www.zob.berlin). **Flix-Bus, MeinFern,** and **Eurolines** all operate from here to locations around Germany and Europe.

BEST OF THE REST

Dresden

Dresden surprises visitors with fanciful Baroque architecture in a delightful-to-stroll cityscape, a dynamic history that mingles tragedy with inspiration, and some of the best museum-going in Germany. Today's Dresden is an intriguing and fun city. At the peak of its power in the 18th century, this capital of Saxony ruled most of present-day Poland and eastern Germany from the banks of the Elbe River. Augustus the Strong, prince elector

The rebuilt Frauenkirche dominates Dresden's old town.

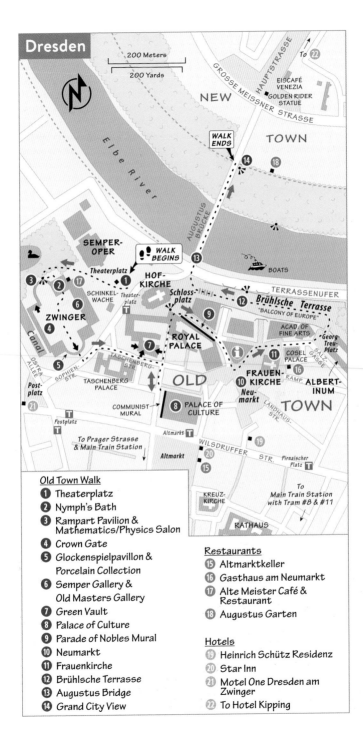

Dresden

200 Meters
200 Yards

NEW TOWN

Elbe River

To 22

EISCAFÉ VENEZIA

GOLDEN RIDER STATUE

GROSSE MEISSNER STRASSE

HAUPTSTRASSE

WALK ENDS

14   18

AUGUSTUS BRÜCKE

SEMPER-OPER

WALK BEGINS

Theaterplatz

13   BOATS

HOF-KIRCHE

SCHINKEL-WACHE

Theater-platz

ZWINGER

Schloss-platz

TERRASSENUFER

12   Brühlsche Terrasse

"BALCONY OF EUROPE"

3   2   17   1

6

4

5

SOPHIEN-STR.

TASCHENBERG-STR.

7

9

ROYAL PALACE

ACAD. OF FINE ARTS

Georg-Treu-Platz

i

11   COSEL PALACE

16   SALZ-GASSE

Canal

OSTRA ALLEE

Postplatz

21

Postplatz

TASCHENBERG PALACE

COMMUNIST MURAL

OLD

8   PALACE OF CULTURE

FRAUEN-KIRCHE   ALBERT-INUM

10

Neu-markt

RAMP.

TOWN

LANDHAUS-STR.

To Prager Strasse & Main Train Station

Altmarkt

Altmarkt

WILSDRUFFER STR.

19

20

15

KREUZ-KIRCHE

Pirnaischer Platz

To Main Train Station with Tram #8 & #11

RATHAUS

Old Town Walk

1 Theaterplatz
2 Nymph's Bath
3 Rampart Pavilion & Mathematics/Physics Salon
4 Crown Gate
5 Glockenspielpavillon & Porcelain Collection
6 Semper Gallery & Old Masters Gallery
7 Green Vault
8 Palace of Culture
9 Parade of Nobles Mural
10 Neumarkt
11 Frauenkirche
12 Brühlsche Terrasse
13 Augustus Bridge
14 Grand City View

Restaurants

15 Altmarktkeller
16 Gasthaus am Neumarkt
17 Alte Meister Café & Restaurant
18 Augustus Garten

Hotels

19 Heinrich Schütz Residenz
20 Star Inn
21 Motel One Dresden am Zwinger
22 To Hotel Kipping

of Saxony and king of Poland, imported artists from all over Europe, peppering his city with fine Baroque buildings and filling his treasury with lavish jewels and artwork.

Dresden is better known outside Germany for its destruction in World War II. American and British bombers firebombed the city on the night of February 13, 1945. More than 25,000 people were killed and 75 percent of the old town center was destroyed. All of the most important historic buildings have been reconstructed.

Day Plan

With one day in Dresden, follow my self-guided walk, and visit your pick of museums. Reserve ahead to visit one of Dresden's top sights, the Historic Green Vault.

Orientation

Dresden's Old Town (Altstadt) hugs a curve on the Elbe River, so most of its sights are within easy strolling distance along the south bank of the river. South of the Old Town (a 5-minute tram ride or 20-minute walk away) is the main train station (Hauptbahnhof). Across the river is the more residential New Town (Neustadt).

Tourist Information: Dresden has a good TI right in the heart of the Old Town (daily, Neumarkt 2—enter under *Passage* sign across from door D of Frauenkirche, and go down escalators). A smaller TI kiosk is in the main train station (tel. 0351/501-501, www.dresden.de/tourismus).

Walking Tours: Dresden Walks is a cooperative of local English-speaking guides who offer daily two-hour walks of the Old Town (€12, just show up at 12:00 and pay the guide, may also run at 14:30 June-Sept, meet at green sign at the bottom of the Brühlsche Terrasse stairs at Schlossplatz, mobile 0163-716-9886, www.dresdenwalks.com).

Getting There

Trains connect Dresden with **Berlin** (every 2 hours, 2 hours), **Hamburg** (5/day, 4.5 hours), **Frankfurt** (hourly, 4.5 hours), **Nürnberg** (hourly, 3.5 hours), and **Munich** (every 2 hours, 5 hours). Dresden has two major train stations: If you're visiting for the day, use the Hauptbahnhof for the easiest access to the sights.

To take a tram to Theaterplatz—the beginning of my self-guided walk—exit the

Theaterplatz leads into Dresden's Old Town.

station following *Ausgang 1* signs, cross the tram tracks, and take tram #11 to Postplatz in the Old Town (three stops) and walk 10 minutes up Sophienstrasse to Theaterplatz. Otherwise, it's a 20-minute **stroll** down Prager Strasse to the Old Town.

The city center has several well-marked **parking garages** with reasonable daytime rates.

Rick's Tip: **Reserve ahead** *for the* **Historic Green Vault** *(closed Tue), where a limited number of people are admitted every half-hour.* **Otherwise, line up early** *to buy a same-day ticket (ticket office opens at 10:00; see listing in "Sights"). Once you have your Historic Green Vault visit time, plan the rest of your day around it.*

○ Dresden Old Town Walk

This ▲▲▲ walk takes about 1.5 hours, not counting museum stops. It passes by three major sights: the Zwinger, the Royal Palace and Green Vault treasuries, and the Frauenkirche. If you visit the sights as you go, this walk will fill your day.

• *Begin at...*

❶ Theaterplatz: In the middle of the square, face the equestrian statue of King John, an intellectual mid-19th-century ruler who recognized and preserved Saxon culture—and paid for the **Semperoper** opera house behind the statue (nicknamed for its architect, Gottfried Semper).

As you face the opera house, the big building to your left is the vast Zwinger museum complex (your next stop). Behind you, across the square from the opera house, are the Hofkirche (with its distinctive green-copper, onion-domed steeple) and the sprawling Royal Palace. All the buildings you see here—Dresden's Baroque treasures—are thorough reconstructions. The originals were destroyed in a single night by American and British bombs, with only walls and sometimes just foundations left standing.

• *Head to the gap between the Semperoper and the Zwinger. Near the recommended Alte Meister Café, go up the stairs and hang a left up the path. Head past the adorable fountain at the top of the path to the balcony with a breathtaking view of the grand...*

Zwinger: This complex of buildings is a Baroque masterpiece. Once the pride and

The Zwinger museums and courtyard

joy of the Wettin dynasty, today it's filled with fine museums. The Wettins ruled Saxony for more than 800 years, right up until the end of the First World War. Saxony was ruled by a prince elector—one of a handful of nobles who elected the Holy Roman Emperor. The prince elector of Saxony was one of Germany's most powerful people. In the 18th century, the larger-than-life Augustus the Strong—who was both prince elector of Saxony and king of Poland—kicked off Saxony's Golden Age.

The word "Zwinger" refers to the no-man's-land moat between the outer and inner city walls. As the city expanded, the pavilions and galleries you see today were built. Although the Zwinger buildings might look like a palace to us commoners, no one ever lived here—they were meant solely for pleasurable pursuits.

• Cross the balcony to the left to enjoy a view of the enclosed Nymphs' Bath from above, then take the small stairs at the top down to its pool.

❷ Nymphs' Bath: Here, at what is perhaps the city's favorite fountain, 18th-century aristocrats relaxed among cascading waterfalls and an open-air grotto, ringed by sexy sandstone nymphs. It's textbook Baroque.

• From the pool, cross through the glassy orangery and all the way into the middle of the huge...

Zwinger Courtyard: Survey the four wings, starting with the ❸ Rampart Pavilion (Wallpavillon)—the one you just came from, marked up top by Hercules hoisting the earth. The first wing of the complex to be built, it includes an orangery capped with a sun pavilion built for Augustus' fruit trees and parties. Hercules—the ultimate strongman (who happens to have Augustus' features)—is a fitting symbol for Augustus the Strong. The other side of this wing (on the left) houses the fun Mathematics-Physics Salon.

Turn farther to the left, facing the ❹ Crown Gate (Kronentor). The gate's

golden crown is topped by four golden eagles supporting a smaller crown—symbolizing Polish royalty (since Augustus was also king of Poland).

Turn again to the left to see the ❺ Glockenspielpavillon. The glockenspiel near the top of the gate has 40 bells made of Meissen porcelain. If you're here when they play, listen to the delightful chimes of the porcelain—far sweeter than a typical metal bell. This wing of the Zwinger also houses Augustus the Strong's Porcelain Collection.

Turn once more to the left (with the Crown Gate behind you) to see the stern facade of the ❻ Semper Gallery. This Zwinger wing was added to the original courtyard 100 years later by Gottfried Semper (of opera house fame). It houses Dresden's best painting collection, the Old Masters Gallery.

You are surrounded by three of Dresden's top museums. Anticipating WWII bombs, Dresdeners preserved their town's art treasures by storing them in underground mines and cellars in the countryside. This saved these great works from Allied bombs...but not from the Russians. Nearly all the city's artwork ended up in Moscow until after Stalin's death in 1953, when it was returned by the communist regime to win over their East German subjects.

• Now's a good time to visit your choice of the Zwinger museums.

When you're ready to move on, exit the courtyard through the Glockenspielpavillon. As you exit the corridor, cross the street and the tram tracks and turn left, then curve right down Taschenberg (yellow Taschenberg Palace on your right). The gate on your left is one of several entrances to the Royal Palace, with its ❼ Green Vault treasuries and other sights.

Ahead of you and to the right, the blocky modern building is the...

❽ Palace of Culture (Kulturpalast): Built by the communist government in 1969, this hall's exterior mural depicts

Augustus the Strong (1670-1733)

Friedrich Augustus I of the Wettin family made Dresden one of Europe's most important cities of culture. As prince elector of Saxony, Augustus wheeled and dealed—and pragmatically converted from his Saxon Protestantism to a more Polish-friendly Catholicism—to become King Augustus II of Poland. (You'll notice the city center features both the fancy Protestant Frauenkirche and the huge, prominent Catholic Hofkirche.) Like most Wettins, Augustus the Strong was unlucky at war, but a clever diplomat and a lover of the arts.

The Polish people blame Augustus and his successors—who were far more concerned with wealth and opulence than with sensible governance—for Poland's precipitous decline after its own medieval Golden Age. According to Poles, the Saxon kings did nothing but "eat, drink, and loosen their belts" (it rhymes in Polish).

Whether you consider them the heroes of history, or the villains, Augustus and the rest of the Wettins—and the nobles who paid them taxes—are to thank for Dresden's rich architectural and artistic heritage.

communist themes: workers, strong women, well-cared-for elders, teachers and students, and—of course—the red star and the seal of the former East Germany. Little of this propagandist art, which once inundated the lives of locals, survives in post-communist Germany (what does survive, like this, is protected).

• Leave the Palace of Culture behind you and walk with the Royal Palace on your left. After passing through a tunnel, you emerge onto **Palace Square.** Ahead and to the left are the ▲ **Katholische Hofkirche** (Dresden's Catholic church; free entry) and another elevated passage, designed to allow royalty to go to church without the hassle of dealing with the public.

Now turn to the right, next to one of the palace's entrances, and walk toward the long, yellow mural called the...

❾ **Parade of Nobles** (Fürstenzug): This mural is painted on 24,000 tiles of Meissen porcelain. Longer than a football field, it illustrates seven centuries of the Saxon dynasty of the House of Wettin. The very last figure in the procession (the first one you see, coming from this direction) is the artist himself, Wilhelm Walther. In front of him are commoners (miners, farmers, carpenters, teachers, students, artists), and

then the royals, with 35 names and dates marking the highlights of Wettin rule. Walk the length of the mural to appreciate the detail (stop at 1694—that's Augustus the Strong). The porcelain tiles are originals (from 1907)—they survived the Dresden bombing. They were fired three times at 2,400 degrees Fahrenheit when created...and then fired again during the 1945 firestorm, at only 1,800 degrees.

• When you're finished looking at the mural, dogleg right and walk into the big square, where a statue of Martin Luther stands tall.

❿ **Neumarkt:** This "New Market Square" was once a central square ringed by the homes of rich merchants. It is once again alive with people and cafés, and even a few frilly facades that help you picture what the square looked like in its heyday. The statue of Martin Luther shows him holding not just any Bible, but the Word of God in German, which he personally translated from Hebrew and ancient Greek so that regular people could wrestle with it directly (this is, in a sense, what the Protestant Reformation was all about).

• The big church looming over the square is the...

⓫ **Frauenkirche** (Church of Our Lady): This church is the symbol and soul of

Frauenkirche dome

(an ▲▲ art gallery with the city's best collection of 19th- and 20th-century art; closed Mon, www.skd.museum).

Walk through the square and climb the ramparts for an Elbe River view and a chance to stroll the length of the...

⓬ **Brühlsche Terrasse:** This delightful promenade overlooking the river was once a defensive rampart—look along the side of the terrace facing the Elbe River to see openings for cannons. In the early 1800s, it was turned into a public park, with a leafy canopy of linden trees.

• At the far end of the terrace, stop at the grove of linden trees with a fountain at the center, and look out at the...

⓭ **Augustus Bridge:** The Augustus-brücke has connected Dresden's old and new towns since 1319, when it was the first stone bridge over the river. At the far end of the bridge is a golden equestrian statue, a symbol of Dresden. It's Augustus the Strong, nicknamed the **"Golden Rider"** (Goldene Reiter).

• We're back near where we started, which makes this a good stopping point. But if you have time, walk out to enjoy the ⓮ grand city view from the bridge—of the glass dome of the Academy of Fine Arts, capped by a trumpeting gold angel, and the other venerable facades, domes, and spires of regal Dresden.

Sights
ZWINGER MUSEUMS

Three museums are located off the Zwinger courtyard: the Old Masters Gallery, Mathematics-Physics Salon, and Porcelain Collection. All exhibits are well described in English, but their audioguides will enrich your visit.

Cost: €12 combo-ticket covers all three museums; €6 to visit either the Mathematics-Physics Salon or the Porcelain Collection; Old Masters Gallery requires the €12 combo-ticket (whether you visit the others or not).

Hours: Tue-Sun 10:00-18:00, closed Mon.

the city. When completed in 1743, this was Germany's tallest Protestant church (310 feet high). This building garners the world's attention primarily because of its tragic history and phoenix-like resurrection: On the night of February 13, 1945, the firebombs came. When the smoke cleared the next morning, the Frauenkirche was smoldering but still standing. It burned for two days before finally collapsing. After the war, the Frauenkirche was left a pile of rubble and turned into a peace monument. Only after reunification was the decision made to rebuild it completely.

Circle around the left side of the church to find a big hunk of the bombed **rubble** (near door E, river side of church). Notice the small metal relief of the dome that shows where this piece came from (free entry but donation requested, climbable dome, www.frauenkirche-dresden.de).

• With your back to the rebuilt church, head right to find the nearby dome nicknamed "the lemon juicer." This caps the exhibition hall of the **Academy of Fine Arts.** Walk past that and hook left into the small, grassy Georg-Treu-Platz. The grand Neo-Renaissance building to the right is the **Albertinum**

Information: Tel. 0351/4914-2000, www.skd.museum.

▲▲OLD MASTERS GALLERY (GEMÄLDEGALERIE ALTE MEISTER)

Dresden's best collection of paintings features works by Raphael, Titian, Rembrandt, Rubens, Vermeer, and more. Augustus the Strong and his son, Augustus III, supported much of the purchasing of the art for this collection. Their agents traveled across Europe to add to their holdings, but they also systematically included German works of the **late Gothic** and **early Renaissance** periods. A visit here feels particularly enjoyable for its "quality, not quantity" approach to showing off great art.

▲MATHEMATICS-PHYSICS SALON (MATHEMATISCH-PHYSIKALISCHER SALON)

This fun collection (at the end of the courtyard with the Hercules-topped pavilion; ascend the staircase in the left corner) features scientific gadgets from the 16th to 19th century, including measuring, timekeeping, and surveying instru-ments, as well as globes and telescopes—all displayed like dazzling works of art. Anyone with even a modest scientific bent will find something of interest.

▲PORCELAIN COLLECTION (PORZELLANSAMMLUNG)

Every self-respecting European king had a porcelain works, and the Wettins had the most famous one, at Meissen (a charming town 10 miles north of here). They inspired other royal courts to get into the art form. They also collected porcelain from around the world—from France to Japan and China. Today it's the largest specialist ceramics collection in the world.

ROYAL PALACE (RESIDENZSCHLOSS)

This palace, the residence of the Saxon prince electors and kings, was one of the finest Renaissance buildings in Germany before its destruction in World War II. It's currently being rebuilt in a years-long project, with galleries opening to the public as they are completed. The palace is highlighted by the Saxon treasuries: the Historic Green Vault (Augustus' goodies displayed in reconstructed Baroque halls)

The inner courtyard of the Royal Palace

and the New Green Vault (more royal treasures in contemporary display cases). Other attractions include the Royal Armory, showing off sumptuous armor for horse and rider, and the Turkish Chamber, one of the oldest collections of Ottoman art outside Turkey.

Cost: All sights in the palace—except the Historic Green Vault—are covered by a €12 ticket. The Historic Green Vault requires a separate ticket, with two choices: the €12 standard, timed-entry ticket (€2 surcharge to book in advance), or the €20 VIP-Ticket (which lets you skip the line anytime).

Hours: The entire complex is open Wed-Mon 10:00-18:00, closed Tue.

Information: Tel. 0351/4914-2000, www.skd.museum.

Historic Green Vault Reservations: If you must get in at a certain time, or if you'll be here at a busy period (weekend, holiday, or any time in December), book your ticket in advance online (www.skd.museum) or reserve by email (besucherservice@skd.museum).

Orientation: The palace complex has three entrances, each leading to a glass-domed inner courtyard, where you'll find the ticket windows and restrooms. Inside, the ground floor is home to the Baroque halls of the Historic Green Vault (where bag check is required); the first floor up has the New Green Vault, and the next floor up houses the Giant's Hall, with the bulk of the Royal Armory and the Turkish Chamber.

▲▲HISTORIC GREEN VAULT (HISTORISCHES GRÜNES GEWÖLBE)

This famed, glittering Baroque treasury collection was begun by Augustus the Strong in the early 1700s. Over the years it evolved into the royal family's extravagant trove of ivory, silver, and gold knickknacks, displayed in rooms as opulent as the collection itself.

Following the included audioguide, you'll spend about an hour progressing through the exhibition's rooms. The **Amber Cabinet** serves as a reminder of

just how many different things you can do with fossilized tree sap (in a surprising range of colors), and the **Ivory Room** does the same for elephant tusks. The **White Silver Room,** painted its original vermillion color, holds a chalice carved from a rhino horn, and the **Silver-Gilt Room** displays tableware and gold-ruby glass.

The wide variety of items in the largest room—the aptly named **Hall of Precious Objects**—includes mother-of-pearl sculptures, ostrich-egg and snail-shell goblets, and a model of the Hill of Calvary atop a pile of pearls and polished seashells.

The vault's highlight is the grandly decorated **Jewel Room**—essentially, Saxony's crown jewels. The incredible pieces in here are fine examples of the concept of *Gesamtkunstwerk*—an artwork which has the type of perfection that comes only from the sum of its parts.

▲▲NEW GREEN VAULT (NEUES GRÜNES GEWÖLBE)

This collection shows off more Saxon treasure, but in a modern museum space, arranged chronologically from the Renaissance to the 19th century.

Eating

$$ Altmarktkeller (a.k.a. Sächsisch-Böhmisches Bierhaus) is a festive beer cellar that serves nicely presented Saxon and Bohemian food (Altmarkt 4). **$$ Gasthaus am Neumarkt** has an almost tearoom ambience but dishes up hearty Saxon cuisine (An der Frauenkirche 13, enter on Salzgasse). **$$$ Alte Meister Café and Restaurant** has delightful garden seating (Theaterplatz 1). Just across the Augustus Bridge, **$$ Augustus Garten** beer garden is open only in good weather, offering super-cheap self-service food and a good view back over the river.

Sleeping

$$$ Heinrich Schütz Residenz enjoys a prime location on the Neumarkt square facing the Frauenkirche (Frauenstrasse 14, www.heinrich-schuetz-residenz.de). **$$$ Star Inn** fills a stately old building on the Altmarkt (Altmarkt 4, www.starinnhotels.com). **$ Motel One Dresden am Zwinger** is within cherub-fountain-spitting distance of the Zwinger (Postplatz 5, www.motel-one.com). Family-run **$$ Hotel Kipping** is just behind the Hauptbahnhof (Winckelmannstrasse 6, www.hotel-kipping.de).

BEST OF THE REST

Hamburg

Hamburg is Germany's second-largest city, the richest judged by per-capita income, and its most important port. The city's fishy maritime atmosphere—with a constant breeze and the evocative cries of seagulls—gives Hamburg an almost Scandinavian feel.

The city lacks a quaint medieval center because Ye Olde Hamburg was flattened by a one-two punch that occurred over a 101-year span: A devastating 1842 fire that gutted the town center, and then an equally devastating firebombing by Allied forces in 1943. Today the revitalized city is expanding rapidly as it focuses on redeveloping its old docklands, especially the burgeoning HafenCity district and its spectacular Elbphilharmonie concert hall.

Day Plan

Hamburg can easily fill a rewarding day of sightseeing. Toss your bag in a train-station locker and take a 1.5-hour orientation bus tour, which leaves from the station. Get off at Landungsbrücken in time to catch the 12:00 harbor cruise, or, to go up to the Elbphilharmonie's Plaza viewing platform, get on the #72 public ferry (details on all these options are below). With more time, visit the St. Nikolai Memorial and Hamburg History Museum.

Hamburg is revitalizing its harborfront.

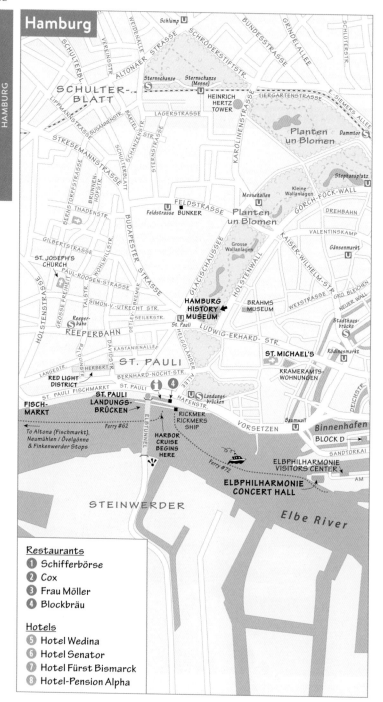

Hamburg

Schlump Ⓤ

SCHULTER-BLATT

Sternschanze Ⓢ

Sternschanze (Messe)

HEINRICH HERTZ TOWER

TIERGARTENSTRASSE

LAGERSTRASSE

Planten un Blomen

Dammtor Ⓤ

Stephansplatz Ⓤ

FELDSTRASSE
Feldstrasse Ⓤ BUNKER

Messehallen Ⓤ

Kleine Wallanlagen

GORCH-FOCK-WALL

DREHBAHN

VALENTINSKAMP

Planten un Blomen

Grosse Wallanlagen

Gänsemarkt Ⓤ

ST. JOSEPH'S CHURCH

HAMBURG HISTORY MUSEUM

BRAHMS MUSEUM

NEUER WALL

Stadthaus-brücke

Reeper-bahn Ⓢ
REEPERBAHN

St. Pauli Ⓤ

LUDWIG-ERHARD- STR.

ST. MICHAEL'S

Rödingsmarkt Ⓤ

ST. PAULI

RED LIGHT DISTRICT

BERNHARD-NOCHT-STR.

KRAMERAMTS-WOHNUNGEN

ST. PAULI Ⓘ ❹

FISCH-MARKT

ST. PAULI LANDUNGS-BRÜCKEN →

Landungs-brücken Ⓤ

To Altona (Fischmarkt), Neumühlen / Övelgönne & Finkenwerder Stops

Ferry #62

HARBOR CRUISE BEGINS HERE

RICKMER RICKMERS SHIP

VORSETZEN

Baumwall Ⓤ

Binnenhafen

BLOCK D →

SANDTORKAI

Ferry #72

ELBPHILHARMONIE VISITORS CENTER

AM

ELBPHILHARMONIE CONCERT HALL

STEINWERDER

Elbe River

Restaurants
❶ Schifferbörse
❷ Cox
❸ Frau Möller
❹ Blockbräu

Hotels
❺ Hotel Wedina
❻ Hotel Senator
❼ Hotel Fürst Bismarck
❽ Hotel-Pension Alpha

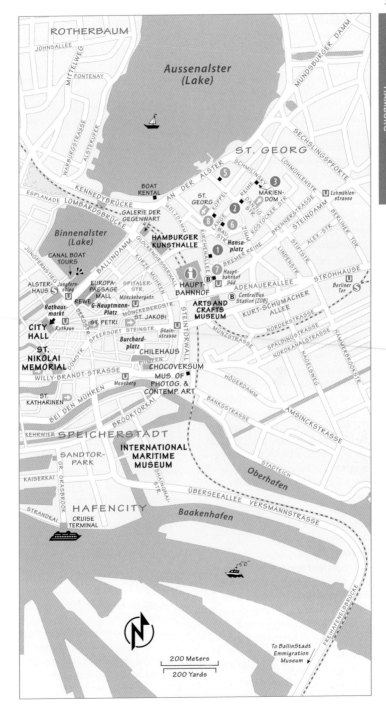

ROTHERBAUM

JOHNSALLEE

MITTELWEG

FONTENAY

WARBURGSTRASSE

ALSTERUFER

*Aussenalster
(Lake)*

MUNDSBURGER DAMM

SECHSLINGSPFORTE

ST. GEORG

SCHMILINSKY

LOHMÜHLENSTR.

KENNEDYBRÜCKE

AN DER ALSTER

5

REIHE

GÄNSE

3

ESPLANADE LOMBARDSBRÜCKE

BOAT
RENTAL

HOLZDAMM

ST.
GEORG

KOPPEL

2

MARIEN-
DOM

ROSTOCKER STR.

BRENNERS STRASSE

STEINDAMM

BERLINER TOR

U Lohmühlen-
strasse

GALERIE DER
GEGENWART

*Binnenalster
(Lake)*

CANAL BOAT
TOURS

BALLINDAMM

KURZE MÜHREN

GLOCKENGIESSERWALL

KIRCHENALLEE

8

LANGE
STR.

BAU.
STR.

6

ZIMM.

LINDENSTR.

ALEX-STR.

HAMBURGER
KUNSTHALLE

1

Hansa-
platz

STIFTSTR.

JUNGERNSTIEG

ALSTER-
HAUS S

Jungfern-
stieg

EUROPA-
PASSAGE
MALL

SPITALER-
STR.

Mönckebergstr.

BREMER REIHE

7

HAUPT-
BAHNHOF

i

U

B

Haupt-
bahnhof
Süd

ADENAUERALLEE

STROHHAUSE

Berliner
Tor S

REWE

G-Hauptmann-
Platz U

MÖNCKEBERGSTR.

ST. JAKOBI

ARTS AND
CRAFTS
MUSEUM

B CentralBus
Station (ZOB)

KURT-SCHUMACHER-
ALLEE

NORDERSTRASSE

Rathaus-
markt

BERGSTR.

ST. PETRI

CITY
HALL

U
Rathaus

DOMSTR.

SPEERSORT

STEINSTR.

Burchard-
platz

Stein-
strasse

STEINTORWALL

MÜNZSTRASSE

SPALDINGSTRASSE

NORDKANALSTRASSE

HAMMERBROOKSTR.

NAGELSWEG

ST.
NIKOLAI
MEMORIAL

WILLY-BRANDT-STRASSE

PUMPEN

CHILEHAUS

CHOCOVERSUM

U
Messberg

MUS. OF
PHOTOG. &
CONTEMP. ART

HÖGERDAMM

ST.
KATHARINEN

BEI DEN MÜHREN

BROOKTORKAI

BANKSSTRASSE

AMSINCKSTRASSE

KEHRWIER SPEICHERSTADT

SANDTOR-
PARK

INTERNATIONAL
MARITIME
MUSEUM

SHANGHAI-
STR.

STADTTEICH

Oberhafen

KAISERKAI

ÜBERSEEALLEE VERSMANNSTRASSE

STRANDKAI

GR. GRASBROOK

HAFENCITY

CRUISE
TERMINAL

Baakenhafen

FREIHAFENELBBRÜCKE

N

200 Meters

200 Yards

To BallinStadt
Emmigration
Museum

Orientation

The city center sits between the Elbe River to the south and Binnenalster lake to the north, and is surrounded by a ring road. Most places of interest are just outside the downtown core: The train station is east of the center; the harbor, and the new HafenCity zone are to the south along the Elbe; the St. Pauli waterfront district lies to the west.

Tourist Information: Hamburg's main TI is in the train station (daily, tel. 040/3005-1701—not answered Sun, www.hamburg-travel.com); there's another at the St. Pauli Landungsbrücken harborfront.

Hamburg Card: If you plan to see at least two or three museums, especially with a travel partner (or two), this card is a sound investment. Sold at TIs and public-transit ticket machines, it covers a full day of public transit plus reduced-priced entry to many sights (€10.50/day).

▲▲**Hop-On Hop-Off Bus Tours:** With its most interesting sights scattered on the perimeter, Hamburg lends itself to orientation by bus. Several companies run circular city bus tours (€17-19 for 1.5 hours, discount with Hamburg Card). The most logical starting points are at the train station and near the Landungsbrücken pier. One company with frequent departures and good English guides is **Die Roten Doppeldecker** (www.die-roten-doppeldecker.de); a €30 combo-ticket adds the recommended Rainer Abicht harbor boat tour.

Getting There

Trains connect Hamburg with **Berlin** (1-2/hour, 2 hours), **Cologne** (hourly, 4 hours), **Frankfurt** (hourly, 4 hours), and **Munich** (hourly, 6.5 hours). From the station, you can catch a bus orientation tour or use the subway to get directly to the sights.

Hamburg's airport (code: HAM, www.hamburg-airport.de) is a simple ride from the train station on the S-1 subway line.

Getting Around

Public transport—subway, buses, and ferries—makes sightseeing efficient in this spread-out city. Buy tickets from machines marked *HVV* at any U-Bahn or S-Bahn stop (use coins and small bills). Buy bus tickets from the driver (will make change). **Single ticket** prices vary with ride length; key your destination into a ticket machine, and it will tell you the price of the ticket (www.hvv.de).

Sights

▲▲ST. NIKOLAI MEMORIAL (MAHNMAL ST. NIKOLAI)

Before the mid-20th century, downtown Hamburg's skyline had five main churches, each with a bold tower. Today there are still five towers...but only four churches. The missing church is St. Nikolai. It was designed in the Neo-Gothic style by British architect George Gilbert Scott, and for a brief time after its completion in 1874, it was the world's tallest church (at 483 feet; its spire is still the fifth tallest in the world). The church was destroyed by WWII firebombing in 1943. Its tower (open to visitors) and a few charred walls have been left as a ruin to commemorate those lost and as an evocative reminder of the horrors of war.

Cost and Hours: Ruins-free to explore and always viewable; tower and museum-€5, daily 10:00-18:00, Oct-April until 17:00; Willy-Brandt-Strasse 60, tel. 040/371125, www.mahnmal-st-nikolai.de. It's a five-minute walk from the Rödingsmarkt U-Bahn station—just follow busy Willy-Brandt-Strasse toward the tower.

▲▲HAMBURG HISTORY MUSEUM (MUSEUM FÜR HAMBURGISCHE GESCHICHTE)

Like the history of the city it covers, this museum is long, complex, and multilayered. Filling a giant old building, the modern, thoughtful exhibits work together to illuminate the full story of Hamburg (with an emphasis on its status as one of

St. Pauli Landungsbrücken harborfront

the world's biggest shipping ports). You'll learn about the city's industrial growth, devastating 1842 fire, WWII firebombing, development of its excellent infrastructure, and environmental conditions of the Elbe River. A highlight is the preserved bridge of an old steamship showing what life was like for the officers on board. Multiple large models of the city at various points in its history help you track how the place changed over time.

Cost and Hours: €9.50, includes audioguide; Mon and Wed-Fri 10:00-17:00, Sat-Sun until 18:00, closed Tue; Holstenwall 24, tel. 040/428-132-100, www.hamburgmuseum.de.

Rick's Tip: *The wide strip of* **parkland** *called* **Planten un Blomen** *stretches from the harbor to the Binnenalster lake. Of the park's varied sections, the most worthwhile is the northern stretch, an oasis of calm ponds, playful fountains, and colorful gardens.*

ST. PAULI LANDUNGSBRÜCKEN HARBORFRONT

Once Hamburg's passenger ship terminal, this half-mile-long floating dock, which parallels the waterfront, is now a thriving, touristy, borderline-tacky wharf. A visit is worth ▲▲. From here you can inhale the inviting aroma of herring and French fries while surveying the harbor and the city's vast port.

▲▲▲ Harbor and Port Guided Boat Tour: Of the hundred or so big-boat harbor tours that go daily here, the best is **Rainer Abicht,** whose excellent tour (once a day in English) gives you a view from the water of all the construction in Hamburg (one-hour harbor tour-€20, €30 combo-ticket with Roten Doppeldecker bus tour, English tour runs April-Oct daily at 12:00, few or no English tours off-season, tel. 040/317-8220, www.abicht.de).

Hop-On, Hop-Off Boat Trip: Maritime Circle Line operates a 1.5-hour journey with English narration three times a day covering the basic harbor highlights (€16, €30 combo-ticket with Roten Doppeldecker bus tour, discounts with Hamburg Card, April-Oct daily at 11:00, 13:00, and 15:00, some off-season tours with fewer stops, tel. 040/2849-3963, www.maritime-circle-line.de).

HAFENCITY PORT DISTRICT

A century ago, Hamburg's port was the world's third-largest, and in Europe it's still second only to Rotterdam's. The port was built right up next to the city center, as the small city-state of Hamburg couldn't defend a remote harbor. But with the advent of huge modern container ships, most marine business shifted to a larger and more modern port nearby (you'll see these big container ships docking under the huge cranes after their North Sea voyage). All this prime real estate suddenly became available and is now being redeveloped.

The result is HafenCity, Europe's biggest urban development project. When it's done, downtown Hamburg will be 40 percent bigger. Planners hope that 45,000 people will eventually work here and 12,000 will call it home. The area feels like a city in itself, with a maritime touch, interesting modern architecture, and a mix of business, culture, and leisure. On weekends locals flock here to take a stroll, bask in the sun, and enjoy a break from the city.

Getting There: For an atmospheric approach, go to the Landungsbrücken

S- and U-Bahn stop and take public ferry #72 one stop upstream. You'll disembark by HafenCity's landmark Elbphilharmonie concert hall.

▲▲▲ELBPHILHARMONIE CONCERT HALL

The centerpiece of the HafenCity development is the jaw-dropping Elbphilharmonie—a combination concert hall, hotel, and apartment complex, all contained in a towering and wildly beautiful piece of architecture. Its daring design and huge size fit in well with the massive scale of the port around it—and when approached by water, it calls to mind the looming prows of the steamer ships that first put Hamburg on the world map.

For visitors, the heart of the complex is the Plaza level, which connects the renovated old harbor warehouse below with the modern glass tower above. From the main entrance, visitors ride a 270-foot-long escalator (dubbed the "Tube"). At the top you'll enjoy a spectacular view down the Elbe toward the harbor and docks. A second, shorter escalator takes you to the Plaza level, where you'll find an outdoor promenade that wraps around the entire level (plus a café and souvenir shop).

Cost and Hours: The Plaza level is open daily 9:00-24:00 to anyone with a Plaza ticket. Tickets are free for same-day visits but subject to availability (get tickets from machines in the entrance foyer, open daily 11:00-20:00). To guarantee you'll get in, buy timed-entry tickets a day or more in advance (€2, buy online or at the ground-floor ticket office, tel. 040/3576-6660, www.elbphilharmonie.de).

Concerts: Tickets for events and concerts at the Elbphilharmonie can be booked by telephone, online, or by email (ticket tel. 040/3576-6666, www.elbphilharmonie.de, tickets@ elbphilharmonie.de), or in person at the visitors center.

Guided Tours: Hour-long tours of the complex run in English daily. Tickets are released roughly 12 weeks out and can be purchased online or in person at the ground-floor ticket office (€15, schedule varies—check online, www. elbphilharmonie.de/tours).

▲MINIATUR WUNDERLAND

Miniatur Wunderland claims to have the world's largest model railway, covering over 16,000 square feet with more than 9.5 miles of track. Marvel at the tiny airport (with model planes taking off), and watch night fall every 15 minutes. Visit the Alps, Scandinavia, Italy, and the US in miniature (the latter complete with a shootout and Area 51). Little bits come to life with a press of a green-lit button—bungee jumpers leap, the drive-in plays a movie, and tiny Bavarians hoist teeny beer mugs to their mini mouths. Hamburg's harbor is lovingly rendered—including the building you're standing in—with a model of the Elbphilharmonie that lets you peek inside.

Cost and Hours: €15, daily 9:30-18:00, longer hours in peak season, Kehrwieder 4, Block D, tel. 040/300-6800, www. miniatur-wunderland.com.

Elbphilharmonie complex on the harbor

Miniatur Wunderland hosts an amazing model railway.

Rick's Tip: *The* **Miniatur Wunderland model railway** *is wildly popular:* **Reserve online or via phone** *at least a couple of days in advance.*

▲▲INTERNATIONAL MARITIME MUSEUM (INTERNATIONALES MARITIMES MUSEUM)

This state-of-the-art exhibit fills nine floors of a towering brick ex-warehouse with thousands of maritime artifacts. Ride the lift to the ninth "deck" (floor) to start with the world's biggest collection of miniature ship models, and then work your way down—each floor has a different military or civilian maritime theme. Between the first and second decks is an enormous model of the RMS *Queen Mary 2*...made entirely of Legos.

Cost and Hours: €13, daily 10:00-18:00, audioguide-€3.50, Koreastrasse 1, Kaispeicher B, tel. 040/3009-2300, www.imm-hamburg.de.

Eating

At $$$ **Schifferbörse** (right across from the train station) the service is surly, but they cook up solid northern German food (Kirchenallee 46). $$$ **Cox** is a well-regarded bistro, which has a menu that leans toward culinary fusion (Lange Reihe 682). $ **Frau Möller** is a rollicking bar serving up very affordable, hearty Alsatian and Hamburger classics (Lange Reihe 96). On the harbor, $$ **Blockbräu** features local cuisine and a great rooftop terrace with harbor views (Landungsbrücken 3).

Sleeping

$$$$ **Hotel Wedina** is hip, full of character, and in a people-friendly neighborhood (Gurlittstrasse 23, www.hotelwedina.de). $$$ **Hotel Senator** is a dated but quiet oasis (Lange Reihe 18, www.hotel-senator-hamburg.de). $$ **Hotel Fürst Bismarck** is old-fashioned and Old World (Kirchenallee 49, www.fuerstbismarck.de) $ **Hotel-Pension Alpha** is a decent budget choice (Koppel 4, www.alphahotel.biz).

German History

A united Germany has only existed since 1871, but the cultural heritage of the German-speaking people stretches back 2,000 years.

Romans
(AD 1-500)

German history begins in AD 9, when Roman troops were ambushed and driven back by the German chief Arminius. For the next 250 years, the Rhine and Danube rivers marked the border between civilized Roman Europe (to the southwest) and "barbarian" German lands (to the northeast). While the rest of Western Europe's future would be Roman, Christian, and Latin, most of Germany followed a separate, pagan path.

In AD 476, Rome fell to the Germanic chief Theodoric the Great (a.k.a. Dietrich of Bern). After that, Germanic Franks controlled northern Europe, ruling a mixed population of Romanized Christians and tree-worshipping pagans.

Charlemagne
(AD 500-1000)

For Christmas in AD 800, the pope gave Charlemagne the title of Holy Roman Emperor. Charlemagne (768-814), the king of the Franks, was the first of many German kings to be called *Kaiser* ("emperor," from "Caesar") over the next thousand years. Allied with the pope, Charlemagne ruled an empire that included Germany, Austria, France, the Low Countries, and northern Italy, but he lacked a clear heir. His united empire was divided into (what would become) Germany, France, and the lands in between (Treaty of Verdun, 843). As this treaty was signed not in Latin, but in the local languages, many mark 843 as the year Europe was born.

Holy Roman Empire
(1000-1500)

Chaotic medieval Germany was made up of more than 300 small, quarreling dukedoms ruled by the Holy Roman Emperor. The title was pretty bogus, implying that the German king ruled the same huge empire as the ancient Romans. In fact, he was "Holy" because he was blessed by the pope, "Roman" to recall ancient grandeur, and the figurehead "Emperor" of what was an empire in name only.

Holy Roman Emperors had less hands-on power than other kings around

Europe. Because of the custom of electing emperors by nobles and archbishops, rather than by bestowing the title through inheritance, they couldn't pass the crown from father to son. While France, England, and Spain were centralizing power around a single ruling family to create nation-states, Germany lagged behind as a decentralized, backward, feudal battleground.

Medieval Growth

Nevertheless, Germany was strategically located at the center of Europe, and trading towns prospered. Several northern towns banded together into the Hanseatic League, promoting open trade around the Baltic Sea. To curry favor at election time, emperors granted powers and privileges to certain towns, which were designated "free imperial cities." Some towns, such as Cologne, held higher status than many nobles, as hosts of one of the seven "electors" of the emperor.

Textiles, mining, and the colonization of lands to the east made German states relatively wealthy and enabled the growth of a thriving middle class. In towns, middle-class folks (burghers), not aristocrats, began running things. In about 1450, Johann Gutenberg of Mainz figured out how to use moveable type for printing, an innovation that would allow the export of a new commodity: ideas.

Luther and the Thirty Years' War
(1500-1700)

Martin Luther—German monk, fiery orator, and religious whistle-blower—sparked a century of European wars by speaking out against the Catholic Church. Luther's protests ("Protestantism") threw Germany into a century of turmoil, as each local prince took sides between Catholics and Protestants.

The Holy Roman Emperor, Charles V (r. 1519-1556), sided with the pope. Charles was the most powerful man in Europe, having inherited an empire that included Germany and Austria, plus the Low Countries, much of Italy, Spain, and Spain's New World possessions. But many local German nobles took the opportunity to go Protestant—some for religious reasons, but also as an excuse to seize Church assets and powers.

The 1555 Peace of Augsburg allowed each local noble to decide the religion of his realm. In general, the northern and eastern lands became Protestant, while the south (today's Bavaria, along with Austria) and west remained Catholic.

Unresolved religious and political differences eventually expanded into the Thirty Years' War (1618-1648). This Europe-wide war was one of history's bloodiest wars, fueled by religious extremism and political opportunism.

By the war's end (Treaty of Westphalia, 1648), a third of all Germans had died, France was the rising European power, and the Holy Roman Empire was a medieval mess of scattered feudal states. In 1689, France's Louis XIV swept down the Rhine, gutting and leveling its once-great castles, and Germany ceased to be a major player in European politics until the modern era.

(For an entertaining one-hour education on Luther, the Reformation, and the wars of religion, see my public-television special, "Rick Steves' Luther and the Reformation" on YouTube or at www.ricksteves.com.)

Austria and Prussia
(1700s)

The German-speaking lands now consisted of three "Germanys": Austria in the south, Prussia in the north, and the rest in between.

Prussia—originally a largely Slavic region—was forged into a unified state by two strong kings. Frederick I (r. 1701-1713) built a modern state around a highly disciplined army, a centralized government, and national pride. His grandson,

Frederick II "The Great" (r. 1740-1786), added French culture and worldliness, preparing militaristic Prussia to enter the world stage.

Meanwhile, Austria thrived under the laid-back rule of the Habsburg family, who gained power in Europe by marrying into it. They acquired the Netherlands, Spain, and Bohemia that way (a strategy that didn't work so well for Marie-Antoinette, who wed the doomed king of France).

In the 1700s, the Germanic lands became a cultural powerhouse, producing musicians (Bach, Haydn, Mozart, Beethoven), writers (Goethe, Schiller), and thinkers (Kant, Leibniz). But politically, fragmented Germany was no match for the modern powers.

After the French Revolution (1789), Napoleon swept through Germany with his armies, forcing the Holy Roman Emperor to hand over his crown (1806). After a thousand years, the Holy Roman Empire was dead.

German Unification
(1800s)

Napoleon's invasion helped unify the German-speaking peoples by rallying them against a common foreign enemy. After Napoleon's defeat, the Congress of Vienna (1815), presided over by the Austrian Prince Metternich, realigned Europe's borders. The idea of unifying the three Germanic nations began to grow. By mid-century, most German-speaking people favored forming a modern nation-state.

Energetic Prussia took the lead in unifying the country. Otto von Bismarck (served 1862-1890), the strong minister of Prussia's weak king, used cunning politics to engineer a unified Germany under Prussian dominance. First, he started a war with Austria, ensuring that any united Germany would be under Prussian control. Next, Bismarck provoked a war with France (the Franco-Prussian War, 1870-1871), which united Prussia and the Ger-man Confederation against their common enemy, France.

Fueled by hysterical patriotism, German armies swept through France and, in the Hall of Mirrors at Versailles, crowned Prussia's Wilhelm I as Emperor (*Kaiser*) of a new German Empire, uniting Prussia and the German Confederation. This Second Reich (1871-1918) featured elements of democracy (an elected *Reichstag*—parliament), offset by a strong military and an emperor with veto powers.

A united and resurgent Germany was suddenly flexing its muscles in European politics. With strong industry, war spoils, overseas colonies, and a large and disciplined military, Germany sought its rightful place at the global table.

World Wars
(1914-1939)

When Archduke Franz Ferdinand, the heir to the Austro-Hungarian Empire, was assassinated in 1914, all of Europe took sides as the political squabble quickly escalated into World War I. Germany and Austria-Hungary attacked British and French troops in France, but were stalled at the Battle of the Marne. Both sides dug defensive trenches, then settled in for four brutal years of bloodshed, boredom, mud, machine-gun fire, disease, and mustard gas.

More than four years later, at 11:00 in the morning of November 11, 1918, the fighting finally ceased. Germany surrendered, signing the Treaty of Versailles.

A new democratic government called the Weimar Republic (1919) dutifully abided by the Treaty of Versailles, and tried to maintain order among Germany's many divided political parties. But the country was in ruins, its economy a shambles, and the war's victors demanded heavy reparations. Communists rioted in the streets, fascists plotted coups, and inflation drove the price of a loaf of bread to a billion marks. When the worldwide depression of 1929 hit Germany with brutal force, the nation was desperate for a strong leader with answers.

Adolf Hitler (1889-1945), in Munich, joined other disaffected Germans to form the National Socialist German Workers' (Nazi) Party. He promised to restore Germany to its rightful glory, blaming the country's current problems on communists, foreigners, and Jews.

By 1930, the Nazis had become a formidable political party in Germany's democracy. They won 38 percent of the seats in the Reichstag in 1932, and Hitler was appointed chancellor (1933).

For the next decade, an all-powerful Hitler revived Germany's economy, building the autobahns and rebuilding the military. Defying the Treaty of Versailles and world opinion, Hitler occupied the Saar region (1935) and the Rhineland (1936), annexed Austria and the Sudetenland (1938), and invaded Czechoslovakia (March 1939). The rest of Europe finally reached its appeasement limit—and World War II began—when Germany invaded Poland in September 1939. When the war was over (1945), countless millions were dead and most German cities had been bombed beyond recognition. The Third Reich was over.

(For a one-hour program on this topic, see my public-television special, "The Story of Fascism in Europe" on YouTube and at www.ricksteves.com.)

Two Germanys
(1945-2000)

After World War II, the Allies divided occupied Germany into two halves, split down the middle by an 855-mile border that Winston Churchill called an "Iron Curtain." By 1949, Germany was officially two separate countries. West Germany (the Federal Republic of Germany) was democratic and capitalist, allied with the powerful United States. East Germany (the German Democratic Republic, or DDR) was a communist state under Soviet control. The Berlin Wall came to symbolize a divided Germany.

After the war, thanks to US aid from the Marshall Plan, West Germany was rebuilt, democracy was established, and its "economic miracle" quickly exceeded pre-WWII levels. Meanwhile, East Germany was ruled with an iron fist under Soviet control.

On November 9, 1989, East Germany unexpectedly opened the Berlin Wall. At first, most Germans—West and East— simply looked forward to free travel and better relations between two distinct nations. But before the month was out, negotiations and elections to reunite the two Germanys had begun. October 3, 1990 was proclaimed German Unity Day, and Berlin reassumed its status as the German capital in 1991.

Germany Today
(2000-PRESENT)

Today Germany is a major economic and political force in Europe. It's a powerful member of the European Union—an organization with its original chief aim to avoid future wars by embracing Germany in the economic web of Europe. Recently, however, Germany has outgrown its role as a mere member state to become, thanks to its economic might, the EU's de facto leader.

The popularlity of Germany's Chancellor Angela Merkel took a hit in 2015 after she welcomed about a million Syrian refugees. Isolated terrorist events have increased pressure on Germany's leaders to take a tougher stance on immigration.

The long-term viability of the EU is another challenge facing Germany. As the biggest and staunchiest EU booster, Germany must grapple with the implications of Brexit (Britain's decision to withdraw from the EU) and the rise of other European anti-EU movements.

For the latest, travel to Germany, buy someone a beer, and ask, "So what's going on in Germany?"

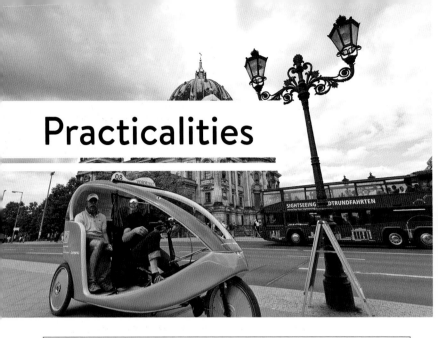

Practicalities

Tourist Information 372
Help!......................... 372
Travel Tips 373
Money........................ 373
Sightseeing................... 376
Eating........................ 377
Sleeping 381

Staying Connected............ 385
Transportation 386
Holidays and Festivals........ 400
Conversions and Climate...... 402
Packing Checklist 403
German Survival Phrases 405

TOURIST INFORMATION

Germany's national tourist office **in the US** is a wealth of information. Before your trip, scan their website (www.germany.travel) for maps and Rhine boat schedules, as well as information on festivals, castles, biking, and regions. Travel brochures can also be downloaded from their website.

In Germany, a good first stop is generally the tourist information office (abbreviated **TI** in this book). Throughout Germany, you'll find TIs are usually well-organized and have English-speaking staff. Swing by the local TI to confirm sightseeing plans, pick up a city map, and get information on public transit, walking tours, special events, and nightlife.

HELP!

Emergency and Medical Help: For any emergency service—ambulance, police, or fire—call **112** from a mobile phone or landline. If you get sick, do as the Germans do and go to a pharmacist for advice. Or ask at your hotel for help—they'll know the nearest medical and emergency services. The US Embassy & Consulates website for Germany has a list of English-speaking doctors (tel. 030/83050, https://de.usembassy.gov, search for "Medical Assistance").

Theft or Loss: To replace a passport, you'll need to go in person to an embassy. If your credit and debit cards disappear, cancel and replace them (see "Damage Control for Lost Cards" on page 375). File a police report, either on the spot or within a day or two; you'll need it to submit an insurance claim for lost or stolen rail passes or travel gear, and it can help with replacing your passport or credit and debit cards. For more information, see www.ricksteves.com/help.

US Embassy in Berlin: Clayallee 170, tel. 030/83050, http://de.usembassy.gov.

Canadian Embassy in Berlin: Leipziger Platz 17, tel. 030/2031-2470, www.germany.gc.ca.

TRAVEL TIPS

Time Zones: Germany, like most of continental Europe, is generally six/nine hours ahead of the East/West Coasts of the US. The exceptions are the beginning and end of Daylight Saving Time: Europe "springs forward" the last Sunday in March (two weeks after most of North America) and "falls back" the last Sunday in October (one week before North America). For a handy time converter, use the world clock app on your mobile phone or download one (see www.timeanddate.com).

Business Hours: In Germany, most shops are open from about 9:00 until 18:00-20:00 on weekdays; smaller stores generally close earlier on Saturdays, and most stores are closed all day Sunday (shops and grocery stores in train stations often have longer hours). In small towns, shops may take a midafternoon break (roughly between 12:00 and 14:00 or 15:00). Banks are generally open Monday to Friday from 9:00 to 15:00 (or later, up to 19:00). Many museums and sights are closed on Monday. Catholic regions, including Bavaria, shut down during religious holidays.

Watt's Up? Europe's electrical system is 220 volts, instead of North America's 110 volts. Most newer electronics (such as laptops, battery chargers, and hair dryers) convert automatically, so you won't need a converter, but you will need an adapter plug with two round prongs, sold inexpensively at travel stores in the US.

Discounts: Discounts for sights are generally not listed in this book. However, seniors (age 60 and over), youths under 18, and students and teachers with proper identification cards (www.isic.org) can get discounts at many sights—always ask. Some discounts are available only to European citizens.

MONEY

Here's my basic strategy for using money in Europe:

- Upon arrival, head for a cash machine (ATM) at the airport and withdraw some local currency, using a debit card

Avoiding Theft

Like anywhere in Europe, thieves target tourists, especially in bigger cities and towns. Pickpockets often stage a commotion or a fight to enable them to work unnoticed. Someone in a small group pushing you as you enter or exit a crowded subway car may slip a hand in your pocket or daybag.

Be on guard, and treat any disturbance around you as a smoke screen for theft. Remember to wear a money belt (tucked under your clothes) to keep your cash, credit cards, and passport secure; carry only the money you need for the day in your front pocket. Keep hold of your daybag, leave nothing of value in your car, and keep your luggage in sight on trains.

There's no need to be scared; just be smart and prepared.

with low international transaction fees.

- Save money by minimizing your credit and debit card exchange fees. The trend is for bigger expenses to be paid by credit card, but cash is still the standby for small purchases and tips.
- Keep your cards and cash safe in a money belt.

What to Bring

I pack the following (in my money belt):

Debit Card: Use this at ATMs to withdraw local cash.

Credit Card: Handy for bigger purchases (at hotels, shops, restaurants, travel agencies, car-rental agencies, and so on), payment machines, and ordering online.

Backup Card: Some travelers carry a third card (debit or credit; ideally from a different bank), in case one gets lost or simply doesn't work.

A Stash of Cash: I always carry $100-200 as a cash backup. A stash of cash comes in handy for emergencies, such as if your ATM card stops working.

What NOT to Bring: Resist the urge to buy euros before your trip or you'll pay the price in bad stateside exchange rates. Wait until you arrive to withdraw money. I've yet to see a European airport that didn't have plenty of ATMs.

Before You Go

Know your PIN. Make sure you know the numeric, four-digit PIN for all of your cards, both debit and credit. Request it if you don't have one and allow time to receive the information by mail.

Report your travel dates. Let your bank know that you'll be using your debit and credit cards in Europe, and when and where you're headed.

Adjust your ATM withdrawal limit. Find out how much you can take out daily and ask for a higher daily withdrawal limit if you want to get more cash at once. Note that European ATMs will withdraw funds only from checking accounts; you're unlikely to have access to your savings account.

Exchange Rate

1 euro (€) = about $1.20

To convert prices in euros to dollars, add about 20 percent: €20 = about $24, €50 = about $60. (Check www.oanda. com for the latest exchange rates.) Just like the dollar, one euro (€) is broken down into 100 cents.

Ask about fees. For any purchase or withdrawal made with a card, you may be charged a currency conversion fee (1-3 percent) and/or a Visa or MasterCard international transaction fee (1 percent).

In Europe

Using Cash Machines: European cash machines have English-language instructions and work just like they do at home—except they spit out local currency instead of dollars, calculated at the day's standard bank-to-bank rate.

In most places, ATMs are easy to locate—in Germany ask for a *Geldautomat*. When possible, withdraw cash from a bank-run ATM located just outside that bank.

If your debit card doesn't work, try a lower amount—your request may have exceeded your withdrawal limit or the ATM's limit.

Avoid "independent" ATMs, such as Travelex, Euronet, Moneybox, Cardpoint, and Cashzone. These have high fees, can be less secure than a bank ATM, and may try to trick users with "dynamic currency conversion" (see below).

Exchanging Cash: Avoid exchanging money in Europe; it's a big rip-off. In a pinch you can always find exchange desks at major train stations or airports—convenient but with crummy rates. Banks generally do not exchange money unless you have an account with them.

Using Credit Cards: US cards no longer require a signature for verification, but don't be surprised if a European card reader generates a receipt for you to sign. Some card readers will accept your card as is; others may prompt you to enter your PIN (so it's important to know it for each of your cards). If a cashier is present, you should have no problems. At self-service payment machines (transit-ticket kiosks, parking, etc.), results are mixed, as US cards may not work in unattended transactions. If your card won't work, look for a cashier who can process your card manually—or pay in cash.

Drivers Beware: Be aware of potential problems using a US credit card to fill up at an unattended gas station, enter a parking garage, or exit a toll road. Carry cash and be prepared to move on to the next gas station if necessary. When approaching a toll plaza, use the "cash" lane.

Dynamic Currency Conversion: If merchants offer to convert your purchase price into dollars (called dynamic currency conversion, or DCC), refuse this "service." You'll pay extra for the expensive convenience of seeing your charge in dollars.

Security Tips: Don't use a debit card for purchases. Because a debit card pulls funds directly from your bank account, potential charges incurred by a thief will stay on your account while the fraudulent use is investigated by your bank.

To access your accounts online while traveling, be sure to use a secure connection (see the "Tips on Internet Security" sidebar, later).

Damage Control for Lost Cards: If you lose your credit or debit card, report the loss immediately to the respective global customer-assistance centers. Call these 24-hour US numbers collect: Visa (tel. 303/967-1096), MasterCard (tel. 636/722-7111), and American Express (tel. 336/393-1111). In Germany, to make a collect call to the US, dial 0-800-225-5288; press zero or stay on the line for an English-speaking operator. You can generally receive a temporary card within two or three business days in Europe (see www.ricksteves.com/help for more).

Tipping

Tipping in Germany isn't as automatic and generous as it is in the US. For special service, tips are appreciated, but not expected. As in the US, the proper amount depends on your resources, tipping philosophy, and the circumstances, but some general guidelines apply.

Restaurants: You don't need to tip if you order your food at a counter. At German restaurants that have a wait staff, it's common to tip by rounding up (about 10 percent) after a good meal. For details on tipping in restaurants, see page 378.

Taxis: For a typical ride, round up your fare a bit (for instance, if your fare is €4.70, pay €5).

Services: In general, if someone in the service industry does a super job for you, a small tip of a euro or two is appropriate... but not required. If you're not sure whether (or how much) to tip, ask a local for advice.

Getting a VAT Refund

Wrapped into the purchase price of your German souvenirs is a value-added tax (VAT) of 19 percent. You're entitled to get most of that tax back if you purchase more than €25 (about $30) worth of goods at a store that participates in the VAT-refund scheme.

Get the paperwork. Have the merchant completely fill out the necessary refund document, called a "Tax-Free Shopping Check." You'll have to present your passport. Get the paperwork done before you leave the store to ensure you'll have everything you need (including your original sales receipt).

Hurdling the Language Barrier

German—like English, Dutch, Swedish, and Norwegian—is a Germanic language, making it easier on most American ears than Romance languages (such as Italian and French). These tips will help you pronounce German words: The letter *w* is always pronounced as "v" (e.g., the word for "wonderful" is *wunderbar,* pronounced VOON-der-bar). The vowel combinations *ie* and *ei* are pronounced like the name of the second letter—so *ie* sounds like a long *e* (as in *hier* and *Bier,* the German words for "here" and "beer"), while *ei* sounds like a long *i* (as in *nein* and *Stein,* the German words for "no" and "stone"). The vowel combination *au* is pronounced "ow" (as in *Frau*). The vowel combinations *eu* and *äu* are pronounced "oy" (as in *neu, Deutsch,* and *Bräu,* the words for "new," "German," and "brew"). To pronounce *ö* and *ü,* purse your lips when you say the vowel; the other vowel with an umlaut, *ä,* is pronounced the same as *e* in "men." (In written German, these can be depicted as the vowel followed by an *e—oe, ue,* and *ae,* respectively.) The letter Eszett (ß) represents *ss.* Written German capitalizes all nouns.

Though most young or well-educated Germans—especially those in the tourist trade and in big cities—speak at least some English, you'll get more smiles if you learn and use German pleasantries. Study the German survival phrases on page 405.

Get your stamp at the border or airport. Process your VAT document at your last stop in the European Union (such as at the airport) with the customs agent who deals with VAT refunds. Arrive an additional hour before you need to check in to allow time to find the customs office—and wait.

Collect your refund. You can claim your VAT refund from refund companies, such as Global Blue or Planet, with offices at major airports, ports, or border crossings (either before or after security, probably strategically located near a duty-free shop). These services (which extract a 4 percent fee) can refund your money in cash immediately or credit your card (within two billing cycles).

Customs for American Shoppers

You can take home $800 worth of items per person duty-free, once every 31 days. Many processed and packaged foods are allowed, including vacuum-packed cheeses, dried herbs, jams, baked goods, candy, chocolate, oil, vinegar, mustard, and honey. Fresh fruits and vegetables and most meats are not allowed, with exceptions for some canned items. As for alcohol, you can bring in one liter duty-free.

To bring alcohol (or liquid-packed foods) in your carry-on bag on your flight home, buy it at a duty-free shop at the airport. You'll increase your odds of getting it onto a connecting flight if it's packaged in a "STEB"—a secure, tamper-evident bag.

For details on allowable goods, customs rules, and duty rates, visit http://help.cbp.gov.

SIGHTSEEING

Sightseeing can be hard work. Use these tips to make your visits to Germany's finest sights meaningful, fun, efficient, and painless.

Plan Ahead

Set up an itinerary that allows you to fit in all your must-see sights. Given how precious your vacation time is, I recommend getting reservations for any must-see sight that offers them. Many museums are closed or have reduced hours at least a few days a year, especially on holidays such as Christmas, New Year's, and Labor Day (May 1). A list of holidays is at the end of this chapter; check online for possible museum closures during your trip.

At Sights

Here's what you can typically expect:

Entering: Be warned that you may not be allowed to enter if you arrive less than 30-60 minutes before closing time. And guards start ushering people out well before the actual closing time, so don't save the best for last.

Many sights have a security check. Allow extra time for these lines. Most museums in Germany require you to check any bag bigger than a purse, and sometimes even purses. Museum lockers are free, but be prepared to pay a €1-2 deposit.

Photography: If the museum's photo policy isn't clearly posted, ask a guard. Generally, taking photos without a flash or tripod is allowed. Some sights ban selfie sticks; others ban photos altogether.

Expect Changes: Artwork can be on tour, on loan, out sick, or shifted at the whim of the curator. Pick up a floor plan as you enter, and ask museum staff if you can't find a particular item.

Audioguides and Apps: Many sights rent audioguides, which generally offer useful recorded descriptions in English (about €2-5; often included with admission). Most of Berlin's top museums are run by the government, and include excellent audioguides with admission (you'll need to leave an ID as a deposit). Museums and sights often offer free apps that you can download to your mobile device (check their websites).

EATING

Germanic cuisine is heavy, hearty, and—by European standards—inexpensive. Each region has its specialties, which are often good values. Order house specials whenever possible. Though it's tasty, German food can get monotonous unless you look beyond the schnitzel and wurst. Fortunately, German chefs—especially in big cities—are increasingly adopting international influences, picking up previously unknown spices and ingredients to jazz up "Modern German" cuisine. Be adventurous.

Breakfast

Most German hotels and pensions include breakfast in the room price and pride themselves on laying out an attractive buffet spread. Even if you're not a big breakfast eater, take advantage of the buffet to fortify yourself for a day of sightseeing. Expect sliced bread, rolls, pastries, cereal, yogurt (both plain and with fruit), eggs, cold cuts, cheese, and fruit. You'll always find coffee, tea, and some sort of *Saft* (juice).

For breakfast, most Germans prefer a sandwich with cold cuts and/or a bowl of *Müsli* (an oat cereal like granola, but less sweet). Instead of pouring milk over cereal, most Germans begin with a dollop of yogurt (or *Quark*—sweet curds that resemble yogurt), then sprinkle the cereal on top. *Bircher Müsli* is a healthy mix of oats, nuts, yogurt, and fruit. To make a German-style sandwich for breakfast, layer *Aufschnitt* (cold cuts), *Schinken* (ham), *Streichwurst* (meat spread, most often *Leberwurst*—liver spread), and *Käse* (cheese) on a slice of bread or a roll.

Lunch and Dinner

Traditional restaurants go by many names. For basic, stick-to-the-ribs meals— and plenty of beer—look for a beer hall (*Brauhaus*) or beer garden (*Biergarten*). *Gasthaus, Gasthof, Gaststätte,* and *Gaststube* all loosely describe an informal, inn-type eatery. A *Kneipe* is a bar, and a *Keller* (or *Ratskeller*) is a restaurant or tavern located in a cellar. A *Weinstube* serves wine and usually traditional food as well.

Most eateries have menus tacked onto their front doors, with an English menu inside. If you see a *Stammtisch* sign hanging over a table at a restaurant or pub, it means that it's reserved for regulars— don't sit here unless invited.

Tipping: You only need to tip at restaurants that have table service. If you order your food at a counter, don't tip. At restaurants with wait staff, it's common to tip after a good meal by rounding up (roughly 10 percent). Rather than leaving coins behind on the table (considered slightly rude), Germans usually pay

directly: When the server comes by with the bill, simply hand over paper money, stating the total you'd like to pay. For example, if paying for a €10 meal with a €20 bill, while handing your money to the server, say "Eleven, please" (or *"Elf, bitte"* if you've got your German numbers down). The server will keep a €1 tip and give you €9 in change.

Budget Tips: It's easy to eat a meal for €10 or less here. Department-store cafeterias (usually on the top floor with a view) are common and handy, and they bridge the language barrier by letting you see your options. A *Schnellimbiss*—or simply *Imbiss*—is a small fast-food takeaway stand where you can get a bratwurst or other grilled sausage (usually less than €2, including a roll). Turkish-style shops and stands selling *döner kebab*—gyro-like, pita-wrapped rotisserie meat—are common (€4 at any time of day).

Some restaurants offer inexpensive €7-10 weekday hot-lunch specials that aren't listed on the regular menu (look for the *Tageskarte* or *Tagesangebot,* or just ask—sometimes available at dinner, too). For smaller portions, order from the *kleine Hunger* (small hunger) section of the menu. Simple dishes of wurst with sauerkraut and bread tend to run €6-8.

Traditional German Fare
Specialties

Here are some typical dishes you'll see at German eateries.

Dampfnudeln: Steamed bread roll with various toppings

Flammkuchen (or *Dünnele*): German version of white pizza, on a thin, yeastless dough; the classic version is topped with bacon and onions

Frikadellen (also called *Klopse;* in Berlin, *Buletten;* and in Bavaria, *Fleischpfanzerl*): Giant meatball, sometimes flattened like a hamburger

Geschnetzeltes: Strips of veal or chicken braised in a rich sauce and served with noodles

Kassler (or **Kasseler**): Salted, slightly smoked pork

Kohlrouladen: Cabbage rolls stuffed with minced meat

Königsberger Klopse (or **Sossklopse**): Meatball with capers and potatoes in a white sauce

Kümmelbraten: Crispy roast pork with caraway

Labskaus: Mushy mix of salted meat, potatoes, often beets, and sometimes herring, onions, and sour cream

Rostbrätel: Marinated and grilled pork neck

Rouladen (or **Rinderrouladen**): Strip of beef rolled up with bacon, onion, and pickles, then braised

Sauerbraten: "Sour"-marinated and roasted cut of beef (sometimes pork), typically served with red cabbage and potato dumplings

Saure Zipfel: Bratwurst cooked in vinegar and onions

Schlachtplatte (or **Schlachtschüssel**): "Butcher's plate"—usually blood sausage, *Leberwurst,* and other meat over hot sauerkraut

Schweinebraten (or **Schweinsbraten**): Roasted pork with gravy

Speckpfannkuchen: Large, savory crêpe with bacon

Stolzer Heinrich: Grilled sausage in beer sauce

Best of the Wurst

The generic term *Bratwurst* (or *Rostbratwurst*) simply means "grilled sausage." *Brühwurst* means boiled.

Blutwurst (or **Blunzen**): Made from congealed blood; variations include *Schwarzwurst, Rotwurst,* and *Beutelwurst*

Bockwurst: Thick pork-and-veal sausage with a mild, grassy flavor and a smoky casing

Currywurst: Grilled pork sausage (usually *Bockwurst*)

Frankfurter: A skinny, pink, boiled sausage

Jagdwurst: Baloney-like smoked pork

Knackwurst (or **Knockwurst**): Stubby, garlicky beef or pork sausage

Landjäger: Skinny, spicy, air-dried salami

Leberkäse: Finely ground corned beef, pork, bacon, and onions baked as a loaf

Leberwurst: Usually made from pig or calf livers and served as a spread on open-face sandwiches

Mettwurst: Made of minced pork that's cured and smoked

Nürnberger: Short and spicy grilled pork sausage from Nürnberg

Saumagen: "Sow's stomach" stuffed with meat, vegetables, and spices

Teewurst: Air-dried, often smoked pork sausage similar to prosciutto

Thüringer: Long, skinny, peppery sausage

Weisswurst: Boiled white sausage

Zwiebelmettwurst: Spicy, soft sausage made with raw pork and onions

Starches

Besides bread (*Brot*) and potatoes (*Kartoffeln*), other typical starches include:

Kartoffelsalat: Potato salad

Knödel: Large dumplings, usually potato

Schupfnudeln: Stubby potato noodles

Spätzle: Little egg noodles; often served with melted cheese and fried onions (*Käsespätzle*)

Salads

Bauernsalat: Greek salad, sometimes with sausage

Bohnensalat: Bean salad

Fleischsalat: Chopped cold cuts mixed with pickles and mayonnaise

Gemischter Salat (or **Bunter Salat**): A mix of lettuce, pickled veggies, and a tasty dressing

Gurkensalat: Cucumber salad

Nudelsalat: Pasta salad

Oliviersalat: Russian-style salad—potatoes, eggs, vegetables, and mayonnaise

Wurstsalat: Chopped sausage in onion and vinegar

Sweets

Make sure to visit a bakery (*Bäckerei*) or pastry shop (*Konditorei*) to browse the selection of fresh pastries (*Feingebäck*) and cakes (*Kuchen*).

Amerikaner: Flat, round doughnut with glazed frosting

Berliner: A jelly-filled doughnut (*Krapfen* in Bavaria, *Berliner Pfannkuchen* in Berlin)

Rohrnudel: Roll-like sweet dumpling with raisins

Schnecken: "Snail"-shaped pastry roll with raisins and nuts

Beverages
Water, Juice, and Soft Drinks

At restaurants, waiters aren't exactly eager to bring you *Leitungswasser* (tap water), preferring that you buy *Mineralwasser* (*mit/ohne Gas*—with/without carbonation).

Popular soft drinks include *Apfelschorle* (half apple juice, half sparkling water) and *Spezi* (cola and orange soda). Menus list drink sizes by the tenth of a liter, or deciliter (dl): 0.2 liters is a small glass, and 0.4 or 0.5 is a larger one.

At stores, most bottled water and soft drinks require a deposit (*Pfand*; usually €0.15 or €0.25), which is refunded if you return the bottle for recycling.

Beer

The average German drinks 40 gallons of beer a year and has a tremendous variety to choose from. *Flaschenbier* is bottled, and *vom Fass* is on tap. When ordering beer in Bavaria, the standard order is *eine Mass* (a whole liter, or about a quart); for something smaller, ask for *eine Halbe* (a half-liter, not always available). For tips on visiting a *Biergarten*, see page 82.

Broadly speaking, most German beers fall into four main categories:

Helles Bier: Closest to American-style beer, this is the generic name for pale lager. Light-colored, a *helles Bier* is similar to a *Pilsner*, but with more malt.

Dunkles Bier: Dark beer. Munich-style *dunkles* is sweet and malty, while farther north it's drier and hoppier.

Weissbier or **Weizenbier:** "White" or "wheat" beer is a yeasty, highly caloric beer. Unfiltered *Weissbier*, especially common in the south, is cloudy (and usually called *Hefeweizen*). *Kristallweizen* is a clear, filtered, yeast-free wheat beer. *Roggenbier* is darker colored and made with rye.

Pilsner (a.k.a. **Pilsener** or simply **Pils**): Barley-based, hoppy, light-colored beer, particularly common in the north.

Wine

Though famous for its beer, Germany also has excellent wine. The best-known white wines are from the Rhine and Mosel, and there are some good reds (usually from the south), including *Dornfelder* (velvety, often oaky, sometimes sweet) and *Spätburgunder* (or *Blauburgunder*; German for "pinot noir").

Wein is commonly sold by the deciliter, with prices listed per 1 dl (sometimes written as 0.1 L on menus; 1 dl is about 3.5 ounces). You can order by the glass simply by asking for *ein Glas*, or to clarify that you don't want much, *eine Dezi* (one deciliter). For white wine, ask for *Weisswein*; red wine is *Rotwein*. Order your wine *lieblich* (sweet), *halbtrocken* (medium), or *trocken* (dry).

Many hotels serve the inexpensive *Sekt*, or German champagne, at breakfast. Also keep an eye out for *Apfelwein* ("apple wine"—hard cider, especially popular in Frankfurt). In winter, *Glühwein* (hot mulled wine) is popular.

Here are some of the white wines you may see:

Eiswein: Ultra-sweet dessert white

Gewürztraminer: Aromatic, intense, and "spicy"

Grauburgunder: German for "pinot gris"—a soft, full-bodied white

Liebfraumilch: Semisweet blending Riesling with Silvaner and Müller-Thurgau

Müller-Thurgau: Light, flowery, smooth, and semisweet

Riesling: Fruity, fragrant, elegant

Silvaner (or *Grüner Silvaner*): Acidic and fruity white

Weinschorle: A spritzer of white wine

SLEEPING

Extensive and opinionated listings of good-value rooms are a major feature of this book's Sleeping sections. Rather than list accommodations scattered throughout a town, I choose hotels in my favorite neighborhoods that are convenient to your sightseeing.

Book your accommodations as soon as your itinerary is set, especially if you want to stay at one of my top listings or if you'll be traveling during busy times. See a list of major holidays and festivals later in this chapter.

Rates and Deals

I've categorized my recommended accommodations based on price, indicated with a dollar-sign rating (see sidebar). The price ranges suggest an estimated cost for a one-night stay in a standard double room with a private toilet and shower in high season, include breakfast, and assume you're booking directly with the hotel.

Booking Direct: To get the best deal, contact family-run hotels directly by phone or email. When you go direct, the owner avoids the commission paid to booking sites, thereby leaving enough wiggle room to offer you a discount, a nicer room, or a free breakfast (if it's not already included). If you prefer to book online or are considering a hotel chain,

it's to your advantage to use the hotel's website.

Getting a Discount: Some hotels extend a discount to those who pay cash or stay longer than three nights. And some accommodations offer a special discount for Rick Steves readers, indicated in this guidebook by the abbreviation "RS%." Discounts vary: Ask for details when you reserve.

Room Taxes: Some cities require hoteliers to charge a daily tourist tax (about €1-5/person per night; in Berlin, it's 5 percent of the room rate). This may be included in the room price or may appear as an extra charge on your bill. In resort towns such as Baden-Baden, visitors pay a small spa tax (per person and per night) that's added to their bill.

Types of Accommodations
Hotels

While I favor smaller, family-run hotels, occasionally a chain hotel can be a good value; the Europe-wide Ibis/Mercure chain has many options (www.accorhotels.com). I'm also impressed with the homegrown, Hamburg-based German chain called Motel One, which specializes in affordable style and has branches

Sleep Code

Hotels in this book are categorized according to the average price of a standard double room with breakfast in high season.

$$$$	**Splurge:** Most rooms over €170
$$$	**Pricier:** €130-170
$$	**Moderate:** €90-130
$	**Budget:** €50-90
¢	**Backpacker:** Under €50
RS%	**Rick Steves discount**

Unless otherwise noted, credit cards are accepted, hotel staff speak basic English, and free Wi-Fi is available. Comparison-shop by checking prices at several hotels (on each hotel's own website, on a booking site, or by email). For the best deal, *book directly with the hotel.* Ask for a discount if paying in cash; if the listing includes RS%, request a Rick Steves discount.

in Berlin, Munich, Nürnberg, Frankfurt, Cologne, and other cities (www.motel-one.com).

Because the train system in Germany is convenient and popular, both locals and foreigners have discovered that staying near the station saves hauling luggage. The concept of the train-station hotel, which went out of favor during the 20th century, is making a big comeback in Germany.

Breakfast is generally included in the quoted rate (except in Berlin), but you can usually add or remove a breakfast option when booking (sometimes continental, but often buffet).

Some hotels can add an extra bed (for a small charge) to turn a double into a triple; some offer larger rooms for four or more people (I call these "family rooms" in the listings). In general, a triple room is cheaper than the cost of a double and a single. Three or four people can economize by requesting one big room.

In Germany, a double bed frequently has two separate mattresses and sometimes two separate (but adjacent) frames—even if the bed is intended for couples. A "real" double bed with a single mattress is called a *Französisches Bett*—a French bed. Rooms

with truly separate twin beds are less common in German hotels.

The EU requires that hotels collect your name, nationality, and ID number. When you check in, the receptionist will normally ask for your passport and may keep it for anywhere from a couple of minutes to a couple of hours. (If you're not comfortable leaving your passport at the desk for a long time, ask when you can pick it up.)

Air-conditioning is rarely needed, and rare at smaller hotels. If you're here during a heat spell, ask to borrow a fan. Learn how the windows work: You'll often find the windows tipped open from the top to air out the room, with the window handle pointing up. To close the window, push it in and rotate the handle so it points down. The third handle position is horizontal, which lets you swing the entire window open.

Even at the best places, mechanical breakdowns occur: Sinks leak, hot water turns cold, toilets may gurgle or smell, the Wi-Fi goes out, or the air-conditioning dies when you need it most. Report your concerns clearly and calmly at the front desk.

If you find that night noise is a problem (if, for instance, your room is over a nightclub), ask for a quieter room in the back or

Using Online Services to Your Advantage

From booking services to user reviews, online businesses are playing a greater role in travelers' planning than ever before. Take advantage of their pluses—and be wise to their downsides.

Booking Sites

Booking websites, including Booking.com and Hotels.com, offer one-stop shopping for hotels. To be listed, a hotel must pay a sizeable commission...and promise that its own website won't undercut the price on the booking-service site.

Remember: When you use an online booking service, you're adding a middleman. To support small, family-run hotels whose world is more difficult than ever, book direct.

Short-Term Rental Sites

Rental juggernaut Airbnb and other short-term rental sites allow travelers to rent rooms and apartments directly from locals. Airbnb fans appreciate feeling part of a real neighborhood as "temporary Europeans."

Critics view Airbnb as creating unfair competition for established guesthouse owners. As a lover of Europe, I share the worry of those who see residents nudged aside by tourists. But as an advocate for travelers, I appreciate the value and cultural intimacy Airbnb provides.

User Reviews

User-generated review sites and apps such as Yelp and TripAdvisor can give you a consensus of opinions about everything from hotels and restaurants to sights and nightlife. But a user-generated review is based on the limited experience of one person, while a guidebook is the work of a trained researcher who visits many restaurants and hotels year after year.

Both types of information have their place, and in many ways, they're complementary. If something is well reviewed in a guidebook and it also gets good online reviews, it's likely a winner.

on an upper floor. To guard against theft in your room, keep valuables out of sight. Some rooms come with a safe, and other hotels have safes at the front desk.

For more complicated problems, don't expect instant results. Above all, keep a positive attitude. Remember, you're on vacation. If your hotel is a disappointment, spend more time out enjoying the place you came to see.

Guesthouses

Compared to hotels, guesthouses (*Pensionen, Gasthäuser,* or *Gasthöfe* in German) give you double the cultural intimacy for half the price. While you may lose some of the conveniences of a hotel, I happily make the trade-off for the lower rates and personal touches. If you have a reasonable but limited budget, skip hotels and look for smaller, family-run places.

The smallest establishments are private homes with rooms (*Zimmer*) rented out to travelers for as little as €20 per person. Rooms can run the gamut. Some are suite-like, with multiple rooms, separate entrances, and private baths. Others are spare bedrooms in family homes,

Making Hotel Reservations

Requesting a Reservation: For family-run hotels, it's generally cheaper to book your room directly via email or a phone call. For business-class hotels, or if you'd rather book online, reserve directly through the hotel's official website (not a booking website). For complicated requests, send an email. Almost all of my recommended hotels take reservations in English.

Here's what the hotelier wants to know:
- Type(s) of rooms you want and size of your party
- Number of nights you'll stay
- Your arrival and departure dates, written European-style as day/month/year (18/06/20 or 18 June 2020)
- Special requests (en suite bathroom, cheapest room, twin beds vs. double bed, quiet room)
- Applicable discounts (such as a Rick Steves reader discount, cash discount, or promotional rate)

Confirming a Reservation: Most places will request a credit-card number to hold your room. If you're using an online reservation form, look for the *https* or a lock icon at the top of your browser. If you book direct, you can email, call, or fax this information.

Canceling a Reservation: If you must cancel, it's courteous—and smart—to do so with as much notice as possible, especially for smaller family-run places. Cancellation policies can be strict; read the fine print before you book. Many discount deals require prepayment, with cancellation refunds.

Reconfirming a Reservation: Always call or email to reconfirm your room reservation a few days in advance. For B&Bs or very small hotels, I call again on my day of arrival to tell my host what time to expect me (especially important if arriving late—after 17:00).

Phoning: For tips on how to call hotels overseas, see page 387.

with no in-room plumbing (but you have access to the bathroom and shower in the home). Finding and booking a guesthouse is no different than reserving a hotel. Even most smaller places are listed on hotel-booking websites—but a direct booking is especially appreciated at mom-and-pop places, and will likely net you a better price. Private rooms are also available through Airbnb-type services. If you haven't booked ahead, look for signs that say *Zimmer frei* (green), which means rooms are available; *Zimmer belegt* (orange) means no vacancy.

Short-Term Rentals

A short-term rental—whether an apartment, house, or room in a local's home—is an increasingly popular alternative, especially if you plan to settle in one location for several nights. For stays longer than a few days, you can usually find a rental that's comparable to—and cheaper than—a hotel room with similar amenities. Many places require a minimum stay and have strict cancellation policies. And you're generally on your own: There's no hotel reception desk, breakfast, or daily cleaning service.

Aggregator websites such as Airbnb, FlipKey, Booking.com, and the HomeAway family of sites (HomeAway, VRBO, and VacationRentals) let you browse properties and correspond directly with European property owners or managers.

Hostels

A hostel (*Jugendherberge*) provides cheap beds where you sleep alongside strangers for about €25 per night. Travelers of any age are welcome if they don't mind dorm-style accommodations and meeting other travelers. Most hostels offer kitchen facilities, guest computers, Wi-Fi, and a self-service laundry. Hostels almost always provide bedding, but the towel's up to you (though you can usually rent one for a small fee). Family and private rooms are often available.

Independent hostels tend to be easygoing, colorful, and informal (no membership required; www.hostelworld.com). You may pay slightly less by booking directly with the hostel. **Official hostels** are part of Hostelling International (HI) and share an online booking site (www.hihostels.com). HI hostels typically require that you be a member or pay a bit more per night.

STAYING CONNECTED

One of the most common questions I hear from travelers is, "How can I stay connected in Europe?" The short answer is: more easily and cheaply than you might think.

The simplest solution is to bring your own device—mobile phone, tablet, or laptop—and use it just as you would at home (following the tips below). For more details, see www.ricksteves.com/phoning. For a practical one-hour talk covering tech issues for travelers, see www.ricksteves.com/mobile-travel-skills.

Using a Mobile Phone in Europe

Sign up for an international plan. To stay connected at a lower cost, sign up for an international service plan through your carrier. Most providers offer a simple bundle that includes calling, messaging, and data. Your normal plan may already include international coverage (T-Mobile's does).

Use free Wi-Fi whenever possible. Unless you have an unlimited-data plan, you're best off saving most online tasks for Wi-Fi. You can access the internet, send texts, and even make voice calls over Wi-Fi.

Minimize the use of your cellular network. Even with an international data plan, wait until you're on Wi-Fi to Skype, download apps, stream videos, or do other megabyte-greedy tasks. Using a navigation app such as Google Maps over a cellular network can take lots of data, so do this sparingly or use it offline. Disable automatic updates so your apps will only update when you're on Wi-Fi. Also change your device's email settings from "auto-retrieve" to "manual" (or from "push" to "fetch").

Use Wi-Fi calling and messaging apps. Skype, WhatsApp, FaceTime, and Google Hangouts are great for making free or low-

Tips on Internet Security

Make sure that your device is running the latest versions of its operating system, security software, and apps. Next, ensure that your device and key programs (like email) are password-protected. On the road, use only secure Wi-Fi hotspots. Ask the hotel or café staff for the specific name of their Wi-Fi network, and make sure you log on to that exact one.

If you must access your financial info online, use a banking app rather than accessing your account via a browser. A cellular connection is more secure than Wi-Fi. Avoid logging onto personal finance sites on a public computer.

Never share your credit-card number (or any other sensitive information) online unless you know that the site is secure. A secure site displays a little padlock icon, and the URL begins with *https* (instead of the usual *http*).

card (usually available at newsstands, tobacco shops, and train stations) to call out from your hotel. Dial the toll-free access number, enter the card's PIN code, then dial the number. Even small hotels in Germany tend to have a direct-dial system, so callers can reach you without going through reception. Ask the staff for your room's specific telephone number.

Some hotels have **public computers** in their lobbies for guests to use; otherwise you may find them at public libraries (ask your hotelier or the TI for the nearest location). On a European keyboard, use the "Alt Gr" key to the right of the space bar to insert the extra symbol that appears on some keys. If you can't locate a special character (such as @), simply copy and paste it from a web page.

Mail

You can mail one package per day to yourself worth up to $200 duty-free from Europe to the US (mark it "personal purchases"). If you're sending a gift to someone, mark it "unsolicited gift." For details, visit www.cbp.gov, select "Travel," and search for "Know Before You Go."

The German postal service works fine, but for quick transatlantic delivery (in either direction), consider services such as DHL (www.dhl.com).

TRANSPORTATION

This section covers the basics on trains, buses, rental cars, and flights. Considering the efficiency of Germany's trains and buses, you'd never need to use a car.

You can follow my recommended two-week itinerary (page 26) by public transit, but renting a car for a few days makes it possible for you to get more out of your visit to the Bavarian Alps, where sights are scattered and the public transit is sparse. Other regions worth a joyride are the Romantic Road and the Rhine Valley (particularly if you want to explore more than this book covers). A car is an expensive

cost calls or sending texts over Wi-Fi. With an app installed on your phone, tablet, or laptop, you can log on to a Wi-Fi network and contact friends or family members who use the same service. If you buy credit in advance, with some of these services you can call or send a text anywhere for just pennies per minute.

Without a Mobile Phone

It's possible to travel in Europe without a mobile device. You can make calls from your hotel and check email or browse websites using public computers.

Most **hotels** charge a fee for placing calls—ask for rates before you dial. You can use a prepaid international phone

How to Dial

To make an international call, follow the dialing instructions below. Drop an initial zero, if present, when dialing a European phone number—except when calling Italy. I've used the telephone number of one of my recommended Berlin hotels as an example (tel. 030/780-089-760).

From a Mobile Phone

It's easy to dial with a mobile phone. Whether calling from the US to Europe, country to country within Europe, or from Europe to the US, it's all the same. Press zero until you get a + sign, enter the country code (49 for Germany), then dial the phone number.

▶ To call the Berlin hotel from any location, dial +49-30/780-089-760.

From a US Landline to Europe

Dial 011 (US/Canada access code), country code (49 for Germany), and phone number.

▶ To call the Berlin hotel from your home phone, dial 011-49-30/780-089-760.

From a European Landline to the US or Europe

Dial 00 (Europe access code), country code (1 for the US, 49 for Germany), and phone number.

▶ To call my US office from Germany, dial 00-1-425-771-8303.
▶ To call the Berlin hotel from France, dial 00-49-30/780-089-760.

For a complete list of European country codes and more phoning help, see www.howtocallabroad.com.

headache in big cities such as Munich, Frankfurt, and Berlin (park it).

For more detailed information on transportation throughout Europe, see www.ricksteves.com/transportation.

Trains

German trains—most operated by the Deutsche Bahn (DB), Germany's national railway—are speedy and comfortable. They cover cities and small towns well. Though German trains are fairly punctual, very tight connections can be a gamble. Once the obvious choice for long-distance travel within Germany, trains now face competition from buses offering ultra-low fares (described later).

If you have a rail pass, you can hop on any train without much forethought (though for a small fee, you can reserve a seat on a fast train). Without a rail pass, you can save a lot of money by understanding the difference between fast trains and cheaper "regional" trains.

Types of Trains

Germany's three levels of trains differ in price, speed, and comfort. **ICE** trains are the fastest, zipping from city to city in air-conditioned comfort, and costing proportionately more. Midlevel **IC** and **EC** trains look older than the ICEs. **Regional trains** (labeled RB, RE, IRE, or S on schedules) are slowest but cost much less. Milk-run S and RB trains stop at every station.

If you have a rail pass, take the fastest

train available; rail-pass holders don't pay a supplement for the fast ICE trains. If you're buying point-to-point tickets, taking a slower train can save a lot of money. You also save with day-pass deals valid only on slower trains.

Schedules

Schedules change by season, weekday, and weekend. Verify train times listed in this book at www.bahn.com. This website also includes public transport in cities (buses, trams, and subways). The handy DB Navigator app is also a useful tool for schedules.

At staffed train stations, attendants will print out a step-by-step itinerary for you, free of charge. You can also produce an itinerary yourself by using the trackside machines marked *Fahrkarten* (usually silver, red, and blue). The touch-screen display gives you an English option; choose "Timetable Information," indicate your point of departure and destination, and then hit "Print" for a personalized schedule, including transfers and track numbers.

If you're changing trains en route and have a tight connection, note the numbers of the platforms (*Bahnsteig* or *Gleis*) where you will arrive and depart (listed on itineraries). This will save you precious time hunting for your connecting train.

Rail Passes

The single-country German Rail Pass can be a great value, often saving money while allowing you to hop on trains at your convenience (since most daytime routes in Germany, including fast ICE trains, do not require seat reservations). Rail passes are an even better deal if you're under 28 (you qualify for a youth pass) or traveling with a companion (you save with the "twin" rate). For only shorter hops, a rail pass probably isn't worth it, especially if you get discounts on point-to-point tickets and day passes.

If you're traveling beyond Germany (and beyond the international bus and train coverage of the German Rail Pass), consider the Eurail Global Pass, covering most of Europe. If you buy separate passes for neighboring countries, note that you'll use a travel day on each when crossing the border.

When choosing how many travel days you need for your rail pass, it can be worthwhile to buy an extra day (about $15-20 per person) even to cover short trips on regional trains simply for the convenience of not having to buy tickets. Your rail pass covers certain extras, including travel on city S-Bahn systems (except in

Rail Pass or Point-to-Point Tickets?

Rail Passes

A German Rail Pass lets you travel by train in Germany for three to fifteen days (consecutively or not) within a one-month period. Discounted "Twin" rates are offered for two people traveling together. Germany is also covered (along with most of Europe) by the classic Eurail Global Pass.

Discounted rates are offered for seniors (age 60 and up) and youths (ages 12-27). Up to two kids (ages 4-11) can travel free with each adult-rate pass (including the German Twin pass, but not with Eurail senior rates). All passes offer a choice of first or second class for all ages.

While most rail passes are best purchased outside Europe (through travel agents or Rick Steves' Europe), the German Rail Pass is also sold at main train stations and airports in Germany. For more on rail passes, including current prices, go to www.ricksteves.com/rail.

Point-to-Point Tickets

If you're taking just a couple of train rides, buying individual point-to-point tickets may save you money over a pass. Use this map to add up approximate pay-as-you-go fares for your itinerary, and compare that to the price of a rail pass. Keep in mind that significant discounts on point-to-point tickets may be available with advance purchase.

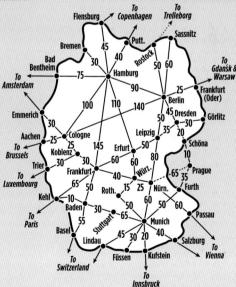

Map shows approximate costs, in USD, for one-way, second-class tickets on faster trains.

Germany's Public Transportation

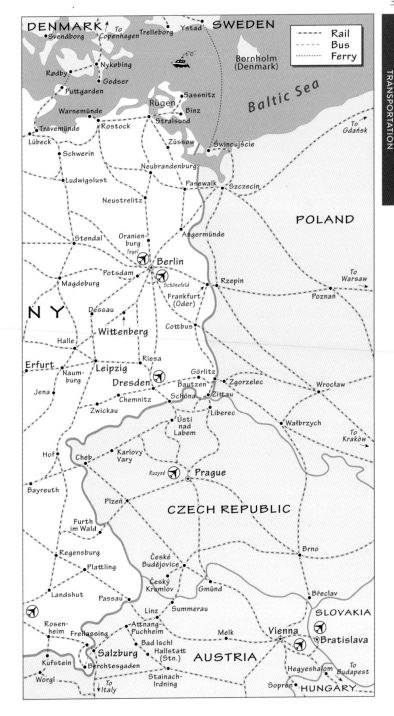

Berlin, where it's only good on S-Bahn lines between major train stations), German buses marked "Deutsche Bahn" or "DB" (run by the train company), and international express buses operated by Deutsche Bahn (covered by either a German Rail Pass or a pass for both countries of travel). Rail passes also get you a 20 percent discount on K-D Line boats on the Rhine and Mosel Rivers and the Romantic Road bus.

Because Salzburg, Austria is so close to the German border, traveling to or from the city on the main line from Munich counts as traveling within Germany, as far as your rail pass is concerned (Salzburg is the official border station on that line).

For more detailed advice on figuring out the smartest rail-pass options for your train trip, visit www.ricksteves.com/rail.

Point-to-Point Tickets

First Class vs. Second Class: First-class tickets usually cost 50 percent more than second-class tickets. While first-class cars are a bit more spacious and quieter than second class, the main advantage of a first-class ticket is the lower chance that the cars will fill up. Riding in second class gets you there at the same time, and with the same scenery. As second-class seating is still comfortable and quiet, most of my readers find the extra cost of first class isn't worth it. Germans tell me they never ride in first class unless someone else is paying for it.

Full-Fare Tickets (*Normalpreis*): The most you'll ever have to pay for a journey is the unrestricted *Normalpreis*. This full-fare ticket allows you to easily change your plans and switch to an earlier or later train, without paying a penalty. (If you buy a *Normalpreis* ticket for a slower train, though, you can't use it on a fast one without paying extra.)

Discount Fares (*Sparpreis*): If you reserve a ticket on a fast train at least a day in advance and are comfortable committing to specific departure times, you can usually save 25-75 percent over the *Nor-*

malpreis. These tickets are more restrictive; you must take the train listed on the ticket.

Day Passes

You may save even more with three types of extremely popular day passes valid only on slow trains: the various Länder-Tickets, the Schönes-Wochenende-Ticket, and the Quer-durchs-Land-Ticket. They are most cost-effective for groups of two to five people, but single travelers can benefit from them, too.

With a **Länder-Ticket,** up to five people traveling together get unlimited travel in second class on regional trains for one day at a very cheap price (generally €23-25 for the first person plus €4-6 for each additional person). There are a few restrictions: A Länder-Ticket only covers travel within a certain *Land* (Germany's version of a US state; Bavaria, Baden-Württemberg, Saxony, or Rheinland-Pfalz), doesn't work for the fastest classes of trains (ICE, IC, EC), and doesn't cover travel on weekdays before 9:00. Still, Länder-Tickets offer big savings, don't require advance purchase, and are also valid on local transit.

The **Quer-durchs-Land-Ticket** works like a Länder-Ticket, but gives you the run of the whole country. It's valid on any regional train anywhere in Germany, but doesn't include city transit (€44, each additional passenger-€8, maximum of 5 travelers, only valid weekdays after 9:00).

The **Schönes-Wochenende-Ticket** is a cheaper weekend version of the Quer-durchs-Land Ticket, with looser conditions: It's valid on all regional trains on a Saturday or Sunday (starting at midnight), it does cover local transit in some areas (check specifics when you buy), and additional travelers pay only €4 extra (first person-€40, maximum 5 travelers).

Buying Tickets

Online: You can buy German train tickets online and print them out, or have them sent to your phone as an eticket; visit www.

bahn.com and create a login and password. If you print out your ticket, the conductor may also ask to see your passport. Another option is to use the DB Navigator app, which lets you buy tickets with your credit card—even for the same day of travel.

At the Station: Major German stations have a handy *Reisezentrum* (travel center) where you can ask questions and buy tickets (with a €2 markup for the personal service). You can also buy tickets from machines. The silver, red, and blue touch-screen machines (marked with the Deutsche Bahn logo and *Fahrkarten,* which means "tickets") are user-friendly. They sell both short- and long-distance train tickets, and print schedules for free. You can pay with bills, coins, or credit cards—but US credit cards may not work. There's one exception: Any trip that is entirely within the bounds of a regional transport network (i.e., Frankfurt-Bacharach or Nürnberg-Rothenburg) is considered local: Tickets can only be bought on the day of travel, and you must pay cash.

Each German city and region also has its own machines that sell only same-day tickets to nearby destinations (usually including Länder-Ticket day passes). In cities, these machines also sell local public transit tickets. At some smaller, unstaffed stations, these machines are the only ticket-buying option.

On the Train: You can buy a ticket on board from the conductor for a long-distance journey by paying a small markup. But if you're riding a local (short distance) train, you're expected to board with a valid ticket...or you can get fined. Note that ticket checkers on local trains aren't necessarily in uniform.

Getting a Seat

On the faster ICE, IC, and EC trains, it costs €4.50 extra per person to reserve a seat, which you can do at a station ticket desk, a touch-screen machine, or online (especially useful with a rail pass or a second-class ticket). If buying a first-class ticket on these trains, you can add a seat assignment for free at the time of purchase. German trains generally offer ample seating, but popular routes do fill up, especially on holiday weekends. If your itinerary is set, and you don't mind the small fee, seat reservations can be worth it for the peace of mind. They're especially smart for small groups and families (€9 reservation cap for families).

If you have a seat reservation, while waiting for your train to arrive, note the departure time and *Wagen* (car) number and look along the train platform for the diagram (*Wagenstandanzeiger*) showing what sector of the platform the car will arrive at (usually A through F). Stand in that sector to avoid a last-minute dash to the right car or a long walk through the train to your seat. This is especially important for ICE trains, which are often divided into two unconnected parts.

If you're traveling without a reservation and are looking for an open seat, check the displays (or, in older trains, the slips of paper) that mark reserved seats. If you have a hard time finding an unreserved seat, take a closer look at the reservations—if you find a seat that's reserved for a leg of the journey that doesn't overlap with yours, you're free to take the seat.

Long-Distance Buses

While most travelers still find the train to be the better option (mainly because rail passes make German train travel affordable and no-hassle), ultra-low-fare long-distance buses are worth considering. While buses don't offer as extensive a network as trains, they do cover the most popular cities for travelers, often with a direct connection. The primary disadvantage to buses is a lack of travel flexibility: Buses are far less likely than trains to have a seat available for those who show up sans ticket (especially on either end of a weekend). And compared to trains, buses also offer fewer departures per day, though your options probably aren't too shabby on major routes served by multiple operators.

Trains also beat buses in travel time and convenience, although often not by much.

Bus tickets are sold on the spot (on board and/or at kiosks at some bus terminals), but because the cheapest fares often sell out, it's best to book online as soon as you're sure of your plans (at a minimum, book a few days ahead to nab the best prices). The main bus operator is FlixBus (www.flixbus.de).

Renting a Car

Most of the major US rental agencies (including Avis, Budget, Enterprise, Hertz, and Thrifty) have offices throughout Europe. Also consider the two major Europe-based agencies, Europcar and Sixt. Consolidators such as Auto Europe/Kemwel (www.autoeurope.com—or the sometimes cheaper www.autoeurope.eu) compare rates at several companies to get you the best deal.

Wherever you book, always read the fine print. Ask about add-on charges—such as one-way drop-off fees, airport surcharges, or mandatory insurance policies—that aren't included in the "total price."

Rental Costs and Considerations

Figure on paying roughly $250 for a one-week rental for a basic compact car. Allow extra for supplemental insurance, fuel, tolls, and parking.

Manual vs. Automatic: Almost all rental cars in Europe are manual by default—and cars with a stick shift are generally cheaper. If you need an automatic, request one in advance. When selecting a car, don't be tempted by a larger model, as it won't be as maneuverable on narrow, winding roads or when squeezing into tight parking lots.

Age Restrictions: Some rental companies impose minimum and maximum age limits. Young drivers (25 and under) and seniors (69 and up) should check the rental policies and rules section of car rental websites.

Choosing Pick-up/Drop-off Locations:

Always check the hours of the location you choose: Many rental offices close from midday Saturday until Monday morning and, in smaller towns, at lunchtime.

Wherever you select, get precise details on the location and allow ample time to find it.

Crossing Borders in a Rental Car: Be aware that international trips—say, picking up in Berlin and dropping off in Prague—can be expensive if the rental company assesses a drop-off fee for crossing a border. Always tell your car-rental company exactly which countries you'll be entering. Double-check with your rental agent that you have all the documentation you need before you drive off (especially if you're crossing borders into non-Schengen countries, such as Croatia, where you might need to present proof of insurance).

Picking Up Your Car: Before driving off in your rental car, check it thoroughly and make sure any damage is noted on your rental agreement. Rental agencies in Europe tend to charge for even minor damage, so be sure to mark everything. Find out how your car's gearshift, lights, turn signals, wipers, radio, and fuel cap function, and know what kind of fuel the car takes (diesel vs. unleaded). When you return the car, make sure the agent verifies its condition with you. Some drivers take pictures of the returned vehicle as proof of its condition.

Car Insurance Options

When you rent a car in Europe, the price typically includes liability insurance, which covers harm to other cars or motorists—but not the rental car itself. To limit your financial risk in case of damage to the rental, choose one of these options: Buy a Collision Damage Waiver (CDW) with a low or zero deductible from the car-rental company (roughly 30-40 percent extra), get coverage through your credit card (free, but more complicated), or get collision insurance as part of a larger travel-insurance policy. For more on car-rental insurance, see www.ricksteves.com/cdw.

Navigation Options

If you'll be navigating using your phone or a GPS unit from home, remember to bring a car charger and device mount.

Your Mobile Phone: The mapping app on your phone works fine for navigation in Europe, but for real-time turn-by-turn directions and traffic updates, you'll need mobile data access. And driving all day can burn through a lot of very expensive data. The economical workaround is to use map apps that work offline. By downloading in advance from Google Maps, Apple Maps, Here WeGo, or Navmii, you can still have turn-by-turn voice directions and maps that recalibrate even though they're offline.

You must download your maps before you go offline—and it's smart to select large regions. Then turn off your data connection so you're not charged for roaming. Call up the map, enter your destination, and you're on your way. Even if you don't have to pay extra for data roaming, this option is great for navigating in areas with poor connectivity.

GPS Devices: If you want the convenience of a dedicated GPS unit, consider renting one with your car ($10-30/day). These units offer real-time turn-by-turn directions and traffic without the data requirements of an app. The unit may come loaded only with maps for its home country; if you need additional maps, ask. Also make sure your device's language is set to English before you leave.

Maps and Atlases: Even when navigating primarily with a mobile app or GPS, I always make it a point to have a paper map. It's invaluable for getting the big picture, understanding alternate routes, and filling in when my phone runs out of juice. It's smart to buy a better map before you go, or pick one up at European gas stations, bookshops, newsstands, and tourist shops.

Driving

Road Rules: Be aware of typical European road rules; for example, many countries require headlights to be turned on at all times, and nearly all forbid handheld mobile-phone use. In Germany, kids under age 12 (or less than about 5 feet tall) must ride in an appropriate child-safety seat. Seat belts are mandatory for all, and two beers under those belts are enough to land you in jail. You're required to use low-beam headlights if it's overcast, raining, or snowing. In Europe, you're not allowed to turn right on a red light, unless a sign or signal specifically authorizes it, and on expressways it's illegal to pass drivers on the right. Ask your car-rental company about these rules, or check the "International Travel" section of the US State Department website (www.travel.state.gov).

Fuel: Unleaded gasoline comes in "Super" (95 octane) and "Super Plus" (98 octane). Pumps marked "E10" or "Super E10" mean the gas contains 10 percent ethanol—make sure your rental can run on this mix. Your US credit and debit cards may not work at self-service gas pumps. Pay the attendant or carry enough euros.

Navigation: Use good local maps and study them before each drive. Learn which exits you need to look out for, which major cities you'll travel toward, where the ruined castles lurk, and so on. Every long drive between my recommended destinations is via the autobahn (super-freeway), and nearly every scenic backcountry drive is paved and comfortable. Learn the universal road signs (explained in charts in most road atlases and at service stations). To get to the center of a city, follow signs for *Zentrum* or *Stadtmitte*.

The Autobahn: Blue signs direct you to the autobahn, which generally provides the shortest trip between any two points (no speed limit in many sections, toll-free within Germany). To understand this complex but super-efficient freeway, look for the *Autobahn Service* booklet at any autobahn rest stop (free, lists all stops,

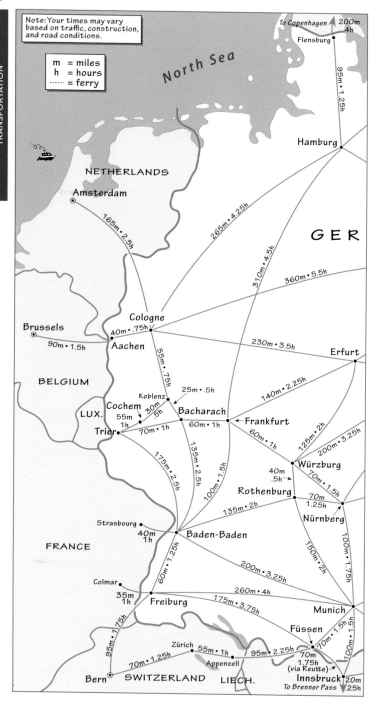

Note: Your times may vary based on traffic, construction, and road conditions.

m = miles
h = hours
...... = ferry

North Sea

To Copenhagen 200m 4h
Flensburg
95m • 1.25h
Hamburg

NETHERLANDS
Amsterdam
165m • 2.5h
265m • 4.25h
310m • 4.5h
360m • 5.5h

GER

Cologne
Brussels
90m • 1.5h
40m • .75h
Aachen
230m • 3.5h
Erfurt

BELGIUM
55m • .75h
25m • .5h
140m • 2.25h
Koblenz
Cochem
30m .5h
55m 1h
Bacharach
70m • 1h
60m • 1h
Frankfurt
LUX.
Trier
175m • 2.5h
135m • 2.5h
100m • 1.5h
60m • 1h
125m • 2h
200m • 3.25h
Würzburg
40m .5h
70m • 1.5h
Rothenburg
70m 1.25h
Strasbourg
135m • 2h
Nürnberg
40m 1h
Baden-Baden
200m • 3.25h
150m • 2h
100m • 1.75h
FRANCE
Colmar
35m 1h
60m • 1.25h
260m • 4h
Freiburg
175m • 3.75h
Munich
Füssen
95m • 1.75h
Zürich
55m • 1h
95m • 2.25h
70m 1.5h
100m • 1.5h
70m • 1.25h
Appenzell
70m 1.75h (via Reutte)
Bern
SWITZERLAND
LIECH.
Innsbruck 20m .25h
To Brenner Pass

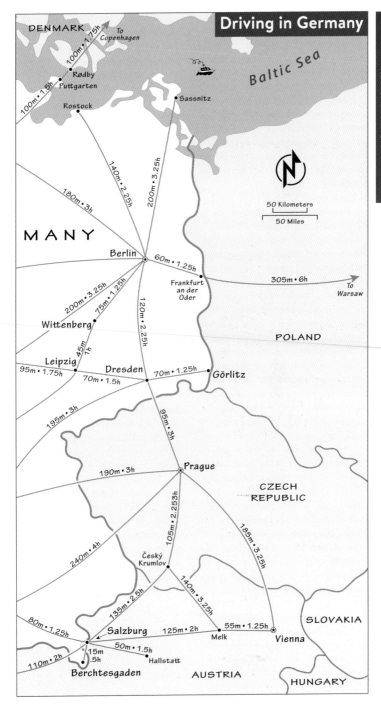

DENMARK

100m • 1.75h   To Copenhagen

Rødby
Puttgarten

100m • 1.5h

Rostock

Sassnitz

Baltic Sea

Driving in Germany

140m • 2.25h

200m • 3.25h

180m • 3h

MANY

50 Kilometers

50 Miles

Berlin   60m • 1.25h

Frankfurt
an der
Oder

305m • 6h   To Warsaw

200m • 3.25h   75m • 1.25h

120m • 2.25h

Wittenberg

POLAND

45m • 1h

Leipzig

95m • 1.75h   Dresden   70m • 1.25h   Görlitz

70m • 1.5h

195m • 3h

95m • 3h

190m • 3h   Prague

CZECH
REPUBLIC

105m • 2.253h

185m • 3.25h

240m • 4h

Český
Krumlov

140m • 3.25h

SLOVAKIA

80m • 1.25h   135m • 2.5h   125m • 2h   55m • 1.25h

Salzburg   Melk   Vienna

110m • 2h   15m
.5h

50m • 1.5h   Hallstatt

Berchtesgaden   AUSTRIA

HUNGARY

services, road symbols, and more). Exits are spaced about every 20 miles and often have a gas station, a restaurant, a mini-market, and sometimes a tourist information desk. Know what you're looking for—miss it, and you're long autobahn-gone.

Autobahns in Germany are famous for having no speed limit, but some sections do have a limit, particularly in urban areas and near complicated interchanges. There are also cameras that take pictures of the speeder's license plate—so obey the law or be prepared to pay.

It's important to stay alert on the autobahn: Everything happens much more quickly, and the speed differential between lanes can be dangerous for unaccustomed drivers. Watch for potential lane changers, whether from your right or from behind—a roaring Mercedes can appear out of thin air in your rearview mirror. Even if you're obeying posted limits, don't cruise in the left lane—it's not only dangerous, it can earn you a big ticket.

Umweltplakette for Driving in German Cities: To drive into specially designated "environmental zones" (Umweltzone) in the centers of many German cities you are required to display an Umweltplakette sticker. Literally "environmental sticker," these come standard with most German rental cars (ask when you pick up your car).

Parking: To park on the street, pick up a plastic clock (Parkscheibe, available free at gas stations, police stations, and Tabak shops). Display your arrival time on the clock and put it on the dashboard, so parking attendants can see you've been there less than the posted maximum stay.

Theft: Thieves easily recognize rental cars and assume they are filled with a tourist's gear. Be sure all your valuables are out of sight and locked in the trunk, or even better, with you or in your room.

Driving in Austria: If you side-trip by car into Austria, bring your US driver's license and get an International Driving Permit (sold at local AAA offices in the US, www.aaa.com). Austria charges drivers who use their expressways. You'll need to have a Vignette sticker stuck to the inside of your rental car's windshield (€9 for 10 days, buy at border crossing, big gas stations near borders, or a rental-car agency). Dipping into the country on regular roads—such as around Reutte, or the less-direct route between the German border and Salzburg—requires no special payment.

Flights

To compare flight costs and times, begin with a travel search engine: Kayak.com is the top site for flights to and within Europe, easy-to-use Google Flights has price alerts, and Skyscanner.com includes many inexpensive flights within Europe.

Flights to Europe: Start looking for international flights about four to six months before your trip, especially for peak-season travel. Depending on your itinerary, it can be efficient and no more expensive to fly into one city and out of another. If your flight requires a connection in Europe, see my hints on navigating Europe's top hub airports at www.ricksteves.com/hub-airports.

Flights within Europe: Flying between European cities has become surprisingly affordable. Before buying a long-distance train or bus ticket, first check the cost of a flight on one of Europe's airlines, whether a major carrier or a no-frills outfit like EasyJet and Ryanair. Others with strong presence in Germany are Eurowings, Condor, WizzAir, and TUIfly. Be aware of the potential drawbacks of flying with a discount airline: nonrefundable and nonchangeable tickets, minimal customer service, time-consuming treks to secondary airports, and stingy baggage allowances.

Flying to the US and Canada: Because security is extra tight for flights to the US, be sure to give yourself plenty of time at the airport. It's also important to charge your electronic devices before you board because security checks may require you to turn them on (see www.tsa.gov for the latest rules).

Resources from Rick Steves

Begin Your Trip at RickSteves.com

My mobile-friendly **website** is *the* place to explore Europe in preparation for your trip. You'll find thousands of fun articles, videos, and radio interviews; a wealth of money-saving tips for planning your dream trip; travel news dispatches; a video library of my travel talks; my travel blog; and my latest guidebook updates (www.ricksteves.com/update).

Our **Travel Forum** is a well-groomed collection of message boards where our travel-savvy community answers questions and shares personal travel experiences—and our well-traveled staff chimes in when they can be helpful.

Our **online Travel Store** offers bags and accessories that I've designed to help you travel smarter and lighter. These include my popular carry-on bags (which I live out of four months a year), money belts, totes, toiletries kits, adapters, guidebooks, and planning maps.

Our website can also help you find the perfect **rail pass** for your itinerary and your budget.

Rick Steves' Tours, Guidebooks, TV Shows, and More

Small Group Tours: Want to travel with greater efficiency and less stress? We offer more than 40 itineraries reaching the best destinations in this book...and beyond. You'll enjoy great guides and a fun bunch of travel partners. For all the details, and to get our tour catalog, visit www.ricksteves.com/tours or call us at 425/608-4217.

Books: This book is just one of many in my series on European travel, which includes country and city guidebooks, Snapshots (excerpted chapters from bigger guides), Pocket guides (full-color little books on big cities), and my budget-travel skills handbook, *Rick Steves Europe Through the Back Door.* A more complete list of my titles appears near the end of this book.

TV Shows and Travel Talks: My public television series, *Rick Steves' Europe,* covers Europe from top to bottom with over 100 half-hour episodes (watch full episodes at my website). Or, to raise your travel I.Q., check out the video versions of our popular classes (covering most European countries as well as travel skills).

Radio: My weekly public radio show, *Travel with Rick Steves,* features interviews with travel experts from around the world. It airs on 400 public radio stations across the US, or you can hear it as a podcast. A complete archive of programs is available on my website.

Audio Tours on My Free App: I've produced dozens of free, self-guided audio tours of the top sights in Europe. For those tours and other audio content, get my free **Rick Steves Audio Europe app,** an extensive online library organized by destination. For more on the app, see page 29.

HOLIDAYS AND FESTIVALS

This list includes selected festivals in major cities, plus national holidays observed throughout Germany (when many sights and banks close). Before planning a trip around a festival, verify the dates with the festival website, the national tourist office (www.germany.travel), or RickSteves.com.

Jan 1	New Year's Day
Jan 6	Epiphany (Heilige Drei Könige)
Late Feb-early March	Fasching (carnival season leading up to Ash Wednesday)
March/April	Easter weekend (Good Friday-Easter Monday)
Mid-April-early May	Spring Festival, Munich (Frühlingsfest, the "little sister of Oktoberfest") and Nürnberg
May 1	May Day with maypole dances
Mid-May	International Dixieland Festival (www.dixielandfestival-dresden.com), Dresden
40th Day after Easter	Ascension
Late May-early June	Fressgass' Fest, Frankfurt

May/June (Pentecost weekend)	Carnival of Cultures (www.karneval-berlin.de), Berlin; Meistertrunk Show (play and market, medieval costumes, Biergarten parties, www.meistertrunk.de), Rothenburg
Mid-June	Stadtteilfest Bunte Republik Neustadt, Dresden (counterculture block party, www.brn-dresden.de)
June (one week after Pentecost Sunday)	Corpus Christi (Fronleichnam)
Mid-June–mid-July	Tollwood, Munich (art, concerts, street theater, www.tollwood.de)
Late June	City Festival (www.elbhangfest.de), Dresden
July	Kiliani Volksfest, Würzburg (county fair-type folk festival)
Early July	Open Air Festival, Berlin (www.classicopenair.de)
Late July–early Aug	Klassik Open Air (fireworks and classical music, www.klassikopenair.de), Nürnberg
Early Aug	International Beer Festival, Berlin (www.bierfestival-berlin.de)
Aug 15	Assumption (Mariä Himmelfahrt)
Late Aug	Museum Riverbank Festival, Frankfurt
Late Aug–early Sept	Rheingau Wine Festival, Frankfurt
Early Sept	Reichsstadt Festival (fireworks), Rothenburg
Late Sep-early Oct	Oktoberfest (www.oktoberfest.de), Munich
Oct 3	German Unity Day (Tag der Deutschen Einheit)
Mid-Oct	Festival of Lights, Berlin (landmark buildings artistically lit, www.festival-of-lights.de)
Nov	Jazzfest Berlin (www.berlinerfestspiele.de)
Nov 1	All Saints' Day (Allerheiligen)
Nov 11	St. Martin's Day (Martinstag)
Dec	Christmas markets, good ones in Nürnberg, Munich, and Rothenburg
Dec 6	St. Nikolaus Day (parades)
Dec 24	Christmas Eve (Heiliger Abend), when Germans celebrate the holiday
Dec 25	Christmas
Dec 31	New Year's Eve ("Silvester")

CONVERSIONS AND CLIMATE

Numbers and Stumblers

- Europeans write a few of their numbers differently than we do. 1 = 1, 4 = 4, 7 = 7.
- In Europe, dates appear as day/month/year, so Christmas 2020 is 25/12/20.
- Commas are decimal points and decimals are commas. A dollar and a half is 1,50, one thousand is 1.000, and there are 5.280 feet in a mile.
- When counting with fingers, start with your thumb. If you hold up your first finger to request one item, you'll probably get two.
- What Americans call the second floor of a building is the first floor in Europe.
- On escalators and moving sidewalks, Europeans keep the left "lane" open for passing. Keep to the right.

Metric Conversions

A **kilogram** equals 1,000 grams (about 2.2 pounds). One hundred **grams** (a common unit at markets) is about a quarter-pound.

One **liter** is about a quart, or almost four to a gallon. A **kilometer** is six-tenths of a mile. To convert kilometers to miles, cut the kilometers in half and add back 10 percent of the original (120 km: 60 + 12 = 72 miles). One **meter** is 39 inches—just over a yard.

Clothing Sizes

When shopping for clothing, use these US-to-European comparisons as general guidelines (but note that no conversion is perfect).

Women: For pants and dresses, add 30 in Germany (US 10 = German 40). For blouses and sweaters, add 8 for most of Europe (US 32 = European 40). For shoes, add 30-31 (US 7 = European 37/38).

Men: For shirts, multiply by 2 and add about 8 (US 15 = European 38). For jackets and suits, add 10. For shoes, add 32-34.

Children: Clothing is sized by height—in centimeters (2.5 cm = 1 inch), so a US size 8 roughly equates to 132-140. For shoes up to size 13, add 16-18, and for sizes 1 and up, add 30-32.

Germany's Climate

First line, average daily high; second line, average daily low; third line, average days without rain. For more detailed weather statistics for destinations in this book (as well as the rest of the world), check www.wunderground.com.

Munich

J	F	M	A	M	J	J	A	S	O	N	D
35°	38°	48°	56°	64°	70°	74°	73°	67°	56°	44°	36°
23°	23°	30°	38°	45°	51°	55°	54°	48°	40°	33°	26°
15	12	18	15	16	13	15	15	17	18	15	16

Berlin

J	F	M	A	M	J	J	A	S	O	N	D
35°	37°	46°	56°	66°	72°	75°	74°	68°	56°	45°	38°
26°	26°	31°	39°	47°	53°	57°	56°	50°	42°	36°	29°
14	13	19	17	19	17	17	17	18	17	14	16

Packing Checklist

Whether you're traveling for five days or five weeks, you won't need more than this. Pack light to enjoy the sweet freedom of true mobility.

Clothing

- ❏ 5 shirts: long- & short-sleeve
- ❏ 2 pairs pants (or skirts/capris)
- ❏ 1 pair shorts
- ❏ 5 pairs underwear & socks
- ❏ 1 pair walking shoes
- ❏ Sweater or warm layer
- ❏ Rainproof jacket with hood
- ❏ Tie, scarf, belt, and/or hat
- ❏ Swimsuit
- ❏ Sleepwear/loungewear

Money

- ❏ Debit card(s)
- ❏ Credit card(s)
- ❏ Hard cash (US $100-200)
- ❏ Money belt

Documents

- ❏ Passport
- ❏ Tickets & confirmations: flights, hotels, trains, rail pass, car rental, sight entries
- ❏ Driver's license
- ❏ Student ID, hostel card, etc.
- ❏ Photocopies of important documents
- ❏ Insurance details
- ❏ Guidebooks & maps

Toiletries Kit

- ❏ Basics: soap, shampoo, toothbrush, toothpaste, floss, deodorant, sunscreen, brush/comb, etc.
- ❏ Medicines & vitamins
- ❏ First-aid kit
- ❏ Glasses/contacts/sunglasses
- ❏ Sewing kit
- ❏ Packet of tissues (for WC)
- ❏ Earplugs

Electronics

- ❏ Mobile phone
- ❏ Camera & related gear
- ❏ Tablet/ebook reader/laptop
- ❏ Headphones/earbuds
- ❏ Chargers & batteries
- ❏ Phone car charger & mount (or GPS device)
- ❏ Plug adapters

Miscellaneous

- ❏ Daypack
- ❏ Sealable plastic baggies
- ❏ Laundry supplies: soap, laundry bag, clothesline, spot remover
- ❏ Small umbrella
- ❏ Travel alarm/watch
- ❏ Notepad & pen
- ❏ Journal

Optional Extras

- ❏ Second pair of shoes (flip-flops, sandals, tennis shoes, boots)
- ❏ Travel hairdryer
- ❏ Picnic supplies
- ❏ Water bottle
- ❏ Fold-up tote bag
- ❏ Small flashlight
- ❏ Mini binoculars
- ❏ Small towel or washcloth
- ❏ Inflatable pillow/neck rest
- ❏ Tiny lock
- ❏ Address list (to mail postcards)
- ❏ Extra passport photos

German Survival Phrases

When using the phonetics, pronounce ī like the long i in "light." Bolded syllables are stressed.

English	German	Pronunciation
Good day.	Guten Tag.	**goo**-tehn tahg
Do you speak English?	Sprechen Sie Englisch?	**shprehkh**-ehn zee **ehgn**-lish
Yes. / No.	Ja. / Nein.	yah / nīn
I (don't) understand.	Ich verstehe (nicht).	ikh fehr-**shtay**-heh (nikht)
Please.	Bitte.	**bit**-teh
Thank you.	Danke.	**dahng**-keh
I'm sorry.	Es tut mir leid.	ehs toot meer līt
Excuse me.	Entschuldigung.	ehnt-**shool**-dig-oong
(No) problem.	(Kein) Problem.	(kīn) proh-**blaym**
(Very) good.	(Sehr) gut.	(zehr) goot
Goodbye.	Auf Wiedersehen.	owf **vee**-der-zayn
one / two	eins / zwei	īns / tsvī
three / four	drei / vier	drī / feer
five / six	fünf / sechs	fewnf / zehkhs
seven / eight	sieben / acht	**zee**-behn / ahkht
nine / ten	neun / zehn	noyn / tsayn
How much is it?	Wieviel kostet das?	**vee**-feel **kohs**-teht dahs
Write it?	Schreiben?	**shrī**-behn
Is it free?	Ist es umsonst?	ist ehs oom-**zohnst**
Included?	Inklusive?	in-kloo-**zee**-veh
Where can I buy / find...?	Wo kann ich kaufen / finden...?	voh kahn ikh **kow**-fehn / **fin**-dehn
I'd like / We'd like...	Ich hätte gern / Wir hätten gern...	ikh **heh**-teh gehrn / veer **heh**-tehn gehrn
...a room.	...ein Zimmer.	īn **tsim**-mer
...a ticket to _____.	...eine Fahrkarte nach _____.	**ī**-neh **far**-kar-teh nahkh
Is it possible?	Ist es möglich?	ist ehs **mur**-glikh
Where is...?	Wo ist...?	voh ist
...the train station	...der Bahnhof	dehr **bahn**-hohf
...the bus station	...der Busbahnhof	dehr **boos**-bahn-hohf
...the tourist information office	...das Touristen-informations-büro	dahs too-**ris**-tehn-in-for-maht-see-**ohns**-**bew**-roh
...the toilet	...die Toilette	dee toh-**leh**-teh
men	Herren	**hehr**-rehn
women	Damen	**dah**-mehn
left / right	links / rechts	links / rehkhts
straight	geradeaus	geh-**rah**-deh-**ows**
What time does this open / close?	Um wieviel Uhr wird hier geöffnet / geschlossen?	oom **vee**-feel oor veerd heer geh-**urf**-neht / geh-**shloh**-sehn
At what time?	Um wieviel Uhr?	oom **vee**-feel oor
Just a moment.	Moment.	moh-**mehnt**
now / soon / later	jetzt / bald / später	yehtst / bahld / **shpay**-ter
today / tomorrow	heute / morgen	**hoy**-teh / **mor**-gehn

In a German Restaurant

English	German	Pronunciation
I'd like / We'd like...	Ich hätte gern / Wir hätten gern...	ikh **heh**-teh gehrn / veer **heh**-tehn gehrn
...a reservation for...	...eine Reservierung für...	**ī**-neh reh-zer-**feer**-oong fewr
...a table for one / two.	...einen Tisch für eine Person / zwei Personen.	**ī**-nehn tish fewr **ī**-neh pehr-zohn / tsvī pehr-**zoh**-nehn
Nonsmoking.	Nichtraucher.	**nikht**-rowkh-er
Is this seat free?	Ist hier frei?	ist heer frī
Menu (in English), please.	Speisekarte (auf Englisch), bitte.	**shpī**-zeh-kar-teh (owf **ehng**-lish) **bit**-teh
service (not) included	Trinkgeld (nicht) inklusive	**trink**-gehlt (nikht) in-kloo-**zee**-veh
cover charge	Eintritt	**īn**-trit
to go	zum Mitnehmen	tsoom **mit**-nay-mehn
with / without	mit / ohne	mit / **oh**-neh
and / or	und / oder	oont / **oh**-der
menu (of the day)	(Tages-) Karte	(**tah**-gehs-) **kar**-teh
set meal for tourists	Touristenmenü	too-**ris**-tehn-meh-**new**
specialty of the house	Spezialität des Hauses	**shpayt**-see-ah-lee-**tayt** dehs **how**-zehs
appetizers	Vorspeise	**for**-shpī-zeh
bread / cheese	Brot / Käse	broht / **kay**-zeh
sandwich	Sandwich	**zahnd**-vich
soup	Suppe	**zup**-peh
salad	Salat	zah-**laht**
meat	Fleisch	flīsh
poultry	Geflügel	geh-**flew**-gehl
fish	Fisch	fish
seafood	Meeresfrüchte	**meh**-rehs-**frewkh**-teh
fruit	Obst	ohpst
vegetables	Gemüse	geh-**mew**-zeh
dessert	Nachspeise	**nahkh**-shpī-zeh
mineral water	Mineralwasser	min-eh-**rahl**-vah-ser
tap water	Leitungswasser	**lī**-toongs-vah-ser
milk	Milch	milkh
(orange) juice	(Orangen-) Saft	(oh-**rahn**-zhehn-) zahft
coffee / tea	Kaffee / Tee	kah-**fay** / tay
wine	Wein	vīn
red / white	rot / weiß	roht / vīs
glass / bottle	Glas / Flasche	glahs / **flah**-sheh
beer	Bier	beer
Cheers!	Prost!	prohst
More. / Another.	Mehr. / Noch eins.	mehr / nohkh īns
The same.	Das gleiche.	dahs **glīkh**-eh
Bill, please.	Rechnung, bitte.	**rehkh**-noong **bit**-teh
tip	Trinkgeld	**trink**-gehlt
Delicious!	Lecker!	**lehk**-er

For more user-friendly German phrases, check out *Rick Steves' German Phrase Book and Dictionary* or *Rick Steves' French, Italian & German Phrase Book.*

INDEX

A

Academy of Arts (Berlin): 304
Academy of Fine Arts (Dresden): 358
Accommodations: See Sleeping; and specific destinations
Ägyptisches Museum (Berlin): See Egyptian Collection
Airbnb: 383, 384–385
Airports: Berlin, 351; Frankfurt, 283; Munich, 95; Salzburg, 145
Air travel: 25, 29, 398
Albertinum (Dresden): 358
Albrecht Dürer House (Nürnberg): 227, 229
Alexanderplatz (Berlin): 293, 312–313
Alm River Canal Exhibit (Salzburg): 129
Alois Dallmayr Delicatessen (Munich): 53, 89
Alps: See Bavarian Alps
Altdorfer, Albrecht: 67
Alte Nationalgalerie (Berlin): 321
Alte Oper (Frankfurt): 287
Alte Pinakothek (Munich): 38, 66–69
Alter Markt (Salzburg): 122–123
Altes Haus (Bacharach): 250, 252–253
Altstadt (Frankfurt): 289
Amalienburg (Munich): 78–79
Ampelmännchen: 311, 336
Ancient Spa Museum (Baden-Baden): 276
Apartment rentals: 383, 384–385
Apfelwein (apple wine): 289, 380
Apps: 29, 385–386; navigation, 395; sightseeing, 377
Asam Church (Munich): 39, 49–50
ATMs: 373–375
Audio Europe, Rick Steves: 29, 399
Augustiner Beer Garden (Munich): 50, 85
Augustiner Bräustübl (Salzburg): 138
Auguststrasse (Berlin): 347
Augustus Bridge (Dresden): 358
Augustus II (the Strong): 352, 354, 357–360
Austria: 104–145. See also Salzburg
Autobahn: about, 395, 398

B

Bacharach: 240, 244–255; eating, 252–253; experiences, 251–252; map, 246–247; orientation, 244–245; shopping, 252; sleeping, 253–254; tourist information, 245; transportation,
254–255; walking tour, 245–251
Bacharach Old Town Walls: 248, 249, 252
Bacharach Protestant Church: 249
Bacharach Tall Tower: 250–251
Baden-Baden: 275–282; baths, 277, 279–280; eating, 282; map, 278; orientation, 275; sights/activities, 277–281; sleeping, 282; walking tour, 276–277
Baden-Baden Casino: 276, 280–281
Baden-Baden Catholic Church: 276
Banking District (Frankfurt): 286
Banks (banking): alerting to travel, 29. See also Money
Baths, in Baden-Baden: 277, 279–280
Baths of Caracalla (Baden-Baden): 279–280
Baumeister Haus (Rothenburg): 197, 204
Baumgarten (Füssen): 159–160
Bavarian Alps: 148–185; at a glance, 150–151; best of, 14–15; itineraries, 148–149; map, 152–153. See also Füssen; Nürnberg
Bavarian craftsmanship: 159, 176
Bavarian Terrace (Zugspitze): 184–185
Bayerisch Staatsoper (Munich): 82
Bebelplatz (Berlin): 307–308
Beer: 380; Munich, 84; guided tours, 35; Oktoberfest, 80–81, 400. See also Beer gardens/halls
Beer and Oktoberfest Museum (Munich): 81
Beer gardens/halls: Berlin, 339, 342; Cologne, 274; Dresden, 360; Frankfurt, 289; Munich, 38, 47, 53–54, 81–85; Rothenburg, 210–211; St. Goar, 262; Salzburg, 136, 138, 139
Beer Hall Putsch of 1923: 47, 55, 65
Beer steins, shopping for: 82, 208, 252
Bell tower: See Glockenspiel
Benedictine Monastery (Füssen): 158
Benedict XVI, Pope: 52, 183
Berlin: 292–352; at a glance, 296–297; best of, 20–21; eating, 338–343; experiences, 336–338; helpful hints, 295, 298; itineraries, 292–293; maps, 294–295, 302–303, 316–317, 319, 326, 340–341, 344–345; nightlife, 337–338; orientation, 293–294; shopping, 336–337; sights, 313–336; sleeping, 343–347; tourist information, 294–295; tours, 298–299; transportation, 347–352; walking tour, 299–313
Berlin Cathedral: 310

Berlin City Hall: 311

Berlin courtyards *(Höfe):* 297, 323

Berliner Ensemble: 338

Berlin Hauptbahnhof: 292, 300, 351–352

Berlin Wall: 292, 330; Checkpoint Charlie, 297, 328–331; Documentation Center, 327; Victims Memorial, 301

Berlin Wall Memorial: 297, 324–328; map, 326; self-guided tour, 325–328

Beverages: 380–381. *See also* Beer; Wine and vineyards

Biergartens: *See* Beer gardens/halls

Biking (bike rentals): Bacharach, 245; Berlin, 351; Füssen, 149, 154; Munich, 35, 40, 72, 95; Rhine Valley, 242, 244; Rothenburg, 194; St. Goar, 255; Salzburg, 112, 133, 144

Bingen: 235

Binnenalster (Hamburg): 364

Blaue Reiter: 38, 69–70

BMW-Welt and Museum (Munich): 29, 39, 79–80

Boat cruises: Berlin, 298; Hamburg, 365; Rhine River, 241–242

Boppard: 236

Brandenburg Gate (Berlin): 293, 296, 301–303, 315

Brandenburg Tor (Berlin): 306–307

Braubach: 262–265

Bread Market Square (Füssen): 158

Brienner Strasse (Munich): 55, 88

British Embassy (Berlin): 306

Brühlsche Terrasse (Dresden): 358

Budgeting: 25, 28

Burg Eltz: 233, 266–268; map, 267

Burggarten: *See* Castle Garden

Burggasse (Rothenburg): 202, 204

Burgtor Gate (Rothenburg): 203

Business hours: 373

Bus travel (buses): 393–394; map, 390–391. *See also specific destinations*

C

Cable cars: *See* Funiculars

Café Tomaselli (Salzburg): 124, 136

Campground, in Bacharach: 248

Caracalla Baths (Baden-Baden): 279–280

Car insurance: 394–395

Car rentals: 25, 394

Car travel (driving): 395–398; distances and time, 396–397. *See also specific destinations*

Casino, in Baden-Baden: 276, 280–281

Castle Garden (Nurnberg), 227; (Rheinfels Castle), 260; (Rothenburg), 202–203

Castles: Ehrenfels Castle, 240; Füssen High Castle, 159; Gutenfels Castle, 239; Hohenschwangau Castle, 150, 168–169; Katz Castle, 327; Lahneck Castle, 236; Liebenstein Castle, 236–237; Linderhof Castle, 151, 180–182; Marksburg Castle, 233, 236, 262–265; Maus Castle, 237; Neuschwanstein Castle, 150, 169–171; Nürnberg Imperial Castle, 226–227; Pfalz Castle, 239; Reichenstein Castle, 240; Rheinfels Castle, 256, 258–260; Rheinstein Castle, 240; Sooneck Castle, 240; Stahleck Castle, 240; Sterrenberg Castle, 236–237

Cell phones: 29, 385–386

Chancellery (Berlin): 300

Chapel of Reconciliation (Berlin): 327–328

Chapel of the Three Magi (Cologne): 273

Chapel of the Virgin (Cologne): 273

Checkpoint Charlie (Berlin): 297, 307, 328–331

Chinese Tower Beer Garden (Munich): 71, 85

Chocolate: 211, 336

Christmas Headquarters (Rothenburg): 208

Christmas markets: 24, 401; Munich, 81; Nürnberg, 226; Rothenburg, 208; Salzburg, 105

Christmas Museum (Rothenburg): 193, 207

Church of Our Lady: *See* Frauenkirche

Climate: 402

Clothing sizes: 402

Cologne: 268–274; eating, 274; map, 269; sights, 270–274; sleeping, 274

Cologne Cathedral: 233, 270–274; map, 271

Concentration camp: *See* Dachau Concentration Camp Memorial

Convent Garden (Rothenburg): 202

Costs of trip: 25, 28

Courtyards *(Höfe)* of Berlin: 297, 323

Cranach, Lucas: 227–228, 334

Credit cards: 29, 374–375

Creglingen: 193, 214

Crown Gate (Dresden): 356

Cuckoo clocks, shopping for: 252, 261

Cuisine: 377–380; Berlin, 339; Munich, 82–83; Rothenburg, 209

Currency and exchange: 373–375

Customs regulations: 376

Cuvilliés Theater (Munich): 57, 64

Cycling: *See* Biking

D

Dachau Concentration Camp Memorial: 39, 98–101; map, 100; self-guided tour, 99–101

Dallmayr Delicatessen (Munich): 53, 89

Da Vinci, Leonardo: 68

DDR Museum (Berlin): 297, 323

Debit cards: 29, 374–375

Deutscher Dom (Berlin): 315

Deutsches Historisches Museum (Berlin): 297, 322–323

Deutsches Museum (Munich): 39, 72–73

Deutsches Theatre (Munich): 82

Dining: *See* Eating; *and specific destinations*

Dinkelsbühl: 193, 216

Dinkelsbühl City History Museum: 216

Dirndls, shopping for: 82

Dresden: 22, 352–361; eating, 360; map, 353; orientation, 354; sights, 358–360; sleeping, 360–361; tourist information, 354; transportation, 354–355; walking tour, 355–358

Drinks: 380–381. *See also* Beer; Wine and vineyards

Dürer, Albrecht: 67–68, 227, 258, 334; House (Nürnberg), 227, 229

Dwarf Park (Munich): 130

DZ Bank Building (Berlin): 304

E

Eataly (Munich): 88

Eating: 377–380; budgeting, 28; restaurant phrases, 406; tipping, 375, 378. *See also specific destinations*

Egyptian Collection (Berlin): 320–321

Egyptian Museum (Munich): 38, 69

Ehrenfels Castle: 240

Ehrwald: 183, 184

Eibsee: 183

Eiserner Steg Bridge (Frankfurt): 289

Elbphilharmonie Concert Hall (Hamburg): 366

Electricity: 373

Embassies, in Berlin: 304, 306, 307, 373

Emergencies: 372

Engels, Friedrich: 310–311

English Conversation Club (Rothenburg): 210

English Garden (Munich): 39, 71–72, 85

EurAide: 35, 351

Euro currency: 374–375

F

Fachwerkhäuser: 159

Fernsehturm (Berlin): 312

Festival Hall (Salzburg): 110, 120

Festival of Lights (Berlin): 401

Festivals: 400–401

Festung Marienberg (Würzburg): 222–223

Fingerhut Museum (Creglingen): 214

Fortress Museum (Munich): 128, 129

Franciscan Church (Rothenburg): 203

Franciscan Monastery (Füssen): 155

Frankfurt: 22, 282–289; eating, 289; map, 284–285; orientation, 282; sleeping, 289; walking tour, 283, 286–289

Frankfurt City Model: 289

Frankfurt Opera House: 287

Franziskanerkloster (Füssen): 155

Frauenkirche (Dresden), 357–358; (Munich), 51–52; (Nürnberg), 226

Frederick II (the Great): 306, 307, 308, 315, 322, 369–370

French Cathedral (Berlin): 315

Fressgass' (Frankfurt): 287

Friedrich, Caspar David: 321

Friedrichsbad (Baden-Baden): 277, 279

Friedrichstrasse (Berlin): 307

Friedrichstrasse Station (Berlin): 324

Friese (Rothenburg): 208

Fünf Höfe Passage (Munich): 52, 81

Funiculars (gondolas): Baden-Baden, 281; Oberammergau, 178; Salzburg, 125, 129; Tegelberg, 150, 172–173; Zugspitze, 182–183, 185

Füssen: 149, 154–164; eating, 161–162; experiences, 160–161; helpful hints, 149, 154; map, 156–157; nightlife, 162; orientation, 149; sleeping, 162–163; tourist information, 149; tours, 154; transportation, 163–164; walking tour, 154–160

Füssen Benedictine Monastery: 158

Füssen Franciscan Monastery: 155

Füssen Heritage Museum: 158

Füssen High Castle: 159

Füssen Treetop Walkway: 160–161

G

Galeries Lafayette (Berlin): 307, 336–337, 339

Garmisch: 183

Geburtshaus (Salzburg): 108, 123–125

INDEX

Gedenkstätte Berliner Mauer: 297, 324–328; map, 326
Gehry, Frank: 304
Gemäldegalerie (Berlin): 297, 333–336
Gemäldegalerie Alte Meister (Dresden): 359
Gendarmenmarkt (Berlin): 297, 315, 336
German Cathedral (Berlin): 315
German Christmas Museum (Rothenburg): 193, 207
German History Museum (Berlin): 297, 322–323
German Hunting and Fishing Museum (Munich): 51
Germanic National Museum (Nürnberg): 227–228
German Parliament (Berlin): See Reichstag
German Railway Museum (Nürnberg): 228
German State Opera (Berlin): 308
Gernsbacher Strasse (Baden-Baden): 276–277
Getreidegasse (Salzburg): 108, 121–122
Ghost Subway Station (Berlin): 306–307
Gliding: 172
Glockenspiel (Dresden), 356; (Munich), 41; (Salzburg), 115
Gondolas: See Funiculars
Green Market (Rothenburg): 198–199
Green Vault (Dresden): 355, 356, 360
Guesthouses: overview, 383–384
Guidebooks, Rick Steves: 399
Gutenfels Castle: 239

H

Hackesche Höfe (Berlin): 323, 336
Hackescher Markt (Berlin): 323; eating, 343; market, 336; sleeping, 346–347
HafenCity Port District (Hamburg): 365–366
Hallein: 112
Hamburg: 22, 361–367; eating, 367; map, 362–363; sights, 364–367; sleeping, 367
Hamburg Card: 364
Hamburg History Museum: 364–365
Hang gliding: 172
Hauptmarkt (Nürnberg): 226
Hauptwache (Frankfurt): 287
Haus Schwarzenberg (Berlin): 323
Heinrich Heine Viewpoint (Bacharach): 246–247
Hellbrunn Palace and Gardens (Salzburg): 108, 110, 131–133
Herrgottskirche Church (Creglingen): 193, 214

Herrngasse (Rothenburg): 197–198, 203
Hiking: Burg Eltz, 266; Rothenburg, 192, 202, 205–206; St. Goar, 256, 258
Historic Green Vault (Dresden): 355, 356, 360
Historiengewölbe (Rothenburg): 193, 198
History: 368–371
Hitler, Adolf: 47, 48–49, 55, 65, 100, 228, 299–300, 301, 304, 308, 310, 323, 331–332, 371; bunker site, in Berlin, 305
Hofbräuhaus (Munich): 38, 53–54, 83
Hofgarten (Munich): 56, 89
Hofkirche (Dresden), 357; (Würzburg), 222
Hohensalzburg Fortress (Salzburg): 108, 117, 125–129; concerts, 126, 134; map, 126–127; self-guided tour, 127–129
Hohenschwangau Castle: 150, 168–169
Holbein, Hans: 333–334
Holidays: 400–401
Holocaust memorial (Berlin): 296, 304–305, 315
Holy Spirit Church (Füssen): 158
Hostels: overview, 385. See also specific destinations
Hotel Adlon (Berlin): 304
Hotel de Rome (Berlin): 307–308
Hotel Hirsch (Füssen): 154, 162
Hotels: budgeting, 28; online reviews, 383; overview, 381–383; reservations, 29, 383, 384. See also specific destinations
Hot springs, in Baden-Baden: 277, 279–280
Humboldt Forum (Berlin): 309
Humboldt University (Berlin): 307

I

Imperial Castle (Nürnberg): 226–227
Imperial Chapel: See Hofkirche
International Maritime Museum (Hamburg): 367
Internet security: 386
Ishtar Gate: 318–319
Itineraries: Bavarian Alps, 148–149; Berlin, 292–293; best two-week trip, 26–27; designing your own, 24–25; Munich, 34; Rhine Valley, 233; Romantic Road, 188; Rothenburg, 188; Salzburg, 104–105

J

Jackson (Michael) Memorial (Munich): 52
Jazz music: 82, 135, 337–338
Jewish History Museum (Munich): 49

Jewish Holocaust Memorial (Frankfurt): 289

Jewish Museum Berlin: 297, 332–333

Jewish Quarter (Berlin): 293, 323–324; eating, 342; sleeping, 346

K

Kaiserburg (Nürnberg): 226–227

Kaiser-Maximilian-Platz (Füssen): 154

Kaiserstrasse (Frankfurt): 283, 286

Kaiviertel (Salzburg): 136

Kapitelplatz (Munich): 117–118

Kardinal-Faulhaber-Strasse (Munich): 52

Karl-Liebknecht-Strasse (Berlin): 311

Käthe Kollwitz Museum (Cologne): 274

Käthe Wohlfahrt (Rothenburg): 204–205, 208

Katz Castle: 327

Kaub: 239

Kaufingerstrasse (Munich): 50

King's Castles: See Ludwig II castles

Kleinmarkthalle (Frankfurt): 287, 289

Klingentor (Rothenburg): 201

Kloster St. Mang (Füssen): 158

Koblenz: 236

Kolbensattel: 178

Kollegienkirche (Salzburg): 120

Kollwitz, Käthe: 309, 322; Museum (Cologne), 274

Köln: See Cologne

Königliche Kristall-Therme (Füssen): 160

Kuenburg Bastion (Salzburg): 128

Kulturforum (Berlin): 297, 333–336

Kurfürstendamm (Berlin): 294

Kurhaus (Baden-Baden): 276

KZ-Gedenkstätte Dachau: See Dachau Concentration Camp Memorial

L

Laber Bergbahn: 178

Lahneck Castle: 236

Language: restaurant phrases, 406; survival phrases, 405

Language barrier: 376

Lech Falls: 149, 159–160

Lech River: 149, 155

Lenbachhaus (Munich): 38, 69–70

Leopoldskron Palace (Salzburg): 110

Leopoldsplatz (Baden-Baden): 277

Lermoos: 184

Lichtentaler Allee (Baden-Baden): 281

Liebenstein Castle: 236–237

Linderhof Castle: 151, 180–182

Loden-Frey Verkaufshaus (Munich): 82

Lorch: 240

Loreley, the: 237–239

Lorenzkirche (Nürnberg): 224, 226

Ludwig Beck (Munich): 82

Ludwig II ("Mad King"): 46, 64, 74, 168–171; biographical sketch, 167; tomb, in Munich, 51

Ludwig II ("Mad King") castles: 150, 164–171, 180–182; maps, 165, 169; orientation, 164–167; reservations, 165–166; sights near, 171–174; tours, 164; transportation, 164, 166

Ludwig Museum (Cologne): 274

Ludwigstrasse (Munich): 56

Lüftlmalerei: 159, 175

Luges: 151, 173–174, 178; about, 173

Lustgarten (Berlin): 309–310

Luther, Martin: 44, 46, 66, 228, 311, 357, 369

M

Mail: 386

Mainfränkisches Museum (Würzburg): 223

Main Tower (Frankfurt): 286–287

Marienberg Fortress (Würzburg): 222–223

Marienbrücke: 150, 171–172

Marien Church (Berlin): 311–312

Marienhof (Munich): 53

Marienplatz (Munich): 38, 41, 44; beer halls/gardens, 83–85; eating, 85, 88; shopping, 82

Marionettes: 65, 129, 134

Markets: Berlin, 336; Frankfurt, 287, 289; Füssen, 161–162; Munich, 38, 46–48; Salzburg, 120, 138. See also Christmas markets

Market Square (Rothenburg): 192, 196–198, 206–207

Marksburg Castle: 233, 236, 262–265

Marktplatz (Baden-Baden): 276

Markt Tower (Bacharach): 249

Marstallmuseum (Munich): 78

Marx-Engels-Forum (Berlin): 310–311

Mary's Bridge: 150, 171–172

Mathematics-Physics Salon (Dresden): 356, 359

Mauerpark (Berlin): 336

Maus Castle: 237

Maximilianstrasse (Munich): 54

Max-Joseph-Platz (Munich): 54–55

Maypoles: 47–48

Medical help: 372

Medieval Crime and Punishment Museum (Rothenburg): 192, 206–207

Meistertrunk Show (Rothenburg): 196–197, 208, 401

Memorial to Politicians Who Opposed Hitler (Berlin): 301

Memorial to the Homosexuals Persecuted Under the National Socialist Regime (Berlin): 315

Memorial to the Murdered Jews of Europe (Berlin): 296, 304–305, 315

Merkur (Baden-Baden): 281

Metric conversions: 402

Michael Jackson Memorial (Munich): 52

Michaelskirche (Munich): 50–51

Miniatur Wunderland (Hamburg): 366–367

Mirabell Gardens and Palace (Salzburg): 109, 110, 130, 134

Mobile phones: 29, 385–386

Mönchsberg (Salzburg): 105, 121, 125–129; eating, 136–137

Money: 373–376; average daily expenses, 25; budgeting, 25, 28

Money-saving tips: 28, 373; Berlin, 295, 298; eating, 378; Füssen, 149; Hamburg, 364; Salzburg, 105; sleeping, 381

Monument to the Murdered Sinti and Roma of Europe (Berlin): 314–315

Moselkern: 266

Mozart, Wolfgang Amadeus: 64, 73–74, 114, 117, 125, 135; Birthplace (Salzburg), 108, 123–125; concerts, 134–135, 136; Residence (Salzburg), 109, 130–131

Mozartplatz (Salzburg): 114

Mozartsteg (Salzburg): 112

Münchner Kindl: 41, 44

Münchner Stadtmuseum: 39, 49, 64–65

Munich: 34–98; at a glance, 38–39; best of, 10–11; eating, 82–89; excursion areas, 98–101; experiences, 80–82; helpful hints, 35; history of, 46–47; itineraries, 34; maps, 36–37, 42–43, 66, 72, 86–87, 90–91, 96–97, 126–127; nightlife, 82; orientation, 34–35; shopping, 81–82; sights, 56–80; sleeping, 89–93; tourist information, 35; tours, 35, 40; transportation, 94–98; walking tour, 40–56

Munich City Museum: 39, 49, 64–65

Munich New Town Hall: 41, 44

Munich Old Town Hall: 44

Museum Island (Berlin): 293, 296–297, 309–310, 318–321; eating near, 338–339; map, 319

Museum Ludwig (Cologne): 274

Museum of the Wall at Checkpoint Charlie (Berlin): 297, 329, 331

Museum Quarter (Munich): 66–71; map, 66

Museums: sightseeing tips, 376–377. See also specific museums

Music: Berlin, 337–338; Hamburg, 366; Munich, 82; Salzburg, 126, 133–135. See also Mozart, Wolfgang Amadeus; Opera; Sound of Music

N

National Theater (Munich): 54–55

Nazi Documentation Center (Munich), 39, 71; (Nürnberg), 228, 229

Nazi Rally Grounds (Nurnberg): 228, 229

Nazis (Nazism): 371; Berlin, 301, 304–306, 308–309, 314–315, 322–323, 331–332; Dachau Memorial, 39, 98–101; Munich, 47, 55, 65, 71; Nürnberg, 223, 228. See also Hitler, Adolf

Nefertiti, Queen, bust: 321

Neue Residenz (Salzburg): 115

Neues Museum (Berlin): 297, 320–321

Neue Synagogue (Berlin): 323–324

Neue Wache (Berlin): 308–309

Neugasse (Rothenburg): 205

Neumarkt (Dresden): 357

Neuschwanstein Castle: 150, 169–171; orientation, 164–167; reservations, 165–166; tours, 164; transportation, 166

New Green Vault (Dresden): 360

New Guardhouse (Berlin): 308–309

New Museum (Berlin): 297, 320–321

New Old Town (Frankfurt): 289

New Residenz (Salzburg): 115

New Synagogue (Berlin): 297, 323–324

Niederwald Monument: 240–241

Night Watchman's Tour (Rothenburg): 192, 194, 196

Nonnberg Abbey (Salzburg): 110

Nordbahnhof (Berlin): 325, 326, 328

Nördlingen: 193, 216–217

Nürnberg: 22, 223–229; eating, 229; maps, 225, 229; sights, 224–228; sleeping, 229

Nurnberg Main Market Square: 226

Nürnberg Transport Museum: 228

Nymphenburg Palace (Munich): 39, 73–79; map, 75

Nymphenburg porcelain: 63, 78, 82
Nymphs' Bath (Dresden): 356

O

Oberammergau: 151, 175–180; map, 177
Oberammergau Museum: 176
Oberwesel: 239
Odeonsplatz (Munich): 55–56
Oktoberfest (Munich): 80–81, 400
Oktoberfest Museum (Munich): 81
Old Jewish Quarter (Berlin): 293, 323–324; eating, 342; sleeping, 346
Old Masters Gallery (Dresden): 359
Old Mint (Bacharach): 250
Old National Gallery (Berlin): 321
Old Town (Dresden): 354, 355–358
Old Town (Nürnberg): 224, 226
Old Town (Rothenburg): 189, 196–206; eating, 209–211; guided tours, 194, 196–206; map, 195; sleeping, 211–213; walking tour, 196–206
Old Town (Salzburg): 105, 108, 123–125; eating, 135–138; map, 113; sleeping, 144; walking tour, 112–123
Onel Jakob Synagogue (Munich): 48–49
Opera: Berlin, 308; Dresden, 355; Frankfurt, 287; Munich, 82

P

Packing tips and checklist: 29, 403
"Painters' Corner" (Bacharach): 251
Palace of Culture (Dresden): 356–357
Palace of Tears (Berlin): 324
Parade of Nobles (Dresden): 357
Pariser Platz (Berlin): 304
Parliament (Berlin): See Reichstag
Passion Play (Oberammergau): 175, 177–178
Passports: 29, 373
Paulskirche (Frankfurt): 287–288
Pergamon Museum (Berlin): 296, 318–320
Pfalz Castle: 239
Phones: 385–386
Pilatus House (Oberammergau): 176
Platz der Republik (Berlin): 299
Platzl (Munich): 53
Police: 372
Pöllat Gorge: 150, 172
Porcelain Collection (Dresden): 356, 359
Posthof (Bacharach): 249
Post offices: 386

Prenzlauer Berg (Berlin): 293, 297; eating, 339, 342; market, 336; music, 338; sights, 324–328; sleeping, 343, 346
Promenadeplatz (Munich): 52
Prostitution: 283, 286
Puppets: 65, 129, 134

R

"Raft Busters": 239–240
Rail passes: 25, 388, 389, 392, 399
Rail travel: See Train travel
Railway Museum (Nürnberg): 228
Rainer Regiments Museum (Munich): 129
Rally Grounds (Nürnberg): 228, 229
Raphael: 68, 359
Reichenstein Castle: 240
Reichsstadt Festival (Rothenburg): 208, 401
Reichstag (Berlin): 296, 299–300, 313–314; climbing cupola, 314; memorials near, 314–315; reservations, 29, 313–314
Rembrandt van Rijn: 69, 335, 359
Rental properties: 383, 384–385
Residenz (Dresden), 359–360; (Munich), 38, 54, 57–64; map, 61; (Salzburg), 115; (Würzburg), 218–222
Residenz Garden (Würzburg): 222
Residenz Museum (Munich): 57, 59–64
Residenzplatz (Salzburg): 114–115
Residenz Treasury (Munich): 57, 58–59
Resources from Rick Steves: 399
Restaurants: See Eating; and specific destinations
Reutte: 183, 184
Rheinfels Castle: 233, 237, 256, 258–261; map, 259; orientation, 233, 256, 258; self-guided tour, 258, 260–261
Rheinstein Castle: 240
Rhine in Flames Festival: 241
Rhine River: 233–248, 251; barge trade on, 238; cruises, 241–242; ferries, 242; festivals, 241; history of castles of, 235; maps, 234, 243
Rhine Valley: 232–265; at a glance, 233; best of, 18–19; itineraries, 233; maps, 234, 243; self-guided tour, 234–241; transportation, 241–242, 244
Riemenschneider, Tilman: 200–201, 214, 223, 228
Ries crater: 216
Roman-Germanic Museum (Cologne): 273–274
Roman-Irish Bath (Baden-Baden): 277, 279
Romantic Road: 188, 214–217; at a glance, 193;

INDEX

best of, 16–17; buses, 214; itineraries, 188; map, 215
Römerberg (Frankfurt): 288
Room and board: See Eating; Sleeping; and specific destinations
Rosenthaler Platz (Berlin): 343
Rothenberg Historical Town Hall Vaults: 193, 198
Rothenburg City Territory, Map of: 198
Rothenburg Franciscan Church: 203
Rothenburg Market Square: 192, 196–198, 206–207
Rothenburg Museum: 192, 201–202
Rothenburg ob der Tauber: 189–213; at a glance, 192–193; best of, 16–17; eating, 209–211; festivals, 208; itineraries, 188; maps, 190–191, 195; orientation, 189, 194; shopping, 204–205, 208; sights, 206–207; sleeping, 211–213; tourist information, 194; tours, 194; transportation, 213; walking tour, 196–206
Rothenburg Town Hall and Tower: 193, 196, 206
Rothenburg Town Wall: 192, 202, 205–206
Royal Crystal Baths (Füssen): 150, 160
Royal Stables Museum (Munich): 78
Rubens, Peter Paul: 68–69, 335, 359
Rupert, Saint: 119
Rupertgasse (Salzburg): 139, 143
Russian Embassy (Berlin): 307

S
Sachsenhausen (Frankfurt): 289
St. Anna Chapel (Füssen): 158
St. Bartholomew's Cathedral (Frankfurt): 288–289
St. George's Fountain (Rothenburg): 197
St. Georg's Cathedral (Dinkelsbühl): 216
St. Georg's Church (Nördlingen): 216
St. Goar: 237, 255–262; eating, 261–262; map, 257; shopping, 261; sights, 256–261; sleeping, 262–263
St. Hedwig's Church (Berlin): 308
St. Jakob's Church (Rothenburg): 192, 199–201
St. Lawrence Church (Nürnberg): 224, 226
St. Magnus Basilica (Füssen): 159
St. Magnus Monastery (Füssen): 158
St. Michael's Church (Munich): 50–51
St. Nikolai Memorial (Hamburg): 364
St. Pauli Landungsbrücken Harborfront (Hamburg): 365
St. Paul's Church (Frankfurt): 287–288

St. Peter's Cemetery (Salzburg): 110, 118–119
St. Peter's Church (Munich), 44–45; (Salzburg), 119–120, 135
St. Sebastian Cemetery (Füssen), 154–155; (Salzburg), 131
Salzach River: 105, 114, 118, 133
Salzburg: 104–145; at a glance, 108–109; best of, 12–13; eating, 135–139; history of, 124; itineraries, 104–105; maps, 106–107, 113, 132, 140–141; music, 126, 133–135; orientation, 105; sights/activities, 123–135; sleeping, 139–144; tourist information, 105; tours, 105, 110–112; transportation, 144–145; walking tour, 112–123
Salzburg Card: 105
Salzburg Cathedral: 108, 115–117, 135
Salzburg Festival: 29, 105, 135, 401
Salzburg Museum: 108, 123
Sausage (wurst): about, 379
Sausage stands: 137–138, 339, 342
Saxony: See Dresden
Schatzkammer (Munich): 57, 58–59
Schatz Konditorei (Salzburg): 122
Schmiedgasse (Rothenburg): 192, 204–205
Schönefeld Airport (Berlin): 351
Schrannenhalle (Munich): 48, 88
Schwangau: 160
Sebastiansplatz (Munich): 48
Semperoper (Dresden): 355
Seven Maidens: 239
Shell Grotto (Munich): 59
Shopping: hours, 373; VAT refunds, 375–376. See also specific destinations
Shrine of the Magi (Cologne): 272–273
Sights (sightseeing): best two-week trip, 26–27; general tips, 376–377. See also Itineraries; and specific sights destinations
Sleep code: 382
Sleeping: 381–385; budgeting, 25; online reviews, 383; reservations, 29, 383, 384. See also specific destinations
Smartphones: 29, 385–386
Sommerrodelbahn Steckenberg (Unterammergau): 178
Sony Center (Berlin): 337
Sooneck Castle: 240
Sophienstrasse (Baden-Baden): 277
Sound of Music: 118, 120, 129, 130, 132–133, 134; debunking myths, 110–111; tours, 105, 110–112
Soviet War Memorial (Berlin): 315

Spitalgasse (Rothenburg): 192, 204-205
Spitaltor (Rothenburg): 192, 204, 206
Spree River: 310, 338; cruises, 298
Staatliches Museum Ägyptischer Kunst (Munich): 38, 69
Stahleck Castle: 240
Steingasse (Salzburg): 109, 139
Sterrenberg Castle: 236-237
Stiftskeller St. Peter (Salzburg): 134, 136
Stolpersteine (stumbling stones): 308
Swimming: 160, 178
Synagogues: 48-49, 297, 323-324

T
Taunusstrasse (Frankfurt): 283, 286
Taxes: VAT refunds, 375-376
Tegel Airport (Berlin): 351
Tegelberg Cable Car: 150, 172-173
Tegelberg Luge: 151, 173-174
Telephones: 385-386, 387; Austria, 105
Temperatures, average monthly: 402
Teufelsberg (Berlin): 314
Theaterplatz (Dresden): 355
Theatinerkirche (Munich): 55
Theft alerts: 30, 373
Tiepolo, Giovanni Battista: 219-220, 222
Tiergarten (Berlin): 294, 303-304
Tipping: 375, 378
Tirolean Terrace (Zugspitze): 183-184
Topography of Terror (Berlin): 297, 331-332
Toscaninihof (Salzburg): 120
Tourist information: 372. See also specific destinations
Tours: Rick Steves, 399. See also specific destinations
Train travel: 387-393; budgeting, 25, 28; getting a seat, 393; map, 390-391; schedules, 388; tickets, 392-393. See also specific destinations
Transportation: 386-398; budgeting, 25, 28; map, 390-391. See also specific destinations
Transport Museum (Nürnberg): 228
Travel smarts: 24-25
Travel strategies: 29-30
Travel tips: 373
Treetop Walkway (Füssen): 160-161
Trinkhalle (Baden-Baden): 276
Trip costs: 25, 28
TV Tower (Berlin): 312

U
Unity Day: 371, 401
Universitätsplatz (Salzburg): 120-121
Unterammergau: 178
Unter den Linden (Berlin): 293, 296, 306, 315; eating, 339
US Embassy (Berlin): 304, 373

V
VAT refunds: 375-376
Victory Column (Berlin): 303-304
Viktualienmarkt (Munich): 38, 46-48; eating near, 88
Viscardigasse (Munich): 55
Visitor information: 372. See also specific destinations
Von Trapp family: See Sound of Music

W
Wagner, Richard: 64
Walderlebniszentrum Ziegelwies (Füssen): 160-161
Wallraf-Richartz Museum (Cologne): 274
Weather: 402
Weikersheim: 193, 214-215
Weinbergsweg (Berlin): 343
Wellenberg Swimming Pool: 178
Wieskirche: 151, 174-175, 193, 217
Wilhelmstrasse (Berlin): 305-306
Willy Brandt Berlin-Brandenburg International Airport: 351
Wine and vineyards: 380-381; Rhine Valley, 240, 241, 251-252; Rothenburg, 204, 208
Wohnhaus (Salzburg): 109, 130-131
Women's Protest Memorial (Berlin): 312
Woodcarving: 176, 178
Wood Market Tower (Bacharach): 251
World Time Clock (Berlin): 312
World War II: 47, 247-248, 268, 322-323, 371. See also Nazis
Wurst (sausage): See Sausage
Würzburg: 22, 217-223; eating, 223; map, 220-221; sights, 218-223; sleeping, 223

Z
Zeil (Frankfurt): 287
Zugspitze: 151, 182-185; map, 184
Zwinger (Dresden): 355-356, 358-359

INDEX

MAP INDEX

FRONT MAP
Germany: 4

INTRODUCTION
Top Destinations in Germany: 9
The Best of Germany in 2 Weeks: 27

MUNICH
Munich: 36
Munich City Walk: 43
Residenz Tour: 61
Museum Quarter: 66
Alte Pinakothek: 67
Greater Munich: 72
Nymphenburg Palace Complex: 75
Munich Restaurants: 86
Munich Hotels: 90
Munich Transportation: 96

Near Munich
Dachau: 100

SALZBURG
Salzburg: 106
Salzburg Town Walk: 113
Hohensalzburg Fortress: 127
Near Salzburg: 132
Salzburg Restaurants & Hotels: 140

BAVARIAN ALPS
Bavarian Alps: 152
Füssen: 157
The King's Castles Area: 165
The King's Castles: 169
Oberammergau: 177
Zugspitze Area: 184

ROTHENBURG AND THE ROMANTIC ROAD
Rothenburg: 191
Rothenburg Walks: 195

Near Rothenburg
The Romantic Road: 215

Best of the Rest: Würzburg
Würzburg: 221

Best of the Rest: Nürnberg
Nürnberg: 225
Nazi Documentation Center & Rally Grounds: 229

RHINE VALLEY
Rhine Overview: 234
The Best of the Rhine: 243
Bacharach: 247
St. Goar: 257
St. Goar's Rheinfels Castle: 259

Near the Rhine Valley
Burg Eltz Area: 267
Cologne: 269
Cologne Cathedral: 271

Best of the Rest: Baden-Baden
Central Baden-Baden: 278

Best of the Rest: Frankfurt
Frankfurt: 284

BERLIN
Berlin Overview: 294
Berlin City Walk: 302
Berlin: 316
Museum Island: 319
Berlin Wall Memorial Area: 326
Near Checkpoint Charlie: 329
Berlin Eateries & Nightlife: 340
Berlin Hotels: 344
Berlin Public Transportation: 348

Best of the Rest: Dresden
Dresden: 353

Best of the Rest: Hamburg
Hamburg: 362

PRACTICALITIES
Rail Passes or Point-to-Point Tickets?: 389
Germany's Public Transportation: 390
Driving in Germany: 397

Start your trip at

Our website enhances this book and turns

Explore Europe

At ricksteves.com you can browse through thousands of articles, videos, photos and radio interviews, plus find a wealth of money-saving travel tips for planning your dream trip. And with our mobile-friendly website, you can easily access all this great travel information anywhere you go.

TV Shows

Preview the places you'll visit by watching entire half-hour episodes of Rick Steves' Europe (choose from all 100 shows) on-demand, for free.

ricksteves.com

your travel dreams into affordable reality

Radio Interviews

Enjoy ready access to Rick's vast library of radio interviews covering travel tips and cultural insights that relate specifically to your Europe travel plans.

Travel Forums

Learn, ask, share! Our online community of savvy travelers is a great resource for first-time travelers to Europe, as well as seasoned pros.

Travel News

Subscribe to our free Travel News e-newsletter, and get monthly updates from Rick on what's happening in Europe.

Classroom Europe

Check out our free resource for educators with 300+ short video clips from the Rick Steves' Europe TV show.

Audio Europe™

Rick's Free Travel App

Get your FREE Rick Steves Audio Europe™ app to enjoy…

- Dozens of self-guided tours of Europe's top museums, sights and historic walks
- Hundreds of tracks filled with cultural insights and sightseeing tips from Rick's radio interviews
- All organized into handy geographic playlists
- For Apple and Android

With Rick whispering in your ear, Europe gets even better.

Pack Light and Right

Gear up for your next adventure at ricksteves.com

Light Luggage
Pack light and right with
Rick Steves' affordable,
custom-designed rolling
carry-on bags, backpacks,
day packs and shoulder bags.

Accessories
From packing cubes to
moneybelts and beyond,
Rick has personally selected
the travel goodies that will help
your trip go smoother.

Shop at ricksteves.com

Rick Steves has

Experience maximum Europe

Save time and energy

This guidebook is your independent-travel toolkit. But for all it delivers, it's still up to you to devote the time and energy it takes to manage the preparation and logistics that are essential for a happy trip. If that's a hassle, there's a solution.

Rick Steves Tours

A Rick Steves tour takes you to Europe's most

great tours, too!

with minimum stress

interesting places with great guides and small groups of 28 or less. We follow Rick's favorite itineraries, ride in comfy buses, stay in family-run hotels, and bring you intimately close to the Europe you've traveled so far to see. Most importantly, we take away the logistical headaches so you can focus on the fun.

travelers—nearly half of them repeat customers—along with us on four dozen different itineraries, from Ireland to Italy to Athens.

Is a Rick Steves tour the right fit for your travel dreams? Find out at ricksteves.com, where you can also request Rick's latest tour catalog.

Join the fun

This year we'll take thousands of free-spirited travelers—

Europe is best experienced with happy travel partners. We hope you can join us.

See our itineraries at ricksteves.com

A Guide for Every Trip

BEST OF GUIDES

Full color easy-to-scan format, focusing on Europe's most popular destinations and sights

Best of England
Best of Europe
Best of France
Best of Germany
Best of Ireland
Best of Italy
Best of Scotland
Best of Spain

COMPREHENSIVE GUIDES

City, country, and regional guides with detailed coverage for a multi-week trip exploring the most iconic sights and venturing off the beaten track

Amsterdam & the Netherlands
Barcelona
Belgium: Bruges, Brussels,
    Antwerp & Ghent
Berlin
Budapest
Croatia & Slovenia
Eastern Europe
England
Florence & Tuscany
France
Germany
Great Britain
Greece: Athens & the Peloponnese
Iceland
Ireland
Istanbul
Italy
London
Paris
Portugal
Prague & the Czech Republic
Provence & the French Riviera
Rome
Scandinavia
Scotland
Sicily
Spain
Switzerland
Venice
Vienna, Salzburg & Tirol

THE BEST OF ROME

me, Italy's capital, is studded with
man remnants and floodlit-fountain
ares. From the Vatican to the Colos-
m, with crazy traffic in between, Rome
onderful, huge, and exhausting. The
ods, the heat, and the weighty history

of the Eternal City where Caesars walked
can make tourists wilt. Recharge by taking siestas, gelato breaks, and after-dark
walks, strolling from one atmospheric
square to another in the refreshing evening air.

red **Pantheon**—which
rgest dome until the
arly 2,000 years old
day over 1,500).

l of Athens in the **Vat-**
odies the humanistic
ance.

, gladiators fought
another, entertaining
0,
is Rome

POCKET GUIDES

Compact, full color city guides with the essentials for shorter trips

Amsterdam	Munich & Salzburg
Athens	Paris
Barcelona	Prague
Florence	Rome
Italy's Cinque Terre	Venice
London	Vienna

SNAPSHOT GUIDES

Focused single-destination coverage

Basque Country: Spain & France
Copenhagen & the Best of Denmark
Dublin
Dubrovnik
Edinburgh
Hill Towns of Central Italy
Krakow, Warsaw & Gdansk
Lisbon
Loire Valley
Madrid & Toledo
Milan & the Italian Lakes District
Naples & the Amalfi Coast
Nice & the French Riviera
Normandy
Northern Ireland
Norway
Reykjavík
Rothenburg & the Rhine
Sevilla, Granada & Southern Spain
St. Petersburg, Helsinki & Tallinn
Stockholm

Rick Steves books are available
from your favorite bookseller.
Many guides are available as ebooks.

CRUISE PORTS GUIDES

Reference for cruise ports of call

Mediterranean Cruise Ports
Northern European Cruise Ports

Complete your library with...

TRAVEL SKILLS & CULTURE

Study up on travel skills before visiting "Europe through the back door" or gain insight on European history and culture

Europe 101
Europe Through the Back Door
European Christmas
European Easter
European Festivals
Postcards from Europe
Travel as a Political Act

PHRASE BOOKS & DICTIONARIES

French
French, Italian & German
German
Italian
Portuguese
Spanish

PLANNING MAPS

Britain, Ireland & London
Europe
France & Paris
Germany, Austria & Switzerland
Iceland
Ireland
Italy
Spain & Portugal

PHOTO CREDITS

Avalon Travel
Hachette Book Group
1700 Fourth Street
Berkeley, CA 94710

Text © 2019 by Rick Steves' Europe, Inc. All rights reserved.
Maps © 2019 by Rick Steves' Europe, Inc. All rights reserved.

Printed in China
First printing November 2019.

ISBN 978-1-64171-112-8

For the latest on Rick's lectures, guidebooks, tours, public radio show, and public television series, contact Rick Steves' Europe, 130 Fourth Avenue North, Edmonds, WA 98020, 425/771-8303, www.ricksteves.com, rick@ricksteves.com.

RICK STEVES' EUROPE
Special Publications Manager: Risa Laib
Managing Editor: Jennifer Madison Davis
Assistant Managing Editor: Cathy Lu
Project Editor: Suzanne Kotz
Editors: Glenn Eriksen, Tom Griffin, Rosie Leutzinger, Jessica Shaw, Carrie Shepherd
Editorial & Production Assistant: Megan Simms
Graphic Content Director: Sandra Hundacker
Maps & Graphics: David C. Hoerlein, Lauren Mills, Mary Rostad
Digital Asset Coordinator: Orin Dubrow

AVALON TRAVEL
Editorial Director: Kevin McLain
Senior Editor and Series Manager: Madhu Prasher
Editors: Jamie Andrade, Sierra Machado
Copy Editor: Kelly Lydick
Proofreader: Patrick Collins
Indexer: Stephen Callahan
Interior Design & Layout: McGuire Barber Design
Cover Design: Kimberly Glyder Design
Maps & Graphics: Kat Bennett

Let's Keep on Travelin'

Your trip doesn't need to end.

Follow Rick on social media!

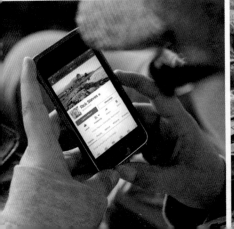